CWNA®

Certified Wireless Network Administrator

Official Study Guide

Fourth Edition

David A. Westcott, CWNE #7

David D. Coleman, CWNE #4

SYBEX®
A Wiley Brand

Senior Acquisitions Editor: Jeff Kellum
Development Editor: Mary Ellen Schutz
Technical Editors: Andrew von Nagy and Marcus Burton
Production Editor: Eric Charbonneau
Copy Editor: Judy Flynn
Editorial Manager: Pete Gaughan
Vice President and Executive Group Publisher: Richard Swadley
Associate Publisher: Chris Webb
Media Project Manager 1: Laura Moss-Hollister
Media Associate Producer: Josh Frank
Media Quality Assurance: Doug Kuhn
Book Designer: Judy Fung
Proofreader: Nancy Bell
Indexer: Jack Lewis
Project Coordinator, Cover: Patrick Redmond
Cover Designer: Wiley

Dear Reader,

Thank you for choosing *CWNA: Certified Wireless Network Administrator, Fourth Edition*. This book is part of a family of premium-quality Sybex books, all of which are written by outstanding authors who combine practical experience with a gift for teaching.

Sybex was founded in 1976. More than 30 years later, we're still committed to producing consistently exceptional books. With each of our titles, we're working hard to set a new standard for the industry. From the paper we print on to the authors we work with, our goal is to bring you the best books available.

I hope you see all that reflected in these pages. I'd be very interested to hear your comments and get your feedback on how we're doing. Feel free to let me know what you think about this or any other Sybex book by sending me an email at contactus@sybex.com. If you think you've found a technical error in this book, please visit http://sybex.custhelp.com. Customer feedback is critical to our efforts at Sybex.

Best regards,

Chris Webb
Associate Publisher, Sybex, an Imprint of Wiley

Acknowledgments

When we wrote the first edition of the CWNA Study Guide, David Coleman's children, Brantley and Carolina, were young teenagers. David would like to thank his now adult children for their years of support and for making their dad very proud. David would also like to thank his mother, Marjorie Barnes, and his stepfather, William Barnes, for many years of support and encouragement.

David Coleman would also like to thank the entire Aerohive Networks training department: Paul Levasseur, Bryan Harkins, Metka Dragos, Gregor Vucajnk, Roslyn Rissler, and Yuki Fraher. We have built a fantastic team! David Coleman would also like to thank Abby Strong and all of his co-workers at Aerohive Networks (www.aerohive.com). It has been one wild ride the past four years!

David Westcott would like to thank his parents, Kathy and George, who have provided so much support and love and from whom he has learned so much. He would also like to thank Janie, Jennifer, and Samantha for their patience and understanding of life on the road and for their support throughout the writing of this book. And special thanks to Savannah Grace, for providing me with the joy of seeing and experiencing life from a new perspective.

David Westcott also would like to thank the training department at Aruba Networks. More than 10 years ago, Chris Leach hired him as a contract trainer. Much has changed over the years, but thanks to Chris, Carolyn Cutler, Susan Wells, Kevin Hamilton, Ramon Pastor, and Stewart Trammell, it has been a fun and exciting journey.

Together, we must first thank Sybex acquisitions editor Jeff Kellum for initially finding us and bringing us to this project. Jeff is an extremely patient and understanding editor who has now survived publishing six books with us. We would also like to thank our development editor, Mary Ellen Schutz. Mary Ellen did a great job keeping us focused and motivated. We also need to send special thanks to our editorial manager, Pete Gaughan; our production editor, Eric Charbonneau; Judy Flynn, our copyeditor; Nancy Bell, our proofreader; and Jack Lewis, our indexer.

We also need to give a big shout-out to our technical editor, Marcus Burton of Ruckus Networks (www.ruckuswireless.com). The feedback and input provided by Marcus was invaluable. Special thanks also goes to Andrew vonNagy of Revolution Wi-Fi (www.revolutionwifi.net) for his feedback and content review. Andrew is a well-known Wi-Fi superstar who writes the best vendor-neutral Wi-Fi blog.

Thanks very much to Matthew Gast for the heartfelt foreword. Matthew, an author himself, has written numerous books about 802.11 technology. A simple Google search on Matthew Gast's name reveals why he is considered an utmost authority on 802.11 technology.

We would also like to thank Brad Crump, Tom Carpenter, and Julia Baldini of the CWNP program (www.cwnp.com). All CWNP employees, past and present, should be proud of the internationally renowned wireless certification program that sets the education standard within the enterprise Wi-Fi industry. It has been a pleasure working with all of you for over a decade.

Andrew Crocker has again provided us with wonderful photographs and some amazing editing of some not so wonderful photographs that we provide him. You can see much more of his work and talent at www.andrew-crocker.com.

Thanks to Proxim and to Ken Ruppel (kenruppel@gmail.com) for allowing us to include the video *Beam Patterns and Polarization of Directional Antennas* with the book's online resources, which can be accessed at www.sybex.com/go/cwna4e.

Special thanks goes to Andras Szilagyi, not only for creating the EMANIM software program but for all the extra assistance he provided over the past eight years by creating customized versions of the program for the different editions of the book.

We would also like to thank the following individuals and companies for their support and contributions to the book:

Caster Tray

(www.castertray.com) —Joel Baldevarona

Divergent Dynamics

(www.divergentdynamics.com) —Devin Akin

Ekahau

(www.ekahau.com) —Jussi Kiviniemi

Fluke Networks

(www.flukenetworks.com) —Dilip Advani, Karthik Krishnaswamy

Metageek

(www.metageek.com) —Mark Jensen

WLAN Professionals

(www.wlanpros.com) —Keith Parsons

Welch Allyn

(www.welchallyn.com) —Jeffrey Walker

Wi-Fi Alliance

(www.wi-fi.org) —Trisha Campbell

Xirrus

(www.xirrus.com) —Bruce Miller

About the Authors

David D. Coleman is the Global Training Manager for Aerohive Networks, www.aerohive.com, creators of the award-winning cooperative control wireless LAN (WLAN) architecture. David is in charge of Aerohive training programs for all partners and customers. He has instructed IT professionals from around the globe in wireless networking administration, wireless security, and wireless frame analysis. David has written multiple books, blogs, and white papers about wireless networking. Prior to working at Aerohive, he specialized in corporate and government Wi-Fi training. In the past, he provided WLAN training for numerous private corporations, the US Army, the US Navy, the US Air Force, and other federal and state government agencies. When he is not traveling, David resides in Atlanta, Georgia. David is CWNE #4, and he can be reached via email at mistermultipath@gmail.com. You can also follow David online via Twitter at www.twitter.com/mistermultipath.

David Westcott is an independent consultant and technical trainer with more than 25 years of experience in information technology, specializing in wireless networking and security. In addition to providing advice and direction to corporate clients, David has been a certified trainer for more than 21 years, providing training around the world to government agencies, corporations, and universities. He has provided training on six continents and in over 45 US states. David was an adjunct faculty member for Boston University's Corporate Education Center for more than 10 years. He has co-authored six books about wireless networking as well as numerous white papers and best practices documents. He has also developed courseware and training videos for clients on wireless networking, wireless mesh networking, wireless packet analysis, wired networking, and security. David especially enjoys providing custom onsite training, which focuses on teaching his clients how to apply product and technical knowledge to address their support and troubleshooting needs.

Since installing his first wireless network in 1999, David has become a Certified Wireless Network Trainer, Administrator, Security Professional, and Analysis Professional. He has earned certifications from Cisco, Aruba Networks, Microsoft, EC-Council, CompTIA, and Novell. When not traveling, David lives in Concord, Massachusetts. David is CWNE #7 and can be reached via email at david@westcott-consulting.com.

Contents at a Glance

Contents

Table of Exercises

Foreword

My first formative experience with networking was installing Linux on a 386 laptop. In the days before PC Cards, getting computers on a network was not a plug-and-play task. My first experience with Wi-Fi required going to war with Windows device drivers, and I expended all that effort so I could walk up to my co-workers and ask them, "What is your favorite website?" and then proceed to call it up without having the computer plugged into anything. Such a simple shtick is what passed for a Wi-Fi demo at the time, and the novelty delighted and amazed people more than many demos I have done since.

The years since then have been an interesting journey. I didn't know it at the time, but my after-hours fighting with that old beat-up laptop had nudged me in a new direction. As I traveled the world volunteering in industry groups that were developing the technology, I would visit many interesting locations, hoping that our protocols would stand the test of time while wandering the Acropolis in Athens or lost in the back streets of Venice, wondering whether the jumbled Venetian streets were more or less confusing than the Wi-Fi security architecture, and reveling in the electronic culture of Tokyo while contemplating the obvious challenges to building Wi-Fi networks in such a dense and thriving city.

Providing freely flowing connectivity is a challenge, and many technologies contended to be the prime mover of that ubiquitous connectivity. Wi-Fi provided such a blend of high speeds and good capacity with good economics that it became the default way to connect to a network.

Wi-Fi has grown from an interesting curiosity used by the networking elite into a technology so woven into the fabric of our lives that it has erased Ethernet from our collective memory. Starting with the introduction of the first MacBook Air in 2008, everything became connected primarily by Wi-Fi. Without the ability to offer continuous connectivity, rich media experiences on phones would not have happened. Tablets are possible because so much content and data is accessible through networks that the mass storage can be held outside the device, accessible through a robust network connection.

Our first great wave of connectivity is now coming to a close. Wi-Fi's first act—connecting people—is over. We turned desktops into laptops and then turned laptops into bulky accessories that we used only when our phones and tablets would not suffice. It is now time for the second act—connecting everything else. Making the world around us more aware and responsive requires that new sensors just power up, tune in, and start reporting on the world around them. Instrumenting everything will unleash a flood of data, and tomorrow's Wi-Fi networks need to handle that data without a hitch. Underpinning every API, every service, and all of the instrumentation needed to make it all work is a solid foundation of connectivity. Interacting with and controlling the world requires a bigger network than we have ever seen, and Wi-Fi will be one of the pillars of our brave new data-driven world.

The only thing worse than missing the last decade of innovation in Wi-Fi would be to miss the next innovation. Reading this book is an excellent first step in participating in the decade yet to come. As you take those first steps, halting as they may seem, trust in your guides. Both David and Dave have been in Wi-Fi as long as I have, and their practical knowledge and expertise are the best introduction to the technology you could ask for.

—*Matthew Gast*
Former chair, 802.11-2012 & Wi-Fi Alliance task group leader
San Francisco, California
April 2014

Introduction

If you have purchased this book or if you are thinking about purchasing this book, you probably have some interest in taking the CWNA® (Certified Wireless Network Administrator) certification exam or in learning more about what the CWNA certification exam encompasses. We would like to congratulate you on this first step, and we hope that our book can help you on your journey. Wireless networking is one of the hottest technologies on the market. As with many fast-growing technologies, the demand for knowledgeable people is often greater than the supply. The CWNA certification is one way to prove that you have the knowledge and skills to support this growing industry. This Study Guide was written with that goal in mind.

This book was written to help teach you about wireless networking so that you have the knowledge needed not only to pass the CWNA certification test but also to be able to design, install, and support wireless networks. We have included review questions at the end of each chapter to help you test your knowledge and prepare for the test. We have also included labs, videos, and presentations on the book's website (www.sybex.com/go/cwna4e) to further facilitate your learning.

Before we tell you about the certification process and requirements, we must mention that this information may have changed by the time you take your test. We recommend that you visit www.cwnp.com as you prepare to study for your test to determine what the current objectives and requirements are.

Do not just study the questions and answers! The practice questions in this book are designed to test your knowledge of a concept or objective that is likely to be on the CWNA exam. The practice questions will be different from the actual certification exam questions. If you learn and understand the topics and objectives, you will be better prepared for the test.

About CWNA® and CWNP®

If you have ever prepared to take a certification test for a technology that you are unfamiliar with, you know that you are not only studying to learn a different technology but probably also learning about an industry that you are unfamiliar with. Read on and we will tell you about CWNP.

CWNP is an abbreviation for *Certified Wireless Network Professional*. There is no CWNP test. The CWNP program develops courseware and certification exams for wireless LAN technologies in the computer networking industry. The CWNP certification program is a vendor-neutral program.

The objective of CWNP is to certify people on wireless networking, not on a specific vendor's product. Yes, at times the authors of this book and the creators of the certification will talk about, demonstrate, or even teach how to use a specific product; however, the goal is the overall understanding of wireless, not the product itself. If you learned to drive a car, you had to physically sit and practice in one. When you think back and reminisce, you probably do not tell someone you learned to drive a Ford; you probably say you learned to drive using a Ford.

There are seven wireless certifications offered by the CWNP program:

CWTS: Certified Wireless Technology Specialist   CWTS is an entry-level WLAN certification exam (PW0-071). This certification is geared specifically toward both WLAN sales and support staff for the enterprise WLAN industry. The CWTS certification verifies that sales and support staff are specialists in WLAN technology and have all the fundamental knowledge, tools, and terminology to more effectively sell and support WLAN technologies.

CWNA: Certified Wireless Network Administrator   The CWNA certification is a foundation-level Wi-Fi certification; however, it is not considered an entry-level technology certification. Individuals taking this exam (CWNA 106) typically have a solid grasp on network basics such as the OSI model, IP addressing, PC hardware, and network operating systems. Many candidates already hold other industry-recognized certifications, such as the CompTIA Network+ or Cisco CCNA, and are looking for the CWNA certification to enhance or complement existing skills.

CWSP: Certified Wireless Security Professional   The CWSP certification exam (PW0-204) is focused on standards-based wireless security protocols, security policy, and secure wireless network design. This certification introduces candidates to many of the technologies and techniques that intruders use to compromise wireless networks and that administrators use to protect wireless networks. With recent advances in wireless security, WLANs can be secured beyond their wired counterparts.

CWDP: Certified Wireless Design Professional   The CWDP certification exam (PW0-250) is a professional-level career certification for networkers who are already CWNA certified and have a thorough understanding of RF technologies and applications of 802.11 networks. This certification prepares WLAN professionals to properly design wireless LANs for different applications to perform optimally in different environments.

CWAP: Certified Wireless Analysis Professional   The CWAP certification exam (PW0-270) is a professional-level career certification for networkers who are already CWNA certified and have a thorough understanding of RF technologies and applications of 802.11 networks. This certification provides an in-depth look at 802.11 operations and prepares WLAN professionals to be able to perform, interpret, and understand wireless packet and spectrum analysis.

CWNE: Certified Wireless Network Expert   The CWNE certification is the highest-level certification in the CWNP program. By successfully completing the CWNE requirements, you will have demonstrated that you have the most advanced skills available in today's wireless LAN market. The CWNE certification requires CWNA, CWAP, CWDP, and CWAP certifications. To earn the CWNE certification, a rigorous application must be submitted and approved by CWNP's review team.

CWNT: Certified Wireless Network Trainer   Certified Wireless Network Trainers are qualified instructors certified by the CWNP program to deliver CWNP training courses to IT professionals. CWNTs are technical and instructional experts in wireless technologies, products, and solutions. To ensure a superior learning experience for our customers, CWNP Education Partners are required to use CWNTs when delivering training using official CWNP courseware. More information about becoming a CWNT is available on the CWNP website.

How to Become a CWNA

To become a CWNA, you must do the following two things: agree that you have read and will abide by the terms and conditions of the CWNP Confidentiality Agreement and pass the CWNA certification test.

 A copy of the CWNP Confidentiality Agreement can be found online at the CWNP website.

When you sit to take the test, you will be required to accept this confidentiality agreement before you can continue with the test. After you have agreed, you will be able to continue with the test, and if you pass it, you are then a CWNA.

The information for the exam is as follows:

Exam name: Wireless LAN Administrator

Exam number: CWNA 106

Cost: $175 (in US dollars)

Duration: 90 minutes

Questions: 60

Passing score: 70 percent (80 percent for instructors)

Available languages: English

Availability: Register at Pearson VUE (www.vue.com/cwnp)

When you schedule the exam, you will receive instructions regarding appointment and cancellation procedures, ID requirements, and information about the testing center location. In addition, you will receive a registration and payment confirmation letter. Exams can be scheduled weeks in advance or, in some cases, even as late as the same day. Exam vouchers can also be purchased at the CWNP website.

After you have successfully passed the CWNA exam, the CWNP program will award you a certification that is good for three years. To recertify, you will need to pass the current CWNA exam, the CWSP exam, the CWDP exam, or the CWAP exam that is current at that time. If the information you provided to the testing center is correct, you will receive an email from CWNP recognizing your accomplishment and providing you with a CWNP certification number. After you earn any CWNP certification, you can request a certification kit. The kit includes a congratulatory letter, a certificate, and a wallet-sized personalized ID card. You will need to log in to the CWNP tracking system, verify your contact information, and request your certification kit.

Who Should Buy This Book?

If you want to acquire a solid foundation in wireless networking and your goal is to prepare for the exam, this book is for you. You will find clear explanations of the concepts you need to grasp and plenty of help to achieve the high level of professional competency you need in order to succeed.

If you want to become certified as a CWNA, this book is definitely what you need. However, if you just want to attempt to pass the exam without really understanding wireless, this Study Guide is not for you. It is written for people who want to acquire hands-on skills and in-depth knowledge of wireless networking.

How to Use This Book and the Companion Website

We have included several testing features in the book and on the book's website (www .sybex.com/go/cwna4e). These tools will help you retain vital exam content as well as prepare you to sit for the actual exam.

Before You Begin   At the beginning of the book (right after this introduction) is an assessment test that you can use to check your readiness for the exam. Take this test before you start reading the book; it will help you determine the areas that you may need to brush up on. The answers to the assessment test appear on a separate page after the last question of the test. Each answer includes an explanation and a note telling you the chapter in which the material appears.

Chapter Review Questions   To test your knowledge as you progress through the book, there are review questions at the end of each chapter. As you finish each chapter, answer the review questions and then check your answers. You can go back and reread the section that deals with each question you answered incorrectly to ensure that you answer correctly the next time you are tested on the material.

Electronic Flashcards   You will find flashcard questions on the book's website (www .sybex.com/go/cwna4e). These are short questions and answers, just like the flashcards you probably used in school. You can answer them on your PC or download them onto a smartphone for quick and convenient reviewing.

Test Engine   The book's website (www.sybex.com/go/cwna4e) also contains the Sybex Test Engine. With this custom test engine, you can identify weak areas up front and then develop a solid studying strategy that includes each of the robust testing features described previously. Our thorough ReadMe file will walk you through the quick, easy installation process.

In addition to the assessment test and the chapter review questions, you will find three bonus exams. Use the test engine to take these practice exams just as if you were taking the actual exam (without any reference material). When you have finished the first exam, move on to the next one to solidify your test-taking skills. If you answer more than 95 percent of the questions correctly, you are ready to take the certification exam.

Labs and Exercises   Several chapters in this book have labs that use software, spreadsheets, and videos that are also provided on the book's website (www.sybex.com/go/cwna4e). These labs and exercises will provide you with a broader learning experience by supplying hands-on experience and step-by-step problem solving.

White Papers   Several chapters in this book reference wireless networking white papers that are available from the referenced websites. These white papers serve as additional reference material for preparing for the CWNA exam.

CWNA Exam (CWNA-106) Objectives

The CWNA exam measures your understanding of the fundamentals of RF behavior, your ability to describe the features and functions of wireless LAN components, and your knowledge of the skills needed to install, configure, and troubleshoot wireless LAN hardware peripherals and protocols.

The skills and knowledge measured by this exam were derived from a survey of wireless networking experts and professionals. The results of this survey were used in weighing the subject areas and ensuring that the weighting is representative of the relative importance of the content.

The following chart provides the breakdown of the exam, showing you the weight of each section:

Subject area	% of exam
Radio frequency (RF) technologies	21%
IEEE 802.11 regulations and standards	17%
IEEE 802.11 protocols and devices	17%
IEEE 802.11 network implementation	25%
IEEE 802.11 network security	8%
IEEE 802.11 RF site surveying	12%
Total	**100%**

Radio Frequency (RF) Technologies—21%

1.1. RF Fundamentals

1.1.1. Define and explain the basic concepts of RF behavior.

- Gain and loss
- Reflection, refraction, diffraction, and scattering
- VSWR
- Return loss
- Amplification
- Attenuation
- Absorption
- Wave propagation including free space path loss (FSPL) and delay spread

1.2. RF Mathematics

1.2.1. Understand and apply the basic components of RF mathematics and measurement.

- Watt and milliwatt
- Decibel (dB)
- dBm, dBi and dBd
- SNR
- RSSI
- System operating margin (SOM), fade margin and link budget
- Intentional radiator compared with equivalent isotropically radiated power (EIRP)

1.3. RF Signal and Antenna Concepts

1.3.1. Identify RF signal characteristics, the applications of basic RF antenna concepts, and the implementation of solutions that require RF antennas.

- Line of sight and Fresnel zone issues
- Beamwidths
- Azimuth and elevation charts
- Passive gain vs. active gain
- Isotropic radiator
- Polarization
- Antenna diversity types

- Radio chains
- Spatial multiplexing (SM)
- Transmit beamforming (TxBF) (as defined by the 802.11 standard)
- Maximal ratio combining (MRC)
- Space-time block coding (STBC)
- Cyclic shift diversity (CSD)
- Multi-user MIMO (MU-MIMO)
- Wavelength, frequency, amplitude, and phase

1.3.2. Explain the applications of physical RF antenna and antenna system types and identify their basic attributes, purpose, and function.

- Omni-directional/dipole antennas
- Semi-directional antennas
- Highly directional antennas
- Sectorized antennas and antenna arrays

1.3.3. Describe the proper locations and methods for installing RF antennas.

- Pole/mast mount
- Ceiling mount
- Wall mount
- Outdoor/indoor mounting considerations

1.4. RF Antenna Accessories

1.4.1. Identify the use of the following WLAN accessories.

- RF cables, connectors, and signal splitters
- Amplifiers and attenuators
- Lightning arrestors and grounding rods/wires
- Mounting systems
- Towers, safety equipment, and related concerns

IEEE 802.11 Regulations and Standards—17%

2.1. Spread Spectrum Technologies

2.1.1. Identify some of the uses for wireless networking technologies.

- Wireless LANs
- Wireless PANs
- Wireless bridging

2.1.2. Comprehend the differences between, and explain the different types of, spread spectrum technologies and how they relate to the IEEE 802.11-2012 standard's (as amended and including IEEE 802.11ac) PHY clauses.

- DSSS
- HR-DSSS
- ERP
- OFDM
- HT
- VHT

2.1.3. Identify the basic underlying concepts of how spread spectrum technology works.

- Modulation
- Coding

2.1.4. Identify and apply the concepts that make up the functionality of spread spectrum technology.

- Co-location
- Channel centers and widths (all PHYs)
- Primary and secondary channels
- Adjacent overlapping and nonoverlapping channels
- Carrier frequencies
- Throughput vs. data rate
- Bandwidth
- Communication resilience
- Carrier Sense Multiple Access with Collision Avoidance (CSMA/CA)
- Physical carrier sense – clear channel assessment (CCA)
- Virtual carrier sense (NAV)

2.2. IEEE 802.11-2012 Standard (as amended and including 802.11aa, 802.11ac, 802.11ad, 802.11ae, and 802.11af)

2.2.1. Identify, explain, and apply the frame types and frame exchange sequences covered by the IEEE 802.11-2012 standard.

2.2.2. Identify and apply regulatory domain requirements.

- Dynamic frequency selection (DFS)
- Transmit power control (TPC)
- Available channels
- Output power

2.2.3. Understand the OSI model layers affected by the 802.11-2012 standard and amendments.

2.2.4. Use of ISM, U-NII and licensed bands in Wi-Fi networks.

2.2.5. Supported data rates for each IEEE 802.11-2012 (as amended to include 802.11ac) PHY.

2.2.6. Understand the IEEE standard creation and ratification process and identify IEEE standard naming conventions.

2.3. 802.11 Industry Organizations and Their Roles

2.3.1. Define the roles of the following organizations in providing direction, cohesion, and accountability within the WLAN industry.

- Regulatory domain governing bodies
- IEEE
- Wi-Fi Alliance
- IETF

IEEE 802.11 Protocols and Devices—17%

3.1. IEEE 802.11 Protocol Architecture

3.1.1. Summarize the processes involved in authentication and association.

- The 802.11 state machine
- Open System authentication, Shared Key authentication, and deauthentication
- Association, reassociation, and disassociation

3.1.2. Define, describe, and apply the following concepts associated with WLAN service sets.

- Stations
- BSSs
- Basic service area (BSA)
- Starting and joining a BSS
- BSSID
- SSID
- Ad Hoc mode and IBSS
- Infrastructure mode and ESS
- Distribution system (DS)
- Distribution system medium (DSM)
- Layer 2 and layer 3 roaming

3.1.3. Explain and apply the following power-management features of WLANs.

- Active mode
- Power Save mode
- Unscheduled automatic power save delivery (U-APSD)
- WMM Power Save (WMM-PS)
- Power Save Multi-Poll (PSMP)
- Spatial multiplexing power save (SMPS)
- TIM/DTIM/ATIM
- VHT TXOP

3.2. IEEE 802.11 MAC and PHY Layer Technologies

3.2.1. Describe and apply the following concepts surrounding WLAN frames.

- IEEE 802.11 frame format vs. IEEE 802.3 frame format
- Define terminology related to the MAC and PHY
  - Guard interval (GI)
  - PSDU, PPDU, and PPDU formats
  - MSDU, MPDU
  - A-MPDU vs. A-MSDU
  - 802.11 frame format and types
  - Interframe spaces (RIFS, SIFS, PIFS, DIFS, AIFS, EIFS)
  - Block acknowledgments
  - Fragmentation
- Jumbo frame support (layer 2)
- MTU discovery and functionality (layer 3)

3.2.2. Identify methods described in the IEEE 802.11-2012 standard for locating, joining, and maintaining connectivity with an 802.11 WLAN.

- Active scanning (probes)
- Passive scanning (beacons)
- Dynamic rate switching (DRS)

3.2.3. Define, describe, and apply IEEE 802.11 coordination functions and channel access methods and features available for optimizing data flow across the RF medium.

- DCF and HCF coordination functions
- EDCA channel access method
- RTS/CTS and CTS-to-Self protocols
- HT channel width operation

- HT protection mechanisms
- HT operation modes (0, 1, 2, 3)
- VHT channel width operation
- VHT protection mechanisms
- VHT Operating Mode field

3.3 WLAN Infrastructure and Client Devices

3.3.1. Identify the purpose of the following WLAN infrastructure devices and describe how to install, configure, secure, and manage them.

- Autonomous access points
- Controller-based access points
- Mesh access points/routers
- Enterprise WLAN controllers
- Distributed WLAN architectures
- Remote office WLAN controllers and/or APs
- PoE injectors (single and multiport) and PoE-enabled Ethernet switches
- WLAN bridges
- Home and branch WLAN routers

3.3.2. Describe the purpose of the following WLAN client devices and explain how to install, configure, secure, and manage them.

- PC Cards (ExpressCard, CardBus, and PCMCIA)
- USB2/3
- PCI, Mini PCI, Mini PCIe, and Half Mini PCIe cards
- Workgroup bridges

IEEE 802.11 Network Implementation—25%

4.1. 802.11 Network Design, Implementation, and Management

4.1.1. Identify technology roles for which WLAN technology is appropriate and describe implementation of WLAN technology in those roles.

- Corporate data access and end-user mobility
- Network extension to remote areas
- Building-to-building connectivity (bridging)
- Last-mile data delivery—wireless ISP
- Small office/home office (SOHO) use
- Mobile office networking

- Educational/classroom use
- Industrial—warehousing and manufacturing
- Healthcare—hospitals and offices
- Hotspots—public network access
- Transportation networks (trains, planes, automobiles)
- Law enforcement networks

4.2. 802.11 Network Troubleshooting

4.2.1. Identify and explain how to solve the following WLAN implementation challenges by using features available in enterprise-class WLAN equipment.

- System throughput
- Co-channel and adjacent-channel interference
- RF noise and noise floor
- Narrowband and wideband RF interference
- Multipath (in SISO and MIMO environments)
- Hidden nodes, near/far, weather, and possible solutions

4.3 Power over Ethernet (PoE)

4.3.1. IEEE 802.3-2012, Clause 33 Powering 802.11 devices

- Proprietary midspan and endpoint PSEs
- IEEE 802.3 at midspan and endpoint PSEs

4.4. WLAN Architectures - Configuration, Installation and Management

4.4.1. Define, describe, and implement autonomous APs with network connectivity and common features including control, management and data planes

4.4.2. Define, describe, and implement WLAN controllers that use centralized and/or distributed forwarding with network connectivity and common features including control, management and data planes

- Core, distribution, and access layer forwarding
- Controller-based, mesh, and portal APs
- Scalability
- Intra- and inter-controller station handoffs
- Advantages and limitations
- Tunneling, QoS, and VLANs

4.4.3. Define, describe, and implement distributed and controller-less WLAN architectures with network connectivity and common features including control, management and data planes.

- Scalability
- Inter-AP handoffs
- Advantages and limitations
- Tunneling, QoS, and VLANs

4.4.4. Define, describe, and implement a WNMS that manages APs and WLAN controllers with network connectivity and common features including control, management, and data planes.

4.4.5. Define, describe, and implement a multiple-channel architecture (MCA) network model.

- BSSID/ESSID configuration
- Site surveying methodology
- Network throughput capacity
- Co-channel and adjacent-channel interference
- Cell sizing (including micro-cell)

4.4.6. Define, describe, and implement a single channel architecture (SCA) network model.

- BSSID/ESSID configuration (including virtual BSSIDs)
- Site surveying methodology
- Network throughput capacity
- Co-channel and adjacent-channel interference
- Cell sizing
- Transmission coordination

4.4.7. Define and describe alternative WLAN architectures including control, management, and data planes.

- WLAN arrays
- Mesh networks
- Cloud management

4.5. WLAN Deployment Types

4.5.1. Understand WLAN design and deployment considerations for commonly supported WLAN applications and devices.

- Data
- Voice
- Video
- Real-Time Location Services (RTLS)
- Mobile devices (tablets and smartphones)

- High Density
- Airtime fairness
- Band steering

4.6. WLAN Access and Deployment Technologies

- Bring your own device (BYOD)
- Guest access
- Mobile device management (MDM)
- Network access control (NAC)

IEEE 802.11 Network Security—8%

5.1. IEEE 802.11 Network Security Architecture

5.1.1. Identify and describe the strengths, weaknesses, appropriate uses, and implementation of the following IEEE 802.11 security-related items.

- Weak security mechanisms
  - WEP cipher suite
  - Open System authentication
  - Shared Key authentication
  - MAC filtering
  - SSID hiding
- Effective security mechanisms
  - WPA-/WPA2-Enterprise
  - WPA-/WPA2-Personal
  - TKIP and CCMP cipher suites
  - 802.1X/EAP framework
  - Preshared key (PSK)/passphrase authentication
  - Per-user preshared keys (PPSK)
  - Wi-Fi Protected Setup (WPS)
- Additional mechanisms
  - Secure device management protocols (HTTPS, SNMPv3, SSH2)
  - Role-based access control (RBAC)
  - Captive portals and guest networks
  - Protected management Frames (802.11w)
  - Fast secure roaming methods

5.2. 802.11 Network Security Analysis, Performance Analysis, and Troubleshooting

5.2.1. Describe, explain, and illustrate the appropriate applications for the following wireless security solutions from a monitoring, containment, and reporting perspective.

- Wireless intrusion protection system (WIPS)
- Protocol and spectrum analyzers

IEEE 802.11 RF Site Surveying—12%

6.1. IEEE 802.11 Network Site Survey Fundamentals

6.1.1. Explain the importance of and the processes involved in information collection for manual and predictive RF site surveys.

- Gathering business requirements
- Interviewing managers and users
- Defining physical and data security requirements
- Gathering site-specific documentation
- Documenting existing network characteristics
- Gathering permits and zoning requirements
- Indoor- or outdoor-specific information
- Identifying infrastructure connectivity and power requirements
- Understanding RF coverage requirements
- Understanding data capacity and client density requirements
- VoWiFi considerations for delay and jitter
- Client connectivity requirements
- Antenna use considerations
- Aesthetics requirements
- Tracking system considerations
- WIPS sensor considerations

6.1.2. Explain the technical aspects involved in performing manual and predictive RF site surveys.

- Locating and identifying RF interference sources
- Defining AP and antenna types to be used
- Defining AP and antenna placement locations
- Defining AP output power and channel assignments
- Defining co-channel and adjacent-channel interference

- Testing applications for proper operation
- Measuring performance metrics according to design requirements

6.1.3. Describe site survey reporting and follow-up procedures for manual and predictive RF site surveys

- Reporting methodology
- Customer reporting requirements
- Hardware recommendations and bills of material
- Application analysis for capacity and coverage verification

6.2. IEEE 802.11 Network Site Survey Systems and Devices

6.2.1. Identify the equipment, applications, and system features involved in performing predictive site surveys.

6.2.2. Identify the equipment, applications, and methodologies involved in performing manual site surveys.

6.2.3. Identify the equipment, applications, and methodologies involved in self-managing RF technologies (automated RF resource management).

CWNA Exam Terminology

The CWNP program uses specific terminology when phrasing the questions on any of the CWNP exams. The terminology used most often mirrors the same language that is used by the Wi-Fi Alliance and in the IEEE 802.11-2012 standard. The most current IEEE version of the 802.11 standard is the IEEE 802.11-2012 document, which includes all the amendments that have been ratified prior to the document's publication. Standards bodies such as the IEEE often create several amendments to a standard before "rolling up" the ratified amendments (finalized or approved versions) into a new standard.

 To properly prepare for the CWNA exam, any test candidate should become 100 percent familiar with the terminology used by the CWNP program. This book defines and covers all terminology including acronyms, terms, and definitions.

CWNP Authorized Materials Use Policy

CWNP does not condone the use of unauthorized training materials, aka brain dumps. Individuals who utilize such materials to pass CWNP exams will have their certifications revoked. In an effort to more clearly communicate CWNP's policy on use of unauthorized study materials, CWNP directs all certification candidates to the CWNP Candidate

Conduct Policy, which is available on the CWNP website. Please review this policy before beginning the study process for any CWNP exam. Candidates will be required to state that they understand and have abided by this policy at the time of exam delivery.

Tips for Taking the CWNA Exam

Here are some general tips for taking your exam successfully:

- Bring two forms of ID with you. One must be a photo ID, such as a driver's license. The other can be a major credit card or a passport. Both forms must include a signature.

- Arrive early at the exam center so you can relax and review your study materials, particularly tables and lists of exam-related information.

- Read the questions carefully.

- Do not be tempted to jump to an early conclusion. Make sure you know exactly what the question is asking.

- There will be questions with multiple correct responses.

- When there is more than one correct answer, a message at the bottom of the screen will prompt you to either "choose two" or "choose all that apply." Be sure to read the messages displayed to know how many correct answers you must choose.

- When answering multiple-choice questions you are not sure about, use a process of elimination to get rid of the obviously incorrect answers first. Doing so will improve your odds if you need to make an educated guess.

- Do not spend too much time on one question.

- This is a form-based test; however, you cannot move backward through the exam. You must answer the current question before you can move to the next question, and after you have moved to the next question, you cannot go back and change your answer on a previous question.

- Keep track of your time.

- Because this is a 90-minute test consisting of 60 questions, you have an average of 90 seconds to answer each question. You can spend as much or as little time on any one question, but when 90 minutes is up, the test is over. Check your progress. After 45 minutes, you should have answered at least 30 questions. If you have not, do not panic. You will simply need to answer the remaining questions at a faster pace. If on average you can answer each of the remaining 30 questions 4 seconds quicker, you will recover 2 minutes. Again, do not panic; just pace yourself.

- For the latest pricing on the exams and updates to the registration procedures, visit CWNP's website at www.cwnp.com.

CWNA: Certified Wireless Network Administrator Exam (CWNA-106) Objectives

The CWNA: *Certified Wireless Network Administrator Official Study Guide, Fourth Edition*, was written to cover every CWNA-106 exam objective at a level appropriate to its exam weighting. The following sections provide a breakdown of this book's exam coverage, showing you the weight of each section and listing the chapter where each objective or subobjective is covered:

Subject area	% of exam
Radio frequency (RF) technologies	21%
IEEE 802.11 regulations and standards	17%
IEEE 802.11 protocols and devices	17%
IEEE 802.11 network implementation	25%
IEEE 802.11 network security	8%
IEEE 802.11 RF site surveying	12%
Total	**100%**

Radio Frequency (RF) Technologies

Objective	Chapter
1.1. RF Fundamentals	2, 4

        1.1.1.   Define and explain the basic concepts of RF behavior:
- ❖ gain and loss
- ❖ reflection, refraction, diffraction, and scattering
- ❖ VSWR
- ❖ return loss
- ❖ amplification
- ❖ attenuation
- ❖ absorption
- ❖ wave propagation including free space path loss and delay spread

1.3.3. Describe the proper locations and methods for installing RF antennas:

❖ pole/mast mount

❖ ceiling mount

❖ wall mount

❖ outdoor/indoor mounting considerations

1.4.   RF Antenna Accessories   4

1.4.1. Identify the use of the following WLAN accessories:

❖ RF cables, connectors, and signal splitters

❖ amplifiers and attenuators

❖ lightning arrestors and grounding rods/wires

❖ mounting systems

❖ towers, safety equipment, and related concerns

IEEE 802.11 Regulations and Standards

Objective	Chapter
2.1. Spread Spectrum Technologies	6, 7, 8, 18, 19

2.1.1. Identify some of the uses for spread spectrum technologies:

❖ wireless LANs

❖ wireless PANs

❖ wireless bridging

2.1.2. Comprehend the differences between, and explain the different types of spread spectrum technologies and how they relate to the IEEE 802.11-2012 standard's (as amended and including 802.11ac) PHY clauses:

❖ DSSS

❖ HR-DSSS

❖ ERP

❖ OFDM

❖ HT

❖ VHT

2.1.3.   Identify the basic underlying concepts of how spread spectrum technology works, including modulation and coding.

2.1.4.   Identify and apply the concepts that make up the functionality of spread spectrum technology:
- ❖ co-location
- ❖ channel centers and widths (all PHYs)
- ❖ primary and secondary channels
- ❖ adjacent overlapping and non-overlapping channels
- ❖ carrier frequencies
- ❖ throughput vs. data rate
- ❖ bandwidth
- ❖ communication resilience
- ❖ Carrier Sense Multiple Access with Collision Avoidance (CSMA/CA)
- ❖ Physical carrier sense – clear channel assessment (CCA)
- ❖ virtual carrier sense (NAV)

2.2.   IEEE 802.11-2012 standard (as amended and including 802.11aa,   5, 6, 9, 19
802.11ac, 802.11ad, 802.11ae, and 802.11af).

2.2.1.   Identify, explain, and apply the basic frame types and frame exchange sequences covered by the IEEE 802.11-2012 standard.

2.2.2.   Identify and apply regulatory domain requirements:
- ❖ dynamic frequency selection (DFS)
- ❖ transmit power control (TPC)
- ❖ available channels
- ❖ output power

2.2.3.   Understand the OSI model layers affected by the 802.11-2012 standard and amendments.

2.2.4.   Use of ISM, U-NII, and licensed bands in Wi-Fi networks.

2.2.5.   Supported data rates for each IEEE 802.11-2012 (as amended to include 802.11ac) PHY.

2.2.6.   Understand the IEEE standard creation and ratification process and identify IEEE standard naming conventions.

IEEE 802.11 Protocols and Devices

3.1.3. Explain and apply the following power management features of WLANs:

❖ Active mode

❖ Power Save mode

❖ unscheduled automatic power save delivery (U-APSD)

❖ WMM Power Save (WMM-PS)

❖ Power Save Multi-Poll (PSMP)

❖ spatial multiplexing power save (SMPS)

❖ TIM/DTIM/ATIM

❖ VHT TXOP

3.2.   IEEE 802.11 MAC and PHY Layer Technologies   8, 9, 18, 19

3.2.1. Describe and apply the following concepts surrounding WLAN frames:

❖ IEEE 802.11 frame format vs. IEEE 802.3 frame format

❖ Define terminology related to the MAC & PHY

    ❖ Guard Interval (GI)

    ❖ PSDU, PPDU, and PPDU Formats

    ❖ MSDU and MPDU

    ❖ A-MPDU vs. A-MSDU

    ❖ 802.11 Frame Format and Types

    ❖ Interframe spaces (RIFS, SIFS, PIFS, DIFS, AIFS, EIFS)

    ❖ Block acknowledgments

    ❖ Fragmentation

❖ Jumbo frame support (layer 2)

❖ MTU discovery and functionality (layer 3)

3.2.2. Identify methods described in the IEEE 802.11-2012 standard for locating, joining, and maintaining connectivity with an IEEE 802.11 WLAN:

❖ active scanning (probes)

❖ passive scanning (beacons)

❖ dynamic rate switching (DRS)

3.2.3.   Define, describe, and apply IEEE 802.11 coordination functions and channel access methods and features available for optimizing data flow across the RF medium:

❖ DCF and HCF coordination functions

❖ EDCA channel access method

❖ RTS/CTS and CTS-to-Self protocols

❖ HT channel width operation

❖ HT protection mechanisms

❖ HT Operation Modes (0, 1, 2, 3)

❖ VHT channel width operation

❖ VHT protection mechanisms

❖ VHT Operating Mode field

3.3.   WLAN Infrastructure and Client Devices   10, 17

3.3.1.   Identify the purpose of the following WLAN infrastructure devices and describe how to install, configure, secure, and manage them:

❖ autonomous access points

❖ controller-based access points

❖ mesh access points/routers

❖ enterprise WLAN controllers

❖ distributed WLAN architectures

❖ remote office WLAN controllers and/or APs

❖ PoE injectors (single and multi-port) and PoE-enabled Ethernet switches

❖ WLAN bridges

❖ home and branch WLAN routers

3.3.2.   Describe the purpose of the following WLAN client adapters and explain how to install, configure, secure, and manage them:

❖ PC Cards (ExpressCard, CardBus, and PCMCIA)

❖ USB2/3

❖ PCI, Mini PCI, and Mini PCIe, and Half Mini PCIe cards

❖ workgroup bridges

IEEE 802.11 Network Implementation

IEEE 802.11 Network Security

Objective	Chapter

5.1.   IEEE 802.11 Network Security Architecture   13

5.1.1.   Identify and describe the strengths, weaknesses, appropriate uses, and implementation of the following IEEE 802.11 security-related items:

❖ weak security mechanisms
  ❖ WEP cipher suite
  ❖ open system authentication
  ❖ shared key authentication
  ❖ MAC filtering
  ❖ SSID hiding
❖ effective security mechanisms
  ❖ WPA-/WPA2-enterprise
  ❖ WPA-/WPA2-personal
  ❖ TKIP and CCMP cipher suites
  ❖ 802.1X/EAP framework
  ❖ preshared key (PSK)/passphrase authentication
  ❖ per-user preshared keys (PPSK)
  ❖ Wi-Fi protected setup (WPS)
❖ additional mechanisms
  ❖ secure device management protocols (HTTPS, SNMPv3, SSH2)
  ❖ role-based access control (RBAC)
  ❖ captive portals and guest networks
  ❖ protected management frames
  ❖ fast secure roaming methods

5.2.   IEEE 802.11 Network Security Analysis, Performance Analysis, and   14
Troubleshooting

5.2.1.   Describe, explain, and illustrate the appropriate applications for the following wireless security solutions from a monitoring, containment, and reporting perspective:

❖ wireless intrusion protection system (WIPS)
❖ protocol and spectrum analyzers

IEEE 802.11 RF Site Surveying

Objective	Chapter
6.1. IEEE 802.11 Network Site Survey Fundamentals	15

6.1.1.   Explain the importance of and the processes involved in information collection for manual and predictive RF site surveys:
- ❖ gathering business requirements
- ❖ interviewing managers and users
- ❖ defining physical and data security requirements
- ❖ gathering site-specific documentation
- ❖ documenting existing network characteristics
- ❖ gathering permits and zoning requirements
- ❖ indoor- or outdoor-specific information
- ❖ identifying infrastructure connectivity and power requirements
- ❖ understanding RF coverage requirements
- ❖ understanding data capacity and client density requirements
- ❖ VoWiFi considerations for delay and jitter
- ❖ client connectivity requirements
- ❖ antenna use considerations
- ❖ aesthetics requirements
- ❖ tracking system considerations
- ❖ WIPS sensor considerations

6.1.2.   Explain the technical aspects involved in performing manual and predictive RF site surveys:
- ❖ locating and identifying RF interference sources
- ❖ defining AP and antenna types to be used
- ❖ defining AP and antenna placement locations
- ❖ defining AP output power and channel assignments
- ❖ defining co-channel and adjacent-channel interference
- ❖ testing applications for proper operation
- ❖ measuring performance metrics according to design requirements

6.1.3.   Describe site survey reporting and follow-up procedures for manual and predictive RF site surveys:
- ❖ reporting methodology
- ❖ customer reporting requirements
- ❖ hardware recommendations and bills of material
- ❖ application analysis for capacity and coverage verification

Assessment Test

1. At which layers of the OSI model does 802.11 technology operate? (Choose all that apply.)
    A. Data-Link
    B. Network
    C. Physical
    D. Presentation
    E. Transport

2. Which Wi-Fi Alliance certification defines the mechanism for conserving battery life that is critical for handheld devices such as bar code scanners and VoWiFi phones?
    A. WPA2-Enterprise
    B. WPA2-Personal
    C. WMM-PS
    D. WMM-SA
    E. CWG-RF

3. Which of these frequencies has the longest wavelength?
    A. 750 KHz
    B. 2.4 GHz
    C. 252 GHz
    D. 2.4 MHz

4. Which of these terms can best be used to compare the relationship between two radio waves that share the same frequency?
    A. Multipath
    B. Multiplexing
    C. Phase
    D. Spread spectrum

5. A bridge transmits at 10 mW. The cable to the antenna produces a loss of 3 dB, and the antenna produces a gain of 20 dBi. What is the EIRP?
    A. 25 mW
    B. 27 mW
    C. 4 mW
    D. 1,300 mW
    E. 500 mW

6. dBi is an expression of what type of measurement?

   A. Access point gain

   B. Received power

   C. Transmitted power

   D. Antenna gain

7. What are some possible effects of voltage standing wave ratio (VSWR)? (Choose all that apply.)

   A. Increased amplitude

   B. Decreased signal strength

   C. Transmitter failure

   D. Erratic amplitude

   E. Out-of-phase signals

8. When installing a higher-gain omnidirectional antenna, which of the following occurs? (Choose two.)

   A. The horizontal coverage increases.

   B. The horizontal coverage decreases.

   C. The vertical coverage increases.

   D. The vertical coverage decreases.

9. 802.11a OFDM radios are backward compatible with which IEEE 802.11 radios?

   A. 802.11 legacy (FHSS) radios

   B. 802.11g (ERP) radios

   C. 802.11 legacy (DSSS) radios

   D. 802.11b (HR-DSSS) radios

   E. 802.11n (HT) radios

   F. None of the above

10. Which IEEE 802.11 amendment specifies the use of up to eight spatial streams of modulated data bits?

   A. IEEE 802.11n

   B. IEEE 802.11g

   C. IEEE 802.11ac

   D. IEEE 802.11s

   E. IEEE 802.11w

11. The FCC is preparing for the advent of 802.11ac technology that can use 80 MHz and 160 MHz channels, and therefore, more unlicensed spectrum is needed. What are the newly proposed 5 GHz frequency bands? (Choose all that apply.)

    A. U-NII-1

    B. U-NII-2A

    C. U-NII-2B

    D. U-NII-2C

    E. U-NII-3

    F. U-NII-4

12. What signal characteristics are common in spread spectrum signaling methods? (Choose two.)

    A. Narrow bandwidth

    B. Low power

    C. High power

    D. Wide bandwidth

13. A service set identifier is often synonymous with which of the following?

    A. IBSS

    B. ESSID

    C. BSSID

    D. BSS

14. Which ESS design scenario is defined by the IEEE 802.11-2012 standard?

    A. Two or more access points with overlapping coverage cells

    B. Two or more access points with overlapping disjointed coverage cells

    C. One access point with a single BSA

    D. Two basic service sets connected by a DS with co-located coverage cells

    E. None of the above

15. What CSMA/CA conditions must be met before an 802.11 radio can transmit? (Choose all that apply.)

    A. The NAV timer must be equal to zero.

    B. The random backoff timer must have expired.

    C. The CCA must be idle.

    D. The proper interframe space must have occurred.

    E. The access point must be in PCF mode.

16. Beacon management frames contain which of the following information? (Choose all that apply.)

   A. Channel information

   B. Destination IP address

   C. Basic data rate

   D. Traffic indication map (TIM)

   E. Vendor proprietary information

   F. Time stamp

   G. Spread spectrum parameter sets

17. Metka Dragos was hired to perform a wireless packet analysis of your network. While performing the analysis, she noticed that many of the data frames were preceded by an RTS frame followed by a CTS frame. What could cause this phenomenon to occur? (Choose all that apply.)

   A. Because of high RF noise levels, some of the stations have automatically enabled RTS/CTS.

   B. An AP was manually configured with a low RTS/CTS threshold.

   C. A nearby 802.11 FHSS radio is causing some of the nodes to enable a protection mechanism.

   D. The network is a mixed-mode environment.

18. What is another name for an 802.11 data frame that is also known as a PSDU?

   A. PPDU

   B. MSDU

   C. MPDU

   D. BPDU

19. Which WLAN device uses dynamic layer 2 routing protocols?

   A. WLAN switch

   B. WLAN controller

   C. WLAN VPN router

   D. WLAN mesh access point

20. What term best describes the bulk of the data generated on the Internet being created by sensors, monitors, and machines?

   A. Wearables

   B. Cloud-enabled networking (CEN)

   C. Cloud-based networking (CBN)

D. Software as a service (SaaS)

E. Internet of Things (IoT)

21. Wi-Fi technology is used in many different vertical markets. Which of these vertical markets use Wi-Fi for inventory control? (Choose all that apply.)

   A. Retail

   B. Manufacturing

   C. Education

   D. Law enforcement

   E. Hotspots

22. What term best describes how Wi-Fi can be used to identify customer behavior and shopping trends?

   A. Radio analytics

   B. Customer analytics

   C. Retail analytics

   D. 802.11 analytics

23. The hidden node problem occurs when one client station's transmissions are not heard by some of the other client stations in the coverage area of a basic service set (BSS). What are some of the consequences of the hidden node problem? (Choose all that apply.)

   A. Retransmissions

   B. Intersymbol interference (ISI)

   C. Collisions

   D. Increased throughput

   E. Decreased throughput

24. What are some potential causes of layer 2 retransmissions? (Choose all that apply.)

   A. RF interference

   B. Low signal-to-noise ratio (SNR)

   C. Dual-frequency transmissions

   D. Fade margin

   E. Multiplexing

25. Which of these solutions would be considered strong WLAN security?

   A. SSID cloaking

   B. MAC filtering

   C. WEP

   D. Shared Key authentication

   E. CCMP/AES

26. Which security standard defines port-based access control?

    A. IEEE 802.11x

    B. IEEE 802.3b

    C. IEEE 802.11i

    D. IEEE 802.1X

    E. IEEE 802.11s

27. Which is the best tool for detecting an RF jamming denial-of-service attack? (Choose all that apply.)

    A. Time-domain analysis software

    B. Layer 2 distributed WIPS

    C. Spectrum analyzer

    D. Layer 1 distributed WIPS

    E. Oscilloscope

28. Which of these attacks can be detected by a wireless intrusion detection system (WIDS)? (Choose all that apply.)

    A. Deauthentication spoofing

    B. MAC spoofing

    C. Rogue ad hoc network

    D. Association flood

    E. Rogue AP

29. You have been hired by the XYZ Company based in the United States for a wireless site survey. What government agencies need to be informed before a tower is installed of a height that exceeds 200 feet above ground level? (Choose all that apply.)

    A. RF regulatory authority

    B. Local municipality

    C. Fire department

    D. Tax authority

    E. Aviation authority

30. You have been hired by the ABC Corporation to conduct an indoor site survey. What information will be in the final site survey report that is delivered? (Choose two.)

    A. Security analysis

    B. Coverage analysis

    C. Spectrum analysis

    D. Routing analysis

    E. Switching analysis

31. Name potential sources of interference in the 5 GHz U-NII band. (Choose all that apply.)

    A. Perimeter sensors

    B. Nearby OFDM (802.11a) WLAN

    C. FM radio

    D. DSSS access point

    E. Bluetooth

    F. Nearby HT (802.11n) WLAN

32. Which of these measurements are taken for indoor coverage analysis? (Choose all that apply.)

    A. Received signal strength

    B. Signal-to-noise ratio

    C. Noise level

    D. Path loss

    E. Packet loss

33. Many 802.11ac enterprise access points require 802.3at power to be fully functional. What 802.11ac capabilities might be downgraded when using the lower power provided by 802.3af power sourcing equipment? (Choose all that apply.)

    A. MIMO radio chains

    B. 80 MHz channel capability

    C. 256-QAM modulation

    D. 40 MHz channel capability

34. What must a powered device (PD) do to be considered PoE compliant (IEEE 802.3-2005 Clause 33)? (Choose all that apply.)

    A. Be able to accept power in either of two ways (through the data lines or unused pairs).

    B. Reply with a classification signature.

    C. Reply with a 35 ohm detection signature.

    D. Reply with a 25 ohm detection signature.

    E. Receive 30 watts of power from the power sourcing equipment.

35. An 802.11n (HT) network can operate on which frequency bands? (Choose all that apply.)

    A. 902–928 MHz

    B. 2.4–2.4835 GHz

    C. 5.15–5.25 GHz

    D. 5.47–5.725 GHz

36. What are some of the methods used to reduce MAC layer overhead as defined by the 802.11n-2009 amendment? (Choose all that apply.)

    A. A-MSDU

    B. A-MPDU

    C. MCS

    D. PPDU

    E. MSDU

37. How many modulation and coding schemes (MCS) are defined by the 802.11ac-2013 amendment?

    A. 10

    B. 100

    C. 7

    D. 70

    E. 22

38. What capabilities defined by the 802.11n-2009 amendment are no longer defined by the 802.11ac-2013 amendment? (Choose all that apply.)

    A. Equal modulation

    B. Unequal modulation

    C. RIFS

    D. SIFS

    E. 40 MHz channels

39. What can be delivered over-the-air to WLAN mobile devices such as tablets and smart-phones when a mobile device management (MDM) solution is deployed?

    A. Configuration settings

    B. Applications

   C. Certificates

   D. Web clips

   E. All of the above

40. WLAN vendors have begun to offer the capability for guest users to log in to a guest WLAN with preexisting social media credentials, such as Facebook or Twitter usernames and passwords. What authorization framework can be used for social media login to WLAN guest networks?

   A. Kerberos

   B. RADIUS

   C. 802.1X/EAP

   D. OAuth

   E. TACACS

Answers to the Assessment Test

1. A and C. The IEEE 802.11-2012 standard defines communication mechanisms at only the Physical layer and MAC sublayer of the Data-Link layer of the OSI model. For more information, see Chapter 1.

2. C. WMM-PS helps conserve battery power for devices using Wi-Fi radios by managing the time the client device spends in sleep mode. Conserving battery life is critical for handheld devices such as bar code scanners and VoWiFi phones. To take advantage of power-saving capabilities, both the device and the access point must support WMM Power Save. For more information, see Chapter 1.

3. A. A 750 KHz signal has an approximate wavelength of 1,312 feet, or 400 meters. A 252 GHz signal has an approximate wavelength of less than 0.05 inches, or 1.2 millimeters. Remember, the higher the frequency of a signal, the smaller the wavelength property of an electromagnetic signal. For more information, see Chapter 2.

4. C. Phase involves the positioning of the amplitude crests and troughs of two waveforms. For more information, see Chapter 2.

5. E. The 10 mW of power is decreased by 3 dB, or divided by 2, giving 5 mW. This is then increased by 20 dBi, or multiplied by 10 twice, giving 500 mW. For more information, see Chapter 3.

6. D. Theoretically, an isotropic radiator can radiate an equal signal in all directions. An antenna cannot do this because of construction limitations. However, antennas are often referred to as isotropic radiators because they radiate RF energy. The gain, or increase, of power from an antenna when compared to what an isotropic radiator would generate is known as decibels isotropic (dBi). Another way of phrasing this is decibel gain referenced to an isotropic radiator, or change in power relative to an antenna. dBi is a measurement of antenna gain. For more information, see Chapter 3.

7. B, C and D. Reflected voltage caused by an impedance mismatch may cause a degradation of amplitude, erratic signal strength, or even the worst-case scenario of transmitter burnout. See Chapter 4 for more information.

8. A and D. When the gain of an omnidirectional antenna is increased, the vertical coverage area decreases while the horizontal coverage area is increased. See Chapter 4 for more information.

9. F. 802.11a (OFDM) radios transmit in the 5 GHz U-NII bands and are not compatible with 802.11 legacy (FHSS) radios, 802.11 legacy (DSSS) radios, 802.11b (HR-DSSS) radios, or 802.11g (ERP) radios, which transmit in the 2.4 GHz ISM frequency band. 802.11a (OFDM) radios are forward compatible but not backward compatible with 802.11n (HT) radios. 802.11n radios, which can transmit on either frequency band, are backward compatible with 802.11a radios as well as 802.11g (ERP), 802.11b (HR-DSSS), and 802.11 legacy (DSSS) radios. None of these radio technologies are backward compatible with 802.11 legacy (FHSS) radios. For more information, see Chapter 5.

10. C. The 802.11ac-2013 amendment defines the use of 256-QAM modulation, up to eight spatial streams, multiuser MIMO, 80 MHz channels, and 160 MHz channels. 802.11 MIMO technology and 40 MHz channels debuted with the ratification of the 802.11n-2009 amendment. For more information, see Chapter 5.

11. C and F. In January 2013, the FCC announced that 195 MHz of additional spectrum space would be made available for unlicensed use. A new 120 MHz wide band called U-NII-2B, which occupies the frequency space of 5.35 GHz–5.47 GHz, and another new 75 MHz wide band called U-NII-4 occupies the 5.85 GHz–5.925 GHz frequency space. See Chapter 6 for more information.

12. B and D. A spread spectrum signal utilizes bandwidth that is wider than what is required to carry the data and has low transmission power requirements. See Chapter 6 for more information.

13. B. The logical network name of a wireless LAN is often called an ESSID (extended service set identifier) and is essentially synonymous with SSID (service set identifier), which is another term for a logical network name in the most common deployments of a WLAN. For more information, see Chapter 7.

14. E. The scenarios described in options A, B, C, and D are all examples of how an extended service set may be deployed. The IEEE 802.11-2012 standard defines an extended service set (ESS) as "a set of one or more interconnected basic service sets." However, the IEEE 802.11-2012 standard does not mandate any of the examples given in the options. For more information, see Chapter 7.

15. A, B, C and D. Carrier Sense Multiple Access with Collision Avoidance (CSMA/CA) is a medium access method that utilizes multiple checks and balances to try to minimize collisions. These checks and balances can also be thought of as several lines of defense. The various lines of defense are put in place to hopefully ensure that only one radio is transmitting while all other radios are listening. The four lines of defense include the network allocation vector, the random backoff timer, the clear channel assessment, and interframe spacing. For more information, see Chapter 8.

16. A, C, D, E, F and G. The only information not contained in the beacon management frame is the destination IP address. The body of all 802.11 management frames contain only layer 2 information; therefore, IP information is not included in the frame. Other information that is included in a beacon includes security and QoS parameters. For more information, see Chapter 9.

17. B and D. AP radios can be manually configured to use RTS/CTS for all transmissions. This is usually done to diagnose hidden node problems. This network could also be a mixed-mode 802.11b (HR-DSSS) and 802.11g (ERP) network. The 802.11g nodes have enabled RTS/CTS as their protection mechanism. For more information, see Chapter 9.

18. C. The technical name for an 802.11 data frame is MAC Protocol Data Unit (MPDU). An MPDU contains a layer 2 header, a frame body, and a trailer that is a 32-bit CRC known as the frame check sequence (FCS). Inside the frame body of an MPDU is a MAC Service Data Unit (MSDU), which contains data from the LLC and layers 3–7. For more information, see Chapter 9.

19. D. WLAN mesh access points create a self-forming WLAN mesh network that automatically connects access points at installation and dynamically updates routes as more clients are added. Most WLAN mesh networks use dynamic layer 2 routing protocols with metrics such as RSSI, SNR, and client load. For more information, see Chapter 10.

20. E. Over the years, most of the data generated on the Internet has been created by human beings. The theory of Internet of Things (IoT) is that in the future, the bulk of the data generated on the Internet might be created by sensors, monitors, and machines. 802.11 radio NICs used as client devices have begun to show up in many types of machines and devices. For more information, see Chapter 10.

21. A and B. Warehouse, manufacturing, and retail environments often deploy wireless handheld devices, such as bar code scanners, which are used for inventory control. For more information, see Chapter 11.

22. C. To further support and understand customers and their behaviors, retail analytic products are being installed to monitor customer movement and behavior. Strategically placed access points or sensor devices listen for probe frames from Wi-Fi-enabled smartphones. MAC addresses are used to identify each unique device, and signal strength is used to monitor and track the location of the shopper. Retail analytics can identify the path the shopper took while walking through the store, along with the time spent in different areas of the store. This information can be used to identify shopping patterns and to analyze the effectiveness of in-store displays and advertisements. For more information, see Chapter 11.

23. A, C and E. The stations that cannot hear the hidden node will transmit at the same time that the hidden node is transmitting. This will result in continuous transmission collisions in a half-duplex medium. Collisions will corrupt the frames and they will need to be retransmitted. Any time retransmissions are necessary, more overhead is added to the medium, resulting in decreased throughput. Intersymbol interference is a result of multipath and not the hidden node problem. For more information, see Chapter 12.

24. A and B. Layer 2 retransmissions can be caused by many different variables in a WLAN environment. Multipath, RF interference, hidden nodes, adjacent cell interference, and low signal-to-noise ratio (SNR) are all possible causes of layer 2 retransmissions. For more information, see Chapter 12.

25. E. Although you can hide your SSID to cloak the identity of your wireless network from script kiddies and nonhackers, it should be clearly understood that SSID cloaking is by no means an end-all wireless security solution. Because of spoofing and because of all the administrative work that is involved, MAC filtering is not considered a reliable means of security for wireless enterprise networks. WEP and Shared Key authentication are legacy 802.11 security solutions. CCMP/AES is defined as the default encryption type by the IEEE 802.11i security amendment. Cracking the AES cipher would take the lifetime of the sun using the tools that are available today. For more information, see Chapter 13.

26. D. The IEEE 802.1X standard is not specifically a wireless standard and often is mistakenly referred to as IEEE 802.11x. The IEEE 802.1X standard is a port-based access control standard. IEEE 802.1X provides an authorization framework that allows or disallows traffic to pass through a port and thereby access network resources. For more information, see Chapter 13.

27. C and D. Although the layer 2 wireless intrusion detection and prevention products might be able to detect some RF jamming attacks, the only tool that will absolutely identify an interfering signal is a spectrum analyzer. A spectrum analyzer is a frequency domain tool that can detect any RF signal in the frequency range that is being scanned. Layer 1 distributed spectrum analysis is now available in some WIPS enterprise solutions. For more information, see Chapter 14.

28. A, B, C, D and E. 802.11 wireless intrusion detection systems may be able to monitor for as many as 100 or more attacks. Any layer 2 DoS attack and spoofing attack and most rogue devices can be detected. For more information, see Chapter 14.

29. A, B and E. In the United States, if any tower exceeds a height of 200 feet above ground level (AGL), you must contact both the FCC and FAA, which are communications and aviation regulatory authorities. Other countries will have similar height restrictions, and the proper RF regulatory authority and aviation authority must be contacted to find out the details. Local municipalities may have construction regulations and a permit may be required. For more information, see Chapter 15.

30. B and C. The final site survey report, known as the deliverable, will contain spectrum analysis information identifying potential sources of interference. Coverage analysis will also define RF cell boundaries. The final report also contains recommended access point placement, configuration settings, and antenna orientation. Capacity planning is considered to be mandatory when designing a WLAN; however, application throughput testing is often an optional analysis report included in the final survey report. Security, switching, and routing analysis are not included in a site survey report. For more information, see Chapter 15.

31. A, B and F. Nearby 802.11a (OFDM) WLAN and perimeter sensors both transmit in the 5 GHz U-NII bands. 802.11n (HT) WLAN radios can transmit at either 2.4 or 5 GHz. A nearby 802.11n WLAN operating at 5 GHz can potentially be a source of interference. DSSS access points and Bluetooth devices transmit in the 2.4 GHz frequency space. FM radios transmit in licensed frequencies. For more information, see Chapter 16.

32. A, B, C and E. RF coverage cell measurements that are taken during an indoor passive site survey include received signal strength, noise levels, signal-to-noise ratio (SNR), and data rates. Packet loss can be an additional measurement recorded during an active manual site survey. Packet loss is a calculation needed for an outdoor wireless bridging survey. For more information, see Chapter 16.

33. A, B and C. The most common method is to downgrade the MIMO capability of the 802.11ac access points so that 802.3af power can be used. 802.11ac APs with 3×3 transmitter capability might use only one or two transmitters when using 802.3af PoE and therefore conserve power. The downside is that not all of the MIMO transmitter capabilities are being used by the APs. Other vendors have chosen to disable processor-intensive 802.11ac functions such as 80 MHz channel capability and the use of more complex modulation. In other words, the 802.11ac 3×3:3 MIMO radio can still use all three transmitters but effectively the radio functions as an 802.11n radio when using the lower 802.3af power. Newer generation 802.11ac 3×3:3 MIMO radios can be fully powered by 802.3af PoE without any downgrade of functionality. For more information, see Chapter 19.

34. A and D. For a powered device (PD) such as an access point to be considered compliant with the IEEE 802.3-2005 Clause 33 PoE standard, the device must be able to receive power through the data lines or the unused twisted pairs of an Ethernet cable. The PD must also reply to the power-sourcing equipment (PSE) with a 25 ohm detection signature. The PD may reply with a classification signature, but it is optional. The current PoE standard allows for a maximum draw of 12.95 watts by the PD from the power-sourcing equipment. For more information, see Chapter 17.

35. B, C and D. High Throughput (HT) technology is defined by the IEEE 802.11n-2009 amendment and is not frequency dependent. 802.11n (HT) can operate in the 2.4 GHz ISM band as well as all of the 5 GHz U-NII frequency bands. For more information, see Chapter 18.

36. A and B. The 802.11n-2009 amendment introduced two new methods of frame aggregation to help reduce the overhead. Frame aggregation is a method of combining multiple frames into a single frame transmission. The first method of frame aggregation is known as an Aggregate MAC Service Data Unit (A-MSDU). The second method of frame aggregation is known as an Aggregate MAC Protocol Data Unit (A-MPDU). For more information, see Chapter 18.

37. A. The 802.11n-2009 amendment defined over 70 modulation and coding schemes (MCSs). The 802.11ac-2013 amendment lowers the number to 10. The 802.11ac data rates are determined by the number of spatial streams, guard interval, and which one of the 10 MCS is used. For more information, see Chapter 19.

38. B and C. Reduced interframe spacing (RIFS), unequal modulation, Greenfield mode, and implicit beamforming are 802.11n capabilities that are no longer defined with the advent of the 802.11ac amendment. For more information, see Chapter 19.

39. E. Mobile device management (MDM) solutions can be used for both a company-issued device (CID) and a bring your own device (BYOD), which is owned by an employee. MDM solutions offer the capability of over-the-air installation and distribution of security certificates, web clips, applications, and configuration settings. For more information, see Chapter 20.

40. D. The OAuth 2.0 authorization framework enables a third-party application to obtain limited access to an HTTP service and is often used for social login for Wi-Fi guest networks. For more information, see Chapter 20.

Chapter

1

Overview of Wireless Standards, Organizations, and Fundamentals

---

IN THIS CHAPTER, YOU WILL LEARN ABOUT THE FOLLOWING:

✓ **History of WLAN**

✓ **Standards organizations**

  ▪ Federal Communications Commission

  ▪ International Telecommunication Union Radiocommunication Sector

  ▪ Institute of Electrical and Electronics Engineers

  ▪ Internet Engineering Task Force

  ▪ Wi-Fi Alliance

  ▪ International Organization for Standardization

✓ **Core, distribution, and access**

✓ **Communications fundamentals**

Wireless local area network (WLAN) technology has a long history that dates back to the 1970s with roots as far back as the 19th century. This chapter will start with a brief history of WLAN technology. Learning a new technology can seem like a daunting task. There are so many new acronyms, abbreviations, terms, and ideas to become familiar with. One of the keys to learning any subject is to learn the basics. Whether you are learning to drive a car, fly an airplane, or install a wireless computer network, there are basic rules, principles, and concepts that, once learned, provide the building blocks for the rest of your education.

The Institute of Electrical and Electronics Engineers (IEEE) 802.11 technology, more commonly referred to as Wi-Fi, is a standard technology for providing local area network (LAN) communications using radio frequencies (RFs). The IEEE designated the 802.11-2012 standard as a guideline to provide operational parameters for WLANs. There are numerous standards organizations and regulatory bodies that help govern and direct wireless technologies and the related industry. Having some knowledge of these various organizations can provide you with insight as to how IEEE 802.11 functions, and sometimes even how and why the standards have evolved the way they have.

As you become more knowledgeable about wireless networking, you may want or need to read some of the standards documents that are created by the different organizations. Along with the information about the standards bodies, this chapter includes a brief overview of their documents.

In addition to reviewing the various standards organizations that guide and regulate Wi-Fi, this chapter discusses where WLAN technology fits in with basic networking design fundamentals. Finally, this chapter reviews some fundamentals of communications and data keying that are not part of the CWNA exam but that may help you better understand wireless communications.

History of WLAN

In the 19th century, numerous inventors and scientists, including Michael Faraday, James Clerk Maxwell, Heinrich Rudolf Hertz, Nikola Tesla, David Edward Hughes, Thomas Edison, and Guglielmo Marconi, began to experiment with wireless communications. These innovators discovered and created many theories about the concepts of electrical magnetic *radio frequency (RF)*.

Wireless networking technology was first used by the US military during World War II to transmit data over an RF medium using classified encryption technology to send battle plans across enemy lines. The *spread spectrum* radio technologies often used in today's

WLANs were also originally patented during the era of World War II, although they were not implemented until almost two decades later.

In 1970, the University of Hawaii developed the first wireless network, called ALOHAnet, to wirelessly communicate data between the Hawaiian Islands. The network used a LAN communication Open Systems Interconnection (OSI) layer 2 protocol called ALOHA on a wireless shared medium in the 400 MHz frequency range. The technology used in ALOHAnet is often credited as a building block for the Medium Access Control (MAC) technologies of Carrier Sense Multiple Access with Collision Detection (CSMA/CD) used in Ethernet and Carrier Sense Multiple Access with Collision Avoidance (CSMA/CA) used in 802.11 radios. You will learn more about CSMA/CA in Chapter 8, "802.11 Medium Access."

In the 1990s, commercial networking vendors began to produce low-speed wireless data networking products, most of which operated in the 900 MHz frequency band. The Institute of Electrical and Electronics Engineers (IEEE) began to discuss standardizing WLAN technologies in 1991. In 1997, the IEEE ratified the original 802.11 standard that is the foundation of the WLAN technologies that you will be learning about in this book.

This legacy 802.11 technology was deployed between 1997 and 1999 mostly in warehousing and manufacturing environments for the use of low-speed data collection with wireless barcode scanners. In 1999, the IEEE defined higher data speeds with the 802.11b amendment. The introduction of data rates as high as 11 Mbps, along with price decreases, ignited the sales of wireless home networking routers in the small office, home office (SOHO) marketplace. Home users soon became accustomed to wireless networking in their homes and began to demand that their employers also provide wireless networking capabilities in the workplace. After initial resistance to 802.11 technology, small companies, medium-sized businesses, and corporations began to realize the value of deploying 802.11 wireless networking in their enterprises.

If you ask the average user about their 802.11 wireless network, they may give you a strange look. The name that people often recognize for the technology is *Wi-Fi*. Wi-Fi is a marketing term, recognized worldwide by millions of people as referring to 802.11 wireless networking.

What Does the Term *Wi-Fi* Mean?

Many people mistakenly assume that *Wi-Fi* is an acronym for the phrase *wireless fidelity* (much like *hi-fi* is short for *high fidelity*), but Wi-Fi is simply a brand name used to market 802.11 WLAN technology. Ambiguity in IEEE framework standards for wireless communications allowed manufacturers to interpret the 802.11 standard in different ways. As a result, multiple vendors could have IEEE 802.11–compliant devices that did not interoperate with each other. The organization Wireless Ethernet Compatibility Alliance (WECA) was created to further define the IEEE standard in such a way as to force interoperability between vendors. WECA, now known as the Wi-Fi Alliance, chose the term *Wi-Fi* as a marketing brand. The Wi-Fi Alliance champions enforcing interoperability among wireless devices. To be Wi-Fi compliant, vendors must send their products to a Wi-Fi Alliance test lab that thoroughly tests compliance to the Wi-Fi certification. More information about the origins of the term Wi-Fi can be found online at Wi-Fi Net News:

http://wifinetnews.com/archives/2005/11/wi-fi_stands_fornothing_and_everything.html

Wi-Fi radios are used for numerous enterprise applications and can also be found in laptops, smartphones, cameras, televisions, printers, and many other consumer devices. According to the Wi-Fi Alliance, the billionth Wi-Fi chipset was sold in 2009. Less than 4 years later in 2012, annual shipments of Wi-Fi devices are more than 1.75 billion and continuing to grow, with estimates of annual shipments doubling to over 3.5 billion Wi-Fi chipsets by 2017. In a survey that the Wi-Fi Alliance conducted, 68 percent of Wi-Fi users would rather give up chocolate than do without Wi-Fi. Since the original standard was created in 1997, 802.11 technology has grown to enormous proportions; Wi-Fi has become part of our worldwide communications culture. A recent report from Telecom Advisory Services estimates that technologies that rely on unlicensed spectrum adds $222 billion dollars per year to the U.S. economy. Over $91 billion dollars can be attributed to Wi-Fi.

Standards Organizations

Each of the standards organizations discussed in this chapter help to guide a different aspect of the wireless networking industry.

The International Telecommunication Union Radiocommunication Sector (ITU-R) and local entities such as the Federal Communications Commission (FCC) set the rules for what the user can do with a radio transmitter. These organizations manage and regulate frequencies, power levels, and transmission methods. They also work together to help guide the growth and expansion that is being demanded by wireless users.

The Institute of Electrical and Electronics Engineers (IEEE) creates standards for compatibility and coexistence between networking equipment. The IEEE standards must adhere to the rules of the communications organizations, such as the FCC.

The Internet Engineering Task Force (IETF) is responsible for creating Internet standards. Many of these standards are integrated into the wireless networking and security protocols and standards.

The Wi-Fi Alliance performs certification testing to make sure wireless networking equipment conforms to the 802.11 WLAN communication guidelines, which are similar to the IEEE 802.11-2012 standard.

The International Organization for Standardization (ISO) created the Open Systems Interconnection (OSI) model, which is an architectural model for data communications.

You will look at each of these organizations in the following sections.

Federal Communications Commission

To put it simply, the *Federal Communications Commission (FCC)* regulates communications within the United States as well as communications to and from the United States. Established by the Communications Act of 1934, the FCC is responsible for regulating interstate and international communications by radio, television, wire, satellite, and cable. The task of the FCC in wireless networking is to regulate the radio signals that are used for wireless networking. The FCC has jurisdiction over the 50 states, the District of Columbia, and US possessions. Most countries have governing bodies that function similarly to the FCC.

The FCC and the respective controlling agencies in other countries typically regulate two categories of wireless communications: licensed spectrum and unlicensed spectrum. The difference is that unlicensed users do not have to go through the license application procedures before they can install a wireless system. Both licensed and unlicensed communications are typically regulated in the following five areas:

- Frequency
- Bandwidth
- Maximum power of the intentional radiator (IR)
- Maximum equivalent isotropically radiated power (EIRP)
- Use (indoor and/or outdoor)
- Spectrum sharing rules

 Real World Scenario

What Are the Advantages and Disadvantages of Using an Unlicensed Frequency?

As stated earlier, licensed frequencies require an approved license application, and the financial costs are typically very high. One main advantage of an unlicensed frequency is that permission to transmit on the frequency is free. Although there are no financial costs, you still must abide by transmission regulations and other restrictions. In other words, transmitting in an unlicensed frequency may be free, but there still are rules.

The main disadvantage to transmitting in an unlicensed frequency band is that anyone else can also transmit in that same frequency space. Unlicensed frequency bands are often very crowded; therefore, transmissions from other individuals can cause interference with your transmissions. If someone else is interfering with your transmissions, you have no legal recourse as long as the other individual is abiding by the rules and regulations of the unlicensed frequency.

Essentially, the FCC and other regulatory bodies set the rules for what the user can do regarding RF transmissions. From there, the standards organizations create the standards to work within these guidelines. These organizations work together to help meet the demands of the fast-growing wireless industry.

The FCC rules are published in the Code of Federal Regulations (CFR). The CFR is divided into 50 titles that are updated yearly. The title that is relevant to wireless networking is Title 47, *Telecommunications*. Title 47 is divided into many parts; Part 15, "Radio Frequency Devices," is where you will find the rules and regulations regarding wireless networking related to 802.11. Part 15 is further broken down into subparts and sections. A complete reference will look like this example: 47CFR15.3.

International Telecommunication Union Radiocommunication Sector

A global hierarchy exists for management of the RF spectrum worldwide. The United Nations has tasked the *International Telecommunication Union Radiocommunication Sector (ITU-R)* with global spectrum management. The ITU-R strives to ensure interference-free communications on land, sea, and in the skies. The ITU-R maintains a database of worldwide frequency assignments through five administrative regions.

The five administrative regions are broken down as follows:

Region A: The Americas   Inter-American Telecommunication Commission (CITEL)

> www.citel.oas.org

Region B: Western Europe   European Conference of Postal and Telecommunications Administrations (CEPT)

> www.cept.org

Region C: Eastern Europe and Northern Asia   Regional Commonwealth in the field of Communications (RCC)

> www.en.rcc.org.ru

Region D: Africa   African Telecommunications Union (ATU)

> www.atu-uat.org

Region E: Asia and Australasia   Asia-Pacific Telecommunity (APT)

> www.aptsec.org

In addition to the five administrative regions, the ITU-R defines three radio regulatory regions. These three regions are defined geographically, as shown in the following list. You should check an official ITU-R map to identify the exact boundaries of each region.

- Region 1: Europe, Middle East, and Africa
- Region 2: Americas
- Region 3: Asia and Oceania

The ITU-R radio regulation documents are part of an international treaty governing the use of spectrum. Within each of these regions, the ITU-R allocates and allots frequency bands and radio channels that are allowed to be used, along with the conditions regarding their use. Within each region, local government RF regulatory bodies, such as the following, manage the RF spectrum for their respective countries:

Australia   Australian Communications and Media Authority (ACMA)

Japan   Association of Radio Industries and Businesses (ARIB)

New Zealand   Ministry of Economic Development

United States   Federal Communications Commission (FCC)

It is important to understand that communications are regulated differently in many regions and countries. For example, European RF regulations are very different from the regulations used in North America. When deploying a WLAN, please take the time to learn about rules and policies of the local *regulatory domain authority*. However, since the rules vary around the globe, it is beyond the capabilities of this book to reference the different regulations. Additionally, the CWNA exam will not reference the RF regulations of the FCC or those specific to any other country.

> More information about the ITU-R can be found at www.itu.int/ITU-R.

Institute of Electrical and Electronics Engineers

The *Institute of Electrical and Electronics Engineers*, commonly known as the *IEEE*, is a global professional society with about 400,000 members in 160 countries. The IEEE's mission is to "foster technological innovation and excellence for the benefit of humanity." To networking professionals, that means creating the standards that we use to communicate.

The IEEE is probably best known for its LAN standards, the IEEE 802 project.

> The 802 project is one of many IEEE projects; however, it is the only IEEE project addressed in this book.

IEEE projects are subdivided into working groups to develop standards that address specific problems or needs. For instance, the IEEE 802.3 working group was responsible for the creation of a standard for Ethernet, and the IEEE 802.11 working group was responsible for creating the WLAN standard. The numbers are assigned as the groups are formed, so the 11 assigned to the wireless group indicates that it was the 11th working group formed under the IEEE 802 project.

As the need arises to revise existing standards created by the working groups, task groups are formed. These task groups are assigned a sequential single letter (multiple letters are assigned if all single letters have been used) that is added to the end of the standard number (for example, 802.11a, 802.11g, and 802.3at). Some letters are not assigned. For example *o* and *l* are not assigned to prevent confusion with the numbers 0 and 1. Other letters may not be assigned to task groups to prevent confusion with other standards. For example, 802.11x has not been assigned because it can be easily confused with the 802.1X standard and because 802.11*x* has become a common casual reference to the 802.11 family of standards.

> You can find more information about the IEEE at www.ieee.org.

It is important to remember that the IEEE standards, like many other standards, are written documents describing how technical processes and equipment should function. Unfortunately, this often allows for different interpretations when the standard is being implemented, so it is common for early products to be incompatible between vendors, as was the case with some of the early 802.11 products.

> The history of the 802.11 standard and amendments is covered extensively in Chapter 5, "IEEE 802.11 Standards." The CWNA exam (CWNA-106) is based on the most recently published version of the standard, 802.11-2012. The 802.11-2012 standard can be downloaded from
>
> http://standards.ieee.org/about/get/802/802.11.html

Internet Engineering Task Force

The *Internet Engineering Task Force*, commonly known as the *IETF*, is an international community of people in the networking industry whose goal is to make the Internet work better. The mission of the IETF, as defined by the organization in a document known as RFC 3935, is "to produce high quality, relevant technical and engineering documents that influence the way people design, use, and manage the Internet in such a way as to make the Internet work better. These documents include protocol standards, best current practices, and informational documents of various kinds." The IETF has no membership fees, and anyone may register for and attend an IETF meeting.

The IETF is one of five main groups that are part of the Internet Society (ISOC). The ISOC groups include the following:

- Internet Engineering Task Force (IETF)
- Internet Architecture Board (IAB)
- Internet Corporation for Assigned Names and Numbers (ICANN)
- Internet Engineering Steering Group (IESG)
- Internet Research Task Force (IRTF)

The IETF is broken into eight subject matter areas: Applications, General, Internet, Operations and Management, Real-Time Applications and Infrastructure, Routing, Security, and Transport. Figure 1.1 shows the hierarchy of the ISOC and a breakdown of the IETF subject matter areas.

FIGURE 1.1   ISOC hierarchy

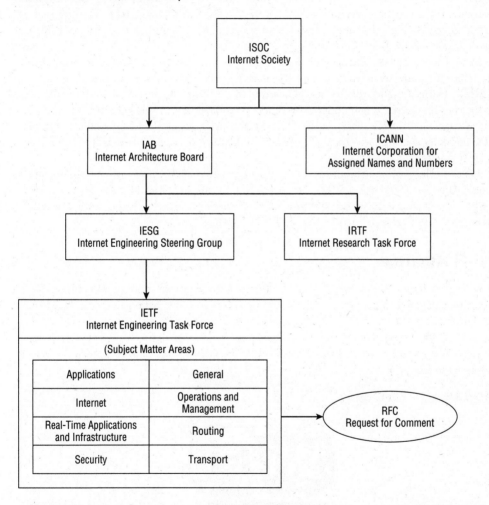

The IESG provides technical management of the activities of the IETF and the Internet standards process. The IETF is made up of a large number of groups, each addressing specific topics. An IETF working group is created by the IESG and is given a specific charter or specific topic to address. There is no formal voting process for the working groups. Decisions in working groups are made by rough consensus, or basically a general sense of agreement among the working group.

The results of a working group are usually the creation of a document known as a *Request for Comments (RFC)*. Contrary to its name, an RFC is not actually a request for comments, but a statement or definition. Most RFCs describe network protocols, services, or policies and may evolve into an Internet standard. RFCs are numbered sequentially, and once a number is assigned, it is never reused. RFCs may be updated or supplemented by higher-numbered RFCs. As an example, Mobile IPv4 was described in RFC 3344 in 2002. This document was updated in RFC 4721. In 2012, RFC 5944 made RFC 3344 obsolete. At the top of the RFC document, it states whether the RFC is updated by another RFC and also if it makes any other RFCs obsolete.

Not all RFCs are standards. Each RFC is given a status, relative to its relationship with the Internet standardization process: Informational, Experimental, Standards Track, or Historic. If it is a Standards Track RFC, it could be a Proposed Standard, Draft Standard, or Internet Standard. When an RFC becomes a standard, it still keeps its RFC number, but it is also given an "STD *xxxx*" label. The relationship between the STD numbers and the RFC numbers is not one-to-one. STD numbers identify protocols, whereas RFC numbers identify documents.

Many of the protocol standards, best current practices, and informational documents produced by the IETF affect WLAN security. In Chapter 13, "802.11 Network Security Architecture," you will learn about some of the varieties of the Extensible Authentication Protocol (EAP) that is defined by the IETF RFC 3748.

Wi-Fi Alliance

The *Wi-Fi Alliance* is a global, nonprofit industry association of more than 550 member companies devoted to promoting the growth of WLANs. One of the primary tasks of the Wi-Fi Alliance is to market the Wi-Fi brand and raise consumer awareness of new 802.11 technologies as they become available. Because of the Wi-Fi Alliance's overwhelming marketing success, the majority of the worldwide Wi-Fi users are likely to recognize the Wi-Fi logo seen in Figure 1.2.

FIGURE 1.2   Wi-Fi logo

The Wi-Fi Alliance's main task is to ensure the interoperability of WLAN products by providing certification testing. During the early days of the 802.11 standard, the Wi-Fi

Alliance further defined some of the ambiguous standards requirements and provided a set of guidelines to ensure compatibility between different vendors. This is still done to help simplify the complexity of the standards and to ensure compatibility. As seen in Figure 1.3, products that pass the Wi-Fi certification process receive a Wi-Fi Interoperability Certificate that provides detailed information about the individual product's Wi-Fi certifications.

FIGURE 1.3   Wi-Fi Interoperability Certificate

The Wi-Fi Alliance, originally named the Wireless Ethernet Compatibility Alliance (WECA), was founded in August 1999. The name was changed to the Wi-Fi Alliance in October 2002.

The Wi-Fi Alliance has certified more than 15,000 Wi-Fi products for interoperability since testing began in April 2000. Multiple Wi-Fi CERTIFIED programs exist that cover basic connectivity, security, quality of service (QoS), and more. Testing of vendor Wi-Fi products is performed in independent authorized test laboratories in eight countries. A listing of these testing laboratories can be found on the Wi-Fi Alliance's website. The guidelines for interoperability for each Wi-Fi CERTIFIED program are usually based on key components and functions that are defined in the IEEE 802.11-2012 standard and various 802.11 amendments. In fact, many of the same engineers who belong to 802.11 task groups are also contributing members of the Wi-Fi Alliance. However, it is important to understand that the IEEE and the Wi-Fi Alliance are two separate organizations. The IEEE 802.11 task group defines the WLAN standards, and the Wi-Fi Alliance defines interoperability certification programs. The Wi-Fi CERTIFIED programs include the following:

Core Technology and Security   The core technology and security program certifies 802.11a, b, g, n, and/or ac interoperability to ensure that the essential wireless data transmission works as expected. Each device is tested according to its capabilities. Table 1.1 lists the five different core Wi-Fi transmission technologies along with the frequencies and maximum data rate that each is capable of.

TABLE 1.1   Five generations of Wi-Fi

Wi-Fi technology	Frequency band	Maximum data rate
802.11a	5 GHz	54 Mbps
802.11b	2.4 GHz	11 Mbps
802.11g	2.4 GHz	54 Mbps
802.11n	2.4 GHz, 5 GHz, 2.4 or 5 GHz (selectable), or 2.4 and 5 GHz (concurrent)	450 Mbps
802.11ac	5 GHz	1.3 Gbps

Each certified product is required to support one frequency band as a minimum, but it can support both.

Although 802.11n specifies data rates of up to 600 Mbps, and 802.11ac specifies data rates of up to 6.93 Gbps, as of this writing, equipment to support these maximum data rates had not been developed yet. Therefore, the Wi-Fi certification tests do not test up to the maximum 802.11n or 802.11ac specified data rates.

In addition to having the required transmission capabilities, each device must support *robust security network (RSN)* capabilities, security mechanisms that were originally defined in the IEEE 802.11i amendment. Devices must support Wi-Fi Protected Access (WPA) and Wi-Fi Protected Access 2 (WPA2) security mechanisms for personal (WPA2-Personal) or enterprise (WPA2-Enterprise) environments. Additionally, enterprise devices must support *Extensible Authentication Protocol (EAP)*, which is used to validate the identity of the wireless device or user. In 2012, support for Protected Management Frames extended WPA2 protection to unicast and multicast management action frames. You will find a more detailed discussion of WPA and WPA2 security in Chapter 13, "802.11 Network Security Architecture."

Wi-Fi Multimedia   Wi-Fi Multimedia (WMM) is based on the QoS mechanisms that were originally defined in the IEEE 802.11e amendment. WMM enables Wi-Fi networks to prioritize traffic generated by different applications. In a network where WMM is supported by both the access point and the client device, traffic generated by time-sensitive applications such as voice or video can be prioritized for transmission on the half-duplex RF medium. WMM certification is mandatory for all core certified devices that support 802.11n. WMM certification is optional for core certified devices that support 802.11 a, b, or g. WMM mechanisms are discussed in greater detail in Chapter 9, "MAC Architecture."

WMM Power Save   WMM Power Save (WMM-PS) helps conserve battery power for devices using Wi-Fi radios by managing the time the client device spends in sleep mode. Conserving battery life is critical for handheld devices such as barcode scanners and voice over Wi-Fi (VoWiFi) phones. To take advantage of power-saving capabilities, both the device and the access point must support WMM Power Save. WMM-PS and legacy power-saving mechanisms are discussed in greater detail in Chapter 9.

Wi-Fi Protected Setup   Wi-Fi Protected Setup defines simplified and automatic WPA and WPA2 security configurations for home and small-business users. Users can easily configure a network with security protection by using either near field communication (NFC), a personal identification number (PIN) or a button located on the access point and the client device.

Wi-Fi Direct   Wi-Fi Direct enables Wi-Fi devices to connect directly without the use of an access point, making it easier to print, share, synch, and display. Wi-Fi Direct is ideal for mobile phones, cameras, printers, PCs, and gaming devices needing to establish a one-to-one connection, or even connecting a small group of devices. Wi-Fi Direct is simple to configure (in some cases as easy as pressing a button), provides the same performance and range as other Wi-Fi certified devices, and is secured using WPA2 security.

Converged Wireless Group-RF Profile   Converged Wireless Group-RF Profile (CWG-RF) was developed jointly by the Wi-Fi Alliance and the Cellular Telecommunications and Internet Association (CTIA), now known as The Wireless Association. CWG-RF defines performance metrics for Wi-Fi and cellular radios in a converged handset to help ensure that both technologies perform well in the presence of the other. All CTIA-certified handsets now include this certification.

Voice Personal   Voice Personal offers enhanced support for voice applications in residential and small-business Wi-Fi networks. These networks include one access point, mixed voice and data traffic from multiple devices (such as phones, PCs, printers, and other consumer electronic devices), and support for up to four concurrent phone calls. Both the access point and the client device must be certified to achieve performance matching the certification metrics.

Voice Enterprise   Voice Enterprise offers enhanced support for voice applications in enterprise Wi-Fi networks. Enterprise-grade voice equipment must provide consistently good voice quality under all network load conditions and coexist with data traffic. Both access point and client devices must support prioritization using WMM, with voice traffic being placed in the highest-priority queue (Access Category Voice, AC_VO). Voice Enterprise equipment must also support seamless roaming between APs, WPA2-Enterprise security, optimization of power through the WMM-Power Save mechanism, and traffic management through WMM-Admission Control.

Tunneled Direct Link Setup   Tunneled Direct Link Setup (TDLS) enables devices to establish secure links directly with other devices after they have joined a traditional Wi-Fi network. This will allow consumer devices such as TVs, gaming devices, smartphones, cameras, and printers to communicate quickly, easily, and securely between each other.

Passpoint   Passpoint is designed to revolutionize the end user experience when connecting to Wi-Fi hotspots. This will be done by automatically identifying the hotspot and connecting to it, automatically authenticating the user to the network using Extensible Authentication Protocol (EAP), and providing secure transmission using WPA2-Enterprise encryption. Passpoint is also known as Hotspot 2.0.

WMM-Admission Control   WMM-Admission Control allows Wi-Fi networks to manage network traffic based upon channel conditions, network traffic load, and type of traffic (voice, video, best effort data, or background data). The access point allows only the traffic that it can support to connect to the network, based upon the available network resources. This allows users to confidently know that, when the connection is established, the resources will be there to maintain it.

IBSS with Wi-Fi Protected Setup   IBSS with Wi-Fi Protected Setup provides easy configuration and strong security for ad hoc (peer-to-peer) Wi-Fi networks. This is designed for mobile products and devices that have a limited user interface, such as smartphones, cameras, and media players. Features include easy push button or PIN setup, task-oriented short-term connections, and dynamic networks that can be established anywhere.

Miracast   Miracast seamlessly integrates the display of streaming video content between devices. Wireless links are used to replace wired connections. Devices are designed to identify and connect with each other, manage their connections, and optimize the transmission of video content. It provides wired levels of capabilities but the portability of Wi-Fi. Miracast provides 802.11n performance, ad hoc connections via Wi-Fi Direct, and WPA2 security.

As 802.11 technologies evolve, new Wi-Fi CERTIFIED programs will be defined by the Wi-Fi Alliance.

Wi-Fi Alliance and Wi-Fi CERTIFIED

Learn more about the Wi-Fi Alliance at www.wi-fi.org. The Wi-Fi Alliance website contains many articles, FAQs, and white papers describing the organization along with additional information about the certification programs. The Wi-Fi Alliance technical white papers are recommended extra reading when preparing for the CWNA exam. The Wi-Fi Alliance white papers can be accessed at www.wi-fi.org/knowledge-center/white-papers.

International Organization for Standardization

The *International Organization for Standardization*, commonly known as the *ISO*, is a global, nongovernmental organization that identifies business, government, and society needs and develops standards in partnership with the sectors that will put them to use. The ISO is responsible for the creation of the Open Systems Interconnection (OSI) model, which has been a standard reference for data communications between computers since the late 1970s.

Why Is It ISO and Not IOS?

ISO is not a mistyped acronym. It is a word derived from the Greek word *isos*, meaning *equal*. Because acronyms can be different from country to country, based on varying translations, the ISO decided to use a word instead of an acronym for its name. With this in mind, it is easy to see why a standards organization would give itself a name that means *equal*.

The OSI model is the cornerstone of data communications, and learning to understand it is one of the most important and fundamental tasks a person in the networking industry can undertake. Figure 1.4 shows the seven layers of the OSI.

The IEEE 802.11-2012 standard defines communication mechanisms only at the Physical layer and MAC sublayer of the Data-Link layer of the OSI model. How 802.11 technology is used at these two OSI layers is discussed in detail throughout this book.

 You should have a working knowledge of the OSI model for both this book and the CWNA exam. Make sure you understand the seven layers of the OSI model and how communications take place at the different layers. If you are not comfortable with the concepts of the OSI model, spend some time reviewing it on the Internet or from a good networking fundamentals book prior to taking the CWNA test. More information about the ISO can be found at www.iso.org.

FIGURE 1.4   The seven layers of the OSI model

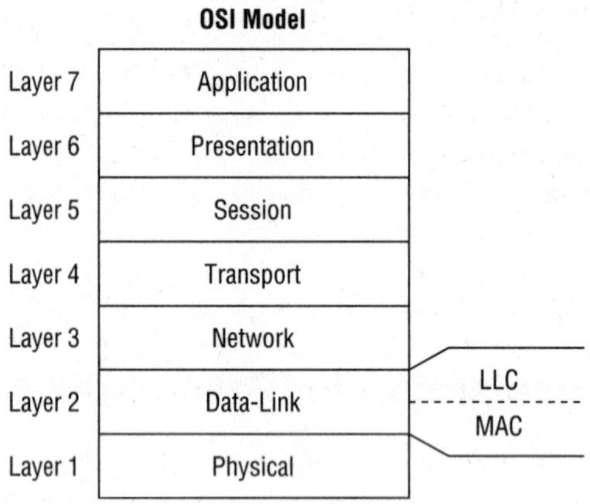

OSI Model

Layer 7	Application
Layer 6	Presentation
Layer 5	Session
Layer 4	Transport
Layer 3	Network
Layer 2	Data-Link — LLC / MAC
Layer 1	Physical

Core, Distribution, and Access

If you have ever taken a networking class or read a book about network design, you have probably heard the terms *core*, *distribution*, and *access* when referring to networking architecture. Proper network design is imperative no matter what type of network topology is used. The core of the network is the high-speed backbone or the superhighway of the network. The goal of the core is to carry large amounts of information between key data centers or distribution areas, just as superhighways connect cities and metropolitan areas.

The core layer does not route traffic or manipulate packets but rather performs high-speed switching. Redundant solutions are usually designed at the core layer to ensure the fast and reliable delivery of packets. The distribution layer of the network routes or directs traffic toward the smaller clusters of nodes or neighborhoods of the network.

The distribution layer routes traffic between virtual LANs (VLANs) and subnets. The distribution layer is akin to the state and county roads that provide medium travel speeds and distribute the traffic within the city or metropolitan area.

The access layer of the network is responsible for slower delivery of the traffic directly to the end user or end node. The access layer mimics the local roads and neighborhood streets that are used to reach your final address. The access layer ensures the final delivery of packets to the end user. Remember that speed is a relative concept.

Because of traffic load and throughput demands, speed and throughput capabilities increase as data moves from the access layer to the core layer. The additional speed and throughput tends to also mean higher cost.

Just as it would not be practical to build a superhighway so that traffic could travel between your neighborhood and the local school, it would not be practical or efficient to build a two-lane road as the main thoroughfare to connect two large cities such as

New York and Boston. These same principles apply to network design. Each of the network layers—core, distribution, and access—is designed to provide a specific function and capability to the network. It is important to understand how wireless networking fits into this network design model.

Wireless networking can be implemented as either point-to-point or point-to-multipoint solutions. Most wireless networks are used to provide network access to the individual client stations and are designed as point-to-multipoint networks. This type of implementation is designed and installed on the access layer, providing connectivity to the end user. 802.11 wireless networking is most often implemented at the access layer. In Chapter 10, "WLAN Architecture," you will learn about the difference between autonomous access points, cooperative access points, and controller-based access points. All access points are deployed at the access layer; however, controller-based access points commonly tunnel 802.11 wireless traffic to WLAN controllers, which are normally deployed at the distribution or core layer.

Wireless bridge links are typically used to provide connectivity between buildings in the same way that county or state roads provide distribution of traffic between neighborhoods. The purpose of wireless bridging is to connect two separate, wired networks wirelessly. Routing data traffic between networks is usually associated with the distribution layer. Wireless bridge links cannot usually meet the speed or distance requirements of the core layer, but they can be very effective at the distribution layer. An 802.11 bridge link is an example of wireless technology being implemented at the distribution layer.

Although wireless is not typically associated with the core layer, you must remember that speed and distance requirements vary greatly between large and small companies and that one person's distribution layer could be another person's core layer. Very small companies may even implement wireless for all end-user networking devices, forgoing any wired devices except for the connection to the Internet. Higher-bandwidth proprietary wireless bridges and some 802.11 mesh network deployments could be considered an implementation of wireless at the core layer.

Communications Fundamentals

Although the CWNA certification is considered one of the entry-level certifications in the Certified Wireless Network Professional (CWNP) wireless certification program, it is by no means an entry-level certification in the computing industry. Most of the candidates for the CWNA certificate have experience in other areas of information technology. However, the background and experience of these candidates varies greatly.

Unlike professions for which knowledge and expertise is learned through years of structured training, most computer professionals have followed their own path of education and training.

When people are responsible for their own education, they typically will gain the skills and knowledge that are directly related to their interests or their job. The more fundamental knowledge is often ignored because it is not directly relevant to the tasks at hand. Later, as their knowledge increases and they become more technically proficient, people realize that they need to learn about some of the fundamentals.

Many people in the computer industry understand that, in data communications, bits are transmitted across wires or waves. They even understand that some type of voltage change or wave fluctuation is used to distinguish the bits. When pressed, however, many of these same people have no idea what is actually happening with the electrical signals or the waves.

In the following sections, you will review some fundamental communications principles that directly and indirectly relate to wireless communications. Understanding these concepts will help you to better understand what is happening with wireless communications and to more easily recognize and identify the terms used in this profession.

Understanding Carrier Signals

Because data ultimately consists of bits, the transmitter needs a way of sending both 0s and 1s to transmit data from one location to another. An AC or DC signal by itself does not perform this task. However, if a signal fluctuates or is altered, even slightly, the signal can be interpreted so that data can be properly sent and received. This modified signal is now capable of distinguishing between 0s and 1s and is referred to as a *carrier signal*. The method of adjusting the signal to create the carrier signal is called *modulation*.

Three components of a wave that can fluctuate or be modified to create a carrier signal are amplitude, frequency, and phase.

This chapter reviews the basics of waves as they relate to the principles of data transmission. Chapter 2, "Radio Frequency Fundamentals," covers radio waves in much greater detail.

All radio-based communications use some form of modulation to transmit data. To encode the data in a signal sent by AM/FM radios, mobile telephones, and satellite television, some type of modulation is performed on the radio signal that is being transmitted. The average person typically is not concerned with how the signal is modulated, only that the device functions as expected. However, to become a better wireless network administrator, it is useful to have a better understanding of what is actually happening when two stations communicate. The rest of this chapter provides an introduction to waves as a basis for understanding carrier signals and data encoding and introduces you to the fundamentals of encoding data.

Amplitude and Wavelength

RF communication starts when radio waves are generated from an RF transmitter and picked up, or "heard," by a receiver at another location. RF waves are similar to the waves that you see in an ocean or lake. Waves are made up of two main components: wavelength and amplitude (see Figure 1.5).

FIGURE 1.5   This drawing shows the wavelength and amplitude of a wave

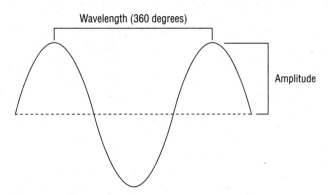

Amplitude   *Amplitude* is the height, force, or power of the wave. If you were standing in the ocean as the waves came to shore, you would feel the force of a larger wave much more than you would a smaller wave. Transmitters do the same thing, but with radio waves. Smaller waves are not as noticeable as bigger waves. A bigger wave generates a much larger electrical signal picked up by the receiving antenna. The receiver can then distinguish between highs and lows.

Wavelength   *Wavelength* is the distance between similar points on two back-to-back waves. When measuring a wave, the wavelength is typically measured from the peak of a wave to the peak of the next wave. Amplitude and wavelength are both properties of waves.

Frequency

Frequency describes a behavior of waves. Waves travel away from the source that generates them. How fast the waves travel, or more specifically, how many waves are generated over a 1-second period of time, is known as frequency. If you were to sit on a pier and count how often a wave hits it, you could tell someone how frequently the waves were coming to shore. Think of radio waves in the same way; however, radio waves travel much faster than the waves in the ocean. If you were to try to count the radio waves that are used in wireless networking, in the time it would take for one wave of water to hit the pier, several billion radio waves would have also hit the pier.

Phase

Phase is a relative term. It is the relationship between two waves with the same frequency. To determine phase, a wavelength is divided into 360 pieces referred to as *degrees* (see Figure 1.6). If you think of these degrees as starting times, then if one wave begins at the 0 degree point and another wave begins at the 90 degree point, these waves are considered to be 90 degrees out of phase.

FIGURE 1.6   This drawing shows two waves that are identical; however, they are 90 degrees out of phase with each other.

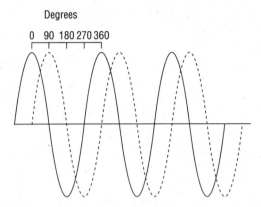

In an ideal world, waves are created and transmitted from one station and received perfectly intact at another station. Unfortunately, RF communications do not occur in an ideal world. There are many sources of interference and many obstacles that will affect the wave in its travels to the receiving station. In Chapter 2, we will introduce you to some of the outside influences that can affect the integrity of a wave and your ability to communicate between two stations.

Time and Phase

Suppose you have two stopped watches and both are set to noon. At noon you start your first watch, and then you start your second watch 1 hour later. The second watch is 1 hour behind the first watch. As time goes by, your second watch will continue to be 1 hour behind. Both watches will maintain a 24-hour day, but they are out of sync with each other. Waves that are out of phase behave similarly. Two waves that are out of phase are essentially two waves that have been started at two different times. Both waves will complete full 360-degree cycles, but they will do it out of phase, or out of sync with each other.

Understanding Keying Methods

When data is sent, a signal is transmitted from the transceiver. In order for the data to be transmitted, the signal must be manipulated so that the receiving station has a way of distinguishing 0s and 1s. This method of manipulating a signal so that it can represent multiple pieces of data is known as a *keying method*. A keying method is what changes a signal into a carrier signal. It provides the signal with the ability to encode data so that it can be communicated or transported.

There are three types of keying methods that are reviewed in the following sections: amplitude-shift keying (ASK), frequency-shift keying (FSK), and phase-shift keying (PSK). These keying methods are also referred to as *modulation techniques*. Keying methods use two different techniques to represent data:

Current State   With current state techniques, the current value (the current state) of the signal is used to distinguish between 0s and 1s. The use of the word *current* in this context does not refer to current as in voltage but rather to current as in the present time. Current state techniques will designate a specific or current value to indicate a binary 0 and another value to indicate a binary 1. At a specific point in time, it is the value of the signal that determines the binary value. For example, you can represent 0s and 1s by using an ordinary door. Once a minute you can check to see whether the door is open or closed. If the door is open, it represents a 0, and if the door is closed, it represents a 1. The current state of the door, open or closed, is what determines 0s or 1s.

State Transition   With state transition techniques, the change (or transition) of the signal is used to distinguish between 0s and 1s. State transition techniques may represent a 0 by a change in a wave's phase at a specific time, whereas a 1 would be represented by no change in a wave's phase at a specific time. At a specific point in time, it is the presence of a change or the lack of presence of a change that determines the binary value. The upcoming section "Phase-Shift Keying" provides examples of this in detail, but a door can be used again to provide a simple example. Once a minute you check the door. In this case, if the door is moving (opening or closing), it represents a 0, and if the door is still (either open or closed), it represents a 1. In this example, the state of transition (moving or not moving) is what determines 0s or 1s.

Amplitude-Shift Keying

Amplitude-shift keying (ASK) varies the amplitude, or height, of a signal to represent the binary data. ASK is a current state technique, where one level of amplitude can represent a 0 bit and another level of amplitude can represent a 1 bit. Figure 1.7 shows how a wave can modulate an ASCII letter *K* by using amplitude-shift keying. The larger amplitude wave is interpreted as a binary 1, and the smaller amplitude wave is interpreted as a binary 0.

FIGURE 1.7   An example of amplitude-shift keying (ASCII code of an uppercase *K*)

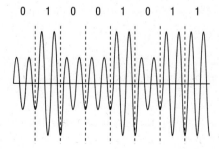

This shifting of amplitude determines the data that is being transmitted. The way the receiving station performs this task is to first divide the signal being received into periods of time known as *symbol periods*. The receiving station then samples or examines the wave during this symbol period to determine the amplitude of the wave. Depending on the value of the wave's amplitude, the receiving station can determine the binary value.

As you will learn later in this book, wireless signals can be unpredictable and also subjected to interference from many sources. When noise or interference occurs, it usually affects the amplitude of a signal. Because a change in amplitude due to noise could cause the receiving station to misinterpret the value of the data, ASK has to be used cautiously.

Frequency-Shift Keying

Frequency-shift keying (FSK) varies the frequency of the signal to represent the binary data. FSK is a current state technique, where one frequency can represent a 0 bit and another frequency can represent a 1 bit (Figure 1.8). This shifting of frequency determines the data that is being transmitted. When the receiving station samples the signal during the symbol period, it determines the frequency of the wave, and depending on the value of the frequency, the station can determine the binary value.

FIGURE 1.8   An example of frequency-shift keying (ASCII code of an uppercase *K*)

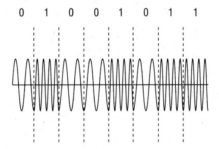

Figure 1.8 shows how a wave can modulate an ASCII letter *K* by using frequency-shift keying. The faster frequency wave is interpreted as a binary 1, and the slower frequency wave is interpreted as a binary 0.

FSK is used in some of the legacy deployments of 802.11 wireless networks. With the demand for faster communications, FSK techniques would require more expensive technology to support faster speeds, making it less practical.

Why Have I Not Heard about Keying Methods Before?

You might not realize it, but you *have* heard about keying methods before. AM/FM radio uses amplitude modulation (AM) and frequency modulation (FM) to transmit the radio stations that you listen to at home or in your automobile. The radio station modulates the voice and music into its transmission signal, and your home or car radio demodulates it.

Phase-Shift Keying

Phase-shift keying (PSK) varies the phase of the signal to represent the binary data. PSK is can be a state transition technique, where the change of phase can represent a 0 bit and the lack of a phase change can represent a 1 bit, or vice versa. This shifting of phase determines the data that is being transmitted. PSK can also be a current state technique, where the value of the phase can represent a 0 bit or a 1 bit. When the receiving station samples the signal during the symbol period, it determines the phase of the wave and the status of the bit.

Figure 1.9 shows how a wave can modulate an ASCII letter *K* by using phase-shift keying. A phase change at the beginning of the symbol period is interpreted as a binary 1, and the lack of a phase change at the beginning of the symbol period is interpreted as a binary 0.

FIGURE 1.9　An example of phase-shift keying (ASCII code of an uppercase *K*)

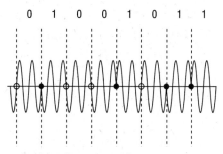

PSK technology is used extensively for radio transmissions as defined by the 802.11-2012 standard. Typically, the receiving station samples the signal during the symbol period, compares the phase of the current sample with the previous sample, and determines the difference. This degree of difference, or *differential*, is used to determine the bit value.

More advanced versions of PSK can encode multiple bits per symbol. Instead of using two phases to represent the binary values, you can use four phases. Each of the four phases is capable of representing two binary values (00, 01, 10, or 11) instead of one (0 or 1), thus shortening the transmission time. When more than two phases are used, this is referred to as *multiple phase-shift keying (MPSK)*. Figure 1.10 shows how a wave can modulate an ASCII letter *K* by using a multiple phase-shift keying method. Four possible phase changes can be monitored, with each phase change now able to be interpreted as 2 bits of data instead of just 1. Notice that there are fewer symbol times in this figure than there are in Figure 1.9.

FIGURE 1.10   An example of multiple phase-shift keying (ASCII code of an uppercase *K*)

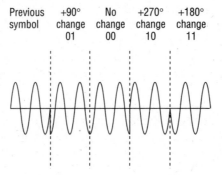

| Previous symbol | +90° change 01 | No change 00 | +270° change 10 | +180° change 11 |

Where Else Can I Learn More about 802.11 Technology and the Wi-Fi Industry?

Reading this book from cover to cover is a great way to start understanding Wi-Fi technology. In addition, because of the rapidly changing nature of 802.11 WLAN technologies, the authors of this book recommend these additional resources:

Wi-Fi Alliance   As mentioned earlier in this chapter, the Wi-Fi Alliance is the marketing voice of the Wi-Fi industry and maintains all the industry's certifications. The knowledge center section of the Wi-Fi Alliance website, www.wi-fi.org, is an excellent resource.

CWNP   The Certified Wireless Networking Professional program maintains learning resources such as user forums and a WLAN white paper database. The website www .cwnp.com is also the best source of information about all the vendor-neutral CWNP wireless networking certifications.

WLAN Vendor Websites   Although the CWNA exam and this book take a vendor-neutral approach about 802.11 education, the various WLAN vendor websites are often excellent resources for information about specific Wi-Fi networking solutions. Many of the major WLAN vendors are mentioned throughout this book, and a listing of most of the major WLAN vendor websites can be found in Chapter 11, "WLAN Deployment and Vertical Markets."

Wi-Fi Blogs   In recent years, numerous personal blogs about the subject of Wi-Fi have sprung up all over the Internet. One great example is the Revolution Wi-Fi blog written by CWNE #84, Andrew vonNagy, at

    http://revolutionwifi.blogspot.com

Summary

This chapter explained the history of wireless networking and the roles and responsibilities of key organizations involved with the wireless networking industry:

- FCC and other regulatory domain authorities
- IEEE
- IETF
- Wi-Fi Alliance

To provide a basic understanding of the relationship between networking fundamentals and 802.11 technologies, we discussed these concepts:

- OSI model
- Core, distribution, and access

To provide a basic knowledge of how wireless stations transmit and receive data, we introduced some of the components of waves and modulation:

- Carrier signals
- Amplitude
- Wavelength
- Frequency
- Phase
- Keying methods, including ASK, FSK, and PSK

When you are troubleshooting RF communications, having a solid knowledge of waves and modulation techniques can help you understand the fundamental issues behind communications problems and help lead you to a solution.

Exam Essentials

Know the four industry organizations.   Understand the roles and responsibilities of the regulatory domain authorities, the IEEE, the IETF, and the Wi-Fi Alliance.

Understand core, distribution, and access.   Know where 802.11 technology is deployed in fundamental network design.

Understand wavelength, frequency, amplitude, and phase.   Know the definitions of each RF characteristic.

Understand the concepts of modulation.   ASK, FSK, and PSK are three carrier signal modulation techniques.

Review Questions

1. 802.11 technology is typically deployed at which fundamental layer of network architecture?

   A. Core

   B. Distribution

   C. Access

   D. Network

2. Which organization is responsible for enforcing maximum transmit power rules in an unlicensed frequency band?

   A. IEEE

   B. Wi-Fi Alliance

   C. ISO

   D. IETF

   E. None of the above

3. 802.11 wireless bridge links are typically associated with which network architecture layer?

   A. Core

   B. Distribution

   C. Access

   D. Network

4. The 802.11-2012 standard was created by which organization?

   A. IEEE

   B. OSI

   C. ISO

   D. Wi-Fi Alliance

   E. FCC

5. What organization ensures interoperability of WLAN products?

   A. IEEE

   B. ITU-R

   C. ISO

   D. Wi-Fi Alliance

   E. FCC

6. What type of signal is required to carry data?

    A. Communications signal

    B. Data signal

    C. Carrier signal

    D. Binary signal

    E. Digital signal

7. Which keying method is most susceptible to interference from noise?

    A. FSK

    B. ASK

    C. PSK

    D. DSK

8. Which sublayer of the OSI model's Data-Link layer is used for communication between 802.11 radios?

    A. LLC

    B. WPA

    C. MAC

    D. FSK

9. While performing some research, Janie comes across a reference to a document titled RFC 3935. Which of the following organization's website would be best to further research this document?

    A. IEEE

    B. Wi-Fi Alliance

    C. WECA

    D. FCC

    E. IETF

10. The Wi-Fi Alliance is responsible for which of the following certification programs?

    A. 802.11i

    B. WEP

    C. 802.11-2012

    D. WMM

    E. PSK

11. Which wave properties can be modulated to encode data? (Choose all that apply.)

    A. Amplitude

    B. Frequency

   C. Phase

   D. Wavelength

12. The IEEE 802.11-2012 standard defines communication mechanisms at which layers of the OSI model? (Choose all that apply.)

   A. Network

   B. Physical

   C. Transport

   D. Application

   E. Data-Link

   F. Session

13. The height or power of a wave is known as what?

   A. Phase

   B. Frequency

   C. Amplitude

   D. Wavelength

14. Samantha received a gaming system as a gift. She would like to have it communicate with her sister Jennifer's gaming system so that they can play against each other. Which of the following technologies, if deployed in the two gaming systems, should provide for the easiest configuration of the two systems to communicate with each other?

   A. Wi-Fi Personal

   B. Wi-Fi Direct

   C. 802.11n

   D. CWG-RF

   E. Wi-Fi Protected Setup

15. What other Wi-Fi Alliance certifications are required before a Wi-Fi radio can also be certified as Voice Enterprise compliant? (Choose all that apply.)

   A. WMM-Power Save

   B. Wi-Fi Direct

   C. WPA2-Enterprise

   D. Voice Personal

   E. WMM-Admission Control

16. Which of the following wireless communications parameters and usage are typically governed by a local regulatory authority? (Choose all that apply.)

   A. Frequency

   B. Bandwidth

C. Maximum transmit power

D. Maximum EIRP

E. Indoor/outdoor usage

17. The Wi-Fi Alliance is responsible for which of the following certification programs? (Choose all that apply.)

    A. WECA

    B. Voice Personal

    C. 802.11v

    D. WAVE

    E. WMM-PS

18. A wave is divided into degrees. How many degrees make up a complete wave?

    A. 100

    B. 180

    C. 212

    D. 360

19. What are the advantages of using unlicensed frequency bands for RF transmissions? (Choose all that apply.)

    A. There are no government regulations.

    B. There is no additional financial cost.

    C. Anyone can use the frequency band.

    D. There are no rules.

20. The OSI model consists of how many layers?

    A. Four

    B. Six

    C. Seven

    D. Nine

Chapter

2

Radio Frequency Fundamentals

IN THIS CHAPTER, YOU WILL LEARN ABOUT THE FOLLOWING:

✓ **Definition of radio frequency signal**

✓ **Radio frequency characteristics**

  ▪ Wavelength

  ▪ Frequency

  ▪ Amplitude

  ▪ Phase

✓ **Radio frequency behaviors**

  ▪ Wave propagation

  ▪ Absorption

  ▪ Reflection

  ▪ Scattering

  ▪ Refraction

  ▪ Diffraction

  ▪ Loss (attenuation)

  ▪ Free space path loss

  ▪ Multipath

  ▪ Gain (amplification)

In addition to understanding the OSI model and basic networking concepts, you must broaden your understanding of many other networking technologies in order to properly design, deploy, and administer an 802.11 wireless network. For instance, when administering an Ethernet network, you typically need a comprehension of TCP/IP, bridging, switching, and routing. The skills to manage an Ethernet network will also aid you as a WLAN administrator because most 802.11 wireless networks act as "portals" into wired networks. The IEEE defines the 802.11 communications at the Physical layer and the MAC sublayer of the Data-Link layer.

To fully understand the 802.11 technology, you need to have a clear concept of how wireless works at the first layer of the OSI model, and at the heart of the Physical layer is *radio frequency (RF)* communications.

In a wired LAN, the signal is confined neatly inside the wire, and the resulting behaviors are anticipated. However, just the opposite is true for a wireless LAN. Although the laws of physics apply, RF signals move through the air in a sometimes unpredictable manner. Because RF signals are not saddled inside an Ethernet wire, you should always try to envision a wireless LAN as an "ever changing" network.

Does this mean that you must be an RF engineer from Stanford University to perform a WLAN site survey or monitor a Wi-Fi network? Of course not, but if you have a good grasp of the RF characteristics and behaviors defined in this chapter, your skills as a wireless network administrator will be ahead of the curve. Why does a wireless network perform differently in an auditorium full of people than it does inside an empty auditorium? Why does the range of a 5 GHz radio transmitter seem shorter than the range of a 2.4 GHz radio transmitter? These are the types of questions that can be answered with some basic knowledge of how RF signals work and perform.

 Wired communications travel across what is known as *bounded medium*. Bounded medium contains or confines the signal (small amounts of signal leakage can occur). Wireless communications travel across what is known as *unbounded medium*. Unbounded medium does not contain the signal, which is free to radiate into the surrounding environment in all directions (unless restricted or redirected by some outside influence).

In this chapter, we first define what an RF signal does. Then, we discuss both the properties and the behaviors of RF.

What Is a Radio Frequency Signal?

This book is by no means intended to be a comprehensive guide to the laws of physics, which is the science of motion and matter. However, a basic understanding of some of the concepts of physics as they relate to radio frequency (RF) is important for even an entry-level wireless networking professional.

The *electromagnetic (EM) spectrum*, which is usually simply referred to as *spectrum*, is the range of all possible electromagnetic radiation. This radiation exists as self-propagating electromagnetic waves that can move through matter or space. Examples of electromagnetic waves include gamma rays, X-rays, visible light, and radio waves. Radio waves are electromagnetic waves occurring on the radio frequency portion of the electromagnetic spectrum, as pictured in Figure 2.1.

FIGURE 2.1   Electromagnetic spectrum

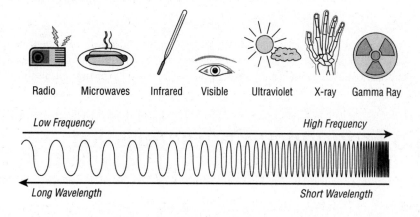

An RF signal starts out as an electrical *alternating current (AC)* signal that is originally generated by a transmitter. This AC signal is sent through a copper conductor (typically a coaxial cable) and radiated out of an antenna element in the form of an electromagnetic wave. This electromagnetic wave is the wireless signal. Changes of electron flow in an antenna, otherwise known as *current*, produce changes in the electromagnetic fields around the antenna.

An alternating current is an electrical current with a magnitude and direction that varies cyclically, as opposed to direct current, the direction of which stays in a constant form. The shape and form of the AC signal—defined as the *waveform*—is what is known as a sine wave, as shown in Figure 2.2. Sine wave patterns can also be seen in light, sound, and the ocean. The fluctuation of voltage in an AC current is known as cycling, or *oscillation*.

FIGURE 2.2   A sine wave

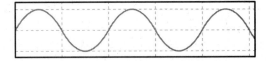

An RF electromagnetic signal radiates away from the antenna in a continuous pattern that is governed by certain properties such as wavelength, frequency, amplitude, and phase. Additionally, electromagnetic signals can travel through mediums of different materials or travel in a perfect vacuum. When an RF signal travels through a vacuum, it moves at the speed of light, which is 299,792,458 meters per second, or 186,000 miles per second.

To simplify mathematical calculations that use the speed of light, it is common to approximate the value by rounding it up to 300,000,000 meters per second. Any references to the speed of light in this book will use the approximate value.

RF electromagnetic signals travel using a variety or combination of movement behaviors. These movement behaviors are referred to as *propagation behaviors*. We discuss some of these propagation behaviors, including absorption, reflection, scattering, refraction, diffraction, amplification, and attenuation, later in this chapter.

Radio Frequency Characteristics

These characteristics, defined by the laws of physics, exist in every RF signal:

- Wavelength
- Frequency
- Amplitude
- Phase

You will look at each of these in more detail in the following sections.

Wavelength

As stated earlier, an RF signal is an alternating current (AC) that continuously changes between a positive and negative voltage. An oscillation, or cycle, of this alternating current is defined as a single change from up to down to up, or as a change from positive to negative to positive.

A *wavelength* is the distance between the two successive crests (peaks) or two successive troughs (valleys) of a wave pattern, as pictured in Figure 2.3. In simpler words, a wavelength is the distance that a single cycle of an RF signal actually travels.

FIGURE 2.3   Wavelength

Distance (360 degrees)

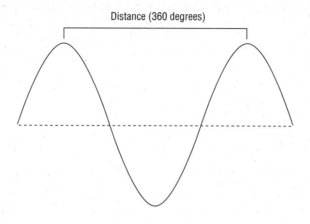

The Greek symbol λ represents wavelength. Frequency is usually denoted by the Latin letter *f*. The Latin letter *c* represents the speed of light in a vacuum. This is derived from *celeritas*, the Latin word meaning speed.

It is very important to understand that there is an inverse relationship between wavelength and frequency. The three components of this inverse relationship are frequency (f, measured in hertz, or Hz), wavelength (λ, measured in meters, or m), and the speed of light (c, which is a constant value of 300,000,000 m/sec). The following reference formulas illustrate the relationship: λ = c/f and f = c/λ. A simplified explanation is that the higher the frequency of an RF signal, the smaller the wavelength of that signal. The larger the wavelength of an RF signal, the lower the frequency of that signal.

AM radio stations operate at much lower frequencies than WLAN 802.11 radios, while satellite radio transmissions occur at much higher frequencies than WLAN radios. For instance, radio station WSB-AM in Atlanta broadcasts at 750 KHz and has a wavelength of 1,312 feet, or 400 meters. That is quite a distance for one single cycle of an RF signal to travel. In contrast, some radio navigation satellites operate at a very high frequency, near 252 GHz, and a single cycle of the satellite's signal has a wavelength of less than 0.05 inches, or 1.2 millimeters. Figure 2.4 displays a comparison of these two extremely different types of RF signals.

As RF signals travel through space and matter, they lose signal strength (attenuate). It is often thought that a higher frequency electromagnetic signal with a smaller wavelength will attenuate faster than a lower frequency signal with a larger wavelength. In reality, the frequency and wavelength properties of an RF signal do not cause attenuation. Distance is the main cause of attenuation. All antennas have an effective area for receiving power known as the aperture. The amount of RF energy that can be captured by the aperture of an antenna is smaller with higher frequency antennas. Although wavelength and frequency do not cause attenuation, the perception is that higher frequency signals with smaller wavelengths attenuate faster than signals with a larger wavelength. Theoretically, in a vacuum, electromagnetic signals will travel forever. However, as a signal travels through our atmosphere, the signal will attenuate to amplitudes below the receive sensitivity threshold of a receiving radio. Essentially, the signal will arrive at the receiver, but it will be too weak to be detected.

FIGURE 2.4 750 KHz wavelength and 252 GHz wavelength

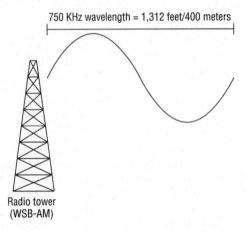

750 KHz wavelength = 1,312 feet/400 meters

Radio tower
(WSB-AM)

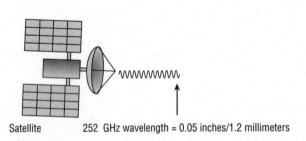

Satellite   252 GHz wavelength = 0.05 inches/1.2 millimeters

The perception is that the higher frequency signal with smaller wavelength will not travel as far as the lower frequency signal with larger wavelength. The reality is that the amount of energy that can be captured by the aperture of a high frequency antenna is smaller than the amount of RF energy that can be captured by a low frequency antenna. A good analogy to a receiving radio would be the human ear. The next time you hear a car coming down the street with loud music, notice that the first thing you hear will be the bass (lower frequencies). This practical example demonstrates that the lower frequency signals with the larger wavelength will be heard from a greater distance than the higher frequency signal with the smaller wavelength.

The majority of wireless LAN (WLAN) radios operate in either the 2.4 GHz frequency range or the 5 GHz range. In Figure 2.5, you see a comparison of a single cycle of the two waves generated by different frequency WLAN radios.

FIGURE 2.5   2.45 GHz wavelength and 5.775 GHz wavelength

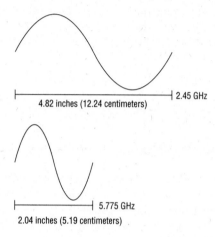

Higher frequency signals will generally attenuate faster than lower frequency signals as they pass through various physical mediums such as brick walls. This is important for a wireless engineer to know for two reasons. First, the coverage distance is dependent on the attenuation through the air (referred to as free space path loss, discussed later in this chapter). Second, the higher the frequency, typically the less the signal will penetrate through obstructions. For example, a 2.4 GHz signal will pass through walls, windows, and doors with greater amplitude than a 5 GHz signal. Think of how much farther you can receive an AM station's signal (lower frequency) versus an FM station's signal (higher frequency).

Note that the length of a 2.45 GHz wave is about 4.8 inches, or 12 centimeters. The length of a 5.775 GHz wave is a distance of only about 2 inches, or 5 centimeters.

As you can see in Figure 2.4 and Figure 2.5, the wavelengths of the different frequency signals are different because, although each signal cycles only one time, the waves travel dissimilar distances. In Figure 2.6, you see the formulas for calculating wavelength distance in either inches or centimeters.

FIGURE 2.6   Wavelength formulas

Wavelength (inches) = 11.811/frequency (GHz)

Wavelength (centimeters) = 30/frequency (GHz)

Throughout this study guide, you will be presented with various formulas. You will not need to know these formulas for the CWNA certification exam. The formulas are in this study guide to demonstrate concepts and to be used as reference material.

Real World Scenario

How Does the Wavelength of a Signal Concern Me?

It is often thought that a higher frequency electromagnetic signal with a smaller wavelength will attenuate faster than a lower frequency signal with a larger wavelength. In reality, the frequency and wavelength properties of an RF signal do not cause attenuation. Distance is the main cause of attenuation. All antennas have an effective area for receiving power known as the aperture. The amount of RF energy that can be captured by the aperture of an antenna is smaller with higher frequency antennas. Although wavelength and frequency do not cause attenuation, the perception is that higher frequency signals with smaller wavelengths attenuate faster than signals with a larger wavelength. When all other aspects of the wireless link are similar, Wi-Fi equipment using 5 GHz radios will have shorter range and a smaller coverage area than Wi-Fi equipment using 2.4 GHz radios.

Part of the design of the WLAN includes what is called a *site survey*. The site survey is responsible for determining zones, or cells, of usable received signal coverage in your facilities. If single radio access points are being used, the 2.4 GHz access points can typically provide greater RF footprints (coverage area) for client stations than the higher frequency equipment. More 5 GHz access points would have to be installed to provide the same coverage that can be achieved by a lesser number of 2.4 GHz access points. The penetration of these signals will also reduce coverage for 5 GHz more than it will for 2.4 GHz. Most enterprise Wi-Fi vendors sell dual-frequency access points (APs) with both 2.4 GHz and 5 GHz radios. Site survey planning and coverage analysis for dual-frequency APs should initially be based on the higher frequency 5 GHz signal which effectively provides a smaller coverage area.

Frequency

As previously mentioned, an RF signal cycles in an alternating current in the form of an electromagnetic wave. You also know that the distance traveled in one signal cycle is the wavelength. But what about how often an RF signal cycles in a certain time period?

Frequency is the number of times a specified event occurs within a specified time interval. A standard measurement of frequency is *hertz (Hz)*, which was named after the German physicist Heinrich Rudolf Hertz. An event that occurs once in 1 second has a frequency of 1 Hz. An event that occurs 325 times in 1 second is measured as 325 Hz. The frequency at which electromagnetic waves cycle is also measured in hertz. Thus, the number of times an RF signal cycles in 1 second is the frequency of that signal, as pictured in Figure 2.7.

Different metric prefixes can be applied to the hertz (Hz) measurement of radio frequencies to make working with very large frequencies easier:

1 hertz (Hz) = 1 cycle per second

1 kilohertz (KHz) = 1,000 cycles per second

1 megahertz (MHz) = 1,000,000 (million) cycles per second

1 gigahertz (GHz) = 1,000,000,000 (billion) cycles per second

FIGURE 2.7   Frequency

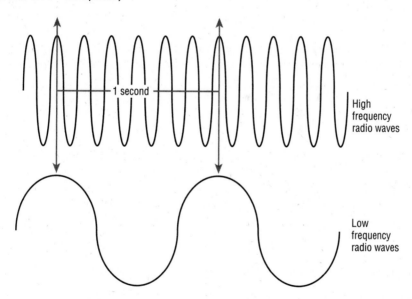

So when we are talking about 2.4 GHz WLAN radios, the RF signal is oscillating 2.4 billion times per second!

Inverse Relationship

Remember that there is an inverse relationship between wavelength and frequency. The three components of this inverse relationship are frequency (f, measured in hertz, or Hz), wavelength (λ, measured in meters, or m), and the speed of light (c, which is a constant value of 300,000,000 m/sec). The following reference formulas illustrate the relationship: λ = c/f and f = c/λ. A simplified explanation is that the higher the frequency of an RF signal, the shorter the wavelength will be of that signal. The longer the wavelength of an RF signal, the lower the frequency will be of that signal.

Amplitude

Another very important property of an RF signal is the *amplitude*, which can be characterized simply as the signal's strength, or power. When speaking about wireless transmissions, this is often referenced as how loud or strong the signal is. *Amplitude* can be defined as the maximum displacement of a continuous wave. With RF signals, the amplitude corresponds to the electrical field of the wave. When you look at an RF signal using an oscilloscope, the amplitude is represented by the positive crests and negative troughs of the sine wave.

In Figure 2.8, you can see that λ represents wavelength and a represents amplitude. The first signal's crests and troughs have more magnitude; thus the signal has more amplitude. The second signal's crests and troughs have decreased magnitude, and therefore the signal has less amplitude.

FIGURE 2.8   Amplitude

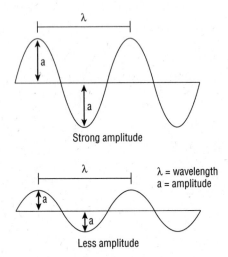

NOTE   Although the signal strength (amplitude) is different, the frequency and wavelength of the signal remains constant. A variety of factors can cause an RF signal to lose amplitude, otherwise known as *attenuation*, which we discuss later in this chapter, in the section "Loss (Attenuation)."

When discussing signal strength in a WLAN, amplitude is usually referred to as either transmit amplitude or received amplitude. *Transmit amplitude* is typically defined as the amount of initial amplitude that leaves the radio transmitter. For example, if you configure an access point to transmit at 50 milliwatts (mW), that is the transmit amplitude. Cables and connectors will attenuate the transmit amplitude while most antenna will amplify the transmit amplitude. When a radio receives an RF signal, the received signal strength is most often referred to as *received amplitude*. RF signal strength measurements taken during a site survey is an example of received amplitude.

Different types of RF technologies require varying degrees of transmit amplitude. AM radio stations may transmit narrow band signals with as much power as 50,000 watts. The radios used in most indoor 802.11 access points have a transmit power range between 1 mW and 100 mW. You will learn later that Wi-Fi radios can receive signals with amplitudes as low as billionths of a milliwatt.

Phase

Phase is not a property of just one RF signal but instead involves the relationship between two or more signals that share the same frequency. The phase involves the relationship between the position of the amplitude crests and troughs of two waveforms.

Phase can be measured in distance, time, or degrees. If the peaks of two signals with the same frequency are in exact alignment at the same time, they are said to be *in phase*. Conversely, if the peaks of two signals with the same frequency are not in exact alignment at the same time, they are said to be *out of phase*. Figure 2.9 illustrates this concept.

What is important to understand is the effect that phase has on amplitude when a radio receives multiple signals. Signals that have 0 (zero) degree phase separation actually combine their amplitude, which results in a received signal of much greater signal strength, potentially as much as twice the amplitude. If two RF signals are 180 degrees out of phase (the peak of one signal is in exact alignment with the trough of the second signal), they cancel each other out and the effective received signal strength is null. Phase separation has a cumulative effect. Depending on the amount of phase separation of two signals, the received signal strength may be either increased or diminished. The phase difference between two signals is very important to understanding the effects of an RF phenomenon known as multipath, which is discussed later in this chapter.

FIGURE 2.9   Phase relationships

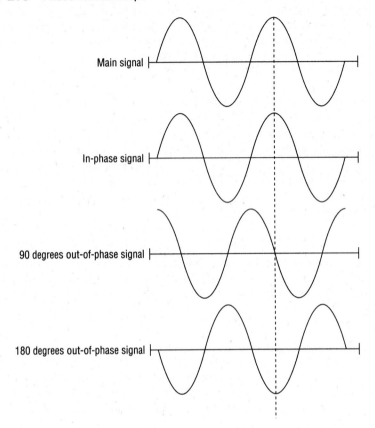

On the book's page at www.sybex.com/go/cwna4e is a freeware Windows-based program called EMANIM. Toward the end of this chapter, you will use this program to execute Exercise 2.1, which is a lab that demonstrates the changes in amplitude due to phase relationships of RF signals.

Radio Frequency Behaviors

As an RF signal travels through the air and other mediums, it can move and behave in different manners. RF propagation behaviors include absorption, reflection, scattering, refraction, diffraction, free space path loss, multipath, attenuation, and gain.

Wave Propagation

Now that you have learned about some of the various characteristics of an RF signal, it is important to understand the way an RF signal behaves as it moves away from an antenna. As stated before, electromagnetic waves can move through a perfect vacuum or pass through materials of different mediums. The way in which the RF waves move—known as wave *propagation*—can vary drastically depending on the materials in the signal's path; for example, drywall will have a much different effect on an RF signal than metal or concrete.

What happens to an RF signal between two locations is a direct result of how the signal propagates. When we use the term *propagate*, try to envision an RF signal broadening or spreading as it travels farther away from the antenna. An excellent analogy is shown in Figure 2.10, which depicts an earthquake. Note the concentric seismic rings that propagate away from the epicenter of the earthquake. Near the epicenter the waves are strong and concentrated, but as the seismic waves move away from the epicenter, the waves broaden and weaken. RF waves behave in much the same fashion. The manner in which a wireless signal moves is often referred to as *propagation behavior*.

 As a WLAN engineer, you should understand RF propagation behaviors for making sure that access points are deployed in the proper location, for making sure the proper type of antenna is chosen, and for monitoring the performance of the wireless network.

FIGURE 2.10   Propagation analogy

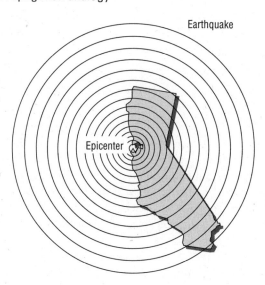

Absorption

The most common RF behavior is *absorption*. If a signal does not bounce off an object, move around an object, or pass through an object, then 100 percent absorption has occurred. Most materials will absorb some amount of an RF signal to varying degrees.

Brick and concrete walls will absorb a signal significantly, whereas drywall will absorb a signal to a lesser degree. A 2.4 GHz signal will be 1/16 the original power after propagating through a brick wall. That same signal will only lose 1/2 the original power after passing though drywall material. Water is another example of a medium that can absorb a signal to a large extent. Absorption is a leading cause of attenuation (loss), which is discussed later in this chapter. The amplitude of an RF signal is directly affected by how much RF energy is absorbed. Even objects with large water content such as paper, cardboard, and fish tanks can absorb signals.

 Real World Scenario

User Density

Mr. Burton performed a wireless site survey at an airport terminal. He determined how many access points were required and their proper placement so that he would have the necessary RF coverage. Ten days later, during a snowstorm, the terminal was crammed with people who were delayed due to the weather. During these delays, the signal strength and quality of the WLAN was less than desirable in many areas of the terminal. What happened? Human bodies!

An average adult body is 50 to 65 percent water. Water causes absorption, which results in attenuation. User density is an important factor when designing a wireless network. One reason is the effects of absorption. Another reason is the amount of available bandwidth, which we discuss in Chapter 15, "Radio Frequency Site Survey Fundamentals."

Reflection

One of the most important RF propagation behaviors to be aware of is reflection. When a wave hits a smooth object that is larger than the wave itself, depending on the media the wave may bounce in another direction. This behavior is categorized as *reflection*. An analogous situation could be a child bouncing a ball off a sidewalk and the ball changing direction. Figure 2.11 depicts another analogy, a laser beam pointed at a single small mirror. Depending on the angle of the mirror, the laser beam bounces or reflects off in a different direction. RF signals can reflect in the same manner, depending on the objects or materials the signals encounter.

There are two major types of reflections: sky wave reflection and microwave reflection. Sky wave reflection can occur in frequencies below 1 GHz, where the signal has a very large wavelength. The signal bounces off the surface of the charged particles of the ionosphere in the earth's atmosphere. This is why you can be in Charlotte, North Carolina, and listen to radio station WLS-AM from Chicago on a clear night.

FIGURE 2.11   Reflection analogy

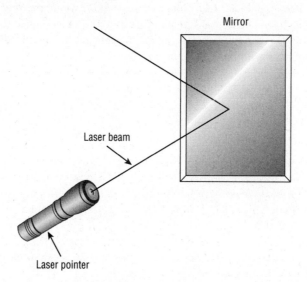

Microwave signals, however, exist between 1 GHz and 300 GHz. Because they are higher frequency signals, they have much smaller wavelengths, thus the term *microwave*. Microwaves can bounce off smaller objects like a metal door. Microwave reflection is what we are concerned about in Wi-Fi environments. In an outdoor environment, microwaves can reflect off large objects and smooth surfaces such as buildings, roads, bodies of water, and even the earth's surface. In an indoor environment, microwaves reflect off smooth surfaces such as doors, walls, and file cabinets. Anything made of metal will absolutely cause reflection. Other materials such as glass and concrete may cause reflection as well.

Reflection Is a Major Source of Poor 802.11a/b/g WLAN Performance

Reflection can be the cause of serious performance problems in a legacy 802.11a/b/g WLAN. As a wave radiates from an antenna, it broadens and disperses. If portions of this wave are reflected, new wave fronts will appear from the reflection points. If these multiple waves all reach the receiver, the multiple reflected signals cause an effect called multipath.

Multipath can degrade the strength and quality of the received signal or even cause data corruption or cancelled signals. (Further discussion of multipath occurs later in this chapter. Hardware solutions to compensate for the negative effects of multipath in this environment, such as directional antennas and antenna diversity, are discussed in Chapter 4, "Radio Frequency Signal and Antenna Concepts.")

Reflection and multipath were often considered primary enemies when deploying legacy 802.11a/b/g radios. 802.11n and 802.11ac radios utilize *multiple-input, multiple-output (MIMO)* antennas and advanced digital signal processing (DSP) techniques to take advantage of multipath. MIMO technology is covered extensively in Chapter 18, "802.11n" and Chapter 19, "Very High Throughput (VHT) and 802.11ac."

Scattering

Did you know that the color of the sky is blue because the molecules of the atmosphere are smaller than the wavelength of light? This blue sky phenomenon is known as Rayleigh scattering (named after the 19th-century British physicist John William Strutt, Lord Rayleigh). The shorter blue wavelength light is absorbed by the gases in the atmosphere and radiated in all directions. This is an example of an RF propagation behavior called *scattering*, sometimes called *scatter*.

Scattering can most easily be described as multiple reflections. These multiple reflections occur when the electromagnetic signal's wavelength is larger than pieces of whatever medium the signal is reflecting from or passing through.

Scattering can happen in two ways. The first type of scatter is on a lower level and has a lesser effect on the signal quality and strength. This type of scattering may manifest itself when the RF signal moves through a substance and the individual electromagnetic waves are reflected off the minute particles within the medium. Smog in our atmosphere and sandstorms in the desert can cause this type of scattering.

The second type of scattering occurs when an RF signal encounters some type of uneven surface and is reflected into multiple directions. Chain link fences, wire mesh in stucco walls or old plaster walls, tree foliage, and rocky terrain commonly cause this type of scattering. When striking the uneven surface, the main signal dissipates into multiple reflected signals, which can cause substantial signal downgrade and may even cause a loss of the received signal.

Figure 2.12 shows a flashlight being shined against a disco mirror ball. Note how the main signal beam is completely displaced into multiple reflected beams with less amplitude and into many different directions.

Refraction

In addition to RF signals being absorbed or bounced (via reflection or scattering), if certain conditions exist, an RF signal can actually be bent in a behavior known as *refraction*. A straightforward definition of refraction is the bending of an RF signal as it passes through a medium with a different density, thus causing the direction of the wave to change. RF refraction most commonly occurs as a result of atmospheric conditions.

FIGURE 2.12   Scattering analogy

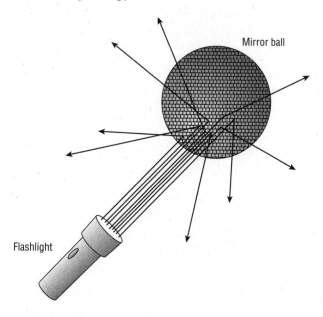

Mirror ball

Flashlight

When you are dealing with long-distance outdoor bridge links, an instance of refractivity change that might be a concern is what is known as the *k-factor*. A k-factor of 1 means there is no bending. A k-factor of less than 1, such as 2/3, represents the signal bending away from the earth. A k-factor of more than 1 represents bending toward the earth. Normal atmospheric conditions have a k-factor of 4/3, which is bending slightly toward the curvature of the earth.

The three most common causes of refraction are water vapor, changes in air temperature, and changes in air pressure. In an outdoor environment, RF signals typically refract slightly back down toward the earth's surface. However, changes in the atmosphere may cause the signal to bend away from the earth. In long-distance outdoor wireless bridge links, refraction can be an issue. An RF signal may also refract through certain types of glass and other materials that are found in an indoor environment. Figure 2.13 shows two examples of refraction.

FIGURE 2.13   Refraction

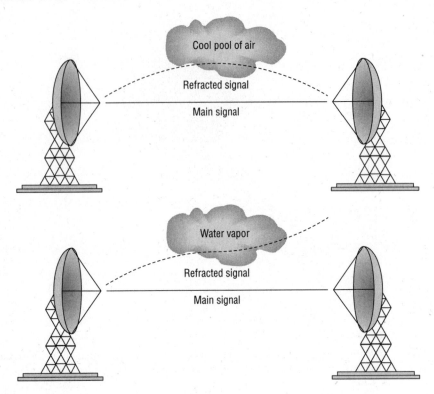

Diffraction

Not to be confused with refraction, another RF propagation behavior exists that also bends the RF signal; it is called *diffraction*. Diffraction is the bending of an RF signal around an object (whereas refraction, as you recall, is the bending of a signal as it passes through a medium). Diffraction is the bending and the spreading of an RF signal when it encounters an obstruction. The conditions that must be met for diffraction to occur depend entirely on the shape, size, and material of the obstructing object, as well as the exact characteristics of the RF signal, such as polarization, phase, and amplitude.

Typically, diffraction is caused by some sort of partial blockage of the RF signal, such as a small hill or a building that sits between a transmitting radio and a receiver. The waves that encounter the obstruction bend around the object, taking a longer and different path. The waves that did not encounter the object do not bend and maintain the shorter and original path. The analogy depicted in Figure 2.14 is a rock sitting in the middle of a river. Most of the current maintains the original flow; however, some of the current that encounters the rock will reflect off the rock and some will diffract around the rock.

FIGURE 2.14   Diffraction analogy

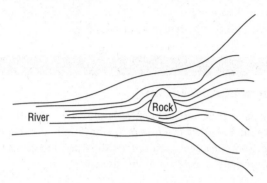

Sitting directly behind the obstruction is an area known as the *RF shadow*. Depending on the change in direction of the diffracted signals, the area of the RF shadow can become a dead zone of coverage or still possibly receive degraded signals. The concept of RF shadows is important when selecting antenna locations. Mounting to a beam or other wall structure can create a virtual RF blind spot.

Loss (Attenuation)

Loss, also known as *attenuation*, is best described as the decrease of amplitude or signal strength. A signal may lose strength when transmitted on a wire or in the air. On the wired portion of the communications (RF cable), the AC electrical signal will lose strength because of the electrical impedance of coaxial cabling and other components such as connectors.

In Chapter 4, we discuss impedance, which is the measurement of opposition to the AC current. You will also learn about impedance mismatches, which can create signal loss on the wired side.

In the past, attenuation was typically not desired; however, as networks are becoming more dense, wireless network designers have moved away from planning for coverage and have moved toward planning for capacity. In many networks, RF engineers desire more attenuation on the wired connections. On rare occasions an RF engineer may add a hardware attenuator device on the wired side of an RF system to introduce attenuation to remain compliant with power regulations or for capacity design purposes.

After the RF signal is radiated into the air via the antenna, the signal will attenuate due to absorption, distance, or possibly the negative effects of multipath. You already know that as an RF signal passes through different mediums, the signal can be absorbed into the medium, which in turn causes a loss of amplitude. Different materials typically yield different attenuation results. A 2.4 GHz RF signal that passes through drywall will attenuate 3 decibels (dB) and lose half of the original amplitude. A 2.4 GHz signal that is absorbed through a brick wall will attenuate 12 dB, which is 16 times less amplitude than the original signal. As discussed earlier, water is a major source of absorption as well as dense materials such as cinder blocks, all of which lead to attenuation.

EXERCISE 2.1

Visual Demonstration of Absorption

In this exercise, you will use a program called EMANIM to view the attenuation effect of materials due to absorption. EMANIM is a free program found on the book's page at www .sybex.com/go/cwna4e. This is a special version of EMANIM that was developed specifically for this book, and contains an extra sf menu choices.

1. Download and install the EMANIM program by double-clicking emanim_setup.exe.

2. From the main EMANIM menu, click Phenomenon.

3. Click Sybex CWNA Study Guide.

4. Click Exercise E.

    When a radio wave crosses matter, the matter absorbs part of the wave. As a result, the amplitude of the wave decreases. The extinction coefficient determines how much of the wave is absorbed by unit length of material.

5. Vary the length of the material and the extinction coefficient for Wave 1 to see how it affects the absorption.

Both loss and gain can be gauged in a relative measurement of change in power called decibels (dB), which is discussed extensively in Chapter 3, "Radio Frequency Components, Measurements, and Mathematics." Table 2.1 shows different attenuation values for several materials.

    Table 2.1 is meant as a reference chart and is not information that will be covered on the CWNA exam. Actual measurements may vary from site to site depending on specific environmental factors.

TABLE 2.1   Attenuation comparison of materials

Material	2.4 GHz
Foundation wall	–15 dB
Brick, concrete, concrete blocks	–12 dB

Material	2.4 GHz
Elevator or metal obstacle	−10 dB
Metal rack	−6 dB
Drywall or sheetrock	−3 dB
Nontinted glass windows	−3 dB
Wood door	−3 dB
Cubicle wall	−2 dB

It is important to understand that an RF signal will also lose amplitude merely as a function of distance due to free space path loss. Also, reflection propagation behaviors can produce the negative effects of multipath and, as a result, cause attenuation in signal strength.

Free Space Path Loss

Because of the laws of physics, an electromagnetic signal will attenuate as it travels, despite the lack of attenuation caused by obstructions, absorption, reflection, diffraction, and so on. *Free space path loss (FSPL)* is the loss of signal strength caused by the natural broadening of the waves, often referred to as *beam divergence*. RF signal energy spreads over larger areas as the signal travels farther away from an antenna, and as a result, the strength of the signal attenuates.

One way to illustrate free space path loss is to use a balloon analogy. Before a balloon is filled with helium, it remains small but has a dense rubber thickness. After the balloon is inflated and has grown and spread in size, the rubber becomes very thin. RF signals lose strength in much the same manner. Luckily, this loss in signal strength is logarithmic and not linear; thus the amplitude does not decrease as much in a second segment of equal length as it decreases in the first segment. A 2.4 GHz signal will change in power by about 80 dB after 100 meters but will lessen only another 6 dB in the next 100 meters.

Here are the formulas to calculate free space path loss:

```
FSPL = 36.6 + (20log₁₀(f)) + (20log₁₀(D))
FSPL = path loss in dB
f = frequency in MHz
D = distance in miles between antennas

FSPL = 32.44+ (20log₁₀(f)) + (20log₁₀(D))
FSPL = path loss in dB
f = frequency in MHz
D = distance in kilometers between antennas
```

Free space path loss formulas are provided as a reference and are not included on the CWNA exam. Many online calculators for FSPL and other RF calculators can also be found with a simple web search.

An even simpler way to estimate free space path loss (FSPL) is called the *6 dB rule* (remember for now that decibels are a measure of gain or loss, and further details of dB are covered extensively in Chapter 3). The 6 dB rule states that doubling the distance will result in a loss of amplitude of 6 dB. Table 2.2 shows estimated path loss and confirms the 6 dB rule.

🌐 Real World Scenario

Why Is Free Space Path Loss Important?

All radio devices have what is known as a receive sensitivity level. The radio receiver can properly interpret and receive a signal down to a certain fixed amplitude threshold. If a radio receives a signal above its amplitude threshold, the signal is powerful enough for the radio to sense and interpret the signal. For example, if you were to whisper a secret to someone, you'd need to make sure that you whisper loud enough for them to hear and understand it.

If the amplitude of a received signal is below the radio's receive sensitivity threshold, the radio can no longer properly sense and interpret the signal. The concept of free space path loss also applies to road trips in your car. When you are in a car listening to an AM radio station, eventually you will drive out of range and the radio will no longer be able to receive and process the music.

In addition to the radio being able to receive and interpret a signal, the received signal must be not only strong enough to be heard but also strong enough to be heard above any RF background noise, typically referred to as the *noise floor*. The signal must be louder than any background noise. In the example of whispering a secret to someone, if you were whispering the secret while an ambulance was driving past with the siren blasting, even though you were whispering loud enough for the person to hear you, the noise from the siren would be too loud for the person to distinguish what you were saying.

When designing both indoor WLANs and outdoor wireless bridge links, you must make sure that the RF signal will not attenuate below the receive sensitivity level of your WLAN radio simply because of free space path loss, and you must make sure that the signal does not attenuate near or below the noise floor. You typically achieve this goal indoors by performing a site survey. An outdoor bridge link requires a series of calculations called a *link budget*. (Site surveys are covered in Chapter 15 and Chapter 16, and link budgets are covered in Chapter 3.)

TABLE 2.2   Attenuation due to free space path loss

Distance (km)	Attenuation (dB)	
	2.4 GHz	**5 GHz**
1	100.0	106.4
2	106.1	112.4
4	112.1	118.5
8	118.1	124.5

Multipath

Multipath is a propagation phenomenon that results in two or more paths of a signal arriving at a receiving antenna at the same time or within nanoseconds of each other. Because of the natural broadening of the waves, the propagation behaviors of reflection, scattering, diffraction, and refraction will occur differently in dissimilar environments. When a signal encounters an object, it may reflect, scatter, refract, or diffract. These propagation behaviors can all result in multiple paths of the same signal.

In an indoor environment, reflected signals and echoes can be caused by long hallways, walls, desks, floors, file cabinets, and numerous other obstructions. Indoor environments with large amounts of metal surfaces such as airport hangars, warehouses, and factories are notoriously high-multipath environments because of all the reflective surfaces. The propagation behavior of reflection is typically the main cause of high-multipath environments. In an outdoor environment, multipath can be caused by a flat road, a large body of water, a building, or atmospheric conditions. Therefore, we have signals bouncing and bending in many different directions. The principal signal will still travel to the receiving antenna, but many of the bouncing and bent signals may also find their way to the receiving antenna via different paths. In other words, multiple paths of the RF signal arrive at the receiver, as seen in Figure 2.15.

It usually takes a bit longer for reflected signals to arrive at the receiving antenna because they must travel a longer distance than the principal signal. The time differential between these signals can be measured in billionths of a second (nanoseconds). The time differential between these multiple paths is known as the *delay spread*. You will learn later in this book that certain spread spectrum technologies are more tolerant than others of delay spread.

So, what exactly happens when multipath presents itself? In television signal transmissions, multipath causes a ghost effect with a faded duplicate image to the right of the main image. With RF signals, the effects of multipath can be either constructive or destructive. Quite often they are destructive. Because of the differences in phase of the multiple paths, the combined signal will often attenuate, amplify, or become corrupted. These effects are sometimes called *Rayleigh fading*, another phenomenon named after British physicist Lord Rayleigh.

FIGURE 2.15   Multipath

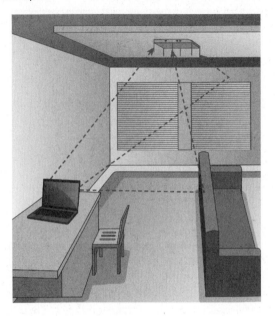

The four possible results of multipath are as follows:

Upfade   This is increased signal strength. When the multiple RF signal paths arrive at the receiver at the same time and are in phase or partially out of phase with the primary wave, the result is an increase in signal strength (amplitude). Smaller phase differences of between 0 and 120 degrees will cause *upfade*. Please understand, however, that the final received signal can never be stronger than the original transmitted signal because of free space path loss. Upfade is an example of constructive multipath.

Downfade   This is decreased signal strength. When the multiple RF signal paths arrive at the receiver at the same time and are out of phase with the primary wave, the result is a decrease in signal strength (amplitude). Phase differences of between 121 and 179 degrees will cause *downfade*. Decreased amplitude as a result of multipath would be considered destructive multipath.

Nulling   This is signal cancellation. When the multiple RF signal paths arrive at the receiver at the same time and are 180 degrees out of phase with the primary wave, the result will be *nulling*. Nulling is the complete cancellation of the RF signal. A complete cancellation of the signal is obviously destructive.

Data Corruption   Because of the difference in time between the primary signal and the reflected signals known as the delay spread, along with the fact that there may be multiple reflected signals, the receiver can have problems demodulating the RF signal's information. The delay spread time differential can cause bits to overlap with each other, and the end result is corrupted data. This type of multipath interference is often known as *intersymbol interference (ISI)*. Data corruption is the most common occurrence of destructive multipath.

The bad news is that high-multipath environments can result in data corruption because of intersymbol interference caused by the delay spread. The good news is that the receiving station will detect the errors through an 802.11-defined cyclic redundancy check (CRC) because the checksum will not calculate accurately. The 802.11 standard requires that most unicast frames be acknowledged by the receiving station with an acknowledgment (ACK) frame; otherwise, the transmitting station will have to retransmit the frame. The receiver will *not* acknowledge a frame that has failed the CRC. Therefore, unfortunately, the frame must be retransmitted, but this is better than it being misinterpreted.

Layer 2 retransmissions negatively affect the overall throughput of any 802.11 WLAN and can also affect the delivery of time-sensitive packets of applications, such as VoIP. In Chapter 12, "WLAN Troubleshooting," we discuss the multiple causes of layer 2 retransmissions and how to troubleshoot and minimize them. Multipath is one of the main causes of layer 2 retransmissions that negatively affect the throughput and latency of a legacy 802.11a/b/g WLAN.

So, how is a hapless WLAN engineer supposed to deal with destructive multipath issues? Multipath can be a serious problem when working with legacy 802.11a/b/g equipment. The use of directional antennas will often reduce the number of reflections, and antenna diversity can also be used to compensate for the negative effects of multipath. Sometimes, reducing transmit power or using a lower-gain antenna can solve the problem as long as there is enough signal to provide connectivity to the remote end. In this chapter, we have mainly focused on the destructive effects that multipath has on legacy 802.11a/b/g radio transmissions. Multipath has a constructive effect with the now prevalent 802.11n and 802.11ac radio transmissions that utilize multiple-input, multiple-output (MIMO) antenna diversity and *maximal ratio combining (MRC)* signal processing techniques.

In the past, data corruption of 802.11a/b/g transmissions caused by multipath had to be dealt with, and using unidirectional antennas to cut down on reflections was commonplace in high-multipath indoor environments. Now that MIMO technology used by 802.11n and 802.11ac radios is commonplace, multipath is now our friend and using unidirectional antennas is rarely needed indoors. However, unidirectional MIMO patch antennas are often used indoors to provide sectored coverage in high-density user environments.

EXERCISE 2.2

Visual Demonstration of Multipath and Phase

In this exercise, you will use a program called EMANIM to view the effect on amplitude due to various phases of two signals arriving at the same time.

1. From the book's page at www.sybex.com/go/cwna4e, download and install the EMANIM program by double-clicking emanim_setup.exe.

2. From the main EMANIM menu, click Phenomenon.

3. Click Sybex CWNA Study Guide.

4. Click Exercise A.

EXERCISE 2.2 *(continued)*

Two identical, vertically polarized waves are superposed (you might not see both of them because they cover each other). The result is a wave having double the amplitude of the component waves.

5. Click Exercise B.

   Two identical, 70-degree out-of-phase waves are superposed. The result is a wave with an increased amplitude over the component waves.

6. Click Exercise C.

   Two identical, 140-degree out-of-phase waves are superposed. The result is a wave with a decreased amplitude over the component waves.

7. Click on Exercise D.

   Two identical, vertically polarized waves are superposed. The result is a cancellation of the two waves.

Gain (Amplification)

Gain, also known as *amplification*, can best be described as the increase of amplitude, or signal strength. The two types of gain are known as active gain and passive gain. A signal's amplitude can be boosted by the use of external devices.

Active gain is usually caused by the transceiver or the use of an amplifier on the wire that connects the transceiver to the antenna. Many transceivers are capable of transmitting at different power levels, with the higher power levels creating a stronger or amplified signal. An amplifier is usually bidirectional, meaning that it increases the AC voltage both inbound and outbound. Active gain devices require the use of an external power source.

Passive gain is accomplished by focusing the RF signal with the use of an antenna. Antennas are passive devices that do not require an external power source. Instead, the internal workings of an antenna focus the signal more powerfully in one direction than another. An increase in signal amplitude is the result of either active gain prior to the signal reaching the antenna or passive gain focusing the signal radiating from the antenna.

 The proper use of antennas is covered extensively in Chapter 4.

Two very different tools can be used to measure the amplitude of a signal at a given point. The first, a frequency domain tool, can be used to measure amplitude in a finite frequency spectrum. The frequency domain tool used by WLAN engineers is called a *spectrum analyzer*. The second tool, a time domain tool, can be used to measure how a signal's amplitude changes over time. The conventional name for a time domain tool is an *oscilloscope*. Figure 2.16 shows how both of these tools can be used to display amplitude. It should be noted that spectrum analyzers are often used by WLAN engineers during site surveys. An oscilloscope is rarely if ever used when deploying a WLAN; however, oscilloscopes are used by RF engineers in laboratory test environments.

FIGURE 2.16   RF signal measurement tools

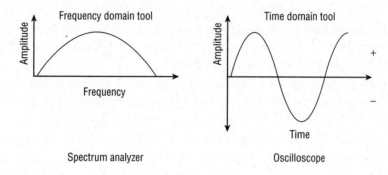

Summary

This chapter covered the meat and potatoes, the basics, of radio frequency signals. To properly design and administer a WLAN network, it is essential to have a thorough understanding of the following principles of RF properties and RF behaviors:

- Electromagnetic waves and how they are generated
- The relationship between wavelength, frequency, and the speed of light
- Signal strength and the various ways in which a signal can either attenuate or amplify
- The importance of the relationship between two or more signals
- How a signal moves by bending, bouncing, or absorbing in some manner

When troubleshooting an Ethernet network, the best place to start is always at layer 1, the Physical layer. WLAN troubleshooting should also begin at the Physical layer. Learning the RF fundamentals that exist at layer 1 is an essential step in proper wireless network administration.

Exam Essentials

Understand wavelength, frequency, amplitude, and phase.   Know the definition of each RF characteristic and how each can affect wireless LAN design.

Remember all the RF propagation behaviors. Be able to explain the differences between each RF behavior (such as reflection, diffraction, scattering, and so on) and the various mediums that are associated with each behavior.

Understand what causes attenuation. Loss can occur either on the wire or in the air. Absorption, free space path loss, and multipath downfade are all causes of attenuation.

Define free space path loss. Despite the lack of any obstructions, electromagnetic waves attenuate in a logarithmic manner as they travel away from the transmitter.

Remember the four possible results of multipath and their relationship to phase. Multipath may cause downfade, upfade, nulling, and data corruption. Understand that the effects of multipath can be either destructive or constructive.

Know the results of intersymbol interference and delay spread. The time differential between a primary signal and reflected signals may cause corrupted bits and affect through- put and latency due to layer 2 retransmissions.

Explain the difference between active and passive gain. Transceivers and RF amplifiers are active devices, whereas antennas are passive devices.

Explain the difference between transmit and received amplitude. Transmit amplitude is typically defined as the amount of initial amplitude that leaves the radio transmitter. When a radio receives an RF signal, the received signal strength is most often referred to as received amplitude.

Review Questions

1. What are some results of multipath interference? (Choose all that apply.)
    A. Scattering delay
    B. Upfade
    C. Excessive retransmissions
    D. Absorption

2. What term best defines the linear distance traveled in one positive-to-negative-to-positive oscillation of an electromagnetic signal?
    A. Crest
    B. Frequency
    C. Trough
    D. Wavelength

3. Which of the following statements are true about amplification? (Choose all that apply.)
    A. All antennas require an outside power source.
    B. RF amplifiers require an outside power source.
    C. Antennas are passive gain amplifiers that focus the energy of a signal.
    D. RF amplifiers passively increase signal strength by focusing the AC current of the signal.

4. A standard measurement of frequency is called what?
    A. Hertz
    B. Milliwatt
    C. Nanosecond
    D. Decibel
    E. K-factor

5. When an RF signal bends around an object, this propagation behavior is known as what?
    A. Stratification
    B. Refraction
    C. Scattering
    D. Diffraction
    E. Attenuation

6. When the multiple RF signals arrive at a receiver at the same time and are _____ with the primary wave, the result can be _____ of the primary signal.
    A. out of phase, scattering
    B. in phase, intersymbol interference

    C. in phase, attenuation

    D. 180 degrees out of phase, amplification

    E. in phase, cancellation

    F. 180 degrees out of phase, cancellation

7. Which of the following statements are true? (Choose all that apply.)

    A. When upfade occurs, the final received signal will be stronger than the original transmitted signal.

    B. When downfade occurs, the final received signal will never be stronger than the original transmitted signal.

    C. When upfade occurs, the final received signal will never be stronger than the original transmitted signal.

    D. When downfade occurs, the final received signal will be stronger than the original transmitted signal.

8. What is the frequency of an RF signal that cycles 2.4 million times per second?

    A. 2.4 hertz

    B. 2.4 MHz

    C. 2.4 GHz

    D. 2.4 kilohertz

    E. 2.4 KHz

9. What is the best example of a time domain tool that could be used by an RF engineer?

    A. Oscilloscope

    B. Spectroscope

    C. Spectrum analyzer

    D. Refractivity gastroscope

10. What are some objects or materials that are common causes of reflection? (Choose all that apply.)

    A. Metal

    B. Trees

    C. Asphalt road

    D. Lake

    E. Carpet floors

11. Which of these propagation behaviors can result in multipath? (Choose all that apply.)

    A. Refraction

    B. Diffraction

    C. Reflection

    D. Scattering

    E. None of the above

12. Which behavior can be described as an RF signal encountering a chain link fence, causing the signal to bounce into multiple directions?

    A. Diffraction

    B. Scatter

    C. Reflection

    D. Refraction

    E. Multiplexing

13. Which 802.11 radio technologies are most impacted by the destructive effects of multipath? (Choose all that apply.)

    A. 802.11a

    B. 802.11b

    C. 802.11g

    D. 802.11n

    E. 802.11i

14. Which of the following can cause refraction of an RF signal traveling through it? (Choose all that apply.)

    A. Shift in air temperature

    B. Change in air pressure

    C. Humidity

    D. Smog

    E. Wind

    F. Lightning

15. Which of the following statements are true about free space path loss? (Choose all that apply.)

    A. RF signals will attenuate as they travel, despite the lack of attenuation caused by obstructions.

    B. Path loss occurs at a constant linear rate.

    C. Attenuation is caused by obstructions.

    D. Path loss occurs at a logarithmic rate.

16. What term is used to describe the time differential between a primary signal and a reflected signal arriving at a receiver?

    A. Path delay

    B. Spread spectrum

    C. Multipath

    D. Delay spread

17. What is an example of a frequency domain tool that could be used by an RF engineer?

    A. Oscilloscope

    B. Spectroscope

    C. Spectrum analyzer

    D. Refractivity gastroscope

18. Using knowledge of RF characteristics and behaviors, which two options should a WLAN engineer be most concerned about during an indoor site survey? (Choose all that apply.)

    A. Brick walls

    B. Indoor temperature

    C. Wood-lath plaster walls

    D. Drywall

19. Which three properties are interrelated?

    A. Frequency, wavelength, and the speed of light

    B. Frequency, amplitude, and the speed of light

    C. Frequency, phase, and amplitude

    D. Amplitude, phase, and the speed of sound

20. Which RF behavior best describes a signal striking a medium and bending in a different direction?

    A. Refraction

    B. Scattering

    C. Diffusion

    D. Diffraction

    E. Microwave reflection

Chapter

3

Radio Frequency Components, Measurements, and Mathematics

IN THIS CHAPTER, YOU WILL LEARN ABOUT THE FOLLOWING:

✓ **Components of RF communications**

  ▪ Transmitter

  ▪ Receiver

  ▪ Antenna

  ▪ Isotropic radiator

  ▪ Intentional radiator (IR)

  ▪ Equivalent isotropically radiated power (EIRP)

✓ **Units of power and comparison**

  ▪ Watt

  ▪ Milliwatt

  ▪ Decibel (dB)

  ▪ dBi

  ▪ dBd

  ▪ dBm

  ▪ Inverse square law

✓ **RF mathematics**

  ▪ Rule of 10s and 3s

✓ **Noise floor**

✓ **Signal-to-noise ratio (SNR)**

✓ Received signal strength indicator (RSSI)

✓ Link budget

✓ Fade margin/system operating margin

To put it simply, data communication is the transferring of information between computers. No matter what form of communication is being used, many components are required to achieve a successful transfer. Before we look at individual components, let us initially keep things simple and look at the three basic requirements for successful communications:

- Two or more devices want to communicate.

- There must be a medium, a means, or a method for them to use to communicate.

- There must be a set of rules for them to use when they communicate. (This is covered in Chapter 8, "802.11 Medium Access.")

These three basic requirements are the same for all forms of communication, whether a group of people are having a conversation at a dinner party, two computers are transmitting data via a dial-up modem, or many computers are communicating via a wireless network.

The existence of a computer network essentially implies that the first requirement is met. If we did not have two or more devices that wanted to share data, we would not need to create the network in the first place. The CWNA certification program also assumes this and is therefore rarely if ever concerned specifically with the data itself. It is assumed that we have data; our concern is to transmit it.

This chapter focuses on the second requirement: the medium, means, or method of communication. We cover the components of radio frequency (RF), which make up what we refer to as the medium for wireless communications. Here we are concerned with the transmission of the RF signal and the role of each device and component along the transmission path. We also show how each device or component affects the transmission.

In Chapter 2, "Radio Frequency Fundamentals," you learned that there are many RF behaviors that affect the signal as it leaves the transmitter and travels toward the receiver. As the signal moves through the various components and then propagates through the air, the signal's amplitude changes. Some components increase the power of the signal (gain), whereas other components decrease the power (loss). In this chapter, you will learn how to quantify and measure the power of the waves and calculate how the waves are affected by both internal and external influences. Through these calculations, you will be able to accurately determine whether you will have the means to communicate between devices.

RF Components

Many components contribute to the successful transmission and reception of an RF signal. Figure 3.1 shows the key components that are covered in the following sections. In addition to knowing the function of the components, it is important to understand how the strength of the signal is specifically affected by each of the components.

FIGURE 3.1:   RF components

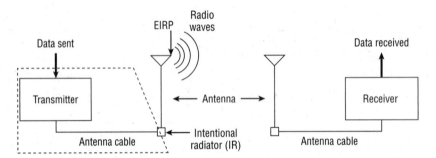

Later in this chapter, when we discuss RF mathematics, we will show you how to calculate the effect that each of the components has on the signal.

Transmitter

The *transmitter* is the initial component in the creation of the wireless medium. The computer hands the data off to the transmitter, and it is the transmitter's job to begin the RF communication.

In Chapter 1, "Overview of Wireless Standards, Organizations, and Fundamentals," you learned about carrier signals and modulation methods. When the transmitter receives the data, it begins generating an alternating current (AC) signal. This AC signal determines the frequency of the transmission. For example, for an 802.11b (HR-DSSS) or 802.11g (ERP) transmission (a 2.4 GHz signal), the AC signal oscillates around 2.4 billion times per second, whereas for an 802.11a (OFDM) transmission (a 5 GHz signal), the AC signal oscillates around 5 billion times per second. This oscillation determines the frequency of the radio wave.

The exact frequencies used are covered in Chapter 6, "Wireless Networks and Spread Spectrum Technologies."

The transmitter takes the data provided and modifies the AC signal by using a modulation technique to encode the data into the signal. This modulated AC signal is now a carrier signal, containing (or carrying) the data to be transmitted. The carrier signal is then transported either directly to the antenna or through a cable to the antenna.

In addition to generating a signal at a specific frequency, the transmitter is responsible for determining the original transmission amplitude, or what is more commonly referred to as the *power level*, of the transmitter. The higher the amplitude of the wave, the more powerful the wave is and the farther it can be received. The power levels that the transmitter is allowed to generate are determined by the local regulatory domain authorities, such as the Federal Communications Commission (FCC) in the United States.

Although we are explaining the transmitter and receiver separately in this chapter, and although functionally they are different components, typically they are one device that is referred to as a *transceiver* (transmitter/ receiver). Typical wireless devices that have transceivers built into them are access points, bridges, and client adapters.

Antenna

An *antenna* provides two functions in a communication system. When connected to the transmitter, it collects the AC signal that it receives from the transmitter and directs, or radiates, the RF waves away from the antenna in a pattern specific to the antenna type. When connected to the receiver, the antenna takes the RF waves that it receives through the air and directs the AC signal to the receiver. The receiver converts the AC signal to bits and bytes. As you will see later in this chapter, the signal that is received is much less than the signal that is generated. This signal loss is analogous to two people trying to talk to each other from opposite ends of a football field. Because of distance alone (free space), the yelling from one end of the field may be heard as barely louder than a whisper on the other end.

The RF transmission of an antenna is usually compared or referenced to an isotropic radiator. An *isotropic radiator* is a *point source* that radiates signal equally in all directions. The sun is probably one of the best examples of an isotropic radiator. It generates equal amounts of energy in all directions. Unfortunately, it is not possible to manufacture an antenna that is a perfect isotropic radiator. The structure of the antenna itself influences the output of the antenna, similar to the way the structure of a light bulb affects the bulb's ability to emit light equally in all directions.

There are two ways to increase the power output from an antenna. The first is to generate more power at the transmitter, as stated in the previous section. The other is to direct, or focus, the RF signal that is radiating from the antenna. This is similar to how you can focus light from a flashlight. If you remove the lens from the flashlight, the bulb is typically not very bright and radiates in almost all directions. To make the light brighter, you could use more powerful batteries, or you could put the lens back on. The lens is not actually creating more light; it is focusing the light that was radiating in all different directions into a narrow area. Some antennas radiate waves as the bulb without the lens does, whereas others radiate focused waves as the flashlight with the lens does.

In Chapter 4, "Radio Frequency Signal and Antenna Concepts," you will learn about the types of antennas and how to properly and most effectively use them.

Receiver

The *receiver* is the final component in the wireless medium. The receiver takes the carrier signal that is received from the antenna and translates the modulated signals into 1s and 0s. It then takes this data and passes it to the computer to be processed. The job of the receiver is not always an easy one. The signal that is received is a much less powerful signal than what was transmitted because of the distance it has traveled and the effects of free space path loss (FSPL). The signal is also often unintentionally altered due to interference from other RF sources and multipath.

Intentional Radiator (IR)

The FCC Code of Federal Regulations (CFR) Part 15 defines an *intentional radiator (IR)* as "a device that intentionally generates and emits radio frequency energy by radiation or induction." Basically, it's something that is specifically designed to generate RF, as opposed to something that generates RF as a by-product of its main function, such as a motor that incidentally generates RF noise.

Regulatory bodies such as the FCC limit the amount of power that is allowed to be generated by an IR. The IR consists of all the components from the transmitter to the antenna but not including the antenna, as shown in Figure 3.1. The power output of the IR is thus the sum of all the components from the transmitter to the antenna, again not including the antenna. The components making up the IR include the transmitter, all cables and connectors, and any other equipment (grounding, lightning arrestors, amplifiers, attenuators, and so forth) between the transmitter and the antenna. The power of the IR is measured at the connecter that provides the input to the antenna. Because this is the point where the IR is measured and regulated, we often refer to this point alone as the IR. This power level is typically measured in milliwatts (mW) or decibels relative to 1 milliwatt (dBm). Using the flashlight analogy, the IR is all of the components up to the lightbulb socket, but not the bulb and lens. This is the raw power, or signal, and now the bulb and lens can focus the signal.

Equivalent Isotropically Radiated Power

Equivalent isotropically radiated power (EIRP) is the highest RF signal strength that is transmitted from a particular antenna. To understand this better, think of our flashlight example for a moment. Let's assume that the bulb without the lens generates 1 watt of power. When you put the lens on the flashlight, it focuses that 1 watt of light. If you were to look at the light now, it would appear much brighter. If you were to measure the brightest point of the light that was being generated by the flashlight, because of the effects of the lens it may be equal to the brightness of an 8-watt bulb. So by focusing the light, you are able to make the equivalent isotropically radiated power of the focused bulb equal to 8 watts.

It is important for you to know that you can find other references to EIRP as *equivalent isotropic radiated power* and *effective isotropic radiated power*. The use of EIRP in this book is consistent with the FCC definition, "equivalent isotropically radiated power, the product of the power supplied to the antenna and the antenna gain in a given direction relative to an isotropic antenna." Even though the terms that the initials stand for at times differ, the definition of EIRP is consistent.

As you learned earlier in this chapter, antennas are capable of focusing, or directing, RF energy. This focusing capability can make the effective output of the antenna much greater than the signal entering the antenna. Because of this ability to amplify the output of the RF signal, regulatory bodies such as the FCC limit the amount of EIRP from an antenna.

In the next section of this chapter, you will learn how to calculate how much power is being provided to the antenna (IR) and how much power is coming out of the antenna (EIRP).

 Real World Scenario

Why Are IR and EIRP Measurements Important?

As you learned in Chapter 1, the regulatory domain authority in an individual country or region is responsible for maximum transmit power regulations. The FCC and other domain authorities usually define maximum power output for the intentional radiator (IR) and a maximum equivalent isotropically radiated power (EIRP) that radiates from the antenna. In laymen's terms, the FCC regulates the maximum amount of power that goes into an antenna and the maximum amount of power that comes out of an antenna.

You will need to know the definitions of IR and EIRP measurements. However, the CWNA exam (CWNA-106) will not test you on any power regulations because they vary from country to country. It is advisable to educate yourself about the maximum transmit power regulations of the country where you plan on deploying a WLAN so that no violations occur. The transmit power of most indoor WLAN radios varies in a range between 1 mW and 100 mW. Therefore, you usually do not need to concern yourself with power regulations when deploying indoor WLAN equipment. However, knowledge of power regulations is important for outdoor WLAN deployments.

Units of Power and Comparison

When an 802.11 wireless network is designed, two key components are coverage and performance. A good understanding of RF power, comparison, and RF mathematics can be very helpful during the network design phase.

In the following sections, we will introduce you to an assortment of *units of power* and *units of comparison*. It is important to know and understand the various types of units of measurement and how they relate to each other. Some of the numbers that you will be working with will represent actual units of power, and others will represent relative units of comparison. Actual units are ones that represent a known or set value.

To say that a man is 6 feet tall is an example of an actual measurement. Since the man's height is a known value, in this case 6 feet, you know exactly how tall he is. Relative units are comparative values comparing one item to a similar type of item. For example, if you wanted to tell someone how tall the man's wife is by using comparative units of measurement, you could say that she is five-sixths his height. You now have a comparative measurement: If you know the actual height of either one, you can then determine how tall the other is.

Comparative units of measurement are useful when working with units of power. As you will see later in this chapter, we can use these comparative units of power to compare the area that one access point can cover vs. another access point. Using simple mathematics, we can determine things such as how many watts are needed to double the distance of a signal from an access point.

Units of power are used to measure transmission amplitude and received amplitude. In other words, units of transmit or received power measurements are *absolute power* measurements. Units of comparison are often used to measure how much gain or loss occurs because of the introduction of cabling or an antenna. Units of comparison are also used to represent a difference in power from point A to point B. In other words, units of comparison are measurements of *change in power*.

Here is a list of the units of power, followed by another list of the units of comparison, all of which are covered in the following sections.

Units of power (absolute)

- watt (W)
- milliwatt (mW)
- decibels relative to 1 milliwatt (dBm)

Units of comparison (relative)

- decibel (dB)
- decibels relative to an isotropic radiator (dBi)
- decibels relative to a half-wave dipole antenna (dBd)

Watt

A *watt (W)* is the basic unit of power, named after James Watt, an 18th-century Scottish inventor. One watt is equal to 1 ampere (amp) of current flowing at 1 volt. To give a better explanation of a watt, we will use a modification of the classic water analogy.

Many of you are probably familiar with a piece of equipment known as a power washer. If you are not familiar with it, it is a machine that connects to a water source, such as a garden hose, and enables you to direct a stream of high-pressure water at an object, with the premise that the fast-moving water will clean the object. The success of a power washer is based on two components: the pressure applied to the water and the volume of water used over a period of time, also known as flow. These two components provide the power of the water stream. If you increase the pressure, you will increase the power of the stream. If you increase the flow of the water, you will also increase the power of the stream. The power of the stream is equal to the pressure times the flow.

A watt is very similar to the output of the power washer. Instead of the pressure generated by the machine, electrical systems have voltage. Instead of water flow, electrical systems have current, which is measured in amps. So the amount of watts generated is equal to the volts times the amps.

Milliwatt (mW)

A *milliwatt (mW)* is also a unit of power. To put it simply, a milliwatt is 1/1,000 of a watt. The reason you need to be concerned with milliwatts is because most of the indoor 802.11 equipment that you will be using transmits at power levels between 1 mW and 100 mW. Remember that the transmit power level of a radio will be attenuated by any cabling and will be amplified by the antenna. Although regulatory bodies such as the FCC may allow intentional radiator (IR) power output of as much as 1 watt, only rarely in point-to-point communications, such as in building-to-building bridge links, would you use 802.11 equipment with more than 300 mW of transmit power.

 Real World Scenario

What Does a Wi-Fi Vendor's Transmit Power Settings Represent?

All Wi-Fi vendors offer the capability to adjust the transmit power settings of an access point. A typical AP radio will usually have transmit power capabilities of 1 mW to 100 mW. However, not every Wi-Fi vendor will represent transmit power values the same way. The transmit power settings of most vendors represent the IR, whereas the transmit power settings of other vendors might actually be the EIRP instead. Furthermore, Wi-Fi vendors might also indicate the transmit amplitude in either milliwatts or dBms—for example, 32 mW or +15 dBm—yet some might simply indicate transmit power in the form of a percentage value, such as 32 percent. You will need to refer to your specific Wi-Fi vendor's deployment guide to fully understand the transmit amplitude value.

Decibel (dB)

The first thing you should know about the *decibel (dB)* is that it is a unit of comparison, not a unit of power. Therefore, it is used to represent a difference between two values. In other words, a dB is a relative expression and a measurement of change in power. In wireless networking, decibels are often used either to compare the power of two transmitters or, more often, to compare the difference or loss between the EIRP output of a transmitter's antenna and the amount of power received by the receiver's antenna.

Decibel is derived from the term *bel*. Employees at Bell Telephone Laboratories needed a way to represent power losses on telephone lines as power ratios. They defined a bel as the ratio of 10 to 1 between the power of two sounds. Let us look at an example: An access point transmits data at 100 mW. Laptop1 receives the signal from the AP at a power level of 10 mW, and laptop2 receives the signal from the AP at a power level of 1 mW. The difference between the signal from the access point (100 mW) to laptop1 (10 mW) is 100:10, or a 10:1 ratio, or 1 bel. The difference between the signal from laptop1 (10 mW) to laptop2 (1 mW) is also a 10:1 ratio, or 1 bel. So the power difference between the access point and laptop2 is 2 bels.

Bels can be looked at mathematically by using logarithms. Not everyone understands or remembers logarithms, so we will review them. First, we need to look at raising a number to a power. If you take 10 and raise it to the third power (10^3 = y), what you are actually doing is multiplying three 10s ($10 \times 10 \times 10$). If you do the math, you will calculate that y is equal to 1,000. So the solution is 10^3 = 1,000. When calculating logarithms, you change the formula to 10^y = 1,000. Here you are trying to figure out what power 10 needs to be raised to in order to get to 1,000. You know in this example that the answer is 3. You can also write this equation as $y = \log_{10}(1,000)$ or $y = \log_{10}1,000$. So the complete equation is $3 = \log_{10}(1,000)$. Here are some examples of power and log formulas:

$10^1 = 10$	$\log_{10}(10) = 1$
$10^2 = 100$	$\log_{10}(100) = 2$
$10^3 = 1,000$	$\log_{10}(1,000) = 3$
$10^4 = 10,000$	$\log_{10}(10,000) = 4$

Now, let's go back and calculate the bels from the access point to the laptop2 example by using logarithms. Remember that bels are used to calculate the ratio between two powers. So let's refer to the power of the access point as P_{AP} and the power of laptop2 as P_{L2}. So, the formula for this example would be $y = \log_{10}(P_{AP}/P_{L2})$. If you plug in the power values, the formula becomes $y = \log_{10}(100/1)$, or $y = \log_{10}(100)$. So this equation is asking, 10 raised to what power equals 100? The answer is 2 bels (10^2 = 100).

OK, so this is supposed to be a section about decibels, but so far we have covered just bels. In certain environments, bels are not exact enough, which is why we use decibels instead. A decibel is equal to 1/10 of a bel. To calculate decibels, all you need to do is multiply bels by 10. So the formulas for bels and decibels are as follows:

bels = $\log_{10}(P_1/P_2)$

decibels = $10 \times \log_{10}(P_1/P_2)$

Now let us go back and calculate the decibels for the example of the access point to laptop2. So the formula now is $y = 10 \times \log_{10}(P_{AP}/P_{L2})$. If you plug in the power values, the formula becomes $y = 10 \times \log_{10}(100/1)$, or $y = 10 \times \log_{10}(100)$. So the answer is +20 decibels. +20 decibels is the equivalent of +2 bels.

 You do not need to know how to calculate logarithms for the CWNA exam. These examples are here only to give you some basic understanding of what they are and how to calculate them. Later in this chapter, you will learn how to calculate decibels without using logarithms.

Now that you have learned about decibels, you are probably still wondering why you cannot just work with milliwatts. You can if you want, but because power changes are calculated using logarithmic formulas, the differences between values can become extremely large and more difficult to deal with. It is easier to say that a 100 mW signal decreased by 70 decibels than to say that it decreased to 0.00001 milliwatts. Because of the scale of the numbers, you can see why decibels can be easier to work with.

 Real World Scenario

Why Should You Use Decibels?

In Chapter 2, you learned that there are many behaviors that can adversely affect a wave. One of the behaviors that you learned about was free space path loss.

If a 2.4 GHz access point is transmitting at 100 mW, and a laptop is 100 meters (0.1 kilometer) away from the access point, the laptop is receiving only about 0.000001 milliwatts of power. The difference between the numbers 100 and 0.000001 is so large that it doesn't have much relevance to someone looking at it. Additionally, it would be easy for someone to accidentally leave out a zero when writing or typing 0.00001 (as we just did).

If you use the FSPL formula to calculate the decibel loss for this scenario, the formula would be

decibels = $32.4 + (20\log_{10}(2,400)) + (20\log_{10}(0.1))$

The answer is a loss of 80.004 dB, which is approximately 80 decibels of loss. This number is easier to work with and less likely to be miswritten or mistyped.

dBi

Earlier in this chapter, we compared an antenna to an isotropic radiator. Theoretically, an isotropic radiator can radiate an equal signal in all directions. An antenna cannot do this because of construction limitations. In other instances, you do not want an antenna to radiate in all directions because you want to focus the signal of the antenna in a particular direction. Whichever the case may be, it is important to be able to calculate the radiating power of the antenna so that you can determine how strong a signal is at a certain distance from the antenna. You may also want to compare the output of one antenna to that of another.

The gain, or increase, of power from an antenna when compared to what an isotropic radiator would generate is known as *decibels isotropic (dBi)*. Another way of phrasing this is *decibel gain referenced to an isotropic radiator* or *change in power relative to an antenna*. Since antennas are measured in gain, not power, you can conclude that dBi is a relative measurement and not an absolute power measurement. dBi is simply a measurement of antenna gain. The dBi value is measured at the strongest point, or the focus point, of the antenna signal. Because antennas always focus their energy more in one direction than another, the dBi value of an antenna is always a positive gain and not a loss. There are, however, antennas with a dBi value of 0, which are often referred to as *no-gain*, or *unity-gain*, antennas.

A common antenna used on access points is the half-wave dipole antenna. The half-wave dipole antenna is a small, typically rubber-encased, general-purpose omnidirectional antenna. A 2.4 GHz half-wave dipole antenna has a dBi value of 2.14.

 Any time you see *dBi*, think *antenna gain*.

dBd

The antenna industry uses two dB scales to describe the gain of antennas. The first scale, which you just learned about, is dBi, which is used to describe the gain of an antenna relative to a theoretical isotropic antenna. The other scale used to describe antenna gain is *decibels dipole (dBd)*, or *decibel gain relative to a dipole antenna*. So a dBd value is the increase in gain of an antenna when it is compared to the signal of a dipole antenna. As you will learn in Chapter 4, dipole antennas are also omnidirectional antennas. Therefore, a dBd value is a measurement of omnidirectional antenna gain and not unidirectional antenna gain. Because dipole antennas are measured in gain, not power, you can also conclude that dBd is a relative measurement and not a power measurement.

The definition of dBd seems simple enough, but what happens when you want to compare two antennas and one is represented with dBi and the other with dBd? This is actually quite simple. A standard dipole antenna has a dBi value of 2.14. If an antenna has a value of 3 dBd, this means that it is 3 dB greater than a dipole antenna. Because the value of a dipole antenna is 2.14 dBi, all you need to do is add 3 to 2.14. So a 3 dBd antenna is equal to a 5.14 dBi antenna.

Don't forget that dB, dBi, and dBd are comparative, or relative, measurements and not units of power.

 Real World Scenario

The Real Scoop on dBd

When working with 802.11 equipment, it is not often that you will have an antenna with a dBd value. 802.11 antennas typically are measured using dBi. On the rare occasion that you do run into an antenna measured with dBd, just add 2.14 to the dBd value and you will know the antenna's dBi value.

dBm

Earlier when you read about bels and decibels, you learned that they measured differences or ratios between two signals. Regardless of the type of power that was being transmitted, all you really knew was that the one signal was greater or less than the other by a particular number of bels or decibels. dBm also provides a comparison, but instead of comparing a signal to another signal, it is used to compare a signal to 1 milliwatt of power. *dBm* means *decibels relative to 1 milliwatt*. So, what you are doing is setting dBm to 0 (zero) and equating that to 1 milliwatt of power. Because dBm is a measurement that is compared to a known value, 1 milliwatt, it is actually a measure of absolute power. Because decibels (relative) are referenced to 1 milliwatt (absolute), think of a dBm as an absolute assessment that measures change of power referenced to 1 milliwatt. You can now state that 0 dBm is equal to 1 milliwatt. Using the formula $dBm = 10 \times \log_{10}(P_{mW})$, you can determine that 100 mW of power is equal to +20 dBm.

If you happen to have the dBm value of a device and want to calculate the corresponding milliwatt value, you can do that too. The formula is $P_{mW} = 10^{(dBm \div 10)}$.

Remember that 1 milliwatt is the reference point and that 0 dBm is equal to 1 mW. Any absolute power measurement of +dBm indicates amplitude greater than 1 mW. Any absolute power measurement of –dBm indicates amplitude less than 1 mW. For example, we stated earlier that the transmission amplitude of most 802.11 radios usually ranges from 1 mW to 100 mW. A transmission amplitude of 100 mW is equal to +20 dBm. Because of FSPL, received signals will always measure below 1 mW. A very strong received signal is –40 dBm, which is the equivalent of 0.0001 mW (1/10,000th of 1 milliwatt).

It might seem a little ridiculous to have to deal with both milliwatts and dBm. If milliwatts are a valid measurement of power, why not just use them? Why do you have to, or want to, also use dBm? These are good questions that are asked often by students. One reason is simply that dBm absolute measurements are often easier to grasp than measurements in the millionths and billionths of a single milliwatt. Most 802.11 radios can interpret received signals from −30 dBm (1/1,000th of 1 mW) to as low as −100 dBm (1/10 of a billionth of 1 mW). The human brain can grasp −100 dBm much easier than 0.0000000001 milliwatts. During a site survey, WLAN engineers will always determine coverage zones by recording the received signal strength in −dBm values.

Another very practical reason to use dBm can be shown using the FSPL formula again. Following are two FSPL equations. The first equation calculates the decibel loss of a 2.4 GHz signal at 100 meters (0.1 kilometer) from the RF source, and the second calculates the decibel loss of a 2.4 GHz signal at 200 meters (0.2 kilometer) from the RF source:

$$FSPL = 32.4 + (20\log_{10}(2{,}400)) + (20\log_{10}(0.1)) = 80.00422 \text{ dB}$$
$$FSPL = 32.4 + (20\log_{10}(2{,}400)) + (20\log_{10}(0.2)) = 86.02482 \text{ dB}$$

In this example, by doubling the distance from the RF source, the signal decreased by about 6 dB. If you double the distance between the transmitter and the receiver, the received signal will decrease by 6 dB. No matter what numbers are chosen, if the distance is doubled, the decibel loss will be 6 dB. This rule also implies that if you increase the amplitude by 6 dB, the usable distance will double. This *6 dB rule* is very useful for comparing cell sizes or estimating the coverage of a transmitter. The 6 dB rule is also useful for understanding antenna gain, because every 6 dB of extra antenna gain will double the usable distance of an RF signal. Remember, if you were working with milliwatts this rule would not be relevant. By converting milliwatts to dBm, you have a more practical way to compare signals.

Remember the *6 dB rule:* +6 dB doubles the distance of the usable signal; −6 dB halves the distance of the usable signal.

Using dBm also makes it easy to calculate the effects of antenna gain on a signal. If a transmitter generates a +20 dBm signal and the antenna adds 5 dBi of gain to the signal, then the power that is radiating from the antenna (EIRP) is equal to the sum of the two numbers, which is +25 dBm.

Inverse Square Law

You just learned about the 6 dB rule, which states that a +6 dB change in signal will double the usable distance of a signal and a −6 dB change in signal will halve the usable distance of a signal. This rule and these numbers are based on the *inverse square law*, originally developed by Isaac Newton.

This law states that the change in power is equal to 1 divided by the square of the change in distance. In other words, as the distance from the source of a signal doubles, the energy is spread out over four times the area, resulting in one-fourth of the original intensity of the signal.

This means that if you are receiving a signal at a certain power level and a certain distance (D) and you double the distance (change in distance = 2), the new power level will change by $1/(2)^2$. To use this principle to calculate the EIRP at a specific distance, the formula is $P/(4 \times pi \times r^2)$, where P equals the initial EIRP power and r equals the original (reference) distance.

Let's also review the formula for free space path loss:

$FSPL = 36.6 + (20\log_{10}(F)) + (20\log_{10}(D))$

FSPL = path loss in dB

F = frequency in MHz

D = distance in miles between antennas

$FSPL = 32.4 + (20\log_{10}(F)) + (20\log_{10}(D))$

FSPL = path loss in dB

F = frequency in MHz

D = distance in kilometers between antennas

The concept of FSPL is also based on Newton's inverse square law. The main variable for the inverse square law is simply distance. The FSPL formula is also based on distance but includes another variable: frequency.

RF Mathematics

When the topic of RF mathematics is discussed, most people cringe and panic because they expect formulas that have logarithms in them. Fear not. You are about to learn RF math without having to use logarithms. If you want to refresh yourself on some of your math skills before going through this section, review the following:

- Addition and subtraction using the numbers 3 and 10
- Multiplication and division using the numbers 2 and 10

No, we are not kidding. If you know how to add and subtract using 3 and 10 and if you know how to multiply and divide using 2 and 10, you have all of the math skills you need to perform RF math. Read on, and we will teach you how.

Rule of 10s and 3s

Before you fully delve into the *rule of 10s and 3s*, it is important to know that this rule may not give you the exact same answers that you would get if you used the logarithmic formulas. The rule of 10s and 3s provides approximate values, not necessarily exact values. If you are an engineer creating a product that must conform to RF regulatory guidelines, you will need to use logarithms to calculate the exact values. However, if you are a network designer planning a network for your company, you will find that the rule of 10s and 3s will provide you with the numbers you need to properly plan your network.

This section will take you step-by-step through numerous calculations. All of the calculations will be based on the following four rules of the 10s and 3s:

- For every 3 dB of gain (relative), double the absolute power (mW).
- For every 3 dB of loss (relative), halve the absolute power (mW).
- For every 10 dB of gain (relative), multiply the absolute power (mW) by a factor of 10.
- For every 10 dB of loss (relative), divide the absolute power (mW) by a factor of 10.

For example, if your access point is configured to transmit at 100 mW and the antenna is rated for 3 dBi of passive gain, the amount of power that will radiate out of the antenna (EIRP) will be 200 mW. Following the rule that you just learned, you will see that the 3 dB of gain from the antenna caused the 100 mW signal from the access point to double. Conversely, if your access point is configured to transmit at 100 mW and is attached to a cable that introduces 3 dB of loss, the amount of absolute amplitude at the end of the cable will be 50 mW. Here you can see that the 3 dB of loss from the cable caused the 100 mW signal from the access point to be halved.

In another example, if your access point is configured to transmit at 40 mW and the antenna is rated for 10 dBi of passive gain, the amount of power that radiates out of the antenna (EIRP) will be 400 mW. Here you can see that the 10 dB of gain from the antenna caused the 40 mW signal from the access point to increase by a factor of 10. Conversely, if your access point is configured to transmit at 40 mW and is attached to a cable that introduces 10 dB of loss, the amount of absolute amplitude at the end of the cable will be 4 mW. Here you can see that the 10 dB of loss from the cable caused the 40 mW signal from the access point to be decreased by a factor of 10.

If you remember these rules, you will be able to quickly perform RF calculations. After reviewing these rules, see Exercise 3.1, which will take you through a step-by-step procedure for using the rule of 10s and 3s. As you work through the step-by-step procedure, remember that dBm is a unit of power and that dB is a unit of change. dB is a value of change that can be applied to dBm. So if you have a +10 dBm signal and it increases by 3 dB, you can add these two numbers together to get a result of +13 dBm signal.

EXERCISE 3.1

Step-by-Step Use of the Rule of 10s and 3s

1. On a sheet of paper, create two columns. The header of the first column should be **dBm**, and the header of the second column should be **mW**.

dBm   mW

2. Next to the dBm header, place a + sign and a – sign, and next to the mW header place a × sign and a ÷ sign.

   These will help you to remember that all math performed on the dBm column is addition or subtraction and all math performed on the mW column is multiplication or division.

+   ×
–   dBm   mW   ÷

3. To the left of the + and – signs, write the numbers **3** and **10**, and to the right of the × and ÷ signs, write the numbers **2** and **10**.

   Any addition or subtraction to the dBm column can be performed using only the numbers 3 and 10. Any multiplication or division to the mW column can be performed using only the numbers 2 and 10.

3   +   ×   2
10 –   dBm   mW   ÷   10

4. If there is a + on the left, there needs to be an x on the right. If there is a – on the left, there needs to be a ÷ on the right.

5. If you are adding or subtracting a 3 on the left, you must be multiplying or dividing by a 2 on the right. If you are adding or subtracting a 10 on the left, you must be multiplying or dividing by a 10 on the right.

6. The last thing you need to do is to put a **0** under the dBm column and a **1** under the mW column.

   Remember that the definition of dBm is *decibels relative to 1 milliwatt*. So now the chart shows that 0 dBm is equal to 1 milliwatt.

3   +   ×   2
10 –   dBm   mW   ÷   10
0   1

Before we continue with other examples, it is important to emphasize that a change of ±3 dB equates to a doubling or halving of the power, no matter what power measurement is being used. In our usage of the rule of 10s and 3s, we are dealing with milliwatts because that is the typical transmission amplitude measurement used by 802.11 equipment. However, it is important to remember that a +3 dB increase means a doubling of the power regardless of the power scale used. So a +3 dB increase of 1.21 gigawatts of power would result in 2.42 gigawatts of power.

An animated explanation of the rule of 10s and 3s—as well as explanations of each of the following examples—has been created using Microsoft PowerPoint and can be downloaded from this book's online resource area that can be accessed at www.sybex.com/go/cwna4e. If you do not have PowerPoint on your computer, you can download from Microsoft's website a PowerPoint Viewer that will allow you to view any PowerPoint file. The names of the PowerPoint files are displayed in the following list.

- `10s and 3s Template.ppt`
- `Rule of 10s and 3s Example 1.ppt`
- `Rule of 10s and 3s Example 2.ppt`
- `Rule of 10s and 3s Example 3.ppt`
- `Rule of 10s and 3s Example 4.ppt`

EXERCISE 3.2

Rule of 10s and 3s, Example 1

In this example, you will begin at 1 mW and double the power three times. In addition to calculating the new power level in milliwatts, you will calculate the power level in dBms.

1. The first thing to do is create the initial chart, as in Exercise 3.1.

$$
\begin{array}{cccc}
3 \ + & & & \times \ 2 \\
10 \ - & & & \div \ 10 \\
& \overline{\text{dBm}} & \overline{\text{mW}} & \\
& 0 & 1 &
\end{array}
$$

EXERCISE 3.2 *(continued)*

2. Now, you want to double the power for the first time. So to the right of the 1 mW and on the next line, write × 2. Then below the 1, perform the calculation.

$$
\begin{array}{ll}
3 \;\; + & \qquad\qquad\qquad\qquad \times \;\; 2 \\
10 \;\; - \quad \underline{\hphantom{xxx}} \qquad \underline{\hphantom{xxx}} \quad \div \;\; 10 \\
\qquad\qquad \text{dBm} \qquad\quad \text{mW} \\
\qquad\qquad\quad 0 \qquad\qquad 1 \\
\qquad\qquad\qquad\qquad\quad = 2 \longleftarrow \times 2
\end{array}
$$

3. You are not finished yet with this new line. Remember that for whatever is done to one side of the chart, there must be a correlative mathematical equation on the other side. Because you multiplied by 2 on the right side, you must add 3 to the left side. So you have just calculated that +3 dBm is equal to 2 mW.

$$
\begin{array}{ll}
3 \;\; + & \qquad\qquad\qquad\qquad \times \;\; 2 \\
10 \;\; - \quad \underline{\hphantom{xxx}} \qquad \underline{\hphantom{xxx}} \quad \div \;\; 10 \\
\qquad\qquad \text{dBm} \qquad\quad \text{mW} \\
\qquad\qquad\quad 0 \qquad\qquad 1 \\
+3 \longrightarrow = 3 \qquad\; = 2 \longleftarrow \times 2
\end{array}
$$

4. You have just completed the first doubling of the power. Now, you will double it two more times and perform the necessary mathematical commands. Since this is the first time using this process, all of the steps have been shown using arrows. Future examples will not contain these arrows.

$$
\begin{array}{ll}
3 \;\; + & \qquad\qquad\qquad\qquad \times \;\; 2 \\
10 \;\; - \quad \underline{\hphantom{xxx}} \qquad \underline{\hphantom{xxx}} \quad \div \;\; 10 \\
\qquad\qquad \text{dBm} \qquad\quad \text{mW} \\
\qquad\qquad\quad 0 \qquad\qquad 1 \\
\qquad\qquad\quad 3 \qquad\qquad 2 \\
+3 \longrightarrow = 6 \qquad\; = 4 \longleftarrow \times 2 \\
+3 \longrightarrow = 9 \qquad\; = 8 \longleftarrow \times 2
\end{array}
$$

You have just calculated that 4 mW = +6 dBm, and 8 mW = +9 dBm. If you had used the conversion formula for dBm instead of the rule of 10s and 3s, the actual answers would be 4 mW = +6.0206 dBm, and 8 mW = +9.0309 dBm. As you can see, this set of rules is accurate but not exact.

EXERCISE 3.3

Rule of 10s and 3s, Example 2

You have a wireless bridge that generates a 100 mW signal. The bridge is connected to an antenna via a cable that creates −3 dB of signal loss. The antenna provides 10 dBi of signal gain. In this example, calculate the IR and EIRP values.

EXERCISE 3.3 *(continued)*

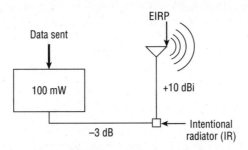

As a reminder, and as seen in the graphic, the IR is the signal up to but not including the antenna, and the EIRP is the signal radiating from the antenna.

1. The first step is to determine whether by using 10 or 2, and × or ÷, you can go from 1 mW to 100 mW.

    It is not too difficult to realize that multiplying 1 by 10 twice will give you 100. So the bridge is generating 100 mW, or +20 dBm, of power.

3 +				× 2
10 −	dBm	mW		÷ 10
	0	1	
+ 10	10	10	× 10
+ 10	20	100	× 10

2. Next you have the antenna cable, which is introducing −3 dB of loss to the signal. After you calculate the effect of the −3 dB loss, you know the value of the IR. You can represent the IR as either +17 dBm or 50 mW.

3 +				× 2
10 −	dBm	mW		÷ 10
	0	1	
+ 10	10	10	× 10
+ 10	20	100	× 10
− 3	17	50	÷ 2

3. Now, all that is left is to calculate the increase of the signal due to the gain from the antenna. Because the gain is 10 dBi, you add 10 to the dBm column and multiply the mW column by 10. This gives you an EIRP of +27 dBm, or 500 mW.

3 +					× 2
10 −		dBm		mW	÷ 10
		0		1	
	+ 10	10		10	× 10
	+ 10	20		100	× 10
	− 3	17		50	÷ 2
	+ 10	27		500	× 10

So far all of the numbers chosen in the examples have been straightforward, using the values that are part of the template. However, in the real world this will not be the case. Using a little creativity, you can calculate gain or loss for any integer. Unfortunately, the rule of 10s and 3s does not work for fractional or decimal numbers. For those numbers, you need to use the logarithmic formula.

dB gain or loss is cumulative. If, for example, you had three sections of cable connecting the transceiver to the antenna and each section of cable provided 2 dB of loss, all three cables would create 6 dB of loss. Using the rule of 10s and 3s, subtracting 6 dBs is equal to subtracting 3 dBs twice. Decibels are very flexible. As long as you come up with the total that you need, they don't care how you do it.

Table 3.1 shows how to calculate all integer dB loss and gain from −10 to +10 by using combinations of just 10s and 3s. Take a moment to look at these values and you will realize that with a little creativity, you can calculate the loss or gain of any integer.

TABLE 3.1   dB Loss and gain (−10 through +10)

Loss or gain (dB)	Combination of 10s and 3s
−10	−10
−9	−3 −3 −3
−8	−10 −10 +3 +3 +3 +3
−7	−10 +3
−6	−3 −3
−5	−10 −10 +3 +3 +3 +3 +3
−4	−10 +3 +3

TABLE 3.1   dB Loss and gain (–10 through +10) *(continued)*

Loss or gain (dB)	Combination of 10s and 3s
–3	–3
–2	–3 –3 –3 –3 +10
–1	–10 +3 +3 +3
+1	+10 –3 –3 –3
+2	+3 +3 +3 +3 –10
+3	+3
+4	+10 –3 –3
+5	+10 +10 –3 –3 –3 –3 –3
+6	+3 +3
+7	+10 –3
+8	+10 +10 –3 –3 –3 –3
+9	+3 +3 +3
+10	+10

EXERCISE 3.4

Rule of 10s and 3s, Example 3

This example is a little more complicated than the previous ones. You have an access point that is transmitting at 50 mW. The signal loss between the access point and the antenna is –1 dB, and the access point is using a +5 dBi antenna. In this example, calculate the IR and the EIRP values.

EXERCISE 3.4 *(continued)*

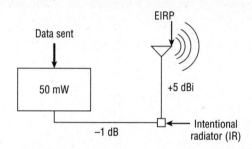

1. The first step after drawing up the template is to convert the 1 mW to 50 mW. This can be done by multiplying the 1 mW by 10 twice and then dividing by 2.

2. The dBm column then needs to be adjusted by adding 10 twice and subtracting 3.

    When the calculations are more complex, it is useful to separate and label the different sections.

		dBm	mW		
3	+			×	2
10	−			÷	10
		0	1		
	+ 10	10	10	× 10	
	+ 10	20	100	× 10	Transmitter
	− 3	17	50	÷ 2	

3. The signal loss between the access point and the antenna is −1 dB. Table 3.1 shows that −1 dB can be calculated by subtracting 10 and adding 3 three times.

4. The mW column will need to be adjusted by dividing by 10 and then multiplying by 2 three times. So the IR is either +16 dBm or 40 mW.

		dBm	mW		
3	+			×	2
10	−			÷	10
		0	1		
	+ 10	10	10	× 10	
	+ 10	20	100	× 10	Transmitter
	− 3	17	50	÷ 2	
	− 10	7	5	÷ 10	
	+ 3	10	10	× 2	Connector
	+ 3	13	20	× 2	
	+ 3	16	40	× 2	

EXERCISE 3.4 *(continued)*

5. The antenna adds a gain of 5 dBi. Table 3.1 shows that +5 dBi can be calculated by adding 10 twice and subtracting 3 five times.

6. The mW column will need to be adjusted by multiplying by 10 twice and dividing by 2 five times. The EIRP is therefore either +21 dBm or 125 mW.

3 + / 10 −	dBm	mW	× 2 / ÷ 10	
	0	1		
+ 10	10	10	× 10	
+ 10	20	100	× 10	Transmitter
− 3	17	50	÷ 2	
− 10	7	5	÷ 10	
+ 3	10	10	× 2	Connector
+ 3	13	20	× 2	
+ 3	16	40	× 2	
+ 10	26	400	× 10	
+ 10	36	4000	× 10	Antenna
− 3	33	2000	÷ 2	
− 3	30	1000	÷ 2	
− 3	27	500	÷ 2	
− 3	24	250	÷ 2	
− 3	21	125	÷ 2	

EXERCISE 3.5

Rule of 10s and 3s, Example 4

In this example, you have an access point that is providing coverage to a specific area of a warehouse via an external directional antenna. The access point is transmitting at 30 mW. The cable and connector between the access point and the antenna creates −3 dB of signal loss. The antenna provides 20 dBi of signal gain. In this example, you will calculate the IR and EIRP values.

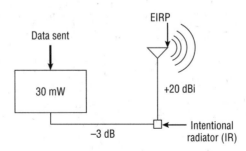

It is not always possible to calculate both sides of the chart by using the rule of 10s and 3s. In some cases, no matter what you do, you cannot calculate the mW value by using 10 or 2. This is one of those cases. You cannot set the mW and dBm values to be equal, but you can still calculate the mW values by using the information provided.

1.   Instead of creating the template and setting 0 dBm equal to 1 mW, enter the value of the transmitter, in this case **30 mW**.

2.   In the dBm column, just enter **unknown**.

Even though you will not know the dBm value, you can still perform all of the necessary mathematics.

```
3   +                        ×    2
10  –                        ÷   10
         dBm          mW

         unknown      30
```

3.   The cable and connectors introduce 3 dB of loss, so subtract 3 from the dBm column and divide the mW column by 2. So the output of the IR is 15 mW.

```
3   +                        ×    2
10  –                        ÷   10
         dBm          mW

         unknown      30
    – 3  unknown – 3   15    ÷ 2
```

4.   The 20 dBi gain from the antenna increases the dBm by 20, so add 10 twice to the dBm column, and multiply the mW column by 10 twice. So the output of the EIRP is 1,500 mW. You can see in the graphic that the 20 dB gain by the antenna and the –3 dB of loss from the cable results in a 17 dB gain from the original dBm. Even though you do not know what the original dBm value is, you can see that it is 17 dB greater.

```
3   +                        ×    2
10  –                        ÷   10
         dBm          mW

         unknown      30
    – 3  unknown – 3   15    ÷ 2
    + 10 unknown + 7   150   × 10
    + 10 unknown + 17  1,500 × 10
```

RF Math Summary

Many concepts, formulas, and examples were covered in the RF mathematics section, so we will bring things together and summarize what was covered. It is important to remember that the bottom line is that you are trying to calculate the power at different points in the RF system and the effects caused by gain or loss. If you want to perform the RF math calculations by using the logarithmic formulas, here they are:

$$dBm = 10 \times \log_{10}(P_{MW})$$

$$mW = 10^{(dBm \div 10)}$$

If you want to use the rule of 10s and 3s, just remember these four simple tasks and you won't have a problem:

- 3 dB gain = mW × 2
- 3 dB loss = mW ÷ 2
- 10 dB gain = mW × 10
- 10 dB loss = mW ÷ 10

Table 3.2 provides a quick reference guide comparing the absolute power measurements of milliwatts to the absolute power dBm values.

TABLE 3.2   dBm and milliwatt conversions

dBm	Milliwatts	Power Level
+ 36 dBm	4,000 mW	4 watts
+ 30 dBm	1,000 mW	1 watt
+ 20 dBm	100 mW	1/10th of 1 watt
+ 10 dBm	10 mW	1/100th of 1 watt
0 dBm	1 mW	1/1,000th of 1 watt
−10 dBm	0.1 mW	1/10th of 1 milliwatt
−20 dBm	0.01 mW	1/100th of 1 milliwatt
−30 dBm	0.001 mW	1/1,000th of 1 milliwatt
−40 dBm	0.0001 mW	1/10,000th of 1 milliwatt
−50 dBm	0.00001 mW	1/100,000th of 1 milliwatt
−60 dBm	0.000001 mW	1 millionth of 1 milliwatt
−70 dBm	0.0000001 mW	1 ten-millionth of 1 milliwatt
−80 dBm	0.00000001 mW	1 hundred-millionth of 1 milliwatt
−90 dBm	0.000000001 mW	1 billionth of 1 milliwatt

Noise Floor

The *noise floor* is the ambient or background level of radio energy on a specific channel. This background energy can include modulated or encoded bits from nearby 802.11 transmitting radios or unmodulated energy coming from non-802.11 devices such as microwave ovens, Bluetooth devices, portable telephones, and so on. Anything electromagnetic has the potential of raising the amplitude of the noise floor on a specific channel.

The amplitude of the noise floor, which is sometimes simply referred to as "background noise," varies in different environments. For example, the noise floor of a 2.4 GHz industrial, scientific, and medical (ISM) channel might be about –100 dBm in a typical environment. However, a noisier RF environment, such as a manufacturing plant, might have a noise floor of –90 dBm because of all the electrical machinery operating within the plant. It should also be noted that the noise floor of 5 GHz channels is almost always lower than the noise floor of 2.4 GHz channels because the 5 GHz frequency bands are less crowded.

Signal-to-Noise Ratio (SNR)

Many Wi-Fi vendors define signal quality as the *signal-to-noise ratio (SNR)*. As shown in Figure 3.2, the SNR is the difference in decibels between the received signal and the background noise level (noise floor), not actually a ratio. For example, if a radio receives a signal of –85 dBm and the noise floor is measured at –100 dBm, the difference between the received signal and the background noise is 15 dB. The SNR is 15 dB.

FIGURE 3.2   Signal-to-noise ratio

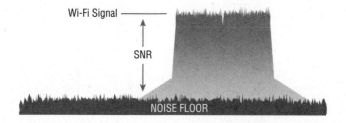

Data transmissions can become corrupted with a very low SNR. If the amplitude of the noise floor is too close to the amplitude of the received signal, data corruption will likely occur and result in layer 2 retransmissions. The retransmissions will negatively affect both throughput and latency. An SNR of 25 dB or greater is considered good signal quality, and an SNR of 10 dB or lower is considered very poor signal quality.

Received Signal Strength Indicator

Receive sensitivity refers to the power level of an RF signal required to be successfully received by the receiver radio. The lower the power level that the receiver can successfully process, the better the receive sensitivity. Think of this as being at a hockey game. There is an ambient level of noise that exists from everything around you. There is a certain volume that you have to speak at for your neighbor to hear you. That level is the receiver sensitivity. It is the weakest signal that the transceiver can decode under normal circumstances. With that said, if the noise in a particular area is louder than normal, then the minimum level you have to yell gets louder.

In WLAN equipment, receive sensitivity is usually defined as a function of network speed. Wi-Fi vendors will usually specify their receive sensitivity thresholds at various data rates; an example vendor specification for a 2.4 GHz radio is listed in Table 3.3. For any given receiver, more power is required by the receiver radio to support the higher data rates. Different speeds use different modulation techniques and encoding methods, and the higher data rates use encoding methods that are more susceptible to corruption. The lower data rates use modulation-encoding methods that are less susceptible to corruption.

TABLE 3.3   Receive sensitivity thresholds (example)

Data rate	Received signal amplitude
MCS7	−77 dBm
MCS6	−78 dBm
MCS5	−80 dBm
MCS4	−85 dBm
MCS3	−88 dBm
MCS2	−90 dBm
MCS1	−90 dBm
MCS0	−90 dBm
54 Mbps	−79 dBm
48 Mbps	−80 dBm
36 Mbps	−85 dBm
24 Mbps	−87 dBm
18 Mbps	−90 dBm

Data rate	Received signal amplitude
12 Mbps	–91 dBm
9 Mbps	–91 dBm
6 Mbps	–91 dBm

The 802.11-2012 standard defines the *received signal strength indicator (RSSI)* as a relative metric used by 802.11 radios to measure signal strength (amplitude). The 802.11 RSSI measurement parameter can have a value from 0 to 255. The RSSI value is designed to be used by the WLAN hardware manufacturer as a relative measurement of the RF signal strength that is received by an 802.11 radio. RSSI metrics are typically mapped to receive sensitivity thresholds expressed in absolute dBm values, as shown in Table 3.4. For example, an RSSI metric of 30 might represent –30 dBm of received signal amplitude. The RSSI metric of 0 might be mapped to –110 dBm of received signal amplitude. Another vendor might use an RSSI metric of 255 to represent –30 dBm of received signal amplitude and 0 to represent –100 dBm of received signal amplitude.

TABLE 3.4   Received signal strength indicator (RSSI) metrics (vendor example)

RSSI	Receive sensitivity threshold	Signal strength (%)	Signal-to-noise ratio	Signal quality (%)
30	–30 dBm	100%	70 dB	100%
25	–41 dBm	90%	60 dB	100%
20	–52 dBm	80%	43 dB	90%
21	–52 dBm	80%	40 dB	80%
15	–63 dBm	60%	33 dB	50%
10	–75 dBm	40%	25 dB	35%
5	–89 dBm	10%	10 dB	5%
0	–110 dBm	0%	0 dB	0%

The 802.11-2012 standard also defines another metric called *signal quality (SQ)*, which is a measure of pseudonoise (PN) code correlation quality received by a radio. In simpler

terms, the signal quality could be a measurement of what might affect coding techniques, such as the Barker code or Complementary Code Keying (CCK), which relates to the transmission speed. In Chapter 6, "Wireless Networks and Spread Spectrum Technologies," you will learn about coding techniques. Anything that might increase the bit error rate (BER), such as a low SNR, might be indicated by SQ metrics.

Information parameters from both RSSI and SQ metrics can be passed along from the PHY layer to the MAC sublayer. Some SQ parameters might also be used in conjunction with RSSI as part of a clear channel assessment (CCA) scheme. Although SQ metrics and RSSI metrics are technically separate measurements, most Wi-Fi vendors refer to both together as simply *RSSI metrics*. For the purposes of this book, whenever we refer to RSSI metrics, we are referring to both SQ and RSSI metrics.

According to the 802.11-2012 standard, "the RSSI is a measure of the RF energy received. Mapping of the RSSI values to actual received power is implementation dependent." In other words, WLAN vendors can define RSSI metrics in a proprietary manner. The actual range of the RSSI value is from 0 to a maximum value (less than or equal to 255) that each vendor can choose on its own (known as RSSI_Max). Many vendors publish their implementation of RSSI values in product documents and/or on the vendor's website. Some WLAN vendors do not publish their RSSI metrics. Because the implementation of RSSI metrics is proprietary, two problems exist when trying to compare RSSI values between different manufacturers' wireless cards. The first problem is that the manufacturers may have chosen two different values as the RSSI_Max. So WLAN vendor A may have chosen a scale from 0 to 100, whereas WLAN vendor B may have chosen a scale from 0 to 30. Because of the difference in scale, WLAN vendor A may indicate a signal with an RSSI value of 25, whereas vendor B may indicate that same signal with a different RSSI value of 8. Also, the radio card manufactured by WLAN vendor A uses more RSSI metrics and is probably more sensitive when evaluating signal quality and SNR.

The second problem with RSSI is that the manufacturer could take their range of RSSI values and compare them to a different range of values. So WLAN vendor A may take its 100-number scale and relate it to dBm values of –110 dBm to –10 dBm, whereas WLAN vendor B may take its 60-number scale and relate it to dBm values of –95 dBm to –35 dBm. So not only do we have different numbering schemes, we also have different ranges of values.

Although the way in which Wi-Fi vendors implement RSSI may be proprietary, most vendors are alike in that they use RSSI thresholds for very important mechanisms, such as roaming and dynamic rate switching. During the *roaming* process, clients make the decision to move from one access point to the next. RSSI thresholds are key factors for clients when they initiate the roaming handoff. RSSI thresholds are also used by vendors to implement *dynamic rate switching (DRS)*, which is a process used by 802.11 radios to shift between data rates. Roaming is discussed in several chapters of this book, and DRS is discussed in greater detail in Chapter 12, "WLAN Troubleshooting."

🌐 Real World Scenario

Can an 802.11 Network Card Truly Measure the Noise Floor and SNR?

It should be understood that the earlier 802.11 wireless network interface cards (NIC) were not spectrum analyzers, and though they could transmit and receive data at a prodigious rate, they could not see raw ambient RF signals. Since the only things getting past the NIC's encoding filter were bits, all of the information reported by the NIC had to come from the bits they received. If you turned on a microwave oven near a wireless NIC, there were no data bits being generated by the microwave, so the NIC would always report a noise variable of zero. In the absence of encoded RF signals coming from other 802.11 devices, the noise variable could not be used to report the noise floor. The only device that could truly measure non-encoded RF energy was a *spectrum analyzer*.

We know that you may have seen many screens generated by your various 802.11 devices that displayed signal (from the RSSI variable) and another value displayed as signal-to-noise ratio (SNR), showing the comparison between the RSSI and the noise floor. The developers of the wireless NICs knew that the RF folks out there "lived, breathed, and died" by signal, noise, and signal-to-noise ratio data.

WLAN professionals demanded a noise variable in order to perform site-survey calculations, so various Wi-Fi vendor organizations came up with unique ways to guess the noise floor. Because 802.11 wireless NICs could only process bits, they needed to come up with algorithms to calculate a noise variable based on the bits going through the NIC.

As with RSSI measurements, different vendors that manufactured 802.11 equipment calculated noise in different ways. Some vendors flatly refused to make up a number for noise only based on bits. Other vendors developed sophisticated algorithms for calculating noise.

More recently 802.11 chip manufactures figured out how to turn off the encoding filters and use the RF signals coming through the antenna to become rudimentary spectrum analyzers. However, this was in lieu of being an 802.11 NIC capable of processing data. Typically, these newer chips could be either a lightweight spectrum analyzer or a Wi-Fi card processing data, but usually not both at the same time, since the front-end filter would identify an 802.11 signal and pass it on to the 802.11 protocol stack, not the spectrum analyzer. Some newer APs can operate in what is sometimes termed "hybrid" mode. These APs can perform both 802.11 and spectrum analysis functions at the same time, although there is often a degradation in WLAN performance. Some of the access point vendors also are using these extra-capable Wi-Fi chips and are adding spectrum analysis as an option for an access point with the appropriate software to take advantage of this extra ability. Please understand that an 802.11 access point is not your best tool to evaluate the noise floor during a site survey. So what is the best tool to measure the noise floor in any environment? A high quality portable spectrum analyzer. A high quality portable spectrum analyzer uses a spectrum analyzer chipset capable of measuring non-encoded RF energy, and the portability of it makes it the best tool to measure the noise floor.

If you would like to learn more about the differences between 802.11 NICs and spectrum analyzers, read *CWAP Certified Wireless Analysis Professional Official Study Guide* (Sybex, 2011).

Link Budget

When radio communications are deployed, a *link budget* is the sum of all the planned and expected gains and losses from the transmitting radio, through the RF medium, to the receiver radio. The purpose of link budget calculations is to guarantee that the final received signal amplitude is above the receiver sensitivity threshold of the receiver radio.

Link budget calculations include original transmit gain, passive antenna gain, and active gain from RF amplifiers. All gain must be accounted for—including RF amplifiers and antennas—and all losses must be accounted for—including attenuators, FSPL, and *insertion loss*. Any hardware device installed in a radio system adds a certain amount of signal attenuation called insertion loss. Cabling is rated for dB loss per 100 feet, and connectors typically add about 0.5 dB of insertion loss.

You have already learned that RF also attenuates as it travels through free space. Figure 3.3 depicts a point-to-point wireless bridge link and shows that loss occurs as the signal moves through various RF components as well as the signal loss caused by FSPL.

FIGURE 3.3   Link budget components

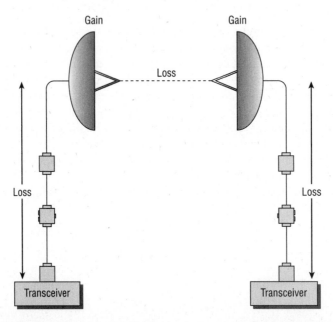

Let's look at the link budget calculations of a point-to-point wireless bridge link, as depicted in Figure 3.4 and Table 3.5. In this case, the two antennas are 10 kilometers apart, and the original transmission is +10 dBm. Notice the amount of insertion loss caused by each RF component, such as the cabling and the lightning arrestors. The antennas passively amplify the signal, and the signal attenuates as it travels through free space. The final received signal at the receiver end of the bridge link is −65.5 dBm.

FIGURE 3.4   Point-to-point link budget gain and loss

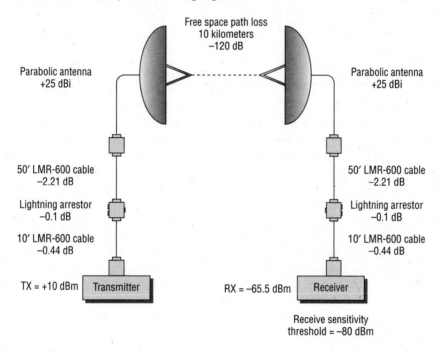

TABLE 3.5   Link budget calculations

Component	Gain or loss	Signal strength
Transceiver (original transmission signal)		+10 dBm
10′ LMR-600 cable	−0.44 dB	+9.56 dBm
Lightning arrestor	−0.1 dB	+9.46 dBm
50′ LMR-600 cable	−2.21 dB	+7.25 dBm
Parabolic antenna	+25 dBi	+32.25 dBm
Free space path loss	−120 dB	−87.75 dBm

TABLE 3.5   Link budget calculations *(continued)*

Component	Gain or loss	Signal strength
Parabolic antenna	+25 dBi	−62.75 dBm
50′ LMR-600 cable	−2.21 dB	−64.96 dBm
Lightning arrestor	−0.1 dB	−65.06 dBm
10′ LMR-600 cable	−0.44 dB	−65.5 dBm
Receiver (final received signal)		−65.5 dBm

Now, let's assume that the receive sensitivity threshold of the receiver radio is −80 dBm. Any signal received with amplitude above −80 dBm can be understood by the receiver radio, whereas any amplitude below −80 dBm cannot be understood. The link budget calculations determined that the final received signal is −65.5 dBm, which is well above the receive sensitivity threshold of −80 dBm. There is almost a 15 dB buffer between the final received signal and the receive sensitivity threshold. The 15 dB buffer that was determined during link budget calculations is known as the *fade margin*, which is discussed in the next section of this chapter.

You may be wondering why these numbers are negative when up until now most of the dBm numbers you have worked with have been positive. Figure 3.5 shows a simple summary of the gains and losses in an office environment. Until now you have worked primarily with calculating the IR and EIRP. It is the effect of FSPL that makes the values negative, as you will see in the calculations based on Figure 3.5. In this example, the received signal is the sum of all components, which is

+20 dBm + 5 dBi − 73.98 dB + 2.14 dBi = −46.84 dBm

FIGURE 3.5   Office link budget gain and loss

Dipole antenna, +5 dBi

Access point,
TX = +20 dBm

Free space path loss
50 meters
−73.98 dB

Integrated antenna
+2.14 dBi

Final signal at the RX = −46.84 dBm

Although the initial transmission amplitude will almost always be above 0 dBm (1 mW), the final received signal amplitude will always be well below 0 dBm (1 mW) because of FSPL.

Fade Margin/System Operating Margin

Fade margin is a level of desired signal above what is required. A good way to explain fade margin is to think of it as a comfort zone. If a receiver has a receive sensitivity of –80 dBm, a transmission will be successful as long as the signal received is greater than –80 dBm. The problem is that the signal being received fluctuates because of many outside influences such as interference and weather conditions. To accommodate for the fluctuation, it is a common practice to plan for a 10 dB to 25 dB buffer above the receive sensitivity threshold of a radio used in a bridge link. The 10 dB to 25 dB buffer above the receive sensitivity threshold is the fade margin.

A fade margin of 10 dB is an absolute minimum. This would only be acceptable for links less than 3 miles or so. Up to 5 miles should have at least a 15 dB fade margin, and links greater than that should be higher. A fade margin of 25 dB is recommended for links greater than 5 miles.

Let's say that a receiver has a sensitivity of –80 dBm, and a signal is typically received at –76 dBm. Then under normal circumstances, this communication is successful. However, because of outside influences, the signal may fluctuate by ± 10 dB. This means that most of the time, the communication is successful, but on those occasions that the signal has fluctuated to –86 dBm, the communication will be unsuccessful. By adding a fade margin of 20 dB in your link budget calculations, you are now stating that for your needs, the receive sensitivity is –60 dBm, and you will plan your network so that the received signal is greater than –60 dBm. If the received signal fluctuates, you have already built in some padding, in this case 20 dB.

If you look back at Figure 3.4, and you required a fade margin of 10 dB above the receive sensitivity of –80 dBm, the amount of signal required for the link would be –70 dBm. Since the signal is calculated to be received at –65.5 dBm, you will have a successful communication. However, if you chose a fade margin of 20 dB, the amount of signal required would be –60 dBm, and based on the configuration in Figure 3.4, you would not have enough signal to satisfy the link budget plus the 20 dB fade margin.

Because RF communications can be affected by many outside influences, it is common to have a fade margin to provide a level of link reliability. By increasing the fade margin, you are essentially increasing the reliability of the link. Think of the fade margin as the buffer or margin of error for received signals that is used when designing and planning an RF system. After the RF link has been installed, it is important to measure the link to see how much buffer or padding there actually is. This functional measurement is known as the *system operating margin (SOM)*. The SOM is the difference between the actual received signal and the signal necessary for reliable communications.

 Real World Scenario

When Are Fade Margin Calculations Needed?

Whenever an outdoor WLAN bridge link is designed, link budget and fade margin calculations will be an absolute requirement. For example, an RF engineer may perform link budget calculations for a 2-mile point-to-point bridge link and determine that the final received signal is 5 dB above the receive sensitivity threshold of a radio at one end of a bridge link. It would seem that RF communications will be just fine; however, because of downfade caused by multipath and weather conditions, a fade margin buffer is needed. A torrential downpour can attenuate a signal as much as 0.08 dB per mile (0.05 dB per kilometer) in both the 2.4 GHz and 5 GHz frequency ranges. Over long-distance bridge links, a fade margin of 25 dB is usually recommended to compensate for attenuation due to changes in RF behaviors such as multipath and due to changes in weather conditions such as rain, fog, or snow.

When deploying a WLAN indoors where high multipath or high noise floor conditions exist, the best practice is to plan for a fade margin of about 5 dB above the vendor's recommended receive sensitivity amplitude. For example, a –70 dBm or stronger signal falls above the RSSI threshold for the higher data rates for most WLAN vendor radios. During the indoor site survey, RF measurements of –70 dBm will often be used to determine coverage areas for higher data rates. In a noisy environment, RF measurements of –65 dBm utilizing a 5 dB fade margin is a recommended best practice.

EXERCISE 3.6

Link Budget and Fade Margin

In this exercise, you will use a Microsoft Excel file to calculate a link budget and fade margin. You will need Excel installed on your computer.

1. From the book's online resource area that can be accessed at www.sybex.com/go/cwna4e, copy the file LinkBudget.xls to your desktop. Open the Excel file from your desktop.

EXERCISE 3.6 *(continued)*

2. In row 10, enter a link distance of **25 kilometers**.

Note that the path loss due to a 25 kilometer link is now 128 dB in the 2.4 GHz frequency.

3. In row 20, enter **128** for path loss in dB.

4. In row 23, change the radio receiver sensitivity to **−80 dBm**.

Notice that the final received signal is now −69 dBm, and the fade margin is only 11 dB.

5. Try increasing the "radio transmitter output power" to see how the connection would fare and to determine how much power would be needed to ensure a fade margin of 20 dB. You can also change the other components such as antenna gain and cable loss to ensure a fade margin of 20 dB.

Summary

This chapter covered six key areas of RF communications:

- RF components
- RF measurements
- RF mathematics
- RSSI thresholds
- Link budgets
- Fade margins

It is important to understand how each of the RF components affects the output of the transceiver. Whenever a component is added, removed, or modified, the output of the RF communications is changed. You need to understand these changes and make sure that the system conforms to regulatory standards. The following RF components were covered in this chapter:

- Transmitter
- Receiver
- Antenna
- Isotropic radiator
- Intentional radiator (IR)
- Equivalent isotropically radiated power (EIRP)

In addition to understanding the components and their effects on the transmitted signal, you must know the different units of power and comparison that are used to measure the output and the changes to the RF communications:

- Units of power
    - Watt
    - Milliwatt
    - dBm
- Units of comparison
    - dB
    - dBi
    - dBd

After you become familiar with the RF components and their effects on RF communications, and you know the different units of power and comparison, you need to understand how to perform the actual calculations and determine whether your RF communication will be successful. It is important to know how to perform the calculations and some of the terms and concepts involved with making sure that the RF link will work properly. These concepts and terms are as follows:

- Rule of 10s and 3s
- Noise floor
- Signal-to-noise ratio (SNR)
- Receive sensitivity
- Received signal strength indicator (RSSI)
- Link budget
- System operating margin (SOM)
- Fade margin

Exam Essentials

Understand the RF components.   Know the function of each of the components and which components add gain and which components add loss.

Understand the units of power and comparison.   Make sure you are comfortable with the difference between units of power (absolute) and units of comparison (relative). Know all of the units of power and comparison, what they measure, and how they are used.

Be able to perform RF mathematics.   There will be no logarithms on the test; however, you must know how to use the rule of 10s and 3s. You will need to be able to calculate a result based on a scenario, power value, or comparative change.

Understand the practical uses of RF mathematics.   When all is said and done, the ultimate question is, Will the RF communication work? This is where an understanding of RSSI, SOM, fade margin, and link budget is important.

Be able to explain the importance of measuring the SNR and the noise floor.   Understand that the ambient background level of radio energy on a specific channel can corrupt 802.11 data transmissions. Understand that the only device that can truly measure unmodulated RF energy is a spectrum analyzer.

Define RSSI.   Understand that RSSI metrics are used by radios to interpret signal strength and quality. 802.11 radios use RSSI metrics for decisions such as roaming and dynamic rate switching.

Understand the necessity of a link budget and fade margin.   A link budget is the sum of all gains and losses from the transmitting radio, through the RF medium, to the receiver radio. The purpose of link budget calculations is to guarantee that the final received signal amplitude is above the receiver sensitivity threshold of the receiver radio. Fade margin is a level of desired signal above what is required.

Review Questions

1. What RF component is responsible for generating the AC signal?

   A. Antenna

   B. Receiver

   C. Transmitter

   D. Transponder

2. A point source that radiates RF signal equally in all directions is known as what?

   A. Omnidirectional signal generator

   B. Omnidirectional antenna

   C. Intentional radiator

   D. Nondirectional transmitter

   E. Isotropic radiator

3. When calculating the link budget and system operating margin of a point-to-point outdoor WLAN bridge link, what factors should be taken into account? (Choose all that apply.)

   A. Distance

   B. Receive sensitivity

   C. Transmit amplitude

   D. Antenna height

   E. Cable loss

   F. Frequency

4. The sum of all the components from the transmitter to the antenna, not including the antenna, is known as what? (Choose two.)

   A. IR

   B. Isotropic radiator

   C. EIRP

   D. Intentional radiator

5. The highest RF signal strength that is transmitted from an antenna is known as what?

   A. Equivalent isotropically radiated power

   B. Transmit sensitivity

   C. Total emitted power

   D. Antenna radiated power

6. Select the absolute units of power. (Choose all that apply.)

   A. Watt

   B. Milliwatt

   C. Decibel

   D. dBm

   E. Bel

7. Select the units of comparison (relative). (Choose all that apply.)

   A. dBm

   B. dBi

   C. Decibel

   D. dBd

   E. Bel

8. 2 dBd is equal to how many dBi?

   A. 5 dBi

   B. 4.41 dBi

   C. 4.14 dBi

   D. The value cannot be calculated.

9. 23 dBm is equal to how many mW?

   A. 200 mW

   B. 14 mW

   C. 20 mW

   D. 23 mW

   E. 400 mW

10. A wireless bridge is configured to transmit at 100 mW. The antenna cable and connectors produce a 3 dB loss and are connected to a 16 dBi antenna. What is the EIRP?

    A. 20 mW

    B. 30 dBm

    C. 2,000 mW

    D. 36 dBm

    E. 8 W

11. A WLAN transmitter that emits a 400 mW signal is connected to a cable with a 9 dB loss. If the cable is connected to an antenna with 19 dBi of gain, what is the EIRP?

    A. 4 W

    B. 3,000 mW

    C. 3,500 mW

    D. 2 W

12. WLAN vendors use RSSI thresholds to trigger which radio card behaviors? (Choose all that apply.)

    A. Receive sensitivity

    B. Roaming

    C. Retransmissions

    D. Dynamic rate switching

13. Received signal strength indicator (RSSI) metrics are used by 802.11 radios to define which RF characteristics?

    A. Signal strength

    B. Phase

    C. Frequency

    D. Modulation

14. dBi is a measure of what?

    A. The output of the transmitter

    B. The signal increase caused by the antenna

    C. The signal increase of the intentional transmitter

    D. The comparison between an isotropic radiator and the transceiver

    E. The strength of the intentional radiator

15. Which of the following are valid calculations when using the rule of 10s and 3s? (Choose all that apply.)

    A. For every 3 dB of gain (relative), double the absolute power (mW).

    B. For every 10 dB of loss (relative), divide the absolute power (mW) by a factor of 2.

    C. For every 10 dB of loss (absolute), divide the relative power (mW) by a factor of 3.

    D. For every 10 mW of loss (relative), multiply the absolute power (dB) by a factor of 10.

    E. For every 10 dB of loss (relative), halve the absolute power (mW).

    F. For every 10 dB of loss (relative), divide the absolute power (mW) by a factor of 10.

16. A WLAN transmitter that emits a 100 mW signal is connected to a cable with a 3 dB loss. If the cable is connected to an antenna with 7 dBi of gain, what is the EIRP at the antenna element?

    A. 200 mW

    B. 250 mW

    C. 300 mW

    D. 400 mW

17. In a normal wireless bridged network, the greatest loss of signal is caused by what component?

    A. Receive sensitivity

    B. Antenna cable loss

    C. Lightning arrestor

    D. Free space path loss

18. To double the distance of a signal, the EIRP must be increased by how many dBs?

    A. 3 dB

    B. 6 dB

    C. 10 dB

    D. 20 dB

19. During a site survey of a point-to-point link between buildings at a manufacturing plant, the WLAN engineer determines that the noise floor is extremely high because of all the machinery that is operating in the buildings. The engineer is worried about a low SNR and poor performance due to the high noise floor. What is a suggested best practice to deal with this scenario?

    A. Increase the access points' transmission amplitude.

    B. Mount the access points higher.

    C. Double the distance of the AP signal with 6 dBi of antenna gain.

    D. Plan for coverage cells with a 5 dB fade margin.

    E. Increase the transmission amplitude of the client radios.

20. Which value should not be used to compare wireless network cards manufactured by different WLAN vendors?

    A. Receive sensitivity

    B. Transmit power range

    C. Antenna dBi

    D. RSSI

Chapter

4

Radio Frequency Signal and Antenna Concepts

IN THIS CHAPTER, YOU WILL LEARN ABOUT THE FOLLOWING:

✓ **Azimuth and elevation charts (antenna radiation envelopes)**

✓ **Interpreting polar charts**

✓ **Beamwidth**

✓ **Antenna types**

- Omnidirectional antennas
- Semidirectional antennas
- Highly directional antennas
- Sector antennas
- Antenna arrays
- Static beamforming
- Dynamic beamforming
- Transmit beamforming

✓ **Visual line of sight**

✓ **RF line of sight**

✓ **Fresnel zone**

✓ **Earth bulge**

✓ **Antenna polarization**

✓ **Antenna diversity**

To be able to communicate between two or more transceivers, the radio frequency (RF) signal must be radiated from the antenna of the transmitter with enough power so that it is received and understood by the receiver. The installation of antennas has the greatest ability to affect whether or not the communication is successful. Antenna installation can be as simple as placing an access point in the middle of a small office to provide full coverage for your company, or it can be as complex as installing an assortment of directional antennas, kind of like piecing together a jigsaw puzzle. Do not fear this process; with proper understanding of antennas and how they function, you may find successfully planning for and installing antennas in a wireless network to be a skillful and rewarding task.

This chapter focuses on the categories and types of antennas and the different ways that they can direct an RF signal. Choosing and installing antennas is like choosing and installing lighting in a home. When installing home lighting, you have many choices: table lamps, ceiling lighting, narrow- or wide-beam directional spotlights. In Chapter 3, "Radio Frequency Components, Measurements, and Mathematics," you were introduced to the concept of antennas focusing RF signal. In this chapter, you will learn about the various types of antennas, their radiation patterns, and how to use the different antennas in different environments. You will also learn that the installation and alignment of omnidirectional antennas should vary depending on whether the access point supports 802.11n, 802.11ac, or legacy physical layer technologies.

You will also learn that even though we often use light to explain RF radiation, differences exist between the way the two behave. You will learn about aiming and aligning antennas, and you will learn that what you see is not necessarily what you will get.

In addition to learning about antennas, you will learn about the accessories that may be needed for proper antenna installation. In office environments, you may simply need to connect the antenna to the access point. In outdoor installations, you will need special cable and connectors, lightning arrestors, and special mounting brackets. In this chapter, we will introduce you to the components necessary for successfully installing an antenna.

To summarize, in this chapter you will gain the knowledge that will enable you to properly select, install, and align antennas. These skills will help you successfully implement a wireless network, whether it is a point-to-point network between two buildings or a network providing wireless coverage throughout an office building.

Azimuth and Elevation Charts (Antenna Radiation Envelopes)

There are many types of antennas designed for many different purposes, just as there are many types of lights designed for many different purposes. When purchasing lighting for your home, it is easy to compare two lamps by turning them on and looking at the way each disperses the light. Unfortunately, it is not possible to compare antennas in the same way.

Actual side-by-side comparison of antennas requires you to walk around the antenna with an RF meter, take numerous signal measurements, and then plot the measurements either on the ground or on a piece of paper that represents the environment. Besides the fact that this is a time-consuming task, the results could be skewed by outside influences on the RF signal, such as furniture or other RF signals in the area. To assist potential buyers with their purchasing decision, antenna manufacturers create *azimuth charts* and *elevation charts*, commonly known as radiation patterns, for their antennas. These radiation patterns are created in controlled environments where the results cannot be skewed by outside influences and represent the signal pattern that is radiated by a particular model of antenna. These charts are commonly known as *polar charts* or *antenna radiation envelopes*.

Figure 4.1 shows the azimuth and elevation charts of an omnidirectional antenna. The azimuth chart, labeled H-plane, shows the top-down view of the radiation pattern of the antenna. Since this is an omnidirectional antenna, as you can see from the azimuth chart, its radiation pattern is almost perfectly circular. The elevation chart, labeled E-plane, shows the side view of the radiation pattern of the antenna. There is no standard that requires the antenna manufacturers to align the degree marks of the chart with the direction that the antenna is facing, so unfortunately it is up to the reader of the chart to understand and interpret it.

Here are a few statements that will help you interpret the radiation charts:

- In either chart, the antenna is placed at the center of the chart.
- Azimuth chart = H-plane = top-down view
- Elevation chart = E-plane = side view

The outer ring of the chart usually represents the strongest signal of the antenna. The chart does not represent distance or any level of power or strength. It represents only the relationship of power between different points on the chart.

One way to think of the chart is to consider the way a shadow behaves. If you were to move a flashlight closer or farther from your hand, the shadow of your hand would grow larger or smaller. The shadow does not represent the size of the hand. The shadow represents the relative shape of the hand. Whether the shadow is large or small, the shape and pattern of the shadow of the hand is identical. With an antenna, the radiation pattern will grow larger or smaller depending on how much power the antenna receives, but the shape and the relationships represented by the patterns will always stay the same.

FIGURE 4.1   Azimuth and elevation charts

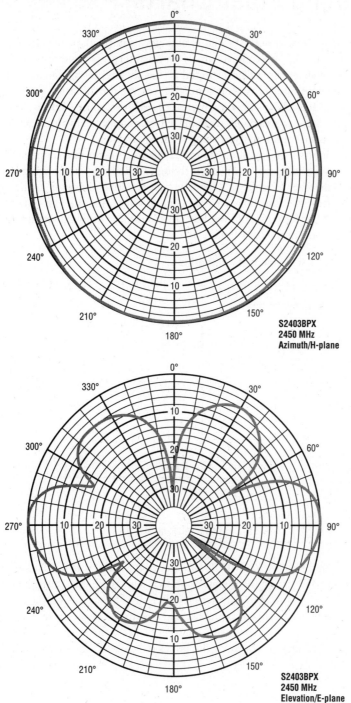

S2403BPX
2450 MHz
Azimuth/H-plane

S2403BPX
2450 MHz
Elevation/E-plane

Interpreting Polar Charts

As we stated, the antenna azimuth (H-plane) and elevation (E-plane) charts are commonly referred to as polar charts. These charts are often misinterpreted and misread. One of the biggest reasons these charts are misinterpreted is that they represent the decibel (dB) mapping of the antenna coverage. This dB mapping represents the radiation pattern of the antenna; however, it does this using a logarithmic scale instead of a linear scale. Remember that the logarithmic scale is a variable scale, based on exponential values, so the polar chart is actually a visual representation using a variable scale.

Take a look at Figure 4.2. The numbers inside the four boxes in the upper-left corner tell you how long and wide each box is. So, even though visually in our drawing we represented the boxes as the same size, in reality each one is twice as long and wide as the previous one. It is easier to draw the four boxes as the same physical size and just put the number in the box to represent the actual size of the box. In the middle drawing, we drew the boxes showing the relative size of the four boxes.

FIGURE 4.2 Logarithmic/linear comparison

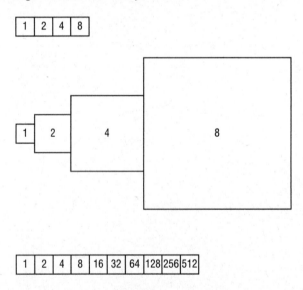

What if we had more boxes, say 10? By representing each box using the same-sized drawing, it is easier to illustrate the boxes, as shown with the boxes in the lower-left corner. In this example, if we tried to show the actual differences in size, as we did in the middle of the drawing, we could not fit this drawing on the page in the book. In fact, the room that you are in may not have enough space for you to even draw this. Because the scale changes so drastically, it is necessary to not draw the boxes to scale so that we can still represent the information.

In Chapter 3, you learned about RF math. In that chapter, one of the rules that you learned was the rule of 6 dB, which indicates that a 6 dB decrease of power decreases the distance the signal travels by half. A 10 dB decrease of power decreases the distance the signal travels by approximately 70 percent. In Figure 4.3, the left polar chart displays the logarithmic representation of the elevation chart of an omnidirectional antenna. This is what you are typically looking at on an antenna brochure or specification sheet. Someone who is untrained in reading these charts would look at the chart and be impressed with how much vertical coverage the antenna provides but would likely be disappointed with the actual coverage. When reading the logarithmic chart, you must remember that for every 10 dB decrease from the peak signal, the actual distance decreases by 70 percent. Each concentric circle on this logarithmic chart represents a change of 5 dB. Figure 4.3 shows the logarithmic pattern of an elevation chart of an omnidirectional antenna along with a linear representation of it's coverage. Notice that the first side lobe is about 10 dB weaker than the main lobe. Remember to compare where the lobes are relative to the concentric circles. This 10 dB decrease on the logarithmic chart is equal to a 70 percent decrease in range on the linear chart. Comparing both charts, you see that the side lobes on the logarithmic chart are essentially insignificant when adjusted to the linear chart. As you can see, this omnidirectional antenna has very little vertical coverage.

FIGURE 4.3   Omnidirectional polar chart (E-plane)

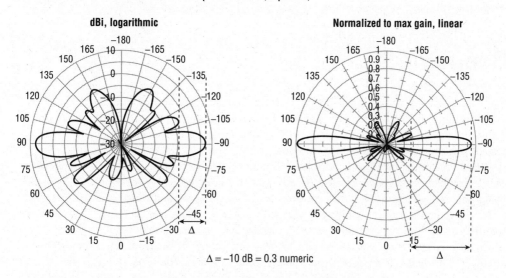

To give you another comparison, Figure 4.4 shows the logarithmic pattern of the elevation chart of a directional antenna along with a linear representation of the vertical coverage area of this antenna. We rotated the polar chart on its side so that you can better visualize the antenna mounted on the side of a building and aiming at another building.

FIGURE 4.4   Directional polar chart (E-plane)

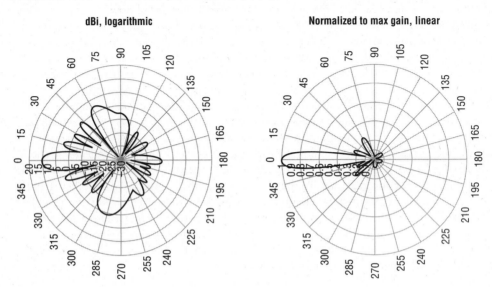

Beamwidth

Many flashlights have adjustable lenses, enabling the user to widen or tighten the concentration of light. RF antennas are capable of focusing the power that is radiating from them, but unlike flashlights, antennas are not adjustable. The user must decide how much focus is desired prior to the purchase of the antenna.

Beamwidth is the measurement of how broad or narrow the focus of an antenna is—and is measured both horizontally and vertically. It is the measurement from the center, or strongest point, of the antenna signal to each of the points along the horizontal and vertical axes where the signal decreases by half power (–3 dB), as seen in Figure 4.5. These –3 dB points are often referred to as *half-power points*. The distance between the two half-power points on the horizontal axis is measured in degrees, giving the horizontal beamwidth measurement. The distance between the two half-power points on the vertical axis is also measured in degrees, giving the vertical beamwidth measurement.

Most of the time when you are deciding which antenna will address your communications needs, you will look at the manufacturer's spec sheets to determine the technical specifications of the antenna. In these brochures, the manufacturer typically includes the numerical values for the horizontal and vertical beamwidths of the antenna. It is important for you to understand how these numbers are calculated. Figure 4.6 illustrates the process.

FIGURE 4.5   Antenna beamwidth

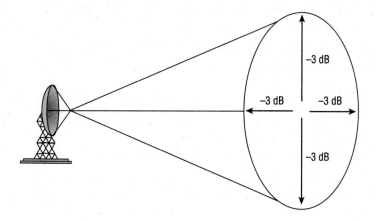

FIGURE 4.6   Beamwidth calculation

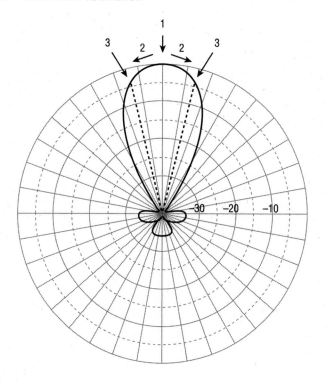

1. First determine the scale of the polar chart.

   On this chart, you can see that the solid circles represent the –10 dB, –20 dB, and –30 dB lines and the dotted circles therefore represent the –5 dB, –15 dB, and –25 dB lines. These represent the dB decrease from the peak signal.

2. To determine the beamwidth of this antenna, first locate the point on the chart where the antenna signal is the strongest.

   In this example, the signal is strongest where the number 1 arrow is pointing.

3. Move along the antenna pattern away from the peak signal (as shown by the two number 2 arrows) until you reach the point where the antenna pattern is 3 dB closer to the center of the diagram (as shown by the two number 3 arrows).

   This is why you needed to know the scale of the chart first.

4. Draw a line from each of these points to the middle of the polar chart (as shown by the dark dotted lines).

5. Measure the distance in degrees between these lines to calculate the beamwidth of the antenna.

   In this example, the beamwidth of this antenna is about 28 degrees.

It is important to realize that even though the majority of the RF signal that is generated is focused within the beamwidth of the antenna, a significant amount of signal can still radiate from outside the beamwidth, from what is known as the antenna's side or rear lobes. As you look at the azimuth charts of different antennas, you will notice that some of these side and rear lobes are fairly significant. Although the signal of these lobes is drastically less than the signal of the main beamwidth, they are dependable, and in certain implementations very functional. It is important when aligning point-to-point antennas that you make sure they are actually aligned to the main lobe and not a side lobe.

Table 4.1 shows the types of antennas that are used in 802.11 communications.

Table 4.1 provides reference information that will be useful as you learn about various types of antennas in this chapter.

TABLE 4.1   Antenna beamwidth

Antenna types	Horizontal beamwidth (in degrees)	Vertical beamwidth (in degrees)
Omnidirectional	360	7 to 80
Patch/panel	30 to 180	6 to 90

Antenna types	Horizontal beamwidth (in degrees)	Vertical beamwidth (in degrees)
Yagi	30 to 78	14 to 64
Sector	60 to 180	7 to 17
Parabolic dish	4 to 25	4 to 21

Antenna Types

There are three main categories of antennas:

Omnidirectional: *Omnidirectional antennas* radiate RF in a fashion similar to the way a table or floor lamp radiates light. They are designed to provide general coverage in all directions.

Semidirectional: *Semidirectional antennas* radiate RF in a fashion similar to the way a wall sconce radiates light away from the wall or the way a street lamp shines light down on a street or a parking lot, providing a directional light across a large area.

Highly directional: *Highly directional antennas* radiate RF in a fashion similar to the way a spotlight focuses light on a flag or a sign.

Each type of antenna is designed with a different objective in mind.

 It is important to keep in mind that this section is discussing types of antennas and not lighting. Although it is useful to refer to lighting to provide analogies to antennas, it is critical to remember that unlike lighting, RF signals can travel through solid objects such as walls and floors.

In addition to antennas acting as radiators and focusing signals that are being transmitted, they focus signals that are received. If you were to walk outside and look up at a star, it would appear fairly dim. If you were to look at that same star through binoculars, it would appear brighter. If you were to use a telescope, it would appear even brighter. Antennas function in a similar way. Not only do they amplify signal that is being transmitted, they also amplify signal that is being received. High-gain microphones operate in the same way, enabling you to not only watch the action of your favorite sport on television but to also hear the action.

Antennas or Antennae?

Although it is not a matter of critical importance, many are often curious whether the plural of *antenna* is *antennas* or *antennae*. The simple answer is both, but the complete answer is it depends. When *antenna* is used as a biological term, the plural is *antennae*, such as the antennae of a bug. When it is used as an electronics term, the plural is *antennas*, such as the antennas on an access point.

Omnidirectional Antennas

Omnidirectional antennas radiate RF signal in all directions. The small, rubber-coated *dipole antenna*, often referred to as a *rubber duck* antenna, is the classic example of an omnidirectional antenna and is the default antenna of many access points, although most of the antennas nowadays are encased in plastic instead of rubber. A perfect omnidirectional antenna would radiate RF signal like the theoretical isotropic radiator from Chapter 3, "Radio Frequency Components, Measurements, and Mathematics." The closest thing to an isotropic radiator is the omnidirectional dipole antenna.

An easy way to explain the radiation pattern of a typical omnidirectional antenna is to hold your index finger straight up (this represents the antenna) and place a bagel on it as if it were a ring (this represents the RF signal). If you were to slice the bagel in half horizontally, as if you were planning to spread butter on it, the cut surface of the bagel would represent the azimuth chart, or H-plane, of the omnidirectional antenna. If you took another bagel and sliced it vertically instead, essentially cutting the hole that you are looking through in half, the cut surface of the bagel would now represent the elevation, or E-plane, of the omnidirectional antenna.

In Chapter 3, you learned that antennas can focus or direct the signal that they are transmitting. It is important to know that the higher the dBi or dBd value of an antenna, the more focused the signal. When discussing omnidirectional antennas, it is not uncommon to initially question how it is possible to focus a signal that is radiated in all directions. With higher-gain omnidirectional antennas, the vertical signal is decreased and the horizontal power is increased.

Figure 4.7 shows the elevation view of three theoretical antennas. Notice that the signal of the higher-gain antennas is elongated, or more focused horizontally. The horizontal beamwidth of omnidirectional antennas is always 360 degrees, and the vertical beamwidth ranges from 7 to 80 degrees, depending on the particular antenna.

Because of the narrower vertical coverage of the higher-gain omnidirectional antennas, it is important to carefully plan how they are used. Placing one of these higher-gain antennas on the first floor of a building may provide good coverage to the first floor, but because of the narrow vertical coverage, the second and third floors may receive minimal signal. In some installations, you may want this; in others, you may not. Indoor installations typically use low-gain omnidirectional antennas with gain of about 2.14 dBi.

FIGURE 4.7   Vertical radiation patterns of omnidirectional antennas

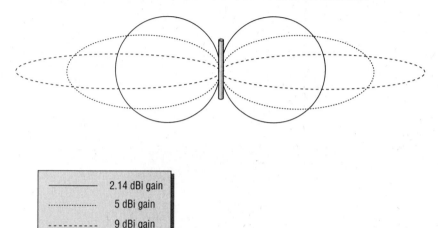

————————	2.14 dBi gain
····················	5 dBi gain
- - - - - - - -	9 dBi gain

Antennas are most effective when the length of the element is an even fraction (such as 1/4 or 1/2) or a multiple of the wavelength (λ). A 2.4 GHz half-wave dipole antenna (see Figure 4.8) consists of two elements, each 1/4 wave in length (about 1 inch), running in the opposite direction from each other. Higher-gain omnidirectional antennas are typically constructed by stacking multiple dipole antennas on top of each other and are known as *collinear antennas.*

Omnidirectional antennas are typically used in point-to-multipoint environments. The omnidirectional antenna is connected to a device (such as an access point) that is placed at the center of a group of client devices, providing central communications capabilities to the surrounding clients. High-gain omnidirectional antennas can also be used outdoors to connect multiple buildings together in a point-to-multipoint configuration. A central building would have an omnidirectional antenna on its roof, and the surrounding buildings would have directional antennas aimed at the central building. In this configuration, it is important to make sure that the gain of the omnidirectional antenna is high enough to provide the coverage necessary but not so high that the vertical beamwidth is too narrow to provide an adequate signal to the surrounding buildings.

Figure 4.9 shows an installation where the gain is too high. The building to the left will be able to communicate, but the building on the right is likely to have problems. To solve the problem that is pictured in Figure 4.9, sector arrays using a down-tilt configuration are used instead of high-gain omnidirectional antennas. Sector antennas are discussed later in this chapter.

FIGURE 4.8 Half-wave dipole antenna

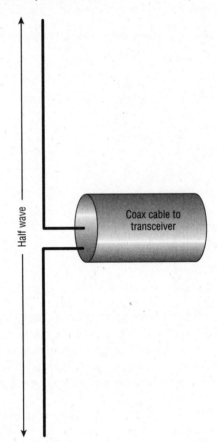

FIGURE 4.9 Improperly installed omnidirectional antenna

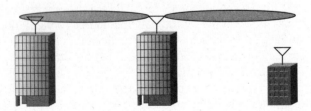

Semidirectional Antennas

Unlike omnidirectional antennas that radiate RF signals in all directions, semidirectional antennas are designed to direct a signal in a specific direction. Semidirectional antennas are used for short- to medium-distance communications, with long-distance communications being served by highly directional antennas.

It is common to use semidirectional antennas to provide a network bridge between two buildings in a campus environment or down the street from each other. Longer distances would be served by highly directional antennas.

Three types of antennas fit into the semidirectional category:

- Patch
- Panel
- Yagi (pronounced *YAH-gee*)

Patch and panel antennas, as shown in Figure 4.10, are more accurately classified or referred to as planar antennas. *Patch* refers to a particular way of designing the radiating elements inside the antenna. Unfortunately, it has become common practice to use the terms *patch antenna* and *panel antenna* interchangeably. If you are unsure of the antenna's specific design, it is better to refer to it as a *planar antenna*.

FIGURE 4.10   The exterior of a patch antenna and the internal antenna element

 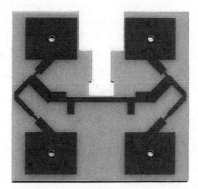

These antennas can be used for outdoor point-to-point communications up to about a mile but are more commonly used as a central device to provide unidirectional coverage from the access point to the clients in an indoor environment. It is common for patch or panel antennas to be connected to access points to provide directional coverage within a building. Planar antennas can be used effectively in libraries, warehouses, and retail stores with long aisles of shelves. Because of the tall, long shelves, omnidirectional antennas often have difficulty providing RF coverage effectively.

In contrast, planar antennas can be placed high on the side walls of the building, aiming through the rows of shelves. The antennas can be alternated between rows, with every other antenna being placed on the opposite wall. Since planar antennas have a horizontal beamwidth of 180 degrees or less, a minimal amount of signal will radiate outside of the building. With the antenna placement alternated and aimed from opposite sides of the building, the RF signal is more likely to radiate down the rows, providing the necessary coverage.

Planar antennas are also often used to provide coverage for long hallways with offices on each side or hospital corridors with patient rooms on each side. A planar antenna can be placed at the end of the hall and aimed down the corridor. A single planar antenna can provide RF signal to some or all of the corridor and the rooms on each side and some coverage to the floors above and below. How much coverage will depend on the power of the transmitter, the gain and beamwidth (both horizontal and vertical) of the antenna, and the attenuation properties of the building.

Before the advent of 802.11 MIMO radios, patch and panel antennas were used indoors with legacy 802.11a/b/g radios to help reduce reflections and hopefully reduce the negative effects of multipath. Semidirectional indoor antennas were often deployed in high multipath environments, such as warehouses or retail stores with a lot of metal racks or shelving. Now that MIMO technology is prevalent, patch and panel antennas are no longer needed to reduce multipath because multipath is constructive with MIMO technology.

802.11n and 802.11ac MIMO patch antennas are still used indoors but for a much different reason. The most common use case for deploying a MIMO patch antenna indoors is a high-density environment. A high-density environment can be described as a small area where numerous Wi-Fi client devices exist. An example might be a gymnasium at a school or a meeting hall packed with people using multiple Wi-Fi radios. In a high-density scenario, an omnidirectional antenna might not be the best solution for coverage. MIMO patch and panel antennas are often mounted from the ceiling downward to provide tight "sectors" of coverage. The most common use of indoor MIMO patch antennas is for high-density environments.

Yagi-Uda antennas, shown in Figure 4.11, are more commonly known as just Yagi antennas. They are typically used for short- to medium-distance point-to-point communications of up to about 2 miles, although high-gain *Yagi antennas* can be used for longer distances.

Another benefit of semidirectional antennas is that they can be installed high on a wall and tilted downward toward the area to be covered. This cannot be done with an omnidirectional antenna without causing the signal on the other side of the antenna to be tilted upward. Since the only RF signal that radiates from the back of a semidirectional antenna is incidental, the ability to aim it vertically is an additional benefit.

Figure 4.12 shows the radiation patterns of a typical semidirectional panel antenna. Remember that these are actual azimuth and elevation charts from a specific antenna and that every manufacturer and model of antenna will have a slightly different radiation pattern.

FIGURE 4.11   The exterior of a Yagi antenna and the internal antenna element

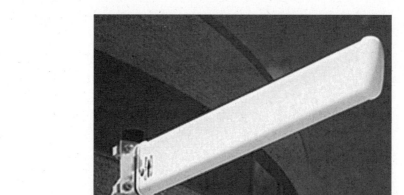

Highly Directional Antennas

Highly directional antennas are strictly used for point-to-point communications, typically to provide network bridging between two buildings. They provide the most focused, narrow beamwidth of any of the antenna types.

There are two types of highly directional antennas: *parabolic dish antennas* and *grid antennas*:

Parabolic Dish Antenna   The parabolic dish antenna is similar in appearance to the small digital satellite TV antennas that can be seen on the roofs of many houses.

Grid Antenna   As pictured in Figure 4.13, the grid antenna resembles the grill of a barbecue, with the edges slightly curved inward. The spacing of the wires on a grid antenna is determined by the wavelength of the frequencies that the antenna is designed for.

Because of the high gain of highly directional antennas, they are ideal for long-distance point-to-point communications.

FIGURE 4.12   Radiation pattern of a typical semidirectional panel antenna

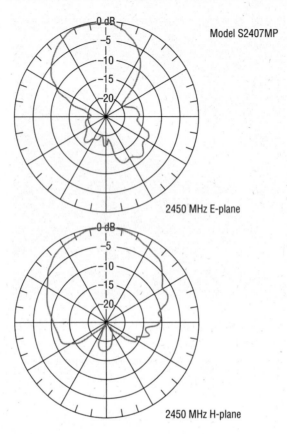

Model S2407MP

2450 MHz E-plane

2450 MHz H-plane

FIGURE 4.13   Grid antenna

Because of the long distances and narrow beamwidth, highly directional antennas are affected more by antenna wind loading, which is antenna movement or shifting caused by wind. Even slight movement of a highly directional antenna can cause the RF beam to be aimed away from the receiving antenna, interrupting RF communications. In high-wind environments, grid antennas, because of the spacing between the wires, are less susceptible to wind load and may be a better choice.

Another option in high-wind environments is to choose an antenna with a wider beamwidth. In this situation, if the antenna were to shift slightly, the signal would still be received because of its wider coverage area. Keep in mind that a wider beam means less gain. If a solid dish is used, it is highly recommended that a protective cover known as a radome be used to help offset some of the effects of the wind. No matter which type of antenna is installed, the quality of the mount and antenna will have a huge effect in reducing wind load.

Sector Antennas

Sector antennas are a special type of high-gain, semidirectional antenna that provides a pie-shaped coverage pattern. These antennas are typically installed in the middle of the area where RF coverage is desired and placed back to back with other sector antennas. Individually, each antenna services its own piece of the pie, but as a group, all of the pie pieces fit together and provide omnidirectional coverage for the entire area. Combining multiple sector antennas to provide 360 degrees of horizontal coverage, as shown in Figure 4.14, is known as a *sectorized array*.

Unlike other semidirectional antennas, a sector antenna generates very little RF signal behind the antenna (*back lobe*) and therefore does not interfere with the other sector antennas that it is working with. The horizontal beamwidth of a sector antenna is from 60 to 180 degrees, with a narrow vertical beamwidth of 7 to 17 degrees. Sector antennas typically have a gain of at least 10 dBi.

Installing a group of sector antennas to provide omnidirectional coverage for an area provides many benefits over installing a single omnidirectional antenna:

- To begin with, sector antennas can be mounted high over the terrain and tilted slightly downward, with the tilt of each antenna at an angle appropriate for the terrain it is covering. Omnidirectional antennas can also be mounted high over the terrain; however, if an omnidirectional antenna is tilted downward on one side, the other side will be tilted upward.

- Since each antenna covers a separate area, each antenna can be connected to a separate transceiver and can transmit and receive independently of the other antennas.

  This provides the capability for all the antennas to be transmitting at the same time, providing much greater throughput. A single omnidirectional antenna is capable of transmitting to only one device at a time.

- The last benefit of the sector antennas over a single omnidirectional antenna is that the gain of the sector antennas is much greater than the gain of the omnidirectional antenna, providing a much larger coverage area.

FIGURE 4.14 Sectorized array

Historically, sector antennas were used extensively for cell phone communications. With the expansion of 802.11 networks in stadiums and outdoor venues, the use of sector antennas has increased.

 Real World Scenario

Cellular Sector Antennas Are Everywhere

As you walk or drive around your town or city, look for radio communications towers. Many of these towers have what appear to be rings of antennas around them. These rings of antennas are sector antennas. If a tower has more than one grouping or ring around it, then multiple cellular carriers are using the same tower.

Antenna Arrays

An *antenna array* is a group of two or more antennas that are integrated together to provide coverage. These antennas operate together to perform what is known as beamforming.

Beamforming is a method of concentrating RF energy. Concentrating a signal means that the power of the signal will be greater and the SNR at the receiver should therefore also be greater, providing a better transmission.

There are three different types of beamforming:

- Static beamforming
- Dynamic beamforming
- Transmit beamforming

Each of these beamforming methods is explained in the following sections.

Static Beamforming

Static beamforming is performed by using directional antennas to provide a fixed radiation pattern. Static beamforming uses multiple directional antennas, all clustered together but aimed away from a center point or location. *Static beamforming* is just another term occasionally used when referring to an indoor sectorized array. Wi-Fi vendor Xirrus manufactures an indoor sectorized array solution that uses directional antennas to create multiple beam sectors.

As shown in Figure 4.15, each beam sector is assigned different nonoverlapping channels. If you want to use 8 antennas to cover a 360 degree area, by dividing 360 by 8, you will determine that each antenna must have at least a 45 degree beamwidth to cover the 360 degree area. Indoor sectorized array solutions are available with as many as 16 unidirectional antennas that together provide 360 degrees of high-density coverage.

FIGURE 4.15   Static beamforming—indoor sectorized array

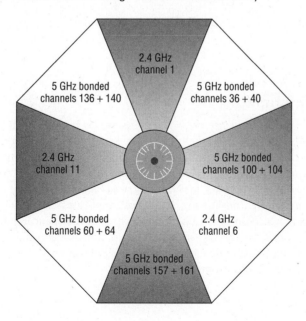

Dynamic Beamforming

Dynamic beamforming focuses the RF energy in a specific direction and in a particular shape. Like static beamforming, the direction and shape of the signal is focused, but unlike static beamforming, the radiation pattern of the signal can change on a frame-by-frame basis. This can provide the optimal power and signal for each station. As shown in Figure 4.16, dynamic beamforming uses an *adaptive antenna array* that maneuvers the beam in the direction of a targeted receiver. The technology is often referred to as *smart antenna technology*, or *beamsteering*. Currently, the only Wi-Fi vendor that offers dynamic beamforming capabilities in its access points is Ruckus Wireless. Dynamic beamforming capabilities are not available on the client side.

FIGURE 4.16   Dynamic beamforming—adaptive antenna array

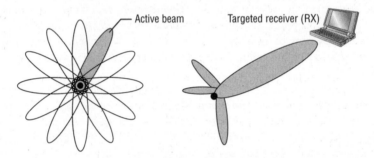

Dynamic beamforming can focus a beam in the direction of an individual client for downstream unicast transmissions between an access point and the targeted client. However, any broadcast frames such as beacons are transmitted using an omnidirectional pattern so that the access point can communicate with all nearby client stations in all directions. Note that Figure 4.16 illustrates the concept; the actual beam is probably more like the signal pattern generated by the antenna in Figure 4.12.

Transmit Beamforming

Transmit beamforming (TxBF) is performed by transmitting multiple phase-shifted signals with the hope and intention that they will arrive in-phase at the location where the transmitter believes that the receiver is located. Unlike dynamic beamforming, TxBF does not change the antenna radiation pattern and an actual directional beam does not exist. In truth, transmit beamforming is not really an antenna technology; it is a digital signal processing technology on the transmitting device that duplicates the transmitted signal on more than one antenna to optimize a combined signal at the client. However, carefully controlling the phase of the signals transmitted from multiple antennas has the effect of improving gain, thus emulating a higher-gain unidirectional antenna. Transmit beamforming is all about adjusting the phase of the transmissions.

The 802.11n amendment defined two types of transmit beamforming, *implicit TxBF* and *explicit TxBF*. Implicit TxBF uses an implicit channel-sounding process to optimize the phase differentials between the transmit chains. Explicit TxBF requires feedback from the stations in order to determine the amount of phase-shift required for each signal. The 802.11ac amendment defines explicit TxBF, requiring the use of channel measurement frames, and both the transmitter and the receiver must support beamforming. 802.11ac will be discussed in greater detail in Chapter 19, "Very-High Throughput (VHT) and 802.11ac."

Visual Line of Sight

When light travels from one point to another, it travels across what is perceived to be an unobstructed straight line, known as the visual *line of sight (LOS)*. For all intents and purposes, it is a straight line, but because of the possibility of light refraction, diffraction, and reflection, there is a slight chance that it is not. If you have been outside on a summer day and looked across a hot parking lot at a stationary object, you may have noticed that, because of the heat rising from the pavement, the object that you were looking at seemed to be moving. This is an example of how visual LOS is sometimes altered slightly. When it comes to RF communications, visual LOS has no bearing on whether the RF transmission is successful.

RF Line of Sight

Point-to-point RF communication also needs to have an unobstructed line of sight between the two antennas. So, the first step for installing a point-to-point system is to make sure that, from the installation point of one of the antennas, you have a clear direct path to the other antenna. Unfortunately, for RF communications to work properly, this is not sufficient. An additional area around the visual LOS needs to remain clear of obstacles and obstructions. This area around the visual LOS is known as the Fresnel zone and is often referred to as RF line of sight.

Fresnel Zone

The *Fresnel zone* (pronounced *FRUH-nel*—the s is silent) is an imaginary, elongated, football-shaped area (American football) that surrounds the path of the visual LOS between two point-to-point antennas. Figure 4.17 shows an illustration of the Fresnel zone's football-like shape.

FIGURE 4.17   Fresnel zone

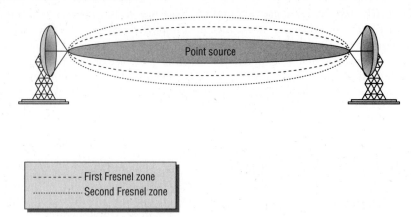

Theoretically, there are an infinite number of Fresnel zones, or concentric ellipsoids (the football shape), that surround the visual LOS. The closest ellipsoid is known as the first Fresnel zone, the next one is the second Fresnel zone, and so on, as depicted in Figure 4.17. For simplicity's sake, and because they are the most relevant for this section, only the first two Fresnel zones are displayed in the figure. The subsequent Fresnel zones have little effect on communications.

If the first Fresnel zone becomes even partly obstructed, the obstruction will negatively influence the integrity of the RF communication. In addition to the obvious reflection and scattering that can occur if there are obstructions between the two antennas, the RF signal can be diffracted or bent as it passes an obstruction of the Fresnel zone. This diffraction of the signal decreases the amount of RF energy that is received by the antenna and may even cause the communications link to fail.

Figure 4.18 illustrates a link that is 1 mile long. The top solid line is a straight line from the center of one antenna to the other. The dotted line shows 60 percent of the bottom half of the first Fresnel zone. The bottom solid line shows the bottom half of the first Fresnel zone. The trees are potential obstructions along the path.

FIGURE 4.18   Fresnel zone clearances of 60 percent and 100 percent

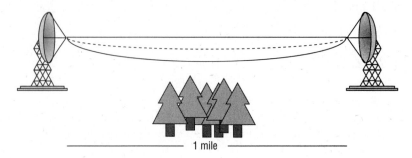

Under no circumstances should you allow any object or objects to encroach more than 40 percent into the first Fresnel zone of an outdoor point-to-point bridge link. Anything more than 40 percent is likely to make the communications link unreliable. Even less than 40 percent obstruction is likely to impair the performance of the link. Therefore, we recommend that you do not allow any obstruction of the first Fresnel zone, particularly in wooded areas where the growth of trees may obstruct the Fresnel zone in the future.

The typical obstacles that you are likely to encounter are trees and buildings. It is important to periodically visually check your link to make sure that trees have not grown into the Fresnel zone or that buildings have not been constructed that encroach into the Fresnel zone. Do not forget that the Fresnel zone exists below, to the sides, and above the visual LOS. If the Fresnel zone does become obstructed, you will need to either move the antenna (usually raise it) or remove the obstacle (usually with a chain saw—just kidding).

To determine whether an obstacle is encroaching into the Fresnel zone, you need to be familiar with a few formulas that enable you to calculate its radius. Don't fret; you will not be tested on these formulas.

The first formula enables you to calculate the radius of the first Fresnel zone at the midpoint between the two antennas. This is the point where the Fresnel zone is the largest. This formula is as follows:

$$radius = 72.2 \times 3 \sqrt{[D \div (4 \times F)]}$$

D = distance of the link in miles

F = transmitting frequency in GHz

This is the optimal clearance that you want along the signal path. Although this is the ideal radius, it is not always feasible. Therefore, the next formula will be very useful. It can be used to calculate the radius of the Fresnel zone that will enable you to have 60 percent of the Fresnel zone unobstructed. This is the minimum amount of clearance you need at the midpoint between the antennas. Here is this formula:

$$radius\ (60\%) = 43.3 \times \sqrt{[D \div (4 \times F)]}$$

D = distance of the link in miles

F = transmitting frequency in GHz

Both of these formulas are useful, but in addition to their benefits, they have major shortcomings. These formulas calculate the radius of the Fresnel zone at the midpoint between the antennas. Since this is the point where the Fresnel zone is the largest, these numbers can be used to determine the minimum height the antennas need to be above the ground. You have to know this number, because if you place the antennas too low, the ground would encroach on the Fresnel zone and cause degradation to the communications. The problem is that if there is a known object somewhere other than the midpoint between the antennas, it is not possible to calculate the radius of the Fresnel zone at that point by using these equations. The following formula can be used to calculate the radius of any Fresnel zone at any point between the two antennas:

$$radius = 72.2 \times \sqrt{[(N \times d1 \times d2) \div (F \times D)]}$$

N = which Fresnel zone you are calculating (usually 1 or 2)

d1 = distance from one antenna to the location of the obstacle in miles

d2 = distance from the obstacle to the other antenna in miles

D = total distance between the antennas in miles (D = d1 + d2)

F = frequency in GHz

Figure 4.19 shows a point-to-point communications link that is 10 miles long. There is an obstacle (tree) that is 3 miles away from one antenna and 40 feet tall. So, the values and the formula to calculate the radius of the Fresnel zone at a point 3 miles from the antenna are as follows:

N = 1 (for first Fresnel zone)

d1 = 3 miles

d2 = 7 miles

D = 10 miles

F = 2.4 GHz

radius at 3 miles = $72.2 \times \sqrt{[(1 \times 3 \times 7) \div (2.4 \times 10)]}$

radius at 3 miles = $72.2 \times \sqrt{[21 \div 24]}$

radius at 3 miles = 67.53 feet

FIGURE 4.19 Point-to-point communication with potential obstacle

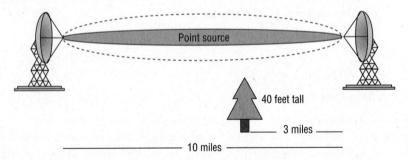

So, if the obstacle is 40 feet tall and the Fresnel zone at that point is 67.53 feet tall, the antennas need to be mounted at least 108 feet (40′ + 67.53′ = 107.53′; we rounded up) above the ground to have complete clearance. If we are willing to allow the obstruction to

encroach up to 40 percent into the Fresnel zone, we need to keep 60 percent of the Fresnel zone clear. So 60 percent of 67.53 feet is 40.52 feet. The absolute minimum height of the antennas will need to be 81 feet (40′ + 40.52′ = 80.52′; again we rounded up). In the next section, you will learn that, because of the curvature of the earth, you will need to raise the antennas even higher to compensate for the earth's bulge.

When highly directional antennas are used, the beamwidth of the signal is smaller, causing a more focused signal to be transmitted. Many people think that a smaller beamwidth would decrease the size of the Fresnel zone. This is not the case. The size of the Fresnel zone is a function of the frequency being used and the distance of the link. Since the only variables in the formula are frequency and distance, the size of the Fresnel zone will be the same regardless of the antenna type or beamwidth. The first Fresnel zone is technically the area around the point source, where the waves are in phase with the point source signal. The second Fresnel zone is then the area beyond the first Fresnel zone, where the waves are out of phase with the point source signal. All of the odd-numbered Fresnel zones are in phase with the point source signal, and all of the even-numbered Fresnel zones are out of phase.

If an RF signal of the same frequency but out of phase with the primary signal intersects the primary signal, the out-of-phase signal will cause degradation or even cancellation of the primary signal (this was covered in Chapter 2 and demonstrated using the EMANIM software). One of the ways that an out-of-phase signal can intercept the primary signal is by reflection. It is, therefore, important to consider the second Fresnel zone when evaluating point-to-point communications. If the height of the antennas and the layout of the geography are such that the RF signal from the second Fresnel zone is reflected toward the receiving antenna, it can cause degradation of the link. Although this is not a common occurrence, the second Fresnel zone should be considered when planning or troubleshooting the connection, especially in flat, arid terrain, like a desert. You should also be cautious of metal surfaces or calm water along the Fresnel zone.

Please understand that the Fresnel zone is three-dimensional. Can something impede on the Fresnel zone from above? Although trees do not grow from the sky, a point-to-point bridge link could be shot under a railroad trestle or a freeway. In these rare situations, consideration would have to be given to proper clearance of the upper radius of the first Fresnel zone. A more common scenario would be the deployment of point-to-point links in an urban city environment. Very often building-to-building links must be shot between other buildings. In these situations, other buildings have the potential of impeding the side radiuses of the Fresnel zone.

Until now, all of the discussion about the Fresnel zone has related to point-to-point communications. The Fresnel zone exists in all RF communications; however, it is in outdoor point-to-point communications where it can cause the most problems. Indoor environments have so many walls and other obstacles where there is already so much reflection, refraction, diffraction, and scattering that the Fresnel zone is not likely to play a big part in the success or failure of the link.

Earth Bulge

When you are installing long-distance point-to-point RF communications, another variable that must be considered is the curvature of the earth, also known as the *earth bulge*. Because the landscape varies throughout the world, it is impossible to specify an exact distance for when the curvature of the earth will affect a communications link. The recommendation is that if the antennas are more than 7 miles away from each other, you should take into consideration the earth bulge, because after 7 miles, the earth itself begins to impede on the Fresnel zone. The following formula can be used to calculate the additional height that the antennas will need to be raised to compensate for the earth bulge:

$H = D^2 \div 8$

H = height of the earth bulge in feet

D = distance between the antennas in miles

You now have all of the pieces to estimate how high the antennas need to be installed. Remember, this is an estimate that is being calculated, because it is assumed that the terrain between the two antennas does not vary. You need to know or calculate the following three things:

- The 60 percent radius of the first Fresnel zone
- The height of the earth bulge
- The height of any obstacles that may encroach into the Fresnel zone, and the distance of those obstacles from the antenna

Taking these three pieces and adding them together gives you the following formula, which can be used to calculate the antenna height:

H = obstacle height + earth bulge + Fresnel zone

$$H = OB + (D^2 \div 8) + (43.3 \times \sqrt{[D \div (4 \times F)]})$$

OB = obstacle height

D = distance of the link in miles

F = transmitting frequency in GHz

Figure 4.20 shows a point-to-point link that spans a distance of 12 miles. In the middle of this link is an office building that is 30 feet tall. A 2.4 GHz signal is being used to communicate between the two towers. Using the formula, we calculate that each of the antennas needs to be installed at least 96.4 feet above the ground:

$$H = 30 + (12^2 \div 8) + (43.3 \times \sqrt{[12 \div (4 \times 2.4)]})$$

$H = 30 + 18 + 48.4$

$H = 96.4$

FIGURE 4.20   Calculating antenna height

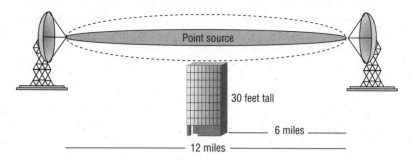

30 feet tall

6 miles

12 miles

Although these formulas are useful, the good news is that you do not need to know them for the test.

Antenna Polarization

Another consideration when installing antennas is antenna polarization. Although it is a lesser-known concern, it is extremely important for successful communications. Proper polarization alignment is vital when installing any type of antenna. As waves radiate from an antenna, the amplitude of the waves can oscillate either vertically or horizontally. It is important to have the polarization of the transmitting and receiving antennas oriented the same in order to receive the strongest possible signal. Whether the antennas are installed with horizontal or vertical polarization is usually irrelevant, as long as both antennas are aligned with the same polarization.

> When discussing antennas, the proper term is antenna *polarization*, which refers to the alignment or orientation of the waves. The use of the term *polarity* is incorrect.

Polarization is not as important for indoor communications because the polarization of the RF signal often changes when it is reflected, which is a common occurrence indoors. Most access points use low-gain omnidirectional antennas, and they should be polarized vertically when mounted from the ceiling. Laptop manufacturers build antennas into the sides of the monitor. When the laptop monitor is in the upright position, the internal antennas are vertically polarized as well.

When aligning a point-to-point or point-to-multipoint bridge, proper polarization is extremely important. If the best received signal level (RSL) you receive when aligning the antennas is 15 dB to 20 dB less than your estimated RSL, there is a good chance you have cross-polarization. If this difference exists on only one side and the other has higher signal, you are likely aligned to a side lobe.

An excellent video, *Beam Patterns and Polarization of Directional Antennas*, is available for download from the book's online resource area, which can be accessed at www.sybex.com/go/cwna4e. This 3-minute video explains and demonstrates the effects of antenna side lobes and polarization. The filename of the video is Antenna Properties.wmv.

Antenna Diversity

Wireless networks, especially indoor networks, are prone to multipath signals. To help compensate for the effects of multipath, antenna diversity, also called spatial diversity, is commonly implemented in wireless networking equipment such as access points. *Antenna diversity* exists when an access point has two or more antennas with a receiver functioning together to minimize the negative effects of multipath.

Because the wavelengths of 802.11 wireless networks are less than 5 inches long, the antennas can be placed very near each other and still allow antenna diversity to be effective. When the access point senses an RF signal, it compares the signal that it is receiving on both antennas and uses whichever antenna has the higher signal strength to receive the frame of data. This sampling is performed on a frame-by-frame basis, choosing whichever antenna has the higher signal strength.

Most pre-802.11n radios use *switched diversity*. When receiving incoming transmissions, switched diversity listens with multiple antennas. Multiple copies of the same signal arrive at the receiver antennas with different amplitudes. The signal with the best amplitude is chosen, and the other signals are ignored. The AP will use one antenna as long as the signal is above a predefined signal level. If the signal degrades below the acceptable level, then the AP will use the signal received on the other antenna.

This method of listening for the best received signal is also known as *receive diversity*. Switched diversity is also used when transmitting, but only one antenna is used. The transmitter will transmit out of the diversity antenna where the best amplitude signal was last heard. The method of transmitting out of the antenna where the last best received signal was heard is known as *transmit diversity*.

When an access point has two antenna ports for antenna diversity, the antennas should have identical gain and should be installed in the same location and with the same orientation. You should not be running antenna cables to antennas in opposite directions to try to provide better coverage. Remember, when diversity is used, the transceiver will switch between the antennas; therefore the antennas need to provide essentially the same coverage. The distance between the antennas should be a factor of the wavelength (1/4, 1/2, 1, 2).

Because the antennas are so close to each other, it is not uncommon to doubt that antenna diversity is actually beneficial. As you may recall from Chapter 3, the amount of RF signal that is received is often less than 0.00000001 milliwatts. At this level of signal, the slightest difference between the signals that each antenna receives can be significant. Other factors to remember are that the access point is often communicating with multiple client devices at different locations. These clients are not always stationary, thus further affecting the path of the RF signal.

The access point has to handle transmitting data differently than receiving data. When the access point needs to transmit data back to the client, it has no way of determining which antenna the client would receive from the best. An access point can handle transmitting data by using the antenna that it used most recently to receive the data. You will remember that this is often referred to as *transmit diversity*. Not all access points are equipped with this capability.

There are many kinds of antenna diversity. Laptops with internal cards usually have diversity antennas mounted inside the laptop monitor. Remember that because of the half-duplex nature of the RF medium, when antenna diversity is used only one antenna is operational at any given time. In other words, a radio card transmitting a frame with one antenna cannot be receiving a frame with the other antenna at the same time.

Multiple-Input, Multiple-Output

Multiple-input, multiple-output (MIMO) is another, more sophisticated form of antenna diversity. Unlike conventional antenna systems, where multipath propagation is an impairment, MIMO (pronounced *MY-moh*) systems take advantage of multipath. MIMO can safely be described as a wireless radio architecture that can receive or transmit using multiple antennas concurrently. Complex signal-processing techniques enable significant enhancements to reliability, range, and throughput in MIMO systems. These techniques send data by using multiple simultaneous RF signals, and the receiver then reconstructs the data from those signals.

802.11n and 802.11ac radios use MIMO technology. One of the key goals when installing a MIMO device is to make sure that each of the signals from the different radio chains travel with different signal polarization. This can be done by aligning or orienting the antennas so that the path that each signal travels is at least slightly different. This will help to introduce delay between the different MIMO signals, which will improve the ability for the MIMO receiver to process the different signals. Different types of MIMO antennas are discussed in the next section and MIMO technology is explored in much further detail in Chapter 18 and Chapter 19, as it is a key component of 802.11n and 802.11ac.

MIMO Antennas

With the need and desire to increase the throughput and capacity of wireless networks, the installation of 802.11n and 802.11ac access points has become the norm. 802.11n has become commonplace not only for indoor networks but also for outdoor networks and point-to-point networks. 802.11ac is quickly supplanting 802.11n networks indoors and will likely become commonplace in outdoor implementations. MIMO antenna selection and placement is important in each of these environments.

Indoor MIMO Antennas

There is usually not much decision making involved regarding the antennas on an indoor MIMO access point. Many of the new enterprise MIMO access points have the antennas integrated into the chassis of the access point, with no antennas protruding from the access point. If the antennas are not integrated in the access point chassis, the MIMO access point likely has three omnidirectional antennas directly attached to it. In some cases the antennas are detachable, allowing you to choose higher gain omnidirectional antennas.

When installing or configuring external MIMO antennas, some vendors require that they all be lined up parallel with each other. If the vendor does not specify this, then you should align them slightly off parallel with each other. One antenna should be aligned vertically, and the other two antennas should be tilted. How much the antennas should be tilted is a topic of much discussion. It is likely that with so many reflective surfaces indoors, the environment itself will provide the necessary multipath for the different signals. While this is likely, it may not be a bad idea to tilt the antennas slightly from an angle of about 15 degrees up to a maximum angle of about 30 degrees off of vertical. None of the antennas should be parallel with any of the other antennas. The goal of tilting the antennas is to help create multipath, but you do not want to change the coverage pattern of the antennas. It is important that all of the antennas are identical. As mentioned earlier, indoor MIMO antennas are often deployed in high-density environments.

Outdoor MIMO Antennas

Most outdoor MIMO access points currently have two antennas per radio, but three radio chain units are becoming more common. As with the indoor access points, multipath provides a benefit for successful and higher data rate communications with outdoor MIMO devices. This benefit may not be realized if the environment does not have reflective surfaces that induce multipath. Therefore, it is important to try to change the radiation path of the two or three antennas while maintaining the same range and coverage with all of the antennas. In the outdoor environment, achieving this goal requires more knowledge and technology than can usually be achieved by leaving the antenna choice and placement up to the designer or installer of the networks. Therefore, many of the access point and antenna manufacturers have designed both omnidirectional and directional MIMO antennas.

To distinguish the different radio chain signals from each other, the directional MIMO antennas incorporate two or three antenna elements within one physical antenna. With a two-element antenna, one of the elements is mounted with vertical polarization and the other with horizontal polarization. The antenna will have two connectors to connect it to the access point. If the access point that the antenna is being connected to is a multi-radio access point, the access point will have two antenna connectors for each radio. It is important to make sure that the two cables from the antenna are connected to the antenna jacks for the same radio. With a three-element antenna, typically two of the elements are mounted 90 degrees off of each other, and the third element is mounted 45 degrees off of the other two elements. The antenna will have three connectors to connect it to the access point. Again, if the access point has two radios, be careful which antenna jacks you use to connect the antenna.

To provide omnidirectional MIMO coverage with two radio chain APs, special pairs of omnidirectional antennas are available. Each pair is made up of an omnidirectional antenna with vertical polarization and a second omnidirectional antenna with horizontal polarization. It is a little strange using these antennas, because in the past with legacy non-802.11n access points, if two omnidirectional antennas were installed on an access point, it was important to purchase identical antennas. With outdoor MIMO omnidirectional antennas, the antennas are purchased as a set, but they are typically of different lengths and widths because of the different polarization that each antenna has. If you are not familiar with these new antenna pairs, you may think that you were shipped the wrong product, due to the antennas not looking the same. When trying to provide omnidirectional coverage using a three-radio-chain AP, special single chassis antennas have begun to appear. One particular type, known as a down-tilt antenna, is made up of three omnidirectional antenna elements, mounted within one antenna body. The antenna is typically mounted in a high location, mounted horizontally above the area of coverage, and is faced down at the floor or ground below. The horizontal coverage area is omnidirectional. The vertical coverage behaves like a typical omnidirectional antenna but with more vertical signal/coverage below the antenna than above.

Antenna Connection and Installation

In addition to the physical antenna being a vital component in the wireless network, the installation and connection of the antenna to the wireless transceiver is critical. If the antenna is not properly connected and installed, any benefit that the antenna introduces to the network can be instantly wiped out. Three key components associated with the proper installation of the antenna are voltage standing wave ratio (VSWR), signal loss, and the actual mounting of the antenna.

Voltage Standing Wave Ratio

Voltage standing wave ratio (VSWR) is a measurement of the change in impedances to an AC signal. Voltage standing waves exist because of impedance mismatches or variations between devices in an RF communications system. Impedance is a value of ohms of electrical resistance to an AC signal. A standard unit of measurement of electrical resistance is the ohm, named after German physicist Georg Ohm. When the transmitter generates the AC radio signal, the signal travels along the cable to the antenna. Some of this incident (or forward) energy is reflected back toward the transmitter because of impedance mismatch.

Mismatches may occur anywhere along the signal path but are usually due to abrupt impedance changes between the radio transmitter and cable and between the cable and the antenna. The amount of energy reflected depends on the level of mismatch between the transmitter, cable, and antenna. The ratio between the voltage of the reflected wave and the voltage of the incident wave, *at the same point along the cable*, is called the *voltage reflection coefficient*, usually designated by the Greek letter rho (ρ).

In an ideal system, where there are no mismatches (the impedance is the same everywhere), all of the incident energy will be delivered to the antenna (except for the resistive losses in the cable itself) and there will be no reflected energy. The cable is said to be *matched*, and the voltage reflection coefficient is exactly zero and the *return loss*, in dB, is infinite. Return loss is essentially the dB difference between the power sent to the antenna and the power reflected back, thus a higher value is better than a lower value. The combination of incident and reflected waves traveling back and forth along the cable creates a resulting *standing wave* pattern along the length of the line. The standing wave pattern is periodic (it repeats) and exhibits multiple peaks and troughs of voltage, current, and power.

VSWR is a numerical relationship between the measurement of the maximum voltage along the line (what is generated by the transmitter) and the measurement of the minimum voltage along the line (what is received by the antenna). VSWR is therefore a ratio of impedance mismatch, with 1:1 (no impedance) being optimal but unobtainable, and typical values range from 1.1:1 to as much as 1.5:1. VSWR military specs are 1.1:1.

$$VSWR = V_{max} \div V_{min}$$

When the transmitter, cable, and antenna impedances are matched (that is, there are no standing waves), the voltage along the cable will be constant. This matched cable is also referred to as a *flat line* because there are no peaks and troughs of voltage along the length of the cable. In this case, VSWR is 1:1. As the degree of mismatch increases, the VSWR increases with a corresponding decrease in the power delivered to the antenna. Table 4.2 shows this effect.

TABLE 4.2   Signal loss caused by VSWR

VSWR	Radiated power	Lost power	Return loss	dB power loss
1:1	100%	0%	Infinite	0 dB
1.5:1	96%	4%	14 dB	Nearly 0 dB
2:1	89%	11%	9.5 dB	< 1 dB
6:1	50%	50%	2.9 dB	3 dB

If VSWR is large, this means that a large amount of voltage is being reflected back toward the transmitter. This of course means a decrease in power or amplitude (loss) of the signal that is supposed to be transmitted. This loss of forward amplitude is known as *return loss* and can be measured in dB. Additionally, the power that is being reflected back is then directed back into the transmitter. If the transmitter is not protected from excessive reflected power or large voltage peaks, it can overheat and fail. Understand that VSWR may cause decreased signal strength, erratic signal strength, or even transmitter failure.

The first thing that can be done to minimize VSWR is to make sure that the impedance of all of the wireless networking equipment is matched. Most wireless networking equipment has an impedance of 50 ohms; however, you should check the manuals to confirm this. When attaching the different components, make sure that all connectors are installed and crimped properly and that they are snugly tightened.

Signal Loss

When connecting an antenna to a transmitter, the main objective is to make sure that as much of the signal that is generated by the transmitter is received by the antenna to be transmitted. To achieve this, it is important to pay particular attention to the cables and connectors that connect the transmitter to the antenna. In the section "Antenna Accessories" later in this chapter, we review the cables, connectors, and many other components that are used when installing antennas. If inferior components are used, or if the components are not installed properly, the access point will most likely function below its optimal capability.

Antenna Mounting

As stated earlier in this chapter, proper installation of the antenna is one of the most important tasks to ensure an optimally functioning network. The following are key areas to be concerned with when installing antennas:

- Placement
- Mounting
- Appropriate use and environment
- Orientation and alignment
- Safety
- Maintenance

Placement

The proper placement of an antenna depends on the type of antenna. When installing omnidirectional antennas, it is important to place the antenna at the center of the area where you want coverage. Remember that lower-gain omnidirectional antennas provide broader vertical coverage, while higher-gain omnidirectional antennas provide wider but much flatter coverage. Be careful not to place high-gain omnidirectional antennas too high above the ground, because the narrow vertical coverage may cause the antenna to provide insufficient signal to clients located on the ground.

When installing directional antennas, make sure you know both the horizontal and vertical beamwidths so that you can properly aim the antennas. Also make sure that you are aware of the amount of gain the antenna is adding to the transmission. If the signal is too strong, it will overshoot the area that you are looking to provide coverage to. This can be a security risk, and you may want to decrease the amount of power that the transceiver is generating to reduce the coverage area, providing of course that this signal decrease does not compromise the performance of your link. Not only can it be a security risk, overshooting your coverage area is considered rude.

If you are installing an outdoor directional antenna, in addition to concerns regarding the horizontal and vertical beamwidths, make sure that you have correctly calculated the Fresnel zone and mounted the antenna accordingly.

Indoor Mounting Considerations

After deciding where to place the antenna, the next step is to decide how to mount it. There are numerous ways of mounting antennas indoors. Most access points have at least a couple of keyhole type mounts for hanging the access point off of a couple of screws on a wall. Most enterprise-class access points have mounting kits that allow you to mount the access point to a wall or ceiling. Many of these kits are designed to easily attach directly to the metal rails of a drop ceiling.

Two common concerns are aesthetics and security. Many organizations, particularly ones that provide hospitality-oriented services such as hotels and hospitals, are concerned about the aesthetics of the installation of the antennas. Specialty enclosures and ceiling tiles can help to hide the installation of the access points and antennas. Other organizations, particularly schools and public environments, are concerned with securing the access points and antennas from theft or vandalism. An access point can be locked in a secure enclosure, with a short cable connecting it to the antenna. There are even ceiling tiles with antennas built into them, invisible to anyone walking by. If security is a concern, mounting the antenna high on the wall or ceiling can also minimize unauthorized access.

If access points or antennas are installed below the ceiling, children or teens will often try to jump up and hit the antennas or throw things at them in an attempt to move them. This also needs to be considered when choosing locations to install antennas.

Outdoor Mounting Considerations

Many antennas, especially outdoor antennas, are mounted on masts or towers. It is common to use mounting clamps and U-bolts to attach the antennas to the masts. For mounting directional antennas, specially designed tilt-and-swivel mounting kits are available to make it easier to aim and secure the antenna. If the antenna is being installed in a windy location (and what rooftop or tower isn't windy?), make sure that you take into consideration wind load and properly secure the antenna.

Appropriate Use and Environment

Make sure that indoor access points and antennas are not used for outdoor communications. Outdoor access points and antennas are specifically built to withstand the wide range of temperatures that they may be exposed to. It is important to make sure that the environment where you are installing the equipment is within the operating temperature range of the access point and antennas. The extreme cold weather of northern Canada may be too cold for some equipment, whereas the extreme heat of the desert in Saudi Arabia may be too hot. Outdoor access points and antennas are also built to stand up to other elements, such as rain, snow, and fog. In addition to installing the proper devices, make sure that the mounts you use are designed for the environment in which you are installing the equipment.

With the expansion of wireless networking, it is becoming more common to not only install wireless devices in harsh environments but also to install them in potentially flammable or combustible environments, such as mines and oil rigs. Installation of access points and antennas in these environments requires special construction of the devices or the installation of the devices in special enclosures.

In the following sections, you will learn about four classification standards. The first two standards designate how a device will stand up to harsh conditions and the following two standards designate the environments in which a device is allowed to operate. These are just four examples of standards that exist and how they apply to equipment and environments. You will need to do research to determine if there are requirements to which you must (or should) adhere to in your country or region when installing equipment.

Ingress Protection Rating

The *Ingress Protection Rating* is sometimes referred to as the International Protection Rating and is commonly referred to as the *IP Code* (not to be confused with Internet Protocol, which is part of TCP/IP). The IP Rating system is published by the International Electrotechnical Commission (IEC). The IP Code is represented by the letters *IP* followed by two digits or a digit and one or two letters, such as IP66.

The first digit of the IP Code classifies the degree of protection that the device provides against the intrusion of solid objects, and the second digit classifies the degree of protection that the device provides against the intrusion of water. If no protection is provided for either of these classifications, the digit is replaced with the letter *X*.

The solids digit can be a value between 0 and 6 with protection ranging from no protection (0) up to dust tight (6). The liquids digit can be a value between 0 and 8, including, for example, no protection (0), dripping water (1), water splashing from any direction (4), powerful water jets (6), and immersion greater than one meter (8).

NEMA Enclosure Rating

The *NEMA Enclosure Rating* is published by the United States National Electrical Manufacturers Association (NEMA). The NEMA ratings are similar to the IP ratings, but the NEMA ratings also specify other features, such as corrosion resistance, gasket aging, and construction practices.

The NEMA enclosure types are defined in the NEMA Standards Publication 250-2008, "Enclosures for Electrical Equipment (1000 Volts Maximum)." This document defines the degree of protection from such things as solid foreign objects like dirt, dust, lint, and fibers along with the ingress of water, oil, and coolant. The rating for the NEMA enclosures is in the form of a number or a number followed by a letter, such as Type 2 or Type 12K.

ATEX Directives

There are two ATEX directives:

ATEX 95   This pertains to equipment and protective systems that are intended to be used in potentially explosive atmospheres.

ATEX 137   This pertains to the workplace and is intended to protect and improve the safety and health of workers at risk from explosive atmospheres.

Organizations in the European Union must follow these directives to protect employees. The ATEX directives inherits their name from the French title of the 94/9/EC directive: "Appareils destinés à être utilisés en ATmosphères EXplosibles."

Employers must classify work areas where explosive atmospheres may exist into different zones. Areas can be classified for gas-vapor-mist environments or dust environments. These regulations apply to all equipment, whether mechanical or electrical, and are categorized for mining and surface industries.

National Electrical Code Hazardous Locations

The *National Electrical Code (NEC)* is a standard for the safe installation of electrical equipment and wiring. The document itself is not a legally binding document, but it can and has been adopted by many local and state governments in the United States, thus making it law in those places. A substantial part of the NEC discusses hazardous locations. The NEC classifies hazardous locations by type, condition, and nature. The hazardous location type is defined as follows:

- Class I—gas or vapor
- Class II—dust
- Class III—fibers and flyings

The type is further subdivided by the conditions of the hazardous location:

- Division 1—normal conditions (for example, a typical day at the loading dock)
- Division 2—abnormal conditions (same loading dock, but a container is leaking its contents)

A final classification defines a group for the hazardous substance, based on the nature of the substance. This value is represented by an uppercase letter ranging from *A* through *G*.

Orientation and Alignment

Before installing an antenna, make sure you read the manufacturer's recommendations for mounting it. This suggestion is particularly important when installing directional antennas.

Since directional antennas may have different horizontal and vertical beamwidths, and because directional antennas can be installed with different polarization, proper orientation can make the difference between being able to communicate or not:

1. Make sure that the antenna polarization is consistent on both ends of a directional link.

2. Decide on the mounting technique and ensure that it is compatible with the mounting location.

3. Align the antennas.

   Remember that you need to align both the direction of the antenna and its vertical tilt.

4. Weatherproof the cables and connectors and secure them from movement.

5. Document and photograph each installation of the access point and antennas. This can help you troubleshoot problems in the future and allows you to more easily determine if there has been movement in the installation or antenna alignment.

As mentioned earlier in this chapter, with the transition to 802.11n, 802.11ac, and MIMO, special two radio chain, outdoor omnidirectional MIMO antennas have been designed to be installed as pairs, with one antenna generating a signal with vertical polarization and the other generating a signal with horizontal polarization.

Safety

We can't emphasize enough the importance of being careful when installing antennas. Most of the time, the installation of an antenna requires climbing ladders, towers, or rooftops. Gravity and wind have a way of making an installation difficult for both the climber and the people below helping.

Plan the installation before you begin, making sure you have all of the tools and equipment that you will need to install the antenna. Unplanned stoppages of the installation and relaying forgotten equipment up and down the ladder add to the risk of injury.

Be careful when working with your antenna or near other antennas. Highly directional antennas are focusing high concentrations of RF energy. This large amount of energy can be dangerous to your health. Do not power on your antenna while you are working on it, and do not stand in front of other antennas that are near where you are installing your antenna. You probably do not know the frequency or power output of these other antenna systems, nor the potential health risks that you might be exposed to.

When installing antennas (or any device) on ceilings, rafters, or masts, make sure they are properly secured. Even a 1-pound antenna can be deadly if it falls from the rafters of a warehouse.

If you will be installing antennas as part of your job, we recommend that you take an RF health and safety course. In the United States, these courses will teach you the FCC and the US Department of Labor Occupational Safety and Health Administration (OSHA) regulations and how to be safe and compliant with the standards. Similar courses can be found in many other countries around the world. We suggest looking for courses that are appropriate to your country or region.

If you need an antenna installed on any elevated structure, such as a pole, tower, or even a roof, consider hiring a professional installer. Professional climbers and installers are trained and, in some places, certified to perform these types of installations. In addition to the training, they have the necessary safety equipment and proper insurance for the job.

If you are planning to install wireless equipment as a profession, you should develop a safety policy that is approved by your local occupational safety representative. You should also receive certified training on climbing safety in addition to RF safety training. First aid and CPR training are also highly recommended.

Maintenance

There are two types of maintenance: preventive and diagnostic. When installing an antenna, it is important to prevent problems from occurring in the future. This seems like simple advice, but since antennas are often difficult to get to after they have been installed, it is especially prudent advice. Two key problems that can be minimized with proper preventative measures are wind damage and water damage. When installing the antenna, make sure all of the nuts, bolts, screws, and so on are installed and tightened properly. Also make sure all the cables are properly secured so that they are not thrashed about by the wind.

To help prevent water damage, cold-shrink tubing or coaxial sealant can be used to minimize the risk of water getting into the cable or connectors. Another common method is a combination of electrical tape and mastic, installed in layers to provide a completely watertight installation. If mastic is used, be sure to first tightly wrap the connection with electrical tape before applying the mastic. If the connection ever needs to be disconnected and reattached, it will be virtually impossible to remove the mastic if it has been applied directly to the connector.

WARNING   Heat-shrink tubing should not be used because the cable can be damaged by the heat that is necessary to shrink the wrapping. Silicone also should not be used, because air bubbles can form under the silicone and moisture can collect.

Another cabling technique is the drip loop. To create a drip loop, when a cable is run down to a connector, run the cable down below the connector and then loop it up to the connector, creating a small loop or "U" of cable below the connector. Drip loops are also used when a cable is run into a building or structure. A drip loop prevents water from flowing down the cable and onto a connector or into the hole where a cable enters the building. Any water that is flowing down the cable will continue to the bottom of the loop and then drip off.

Antennas are typically installed and forgotten about until they break. It is advisable to periodically perform a visual inspection of the antenna and, if needed, verify its status with the installation documentation. If the antenna is not easily accessible, a pair of binoculars or a camera with a very high zoom lens can make this a simple task.

Antenna Accessories

In Chapter 3, we introduced the components of RF communications. In that chapter, the main components were reviewed; however, there are other components that are either not as significant or not always installed as part of the communications link. Important specifications for all antenna accessories include frequency response, impedance, VSWR, maximum input power, and insertion loss. In the following sections we will discuss some of these components and accessories.

Cables

Improper installation or selection of cables can detrimentally affect the RF communications more than just about any other component or outside influence. It is important to remember this fact when installing antenna cables. The following list addresses some concerns when selecting and installing cables:

- Make sure you select the correct cable.

  The impedance of the cable needs to match the impedance of the antenna and transceiver. If there is an impedance mismatch, the return loss from VSWR will affect the link.

- Make sure the cable you select will support the frequencies that you will be using.

  Typically, cable manufacturers list cutoff frequencies, which are the lowest and highest frequencies that the cable supports. This is often referred to as frequency response. For instance, LMR cable is a popular brand of coaxial cable used in RF communications. LMR-1200 will not work with 5 GHz transmissions. LMR-900 is the highest you can use. However, you can use LMR-1200 for 2.4 GHz operations.

- Cables introduce signal loss into the communications link.

  To determine how much loss, cable vendors provide charts or calculators to assist you. Figure 4.21 is an attenuation chart for LMR cable produced by Times Microwave Systems. The left side of the chart lists different types of LMR cable. The farther you move down the list, the better the cable is. The better cable is typically thicker, stiffer, more difficult to work with, and of course, more expensive. The chart shows how much decibel loss the cable will add to the communications link per 100 feet of cable. The column headers list the frequencies that may be used with the cable. For example, 100 feet of LMR-400 cable used on a 2.5 GHz network (2,500 MHz) would decrease the signal by 6.8 dB.

- Attenuation increases with frequency. If you convert from a 2.4 GHz WLAN to a 5 GHz WLAN, the loss caused by the cable will be greater.

- Either purchase the cables precut and preinstalled with the connectors or hire a professional cabler to install the connections (unless you are a professional cabler).

Improperly installed connectors will add more loss to the communications link, which can nullify the extra money you spend for the better-quality cable. It can also introduce return loss in the cable due to reflections.

FIGURE 4.21   Coaxial cable attenuation

Times Microwave Systems (Attenuation dB/100 ft)											
LMR Cable\Frequency	30	50	150	220	450	900	1,500	1,800	2,000	2,500	5,800
100A	3.9	5.1	8.9	10.9	15.8	22.8	30.1	33.2	35.2	39.8	64.1
195	2	2.5	4.4	5.4	7.8	11.1	14.5	16	16.9	19	29.9
195UF	2.3	3	5.3	6.4	9.3	13.2	17.3	19	20.1	22.6	35.6
200	1.8	2.3	4	4.8	7	9.9	12.9	14.2	15	16.9	26.4
200UF	2.1	2.7	4.8	5.8	8.3	11.9	15.5	17.1	18	20.2	31.6
240	1.3	1.7	3	3.7	5.3	7.6	9.9	10.9	11.5	12.9	20.4
240UF	1.6	2.1	3.6	4.4	6.3	9.1	11.8	13	13.8	15.5	24.4
300	1.1	1.4	2.4	2.9	4.2	6.1	7.9	8.7	9.2	10.4	16.5
300UF	1.3	1.6	2.9	3.5	5.1	7.3	9.5	10.5	11.1	12.5	19.8
400	0.7	0.9	1.5	1.9	2.7	3.9	5.1	5.7	6	6.8	10.8
400UF	0.8	1.1	1.8	2.2	3.3	4.7	6.2	6.8	7.2	8.1	13
500	0.5	0.7	1.2	1.5	2.2	3.1	4.1	4.6	4.8	5.5	8.9
500UF	0.6	0.8	1.5	1.8	2.6	3.8	5	5.5	5.8	6.6	10.6
600	0.4	0.5	1	1.2	1.7	2.5	3.3	3.7	3.9	4.4	7.3
600UF	0.5	0.7	1.2	1.4	2.1	3	4	4.4	4.7	5.3	8.7
900	0.3	0.4	0.7	0.8	1.2	1.7	2.2	2.5	2.6	3	4.9
1200	0.2	0.3	0.5	0.6	0.9	1.3	1.7	1.9	2	2.3	not supported
1700	0.1	0.2	0.3	0.4	0.6	0.9	1.3	1.4	1.5	1.7	not supported

UF = Ultraflex (more flexible cable)

Connectors

Many types of connectors are used to connect antennas to 802.11 equipment. Part of the reason for this is that the FCC Report & Order 04-165 requires that amplifiers have either unique connectors or electronic identification systems to prevent the use of noncertified antennas. This requirement was created to prevent people from connecting higher-gain antennas, either intentionally or unintentionally, to a transceiver. An unauthorized high-gain antenna could exceed the maximum equivalent isotropically radiated power (EIRP) that is allowed by the FCC or other regulatory body.

In response to this regulation, cable manufacturers sell *pigtail* adapter cables. These pigtail cables are usually short segments of cable (typically about 2 feet long) with different connectors on each end. They act as adapters, changing the connector and allowing a different antenna to be used.

Many of the same principles of cables apply to the connectors as well as many of the other accessories. RF connectors need to be of the correct impedance to match the other RF equipment. They also support specific ranges of frequencies. The connectors add signal loss to the RF link, and lower-quality connectors are more likely to cause connection or VSWR problems. RF connectors on average add about 1/2 dB of insertion loss.

Splitters

Splitters are also known as signal splitters, RF splitters, power splitters, and power dividers. A splitter takes an RF signal and divides it into two or more separate signals. Only in an unusually special or unique situation would you need to use an RF splitter. One such situation would be if you were connecting sector antennas to one transceiver. If you had three 120-degree antennas aimed away from a central point to provide 360-degree coverage, you could connect each antenna to its own transceiver, or you could use a three-way splitter and equal-length cables to connect the antennas to a single transceiver. When you install a splitter in this type of configuration, not only will the signal be degraded because it is being split three times (known as *through loss*), but also each connector will add its own insertion loss to the signal. There are so many variables and potential problems with this configuration that we recommend this type of installation be attempted only by a very RF-knowledgeable person and only for temporary installations.

A more practical, but again rare, use of a splitter is to monitor the power that is being transmitted. The splitter can be connected to the transceiver and then split to the antenna and a power meter. This approach would enable you to actively monitor the power that is being sent to the antenna.

Amplifiers

An RF *amplifier* takes the signal that is generated by the transceiver, increases it, and sends it to the antenna. Unlike the antenna providing an increase in gain by focusing the signal, an amplifier provides an overall increase in power by adding electrical energy to the signal, which is referred to as *active gain.*

Amplifiers can be purchased as either unidirectional or bidirectional devices. Unidirectional amplifiers perform the amplification in only one direction, either when transmitting or when receiving. Bidirectional amplifiers perform the amplification in both directions.

The amplifier's increase in power is created using one of two methods:

Fixed-Gain   With the fixed-gain method, the output of the transceiver is increased by the amount of the amplifier.

Fixed-Output   A fixed-output amplifier does not add to the output of the transceiver. It simply generates a signal equal to the output of the amplifier regardless of the power generated by the transceiver.

Adjustable variable-gain amplifiers also exist, but using them is not a recommended practice. Unauthorized adjustment of a variable-rate amplifier may result in either violation of power regulations or insufficient transmission amplitude.

Since most regulatory bodies have a maximum power regulation of 1 watt or less at the intentional radiator (IR), the main purpose of using amplifiers is to compensate for cable loss as opposed to boosting the signal for range. Therefore, when installing an amplifier, install it as close to the antenna as possible. Because the antenna cable adds loss to the signal, the shorter antenna cable will produce less loss and allow more signal to the antenna.

Additionally, it is important to note that an amplifier increases noise as well as signal strength. It is not uncommon for an amplifier to raise the noise floor by 10 dB or more.

Amplifiers must be certified with the system in use according to regulatory bodies such as the FCC. If an amplifier is added to a wireless network and it has not been certified, then it is illegal. It is far better to further engineer the system than to use an amplifier.

Attenuators

In some situations, it may be necessary to decrease the amount of signal that is radiating from the antenna. In some instances, even the lowest power setting of the transceiver may generate more signal than you want. In this situation, you can add a fixed-loss or a variable-loss *attenuator*. Attenuators are typically small devices about the size of a C-cell battery, with cable connectors on both sides. Attenuators absorb energy, decreasing the signal as it travels through. Fixed-loss attenuators provide a set amount of dB loss. A variable-loss attenuator has a dial or switch configuration on it that enables you to adjust the amount of energy that is absorbed.

Variable-loss attenuators are often used during outdoor site surveys to simulate loss caused by various grades of cabling and different cable lengths. Another interesting use of a variable attenuator is to test the actual fade margin on a point-to-point link. By gradually increasing the attenuation until there is no more link, you can use that number to determine the actual fade margin of the link.

Lightning Arrestors

The purpose of a *lightning arrestor* is to redirect (shunt) transient currents caused by nearby lightning strikes or ambient static away from your electronic equipment and into the ground. Lightning arrestors are used to protect electronic equipment from the sudden surge of power that a nearby lightning strike or static buildup can cause. You may have noticed the use of the phrase *nearby lightning strike*. This wording is used because lightning arrestors are not capable of protecting against a direct lightning strike. Lightning arrestors can typically protect against surges of up to 5,000 amperes at up to 50 volts. The IEEE specifies that lightning arrestors should be capable of redirecting the transient current in less than 8 microseconds. Most lightning arrestors are capable of doing it in less than 2 microseconds.

The lightning arrestor is installed between the transceiver and the antenna. Any devices that are installed between the lightning arrestor and the antenna will not be protected by the lightning arrestor. Therefore, the lightning arrestor is typically placed closer to the antenna, with all other communications devices (amplifiers, attenuators, etc.) installed between the lightning arrestor and the transceiver. Figure 4.22 shows a properly grounded radio, cabling, and antenna. After a lightning arrestor has performed its job by protecting the equipment from an electrical surge, it will have to be replaced, or it may have a replaceable gas discharge tube (like a fuse). Most installations place the lightning arrestor at the egress to the building. Cable grounding kits can be installed near the antenna and at every 100 feet.

FIGURE 4.22   Installation of lightning protection equipment

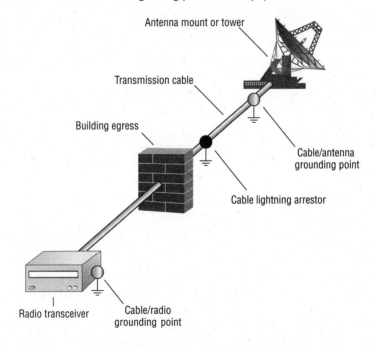

Fiber-optic cable can also be used to provide additional lightning protection. A short piece of fiber-optic cable can be inserted into the Ethernet cable that connects the wireless bridge to the rest of the network. Ethernet-to-fiber adapters, known as transceivers, convert the electrical Ethernet signal to a light-based fiber signal and then back to Ethernet. Because fiber-optic cable is constructed of glass and it uses light and not electricity to transmit data, it does not conduct electricity. It is important to make sure that the power supply for the adapters is protected as well.

The fiber-optic cable acts as a kind of safety net should the lightning arrestor fail due to a much higher transient current or even a direct lightning strike. Realize that if there is a direct lightning strike to the antenna, you can plan on replacing all the components from the fiber-optic cable to the antenna. Furthermore, a direct lightning strike may also arc over the fiber link and still cause damage to equipment on the opposite side of the fiber link. Grounding the RF cables as well can help prevent this from happening.

 Real World Scenario

Not Only Is Lightning Unpredictable, the Results Are Too!

A business in a five-story, 200-year-old brick brownstone in the North End neighborhood of Boston had a lightning strike or a nearby lightning strike. This building was not even one of the tallest buildings in the area, and it was at the bottom of a small hill and surrounded by other similar buildings. An electrical current traveled down the water vent pipe, past a bundle of Ethernet cables. A transient current on the Ethernet cables damaged the transceiver circuits on the Ethernet cards in the PCs and on the individual ports on the Ethernet hub. About half of the Ethernet devices in the company failed, and about half of the ports on the hub were no longer functioning. Yet all of the software recognized the cards, and all of the power and port lights worked flawlessly. The problem appeared to be cabling related.

You often will not know that the problem is lightning related, and the symptoms may be misleading. Testing the lightning arrestors can help with your diagnosis.

Grounding Rods and Wires

When lightning strikes an object, it is looking for the path of least resistance, or more specifically, the path of least impedance. This is where lightning protection and grounding equipment come into play. A grounding system, which is made up of a grounding rod and wires, provides a low-impedance path to the ground. This low-impedance path is installed to encourage the lightning to travel through it instead of through your expensive electronic equipment.

Grounding rods and wires are also used to create what is referred to as a *common ground*. One way of creating a common ground is to drive a copper rod into the ground and connect your electrical and electronic equipment to this rod by using wires or straps (grounding wires). The grounding rod should be at least 6 feet long and should be fully driven into the ground, leaving enough of the rod accessible to attach the ground wires to it. By creating a common ground, you have created a path of least impedance for all of your equipment should lightning cause an electrical surge.

On tower structures, a grounding rod should be placed off of each leg with a No. 2 tinned copper wire. These connections should be exothermically welded to the tower legs. A No. 2 tinned copper wire should also form a ring around the grounding rods, as illustrated in Figure 4.23. The dashed lines are No. 2 tinned copper wire and the circles are grounding rods. Ice bridges and building grounds should also be bonded to this ring to provide equal grounding potentials.

FIGURE 4.23   Grounding ring

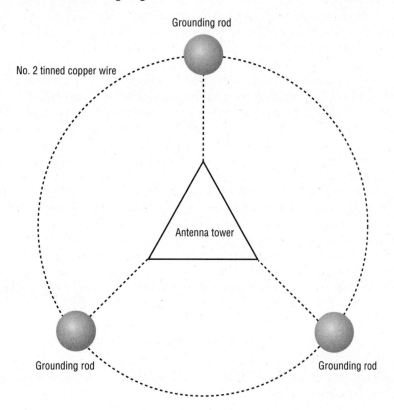

Grounding rod

No. 2 tinned copper wire

Antenna tower

Grounding rod

Grounding rod

Section 12.2 of the EIA/TIA 222F standard states that "a minimum ground shall consist of two 5/8" diameter galvanized steel rods driven not less than 8 feet into the ground.... The ground rods shall be bonded with a lead of not smaller than No. 6 tinned bare copper to the nearest leg or to the metal base of the structure." Current standards dictate a No. 2 solid wire from bus bars and other items to the ground ring. The ground ring is often 2/0 stranded bare wire.

Regulatory Compliance

In Chapter 3, you learned about the RF components along with the concepts of intentional radiator (IR) and equivalent isotropically radiated power (EIRP). In this chapter you learned about antennas and the many aspects of antenna operations and installation. Although there are many antenna, cabling, and component options when you are configuring a wireless network, the reality of it is that you are typically limited as to your antenna choices because of regulatory compliance. Although each regulatory body operates independently, there are similarities between how these organizations operate and certify equipment. This section will briefly explain the process in the United States, as regulated by the FCC.

In order for an access point manufacturer to sell its product within a country or region, it must prove that its product operates within the rules of the relevant regulatory domain, such as the FCC. The FCC creates documents that specify the rules that must be followed by the manufacturer, also referred to as the *responsible party* or the *grant holder.* The manufacturer will send its equipment to be tested by the regulatory body or an authorized testing organization, who will perform the compliance testing on the equipment. If the equipment passes the testing, the device will ultimately be issued an ID number and a *Grant of Certification.*

Most people are not familiar with this process and do not realize that when the company sends its product to be tested, what is submitted is the complete system that the manufacturer will market and sell as the product, which includes the intentional radiator (AP), any cabling and connectors, and the antenna or antennas that it wants to be able to use with the AP. Most companies will have their AP certified with a grouping of antennas that provide different gain and beamwidth characteristics.

An intentional radiator can be operated only with an antenna with which it is authorized. The FCC does allow an antenna to be substituted with a different one, providing two key conditions are met:

- The gain of the new antenna must be the same or lower than the antenna that the system was certified with.

- The new antenna must be of the same type, which means that the antenna must have the same in-band and out-of-band characteristics.

The gain of an antenna is easily identified and provided with most antennas, so the first criteria is relatively simple to meet. However, meeting the second criteria—for example, determining if one antenna is of the same type as another—requires verifying both the in-band and out-of-band characteristics of the antenna. How a new antenna will perform as part of a combined system for out-of-band requirements is very difficult to predict from datasheet information alone. The out-of-band requirements typically include spurious emissions limits over a very wide frequency range (9 KHz to 300 GHz), band edge emissions (a mask-type requirement), limits on harmonics generated, and very low limits on noise in specific restricted bands. Verifying a new antenna against all of these "out-of-band" requirements could require testing as extensive as the original certification testing itself.

Therefore, if you wanted to replace your antenna with an antenna from a third-party manufacturer and wished to claim compliance of the resulting system, you could be asked to provide evidence that the combined system still passes all of these conditions with the new antenna. It is the manufacturer, or grant holder, who is responsible for adhering to the rules of the regulatory domain. Violation of regulatory domain rules could result in a manufacturer being fined or even denied the right to sell its product within the country or region where the violation occurred. Therefore, most manufacturers will not sell or support an antenna that is not on their list of approved antennas.

Summary

This chapter focused on RF signal and antenna concepts. The antenna is a key component of successful RF communications. Four types of antennas are used with 802.11 networks:

- Omnidirectional (dipole, collinear)
- Semidirectional (patch, panel, Yagi)
- Highly directional (parabolic dish, grid)
- Sector

The antenna types produce different signal patterns, which can be viewed on azimuth and elevation charts.

This chapter also reviewed some of the key concerns when installing point-to-point communications:

- Visual LOS
- RF LOS
- Fresnel zone
- Earth bulge
- Antenna polarization

The final section of this chapter covered VSWR and antenna mounting issues, along with antenna accessories and their roles.

Exam Essentials

Know the different categories and types of antennas, how they radiate signals, and what type of environment they are used in.   Make sure you know the three main categories of antennas and the different types of antennas. Know the similarities and differences between them, and understand when and why you would use one antenna over another.

Make sure that you understand azimuth and elevation charts, beamwidth, antenna polarization, and antenna diversity.

Fully understand the Fresnel zone. Make sure you understand all the issues and variables involved with installing point-to-point communications. You are not required to memorize the Fresnel zone or earth bulge formulas; however, you will need to know the principles regarding these topics and when and why you would use the formulas.

Understand the concerns associated with connecting and installing antennas and the antenna accessories. Every cable, connector, and device between the transceiver and the antenna affects the signal that gets radiated from the antenna. Understand which devices provide gain and which provide loss. Understand what VSWR is and what values are good or bad. Know the different antenna accessories, what they do, and why and when you would use them.

Review Questions

1. Which of the following refers to the polar chart of an antenna as viewed from above the antenna? (Choose all that apply)

    A. Horizontal view

    B. Vertical view

    C. H-plane

    D. E-plane

    E. Elevation chart

    F. Azimuth chart

2. The azimuth chart represents a view of an antenna's radiation pattern from which direction?

    A. Top

    B. Side

    C. Front

    D. Both top and side

3. What is the definition of the horizontal beamwidth of an antenna?

    A. The measurement of the angle of the main lobe as represented on the azimuth chart.

    B. The distance between the two points on the horizontal axis where the signal decreases by a third. This distance is measured in degrees.

    C. The distance between the two −3 dB power points on the horizontal axis, measured in degrees.

    D. The distance between the peak power and the point where the signal decreases by half. This distance is measured in degrees.

4. Which antennas are highly directional? (Choose all that apply.)

    A. Omni

    B. Patch

    C. Panel

    D. Parabolic dish

    E. Grid

    F. Sector

5. Semidirectional antennas are often used for which of the following purposes? (Choose all that apply.)

    A. Providing short-distance point-to-point communications

    B. Providing long-distance point-to-point communications

    C. Providing unidirectional coverage from an access point to clients in an indoor environment

    D. Reducing reflections and the negative effects of multipath

6. The Fresnel zone should not be blocked by more than what percentage to maintain a reliable communications link?

    A. 20 percent

    B. 40 percent

    C. 50 percent

    D. 60 percent

7. The size of the Fresnel zone is controlled by what factors? (Choose all that apply.)

    A. Antenna beamwidth

    B. RF line of sight

    C. Distance

    D. Frequency

8. When a long-distance point-to-point link is installed, earth bulge should be considered beyond what distance?

    A. 5 miles

    B. 7 miles

    C. 10 miles

    D. 30 miles

9. A network administrator replaced some coaxial cabling used in an outdoor bridge deployment after water damaged the cabling. After replacing the cabling, the network administrator noticed that the EIRP increased drastically and is possibly violating the maximum EIRP power regulation mandate. What are the possible causes of the increased amplitude? (Choose all that apply.)

    A. The administrator installed a shorter cable.

    B. The administrator installed a lower-grade cable.

    C. The administrator installed a higher-grade cable.

    D. The administrator installed a longer cable.

    E. The administrator used a different-color cable.

10. Which of the following are true for antenna diversity used by 802.11a/b/g access points? (Choose all that apply.)

    A. The transceiver combines the signal from both antennas to provide better coverage.

    B. Transceivers can transmit from both antennas at the same time.

    C. The transceiver samples both antennas and chooses the best received signal from one antenna.

    D. Transceivers can transmit from only one of the antennas at a time.

11. To establish a 4-mile point-to-point bridge link in the 2.4 GHz ISM band, what factors should be taken under consideration? (Choose all that apply.)

    A. Fresnel zone with 40 percent or less blockage

    B. Earth bulge calculations

    C. Minimum of 16 dBi of passive gain

    D. Proper choice of semidirectional antennas

    E. Proper choice of highly directional antennas

12. The ratio between the maximum peak voltage and minimum voltage on a line is known as what?

    A. Signal flux

    B. Return loss

    C. VSWR

    D. Signal incidents

13. What are some of the possible negative effects of an impendence mismatch? (Choose all that apply.)

    A. Voltage reflection

    B. Blockage of the Fresnel zone

    C. Erratic signal strength

    D. Decreased signal amplitude

    E. Amplifier/transmitter failure

14. When determining the mounting height of a long-distance point-to-point antenna, which of the following needs to be considered? (Choose all that apply.)

    A. Frequency

    B. Distance

    C. Visual line of sight

    D. Earth bulge

    E. Antenna beamwidth

    F. RF line of sight

15. Which of the following are true about cables? (Choose all that apply.)

    A. They cause impedance on the signal.

    B. They work regardless of the frequency.

    C. Attenuation decreases as frequency increases.

    D. They add loss to the signal.

16. Amplifiers can be purchased with which of the following features? (Choose all that apply.)

    A. Bidirectional amplification

    B. Unidirectional amplification

    C. Fixed gain

    D. Fixed output

17. The signal between the transceiver and the antenna will be reduced by which of the following methods? (Choose all that apply.)

    A. Adding an attenuator

    B. Increasing the length of the cable

    C. Shortening the length of the cable

    D. Using cheaper-quality cable

18. Lightning arrestors will defend against which of the following?

    A. Direct lightning strikes

    B. Power surges

    C. Transient currents

    D. Improper common grounding

19. The radius of the second Fresnel zone is _____ . (Choose all that apply.)

    A. The area where the signal is out of phase with the point source

    B. The area where the signal is in phase with the point source

    C. Smaller than the first Fresnel zone

    D. Larger than the first Fresnel zone

20. While aligning a directional antenna, you notice that the signal drops as you turn the antenna away from the other antenna, but then it increases a little. This increase in signal is cause by what?

    A. Signal reflection

    B. Frequency harmonic

    C. Side band

    D. Side lobe

IEEE 802.11 Standards

IN THIS CHAPTER, YOU WILL LEARN ABOUT THE FOLLOWING:

✓ **Original IEEE 802.11 standard**

✓ **IEEE 802.11-2007 ratified amendments**

  - 802.11b-1999

  - 802.11a-1999

  - 802.11g-2003

  - 802.11d-2001

  - 802.11h-2003

  - 802.11i-2004

  - 802.11j-2004

  - 802.11e-2005

✓ **IEEE 802.11-2012 ratified amendments**

  - 802.11r-2008

  - 802.11k-2008

  - 802.11y-2008

  - 802.11w-2009

  - 802.11n-2009

  - 802.11p-2010

  - 802.11z-2010

  - 802.11u-2011

  - 802.11v-2011

  - 802.11s-2011

✓ **Post-2012 ratified amendments**

- 802.11ae-2012
- 802.11aa-2012
- 802.11ad-2012
- 802.11ac-2013
- 802.11af-2014

✓ **IEEE 802.11 draft amendments**

- 802.11ah
- 802.11ai
- 802.11aj
- 802.11ak
- 802.11aq

✓ **Defunct amendments**

- 802.11F
- 802.11T

✓ **802.11m Task group**

As discussed in Chapter 1, "Overview of Wireless Standards, Organizations, and Fundamentals," the Institute of Electrical and Electronics Engineers (IEEE) is the professional society that creates and maintains standards that we use for communications, such as the 802.3 Ethernet standard for wired networking. The IEEE has assigned working groups for several wireless communication standards. For example, the 802.15 working group is responsible for personal area network (PAN) communications using radio frequencies. Some of the technologies defined within the 802.15 standard include Bluetooth and ZigBee. Another example is the 802.16 standard, which is overseen by the Broadband Wireless Access Standards working group; this technology is often referred to as WiMAX. The focus of this book is the technology as defined by the IEEE 802.11 standard, which provides for local area network (LAN) communications using radio frequencies (RF).

The 802.11 working group has about 400 active members from more than 200 wireless companies. It consists of standing committees, study groups, and numerous *task groups*. For example, the Standing Committee—Publicity (PSC) is in charge of finding means to better publicize the 802.11 standard. The 802.11 Study Group (SG) is in charge of investigating the possibility of putting new features and capabilities into the 802.11 standard.

IEEE 802.11: More about the Working Group and 2012 Standard

You can find a quick guide to the IEEE 802.11 working group at

```
http://grouper.ieee.org/groups/802/11/QuickGuide_IEEE_802_WG_and_
Activities.htm
```

The 802.11-2012 standard and ratified amendments can be downloaded from

```
http://standards.ieee.org/getieee802/802.11.html
```

Some of the standards and ratified amendment documents are free, and others (particularly recently ratified documents) are available for a fee.

Various 802.11 task groups are in charge of revising and amending the original standard that was developed by the MAC task group (MAC) and the PHY task group (PHY). Each group is assigned a letter from the alphabet, and it is common to hear the term *802.11 alphabet soup* when referring to all the amendments created by the multiple 802.11 task groups. When task groups are formed, they are assigned the next highest available letter in the alphabet, although the amendments may not necessarily be ratified in the same order. Quite a few of the 802.11 task group projects have been completed, and amendments to the original standard have been ratified. Other 802.11 task group projects still remain active and exist as draft amendments.

In this chapter, we discuss the original 802.11 standard, the ratified amendments (many of which are incorporated into the 802.11-2007 standard and the current 802.11-2012 standard), and the draft amendments of various 802.11 task groups.

Original IEEE 802.11 Standard

The original 802.11 standard was published in June 1997 as IEEE Std 802.11-1997, and it is often referred to as 802.11 Prime because it was the first WLAN standard. The standard was revised in 1999, reaffirmed in 2003, and published as IEEE Std 802.11-1999 (R2003). On March 8, 2007, another iteration of the standard was approved, IEEE Std 802.11-2007, and on March 29, 2012, the most recent iteration of the standard was approved, IEEE Std 802.11-2012.

The IEEE specifically defines 802.11 technologies at the Physical layer and the MAC sublayer of the Data-Link layer. By design, the 802.11 standard does not address the upper layers of the OSI model, although there are interactions between the 802.11 MAC layer and the upper layers for parameters such as quality of service (QoS). The PHY task group worked in conjunction with the MAC task group to define the original 802.11 standard. The PHY task group defined three original Physical layer specifications:

Infrared (IR)   *Infrared (IR)* technology uses a light-based medium. Although an infrared medium was indeed defined in the original 802.11 standard, the implementation is obsolete. More information about modern implementations of infrared technology can be found at the Infrared Data Association's website, at www.irda.org. The scope of this book focuses on the 802.11 RF mediums. Infrared devices are known as *Clause 15 devices.*

Frequency Hopping Spread Spectrum (FHSS)   Radio frequency signals can be defined as narrowband signals or as spread spectrum signals. An RF signal is considered *spread spectrum* when the bandwidth is wider than what is required to carry the data. *Frequency hopping spread spectrum (FHSS)* is a spread spectrum technology that was first patented during World War II. Frequency hopping 802.11 radios are also called *Clause 14 devices* because of the clause that references them.

Direct Sequence Spread Spectrum (DSSS)   *Direct sequence spread spectrum (DSSS)* is another spread spectrum technology that uses fixed channels. DSSS 802.11 radios are known as *Clause 16 devices.*

What Is an IEEE Clause?

The IEEE standards are very organized, structured documents. A standards document is hierarchically structured, with each section numbered. The highest level (such as 7) is referred to as a *clause,* with the lower-level sections such as 7.3.2.4 referred to as *subclauses.* As an amendment is created, the sections in the amendment are numbered relative to the latest version of the standard, even though the amendment is a separate document. When a standard and its amendments are rolled into a new version of the standard, as was done with IEEE Std 802.11-2007, the clauses and subclauses of all the individual documents are unique, enabling the documents to be combined without having to change any of the section (clause/subclause) numbers. In 2012, the IEEE revised the standard again and rolled into it a group of 10 amendments. Over the years, as new amendments were ratified, some amendments took longer or shorter times to ratify than other amendments. Therefore, the order of some of the clauses was not chronological. Although this is not a requirement, some of the clauses were reordered and renumbered in the IEEE Std 802.11-2012 so that clauses are listed chronologically. Whenever any clauses are referenced in this book, we will use the new number scheme. Although this book often references clauses in the IEEE 802.11 standard, *you will not be tested on clause numbers* in the CWNA exam (CWNA-106).

As defined by 802.11 Prime, the frequency space in which either FHSS or DSSS radios can transmit is the license-free 2.4 GHz *industrial, scientific, and medical (ISM) band.* DSSS 802.11 radios can transmit in channels subdivided from the entire 2.4 GHz to 2.4835 GHz ISM band. The IEEE is more restrictive for FHSS radios, which are permitted to transmit on 1 MHz subcarriers in the 2.402 GHz to 2.480 GHz range of the 2.4 GHz ISM band.

Chances are that you will not be working with older legacy 802.11 equipment because most WLAN deployments use technologies as defined by newer 802.11 amendments. WLAN vendors had the choice of manufacturing either Clause 14 FHSS radios or Clause 16 DSSS radios. Because these spread spectrum technologies differ, they cannot communicate with each other and often have a hard time coexisting. These spread spectrum signals are analogous to oil and water in that they do not mix well. Therefore, it is important to understand that an 802.11 DSSS (Clause 16) radio cannot communicate with an 802.11 FHSS (Clause 14) radio. The majority of legacy WLAN deployments used frequency hopping, but some DSSS solutions were available as well.

What about the speeds? Data rates defined by the original 802.11 standard were 1 Mbps and 2 Mbps regardless of which spread spectrum technology was used. A *data rate* is the number of bits per second the Physical layer carries during a single-frame transmission, normally stated as a number of millions of bits per second (Mbps). Keep in mind that a data rate is the *speed* and not actual *throughput.* Because of medium access methods and communications overhead, aggregate throughput is typically one-half or less of the available data rate speed when using 802.11a/b/g technology. The medium access methods are more efficient with 802.11n and 802.11ac but there still is 30 percent to 40 percent overhead due to medium contention overhead.

 FHSS and DSSS are discussed in more detail in Chapter 6, "Wireless Networks and Spread Spectrum Technologies."

IEEE 802.11-2007 Ratified Amendments

In the years that followed the publishing of the original 802.11 standard, new task groups were assembled to address potential enhancements to the standard. As of this writing, 22 amendments to the standard have been ratified and published by the distinctive task groups. In 2007, the IEEE consolidated 8 ratified amendments along with the original standard, creating a single document that was published as the *IEEE Std 802.11-2007*.

The following documents were rolled into this revision and provided users with a single document containing all the amendments that had been published at that time. The IEEE Std 802.11-2007 document included the following:

- IEEE Std 802.11-1999 (R2003)
- IEEE Std 802.11a-1999
- IEEE Std 802.11b-1999
- IEEE Std 802.11d-2001
- IEEE Std 802.11g-2003
- IEEE Std 802.11h-2003
- IEEE Std 802.11i-2004
- IEEE Std 802.11j-2004
- IEEE Std 802.11e-2005

This revision also included corrections, clarifications, and enhancements. The 802.11-2007 ratified amendments will now be discussed in a somewhat chronological order.

802.11b-1999

Although the Wi-Fi consumer market continues to grow at a tremendous rate, 802.11b-compatible WLAN equipment gave the industry the first needed huge shot in the arm. In 1999, the IEEE Task Group b (TGb) published the IEEE Std 802.11b-1999, which was later amended and corrected as IEEE Std 802.11b-1999/Cor1-2001. All aspects of the 802.11b ratified amendment can now be found in Clause 17 of the 802.11-2012 standard.

The Physical layer medium that was defined by 802.11b is *High-Rate DSSS (HR-DSSS)*. The frequency space in which 802.11b radio cards can operate is the unlicensed 2.4 GHz to 2.4835 GHz ISM band.

 Real World Scenario

Will 802.11b Devices Work with Legacy 802.11 Devices?

The 802.11b amendment specified the use of only a DSSS-type physical medium and did not specify FHSS. Because a good portion of the legacy 802.11 deployments used FHSS, 802.11b radios are not backward compatible with those systems and cannot be used. However, 802.11b Clause 17 radios are backward compatible with legacy 802.11 DSSS Clause 16 devices. 802.11b HR-DSSS WLAN equipment should be able to communicate with legacy 802.11 DSSS WLAN equipment. The caveat to this is that, depending on the manufacturer, the devices might not use the same interpretation of the IEEE standards. Many of the legacy devices did not undergo any compatibility testing, such as that provided by the Wi-Fi Alliance.

The TGb's main goal was to achieve higher data rates within the 2.4 GHz ISM band. 802.11b radio devices accomplish this feat by using a different spreading/coding technique called *Complementary Code Keying (CCK)* and modulation methods using the phase properties of the RF signal. 802.11 devices used a spreading technique called the *Barker code*. The end result is that 802.11b radio devices support data rates of 1, 2, 5.5, and 11 Mbps. 802.11b systems are backward compatible with the 802.11 DSSS data rates of 1 Mbps and 2 Mbps. The transmission data rates of 5.5 Mbps and 11 Mbps are known as HR-DSSS. Once again, understand that the supported data rates refer to available bandwidth and not aggregate throughput. An optional technology called *Packet Binary Convolutional Code (PBCC)* is also defined under Clause 17.

 The Barker code and CCK spreading techniques, as well as applicable modulation methods, are discussed further in Chapter 6, "Wireless Networks and Spread Spectrum Technologies." A brief examination of PBCC can also be found in Chapter 6.

802.11a-1999

During the same year that the 802.11b amendment was approved, another important amendment was also ratified and published as IEEE Std 802.11a-1999. The engineers in the Task Group a (TGa) set out to define how 802.11 technologies would operate in the 5 GHz frequency space using an RF technology called *Orthogonal Frequency Division*

Multiplexing (OFDM). 802.11a radios initially were meant to transmit in three different 100 MHz unlicensed frequency bands in the 5 GHz range. These three bands are called the *Unlicensed National Information Infrastructure (U-NII)* frequency bands. A total of 12 channels are available in the original three U-NII bands. All aspects of the 802.11a ratified amendment can now be found in Clause 18 of the 802.11-2012 standard.

The 2.4 GHz ISM band is a much more crowded frequency space than the 5 GHz U-NII bands. Bluetooth devices, microwave ovens, cordless phones, and numerous other devices all operate in the 2.4 GHz ISM band and are potential sources of interference. In addition, the sheer number of 2.4 GHz WLAN deployments has often been a problem in environments such as multitenant office buildings.

One big advantage of using 802.11a WLAN equipment is that it operates in the less-crowded 5 GHz U-NII bands. As time passed, the three original U-NII bands also started to become crowded. Regulatory bodies such as the FCC opened up more frequency space in the 5 GHz range, and the IEEE addressed this in the 802.11h amendment. The FCC has also proposed even more 5 GHz spectrum be made available in the near future. Greater detail about all of the 5 GHz U-NII bands can be found in Chapter 6.

Legacy 802.11a radios initially could transmit in the 12 channels of the U-NII-1, U-NII-2, and U-NII-3 bands; however, the 5 GHz frequency range and channels used by 802.11a radios are dependent on the RF regulatory body of individual countries. The amendment was mostly about the introduction of OFDM technology that provided better higher rates.

You'll find further discussion about both the ISM and U-NII bands in Chapter 6.

802.11a radios operating in the 5 GHz U-NII bands are classified as Clause 18 devices. As defined by the 802.11a amendment, these devices are required to support data rates of 6, 12, and 24 Mbps with a maximum of 54 Mbps. With the use of a technology called Orthogonal Frequency Division Multiplexing (OFDM), data rates of 6, 9, 12, 18, 24, 36, 48, and 54 Mbps are supported in most manufacturers' radios.

OFDM is discussed further in Chapter 6.

It should be noted that 802.11a radios cannot communicate with 802.11 legacy, 802.11b, or 802.11g radios for two reasons. First, 802.11a radios use a different RF technology than 802.11 legacy or 802.11b devices. Second, 802.11a devices transmit in the 5 GHz U-NII bands, whereas the 802.11/802.11b/802.11g devices operate in the 2.4 GHz ISM band. The good news is that 802.11a can coexist in the same physical space with 802.11, 802.11b, or 802.11g devices because these devices transmit in separate frequency ranges.

When 802.11a was first ratified, it took almost two years before 802.11a devices were readily available. When 802.11a devices did become available, the radio chipsets using OFDM were quite expensive. Because of these two factors, widespread deployment of 5 GHz WLANs in the enterprise was rare. Eventually the chipsets become affordable and the use of 5 GHz frequency bands has grown considerably over the years. WLAN vendors now manufacture dual-frequency access points (APs) with both 2.4 and 5 GHz radios. Most laptops manufactured since 2007 use 802.11a/b/g or 802.11a/b/g/n radios, meaning they are also dual-frequency capable. The majority of enterprise wireless deployments run both 2.4 GHz and 5 GHz 802.11 wireless networks simultaneously.

802.11g-2003

Another amendment that generated a lot of excitement in the Wi-Fi marketplace was published as IEEE Std 802.11g-2003. 802.11g radios used a new technology called *Extended Rate Physical (ERP)* but were still meant to transmit in the 2.4 GHz to 2.4835 GHz ISM frequency band. All aspects of the 802.11g ratified amendment can now be found in Clause 19 of the 802.11-2012 standard.

The main goal of the Task Group g (TGg) was to enhance the 802.11b Physical layer to achieve greater bandwidth yet remain compatible with the 802.11 MAC. Two mandatory and two optional ERP physical layers (PHYs) were defined by the 802.11g amendment.

The mandatory PHYs are ERP-OFDM and ERP-DSSS/CCK. To achieve the higher data rates, a PHY technology called *Extended Rate Physical OFDM (ERP-OFDM)* was mandated. Data rates of 6, 9, 12, 18, 24, 36, 48, and 54 Mbps are possible using this technology, although once again the IEEE requires only the data rates of 6, 12, and 24 Mbps. To maintain backward compatibility with 802.11 (DSSS only) and 802.11b networks, a PHY technology called *Extended Rate Physical DSSS (ERP-DSSS/CCK)* is used with support for the data rates of 1, 2, 5.5, and 11 Mbps.

What Is the Difference between ERP-DSSS/CCK, DSSS, and HR-DSSS?

From a technical viewpoint, there is no difference between ERP-DSSS/CCK and DSSS and HR-DSSS. A key point of the 802.11g amendment was to maintain backward compatibility with older 802.11 (DSSS only) and 802.11b radios while at the same time achieving higher data rates. 802.11g devices (Clause 19 radios) use ERP-OFDM for the higher data rates. ERP-DSSS/CCK is effectively the same technology as DSSS that is used by legacy 802.11 devices (Clause 16 radios) and HR-DSSS that is used by 802.11b devices (Clause 17 radios). Mandated support for ERP-DSSS/CCK allows for backward compatibility with older 802.11 (DSSS only) and 802.11b (HR-DSSS) radios. The technology is explained further in Chapter 6.

The 802.11g ratified amendment also defined two optional PHYs called *ERP-PBCC* and *DSSS-OFDM*. These optional technologies are beyond the scope of this book and rarely used by WLAN vendors.

What Is the Difference between OFDM and ERP-OFDM?

From a technical viewpoint, there is no difference between OFDM and ERP-OFDM. The only difference is the transmit frequency. OFDM refers to 802.11a devices (Clause 18 radios) that transmit in the 5 GHz U-NII-1, U-NII-2, and U-NII-3 frequency bands. ERP-OFDM refers to 802.11g devices (Clause 19 radios) that transmit in the 2.4 GHz ISM frequency band. The technology is explained further in Chapter 6.

 Real World Scenario

What Are the Vendor Operational Modes of an 802.11g Access Point and What Is the Effective Throughput?

While the 802.11g amendment mandated support for both ERP-DSSS/CCK and ERP-OFDM, Wi-Fi vendors typically allow an 802.11g access point to be configured in three very distinct modes:

B-Only Mode   When an 802.11g AP is running in this operational mode, support for DSSS, HR-DSSS, and ERP-DSSS/CCK technology is solely enabled. Effectively, the access point has been configured to be an 802.11b access point, and clients will only be able to communicate with the AP using data rates of 11, 5.5, 2, and 1 Mbps. Aggregate through-put will be the same as that achieved in an 802.11b network.

G-Only Mode   APs configured as G-Only will communicate with 802.11g client stations using only ERP-OFDM technology. Support for ERP-DSSS/CCK, HR-DSSS, and DSSS is disabled, and therefore 802.11b clients will not be able to associate with the access point. Only ERP capable (802.11g) radios will be able to communicate with the access point using data rates of 6–54 Mbps. The aggregate throughput of an AP with a data rate of 54 Mbps might be about 19 Mbps to 20 Mbps. A *G-Only* WLAN is sometimes referred to as a *Pure G* network.

B/G Mode   This is the default operational mode of most 802.11g access points and is often called *mixed mode*. Support for both ERP-DSSS/CCK and ERP-OFDM is enabled. Therefore, 802.11 DSSS, 802.11b, and 802.11g clients can communicate with the access point. However, a price must be paid for the coexistence of these two very different technologies. As soon as the first 802.11 DSSS or 802.11b HR-DSSS station attempts to associate, the access point signals to all the 802.11g stations to enable "protection." Although the protection mechanism does allow for 802.11 (DSSS only), 802.11b, and 802.11g clients to coexist and transmit data at their native data rates, the cumulative result is an immediate and significant degradation in throughput. An 802.11b/g access point with a data rate of 54 Mbps might see a decrease in aggregate throughput from 20 Mbps down to as little as 8 Mbps the instant the protection mechanism is enabled. A thorough discussion of the protection mechanism can be found in Chapter 9, "802.11 MAC Architecture." It should also be noted that these three 802.11g modes of operation are becoming a non-issue as WLAN customers upgrade to higher-speed 802.11n and 802.11ac technology and legacy devices are replaced.

As you have learned, the 802.11g amendment requires support for both ERP-DSSS/CCK and ERP-OFDM. The good news is that an 802.11g AP can communicate with 802.11g client stations as well as 802.11 (DSSS only) or 802.11b client stations. The ratification of the 802.11g amendment triggered monumental sales of Wi-Fi gear in the small office, home office (SOHO) and enterprise markets because of both the higher data rates and the backward compatibility with older equipment.

As mentioned earlier in this chapter, different spread spectrum technologies cannot communicate with each other, yet the 802.11g amendment mandates support for both ERP-DSSS/CCK and ERP-OFDM. In other words, ERP-OFDM and ERP-DSSS/CCK technologies can coexist, yet they cannot speak to each other. Therefore, the 802.11g amendment calls for a *protection mechanism* that allows the two technologies to coexist. The goal of the protection mechanism is to prevent older 802.11b HR-DSSS or 802.11 DSSS radio cards from transmitting at the same time as 802.11g (ERP) radios. Table 5.1 shows a brief overview and comparison of 802.11, 802.11b, 802.11g, and 802.11a.

TABLE 5.1   Original 802.11 amendments comparison

	802.11 legacy	802.11b	802.11g	802.11a
Frequency	2.4 GHz ISM band	2.4 GHz ISM band	2.4 GHz ISM band	5 GHz U-NII-1, U-NII-2, and U-NII-3 bands
Spread spectrum technology	FHSS or DSSS	HR-DSSS	ERP: ERP-OFDM and ERP-DSSS/CCK are mandatory.	OFDM
		PBCC is optional.	ERP-PBCC and DSSS-OFDM are optional.	
Data rates	1, 2 Mbps	DSSS: 1, 2 Mbps HR-DSSS: 5.5 and 11 Mbps	ERP-DSSS/CCK: 1, 2, 5.5, and 11 Mbps	6, 12, and 24 Mbps are mandatory.
			ERP-OFDM: 6, 12, and 24 Mbps are mandatory.	Also supported are 9, 18, 36, 48, and 54 Mbps.
			Also supported are 9, 18, 36, 48, and 54 Mbps.	
			ERP-PBCC: 22 and 33 Mbps	
Backward compatibility	N/A	802.11 DSSS only	802.11b HR-DSSS and 802.11 DSSS	None
Ratified	1997	1999	2003	1999

802.11d-2001

The original 802.11 standard was written for compliance with the regulatory domains of the United States, Japan, Canada, and Europe. Regulations in other countries might define different limits on allowed frequencies and transmit power. The 802.11d amendment, which was published as IEEE Std 802.11d-2001, added requirements and definitions necessary to allow 802.11 WLAN equipment to operate in areas not served by the original standard.

Country code information is delivered in fields inside two wireless frames called *beacons* and *probe responses*. This information is then used by 802.11d-compliant devices to ensure that they are abiding by a particular country's frequency and power rules. Figure 5.1 shows an AP configured for use in Mongolia and a capture of a beacon frame containing the country code, frequency, and power information.

FIGURE 5.1   802.11d settings

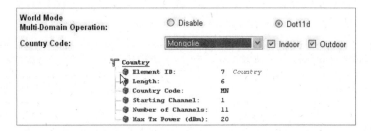

The 802.11d amendment also defines other information specific to configuration parameters of an FHSS access point. FHSS parameters such as hopping patterns might vary from country to country, and the information needs to be once again delivered via the beacon or probe response frames. This information would be useful only in legacy deployments using FHSS technology. All aspects of the 802.11d ratified amendment can now be found in Clause 9.8 of the 802.11-2012 standard.

> A detailed discussion of beacons, probes, and other wireless frames can be found in Chapter 9, "802.11 MAC Architecture."

802.11h-2003

Published as IEEE Std 802.11h-2003, this amendment defines mechanisms for *dynamic frequency selection (DFS)* and *transmit power control (TPC)*. It was originally proposed to satisfy regulatory requirements for operation in the 5 GHz band in Europe and to detect and avoid interference with 5 GHz satellite and radar systems. These same regulatory requirements have also been adopted by the FCC in the United States. The main purpose of DFS and TPC is to provide services where 5 GHz 802.11 radio transmissions will not cause interference with 5 GHz satellite and radar transmissions.

The 802.11h amendment also introduced the capability for 802.11 radios to transmit in a new frequency band called U-NII-2 Extended with 11 more channels, as seen in Table 5.2. The 802.11h amendment effectively is an extension of the 802.11a amendment. OFDM transmission technology is used in all of the U-NII bands. The radar detection and avoidance technologies of DFS and TPC are defined by the IEEE. However, the RF regulatory organizations in each country still define the RF regulations. In the United States and Europe, radar detection and avoidance is required in both the U-NII-2 and U-NII-2 Extended bands.

TABLE 5.2   Unlicensed National Information Infrastructure

Band frequency range	Amendment	Channels
U-NII-1 (lower) 5.150 GHz–5.250 GHz	802.11a	4
U-NII-2 (middle) 5.250 GHz–5.350 GHz	802.11a	4
U-NII-2 Extended 5.47 GHz–5.725 GHz	802.11h	11
U-NII-3 (upper) 5.725 GHz–5.825 GHz	802.11a	4

DFS is used for spectrum management of 5 GHz channels by OFDM radio devices. The European Radiocommunications Committee (ERC) and now the FCC mandate that radio cards operating in the 5 GHz band implement a mechanism to avoid interference with radar systems. DFS is essentially radar-detection and radar-interference avoidance technology. The DFS service is used to meet these regulatory requirements.

The dynamic frequency selection (DFS) service provides for the following:

- An AP will allow client stations to associate based on the supported channel of the access point. The term *associate* means that a station has become a member of the AP's wireless network.

- An AP can quiet a channel to test for the presence of radar.

- An AP may test a channel for the presence of radar before using the channel.

- An AP can detect radar on the current channel and other channels.

- An AP can cease operations after radar detection to avoid interference.

- When interference is detected, the AP may choose a different channel to transmit on and inform all the associated stations.

TPC is used to regulate the power levels used by OFDM radio cards in the 5 GHz frequency bands. The ERC mandates that radio cards operating in the 5 GHz band use TPC to abide by a maximum regulatory transmit power and are able to alleviate transmission power to avoid interference. The TPC service is used to meet the regulatory transmission power requirements.

The transmit power control (TPC) service provides for the following:

- Client stations can associate with an AP based on their transmit power.

- Designation of the maximum transmit power levels permitted on a channel, as permitted by regulations.

- An AP can specify the transmit power of any or all stations that are associated with the AP.

- An AP can change transmission power on stations based on factors of the physical RF environment such as path loss.

The information used by both DFS and TPC is exchanged between client stations and APs inside of management frames. The 802.11h amendment effectively introduced two major enhancements: more frequency space with the introduction of the U-NII-2 Extended band, and radar avoidance and detection technologies. Some aspects of the 802.11h ratified amendment can now be found in Clause 10.8 and Clause 10.9 of the 802.11-2012 standard.

802.11i-2004

From 1997 to 2004, not much was defined in terms of security in the original 802.11 standard. Three key components of any wireless security solution are data privacy (encryption), data integrity (protection from modification) and authentication (identity verification). For seven years, the only defined method of encryption in an 802.11 network was the use of 64-bit static encryption called *Wired Equivalent Privacy (WEP)*.

WEP encryption has long been cracked and is not considered an acceptable means of providing data privacy. The original 802.11 standard defined two methods of authentication. The default method is *Open System authentication*, which effectively allows access to all users regardless of identity. Another defined method is called *Shared Key authentication*, which opens up a whole new can of worms and potential security risks.

The 802.11i amendment, which was ratified and published as IEEE Std 802.11i-2004, defined stronger encryption and better authentication methods. The 802.11i amendment defined a *robust security network (RSN)*. The intended goal of an RSN was to better hide the data flying through the air while at the same time placing a bigger guard at the front door. The 802.11i security amendment is without a doubt one of the most important enhancements to the original 802.11 standard because of the seriousness of properly protecting a wireless network. The major security enhancements addressed in 802.11i are as follows:

Data Privacy   Confidentiality needs have been addressed in 802.11i with the use of a stronger encryption method called *Counter Mode with Cipher Block Chaining Message Authentication Code Protocol (CCMP)*, which uses the *Advanced Encryption Standard (AES)* algorithm. The encryption method is often abbreviated as CCMP/AES, AES CCMP, or often just CCMP. The 802.11i amendment also defines an optional encryption method known as *Temporal Key Integrity Protocol (TKIP)*, which uses the RC-4 stream cipher algorithm and is basically an enhancement of WEP encryption.

Data Integrity   All of the WLAN encryption methods defined by the IEEE employ data integrity mechanisms to ensure that the encrypted data has not been modified. WEP uses a data integrity method called the Initialization Check Value (ICV). TKIIP uses a method known as the Message Integrity Check (MIC). CCMP uses a much stronger MIC as well as other mechanisms for data integrity. Finally, in the trailer of all 802.11 frames is a 32-bit CRC known as the frame check sequence (FCS) which protects the entire body of the 802.11 frame.

Authentication   802.11i defines two methods of authentication using either an *IEEE 802.1X* authorization framework or *preshared keys (PSKs)*. An 802.1X solution requires the use of an *Extensible Authentication Protocol (EAP)*, although the 802.11i amendment does not specify what EAP method to use.

Robust Security Network (RSN)   This defines the entire method of establishing authentication, negotiating security associations, and dynamically generating encryption keys for client stations and access points.

The Wi-Fi Alliance also has a certification known as *Wi-Fi Protected Access 2 (WPA2)*, which is a mirror of the IEEE 802.11i security amendment. WPA version 1 was considered a preview of 802.11i, whereas WPA version 2 is fully compliant with 802.11i. All aspects of the 802.11i ratified security amendment can now be found in Clause 11 of the 802.11-2012 standard.

Wi-Fi security is the top priority when deploying any WLAN, and that is why there is another valued certification called Certified Wireless Security Professional (CWSP). At least 8 percent of the CWNA test will involve questions regarding Wi-Fi security. Therefore, wireless security topics such as 802.1X, EAP, AES CCMP, TKIP, WPA, and others are described in more detail in Chapter 13, "802.11 Network Security Architecture," and Chapter 14, "Wireless Attacks, Intrusion Monitoring, and Policy."

802.11j-2004

The main goal set out by the IEEE Task Group j (TGj) was to obtain Japanese regulatory approval by enhancing the 802.11 MAC and 802.11a PHY to additionally operate in Japanese 4.9 GHz and 5 GHz bands. The 802.11j amendment was approved and published as IEEE Std 802.11j-2004.

In Japan, 802.11a radio cards can transmit in the lower U-NII band at 5.15 GHz to 5.25 GHz as well as a Japanese licensed/unlicensed frequency space of 4.9 GHz to 5.091 GHz.

802.11a radio cards use OFDM technology and are required to support channel spacing of 20 MHz. When 20 MHz channel spacing is used, data rates of 6, 9, 12, 18, 24, 36, 48, and 54 Mbps are possible using OFDM technology. Japan also has the option of using OFDM channel spacing of 10 MHz, which results in available bandwidth data rates of 3, 4.5, 6, 9, 12, 18, 24, and 27 Mbps. The data rates of 3, 6, and 12 Mbps are mandatory when using 10 MHz channel spacing.

802.11e-2005

The original 802.11 standard did not define adequate *quality of service (QoS)* procedures for the use of time-sensitive applications such as *Voice over WiFi*. Voice over WiFi is also known as Voice over Wireless LAN (VoWLAN). The terminology used by most vendors and the CWNP program is Voice over Wi-Fi (VoWiFi). Application traffic such as voice, audio, and video has a lower tolerance for latency and jitter and requires priority before standard application data traffic. The 802.11e amendment defines the layer 2 MAC methods needed to meet the QoS requirements for time-sensitive applications over IEEE 802.11 WLANs.

The original 802.11 standard defined two methods in which an 802.11 radio card may gain control of the half-duplex medium. The default method, *Distributed Coordination Function (DCF)*, is a contention-based method determining who gets to transmit on the wireless medium next. The original standard also defines another medium access control method called *Point Coordination Function (PCF)*, where the access point briefly takes control of the medium and polls the clients. It should be noted that the PCF medium access method was never adopted by WLAN vendors.

Chapter 8, "802.11 Medium Access," describes the DCF and PCF methods of medium access in greater detail.

The 802.11e amendment defines enhanced medium access methods to support QoS requirements. *Hybrid Coordination Function (HCF)* is an additional coordination function that is applied in an 802.11e QoS wireless network. HCF has two access mechanisms to provide QoS. *Enhanced Distributed Channel Access (EDCA)* is an extension to DCF. The EDCA medium access method will provide for the "prioritization of frames" based on upper-layer protocols. Application traffic, such as voice or video, will be transmitted in a timely fashion on the 802.11 wireless medium, meeting the necessary latency requirements.

Hybrid Coordination Function Controlled Channel Access (HCCA) is an extension of PCF. HCCA gives the access point the ability to provide for "prioritization of stations." In other words, certain client stations will be given a chance to transmit before others. Much like PCF, the HCCA medium access method defined by 802.11e has never been adopted by WLAN vendors.

The Wi-Fi Alliance also has a certification known as *Wi-Fi Multimedia (WMM)*. The WMM standard is a "mirror" of 802.11e and defines traffic prioritization in four access categories with varying degrees of importance. Most aspects of the 802.11e ratified QoS amendment can now be found in Clause 9 of the 802.11-2012 standard.

802.11e and WMM are covered in more detail in Chapter 8.

IEEE Std 802.11-2012

In 2012, the IEEE consolidated 10 ratified amendments along with the IEEE Std 802.11-2007 standard, creating a single document that was published as IEEE Std 802.11-2012.

The following documents were rolled into this revision, providing users with a single document containing all the amendments that had been published at that time. The IEEE Std 802.11-2012 document included the following:

▪ IEEE Std 802.11-2007

- IEEE Std 802.11r-2008
- IEEE Std 802.11k-2008
- IEEE Std 802.11y-2008
- IEEE Std 802.11w-2009
- IEEE Std 802.11n-2009
- IEEE Std 802.11p-2010
- IEEE Std 802.11z-2010
- IEEE Std 802.11u-2011
- IEEE Std 802.11v-2011
- IEEE Std 802.11s-2011

In addition to consolidating the ratified amendments and making corrections, clarifications, and enhancements to the document, all of the clauses and annexes were reviewed chronologically. Some of the clauses and annexes were rearranged and renumbered so that they are now listed in the order that they were ratified. All references in this book refer to the clause numbers as published in IEEE Std 802.11-2012. Table 5.3 lists the clause numbers as defined in IEEE Std 802.11-2007 and ratified amendments, along with the clause numbers as currently defined in IEEE Std 802.11-2012. The clauses that are bold did not change. If you want to see the complete renumbering of all clauses and annexes, refer to Figure A on page X of IEEE Std 802.11-2012.

TABLE 5.3   802.11 clause numbers

IEEE Std 802.11-2007	IEEE Std 802.11-2012
Clause 1	**Clause 1**
Clause 2	**Clause 2**
Clause 3	**Clause 3**
Clause 4	Clause 3.3
Clause 5	Clause 4
Clause 6	Clause 5
Clause 10	Clause 6
802.11u: Clause 11B	Clause 6.4
Clause 12	Clause 7
Clause 13	Clause 7.4

TABLE 5.3   802.11 clause numbers *(continued)*

IEEE Std 802.11-2007	IEEE Std 802.11-2012
Clause 7	Clause 8
Clause 9	**Clause 9**
Clause 11	Clause 10
Clause 8	Clause 11
802.11w: Clause 11A	Clause 12
802.11s: Clause 11C	Clause 13
Clause 14	**Clause 14**
Clause 16	Clause 15
Clause 15	Clause 16
Clause 18	Clause 17
Clause 17	Clause 18
Clause 19	**Clause 19**
802.11n: Clause 20	**Clause 20**

The 802.11-2012 ratified amendments will now be discussed in a somewhat chronological order.

CWNA Exam Terminology

In 2012, the IEEE consolidated the 2007 standard along with the ratified amendments into a single document that is now published as the *802.11-2012 standard*. Technically any of the amendments that have been consolidated into the updated standard no longer exist because they have been rolled up into a single document. However, the Wi-Fi Alliance and most WLAN professionals still refer to many of the ratified amendments by name.

Early versions of the CWNA exam did not refer to any of the 802.11 amendments by name and only tested you on the technologies used by each amendment. For example, 802.11b is a ratified amendment that is part of the 802.11-2012 standard. The technology that was originally defined by the 802.11b amendment is called High-Rate DSSS (HR-DSSS). Although the name *802.11b* effectively remains the more commonly used marketing term, older versions of the CWNA exam used only the technical term *HR-DSSS* instead of the more common term *802.11b*. This led to a lot of confusion for many individuals taking the exam because terminology like 802.11a/b/g is widely used by the Wi-Fi Alliance and by the general public. The good news is that the current version of the CWNA exam (CWNA-106) uses the more common 802.11 amendment terminology.

For the CWNA exam (CWNA-106), you should still understand the differences between technologies and how each one works. A good grasp of which technologies are defined by each of the amendments will also be helpful for your career. Remember, the CWNP program maintains an updated current list of the exam terms.

802.11r-2008

The 802.11r-2008 amendment is known as the *fast basic service set transition (FT)* amendment. The technology is more often referred to as *fast secure roaming* because it defines faster handoffs when roaming occurs between cells in a WLAN using the strong security defined by a robust secure network (RSN). Be aware that there are multiple types of fast secure roaming that are implemented by different vendors. These include CCKM, PKC, OKC, and fast session resumption. Some vendors support 802.11r while others do not. 802.11r was proposed primarily because of the time constraints of applications such as VoWiFi. Average time delays of hundreds of milliseconds occur when a client station roams from one access point to another access point.

Roaming can be especially troublesome when using a WPA-Enterprise or WPA2-Enterprise security solution, which requires the use of a RADIUS server for 802.1X/EAP authentication and often takes 700 milliseconds or greater for the client to authenticate. VoWiFi requires a handoff of 100 milliseconds or less to avoid a degradation of the quality of the call or, even worse, a loss of connection.

Under 802.11r, a client station is able to establish a QoS stream and set up a security association with a new access point in an efficient manner that allows bypassing 802.1X authentication when roaming to a new access point. The client station is able to achieve these tasks either over the wire via the original access point or through the air. Eventually, the client station will complete the roaming process and move to the new access point.

Tactical enterprise deployments of this technology will be extremely important for providing more secure communications for VoWiFi. The details of this technology are heavily tested on the CWSP exam.

802.11k-2008

The goal of the 802.11 Task Group k (TGk) was to provide a means of radio resource measurement (RRM). The 802.11k-2008 amendment calls for measurable client statistical information in the form of requests and reports for the Physical layer 1 and the MAC sublayer of the Data-Link layer 2. 802.11k defines mechanisms in which client station resource data is gathered and processed by an access point or *WLAN controller.* (WLAN controllers are covered in Chapter 10, "WLAN Architecture." For now, think of a WLAN controller as a core device that manages many access points.) In some instances, the client may also request information from an access point or WLAN controller. The following are some of the key radio resource measurements defined under 802.11k:

Transmit Power Control (TPC)   The 802.11h amendment defined the use of TPC for the 5 GHz band to reduce interference. Under 802.11k, TPC will also be used in other frequency bands and in areas governed by other regulatory agencies.

Client Statistics   Physical layer information such as signal-to-noise ratio, signal strength, and data rates can all be reported back to the access point or WLAN controller. MAC information such as frame transmissions, retries, and errors may all be reported back to the access point or WLAN controller as well.

Channel Statistics   Clients may gather noise-floor information based on any RF energy in the background of the channel and report this information back to the access point. Channel-load information may also be collected and sent to the AP. The access point or WLAN controller may use this information for channel management decisions.

Neighbor Reports   802.11k gives client stations the ability to learn from access points or WLAN controllers about other access points where the client stations might potentially roam. AP neighbor report information is shared among WLAN devices to improve roaming efficiency. Mobile Assisted Handover (MAHO) is a technique used by digital phones and cellular systems working together to provide better handover between cells.

Using proprietary methods, a client station keeps a table of known access points and makes decisions on when to roam to another access point. Most client stations make a roaming decision based on the received amplitude of known access points. In other words, a client station decides to roam based on its individual perspective of the RF environment. 802.11k mechanisms provide a client station with additional information about the existing RF environment.

As defined by 802.11k, a client station will request information about neighbor access points on other channels from an access point or WLAN controller. The current AP or WLAN controller will then process that information and generate a *neighbor report* detailing available access points from best to worst. Before a station roams, it will request the neighbor report from the current AP or controller and then decide whether to roam to one of the access points on the neighbor report. Neighbor reports effectively give a client station more information about the RF environment from other existing radios. With the additional information, a client station should make a more informed roaming decision. The 802.11k-2008 amendment in conjunction with the ratified 802.11r-2008 "fast roaming" amendment have the potential to greatly improve roaming performance in 802.11 wireless networks.

Most WLAN infrastructure vendors already support 802.11k and 802.11r technology in their APs and controllers; however, most client devices do not. Some aspects of the 802.11r (secure roaming) and 802.11k (resource management) amendments are tested by the Wi-Fi Alliance with a certification called Voice Enterprise. Although the Voice-Enterprise certification is reality, the majority of clients still do not support 802.11k and 802.11r mechanisms. Over time, we can expect more support for 802.11k and 802.11r technology on the client side.

802.11y-2008

Although 802.11 devices mostly operate in unlicensed frequencies, they can also operate on frequencies that are licensed by national regulatory bodies.

The objective of the IEEE Task Group y (TGy) was to standardize the mechanisms required to allow high-powered, shared 802.11 operations with other non-802.11 devices in the 3650 MHz–3700 MHz licensed band in the United States. It should be noted that the mechanisms defined by the 802.11y-2008 amendment can be used in other countries and in other licensed frequencies.

The licensed 3650 MHz to 3700 MHz band requires content-based protocol (CBP) mechanisms to avoid interference between devices. The medium contention method, CSMA/CA (which is used by Wi-Fi radios), can normally accommodate this requirement. However, when standard CSMA/CA methods are not sufficient, the 802.11y-2008 amendment defines *dynamic STA enablement (DSE)* procedures. 802.11 radios broadcast their actual location as a unique identifier in order to help resolve interference with non-802.11 radios in the same frequency.

802.11w-2009

A common type of attack on an 802.11 WLAN is a denial-of-service attack (DoS attack). There are a multitude of DoS attacks that can be launched against a wireless network; however, a very common DoS attack occurs at layer 2 using 802.11 management frames. Currently, it is simple for an attacker to edit deauthentication or disassociation frames and then retransmit the frames into the air, effectively shutting down the wireless network.

The goal of the IEEE Task Group w (TGw) was to provide a way of delivering management frames in a secure manner, therefore preventing the management frames from being able to be spoofed. The 802.11w-2009 amendment provides protection for unicast, broadcast, and multicast management frames.

These 802.11w frames are referred to as *robust management frames*. Robust management frames can be protected by the management frame protection service and include disassociation, deauthentication, and robust action frames. Action frames are used to request a station to take action on behalf of another station, and not all action frames are robust.

When unicast management frames are protected, frame protection is achieved by using CCMP. Broadcast and multicast frames are protected using the *Broadcast/Multicast Integrity Protocol (BIP)*. BIP provides data integrity and replay protection using AES-128 in Cipher-Based Message Authentication Code (CMAC) mode. It should be noted that the 802.11w amendment will not put an end to all layer 2 DoS attacks. However, once vendors begin to implement 802.11w mechanisms, some of the most common layer 2 DoS attacks can be prevented.

 You'll find a discussion about both layer 1 and layer 2 DoS attacks in Chapter 14, "Wireless Attacks, Intrusion Monitoring, and Policy."

802.11n-2009

An event that that had a major impact on the Wi-Fi marketplace was the ratification of the 802.11n-2009 amendment. Since 2004, the 802.11 Task Group n (TGn) worked on improvements to the 802.11 standard to provide for greater throughput. Some of the IEEE 802.11 amendments in the past have addressed bandwidth data rates in the 2.4 GHz frequency bands. However, the specific objective of the 802.11n-2009 amendment was to increase the throughput in both the 2.4 GHz and 5 GHz frequency bands. The 802.11n-2009 amendment defines a new operation known as *High Throughput (HT)*, which provides PHY and MAC enhancements to support data rates of up to 600 Mbps and therefore aggregate throughput above 100 Mbps.

HT clause 20 radios use *multiple-input, multiple-output (MIMO)* technology in unison with OFDM technology. MIMO uses multiple receiving and transmitting antennas and actually capitalizes on the effects of multipath as opposed to compensating for or eliminating them. The beneficial consequences of using MIMO are increased throughput and even greater range. 802.11n radios are also backward compatible with legacy 802.11a/b/g radios.

 Chapter 18, "802.11n," discusses 802.11n and MIMO technology in great detail.

802.11p-2010

The mission of the 802.11 Task Group p (TGp) was to define enhancements to the 802.11 standard to support Intelligent Transportation Systems (ITS) applications. Data exchanges between high-speed vehicles is possible in the licensed ITS band of 5.9 GHz. Additionally, communications between vehicles and roadside infrastructure is supported in the 5 GHz bands, specifically the 5.850 GHz to 5.925 GHz band within North America.

Communications may be possible at speeds of up to 200 kilometers per hour (124 mph) and within a range of 1,000 meters (3,281 feet). Very short latencies will also be needed as some applications must guarantee data delivery within 4 to 50 milliseconds.

802.11p is also known as Wireless Access in Vehicular Environments (WAVE) and is a possible foundation for a US Department of Transportation project called Dedicated Short Range Communications (DSRC). The DSRC project envisions a nationwide vehicle and roadside communication network utilizing applications such as vehicle safety services, traffic jam alerts, toll collections, vehicle collision avoidance, and adaptive traffic light control. In Europe, the ETSI Intelligent Transport System (ITS) is based on IEEE 802.11 and 802.11p technology. This standard is designed to provide vehicle to vehicle and vehicle to infrastructure communication. 802.11p will also be applicable to marine and rail communications.

802.11z-2010

The purpose of IEEE Task Group z (TGz) was to establish and standardize a *Direct Link Setup (DLS)* mechanism to allow operation with non-DLS-capable access points. In most WLAN environments, all frame exchanges between client stations that are associated to the same access point must pass through the access point. DLS allows client stations to bypass the access point and communicate with direct frame exchanges. Some of the earlier amendments have defined DLS communications. The 802.11z-2010 amendment defined enhancements to DLS communications. It should be noted that DLS communications have yet to be used by enterprise WLAN vendors.

802.11u-2011

The primary objective of the 802.11 Task Group u (TGu) was to address interworking issues between an IEEE 802.11 access network and any external network to which it is connected. A common approach is needed to integrate IEEE 802.11 access networks with external networks in a generic and standardized manner. 802.11u is also often referred to as Wireless Interworking with External Networks (WIEN).

The 802.11u-2011 amendment was ratified in February 2011 and it defines functions and procedures for aiding network discovery and selection by STAs, information transfer from external networks using QoS mapping, and a general mechanism for the provision of emergency services.

The 802.11u-2011 amendment is the basis for the Wi-Fi Alliance's Hotspot 2.0 specification and its Passpoint certification. This standard and certification is designed to provide seamless roaming for wireless devices between your Wi-Fi network and other partner networks, similar to how cellular telephone networks provide roaming.

802.11v-2011

The 802.11v-2011 amendment was ratified in February 2011. While 802.11k defines methods of retrieving information from client stations, 802.11v provides for an exchange of information that can potentially ease the configuration of client stations wirelessly from a central point of management. 802.11v-2011 defines *Wireless Network Management (WNM)*, which gives 802.11 stations the ability to exchange information for the purpose of improving the overall performance of the wireless network. Access points and client stations use WNM protocols to exchange operational data so that each station is aware of the network conditions, allowing stations to be more cognizant of the topology and state of the network.

In addition to providing information on network conditions, WNM protocols define mechanisms in which WLAN devices can exchange location information, provide support for the multiple BSSID capability, and offer a new WNM-Sleep mode in which a client station can sleep for long periods of time without receiving frames from the AP.

Some of the 802.11v mechanisms are defined by the Wi-Fi Alliance as optional mechanisms in the Voice-Enterprise certification. Implementation of 802.11v mechanisms in the enterprise is not yet widespread.

802.11s-2011

The 802.11s-2011 amendment was ratified in July 2011. 802.11 access points typically act as portal devices to a *distribution system (DS)* that is usually a wired 802.3 Ethernet medium. The 802.11-2012 standard, however, does not mandate that the distribution system use a wired medium. Access points can therefore act as portal devices to a *wireless distribution system (WDS)*. The 802.11s amendment proposes the use of a protocol for adaptive, autoconfiguring systems that support broadcast, multicast, and unicast traffic over a multihop mesh WDS.

FIGURE 5.2 Mesh points, mesh APs, and mesh portal

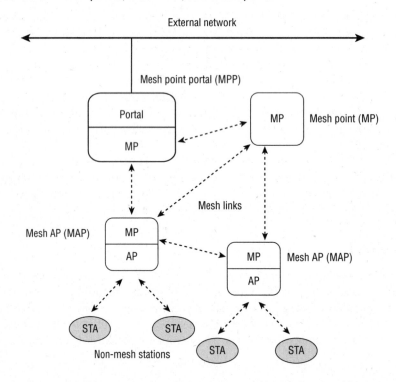

The 802.11 Task Group s (TGs) has set forth the pursuit of standardizing *mesh networking* using the IEEE 802.11 MAC/PHY layers. The 802.11s amendment defines the use of mesh points, which are 802.11 QoS stations that support mesh services. A *mesh point (MP)* is capable of using a mandatory mesh routing protocol called *Hybrid Wireless Mesh Protocol (HWMP)* that uses a default path selection metric. Vendors may also use proprietary mesh routing protocols and metrics. As depicted in Figure 5.2, a *mesh access point (MAP)* is a device that provides both mesh functionalities and AP functionalities simultaneously. A *mesh point portal (MPP)* is a device that acts as a gateway to one or more external networks such as an 802.3 wired backbone.

> Further discussion on distribution systems (DSs) and wireless distribution systems (WDSs) can be found in Chapter 7, "Wireless LAN Topologies." You will learn more about 802.11 mesh networking in Chapter 10.

Post-2012 Ratified Amendments

Since the 802.11-2012 document was published, there have been five more amendments that have been ratified to define further enhancements to 802.11 technology. These amendments—802.11ae-2012, 802.11aa-2012, 802.11ad-2012, 802.11ac-2013, and 802.11af-2014—are discussed in the following sections.

802.11ae-2012

The 802.11ae amendment specifies enhancements to QoS management. A quality-of-service management frame (QMF) service can be enabled, allowing some of the management frames to be transmitted using a QoS access category that is different than the access category that is assigned to voice traffic. This can improve the quality of service of other traffic streams.

802.11aa-2012

The 802.11aa amendment specifies QoS enhancements to the 802.11 Media Access Control (MAC) for robust audio and video streaming for both consumer and enterprise applications. 802.11aa provides improved management, increased link reliability, and increased application performance. The amendment defines Groupcast with retries (GCR), a flexible service to improve the delivery of group addressed frames. GCR can be provided in an infrastructure BSS by the AP to its associated STAs or in a mesh BSS by a mesh STA and its peer mesh STAs.

802.11ad-2012

The 802.11ad amendment defines Very High Throughput (VHT) enhancements using the much higher unlicensed frequency band of 60 GHz. The higher frequency range is big enough to support data rates of up to 7 Gbps. The downside is that 60 GHz will have significantly less effective range than a 5 GHz signal and be limited to line-of-sight communications as the high frequency signal will have difficulty penetrating walls.

The 60 GHz Wi-Fi technology has the potential to be used for wireless docking, wired equivalent data transfers, and streaming of uncompressed video. To provide seamless transition when roaming between the 60 GHz frequency band and legacy 2.4 GHz or 5 GHz bands, a "fast session transfer" feature was added to the specification. Currently there is a debate about whether or not 60 GHz Wi-Fi will be used in high-density deployments with a fallback to 5 GHz.

This VHT technology also required the adoption of a new encryption mechanism. There was concern that the current CCMP encryption methods may not be able to properly process the higher anticipated data rates. CCMP uses two chained-together AES cryptographic modes to process 128-bit blocks of data. The 128-bit blocks of data must also be processed "in order" from the first AES cryptographic mode to the second mode.

The 802.11ad amendment specifies the use of the *Galois/Counter Mode Protocol (GCMP)*, which also uses AES cryptography. However, GCMP calculations can be run in parallel and are computationally less intensive than the cryptographic operations of CCMP.

What Happened to the Wireless Gigabit Alliance?

The Wireless Gigabit Alliance (WiGig) was formed to promote wireless communications among consumer electronics, handheld devices, and PCs using the readily available, unlicensed 60 GHz spectrum. On January 3, 2013, it was announced that the activities of the WiGig Alliance would be consolidated into the Wi-Fi Alliance. Since then, the Wi-Fi Alliance has been actively working toward WiGig branding and product certification testing.

802.11ac-2013

The 802.11ac-2013 amendment defines Very High Throughput (VHT) enhancements below 6 GHz. The technology will only be used in the 5 GHz frequency bands where 802.11a/n radios already operate. 802.11ac will take advantage of the greater spectrum space that the 5 GHz U-NII bands can provide. The 2.4 GHz ISM band cannot provide needed frequency space to take full advantage of 802.11ac technology. To take full advantage of 802.11ac, even more spectrum will be needed in 5 GHz. Fortunately, the FCC has proposed the use of 195 MHz more spectrum in 5 GHz. The new FCC proposals are discussed in Chapter 6. 802.11ac promises Gigabit speeds using four major enhancements:

Wider Channels 802.11n introduced the capability of 40 MHz channels, which effectively doubled the data rates. 802.11ac brings us the capability of 80 MHz and 160 MHz channels. This is the main reason that enterprise 802.11ac radios will operate at 5 GHz as opposed to the 2.4 GHz ISM band.

New Modulation 802.11ac will provide the capability to use 256-QAM modulation, which has the potential to provide a 30 percent increase in speed. 256-QAM modulation will require a very high signal-to-noise (SNR) ratio to be effective.

More Spatial Streams 802.11ac radios could be built to transmit and receive up to eight spatial streams. In reality the first several generations of 802.11ac chipsets will use one to four spatial streams.

Improved MIMO and Beamforming   While 802.11n defined the use of single-user MIMO radios, Very High Throughput (VHT) introduces the use of *multi-user MIMO (MU-MIMO)* technology. An access point with MU-MIMO capability could transmit a signal to multiple client stations on the same channel simultaneously if the client stations are in different physical areas. 802.11ac will utilize a simplified beamforming method called *null data packet (NDP)* beamforming.

The 802.11ac technology will hit the streets in two waves. The first wave of 802.11ac chipsets take advantage of 256-QAM modulation and 80 MHz wide channels. Most of the AP hardware uses 3x3:3 radios. The second wave of 802.11ac chipsets are expected to be able to use MU-MIMO and 160 MHz channels. The AP hardware will also most likely be 4x4:4 radios. Chapter 19, "Very-High Throughput (VHT) and 802.11ac," is an entire chapter about the 802.11ac-2013 amendment and all the underlying technology.

802.11af-2014

The 802.11af amendment allows the use of wireless in the newly opened *TV white space (TVWS)* frequencies between 54 MHz and 790 MHz. This technology is sometimes referred to as White-Fi, or Super Wi-Fi, but we recommend that you shy away from using these terms as this technology is not affiliated with the Wi-Fi Alliance, who is the trademark holder of the term Wi-Fi.

In different regions or TV marketplaces, not all of the available TV channels are used by licensed stations. TVWS is the range of TV frequencies that are not used by any licensed station in a specific area. 802.11af based radios will have to verify what frequencies are available and make sure that they do not cause interference. To achieve this, the 802.11af AP will first need to determine its location, likely through the use of GPS technology. Then the radio device will need to interact with a geographic database to determine the available channels for that given time and location.

The low-bandwidth frequencies that are used mean lower data rates than 802.11a/b/g/n/ac technology. Maximum transmission speed is 26.7 Mbps or 35.6 Mbps, depending upon the width of the channel, which is determined by the regulatory domain. Channel width is between 6 MHz and 8 MHz, and up to 4 channels can be bonded together. 802.11af radios can also support up to 4 spatial streams. Using 4 channels and 4 spatial streams, 802.11af has a maximum data rate of about 426 Mbps or 568 Mbps, depending upon the regulator domain. Although the lower TVWS frequencies mean lower data rates, the lower frequencies will provide longer-distance transmissions, along with better penetration through obstructions such as foliage and buildings. This greater distance could result in coverage that is more pervasive, providing contiguous roaming in outdoor office parks, campuses, or public community networks. Another anticipated use is to provide broadband Internet services to rural areas.

It is important to note that the IEEE 802.22-2011 standard, along with at least one other standard that is in development, also specifies wireless communications using the TV white space frequencies. This may cause coexistence problems in the future between these competing technologies. Also, the existence of multiple technologies in the same frequency space may splinter product development and acceptance.

IEEE 802.11 Draft Amendments

What does the future hold in store for us with 802.11 wireless networking? The draft amendments are a looking glass into the enhancements and capabilities that might be available in the near future for 802.11 wireless networking devices. Even greater throughput as well as operations on higher and lower frequencies await us on the wireless horizon.

It is important to remember that draft amendments are proposals that have yet to be ratified. Although some vendors are already selling products that have some of the capabilities described in the following sections, these features are still considered proprietary. Even though a vendor might be marketing these pre-ratified capabilities, there is no guarantee that their current product will work with future products that are certified as compliant with the forthcoming ratified amendment.

The CWNA exam (CWNA-106) currently covers all of the technologies defined by the 802.11-2012 standard, as well as any amendments ratified since 2012. *You will not be tested on the draft amendments.* Even though you will not be tested on these amendments, we believe it is important for you to be introduced to the technologies that are being planned and developed since they will likely change 802.11 wireless networking in the future.

The ratification of the 802.11n-2009 amendment sparked a major convergence of data, voice, and video over the wireless medium, and the recent ratification of the 802.11ac-2013 amendment is already solidifying and expanding 802.11's role in this environment. The remaining pages of this chapter provide a glimpse into the future of more advanced and sophisticated Wi-Fi products that could bring this technology to even greater heights.

Once again, please remember that because these IEEE amendments are still draft documents, they will likely be different from the final ratified amendments.

802.11ah

The 802.11ah draft amendment defines the use of Wi-Fi in frequencies below 1 GHz. This technology will likely use a new Physical layer that is based upon the technology in 802.11ac. The lower frequencies will mean lower data rates but longer distances. A likely use for 802.11h will be sensor networks along with backhaul for sensor networks and with extended range Wi-Fi. This internetworking of devices is known as *Internet-of-Things (IoT)* or *Machine-to-Machine (M2M)* communications.

The available frequencies will vary between countries. As an example, in the United States, the 902–928 MHz unlicensed ISM frequencies are available, whereas 863–868 MHz would likely be available in Europe and 755–787 would likely be available in China.

802.11ai

The goal of the 802.11ai draft amendment is to provide a *fast initial link setup (FILS)*. This technology could allow a STA to establish a secure link setup in less than 100 ms. The STA would then be able to send valid IP traffic through the AP.

802.11aj

The 802.11aj draft amendment is to provide modifications to the IEEE 802.11ad-2012 amendment's PHY and MAC layer to provide support for operating in the Chinese Milli-Meter Wave (CMMW) frequency bands. The CMMW frequency bands are 59–64 GHz. The amendment will also provide modifications to the IEEE 802.11ad-2012 amendment's PHY and MAC layer to provide support for operating in the Chinese 45 GHz frequency band.

802.11ak

The 802.11ak draft amendment is also referred to as *General Link (GLK)*. The task group is exploring enhancement to 802.11 links for use in bridged networks. These bridged networks will be evaluated as potential support for home entertainment systems, industrial control devices, and other products that have both 802.11 wireless and 802.3 wired capabilities. GLK aims to simplify the use of 802.11 between access points and wireless stations, allowing the stations to provide bridging services.

802.11aq

The 802.11aq Pre Association task group is working to develop an 802.11 amendment that enables delivery of network service information prior to the association of stations on an 802.11 network. This amendment hopes to be able to allow advertisement of services to stations prior to the stations' actual association to the network.

Defunct Amendments

The next two amendments were never ratified and are considered dead in the water. However, the subject matter (roaming and performance testing) of the two amendments is important and therefore we will discuss them in this book.

802.11F

The IEEE Task Group F (TGF) published IEEE Std 802.11F-2003 as a recommended practice in 2003. The amendment was never ratified and was withdrawn in February 2006.

The use of an uppercase letter designation for an IEEE task group, like that in IEEE Task Group F, indicates that this amendment (F) is considered a recommended practice and not part of the 802.11-2012 standard.

The original published 802.11 standard mandated that vendor access points support *roaming*. A mechanism is needed to allow client stations that are already communicating through one AP to be able to jump from the coverage area of the original AP and continue communications through a new AP. A perfect analogy is the roaming that occurs when using a cell phone. When you are talking on a cell phone while inside a moving vehicle, your phone will roam between cellular towers to allow for seamless communications and hopefully an uninterrupted conversation. Seamless roaming allows for mobility, which is the heart and soul of true wireless networking and connectivity.

In Figure 5.3, you see a station downloading a file through AP-1 from an FTP server residing on a wired network backbone. Please note that the access points have overlapping areas of coverage. As the station moves closer to AP-2, which has a stronger signal, the station may roam to AP-2 and continue the FTP transfer through the portal supplied by the new access point.

FIGURE 5.3   Seamless roaming

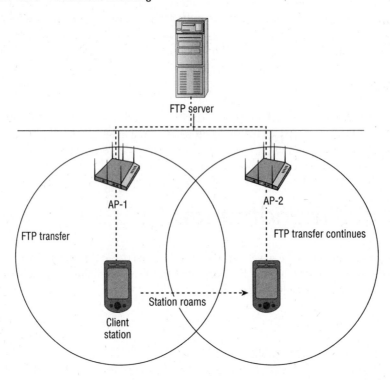

Although the handover that occurs during roaming can be measured in milliseconds, data packets intended for delivery to the station that has roamed to a new access point might still be buffered at the original access point. In order for the buffered data packets to find their way to the station, two things must happen:

1. The new access point must inform the original access point about the station that has roamed and request any buffered packets.

2. The original access point must forward the buffered packets to the new access point via the distribution system for delivery to the client who has roamed.

   Figure 5.4 illustrates these two needed tasks.

FIGURE 5.4   Roaming-distribution system medium

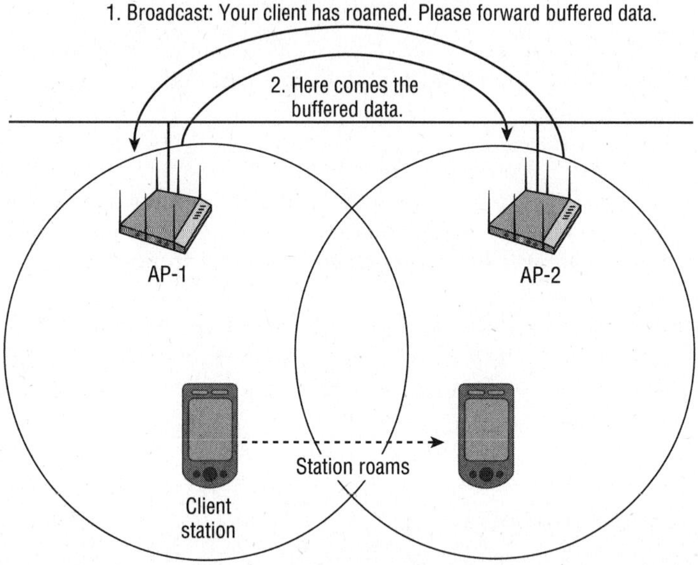

Will Seamless Roaming Work If I Mix and Match Different Vendors' Access Points?

The real-world answer is no. 802.11F was intended to address roaming interoperability between *autonomous access points* from different vendors. The 802.11F amendment was initially only a recommended practice and was eventually withdrawn entirely by the IEEE. WLAN vendors want customers to purchase only the brand of AP that the vendor sells and not the competition's brand of AP. It is the "recommended practice" of this book not to mix different vendors' access points on the same wired network segment. Roaming is discussed in further detail in Chapter 7 and Chapter 9 as well as Chapter 12, "WLAN Troubleshooting."

Although the original 802.11 standard calls for the support of roaming, it fails to dictate how roaming should actually transpire. The IEEE initially intended for vendors to have flexibility in implementing proprietary AP-to-AP roaming mechanisms. The 802.11F amendment was an attempt to standardize how roaming mechanisms work behind the scenes on the distribution system medium, which is typically an 802.3 Ethernet network using TCP/IP networking protocols. 802.11F addressed "vendor interoperability" for AP-to-AP roaming. The final result was a recommended practice to use the *Inter-Access Point Protocol (IAPP)*. IAPP uses announcement and handover processes that result in APs informing other APs about roamed clients as well as delivery of buffered packets. Because the 802.11F amendment was never ratified, the use of IAPP is basically nonexistent.

802.11T

The original goal of the IEEE 802.11 Task Group T (TGT) was to develop performance metrics, measurement methods, and test conditions to measure the performance of 802.11 wireless networking equipment.

The uppercase *T* in the name *IEEE 802.11T* indicates that this amendment was considered a recommended practice and not a standard. The 802.11T amendment was never ratified and has been dropped.

The 802.11T is also called Wireless Performance Prediction (WPP). Its final objective was consistent and universally accepted WLAN measurement practices. These 802.11 performance benchmarks and methods could be used by independent test labs, manufacturers, and even end users.

Real World Scenario

Are Throughput Results the Same among Vendors?

Multiple factors can affect throughput in a wireless network, including the physical environment, range, and type of encryption. Another factor that can affect throughput is simply the vendor radio device that is being used for transmissions. Even though the 802.11-2012 standard clearly defines frequency bandwidths, data rate speeds, and medium access methods, throughput results vary widely from vendor to vendor. A throughput performance test using two radio cards from one vendor will most often yield very different results than the same throughput performance test using two radio cards from another vendor. Typically, you will see better throughput results when sticking with one vendor as opposed to mixing vendor equipment. However, sometimes mixing vendor equipment will produce the unexplained consequence of increased throughput. Although standardized 802.11T metrics were never adopted, the Wi-Fi Alliance defines its own metrics for vendor-neutral lab tests for all of the Wi-Fi Alliance certifications.

802.11m Task Group

The IEEE Task Group m (TGm) started an initiative in 1999 for internal maintenance of the 802.11 standard's technical documentation. 802.11m is often referred to as *802.11 housekeeping* because of its mission of clarifying and correcting the 802.11 standard. Unless you are a member of TGm, this amendment is of little significance. However, this task group also is responsible for "rolling up" ratified amendments into a published document. While this study guide is being written, the most current published version of the WLAN standard is IEEE Std 802.11-2012. The next rolled-up version of the standard is expected in 2015. The 802.11 TGma was responsible for the consolidation of IEEE Std 802.11-2007. The 802.11 TGmb was responsible for the consolidation of the IEEE Std 802.11-2012. The 802.11 TGmc will be responsible for the next standard consolidation, IEEE Std 802.11-2015.

Neither 802.11l nor 802.11o amendments exist because they are considered typologically problematic. The 802.11ab amendment was skipped to avoid confusion with devices that use both 802.11a and 802.11b PHY technologies, which are often called 802.11a/b devices. The 802.11ag amendment was skipped to avoid confusion with devices that use both 802.11a and 802.11g PHY technologies, which are called 802.11a/g devices. Also, it should be noted that there is no amendment with the name of 802.11x. The term *802.11x* sometimes is used to refer to all the 802.11 standards. The IEEE 802.1X standard, which is a port-based access control standard, is often incorrectly called 802.11x.

Summary

This chapter covered the original 802.11 standard, the amendments consolidated into the 802.11-2007 standard, and the amendments consolidated into the 802.11-2012 standard as well as 802.11 amendments ratified since 2012. This chapter also discussed possible future enhancements. We covered the following:

- All the defined PHY and MAC layer requirements of the original 802.11 Prime standard

- All the approved enhancements to the 802.11 standard in the form of ratified amendments, including higher data rates, different spread spectrum technologies, quality of service, and security

- Future capabilities and improvements as proposed in the 802.11 draft documents

Although many proprietary Wi-Fi solutions exist and will continue to exist in the foreseeable future, standardization brings stability to the marketplace. The 802.11-2012 standard and all the future enhanced supplements provide a much needed foundation for vendors, network administrators, and end users.

The CWNA exam will test your knowledge of the 802.11-2012 standard and all the related technologies. Technologies discussed in the 802.11ac-2013 ratified amendment are also covered in the CWNA exam. Your primary focus should be on the 802.11-2012 standard. However, keep in mind that when 802.11 draft amendments become approved, they will be weighted heavier in future versions of the CWNA exam.

Exam Essentials

Know the defined spread spectrum technologies of the original 802.11 standard and the subsequent 802.11-2007 and 802.11-2012 standards.   Although the original 802.11 standard defined infrared, FHSS, and DSSS, later amendments that are now incorporated in the 802.11-2012 standard also define HR-DSSS, OFDM, ERP, HT, and VHT.

Remember both the required data rates and supported data rates of each PHY.   DSSS and FHSS require and support data rates of 1 and 2 Mbps. Other PHYs offer a wider support for data rates. For example, OFDM and ERP-OFDM support data rates of 6, 9, 12, 18, 24, 36, 48, and 54 Mbps, but only the rates of 6, 12, and 24 Mbps are mandatory. With the introduction of 802.11n, it is important to understand the concept of modulation coding schemes (MCSs). Please understand that data rates are transmission speeds and not aggregate throughput.

Know the frequency bands used by each PHY as defined by the 802.11-2012 standard.   802.11a equipment operates in the 5 GHz U-NII bands. DSSS, FHSS, HR-DSSS, and ERP (802.11g) devices transmit and receive in the 2.4 GHz ISM band. Understand that 802.11n devices transmit in either the 2.4 GHz or 5 GHz frequency bands. 802.11ac radios will transmit only in the 5 GHz frequency bands.

Define transmit power control and dynamic frequency selection.   TPC and DFS are typically mandated for use in the 5 GHz band. Both technologies are used as a means to avoid interference with radar transmissions.

Explain the defined wireless security standards, both pre-802.11i and post-802.11i.   Before the passage of 802.11i, WEP encryption and either Open System or Shared Key authentication were defined. The 802.11i amendment calls for the use of CCMP/AES for encryption. For authentication, 802.11i defines either an 802.1X/EAP solution or the use of PSK authentication.

Review Questions

1. An ERP (802.11g) network mandates support for which two spread spectrum technologies?
   - **A.** ERP-OFDM
   - **B.** FHSS
   - **C.** ERP-PBCC
   - **D.** ERP-DSSS/CCK
   - **E.** CSMA/CA

2. The 802.11-2012 standard using an ERP-DSSS/CCK radio supports which data rates?
   - **A.** 3, 6, and 12 Mbps
   - **B.** 6, 9, 12, 18, 24, 36, 48, and 54 Mbps
   - **C.** 6, 12, 24, and 54 Mbps
   - **D.** 6, 12, and 24 Mbps
   - **E.** 1, 2, 5.5, and 11 Mbps

3. Which types of devices were defined in the original 802.11 standard? (Choose all that apply.)
   - **A.** OFDM
   - **B.** DSSS
   - **C.** HR-DSSS
   - **D.** IR
   - **E.** FHSS
   - **F.** ERP

4. Which 802.11 amendment defines wireless mesh networking mechanisms?
   - **A.** 802.11n
   - **B.** 802.11u
   - **C.** 802.11s
   - **D.** 802.11v
   - **E.** 802.11k

5. A robust security network (RSN) requires the use of which security mechanisms? (Choose all that apply.)
   - **A.** 802.11x
   - **B.** WEP
   - **C.** IPsec
   - **D.** CCMP/AES

    E. CKIP

    F. 802.1X

6. An 802.11a radio card can transmit on the _____ frequency and uses _____ spread spectrum technology.

    A. 5 MHz, OFDM

    B. 2.4 GHz, HR-DSSS

    C. 2.4 GHz, ERP-OFDM

    D. 5 GHz, OFDM

    E. 5 GHz, DSSS

7. What are the required data rates of an OFDM station?

    A. 3, 6, and 12 Mbps

    B. 6, 9, 12, 18, 24, 36, 48, and 54 Mbps

    C. 6, 12, 24, and 54 Mbps

    D. 6, 12, and 24 Mbps

    E. 1, 2, 5.5, and 11 Mbps

8. When implementing an 802.1X/EAP RSN network with a VoWiFi solution, what is needed to avoid latency issues during roaming?

    A. Inter-Access Point Protocol

    B. Fast BSS Transition

    C. Distributed Coordination Function

    D. Roaming Coordination Function

    E. Lightweight APs

9. Which new technologies debuted in the 802.11ac-2013 amendment? (Choose all that apply.)

    A. MIMO

    B. MU-MIMO

    C. 256-QAM

    D. 40 MHz channels

    E. 80 MHz channels

10. What is the primary reason that OFDM (802.11a) radios cannot communicate with ERP (802.11g) radios?

    A. 802.11a uses OFDM, and 802.11g uses DSSS.

    B. 802.11a uses DSSS, and 802.11g uses OFDM.

    C. 802.11a uses OFDM, and 802.11g uses CCK.

    D. 802.11a operates at 5 GHz, and 802.11g operates at 2.4 GHz.

    E. 802.11a requires dynamic frequency selection, and 802.11g does not.

11. What two technologies are used to prevent 802.11 radios from interfering with radar and satellite transmissions at 5 GHz?

   A. Dynamic frequency selection

   B. Enhanced Distributed Channel Access

   C. Direct sequence spread spectrum

   D. Temporal Key Integrity Protocol

   E. Transmit power control

12. Which 802.11 amendments provide for throughput of 1 Gbps or higher? (Choose all that apply.)

   A. 802.11aa

   B. 802.11ab

   C. 802.11ac

   D. 802.11ad

   E. 802.11ae

   F. 802.11af

13. As defined by the 802.11-2012 standard, which equipment is compatible? (Choose all that apply.)

   A. ERP and HR-DSSS

   B. HR-DSSS and FHSS

   C. OFDM and ERP

   D. 802.11a and 802.11h

   E. DSSS and HR-DSSS

14. Maximum data rates of _____ are permitted using OFDM radios.

   A. 108 Mbps

   B. 22 Mbps

   C. 24 Mbps

   D. 54 Mbps

   E. 11 Mbps

15. What are the security options available as defined in the original IEEE Std 802.11-1999 (R2003)? (Choose all that apply.)

   A. CCMP/AES

   B. Open System authentication

   C. Preshared keys

   D. Shared Key authentication

   E. WEP

   F. TKIP

16. The 802.11u-2011 amendment is also known as what?

   A. Wireless Interworking with External Networks (WIEN)

   B. Wireless Local Area Networking (WLAN)

   C. Wireless Performance Prediction (WPP)

   D. Wireless Access in Vehicular Environments (WAVE)

   E. Wireless Access Protocol (WAP)

17. The 802.11-2012 standard defines which two technologies for quality of service (QoS) in a WLAN?

   A. EDCA

   B. PCF

   C. Hybrid Coordination Function Controlled Channel Access

   D. VoIP

   E. Distributed Coordination Function

   F. VoWiFi

18. The 802.11h amendment (now part of the 802.11-2012 standard) introduced what two major changes for 5 GHz radios?

   A. U-NII-2 Extended

   B. IAPP

   C. Radar detection

   D. Transmit Frequency Avoidance

   E. Frequency hopping spread spectrum

19. The 802.11b amendment defined which PHY?

   A. HR-DSSS

   B. FHSS

   C. OFDM

   D. PBCC

   E. EIRP

20. Which layers of the OSI model are referenced in the 802.11 standard? (Choose all that apply.)

   A. Application

   B. Data-Link

   C. Presentation

   D. Physical

   E. Transport

   F. Network

Chapter

6

Wireless Networks and Spread Spectrum Technologies

IN THIS CHAPTER, YOU WILL LEARN ABOUT THE FOLLOWING:

✓ **Industrial, Scientific, and Medical bands (ISM)**

- 900 MHz ISM band

- 2.4 GHz ISM band

- 5.8 GHz ISM band

✓ **Unlicensed National Information Infrastructure bands (U-NII)**

- U-NII-1 (lower band)

- U-NII-2 (middle band)

- U-NII-2 Extended

- U-NII-3 (upper band)

- Future U-NII bands

✓ **3.6 GHz band**

✓ **4.9 GHz band**

✓ **Future Wi-Fi frequencies**

- 60 GHz

- White-Fi

✓ **Narrowband and spread spectrum**

- Multipath interference

✓ **Frequency hopping spread spectrum (FHSS)**

- Hopping sequence

- Dwell time

- Hop time
- Modulation

✓ **Direct sequence spread spectrum (DSSS)**

- DSSS data encoding
- Modulation

✓ **Packet Binary Convolutional Code (PBCC)**

✓ **Orthogonal Frequency Division Multiplexing (OFDM)**

- Convolutional coding
- Modulation

✓ **2.4 GHz channels**

✓ **5 GHz channels**

✓ **Adjacent, nonadjacent, and overlapping channels**

✓ **Throughput vs. bandwidth**

✓ **Communication resilience**

In this chapter, you will learn about the different spread spectrum transmission technologies and frequency ranges that are supported by the 802.11 standard and amendments. You will learn how these frequencies are divided into different channels and some of the proper and improper ways of using the channels. Additionally, you will learn about the various types of spread spectrum technologies. You will also learn about Orthogonal Frequency Division Multiplexing (OFDM) and the similarities and differences between OFDM and spread spectrum.

Throughout this chapter are many references to FCC specifications and regulations. The CWNA exam does not test you on any regulatory domain–specific information. Any FCC references are strictly provided to help you understand the technology better. It is important to realize that similarities often exist between the regulations of different regulatory domains. Therefore, understanding the rules of another country's regulatory domain can help you interpret the rules of your regulatory domain.

Industrial, Scientific, and Medical Bands

The IEEE 802.11 standard and the subsequent 802.11b, 802.11g, and 802.11n amendments all define communications in the frequency range between 2.4 GHz and 2.4835 GHz. This frequency range is one of three frequency ranges known as the *industrial, scientific, and medical (ISM) bands*. The frequency ranges of the ISM bands are as follows:

- 902 MHz – 928 MHz (26 MHz wide)
- 2.4 GHz – 2.5 GHz (100 MHz wide)
- 5.725 GHz – 5.875 GHz (150 MHz wide)

The ISM bands are defined by the ITU Telecommunication Standardization Sector (ITU-T) in S5.138 and S5.150 of the Radio Regulations. Although the FCC governs the use of the ISM bands defined by the ITU-T in the United States, their usage in other countries may be different because of local regulations. The 900 MHz band is known as the industrial band, the 2.4 GHz band is known as the scientific band, and the 5.8 GHz band is known as the medical band.

Note that all three of these bands are license-free bands, and there are no restrictions on what types of equipment can be used in any of them. For example, a radio used in medical equipment can be used in the 900 MHz industrial band.

900 MHz ISM Band

The 900 MHz ISM band is 26 MHz wide and spans from 902 MHz to 928 MHz. In the past, this band was used for wireless networking. However, most wireless networks now use higher frequencies, which are capable of faster throughput.

Another factor limiting the use of the 900 MHz ISM band is that in many parts of the world, part of the 900 MHz frequency range has already been allocated to the Global System for Mobile Communications (GSM) for use by mobile phones. Although the 900 MHz ISM band is rarely used for networking, many products such as baby monitors, wireless home telephones, and wireless headphones use this frequency range.

802.11 radios do not operate in the 900 MHz ISM band, but many older legacy deployments of wireless networking did operate in this band. Some vendors still manufacture non-802.11 wireless networking devices that operate in the 900 MHz ISM band. This is a particularly popular frequency that is used for wireless ISPs because of its superior foliage penetration over the 2.4 GHz and 5 GHz frequency ranges.

2.4 GHz ISM Band

The 2.4 GHz ISM band is the most common band used for wireless networking communications. The 2.4 GHz ISM band is 100 MHz wide and spans from 2.4 GHz to 2.5 GHz. Use of the 2.4 GHz ISM for wireless LANs is defined by the IEEE in the 802.11-2012 standard. Even though most of the current 802.11 radio chipsets now include 5 GHz capabilities, the 2.4 GHz ISM band has been the primary band that is used by Wi-Fi devices, often making this band extremely overcrowded. The following wireless radios use this band:

- 802.11 (FHSS radios or DSSS radios)
- 802.11b (HR-DSSS radios)
- 802.11g (ERP radios)
- 802.11n (HT radios)

In addition to being used by 802.11 WLAN equipment, the 2.4 GHz ISM band is also used by microwave ovens, cordless home telephones, baby monitors, and wireless video cameras. The 2.4 GHz ISM band is heavily used, and one of the big disadvantages of using 802.11b/g/n 2.4 GHz radios is the potential for interference.

Please keep in mind that not every country's RF regulatory body will allow for transmissions across the entire 2.4 GHz – 2.5 GHz ISM band. The IEEE 802.11-2012 standard allows for WLAN transmissions in this band across 14 channels. However, each country can determine which channels can be used. A discussion of all the 2.4 GHz channels occurs later in this chapter.

5.8 GHz ISM Band

The 5.8 GHz ISM band is 150 MHz wide and spans from 5.725 GHz to 5.875 GHz. As with the other ISM bands, the 5.8 GHz ISM band is used by many of the same types of consumer products: baby monitors, cordless telephones, and cameras. It is not uncommon for novices to confuse the 5.8 GHz ISM band with the U-NII-3 band, which spans from 5.725 GHz to 5.85 GHz. Both unlicensed bands span the same frequency space. However, the 5.8 GHz ISM band is 25 MHz larger.

The IEEE 802.11a amendment (now part of 802.11-2012 standard) states that "the OFDM PHY shall operate in the 5 GHz band, as allocated by a regulatory body in its operational region." Most countries allow for OFDM transmissions in channels of the various U-NII bands, which are discussed in this chapter. The United States has also always allowed OFDM transmissions on channel 165, which until April of 2014, resided in the 5.8 GHz ISM band. Historically, channel 165 has been sparsely used. In April of 2014, the U-NII-3 band was expanded to include channel 165.

From the perspective of Wi-Fi channels, the 5.8 GHz ISM band is no longer relevant, however, many of the consumer devices that operate in the 5.8 GHz ISM band can cause RF interference with 802.11 radios that transmit in the U-NII-3 band.

Unlicensed National Information Infrastructure Bands

The IEEE 802.11a amendment designated WLAN transmissions within the frequency space of the three 5 GHz bands, each with four channels. These frequency ranges are known as the *Unlicensed National Information Infrastructure (U-NII) bands*. The 802.11a amendment defined three groupings, or bands, of U-NII frequencies, often known as the lower, middle, and upper U-NII bands. These three bands are typically designated as U-NII-1 (lower), U-NII-2 (middle), and U-NII-3 (upper).

When the 802.11h amendment was ratified, the IEEE designated more frequency space for WLAN transmissions. This frequency space, which consists of 12 additional channels, is often referred to as U-NII-2 Extended.

Wi-Fi radios that currently transmit in the 5 GHz U-NII bands include radios that use the following technologies:

- 802.11a (OFDM radios)
- 802.11n (HT radios)
- 802.11ac (VHT radios)

Keep in mind that not every country's RF regulatory body will allow for transmissions in all these bands. The IEEE 802.11-2012 standard allows for WLAN transmissions in all four of the bands across 25 channels. However, each country may be different due to different channel and power regulations. A more detailed discussion of all the 5 GHz channels occurs later in this chapter.

U-NII-1 (Lower Band)

U-NII-1, the lower U-NII band, is 100 MHz wide and spans from 5.150 GHz to 5.250 GHz. A total of four 20 MHz 802.11 channels reside in the U-NII-1 band. In the past, the U-NII-1 band was restricted by the FCC for indoor use only in the United States. As of April 2014, the FCC lifted this restriction. Prior to 2004, the FCC required that all U-NII-1-capable devices have permanently attached antennas. This meant that any 802.11a device that supported U-NII-1 could not have a detachable antenna, even if the device supported other frequencies or standards.

In 2004, the FCC changed the regulations to allow detachable antennas, providing that the antenna connector is unique. This requirement is similar to the antenna requirements for the other U-NII bands and the 2.4 GHz ISM band. Always remember that the 5 GHz power and transmit regulations are often different in other countries. Take care to ensure that you do not exceed the limitations of your local regulatory body.

U-NII-2 (Middle Band)

U-NII-2, the middle U-NII band, is 100 MHz wide and spans from 5.250 GHz to 5.350 GHz. A total of four 20 MHz 802.11 channels reside in the U-NII-2 band. 802.11 radios that transmit in the U-NII-2 band must support dynamic frequency selection (DFS).

U-NII-2 Extended

The U-NII-2 Extended band is 255 MHz wide and spans from 5.470 GHz to 5.725 GHz. Most 5 GHz 802.11 radios can transmit on a total of eleven 20 MHz 802.11 channels that reside in the U-NII-2 band. However, with the advent of 802.11ac technology, a new channel 144 has been added to the U-NII-2 Extended band for a total of twelve channels.

802.11 radios that transmit in the U-NII-2 band must support dynamic frequency selection (DFS). Operations for WLAN communications were first allowed in this band with the ratification of the 802.11h amendment. Prior to the ratification of this amendment, 5 GHz WLAN communications were allowed in only U-NII-1, U-NII-2, and U-NII-3.

Dynamic Frequency Selection and Transmit Power Control

In Chapter 5, "IEEE 802.11 Standards," you learned that the 802.11h amendment defined the use of transmit power control (TPC) and dynamic frequency selection (DFS) to avoid interference with radar transmissions. Any 5 GHz WLAN products manufactured in the United States or Canada on or after July 20, 2007, are required to support dynamic frequency selection if they transmit in the U-NII-2 and U-NII-2 Extended bands. This should be FCC Rule # 15.407(h)(2) requires that WLAN products operating in the U-NII-2 and U-NII-2 Extended bands must support DFS, to protect WLAN communications from interfering with military or weather radar systems. Europe also requires DFS safeguards. DFS is a mechanism that detects the presence of radar signals and dynamically guides a transmitter to switch to another channel. Prior to the start of any transmission, a radio equipped with DFS capability must continually monitor the radio environment for radar's presence. If a radio determines that a radar signal is present, it must either select another channel to avoid interference with radar or go into a "sleep mode" if no other channel is available. TPC is required to protect the Earth exploration satellite service. Once again, the local regulatory agencies determine how TPC and DFS restrictions are imposed in any of the U-NII bands.

U-NII-3 (Upper Band)

U-NII-3, the upper U-NII band, is 125 MHz wide and spans from 5.725 GHz to 5.850 GHz. This band is typically used for outdoor point-to-point communications but can also be used indoors in some countries, including the United States. Many of the countries in Europe do not use the U-NII-3 band for WLAN unlicensed communications. Some European countries allow transmission in the U-NII-3 band with the purchase of an inexpensive license.

In Table 6.1, notice that five 20 MHz 802.11 channels reside in the U-NII-3 band. In April of 2014, the FCC expanded the size of the U-NII-3 band from 100 MHz to 125 MHz. Channel 165, formerly in the 5.8 GHz ISM band, is now available as part of the U-NII-3 band.

TABLE 6.1:   The 5 GHz U-NII bands

Band	Frequency	Channels
U-NII-1	5.15 GHz – 5.25 GHz	4 channels
U-NII-2	5.25 GHZ – 5.35 GHz	4 channels
U-NII-2 Extended	5.47 GHZ – 5.725 GHz	12 channels*
U-NII-3	5.725 GHz – 5.85 GHz	5 channels

*NOTE: With the advent of 802.11ac technology, a new channel 144 has been added to the U-NII-2 Extended band for a total of 12 channels. Currently the majority of 5 GHz radios do not yet transmit on channel 144.

Future U-NII Bands

In January, 2013, the FCC announced that 195 MHz of additional spectrum space would be made available for unlicensed use and promptly released a *Notice of Proposed Rulemaking (NPRM)*, document #13-22, which outlined new rules for how the additional spectrum might be used. FCC #13-22 is available for download at

www.fcc.gov/document/5-ghz-unlicensed-spectrum-unii

It proposes two new U-NII bands as shown in Figure 6.1. A new 120 MHz wide band called U-NII-2B occupies the frequency space of 5.35 GHZ – 5.47 GHz with six potential 20 MHz channels. Another new 75 MHz wide band called U-NII-4 occupies the 5.85 GHZ – 5.925 GHz frequency space with the potential of four more 20 MHz channels.

FIGURE 6.1   Proposed U-NII bands

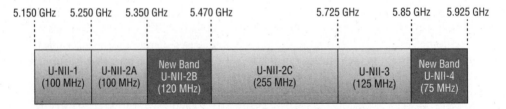

As listed in Table 6.2, the U-NII-2 band would be renamed to U-NII-2A and the U-NII-2 Extended band would be renamed as U-NII-2C. In addition to ten new channels gained from the proposed two new bands, U-NII-2A would gain an extra channel and U-NII-2C would gain an extra channel in frequency space previously used as a guard bands. The FCC is still studying the proposal, but a total of twelve extra 20 MHz channels could become available once approved. Further study of the spectrum sharing and DFS mechanisms may take until late 2014, and we could possibly get approval to use the new spectrum by early 2015.

TABLE 6.2   The new 5 GHz U-NII bands

Old Name	New Name	Frequency	Channels
U-NII-1	U-NII-1	5.15 – 5.25 GHz	4 channels
U-NII-2	U-NII-2A	5.25 – 5.35 GHz	5 channels
	U-NII-2B	5.35 – 5.47 GHz	6 channels
U-NII-2 Extended	U-NII-2C	5.47 – 5.725 GHz	13 channels
U-NII-3	U-NII-3	5.725 – 5.85 GHz	5 channels
	U-NII-4	5.85 – 5.925 GHz	4 channels

The good news is that the FCC recognizes the need for more unlicensed spectrum and the word *Wi-Fi* is mentioned multiple times in NPRM #13-22. The FCC is preparing for the advent of 802.11ac technology that can use 80 MHz and 160 MHz channels and, therefore, more unlicensed spectrum is needed. The FCC has also proposed simplification and standardization of the rules across the entire 5 GHz band. Another reassessment of how to prevent interference with radar satellite transmissions is also part of the proposal. Furthermore, the FCC proposal represents thinking on a global scale, as indicated by the following quote from the proposal: "We are particularly interested in gathering information on ongoing industry standards activity and international efforts to harmonize uses of the 5 GHz band to make more efficient use of the 5 GHz spectrum."

The National Telecommunication and Information Agency (NTIA) is a US government agency that advises the United States President on spectrum policy and they have also made recommendations based on the FCC proposal. The NTIA document is available at

www.ntia.doc.gov/files/ntia/publications/ntia_5_ghz_report_01-25-2013.pdf

The growth and future of Wi-Fi in the years ahead will be significantly affected by the proposed FCC rules when they are implemented.

3.6 GHz Band

In 2008, the 802.11y amendment was ratified. This amendment specified the use of the frequency range of 3.65 GHz to 3.7 GHz. This was approved as a licensed band for use in the United States. Unlike other licensed frequencies, the use of this frequency range was nonexclusive and included limitations when used near certain satellite earth stations. Although the project was designed for use in the United States, it was carefully designed to be able to operate in other countries without the need to ratify a new amendment (a process that can take several years to complete). It was designed to operate in any 5 MHz, 10 MHz, or 20 MHz channel. Regulators can make any frequency range available for use.

4.9 GHz Band

The 802.11-2012 standard defines the frequency range of 4.94 GHz to 4.99 GHz in the United States for public safety organizations to use for the protection of life, health, or property. This band is actually a licensed band and is reserved strictly for public safety. This frequency range has also been approved in other countries, such as Canada and Mexico.

In 2004, the 802.11j amendment was ratified, providing support for the 4.9 GHz to 5.091 GHz frequency range for use in Japan. This amendment was later incorporated in the 802.11-2012 standard.

Because of the proximity of these frequencies to the U-NII-1 band, we are seeing more wireless radios providing support for this band.

Future Wi-Fi Frequencies

The 2.4 GHz ISM band has remained the dominant license-free range of frequencies, known as a *frequency band*, that has been used for Wi-Fi communications since 1997. Although 802.11a was ratified in 1999, the use of the 5 GHz U-NII bands really did not start to catch on until about 2006. Wi-Fi use in the 5 GHz frequency bands continues to expand for a number of reasons: the 2.4 GHz band remains overcrowded, the 5 GHz bands are wider and have more channels, and the advent of 802.11ac will require more frequency space. As mentioned earlier, the FCC has already proposed 195 MHz more frequency space to be made available in two new 5 GHz U-NII bands. In the meantime, the IEEE continues to look toward other spectrum space for future Wi-Fi communications.

60 GHz

As mentioned in Chapter 5, the 802.11ad ratified amendment defines Very High Throughput (VHT) technology that will operate in the unlicensed 60 GHz frequency band. New PHY and MAC layer enhancements have the potential of accomplishing speeds of up to 7 Gbps. Since these ultrahigh frequencies have difficulty penetrating through walls, the technology will most likely be used to provide bandwidth-intensive and short distance communications indoors, such as high definition (HD) video streaming. The technology will not be backward compatible with other 802.11 technology. In September of 2012, the Wi-Fi Alliance designated the WiGig certification to test interoperability of products that operate in the 60 GHz band. The WiGig certification brand was designated with the new logo shown in Figure 6.2.

FIGURE 6.2   WiGig certification logo

Tri-band radios, such as the one in Figure 6.3, will have the capability to provide Wi-Fi access on 2.4 GHz, 5 GHz, and 60 GHz. This tri-band capability should provide for seamless handoff between devices in the short coverage area of the 60 GHz band and the greater coverage area of either the 2.4 GHz or 5 GHz band.

FIGURE 6.3   2.4 GHz, 5 GHz, and 60 GHz tri-band radio card

White-Fi

As mentioned in Chapter 5, *White-Fi* is a term used to describe the use of Wi-Fi technology in the unused television RF spectrum also known as TV white space. The 802.11af draft amendment proposes Wi-Fi operations within these unused frequency ranges. If this technology becomes a reality, one of the immediate gains will be greater range because the white space frequencies are below 1 GHz.

Narrowband and Spread Spectrum

There are two primary radio frequency (RF) transmission methods: *narrowband* and *spread spectrum*. A narrowband transmission uses very little bandwidth to transmit the data that it is carrying, whereas a spread spectrum transmission uses more bandwidth than is necessary to carry its data. Spread spectrum technology takes the data that is to be transmitted and spreads it across the frequencies that it is using. For example, a narrowband radio might transmit data on 2 MHz of frequency space at 80 watts, while a spread spectrum radio might transmit data over a 22 MHz frequency space at 100 milliwatts.

Figure 6.4 shows a rudimentary comparison of how a narrowband and spread spectrum signal relate to each other. Because narrowband signals take up a single or very narrow band of frequencies, intentional jamming or unintentional interference of this frequency range is likely to cause disruption in the signal. Because spread spectrum uses a wider range of frequency space, it is typically less susceptible to intentional jamming or unintentional interference from outside sources, unless the interfering signal was also spread across the range of frequencies used by the spread spectrum communications.

FIGURE 6.4   Overlay of narrowband and spread spectrum frequency use

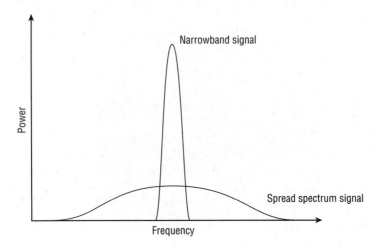

Narrowband signals are typically transmitted using much higher power than spread spectrum signals. Typically, the FCC or other local regulatory bodies require that narrowband transmitters be licensed to minimize the risk of two narrowband transmitters interfering with each other. AM and FM radio stations are examples of narrowband transmitters that are licensed to make sure that two stations in the same or nearby market are not transmitting on the same frequency.

Spread spectrum signals are transmitted using very low power levels.

 Real World Scenario

Who Invented Spread Spectrum?

Spread spectrum was originally patented on August 11, 1942, by actress Hedy Kiesler Markey (Hedy Lamarr) and composer George Antheil and was originally designed to be a radio guidance system for torpedoes, a purpose for which it was never used. The idea of spread spectrum was ahead of its time. It was not until 1957 that further development on spread spectrum occurred, and in 1962 frequency hopping spread spectrum was used for the first time between the US ships at the blockade of Cuba during the Cuban Missile Crisis.

If you would like to learn more about the interesting history of spread spectrum, search the Internet for Lamarr and Antheil. There are many websites with articles about these two inventors and even copies of the original patent. Neither inventor made any money from their patent because it expired before the technology was developed.

Multipath Interference

One of the problems that can occur with RF communications is *multipath* interference. Multipath occurs when a reflected signal arrives at the receiving antenna after the primary signal. Figure 6.5 illustrates a signal traveling from the client to the AP. In this illustration, you can see three different signals, each traveling a different path of different distance and duration. This is similar to the way an echo is heard after the original sound.

FIGURE 6.5   Multipath diagram

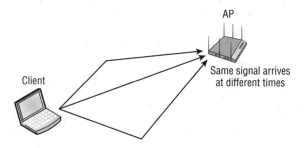

To illustrate multipath further, let us use an example of yelling to a friend across a canyon. Let's assume you are going to yell, "Hello, how are you?" to your friend. To make sure that your friend understands your message, you might pace your message and yell each word 1 second after the previous word. If your friend heard the echo (multipath reflection of your voice) a half-second after the main sound arrived, your friend would hear "HELLO hello HOW how ARE are YOU you" (echoes are represented by lowercase). Your friend would be able to interpret the message because the echo arrived between the main signals, or the sound of your voice. However, if the echo arrived 1 second after the main sound, the echo for the word *hello* would arrive at the same time the word *HOW* arrives. With both sounds arriving at the same time, it may not be possible to understand the message.

RF data communications behave the same way as the sound example. At the receiver, the delay between the main signal and the reflected signal is known as the *delay spread*. A typical delay spread in an indoor environment can vary from 30 to 270 nanoseconds (ns). If the delay spread is too great, data from the reflected signal may interfere with the same data stream from the main signal; this is referred to as *intersymbol interference (ISI)*. Spread spectrum systems are not as susceptible to ISI because they spread their signals across a range of frequencies. These various frequencies produce different delays in multipath, such that some wavelengths may be affected by ISI whereas others may not. Because of this behavior, spread spectrum signals are typically more tolerant of multipath interference than narrowband signals.

802.11 (DSSS), 802.11b (HR-DSSS), and 802.11g (ERP) are tolerant of delay spread only to a certain extent. 802.11 (DSSS) and 802.11b (HR-DSSS) can tolerate delay spread of up to 500 nanoseconds. Even though the delay spread can be tolerated, performance is much better when the delay spread is lower. The 802.11b transmitter will drop to a lower data rate when the delay spread increases. Longer symbols are used when transmitting at the lower data rates. When longer symbols are used, longer delays can occur before ISI occurs. According to some of the 802.11b vendors, 65 nanoseconds or lower delay spread is required for 802.11b at 11 Mbps.

Because of OFDM's greater tolerance of delay spread, an 802.11g transmitter can maintain 54 Mbps with a delay spread of up to about 150 nanoseconds. This depends on the 802.11g chipset that is being used in the transmitter and receiver. Some chipsets are not as tolerant and switch to a lower data rate at a lower delay spread value.

Prior to 802.11n and 802.11ac MIMO technology, multipath had always been a concern. It was a condition that could drastically affect the performance and throughput of the wireless LAN. With the introduction of MIMO, multipath is actually a condition that can now enhance and increase the performance of the wireless LAN. The enhanced digital signal processing techniques of 802.11n and 802.11ac take advantage of multiple simultaneous transmissions and can actually benefit from the effects of multipath. You will learn more about 802.11n and MIMO in Chapter 18, "High Throughput (HT) and 802.11n."

Frequency Hopping Spread Spectrum

Frequency hopping spread spectrum (FHSS) was used in the original 802.11 standard and provided 1 and 2 Mbps RF communications using the 2.4 GHz ISM band for legacy radios. The majority of legacy FHSS radios were manufactured between 1997 and 1999. The IEEE specified that in North America, 802.11 FHSS would use 79 MHz of frequencies, from 2.402 GHz to 2.480 GHz.

Generally, the way FHSS works is that it transmits data by using a small frequency carrier space, then hops to another small frequency carrier space and transmits data, then to another frequency, and so on, as illustrated in Figure 6.6. More specifically, FHSS transmits data by using a specific frequency for a set period of time, known as the *dwell time*. When the dwell time expires, the system changes to another frequency and begins to transmit on that frequency for the duration of the dwell time. Each time the dwell time is reached, the system changes to another frequency and continues to transmit.

FIGURE 6.6 FHSS components

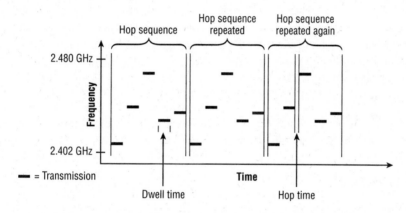

Hopping Sequence

FHSS radios use a predefined *hopping sequence* (also called a hopping pattern or hopping set) comprising a series of small carrier frequencies, or *hops*. Instead of transmitting on one set channel or finite frequency space, an FHSS radio transmits on a sequence of subchannels called hops. Each time the hop sequence is completed, it is repeated. Figure 6.6 shows a make-believe hopping sequence that consists of five hops.

The original IEEE 802.11 standard mandates that each hop is 1 MHz in size. These individual hops are then arranged in predefined sequences. In North America and most of Europe, the hopping sequences contain at least 75 hops, but no greater than 79 hops. Other countries have different requirements; for example, France uses 35 hops, while Spain and Japan use 23 hops in a sequence. For successful transmissions to occur, all FHSS transmitters and receivers must be synchronized on the same carrier hop at the same time. The 802.11 standard defines hopping sequences that can be configured on an FHSS access point, and the hopping sequence information is delivered to client stations via the beacon management frame.

Dwell Time

Dwell time is a defined amount of time that the FHSS system transmits on a specific frequency before it switches to the next frequency in the hop set. The local regulatory body typically limits the amount of dwell time. For example, the FCC specifies a maximum dwell time of 400 milliseconds (ms) per carrier frequency during any 30-second period of time. Typical dwell times are around 100 ms to 200 ms. The IEEE 802.11 standard specifies that a hopping sequence must consist of at least 75 frequencies, 1 MHz wide. Because the standard specifies a maximum bandwidth of 79 MHz, the maximum number of hops possible for a hop set would be 79. With an FHSS hop sequence consisting of 75 hops and a dwell time of 400 ms, it would take about 30 seconds to complete the hop sequence. After the hop sequence is complete, it is repeated.

Hop Time

Hop time is not a specified period of time but rather a measurement of the amount of time it takes for the transmitter to change from one frequency to another. Hop time is typically a fairly small number, often about 200 to 300 microseconds (μs). With typical dwell times of 100 to 200 milliseconds (ms), hop times of 200 to 300 μs are insignificant. Insignificant or not, the hop time is essentially wasted time, or overhead, and is the same regardless of the dwell time. The longer the dwell time, the less often the transmitter has to waste time hopping to another frequency, resulting in greater throughput. If the dwell time is shorter, the transmitter has to hop more frequently, thus decreasing throughput.

Modulation

FHSS uses Gaussian frequency shift keying (GFSK) to encode the data. Two-level GFSK (2GFSK) uses two frequencies to represent a 0 or a 1 bit. Four-level GFSK (4GFSK) uses four frequencies, with each frequency representing 2 bits (00, 01, 10, or 11). Because it takes transmission cycles before the frequency can be determined, the symbol rate (the rate that the data is sent) is only about 1 or 2 million symbols per second, a fraction of the 2.4 GHz carrier frequency.

What Is the Significance of the Dwell Time?

Because FHSS transmissions jump inside a frequency range of 79 MHz, a narrowband signal or noise would disrupt only a small range of frequencies and would produce only a minimal amount of throughput loss. Decreasing the dwell time can further reduce the effect of interference. Conversely, because the radio is transmitting data during the dwell time, the longer the dwell time, the greater the throughput.

802.11 FHSS technology is rarely used anymore, and you will not be tested about FHSS on the CWNA exam. 802.11 vendors stopped manufacturing 802.11 FHSS adapters and access points a long time ago. Most organizations have long since transitioned from 802.11 FHSS to one of the newer and faster transmission methods. It is still important to understand the basics behind FHSS, as there are other technologies, such as Bluetooth, that use FHSS. Be aware that even though Bluetooth uses FHSS, the number of hops, dwell time, and hopping sequence is very different than 802.11 FHSS. It is also important to note that Bluetooth does operate in the 2.4 GHz ISM band, the same band used by 802.11/b/g/n devices.

Direct Sequence Spread Spectrum

Direct sequence spread spectrum (DSSS) was originally specified in the primary, or root, 802.11 standard and provides 1 and 2 Mbps RF communications using the 2.4 GHz ISM band. An updated implementation of DSSS (HR-DSSS) was also specified in the 802.11b addendum and provides 5.5 and 11 Mbps RF communications using the same 2.4 GHz ISM band. The 802.11b 5.5 and 11 Mbps speeds are known as *High-Rate DSSS (HR-DSSS)*.

802.11b devices are backward compatible with the legacy 802.11 DSSS devices. This means that an 802.11b device can transmit using DSSS at 1 and 2 Mbps and using HR-DSSS at 5.5 and 11 Mbps. However, 802.11b devices are not capable of transmitting using FHSS; therefore, they are not backward compatible with 802.11 FHSS devices.

DSSS 1 and 2 Mbps are specified in Clause 16 of the 802.11-2012 standard. HR-DSSS 5.5 and 11 Mbps are specified in Clause 17 of the 802.11-2012 standard.

Unlike FHSS, where the transmitter jumped between frequencies, DSSS is set to one channel. The data that is being transmitted is spread across the range of frequencies that make up the channel. The process of spreading the data across the channel is known as *data encoding*.

DSSS Data Encoding

In Chapter 2, "Radio Frequency Fundamentals," you learned about the many ways that RF signals can get altered or corrupted. Because 802.11 uses an unbounded medium with a huge potential for RF interference, it had to be designed to be resilient enough that data corruption could be minimized. To achieve this, each bit of data is encoded and transmitted as multiple bits of data.

The task of adding additional, redundant information to the data is known as *processing gain*. In this day and age of data compression, it seems strange that we would use a technology that adds data to our transmission, but by doing so, the communication is more resistant to data corruption. The system converts the 1 bit of data into a series of bits that are referred to as *chips*. To create the chips, a Boolean XOR is performed on the data bit and a fixed-length bit sequence pseudorandom number (PN) code. Using a PN code known as the Barker code, the binary data 1 and 0 are represented by the following chip sequences:

Binary data 1 = 1 0 1 1 0 1 1 1 0 0 0

Binary data 0 = 0 1 0 0 1 0 0 0 1 1 1

This sequence of chips is then spread across a wider frequency space. Although 1 bit of data might need only 2 MHz of frequency space, the 11 chips will require 22 MHz of frequency carrier space. This process of converting a single data bit into a sequence is often called *spreading* or *chipping*. The receiving radio converts, or *de-spreads*, the chip sequence back into a single data bit. When the data is converted to multiple chips and some of the chips are not received properly, the radio will still be able to interpret the data by looking at the chips that were received properly. When the Barker code is used, as many as 9 of the 11 chips can be corrupted, yet the receiving radio will still be able to interpret the sequence and convert them back into a single data bit. This chipping process also makes the communication less likely to be affected by intersymbol interference because it uses more bandwidth.

After the Barker code is applied to data, a series of 11 bits, referred to as chips, represent the original single bit of data. This series of encoded bits makes up 1 bit of data. To help prevent confusion, it is best to think of and refer to the encoded bits as *chips*.

The Barker code uses an 11-chip PN; however, the length of the code is irrelevant. To help provide the faster speeds of HR-DSSS, another more complex code, *Complementary Code Keying (CCK)*, is utilized. CCK uses an 8-chip PN, along with using different PNs for different bit sequences. CCK can encode 4 bits of data with 8 chips (5.5 Mbps) and can encode 8 bits of data with 8 chips (11 Mbps). Although it is interesting to learn about, a thorough understanding of CCK is not required for the CWNA exam.

Modulation

After the data has been encoded using a chipping method, the transmitter needs to modulate the signal to create a carrier signal containing the chips. *Differential binary phase shift keying (DBPSK)* utilizes two phase shifts, one that represents a 0 chip and another that represents a 1 chip. To provide faster throughput, *differential quadrature phase shift keying (DQPSK)* utilizes four phase shifts, allowing each of the four phase shifts to modulate 2 chips (00, 01, 10, 11) instead of just 1 chip, doubling the speed.

Table 6.3 shows a summary of the data encoding and modulation techniques used by 802.11 and 802.11b.

TABLE 6.3   DSSS and HR-DSSS encoding and modulation overview

	Data rate (Mbps)	Encoding	Chip length	Bits encoded	Modulation
DSSS	1	Barker coding	11	1	DBPSK
DSSS	2	Barker coding	11	1	DQPSK
HR-DSSS	5.5	CCK coding	8	4	DQPSK
HR-DSSS	11	CCK coding	8	8	DQPSK

Packet Binary Convolutional Code

Packet Binary Convolutional Code (PBCC) is a modulation technique that supports data rates of 5.5, 11, 22, and 33 Mbps; however, both the transmitter and receiver must support the technology to achieve the higher speeds. PBCC was developed by Alantro Communications, which was purchased by Texas Instruments. PBCC modulation was originally defined as optional under the 802.1b amendment. The introduction of the 802.11g amendment allowed for two additional optional ERP-PBCC modulation modes with payload data rates of 22 and 33 Mbps.

PBCC and ERP-PBCC technology was seen for a short time in the SOHO marketplace. However, the technology was rarely deployed in an enterprise environment.

Orthogonal Frequency Division Multiplexing

Orthogonal Frequency Division Multiplexing (OFDM) is one of the most popular communications technologies, used in both wired and wireless communications. The 802.11-2012 standard specifies the use of OFDM at 5 GHz and also specifies the use of ERP-OFDM at 2.4 GHz. As mentioned in Chapter 5, OFDM and ERP-OFDM are the same technology. OFDM is not a spread spectrum technology, even though it has similar properties to spread spectrum, such as low transmit power and using more bandwidth than is required to transmit data. Because of these similarities, OFDM is often referred to as a spread spectrum technology even though technically that reference is incorrect. OFDM actually transmits across 52 separate, closely and precisely spaced frequencies, often referred to as *subcarriers*, as illustrated in Figure 6.7.

FIGURE 6.7   802.11 Channels and OFDM subcarriers

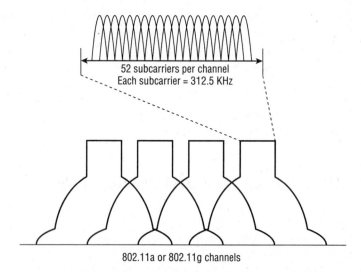

802.11a or 802.11g channels

The frequency width of each subcarrier is 312.5 KHz. The subcarriers are also transmitted at lower data rates, but because there are so many subcarriers, overall data rates are higher. Also, because of the lower subcarrier data rates, delay spread is a smaller percentage of the symbol period, which means that ISI is less likely to occur. In other words, OFDM technology is more resistant to the negative effects of multipath than DSSS and FHSS spread spectrum technologies. Figure 6.8 represents four of the 52 subcarriers. One of the subcarriers is highlighted so that you can more easily understand the drawing. Notice that the frequency spacing of the subcarriers has been chosen so that the harmonics overlap and provide cancellation of most of the unwanted signals.

FIGURE 6.8 Subcarrier signal overlay

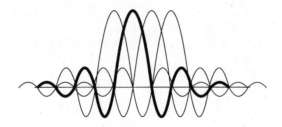

The 52 subcarriers are numbered from –26 to +26. Forty-eight of the subcarriers are used to transmit data. The other four, numbers –21, –7, +7, and +21, are known as *pilot carriers*. These four are used as references for phase and amplitude by the demodulator, allowing the receiver to synchronize itself as it demodulates the data in the other subcarriers.

Convolutional Coding

To make OFDM more resistant to narrowband interference, a form of error correction known as *convolutional coding* is performed. The 802.11-2012 standard defines the use of convolutional coding as the error-correction method to be used with OFDM technology. It is a *forward error correction (FEC)* that allows the receiving system to detect and repair corrupted bits.

There are many levels of convolutional coding. Convolutional coding uses a ratio between the bits transmitted vs. the bits encoded to provide these different levels. The lower the ratio, the less resistant the signal is to interference and the greater the data rate will be. Table 6.4 displays a comparison between the technologies used to create the different data rates of both 802.11a and 802.11g. Notice that the data rates are grouped by pairs based on modulation technique and that the difference between the two speeds is caused by the different levels of convolutional coding. A detailed explanation of convolutional coding is extremely complex and far beyond the knowledge needed for the CWNA exam.

TABLE 6.4 802.11a and 802.11g data rate and modulation comparison

Data rates (Mbps)	Modulation method	Coded bits per subcarrier	Data bits per OFDM symbol	Coded bits per OFDM symbol	Coding rate (data bits/coded bits)
6	BPSK	1	24	48	1/2
9	BPSK	1	36	48	3/4
12	QPSK	2	48	96	1/2
18	QPSK	2	72	96	3/4

TABLE 6.4   802.11a and 802.11g data rate and modulation comparison *(continued)*

Data rates (Mbps)	Modulation method	Coded bits per subcarrier	Data bits per OFDM symbol	Coded bits per OFDM symbol	Coding rate (data bits/ coded bits)
24	16-QAM	4	96	192	1/2
36	16-QAM	4	144	192	3/4
48	64-QAM	6	192	288	2/3
54	64-QAM	6	216	288	3/4

Modulation

OFDM uses binary phase shift keying (BPSK) and quadrature phase shift keying (QPSK) phase modulation for the lower ODFM data rates. The higher OFDM data rates use 16-QAM and 64-QAM modulation. *Quadrature amplitude modulation (QAM)* is a hybrid of phase and amplitude modulation. The 802.11ac amendment also introduced the use of 256-QAM. A *constellation diagram*, also known as a constellation map, is a two-dimensional diagram often used to represent QAM modulation. A constellation diagram is divided into four quadrants, and different locations in each quadrant can be used to represent data bits. Areas on the quadrant relative to the horizontal axis can be used to represent various phase shifts. Areas relative to the vertical axis are used to represent amplitude shifts. A 16-QAM constellation diagram uses sixteen different combinations of phase and amplitude shifts, as shown in Figure 6.9. Each of the sixteen different points within the four quadrants can be used to represent four data bits.

FIGURE 6.9   16-QAM constellation diagram

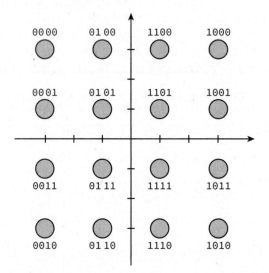

2.4 GHz Channels

To better understand how legacy 802.11 (DSSS), 802.11b (HR-DSSS), and 802.11g (ERP) radios are used, it is important to know how the IEEE 802.11-2012 standard divides the 2.4 GHz ISM band into 14 separate channels, as listed in Table 6.5. Although the 2.4 GHz ISM band is divided into 14 channels, the FCC or local regulatory body designates which channels are allowed to be used. Table 6.5 also shows a sample of how channel support can vary.

TABLE 6.5   2.4 GHz frequency channel plan

Channel ID	Center frequency (GHz)	US (FCC)	Canada (IC)	Many European countries
1	2.412	X	X	X
2	2.417	X	X	X
3	2.422	X	X	X
4	2.427	X	X	X
5	2.432	X	X	X
6	2.437	X	X	X
7	2.442	X	X	X
8	2.447	X	X	X
9	2.452	X	X	X
10	2.457	X	X	X
11	2.462	X	X	X
12	2.467			X
13	2.472			X
14	2.484			

X = supported channel

Channels are designated by their center frequency. How wide the channel is depends on the technology used by the 802.11 transmitter. When DSSS and HR-DSSS 802.11 radios are transmitting, each channel is 22 MHz wide and is often referenced by the center frequency ± 11 MHz. For example, channel 1 is 2.412 GHz ± 11 MHz, which means that channel 1 spans from 2.401 GHz to 2.423 GHz. It should also be noted that within the 2.4 GHz ISM band, the distance between channel center frequencies is only 5 MHz. Because each channel is 22 MHz wide, and because the separation between center frequencies of each channel is only 5 MHz, the channels will have overlapping frequency space. With the introduction of OFDM in 802.11a, along with its expanded use in 802.11g, 802.11n, and 802.11ac, the frequency width used by an OFDM channel is approximately 20 MHz (as defined by the spectral mask, which you will learn about later in this chapter).

Figure 6.10 shows an overlay of all the channels and how they overlap. Channels 1, 6, and 11 have been highlighted because, as you can see, they are separated from each other by enough frequencies that they do not overlap. In order for two channels to not overlap, they must be separated by at least five channels or 25 MHz. Channels such as 2 and 9 do not overlap, but when 2 and 9 are selected, there is no additional legal channel that can be chosen that does not overlap either 2 or 9. In the United States and Canada, the only three simultaneously nonoverlapping channels are 1, 6, and 11. In regions where channels 1 through 13 are allowed to be used, there are different combinations of three nonoverlapping channels, although channels 1, 6, and 11 are commonly chosen. Enterprise deployments of three or more access points in the 2.4 GHz ISM band normally use channels 1, 6, and 11, which are all considered nonoverlapping.

FIGURE 6.10   2.4 GHz channel overlay diagram

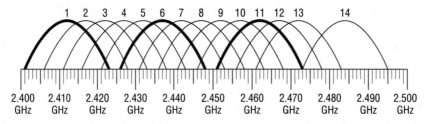

The IEEE 802.11-2012 definitions of nonoverlapping channels in the 2.4 GHz ISM band can be somewhat confusing if not properly explained. Legacy 802.11 (DSSS), 802.11b (HR-DSSS), and 802.11g (ERP) channels all use the same numbering schemes and have the same center frequencies. However, the individual channels' frequency space may overlap. Figure 6.11 shows channels 1, 6, and 11 with 25 MHz of spacing between the center frequencies. These are the most commonly used *nonoverlapping channels* in North America and most of the world for 802.11b/g/n networks.

FIGURE 6.11   HR-DSSS center frequencies

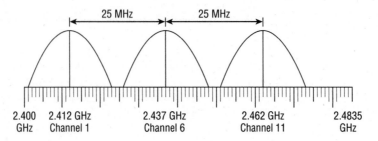

What exactly classifies DSSS or HR-DSSS channels as nonoverlapping? According to the original 802.11 standard, legacy DSSS channels had to have at least 30 MHz of spacing between the center frequencies to be considered nonoverlapping. In a deployment of legacy DSSS equipment using a channel pattern of 1, 6, and 11, the channels were considered overlapping because the center frequencies were only 25 MHz apart. Although DSSS channels 1, 6, and 11 were defined as overlapping, these were still the only three channels used in channel reuse patterns when legacy networks were deployed. This is of little significance anymore because most 2.4 GHz deployments now use 802.11b/g/n technology.

HR-DSSS was introduced under the 802.11b amendment, which states that channels need a minimum of 25 MHz of separation between the center frequencies to be considered nonoverlapping. Therefore, when 802.11b was introduced, channels 1, 6, and 11 were considered nonoverlapping.

The 802.11g amendment, which allows for backward compatibility with 802.11b HR-DSSS, also requires 25 MHz of separation between the center frequencies to be considered nonoverlapping. Under the 802.11g amendment, channels 1, 6, and 11 are also considered nonoverlapping for both ERP-DSSS/CCK and ERP-OFDM.

Although it is very common to represent the RF signal of a particular channel with an arch-type line, this is not a true representation of the signal. As an example, in addition to the main *carrier frequency*, or main frequency, sideband carrier frequencies are generated, as shown in Figure 6.12. In this example, the IEEE defines a *transmit spectrum mask*, specifying that the first sideband frequency (–11 MHz to –22 MHz from the center frequency and +11 MHz to +22 MHz from the center frequency) must be at least 30 dB less than the main frequency. The mask also specifies that any additional sideband carrier frequencies (–22 MHz from the center frequency and beyond and +22 MHz from the center frequency and beyond) must be at least 50 dB less than the main frequency.

FIGURE 6.12   IEEE 802.11b transmit spectrum mask

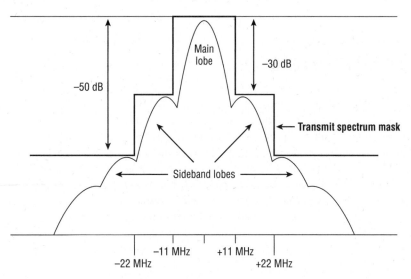

Figure 6.12 illustrates the transmit spectrum mask of an HR-DSSS channel at 2.4 GHz. The transmit spectrum mask is defined to minimize interference between devices on different frequencies. Even though the sideband carrier frequencies are mere whispers of signals compared to the main carrier frequency, even a whisper is noticeable when the person whispering is close to you. This is true for RF devices too.

Figure 6.13 represents 802.11b RF signals on channels 1, 6, and 11. A signal-level line indicates an arbitrary level of reception by the access point on channel 6. At level 1, meaning the AP on channel 6 receives only the signals above the level 1 line, the signals from channel 1 and channel 11 do not intersect (interfere) with the signals on channel 6. However, at the level 2 line, the signals from channel 1 and channel 11 do intersect (interfere) slightly with the signals on channel 6. At the level 3 line, there is significant interference from the signals from channel 1 and channel 11. Because of the potential for this situation, it is important to separate access points (usually 5 to 10 feet is sufficient) so that interference from sideband frequencies does not occur. This separation is important both horizontally and vertically.

FIGURE 6.13 Sideband carrier frequency interference

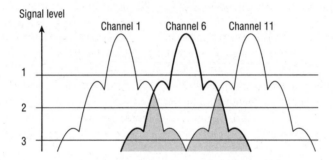

5 GHz Channels

802.11a/n and 802.11ac radios transmit in the 5 GHz U-NII bands: U-NII-1, U-NII-2, U-NII-2 Extended, and U-NII-3. To prevent interference with other possible bands, extra bandwidth is used as a guard. In the U-NII-1 and U-NII-2 bands, the centers of the outermost channels of each band must be 30 MHz from the band's edge. An extra 20 MHz of bandwidth exits in the U-NII-3 band. The unused bandwidth at the edge of each band is known as a *guard band*. The original three U-NII bands each had four nonoverlapping channels with 20 MHz separation between the center frequencies. A fifth channel was recently added to U-NII-3. The U-NII-2 Extended band has twelve nonoverlapping channels with 20 MHz of separation between the center frequencies. The U-NII-2 Extended band was an eleven channel band for many years, but an extra channel, 144, was added to the band with the advent of 802.11ac. If you want to calculate the center frequency of a channel, multiply the channel by 5 and then add 5000 to the result. (e.g. Channel 36 times 5 equals 180, then add 5000, for a center frequency of 5180 MHz, or 5.18 GHz.)

Figure 6.14 shows the eight U-NII-1 and U-NII-2 channels in the top graphic, the twelve U-NII-2 Extended channels in the center graphic, and the five U-NII-3 channels in the bottom graphic. Channel 36 is highlighted so that it is easier to distinguish a single carrier and its sideband frequencies. The IEEE does not specifically define a channel width; however, the spectral mask of an OFDM channel is approximately 20 MHz.

FIGURE 6.14   U-NII channels

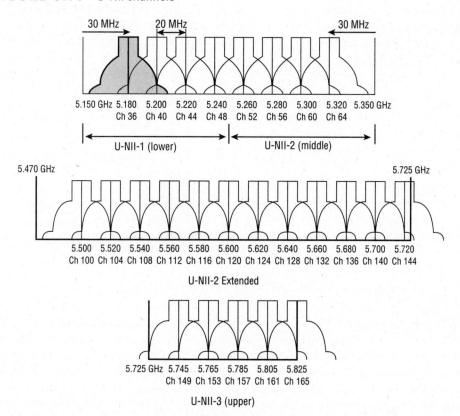

Figure 6.15 depicts a wide overview of all of the 5 GHz channels that can currently be used by 802.11 transmitters. A total of twenty-five 20 MHz channels in the 5 GHz U-NII bands can be used when designing a WLAN with a channel reuse pattern. The channels you can use, of course, depend on the regulations of each country. For example, in most

of Europe, the U-NII-3 band is still considered a licensed band, meaning that only twenty channels are available for a channel reuse pattern. In the United States, all the channels were available until 2009. Notice in Figure 6.15 that DFS is required in U-NII-2 and U-NII-2E channels. In these bands, 802.11 radios are required to use dynamic frequency selection (DFS) to avoid interference with radar. In 2009, the Federal Aviation Authority (FAA) reported interference with *Terminal Doppler Weather Radar (TDWR)* systems. As a result, the FCC suspended certification of 802.11 devices in the U-NII-2 and U-NII-2E bands that required DFS. Eventually, certification was reestablished; however, the rules changed and 802.11 radios were not allowed to transmit in the 5.60 GHz – 5.65 GHz frequency space where TDWR operates. As shown in Figure 6.15, channels 120, 124, and 128 reside in the TDWR frequency space and could not be used for many years in the United States; therefore not all channels were available for a 20 MHz channel reuse. The good news is that as of April 2014, the FCC changed the rules and the TDWR frequency space is once again available. It should also be noted that many enterprise WLAN deployments have completely avoided the use of the DFS channels altogether because many client devices simply have not been certified for any of the DFS channels. A more detailed discussion of 5 GHz Channel reuse patterns and channel planning will be covered in Chapter 12, "WLAN Troubleshooting."

FIGURE 6.15   U-NII channel overview

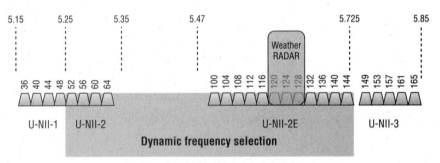

802.11n technology introduced the capability of bonding together two 20 MHz channels to create a larger 40 MHz channel. Channel bonding effectively doubles the frequency bandwidth, meaning double the data rates that can be available to 802.11n radios. 40 MHz channels will be discussed in greater detail in Chapter 18, "802.11n." As shown in Figure 6.16, a total of twelve 40 MHz channels are available to be used in a reuse pattern when deploying an enterprise WLAN. However, in the past, two of the 40 MHz channels have not been used in the United States because they fall within the TDWR band. In Europe, two of the 40 MHz channels cannot be used because they fall within the U-NII-3 band that requires licensing in many countries.

Figure 16.6 also depicts the 80 MHz channels and 160 MHz channels that could possibly be used by 802.11ac radios. In reality, there is not enough frequency space to provide for enough of these channels for proper channel reuse patterns. 802.11ac capabilities, including 80 MHz and 160 MHz channels, are discussed in Chapter 19, "Very High Throughput (VHT) and 802.11ac."

FIGURE 6.16   U-NII 40 MHz, 80 MHz, and 160 MHz channels

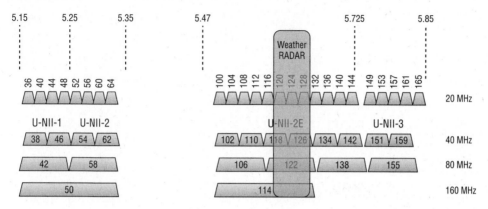

As mentioned earlier in this chapter, the FCC has proposed two more U-NII bands with 195 MHz of frequency space for unlicensed use by 802.11 radios. The FCC has also proposed the simplification and standardization of the rules across the entire 5 GHz band. As of April 2014, DFS rules for radar detection and avoidance have changed and the frequency band used for weather radar is now available for Wi-Fi radios. Should all these proposals be implemented and all the 5 GHz spectrum space be made available, there would be as many as thirty-seven 20 MHz channels that could be used by Wi-Fi radios, as depicted in Figure 6.17.

FIGURE 6.17   Potential U-NII-1 through U-NII-4 20 MHz channels

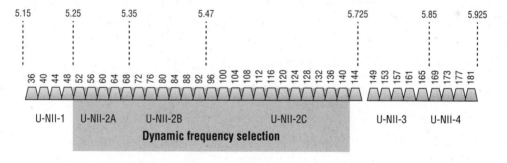

As 802.11ac technology becomes more commonplace, the need for the extra frequency space is even more important. As shown in Figure 6.18, if all the U-NII-1 through U-NII-4 spectrum is indeed made available, channel reuse patterns using larger channels can become a reality. A total of eighteen 40 MHz channels would be available for 802.11n or 802.11ac radios. A reuse pattern of nine 80-MHz channels could be designed for use by 802.11ac radios. There would even be enough frequency space for four 160 MHz channels that could be used by a second generation of 802.11ac radio chipsets in the near future. Please keep in mind that the proposed extra spectrum is still not currently available and that rules and regulations about frequency use can vary from country to country.

FIGURE 6.18 Potential 40 MHz, 80 MHz, and 160 MHz channels

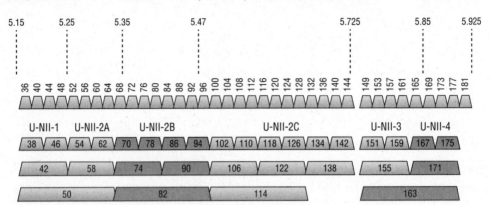

As stated earlier, the IEEE does not specifically define a channel width; however, the spectral mask of an OFDM channel is approximately 20 MHz. The spectral mask of 802.11n or 802.11ac bonded channels is obviously much larger.

As seen in Figure 6.19 of the OFDM spectrum mask, the sideband carrier frequencies do not drop off very quickly, and therefore the sideband frequencies of two adjacent valid channels overlap and are more likely to cause interference. The 802.11a amendment, which originally defined the use of OFDM, required only 20 MHz of separation between the center frequencies for channels to be considered nonoverlapping. All 20 MHz channels in the 5 GHz U-NII bands use OFDM and have 20 MHz of separation between the center frequencies. Therefore, all 5 GHz OFDM channels are considered nonoverlapping by the IEEE. In reality, some sideband carrier frequency overlap exists between any two adjacent 5 GHz channels. Luckily, due to the number of channels and the channel spacing, it is easy to separate adjacent channels and prevent interference with a proper channel reuse plan.

FIGURE 6.19 OFDM spectrum mask

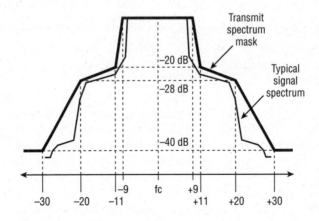

Adjacent, Nonadjacent, and Overlapping Channels

In the preceding paragraphs, you learned how the IEEE 802.11-2012 standard defines nonoverlapping channels. DSSS (legacy) channels require 30 MHz of separation between the center frequencies to be considered nonoverlapping. HR-DSSS (802.11b) and ERP (802.11g) channels require 25 MHz of separation between the center frequencies to be considered nonoverlapping. And finally, 5 GHz OFDM channels require 20 MHz of separation between the center frequencies to be considered nonoverlapping. Why are these definitions important? When deploying a WLAN, it is important to have overlapping cell coverage for roaming to occur. However, it is just as important for these coverage cells not to have overlapping frequency space. A channel reuse pattern is needed because overlapping frequency space causes degradation in performance. The design aspects of channel reuse patterns are discussed in great detail in Chapter 12, "WLAN Troubleshooting."

An often debated topic is what defines an *adjacent channel*. The 802.11-2012 standard loosely defines an adjacent channel as any channel with nonoverlapping frequencies for the DSSS and HR-DSSS PHYs. With ERP and OFDM PHYs, the standard loosely defines an adjacent channel as the first channel with a nonoverlapping frequency space. In other words, the IEEE definition of adjacent channels is almost exactly the same as the definition of nonoverlapping channels that has been discussed earlier. Although not specifically defined, single-channel 2.4 GHz HT (802.11n) devices would follow the 802.11g definitions, and single-channel 5 GHz HT devices would follow the 802.11a definitions. Confused? Table 6.6 illustrates the CWNP program's interpretation of these concepts.

 Real World Scenario

What Is the Significance of Adjacent Channels?

The IEEE's loose definition of adjacent channels contradicts how the term *adjacent channel interference* is used in the WLAN marketplace. Most Wi-Fi vendors use the term *adjacent channel interference* to refer to the degradation of performance resulting from overlapping frequency space that occurs because of an improper channel reuse design. In the WLAN industry, an adjacent channel is considered to be the next or previous numbered channel. For example, channel 3 is adjacent to channel 2. We recommend that you do not get caught up in the IEEE's definition of adjacent channels that was covered earlier in this paragraph and in Table 6.6. The definition of adjacent channels that the Wi-Fi industry has adopted is much more commonplace. The concept of adjacent channel interference is discussed in detail in Chapter 12.

TABLE 6.6   IEEE adjacent and overlapping channels

	DSSS (802.11)	HR-DSSS (802.11b)	ERP (802.11g)	OFDM (802.11a)
Frequency band	2.4 GHz ISM	2.4 GHz ISM	2.4 GHz ISM	U-NII bands
Adjacent	≥ 30 MHz	≥ 25 MHz	= 25 MHz	= 20 MHz
Overlapping	< 30 MHz	< 25 MHz	< 25 MHz	N/A

Throughput vs. Bandwidth

Wireless communication is typically performed within a constrained set of frequencies known as a frequency band. This frequency band is the *bandwidth*. Frequency bandwidth does play a part in the eventual throughput of the data, but many other factors also determine throughput. In addition to frequency bandwidth, data encoding, modulation, medium contention, encryption, and many other factors also play a large part in data throughput.

Care should be taken not to confuse frequency bandwidth with data bandwidth. Data encoding and modulation determine data rates, which are sometimes also referred to as data bandwidth. Simply look at the 5 GHz channels and OFDM as an example. OFDM 802.11a radios can transmit at 6, 9, 12, 18, 24, 36, 48, or 54 Mbps, yet the frequency bandwidth for all the U-NII band channels is the same for all of these speeds. What changes between all of these speeds (data rates) is the modulation and coding technique. The proper term for the changes in speed due to modulation and coding is *data rates*; however, they are also often referred to as *data bandwidth*.

One of the surprising facts when explaining wireless networking to a layperson is the actual throughput that an 802.11 wireless network provides. When novices walk through a computer store and see the packages of 802.11 devices, they likely assume that a device that is labeled as 300 Mbps is going to provide throughput of 300 Mbps. A medium access method known as Carrier Sense Multiple Access with Collision Avoidance (CSMA/CA) attempts to ensure that only one radio device can be transmitting on the medium at any given time. Because of the half-duplex nature of the medium and the overhead generated by CSMA/CA, the actual aggregate throughput is typically 50 percent or less of the data rates for 802.11a/b/g legacy transmissions, and 60-70 percent of the data rates for 802.11n/ac transmissions. In addition to the throughput being affected by the half-duplex nature of 802.11 communications, the throughput is affected differently based on the frequency used. HT and OFDM technologies are used in both the 5 GHz and 2.4 GHz bands. Because of the higher level of RF noise that is typical in the 2.4 GHz ISM band, throughput of 2.4 GHz devices will typically be less than the 5 GHz devices.

It is also very important to understand that the 802.11 RF medium is a *shared* medium, meaning that in any discussion of throughput, it should be thought of as *aggregate throughput*. For example, if a data rate is 54 Mbps, because of CSMA/CA, the aggregate throughput might be about 20 Mbps. If five client stations were all downloading the same file from an FTP server at the same time, the perceived throughput for each client station would be about 4 Mbps under ideal circumstances. When 802.11n and 802.11ac radios are used, the aggregate throughput is typically 65 percent of the advertised data rate. The medium contention overhead created by CSMA/CA is typically about 35 percent of the bandwidth. Medium contention overhead is 50 percent or more when using legacy 802.11a/b/g radios.

RTS/CTS (which you will learn about in Chapter 9, "802.11 MAC Architecture") can also affect throughput by adding communication overhead. In some environments, fragmentation and RTS/CTS can actually increase throughput if the initial throughput was low because of communication problems.

Variables at almost all layers of the OSI model can affect the throughput of 802.11 communications. It is important to understand the different causes, their effects, and what, if anything, can be done to minimize their effect on overall data throughput.

Communication Resilience

Many technologies that have been covered in this chapter either directly or indirectly provide resilience to 802.11 communications. Spread spectrum spreads the data across a range of frequencies, making it less likely for a narrowband RF signal to cause interference. FHSS is inherently more resilient to narrowband interference than OFDM, and OFDM is more resilient to narrowband interference than DSSS. Spread spectrum technology uses a range of frequencies, which inherently adds resilience because delay spread and ISI will vary between the different frequencies. Additionally, data encoding provides error recovery methods, helping to reduce the need for retransmission of the data.

Summary

This chapter focused on the technologies that make up wireless networking and spread spectrum. 802.11, 802.11b, 802.11g, and 802.11n radios use the 2.4 GHz ISM band, while 802.11a/n and 802.11ac radios use 5 GHz U-NII bands. 802.11n HT radios can use both the 2.4 GHz ISM band and the 5 GHz U-NII bands. The ISM and U-NII bands discussed in this chapter are as follows:

- ISM 902 – 928 MHz—industrial
- ISM 2.4 – 2.5 GHz—scientific
- ISM 5.725 – 5.875 GHz—medical
- U-NII-1 5.150 – 5.250 GHz—lower

- U-NII-2 5.250 – 5.350 GHz—middle (also known as U-NII-2A in the proposed frequency updates)
- U-NII-2 extended 5.470 – 5.725 GHz—Extended (also known as U-NII-2C in the proposed frequency updates)
- U-NII-3 5.725 – 5.85 GHz—upper
- Proposed U-NII-2B 5.35 – 5.47 GHz
- Proposed U-NII-4 5.85 – 5.925 GHz

In addition to the ISM and U-NII bands, the following bands were discussed:

- 4.94–4.99 GHz—US public safety
- 4.9–5.091 GHz—Japan
- 60 GHz
- < 1 GHz—White-Fi

Spread spectrum technology was introduced and described in detail along with OFDM and convolutional coding. The following are key spread spectrum technologies and terms that we discussed:

- FHSS
- Dwell time
- Hop time
- DSSS

This chapter ended with a comparison of throughput and bandwidth and a review of the communication resilience of the technologies used in 802.11.

Exam Essentials

Know the technical specifications of all the ISM and U-NII bands.   Make sure that you know all of the frequencies, bandwidth uses, and channels. Be sure to understand the potential effects of the proposed extra 195 MHz of frequency space and what it means for available channels in 5 GHz.

Know spread spectrum.   Spread spectrum can be complicated and has different flavors. Understand FHSS, DSSS, and OFDM (although OFDM is not a spread spectrum technology, it has similar properties and you have to know it). Understand how coding and modulation work with spread spectrum and OFDM.

Understand the similarities and differences between the transmission methods discussed in this chapter.   There are differences and similarities between many of the topics in this chapter. Carefully compare and understand them. Minor subtleties can be difficult to recognize when you are taking the test.

Review Questions

1. Which of the following are valid ISM bands? (Choose all that apply.)
   A. 902 MHz – 928 MHz
   B. 2.4 GHz – 2.5 GHz
   C. 5.725 GHz – 5.85 GHz
   D. 5.725 GHz – 5.875 GHz

2. Which of the following are valid U-NII bands? (Choose all that apply.)
   A. 5.150 GHz – 5.250 GHz
   B. 5.470 GHz – 5.725 GHz
   C. 5.725 GHz – 5.85 GHz
   D. 5.725 GHz – 5.875 GHz

3. Which technologies are used in the 2.4 GHz ISM band? (Choose all that apply.)
   A. FHSS
   B. ERP
   C. DSSS
   D. HR-DSSS

4. 802.11n (HT radios) can transmit in which frequency bands? (Choose all that apply.)
   A. 2.4 GHz – 2.4835 GHz
   B. 5.47 GHz – 5.725 GHz
   C. 902 GHz – 928 GHz
   D. 5.15 GHz – 5.25 GHz

5. In the U-NII-1 band, what is the center frequency of channel 40?
   A. 5.2 GHz
   B. 5.4 GHz
   C. 5.8 GHz
   D. 5.140 GHz

6. What is the channel and band of a Wi-Fi transmission whose center frequency is 5.300 GHz?
   A. U-NII-1 channel 30
   B. U-NII-1 channel 60
   C. U-NII-2 channel 30
   D. U-NII-2 channel 60

7. The 802.11-2012 standard requires how much separation between center frequencies for HR-DSSS channels to be considered nonoverlapping?

   A. 22 MHz

   B. 25 MHz

   C. 30 MHz

   D. 35 MHz

   E. 40 MHz

8. What best describes *hop time*?

   A. The period of time that the transmitter waits before hopping to the next frequency

   B. The period of time that the standard requires when hopping between frequencies

   C. The period of time that the transmitter takes to hop to the next frequency

   D. The period of time the transmitter takes to hop through all of the FHSS frequencies

9. As defined by the IEEE-2012 standard, how much separation is needed between center frequencies of channels in the U–NII-2 Extended band?

   A. 10 MHz

   B. 20 MHz

   C. 22 MHz

   D. 25 MHz

   E. 30 MHz

10. When deploying an 802.11g (ERP-OFDM) wireless network with only two access points, which of these channel groupings would be considered nonoverlapping? (Choose all that apply.)

   A. Channels 1 and 3

   B. Channels 7 and 10

   C. Channels 3 and 8

   D. Channels 5 and 11

   E. Channels 6 and 10

11. Which spread spectrum technology specifies data rates of 22 Mbps and 33 Mbps?

   A. DSSS

   B. ERP-PBCC

   C. OFDM

   D. PPtP

12. If data is corrupted by previous data from a reflected signal, this is known as what?

   A. Delay spread

   B. ISI

    C. Forward error creation

    D. Bit crossover

13. Assuming all channels are supported by a 5 GHz access point, how many possible 20 MHz channels can be configured on the access point?

    A. 4

    B. 11

    C. 12

    D. 25

14. Which of these technologies is the most resilient against the negative effects of multipath?

    A. FHSS

    B. DSSS

    C. HR-DSSS

    D. OFDM

15. HR-DSSS calls for data rates of 5.5 Mbps, and 11 Mbps. What is the average amount of aggregate throughput percentage at any data rate when legacy 802.11a/b/g radios are transmitting?

    A. 80 percent

    B. 75 percent

    C. 50 percent

    D. 100 percent

16. What are the names of the two additional U-NII bands proposed by the FCC that provide for 195 MHz of additional spectrum at 5 GHz? (Choose all that apply.)

    A. U-NII-1

    B. U-NII-2A

    C. U-NII-2B

    D. U-NII-2C

    E. U-NII-3

    F. U-NII-4

17. In the United States, 802.11 radios were not allowed to transmit on which range of frequencies to avoid interference with Terminal Doppler Weather Radar (TDWR) systems?

    A. 5.15 GHz – 5.25 GHz

    B. 5.25 GHz – 5.25 GHz

    C. 5.60 GHz – 5.65 GHz

    D. 5.85 GHz – 5.925 GHz

18. What are the modulation types used by OFDM technology? (Choose all that apply.)

    A. QAM

    B. Phase

    C. Frequency

    D. Hopping

19. The Barker code converts a bit of data into a series of bits that are referred to as what?

    A. Chipset

    B. Chips

    C. Convolutional code

    D. Complementary code

20. A 20 MHz OFDM channel uses how many 312.5 KHz data subcarriers when transmitting?

    A. 54

    B. 52

    C. 48

    D. 36

Chapter

7

Wireless LAN Topologies

IN THIS CHAPTER, YOU WILL LEARN ABOUT THE FOLLOWING:

✓ **Wireless networking topologies**

- Wireless wide area network (WWAN)
- Wireless metropolitan area network (WMAN)
- Wireless personal area network (WPAN)
- Wireless local area network (WLAN)

✓ **802.11 topologies**

- Access point
- Client station
- Integration service (IS)
- Distribution system (DS)
- Wireless distribution system (WDS)
- Service set identifier (SSID)
- Basic service set (BSS)
- Basic service set identifier (BSSID)
- Basic service area (BSA)
- Extended service set (ESS)
- Independent basic service set (IBSS)
- Mesh basic service set (MBSS)
- QoS basic service set (QoS BSS)

✓ **802.11 configuration modes**

- Access point modes
- Client station modes

A computer network is a system that provides communications between computers. Computer networks can be configured as peer to peer, as client-server, or as clustered central processing units (CPUs) with distributed dumb terminals. A networking *topology* is defined simply as the physical and/or logical layout of nodes in a computer network. Any individual who has taken a networking basics class is already familiar with the bus, ring, star, mesh, and hybrid topologies that are often used in wired networks.

All topologies have advantages and disadvantages. A topology may cover very small areas or can exist as a worldwide architecture. Wireless topologies also exist as defined by the physical and logical layout of wireless hardware. Many wireless technologies are available and can be arranged into four major wireless networking topologies. The 802.11-2012 standard defines one specific type of wireless communication. Within the 802.11 standard are four types of topologies, known as *service sets*. Over the years, vendors have also used 802.11 hardware using variations of these topologies to meet specific wireless networking needs. This chapter covers the topologies used by a cross section of RF technologies and covers 802.11-specific WLAN topologies.

Wireless Networking Topologies

Although the main focus of this study guide is 802.11 wireless networking, which is a local area technology, other wireless technologies and standards exist in which wireless communications span either smaller or larger areas of coverage. Examples of other wireless technologies are cellular, Bluetooth, and ZigBee. All of these different wireless technologies can be arranged into four major wireless topologies:

- Wireless wide area network (WWAN)

- Wireless metropolitan area network (WMAN)

- Wireless personal area network (WPAN)

- Wireless local area network (WLAN)

Additionally, although the 802.11-2012 standard is a WLAN standard, the same technology can sometimes be deployed in different wireless network architectures, as discussed in the following sections.

Wireless Wide Area Network (WWAN)

A wide area network (WAN) provides RF coverage over a vast geographical area. A WAN might traverse an entire state, region, or country or even span worldwide. The best example of a WAN is the Internet. Many private and public corporate WANs consist of hardware infrastructure such as T1 lines, fiber optics, and routers. Protocols used for wired WAN communications include Frame Relay, ATM, Multiprotocol Label Switching (MPLS), and others.

A *wireless wide area network (WWAN)* also covers broad geographical boundaries but obviously uses a wireless medium instead of a wired medium. WWANs typically use cellular telephone technologies or proprietary licensed wireless bridging technologies. Cellular providers such as Sprint, Verizon, and Vodafone use a variety of competing technologies to carry data. Some examples of these cellular technologies are general packet radio service (GPRS), code division multiple access (CDMA), time division multiple access (TDMA), Long Term Evolution (LTE), and Global System for Mobile Communications (GSM). Data can be carried to a variety of devices such as smartphones, tablet PCs, and cellular networking cards.

Data rates and bandwidth using these technologies are relatively slow when compared to other wireless technologies, such as 802.11. However, as cellular technologies have improved, so have cellular data-transfer rates. It should be noted, though, that convergence between Wi-Fi technology and cellular technologies is a fast-growing vertical market.

Wireless Metropolitan Area Network (WMAN)

A *wireless metropolitan area network (WMAN)* provides RF coverage to a metropolitan area such as a city and the surrounding suburbs. WMANs have been created for some time by matching different wireless technologies, and recent advancements have made this more practical. One wireless technology that is often associated with a WMAN is defined by the 802.16 standard. This standard defines broadband wireless access and is sometimes referred to as Worldwide Interoperability for Microwave Access (WiMAX). The WiMAX Forum is responsible for compatibility and interoperability testing of wireless broadband equipment such as 802.16 hardware.

802.16 technology are viewed as a direct competitor to other broadband services such as DSL and cable. Although 802.16 wireless networking is typically thought of as a last-mile data-delivery solution, the technology might also be used to provide access to users over citywide areas.

 More information about the 802.16 standard can be found at http:// ieee802.org/16. Learn more about WiMAX at www.wimaxforum.org.

In the past, a lot of press was generated about the possibility of citywide deployments of Wi-Fi networks, giving city residents access to the Internet throughout a metropolitan area. Although 802.11 technology was initially never intended to be used to provide access over such a wide area, many cities had initiatives to achieve this very feat. The equipment that was being used for these large-scale 802.11 deployments was proprietary wireless mesh routers or mesh access points. Many of these cities scrapped their initial plans to deploy 802.11 technology simply because the technology could not scale across an entire city.

However, some WLAN vendors have partnered with 4G/LTE telecommunication companies and have had success with 802.11 WMAN deployments using as many as 100,000 access points for metro access.

Wireless Personal Area Network (WPAN)

A *wireless personal area network (WPAN)* is a wireless computer network used for communication between computer devices within close proximity of a user. Devices such as laptops, gaming devices, tablet PCs, and smartphones can communicate with each other by using a variety of wireless technologies. WPANs can be used for communication between devices or as portals to higher-level networks such as local area networks (LANs) and/or the Internet. The most common technologies in WPANs are Bluetooth and infrared. Infrared is a light-based medium, whereas Bluetooth is a radio-frequency medium that uses frequency hopping spread spectrum (FHSS) technology.

The IEEE 802.15 Working Group focuses on technologies used for WPANs such as Bluetooth and ZigBee. ZigBee is another RF technology that has the potential of low-cost wireless networking between devices in a WPAN architecture.

> You can find further information about the 802.15 WPAN standards at www
> .ieee802.org/15. To learn more about Bluetooth, visit www.bluetooth
> .com. The ZigBee Alliance provides information about ZigBee technology
> at www.zigbee.org. To learn more about infrared communications, visit the
> Infrared Data Association website (www.irda.org).

The best example of 802.11 Wi-Fi radios being used in a wireless personal area networking scenario would be as peer-to-peer connections. We provide more information about 802.11 peer-to-peer networking later in this chapter, in the section entitled "Independent Basic Service Set." Apple's AirDrop technology, which works over Bluetooth and Wi-Fi, is another example of a WPAN used to transfer files between computers or tablets.

Wireless Local Area Network (WLAN)

As you learned in earlier chapters, the 802.11-2012 standard is defined as a *wireless local area network (WLAN)* technology. Local area networks provide networking for a building or campus environment. The 802.11 wireless medium is a perfect fit for local area networking simply because of the range and speeds that are defined by the 802.11-2012 standard and future amendments. The majority of 802.11 wireless network deployments are indeed LANs that provide access at businesses and homes.

WLANs typically use multiple 802.11 access points connected by a wired network backbone. In enterprise deployments, WLANs are used to provide end users with access to network resources and network services and a gateway to the Internet. Although 802.11 hardware can be used in other wireless topologies, the majority of Wi-Fi deployments are

WLANs, which is how the technology was originally defined by the IEEE 802.11 Working Group. The discussion of WLANs usually refers to 802.11 solutions; however, other proprietary and competing WLAN technologies do exist.

Please note that large corporations can deploy and manage 802.11 WLANs on a global scale. Enterprise Wi-Fi networks with many geographical locations can be managed centrally using a network management server (NMS) and might also be connected via virtual private networks (VPNs). A more in-depth discussion of Wi-Fi management and scaling can be found in Chapter 10, "WLAN Architecture."

802.11 Topologies

The main component of an 802.11 wireless network is the radio, which is referred to by the 802.11 standard as a *station (STA)*. The radio can reside inside an access point or be used as a client station. The 802.11-2012 standard defines four separate 802.11 topologies, known as *service sets*, which describe how these radios may be used to communicate with each other. These four 802.11 topologies are known as a basic service set (BSS), extended service set (ESS), independent basic service set (IBSS), and a mesh basic service set (MBSS).

Before we discuss the various 802.11 topologies, let's review a few basic networking terms that are often misunderstood: *simplex*, *half-duplex*, and *full-duplex*. These are three dialog methods that are used for communications between people and also between computer equipment.

Simplex   In simplex communications, one device is capable of only transmitting, and the other device is capable of only receiving. FM radio is an example of simplex communications. Simplex communications are rarely used on computer networks.

Half-Duplex   In half-duplex communications, both devices are capable of transmitting and receiving; however, only one device can transmit at a time. Walkie-talkies, or two-way radios, are examples of half-duplex devices. All RF communications by nature are half-duplex, although recent research at Stanford University claims that full-duplex RF communications are possible with transceivers that might be able to cancel self-interference. IEEE 802.11 wireless networks use half-duplex communications.

Full-Duplex   In full-duplex communications, both devices are capable of transmitting and receiving at the same time. A telephone conversation is an example of a full-duplex communication. Most IEEE 802.3 equipment is capable of full-duplex communications. Currently, the only way to accomplish full-duplex communications in a wireless environment is to have a two-channel bidirectional setup where all transmissions on one channel are transmitted from device A to device B, while all transmissions on the other channel are received on device A from device B. Both device A and device B use two separate radios on different channels.

In the following sections, we cover all the components that make up the four 802.11 service sets.

Access Point

A wired infrastructure device typically associated with half-duplex communications is an Ethernet hub. A wired hub is effectively a shared medium in which only one host device can transmit data at a time. Access points are half-duplex devices because the RF medium uses half-duplex communications that allow for only one radio to transmit at any given time. In reality, an access point is simply a hub with a radio and an antenna. The radio inside an access point must contend for the half-duplex RF medium in the same fashion that the client station radios must contend for the RF medium.

The original CWNP definition of an *access point (AP)* was a half-duplex device with switchlike intelligence. That definition can still be used to characterize *autonomous access points and cooperative access points*. In Chapter 10, "WLAN Architecture," we will discuss three logical planes of network design: management, control, and data. The switchlike intelligence can be defined as both control and data plane mechanisms. Also in Chapter 10, we discuss in detail the differences between access points that do have switchlike intelligence versus *controller-based access points* that do not. WLAN controller-based access points are often called "thin" APs or lightweight APs. With thin access points, the AP configuration and intelligence resides inside a WLAN controller instead of inside the lightweight access points that are managed by the controller. Over the years, many hybrid models have emerged to address where the control plane intelligence actually resides.

The best example of switchlike intelligence used by access points or WLAN controllers is the ability to address and direct wireless traffic at layer 2. Managed wired switches maintain dynamic MAC address tables known as content-addressable memory (CAM) tables that can direct frames to ports based on the destination MAC address of a frame. Similarly, an access point or WLAN controller directs traffic either to the network backbone or back into the wireless medium. The 802.11 header of a wireless frame typically has three MAC addresses, but it can have as many as four in certain situations. The access point uses the layer 2 addressing scheme of the wireless frames to eventually forward the layer 3–7 information either to the integration service or to another wireless client station. The upper-layer information that is contained in the body of an 802.11 wireless data frame is called a *MAC Service Data Unit (MSDU)*. The forwarding of the MSDU is the switchlike intelligence that exists in either standalone APs or WLAN controllers. The intelligence that is often compared to a CAM table is known as the distribution system services (DSS), which are described in more detail later in this chapter.

Many access points also support the use of *virtual local area networks (VLANs)*. For example, although not defined by the 802.11 standard, an access point can support VLANs that can be created on a managed wired switch or a WLAN controller. VLANs are used to reduce the size of broadcast domains on a wired network and to segregate different types of user and management traffic.

Client Station

Any radio that is not used in an access point is typically referred to as a *client station*. Client station radios can be used in laptops, tablets, scanners, smartphones, and many other mobile devices. Client stations must contend for the half-duplex RF medium in the same manner that an access point radio contends for the RF medium. When client stations have a layer 2 connection with an access point, they are known as *associated*.

Integration Service

The 802.11-2012 standard defines an *integration service (IS)* that enables delivery of MSDUs between the distribution system (DS) and a non-IEEE-802.11 LAN via a portal. A simpler way of defining the integration service is to characterize it as a frame format transfer method. The portal is usually either an access point or a WLAN controller. As mentioned earlier, the payload of a wireless 802.11 data frame is the layer 3–7 information known as the MSDU. The eventual destination of this payload is usually to a wired network infrastructure. Because the wired infrastructure is a different physical medium, an 802.11 data frame payload must be effectively transferred into an 802.3 Ethernet frame. For example, a VoWiFi phone sends an 802.11 data frame to a standalone access point. The MSDU payload of the frame is a VoIP packet with a final destination of an IP PBX that resides at the 802.3 network core. The job of the integration service is to remove the 802.11 header and trailer and then encase the MSDU VoIP payload inside an 802.3 frame. The 802.3 frame is then sent on to the Ethernet network. The integration service performs the same actions in reverse when an 802.3 frame payload must be transferred into an 802.11 frame that is eventually transmitted by the access point radio.

It is beyond the scope of the 802.11-2012 standard to define how the integration service operates. Normally, the integration service transfers data frame payloads between an 802.11 and 802.3 medium. However, the integration service could transfer an MSDU between the 802.11 medium and some sort of other medium. If 802.11 user traffic is forwarded at the edge of a network, the integration service exists in an access point. The integration service mechanism normally takes place inside a WLAN controller when 802.11 user traffic is tunneled back to a WLAN controller.

Distribution System

The 802.11-2012 standard also defines a *distribution system (DS)* that is used to interconnect a set of basic service sets (BSSs) via integrated LANs to create an extended service set (ESS). Service sets are described in detail later in this chapter. Access points by their very nature are portal devices. Wireless traffic can be destined back onto the wireless medium or forwarded to the integration service. The DS consists of two main components:

Distribution System Medium (DSM)   A logical physical medium used to connect access points is known as a *distribution system medium (DSM)*. The most common example is an 802.3 medium.

Distribution System Services (DSS)   System services built inside an access point are usually in the form of software. The *distribution system services (DSS)* provide the switchlike intelligence mentioned earlier in this chapter. These software services are used to manage client station associations, reassociations, and disassociations. Distribution system services also use the layer 2 addressing of the 802.11 MAC header to eventually forward the layer 3–7 information (MSDU) either to the integration service or to another wireless client station. A full understanding of DSS is beyond the scope of the CWNA exam but is necessary at the Certified Wireless Analysis Professional (CWAP) certification level.

A single access point or multiple access points may be connected to the same distribution system medium. The majority of 802.11 deployments use an AP as a portal into an 802.3 Ethernet backbone, which serves as the distribution system medium. Access points are usually connected to a switched Ethernet network, which often also offers the advantage of supplying power to the APs via Power over Ethernet (PoE).

An access point may also act as a portal device into other wired and wireless mediums. The 802.11-2012 standard by design does not care, nor does it define, onto which medium an access point translates and forwards data. Therefore, an access point can be characterized as a translational bridge between two mediums. The AP translates and forwards data between the 802.11 medium and whatever medium is used by the distribution system medium. Once again, the distribution system medium will almost always be an 802.3 Ethernet network, as shown in Figure 7.1. In the case of a wireless mesh network, the handoff is through a series of wireless devices, with the final destination typically being an 802.3 network.

FIGURE 7.1 Distribution system medium

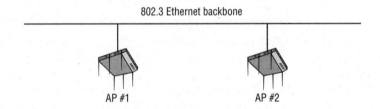

Wireless Distribution System

The 802.11-2012 standard defines a mechanism for wireless communication using a four-MAC-address frame format. The standard describes such a frame format but does not describe how such a mechanism or frame format would be used. This mechanism is known as a *wireless distribution system (WDS)*. Real-world examples of Wi-Fi deployed as a WDS include bridging, repeaters, and mesh networks. Another example of a WDS is when access points are deployed to provide both coverage and backhaul. Although the DS normally uses a wired Ethernet backbone, it is possible to use a wireless connection instead. A WDS can connect access points together using what is referred to as a *wireless backhaul.*

A WDS may operate by using APs with a single 802.11 radio or multiple 802.11 radios. Figure 7.2 depicts two 802.11 APs, each with a single radio. The radios in the APs not only provide access to the client stations but also communicate with each other directly as a WDS. A disadvantage to this solution is that throughput can be adversely affected because of the half-duplex nature of the medium, particularly in a single-radio scenario, where an AP cannot be communicating with a client station and another AP at the same time. The end result is a degradation of throughput.

FIGURE 7.2   Wireless distribution system, single radio

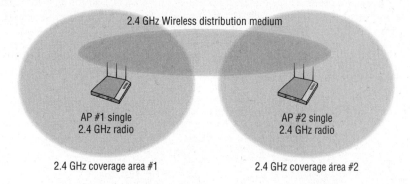

2.4 GHz Wireless distribution medium

AP #1 single
2.4 GHz radio

AP #2 single
2.4 GHz radio

2.4 GHz coverage area #1

2.4 GHz coverage area #2

Which Distribution System Is Most Desirable?

Whenever possible, a wired network will usually be the best option for the distribution system. Because most enterprise deployments already have a wired 802.3 infrastructure in place, integrating a wireless network into an Ethernet network is the most logical solution. A wired distribution system medium does not encounter many of the problems that may affect a WDS, such as physical obstructions and radio frequency interference. A mesh backhaul network is sometimes the better option if cabling is difficult. If the occasion does arise when a wired network cannot connect access points together, a WDS might be a viable alternative. The more desirable WDS solution utilizes different frequencies and radios for client access and distribution.

In Figure 7.3, two dual-radio access points are shown, each with radios operating at different frequencies. The 2.4 GHz radios provide access for the client stations, and the 5 GHz radios serve as the WDS link between the two access points. Throughput is not adversely affected by clients because the 2.4 GHz radio can communicate at the same time as the 5 GHz backhaul radios. Most Wi-Fi vendors now offer mesh networking capabilities that utilize the 5 GHz radios in this manner. Client connectivity could also be permitted on the 5 GHz radios; however, the throughput and performance of the 5 GHz backhaul link will be impacted by extra medium contention overhead caused by the 5 GHz client traffic. The throughput of all mesh networks is negatively impacted if there are multiple hops due to the medium contention overhead.

Wireless repeaters are another example of an 802.11 WDS. Repeaters are used to extend WLAN cell coverage to areas where it is not possible to provide an 802.3 Ethernet cable drop. As illustrated in Figure 7.4, a client station is associated and communicating via a repeater AP. The repeater provides coverage but is not connected to the wired backbone. When a client station sends a frame to the repeater, it is then forwarded to an access point that is connected to the wired backbone. The frame payload is converted into an 802.3 Ethernet frame and sent to a server on the backbone. The 802.11 communications between the repeater and the access point is a WDS. As shown in Figure 7.5, a frame sent within any type of WDS requires four MAC addresses: a source address, a destination address, a transmitter address, and a receiver address.

FIGURE 7.3   Wireless distribution system, dual radios

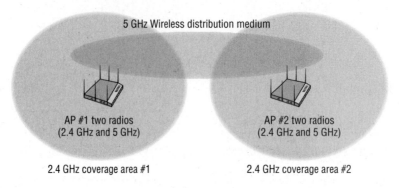

FIGURE 7.4   Repeater cell

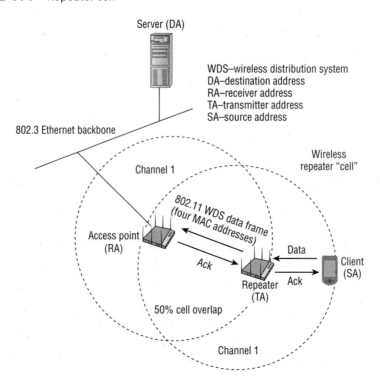

FIGURE 7.5   WDS frame header

```
├···802.11 MAC Header
├···◆ Version:                   0
├···◆ Type:                      %10   Data
├···◆ Subtype:                   %0000  Data Only
├·╤· Frame Control Flags=%00000001
├···◆ Duration:                  213   Microseconds
├···▦ Receiver:                  00:90:96:8A:40:60
├···▦ Transmitter:               00:02:2D:09:73:81
├···▦ Source:                    00:02:2D:74:67:2A
├···▦ Destination:               00:0C:85:62:D2:1D
├···◆ Seq Number:                126
└···◆ Frag Number:               0
```

Repeaters effectively extend the cell coverage of the original access point; therefore, both the repeater and AP must be on the same frequency channel. There must also be at least a 50 percent cell overlap between the coverage cells so that the repeater and AP can communicate with each other. Repeaters do provide coverage into areas where a cable drop is not possible. However, all frame transmissions must be sent twice, first from the client to the repeater and then from the repeater to the AP, which decreases throughput and increases latency. Because the AP cell and the repeater cell are on the same channel and exist in the same layer 1 domain, all radios must contend for the medium. Repeater environments add extra medium contention overhead, which also affects performance.

Most enterprise WLAN vendors no longer offer single radio repeaters that operate on a single frequency. Most enterprise WLAN APs have multiple radio with mesh networking capabilities that can use the 2.4 GHz radios for client access and the 5 GHz radios for backhaul, or vice versa. However, if the radio used for backhaul in a mesh environment also permits client access, it is effectively also performing as a repeater for the client traffic.

Service Set Identifier

The *service set identifier (SSID)* is a logical name used to identify an 802.11 wireless network. The SSID wireless network name is comparable to a Windows workgroup name. "The four 802.11 topologies utilize the SSID so that the radios can identify each other. The radios use this logical name in several different 802.11 frame exchanges." The SSID is a configurable setting on all 802.11 radios, including access points and client stations. The SSID can be made up of as many as 32 characters and is case sensitive. Figure 7.6 shows an SSID configuration of an access point.

FIGURE 7.6   Service set identifier

SSID*	Sybex Wi-Fi	(1-32 characters)
SSID Broadcast Band	2.4 GHz & 5 GHz (11n/a + 11n/b/g) ⬍	

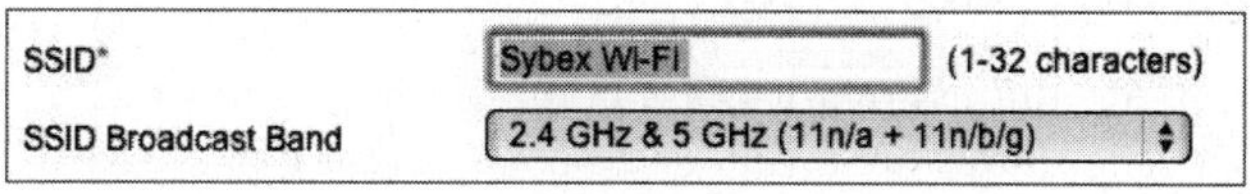

Most access points have the ability to cloak an SSID and keep the network name hidden from illegitimate end users. Hiding the SSID is a very weak attempt at security that is not defined by the 802.11-2012 standard. However, it is an option many administrators still mistakenly choose to implement.

Both active and passive scanning are discussed in detail in Chapter 9, "802.11 MAC Architecture." SSID cloaking is discussed in Chapter 13, "802.11 Network Security Architecture."

Basic Service Set

The *basic service set (BSS)* is the cornerstone topology of an 802.11 network. The communicating devices that make up a BSS consist of one AP radio with one or more client stations. Client stations join the AP wireless domain and begin communicating through the AP. Stations that are members of a BSS have a layer 2 connection and are called *associated*. Figure 7.7 depicts a standard basic service set.

FIGURE 7.7   Basic service set

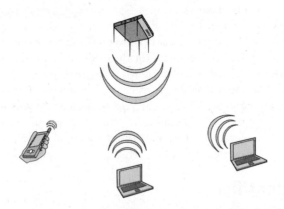

Typically the AP is connected to a distribution system medium, but that is not a requirement of a basic service set. If an AP is serving as a portal to the distribution system, client stations may communicate via the AP with network resources that reside on the DSM. It should also be noted that if client stations wish to communicate with each other, they must relay their data through the AP. In the typical BSS, client stations cannot communicate directly with each other unless they go through the AP. However, client stations could possibly belong to the BSS and communicate directly with each other if they support Wi-Fi Direct.

Basic Service Set Identifier

The 48-bit (6-octet) MAC address of an access point's radio is known as the basic service set identifier (BSSID). The simple definition of a BSSID is that it is the MAC address of the radio network interface in an access point. However, the proper definition is that the BSSID address is the layer 2 identifier of each individual BSS. Most often the BSSID is the MAC address of the radio network interface.

In the previous section, you learned that a basic service set consists of an AP with one or more stations associated with the AP. If you have two BSSs near each other, and they are both advertising the same SSID, a client station needs to identify the one BSS from the other. In order for clients to roam seamlessly, the APs must advertise the same SSID. The client stations, however, still need a unique layer 2 identifier of each AP. The BSSID provides each BSS with a unique identifier, thus the name BSSID.

Do not confuse the BSSID address with the SSID. The service set identifier (SSID) is the logical WLAN name that is user configurable, whereas the BSSID is the layer 2 MAC address of a radio provided by the hardware manufacturer. It should be noted that WLAN vendors offer the functionality to broadcast multiple SSIDs, as well as virtual BSSID capabilities; these capabilities are explained in Chapter 10.

As shown in Figure 7.8, the BSSID address is found in the MAC header of most 802.11 wireless frames and is used for identification purposes of the basic service set. The BSSID address plays a role in directing 802.11 traffic within the basic service set. This address is also used as a unique layer 2 identifier of the basic service set. Furthermore, the BSSID address is needed during the roaming process.

FIGURE 7.8 Basic service set identifier

```
...🖳 802.11 MAC Header
  ┊...🔵 Version:                     0
  ┊...🔵 Type:                        %10    Data
  ┊...🔵 Subtype:                     %0000  Data Only
  ┊ 🖳 Frame Control Flags=%00000010
  ┊...🔵 Duration:                    213    Microseconds
  ┊...🖳 Destination:                 00:02:2D:74:67:2A
  ┊...🖳 BSSID:                       00:0C:85:62:D2:1D
  ┊...🖳 Source:                      00:0C:85:62:D2:1D
  ┊...🔵 Seq Number:                  1653
  ┊...🔵 Frag Number:                 0
```

Basic Service Area

The physical area of coverage provided by an access point in a BSS is known as the *basic service area (BSA)*. Figure 7.9 shows a typical BSA. Client stations can move throughout the coverage area and maintain communications with the AP as long as the received signal between the radios remains above received signal strength indicator (RSSI) thresholds. Client stations can also shift between concentric zones of variable data rates that exist within the BSA. The process of moving between data rates is known as *dynamic rate switching* and is discussed in Chapter 12, "WLAN Troubleshooting."

FIGURE 7.9   Basic service area

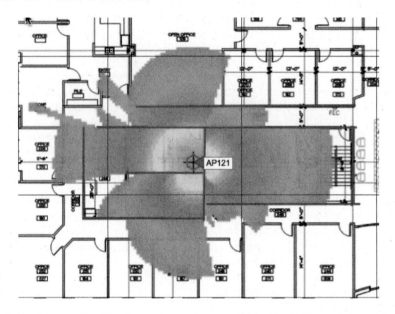

The size and shape of a BSA depends on many variables, including AP transmit power, antenna gain, and physical surroundings. Because environmental and physical surroundings often change, the BSA can often be fluid. When drawing a BSA, it is common to draw a circle around the AP to illustrate the theoretical coverage area. In reality, the real coverage area will have a disproportional shape due to the existing indoor or outdoor environment.

Extended Service Set

While a BSS might be considered the cornerstone 802.11 topology, an *extended service set (ESS)* 802.11 topology is analogous to an entire stone building. An extended service set is two or more basic service sets connected by a distribution system medium. Usually an extended service set is a collection of multiple access points and their associated client stations, all united by a single DSM.

The most common example of an ESS has access points with partially overlapping coverage cells, as shown in Figure 7.10. The purpose behind an ESS with partially overlapping coverage cells is to provide seamless roaming to the client stations. Most vendors recommend cell overlap to achieve successful seamless roaming, although measuring cell overlap is not an exact science. Coverage overlap is really duplicate coverage from the perspective of a Wi-Fi client station and is discussed in greater detail in Chapter 12.

FIGURE 7.10 Extended service set, seamless roaming

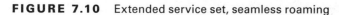
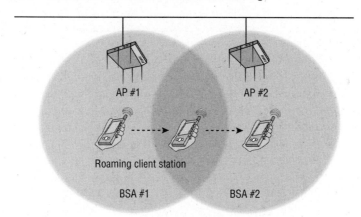

Although seamless roaming is usually a key aspect of WLAN design, there is no requirement for an ESS to guarantee uninterrupted communications. For example, an ESS can utilize multiple access points with nonoverlapping coverage cells, as shown in Figure 7.11. In this scenario, a client station that leaves the basic service area of the first access point will lose connectivity. The client station will later reestablish connectivity as it moves into the coverage cell of the second access point. This method of station mobility between disjointed cells is sometimes referred to as *nomadic roaming*.

FIGURE 7.11 Extended service set, nomadic roaming

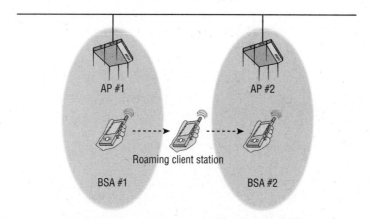

A final example of an ESS deploys multiple access points with overlapping coverage areas, as you can see in Figure 7.12. This 802.11 ESS topology is called *colocation*, and the intended goal is increased client capacity as opposed to roaming. Colocation is one method of providing coverage for a high density of client devices in the same area. Different strategies of high density coverage design are discussed in Chapter 12.

FIGURE 7.12   Extended service set, colocation

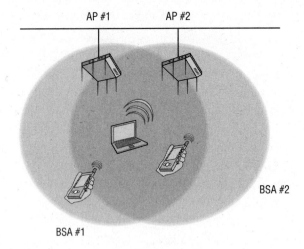

BSA #2

BSA #1

Note that all three of the previously mentioned extended service sets share a distribution system. As stated earlier in this chapter, the distribution system medium is usually an 802.3 Ethernet network; however, the DS may use another type of medium. In the majority of extended service sets, the access points all share the same SSID name. The logical network name of an ESS is often called an *extended service set identifier (ESSID)*. The terminology of ESSID and SSID are synonymous. However, as Figure 7.13 illustrates, access points in an ESS where roaming is required must all share the same logical name (SSID) but have unique layer 2 identifiers (BSSIDs) for each unique BSS coverage cell.

FIGURE 7.13   SSID and BSSIDs within an ESS

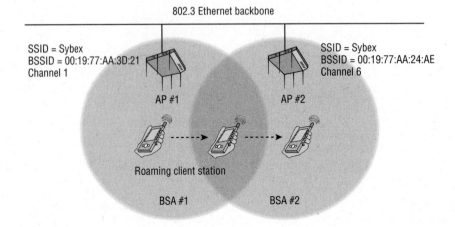

802.3 Ethernet backbone

SSID = Sybex
BSSID = 00:19:77:AA:3D:21
Channel 1

SSID = Sybex
BSSID = 00:19:77:AA:24:AE
Channel 6

AP #1

AP #2

Roaming client station

BSA #1

BSA #2

Independent Basic Service Set

The third service set topology defined by the 802.11 standard is an *independent basic service set (IBSS)*. The radios that make up an IBSS network consist solely of client stations (STAs), and no access point is deployed. An IBSS network that consists of just two STAs is analogous to a wired crossover cable. An IBSS can, however, have multiple client stations in one physical area communicating in an ad hoc fashion. Figure 7.14 depicts four client stations communicating with each other in a peer-to-peer fashion.

FIGURE 7.14   Independent basic service set

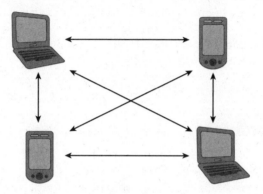

All of the stations transmit frames to each other directly and do not route their frames from one client to another. All client station frame exchanges in an IBSS are peer to peer. All stations in an IBSS must contend for the half-duplex medium, and at any given time only one STA can be transmitting.

The independent basic service set has two other names. Wi-Fi vendors often refer to an IBSS as either a *peer-to-peer network* or an *ad hoc network*.

In order for IBSS communications to succeed, all stations must be transmitting on the same frequency channel. Furthermore, this entire set of standalone wireless stations connected together as a group must share the same SSID WLAN name. Another caveat of an IBSS is that a BSSID address is created. Earlier in this chapter, we defined a BSSID as the MAC address of the radio inside an access point. So, how can an independent basic service set have a BSSID if no access point is used in the IBSS topology? The first station that starts up in an IBSS randomly generates a BSSID in the MAC address format. This randomly generated BSSID is a virtual MAC address and is used for layer 2 identification purposes within the IBSS.

Mesh Basic Service Set

The 802.11 standard has long defined BSS, ESS, and IBSS service sets. The 802.11-2012 standard also defines a service set for an 802.11 mesh topology. When access points support mesh functions, they may be deployed where wired network access is not possible. The mesh functions are used to provide wireless distribution of network traffic, and the set of APs that provide mesh distribution form a *mesh basic service set (MBSS)*. An MBSS requires features that are not necessary in a BSS, ESS, or IBSS because the purpose of an MBSS is different from the other topologies. As shown in Figure 7.15, one or more mesh APs will typically be connected to the wired infrastructure. This mesh AP is known as a mesh point portal, or MPP (sometimes called a mesh root or gateway). The other mesh APs that are not connected to the wired network will form wireless backhaul connections back to the mesh portals to reach the wired network. Mesh APs that are not connected to a wired infrastructure are known as *mesh points*, or MPs. Client stations that are associated to the mesh points have their traffic forwarded through the wireless backhaul. As stated earlier, an MBSS makes use of a wireless distribution system medium for backhaul communications. Usually the MBSS uses the 5 GHz radios for backhaul communications.

FIGURE 7.15   Mesh basic service set

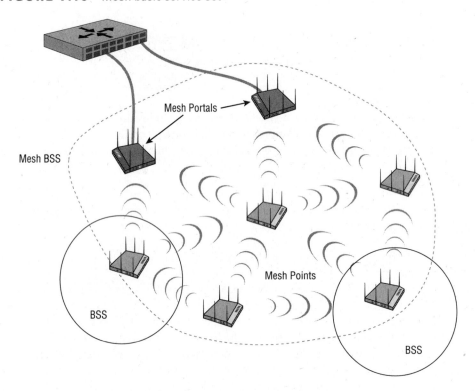

The mesh nodes in an MBSS function much like routers in a network, because their goal is to discover neighbor mesh stations, identify possible and best connections back to the portal, form neighbor links, and share link information. Keep in mind that 802.11 frame exchanges are a layer 2 operation; therefore, mesh routing of 802.11 traffic is based on MAC addresses and not IP addresses. A *hybrid wireless mesh protocol (HWMP)* is defined as the default path selection protocol for an MBSS. HWMP is both proactive and reactive and is effectively a dynamic layer 2 routing protocol. Note that WLAN vendors have offered mesh capabilities for many years using proprietary layer 2 mesh protocols. Most vendors continue to use their own dynamic layer 2 mesh mechanisms utilizing metrics such as RSSI, SNR, client load, and hop counts to determine the best path for the backhaul traffic.

QoS Basic Service Set

Quality of service (QoS) mechanisms can be implemented within all of the 802.11 service sets. The QoS enhancements are available to QoS STAs associated with a QoS access point in a QoS BSS. QoS stations may also belong to the same QoS IBSS. Older radios that do not support quality of service mechanisms are known as non-QoS STAs and non-QoS APs. 802.11 QoS mechanisms are discussed in greater detail in Chapter 8, "802.11 Medium Access."

 Real World Scenario

Vendor Considerations When Deploying and Integrating 802.11 WLAN Infrastructure

When deploying 802.11 infrastructure, the recommended practice is to purchase the equipment from one vendor. A bridge from vendor A is not likely to work with a bridge from vendor B. A mesh point from vendor A most likely will not communicate with a mesh portal from vendor B. Another example of likely interoperability is fast secure roaming. Client stations will probably not be able to roam effectively when using a mix of different WLAN vender access points.

The main purpose of an 802.11 AP is to act as a portal to a wired network infrastructure. Although 802.11 technology operates at layers 1 and 2, there are always higher layer design considerations. All WLAN vendors have different strategies on how to integrate into a pre-existing wired network infrastructure. For that reason, the normal best practice is to stick with one enterprise WLAN vendor when deploying and integrating an 802.11 infrastructure.

802.11 Configuration Modes

While the 802.11-2012 standard defines all radios as stations (STAs), an access point (AP) radio and a client station radio can each be configured in a number of ways. The default configuration of an AP radio is to allow it to operate inside a basic service set (BSS) as a portal device to a wired network infrastructure. However, an AP can be configured to function in other operational modes. Client stations can be configured to participate in either a BSS or an IBSS 802.11 service set.

Access Point Modes

The default configuration of some WLAN vendor access points is known as *root mode*. The main purpose of an AP is to serve as a portal to a distribution system. The normal default setting of an AP is root mode, which allows the AP to transfer data back and forth between the DS and the 802.11 wireless medium. Not all vendors have the same names for this mode of operation. For example, many Wi-Fi vendors use the term AP mode or access mode instead of root mode.

The default root configuration of an AP radio allows it to operate as part of a BSS. There are, however, other operational modes in which an AP may be configured:

Bridge Mode   The AP radio is converted into a wireless bridge. This typically adds extra MAC-layer intelligence to the device and gives the AP the capability to learn and maintain tables about MAC addresses from the wired side of the network.

Workgroup Bridge Mode   The AP radio is transformed into a workgroup bridge which provides wireless backhaul for connected 802.3 wired clients.

Repeater Mode   The AP radio performs as a repeater AP which extends the coverage area of a portal AP on the same channel.

Mesh Mode   The AP radio operates as a wireless backhaul radio for a mesh environment. Depending on the vendor, the backhaul radio may also allow for client access.

Scanner Mode   The AP radio is converted into a sensor radio, allowing the AP to integrate into a wireless intrusion detection system (WIDS) architecture. An AP in scanner mode is in a continuous listening state while hopping between multiple channels. Scanner mode is also often referred to as monitor mode.

The 802.11 standard does not define these AP operational modes; therefore, every WLAN vendor will have different capabilities. These modes of operation are "radio configuration modes" and may be able to be applied to a 2.4 GHz radio in an AP, a 5 GHz radio in an AP, or both radios within an AP. You can see an AP's various configurable modes in Figure 7.16.

FIGURE 7.16   Access point configuration modes

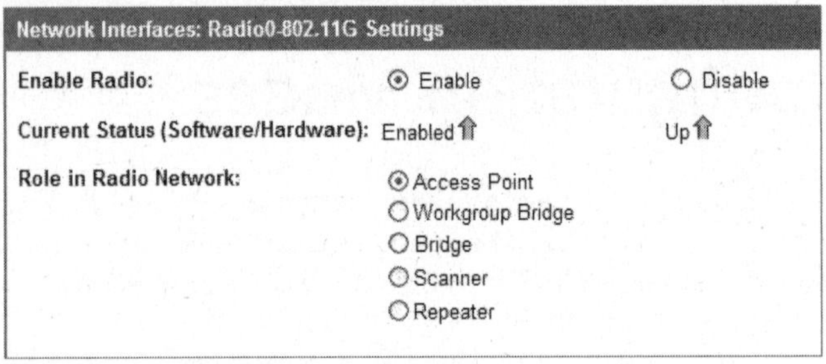

Client Station Modes

A client station may operate in one of two states, as shown in Figure 7.17. The default mode for an 802.11 client radio is typically *infrastructure mode*. When running in Infrastructure mode, the client station will allow communication via an access point. Infrastructure mode allows for a client station to participate in a basic service set or an extended service set. Clients that are configured in this mode may communicate, via the AP, with other wireless client stations within a BSS.

FIGURE 7.17   Client station configuration modes

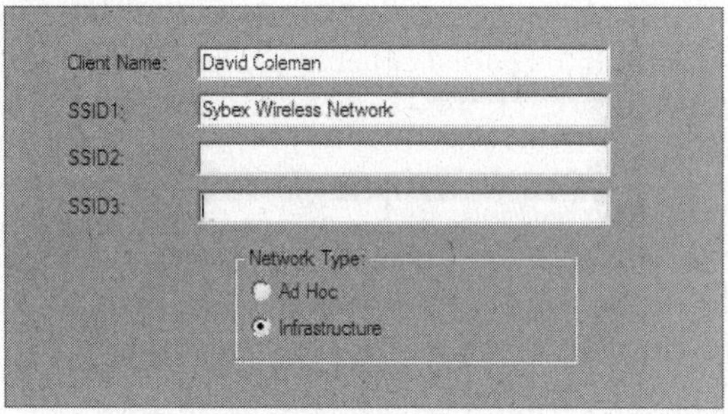

Clients may also communicate through the AP with other networking devices that exist on the distribution system, such as servers or wired desktops.

The second client station mode is called *Ad Hoc mode*. Other vendors may refer to this as Peer-to-Peer mode. 802.11 client stations set to Ad Hoc mode participate in an IBSS topology and do not communicate via an access point. All station transmissions and frame exchanges are peer to peer.

Summary

This chapter covered the major types of generic wireless topologies as well as the topologies specific to 802.11 wireless networking:

- The four wireless architectures that can be used by many different wireless technologies
- The four service sets as defined by the 802.11-2012 standard, and the various aspects and purposes defined for each service set
- Operational configuration modes of both access points and client stations

As a wireless network administrator, you should have a full understanding of the defined 802.11 service sets and how they operate. Administrators typically oversee the design and management of an 802.11 ESS, but there is a good chance that they will also deploy 802.11 radios using a variety of operational modes.

Exam Essentials

Know the four major types of wireless topologies. Understand the differences between a WWAN, WLAN, WPAN, and WMAN.

Explain the four 802.11 service sets. Be able to fully expound on all the components, purposes, and differences of a basic service set, an extended service set, an independent basic service set, and a mesh basic service set. Understand how the 802.11 radios interact with each other in each service set.

Identify the various ways in which an 802.11 radio can be used. Understand that the 802.11 standard expects a radio to be used either as a client station or inside an access point. Also understand that an 802.11 radio can be used for other purposes, such as bridging, repeating, and so on.

Explain the purpose of the distribution system. Know that the DS consists of two pieces: distribution system services (DSS) and the distribution system medium (DSM). Understand that the medium used by the DS can be any type of medium. Explain the functions of a wireless distribution system (WDS).

Define SSID, BSSID, and ESSID. Be able to explain the differences or similarities of all three of these addresses and the function of each.

Describe the various ways in which an ESS can be implemented and the purpose behind each design. Explain the three ways in which the coverage cells of the ESS access points can be designed and the purpose behind each design.

Explain access point and client station configuration modes. Remember all the configuration modes of both an AP and a client station.

Review Questions

1. An 802.11 wireless network name is known as which type of address? (Choose all that apply.)

    A. BSSID

    B. MAC address

    C. IP address

    D. SSID

    E. Extended service set identifier

2. Which two 802.11 topologies require the use of an access point?

    A. WPAN

    B. IBSS

    C. Basic service set

    D. Ad hoc

    E. ESS

3. The 802.11 standard defines which medium to be used in a distribution system (DS)?

    A. 802.3 Ethernet

    B. 802.15

    C. 802.5 token ring

    D. Star-bus topology

    E. None of the above

4. Which option is a wireless computer topology used for communication of computer devices within close proximity of a person?

    A. WWAN

    B. Bluetooth

    C. ZigBee

    D. WPAN

    E. WMAN

5. Which 802.11 service set may allow for client roaming?

    A. ESS

    B. Basic service set

    C. IBSS

    D. Spread spectrum service set

6. What factors might affect the size of a BSA coverage area of an access point? (Choose all that apply.)

    A. Antenna gain

    B. CSMA/CA

    C. Transmission power

    D. Indoor/outdoor surroundings

    E. Distribution system

7. What is the default configuration mode that allows an AP radio to operate in a basic service set?

    A. Scanner

    B. Repeater

    C. Root

    D. Access

    E. Nonroot

8. Which terms describe an 802.11 topology involving STAs but no access points? (Choose all that apply.)

    A. BSS

    B. Ad hoc

    C. DSSS

    D. Infrastructure

    E. IBSS

    F. Peer-to-peer

9. STAs operating in Infrastructure mode may communicate in which of the following scenarios? (Choose all that apply.)

    A. 802.11 frame exchanges with other STAs via an AP

    B. 802.11 frame exchanges with an AP in scanner mode

    C. 802.11 frame peer-to-peer exchanges directly with other STAs

    D. Frame exchanges with network devices on the DSM

    E. All of the above

10. Which of these are included in the four topologies defined by the 802.11-2012 standard? (Choose all that apply.)

    A. DSSS

    B. ESS

    C. BSS

    D. IBSS

    E. FHSS

11. Which wireless topology provides citywide wireless coverage?

    A. WMAN

    B. WLAN

    C. WPAN

    D. WAN

    E. WWAN

12. At which layer of the OSI model will a BSSID address be used?

    A. Physical

    B. Network

    C. Session

    D. Data-Link

    E. Application

13. The basic service set identifier address can be found in which topologies? (Choose all that apply.)

    A. FHSS

    B. IBSS

    C. ESS

    D. HR-DSSS

    E. BSS

14. Which 802.11 service set defines mechanisms for mesh networking?

    A. BSS

    B. DSSS

    C. ESS

    D. MBSS

    E. IBSS

15. What method of dialog communications is used within an 802.11 WLAN?

    A. Simplex communications

    B. Half-duplex communications

    C. Full-duplex communications

    D. Dual-duplex communications

16. What are some operational modes in which an AP radio may be configured? (Choose all that apply.)

    A. Scanner

    B. Root

    C. Bridge

    D. Mesh

    E. Repeater

17. A network consisting of clients and two or more access points with the same SSID connected by an 802.3 Ethernet backbone is one example of which 802.11 topology? (Choose all that apply.)

    A. ESS

    B. Basic service set

    C. Extended service set

    D. IBSS

    E. Ethernet service set

18. What term best describes two access points communicating with each other wirelessly while also allowing clients to communicate through the access points?

    A. WDS

    B. DS

    C. DSS

    D. DSSS

    E. DSM

19. What components make up a distribution system? (Choose all that apply.)

    A. HR-DSSS

    B. Distribution system services

    C. DSM

    D. DSSS

    E. Intrusion detection system

20. What type of wireless topology is defined by the 802.11 standard?

    A. WAN

    B. WLAN

    C. WWAN

    D. WMAN

    E. WPAN

Chapter

8

802.11 Medium Access

IN THIS CHAPTER, YOU WILL LEARN ABOUT THE FOLLOWING:

✓ **CSMA/CA vs. CSMA/CD**

   ▪ Collision detection

✓ **Distributed Coordination Function (DCF)**

   ▪ Interframe space (IFS)

   ▪ Duration/ID field

   ▪ Carrier sense

   ▪ Random backoff timer

✓ **Point Coordination Function (PCF)**

✓ **Hybrid Coordination Function (HCF)**

   ▪ Enhanced Distributed Channel Access (EDCA)

   ▪ HCF Controlled Channel Access (HCCA)

✓ **Block acknowledgment (BA)**

✓ **Wi-Fi Multimedia (WMM)**

✓ **Airtime Fairness**

One of the difficulties we had in writing this chapter was that in order for you to understand how a wireless station gains access to the media, we have to teach more than what is needed for the CWNA exam. The details are needed to grasp the concepts; however, it is the concepts that you will be tested on. If you find the details of this chapter interesting, then after reading this book, you should consider reading *CWAP Certified Wireless Analysis Professional Official Study Guide: Exam PW0-270* by David A. Westcott, David D. Coleman, et al. (Sybex, 2011), which gets into the nitty-gritty details of 802.11 communications. If you decide to take the CWAP exam, at that time you will need to know details far beyond what we have included in this chapter. But for now, take the details for what they are: a foundation for helping you understand the overall process of how a wireless station gains access to the half-duplex medium.

CSMA/CA vs. CSMA/CD

Network communication requires a set of rules to provide controlled and efficient access to the network medium. *Media Access Control (MAC)* is the generic term used when discussing the general concept of access. There are many ways of providing media access. The early mainframes used polling, which sequentially checked each terminal to see whether there was data to be processed. Later, token-passing and contention methods were used to provide access to the media. Two forms of contention that are heavily used in today's networks are *Carrier Sense Multiple Access with Collision Detection (CSMA/CD)* and *Carrier Sense Multiple Access with Collision Avoidance (CSMA/CA)*.

CSMA/CD is well known and is used by Ethernet networks. CSMA/CA is not as well known and is used by 802.11 networks. Stations using either access method must first listen to see whether any other device is transmitting; otherwise, the station must wait until the medium is available. The difference between CSMA/CD and CSMA/CA exists at the point when a client wants to transmit and no other clients are presently transmitting. A CSMA/CD node can immediately begin transmitting. If a collision occurs while a CSMA/CD node is transmitting, the collision will be detected and the node will temporarily stop transmitting. 802.11 wireless radios are not capable of transmitting and receiving at the same time, so they are not capable of detecting a collision during their transmission. For this reason, 802.11 wireless networking uses CSMA/CA instead of CSMA/CD to try to avoid collisions.

When a CSMA/CA station has determined that no other stations are transmitting, the 802.11 radio will choose a random backoff value. The station will then wait an additional period of time, based on that backoff value, before transmitting. During this time, the station continues to monitor to make sure that no other stations begin transmitting. Because of the half-duplex nature of the RF medium, it is necessary to ensure that at any given time only one 802.11 radio has control of the medium. CSMA/CA is a process used to ensure that only one 802.11 radio is transmitting at a time. Is this process perfect? Absolutely not! Collisions still do occur when two or more radios transmit at the same time. However, the IEEE 802.11-2012 standard defines a function called Distributed Coordination Function (DCF) as a medium access method that utilizes multiple checks and balances to try to minimize collisions. These checks and balances can also be thought of as several lines of defense. The various lines of defense are put in place to once again hopefully ensure that only one radio is transmitting while all other radios are listening. CSMA/CA minimizes the risk of collisions without excessive overhead.

The 802.11-2012 standard also defines an optional function called Point Coordination Function (PCF) that allows for the access point (AP) to poll client stations about their need to transmit data. Finally, the 802.11-2012 standard also encompasses a Hybrid Coordination Function (HCF) that specifies advanced *quality of service (QoS)* methods.

This entire process is covered in more detail in the next section of this chapter.

CSMA/CA Overview

Carrier sense determines whether the medium is busy. *Multiple access* ensures that every radio gets a fair shot at the medium (but only one at a time). *Collision avoidance* means only one radio gets access to the medium at any given time, hopefully avoiding collisions.

Collision Detection

In the previous section, we mentioned that 802.11 radios were not able to transmit and receive at the same time and therefore cannot detect collisions. So, if they cannot detect a collision, how do they know whether one occurred? The answer is simple. As shown in Figure 8.1, every time an 802.11 radio transmits a unicast frame, if the frame is received properly, the 802.11 radio that received the frame will reply with an *acknowledgment (ACK)* frame. The ACK frame is a method of delivery verification of unicast frames. 802.11n and 802.11ac radios make use of frame aggregation, which groups multiple unicast frames together. The delivery of aggregated frames is verified using a *block ACK*.

The majority of unicast 802.11 frames must be acknowledged. Broadcast and multicast frames do not require an acknowledgment. If any portion of a unicast frame is corrupted, the *cyclic redundancy check (CRC)* will fail and the receiving 802.11 radio will not send an ACK frame to the transmitting 802.11 radio. If an ACK frame is not received by the original transmitting radio, the unicast frame is not acknowledged and will have to be retransmitted.

FIGURE 8.1   Unicast acknowledgment

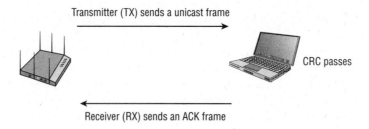

Transmitter (TX) sends a unicast frame

CRC passes

Receiver (RX) sends an ACK frame

This process does not specifically determine whether a collision occurs; in other words, there is no collision detection. However, if an ACK frame is not received by the original radio, there is collision assumption. Think of the ACK frame as a method of delivery verification for unicast 802.11 frames. If no proof of delivery is provided, the original radio assumes there was a delivery failure and retransmits the frame.

Distributed Coordination Function

Distributed Coordination Function (DCF) is the fundamental access method of 802.11 communications. DCF is the mandatory access method of the 802.11 standard. The 802.11 standard also has an optional access method known as *Point Coordination Function (PCF)*, which is covered later in this chapter. With the addition of the 802.11e amendment, which is now part of the 802.11-2012 standard, a third coordination function known as *Hybrid Coordination Function (HCF)* has been added, which also is covered later in this chapter. In the following sections, you will learn about some of the components that are part of the CSMA/CA process. Here are the four main components of DCF:

- Interframe space
- Duration/ID field
- Carrier sense
- Random backoff timer

Think of these four components as checks and balances that work together at the same time to ensure that only one 802.11 radio is transmitting on the half-duplex medium. These four components will be explained separately, but it is important to understand that all four mechanisms are functioning at the same time.

Interframe Space (IFS)

Interframe space (IFS) is a period of time that exists between transmissions of wireless frames. There are six types of interframe spaces, which are listed here in order of shortest to longest:

- Reduced interframe space (RIFS), highest priority
- Short interframe space (SIFS), second highest priority

- PCF interframe space (PIFS), middle priority
- DCF interframe space (DIFS), lowest priority
- Arbitration interframe space (AIFS), used by QoS stations
- Extended interframe space (EIFS), used after receipt of corrupted frames

The actual length of time of each of the interframe spaces varies depending on the transmission speed of the network. Interframe spaces are one line of defense used by CSMA/CA to ensure that only certain types of 802.11 frames are transmitted following certain interframe spaces. For example, only ACK frames, block ACK frames, data frames, and clear-to-send (CTS) frames may follow a SIFS. The two most common interframe spaces used are the SIFS and the DIFS. As pictured in Figure 8.2, the ACK frame is the highest-priority frame, and the use of a SIFS ensures that it will be transmitted first, before any other type of 802.11 frame. Most other 802.11 frames follow a longer period of time called a DIFS.

FIGURE 8.2   SIFS and DIFS

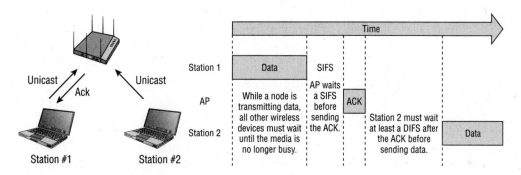

Interframe spaces are all about what type of 802.11 traffic is allowed next. Interframe spacing also acts as a backup mechanism to virtual carrier sense, which is discussed later in this chapter. The main thing that you need to understand at this time is that there are six interframe spaces of different durations of time, and the order is RIFS < SIFS < PIFS < DIFS < AIFS < EIFS.

As you read further in this chapter, you will learn that timing is an important aspect of successful wireless communications. Interframe spaces are just one component of this tightly linked environment.

Duration/ID Field

As pictured in Figure 8.3, one of the fields in the MAC header of an 802.11 frame is the *Duration/ID field*. When a client transmits a unicast frame, the Duration/ID field contains a value from 0 to 32,767. The Duration/ID value represents the time, in microseconds, that is required to transmit an active frame exchange process so that other radios do not interrupt the process. In the example shown in Figure 8.4, the client that is transmitting the data frame calculates how long it will take to receive an ACK frame and includes that length of time in the Duration/ID field in the MAC header of the transmitted unicast data frame.

The value of the Duration/ID field in the MAC header of the ACK frame that follows is 0 (zero). To summarize, the value of the Duration/ID field indicates how long the RF medium will be busy before another station can contend for the medium.

FIGURE 8.3 Duration/ID field

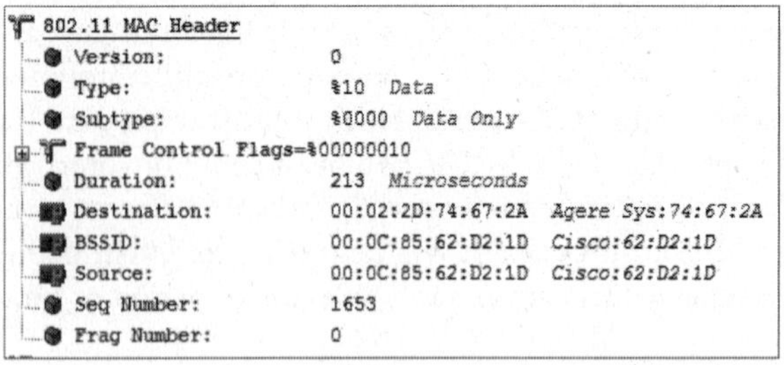

802.11 MAC Header
Version: 0
Type: %10 Data
Subtype: %0000 Data Only
Frame Control Flags=%00000010
Duration: 213 Microseconds
Destination: 00:02:2D:74:67:2A Agere Sys:74:67:2A
BSSID: 00:0C:85:62:D2:1D Cisco:62:D2:1D
Source: 00:0C:85:62:D2:1D Cisco:62:D2:1D
Seq Number: 1653
Frag Number: 0

FIGURE 8.4 Duration value of SIFS + ACK

Time
Data frame
ACK frame
Data
SIFS
ACK
Duration

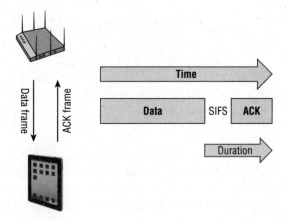

The majority of the time, the Duration/ID field contains a Duration value that is used to reset other stations' network allocation vector (NAV) timers. In the rare case of a PS-Poll frame, the Duration/ID is used as an ID value of a client station using legacy power management. Power management is discussed in Chapter 9, "802.11 MAC Architecture."

Carrier Sense

The first step that an 802.11 CSMA/CA device needs to do to begin transmitting is to perform a carrier sense. This is a check to see whether the medium is busy. Think of it like listening for a busy signal when you call someone on the phone. There are two ways that a carrier sense is performed: virtual carrier sense and physical carrier sense.

Virtual Carrier Sense

Virtual carrier sense uses a timer mechanism known as the *network allocation vector (NAV)*. The NAV timer maintains a prediction of future traffic on the medium based on Duration value information seen in a previous frame transmission. When an 802.11 radio is not transmitting, it is listening. As depicted in Figure 8.5, when the listening radio hears a frame transmission from another station, it looks at the header of the frame and determines whether the Duration/ID field contains a Duration value or an ID value. If the field contains a Duration value, the listening station will set its NAV timer to this value. The listening station will then use the NAV as a countdown timer, knowing that the RF medium should be busy until the countdown reaches 0.

FIGURE 8.5   Virtual carrier sense

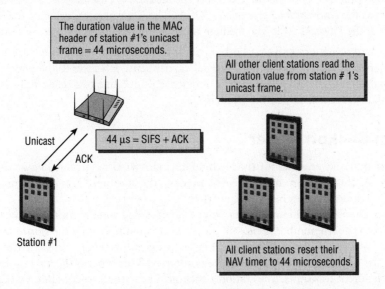

The duration value in the MAC header of station #1's unicast frame = 44 microseconds.

All other client stations read the Duration value from station # 1's unicast frame.

Unicast

44 µs = SIFS + ACK

ACK

Station #1

All client stations reset their NAV timer to 44 microseconds.

This process essentially allows the transmitting 802.11 radio to notify the other stations that the medium will be busy for a period of time (Duration/ID value). The stations that are not transmitting listen and hear the Duration/ID, set a countdown timer (NAV), and wait until their timer hits 0 before they can contend for the medium and eventually transmit on the medium. A station cannot contend for the medium until its NAV timer is 0, nor can a station transmit on the medium if the NAV timer is set to a nonzero value. As stated earlier, there are several lines of defense used by CSMA/CA to prevent collisions, and the NAV timer is often considered the first line of defense. Because the Duration/ID value inside an 802.11 MAC header is used to set the NAV timer, virtual carrier sense is a layer 2 carrier sense mechanism.

Physical Carrier Sense

Virtual carrier sense is one method of keeping other stations from transmitting while another radio has control of the RF medium. However, it is possible that a station did not hear the other radio transmitting and was therefore unable to read the Duration/ID field and set its NAV timer. There could be numerous reasons why, but that is irrelevant at the moment. CSMA/CA utilizes another line of defense to ensure that a station does not transmit while another is already transmitting: The 802.11-2012 standard also defines a *physical carrier sense* mechanism to determine if the medium is busy.

Physical carrier sensing is performed constantly by all stations that are not transmitting or receiving. When a station performs a physical carrier sense, it is actually listening to the channel to see whether any other transmitters are taking up the channel.

Physical carrier sense has two purposes:

- The first purpose is to determine whether a frame transmission is inbound for a station to receive. If the medium is busy, the radio will attempt to synchronize with the transmission.

- The second purpose is to determine whether the medium is busy before transmitting. This is known as the *clear channel assessment (CCA)*. The CCA involves listening for RF transmissions at the Physical layer. The medium must be clear before a station can transmit.

It is important to understand that both virtual carrier sense and physical carrier sense are always happening at the same time. Virtual carrier sense is a layer 2 line of defense, while physical carrier sense is a layer 1 line of defense. If one line of defense fails, hopefully the other will prevent collisions from occurring.

Random Backoff Timer

An 802.11 station may contend for the medium during a window of time known as the *backoff time*. At this point in the CSMA/CA process, the station selects a random backoff value using a pseudo-random backoff algorithm.

The station chooses a random number from a range called a *contention window (CW)* value. After the random number is chosen, the number is multiplied by the *slot time* value. Slot time sizes are dependent on the physical layer specification (PHY) in use (DSSS, OFDM, etc.). This starts a random backoff timer. The random backoff timer is the final timer used by a station before it transmits. The station's backoff timer begins to count down ticks of a clock known as slots. When the backoff time is equal to 0, the client can reassess the channel and, if it is clear, begin transmitting.

If no medium activity occurs during a particular slot time, then the backoff timer is decremented by a slot time. If the physical or virtual carrier sense mechanisms sense a busy medium, the backoff timer decrement is suspended, and the backoff timer value is maintained. When the medium is idle for a duration of a DIFS, AIFS, or EIFS period, the backoff process resumes and continues the countdown from where it left off. When the backoff timer reaches 0, transmission commences. Unsuccessful transmissions cause the CW size to increase exponentially up to a maximum value, as shown in Figure 8.6.

The following example is a simple review of the process:

- An OFDM station selects a random number from a contention window of 0–15. For this example, the number chosen is 4.

- The station multiplies the random number of 4 by a slot time of 9µs.

- The random backoff timer has a value of 36µs (4 slots).

- For every slot time during which there is no medium activity, the backoff time is decremented by a slot time.
- The station decrements the backoff timer until the timer is zero.
- The station transmits if the medium is clear.

FIGURE 8.6   Contention window length

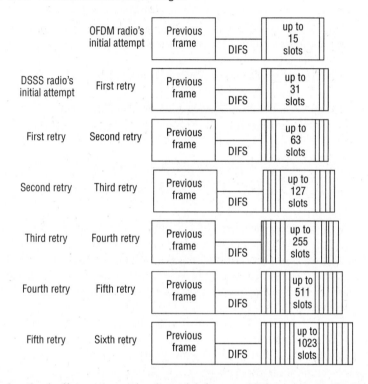

The random backoff timer is another line of defense and helps minimize the likelihood of two stations trying to communicate at the same time, although it does not fully prevent this from occurring. If a station does not receive an ACK, it starts the carrier sense process over again.

Point Coordination Function

In addition to DCF, the IEEE 802.11-2012 standard defines an additional, optional medium access method known as Point Coordination Function (PCF). This access method is a form of polling. The AP performs the function of the *point coordinator (PC)*. Because an AP is taking the role of the point coordinator, the PCF medium access method will work in only a basic service set (BSS). PCF cannot be utilized in an ad hoc network because no AP exists in an independent basic service set (IBSS). Because polling is performed from a central device, PCF provides managed access to the medium.

In order for PCF to be used, both the AP and the station must support it. If PCF is enabled, DCF will still function. The AP will alternate between PCF mode and DCF mode. While the AP is functioning in PCF mode, that time is known as the *contention-free period (CFP)*. During the contention-free period, the AP polls only clients in PCF mode about their intention to send data. This is a method of prioritizing clients. While the AP is functioning in DCF mode, that time is known as the *contention period (CP)*.

If you would like to learn more about PCF, we suggest that you read the 802.11-2012 standard document, which you can download from the IEEE website:

http://standards.ieee.org/about/get/802/802.11.html

As we stated earlier, PCF is an optional access method, and as of this writing, we do not know of any vendor that has implemented it. You will not be tested on PCF.

Hybrid Coordination Function

The 802.11e quality of service amendment added a new coordination function to 802.11 medium contention, known as Hybrid Coordination Function (HCF). The 802.11e amendment and HCF have since been incorporated into the 802.11-2012 standard. HCF combines capabilities from both DCF and PCF and adds enhancements to them to create two channel-access methods: Enhanced Distributed Channel Access (EDCA) and HCF Controlled Channel Access (HCCA).

DCF and PCF medium contention mechanisms discussed earlier allow for an 802.11 radio to transmit a single frame. After transmitting a frame, the 802.11 station must contend for the medium again before transmitting another frame. HCF defines the ability for an 802.11 radio to send multiple frames when transmitting on the RF medium. When an HCF-compliant radio contends for the medium, it receives an allotted amount of time to send frames. This period of time is called a *transmit opportunity (TXOP)*. During this TXOP, an 802.11 radio may send multiple frames in what is called a *frame burst*. A short interframe space (SIFS) is used between each frame to ensure that no other radios transmit during the frame burst.

Enhanced Distributed Channel Access

Enhanced Distributed Channel Access (EDCA) is a wireless media access method that provides differentiated access that directs traffic to four access-category QoS priority queues. EDCA is an extension of DCF. The EDCA medium access method prioritizes traffic using priority tags that are identical to 802.1D priority tags. Priority tags provide a mechanism for implementing QoS at the MAC level.

Different classes of service are available, represented in a 3-bit user priority field in an IEEE 802.1Q header added to an Ethernet frame. 802.1D enables priority queuing (enabling some Ethernet frames to be forwarded ahead of others within a switched Ethernet network). Figure 8.7 depicts 802.1D priority tags from the Ethernet side that are used to direct traffic to access-category queues.

FIGURE 8.7   EDCA and 802.1D priority tags

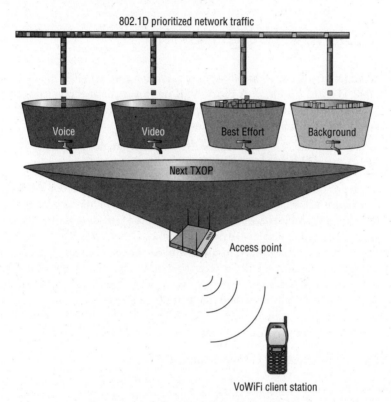

EDCA defines four access categories, based on the eight UPs. The four access categories from lowest priority to highest priority are AC_BK (Background), AC_BE (Best Effort), AC_VI (Video), and AC_VO (Voice). For each access category, an enhanced version of DCF known as *Enhanced Distributed Channel Access Function (EDCAF)* is used to contend for a TXOP. Frames with the highest-priority access category have the lowest backoff values and therefore are more likely to get a TXOP. The specific details of this process are beyond the scope of the CWNA exam.

HCF Controlled Channel Access

HCF Controlled Channel Access (HCCA) is a wireless media access method that uses a QoS-aware centralized coordinator known as a *hybrid coordinator (HC)*, which operates differently than the point coordinator in a PCF network. The HC is built into the AP and has a higher priority of access to the wireless medium. Using this higher priority level, it can allocate TXOPs to itself and other stations to provide a limited-duration controlled access phase (CAP), providing contention-free transfer of QoS data. The specific details of this process are beyond the scope of the CWNA exam. As with PCF, as of this writing we do not know of any vendor that has implemented HCCA.

Block Acknowledgment

The 802.11e amendment also introduced a *Block acknowledgment (BA)* mechanism that is defined in the 802.11-2012 standard. A Block ACK improves channel efficiency by aggregating several acknowledgments into one single acknowledgment frame. There are two types of Block ACK mechanisms: immediate and delayed.

- The immediate Block ACK is designed for use with low-latency traffic.
- The delayed Block ACK is more suitable for latency-tolerant traffic.

For the purposes of this book, we will discuss only the immediate Block ACK.

As pictured in Figure 8.8, an originator station sends a block of QoS data frames to a recipient station. The originator requests acknowledgment of all the QoS data frames by sending a BlockAckReq frame. Instead of acknowledging each unicast frame independently, the block of QoS data frames are all acknowledged by a single Block ACK. A bitmap in the Block ACK frame is used to indicate the status of all the received data frames. If only one of the frames is corrupted, only that frame will need to be retransmitted. The use of a Block ACK instead of a traditional ACK is a more efficient method that cuts down on medium contention overhead. Uses of Block ACK mechanisms are further defined in the 802.11n-2009 amendment for the purposes of frame aggregation. Please see Chapter 18, "802.11n," for more details.

FIGURE 8.8 Immediate Block acknowledgment

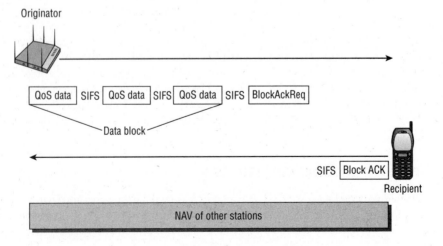

Wi-Fi Multimedia

Prior to the adoption of the 802.11e amendment, no adequate QoS procedures had been defined for the use of time-sensitive applications such as *Voice over Wi-Fi (VoWiFi)*. Application traffic such as voice, audio, and video has a lower tolerance for latency and jitter and requires priority before standard data traffic. The 802.11e amendment defined the layer 2 MAC methods needed to meet the QoS requirements for time-sensitive applications over IEEE 802.11 wireless LANs. The Wi-Fi Alliance introduced the *Wi-Fi Multimedia (WMM)* certification as a partial mirror of 802.11e amendment.

Because WMM is based on EDCA mechanisms, 802.1D priority tags from the Ethernet side are used to direct traffic to four access-category priority queues. The WMM certification provides for traffic prioritization via four access categories, as described in Table 8.1.

TABLE 8.1   Wi-Fi multimedia access categories

Access category	Description	802.1D tags
WMM Voice priority	This is the highest priority. It allows multiple and concurrent VoIP calls with low latency and toll voice quality.	7, 6
WMM Video priority	This supports prioritized video traffic before other data traffic. A single 802.11g or 802.11a channel can support three to four SDTV video streams or one HDTV video stream.	5, 4
WMM Best Effort priority	This is traffic from applications or devices, such as Internet browsing, that cannot provide QoS capabilities, such as legacy devices. This traffic is not as sensitive to latency but is affected by long delays.	0, 3
WMM Background priority	This is low-priority traffic that does not have strict throughput or latency requirements. This traffic includes file transfers and print jobs.	2, 1

The Wi-Fi Alliance also defined *WMM-PS (Power Save)*, which uses 802.11e power-saving mechanisms to increase the battery life via advanced power-saving mechanisms. More information about power management can be found in Chapter 9.

Another Wi-Fi Alliance certification is *WMM-Admission Control*, which defines the use of management frames for the signaling between an AP and a client station. Client stations can request to send a *traffic stream (TS)* of frames of a particular WMM access category. A traffic stream can be unidirectional or bidirectional. An AP will evaluate a request frame from a client station against the network load and channel conditions. If the AP can accommodate the request, it accepts the request and grants the client station the medium time for a traffic stream. If the request is rejected, the client device is not allowed to initiate the requested traffic stream and may decide to delay the traffic stream, associate with a different AP, or establish a best-effort traffic stream outside the operation of WMM-Admission Control. WMM-Admission Control improves the performance for time-sensitive data such as video and voice. WMM-Admission Control improves the reliability of applications in progress by preventing oversubscription of bandwidth.

Important Wi-Fi Alliance White Papers

The Wi-Fi Alliance has two white papers that we recommend you read to learn more about WMM. Both white papers are available for download at the WiFi Alliance website: www.wi-fi.org.

- *Wi-Fi CERTIFIED for WMM—Support for Multimedia Applications with Quality of Service in Wi-Fi Networks*
- *WMM Power Save for Mobile and Portable Wi-Fi CERTIFIED Devices*

Airtime Fairness

One of the important features of 802.11 is its ability to support many different data rates. This allows older technologies to still communicate alongside newer devices, along with enabling devices to maintain communications by shifting to slower data rates as they move away from an access point. The ability to use these slower data rates is paramount to 802.11 communications; however, it can also be a huge hindrance to the overall performance of the network and to individual devices operating at faster data rates.

Since 802.11 is contention based, each radio must contend for its turn to communicate, then transmit, and then go back to the contention process. As each radio takes its turn transmitting, the other 802.11 radios must wait. If the transmitting radio is using a fast data rate, the other radios do not have to wait long. If the transmitting radio is using a slow data rate, the other radios will have to wait a much longer period of time. When 802.11 radios transmit at very low data rates such as 1 Mbps and 2 Mbps, effectively they cause medium-contention overhead for higher data rate transmitters due to the long wait time while the slower devices are transmitting.

To try to understand this, look at Figure 8.9. The top portion of the figure illustrates the normal operation of two stations each sending eight frames. One station is sending eight frames at a higher data rate and the other station is sending eight frames at a lower data rate. If a high-speed and a low-speed device coexist in the same WLAN, they have to share or contend for the time to transmit. In other words, both stations will statistically get an equal number of times to access the RF medium even though one of the stations is capable of transmitting at a higher rate and requires much less airtime to transmit the same amount of data. Because there is no priority given to the station with the higher data rate, both stations finish transmitting their eight frames over the same period of time.

FIGURE 8.9   Airtime fairness example

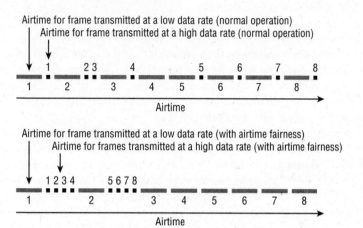

Instead of allocating equal access to the network between devices, the goal of *airtime fairness* is to allocate equal time, as opposed to equal opportunity. Airtime fairness can provide better time management of the RF medium. In the bottom half of Figure 8.9, airtime fairness is enabled; you can see that the station with the higher data rate transmission is given priority before the station with the lower data rates. Effectively this is a much better use of transmission time because the higher data rate station does not have to remain idle waiting during the lower data rate transmission. Notice that the faster station transmitted all eight frames in a much shorter time period, and the slower rate station still sent all eight frames in about the same period as before. Airtime fairness effectively achieves better time management of the medium by cutting down on wait times. The net result is better performance, higher capacity, and more throughput over the Wi-Fi network.

There currently are no 802.11 standards or amendments that define airtime fairness or how to implement it. Nor is there any requirement for a vendor to implement it. Most vendors use airtime fairness mechanisms only for downstream transmissions from an AP to an associated client. Airtime fairness mechanisms are normally used for prioritizing the higher data rate downstream transmissions from an AP over the lower data rate downstream transmissions from an AP. At least one vendor also makes claims of upstream airtime fairness capability. Any implementation of airtime fairness is a proprietary solution developed by each WLAN vendor. No matter how each vendor implements its solution, the underlying goal is essentially the same: to prevent slower devices from bogging down the rest of the network.

Although each WLAN vendor takes its own approach to implementing airtime fairness, it is typical for them to analyze the downstream client traffic and assign different weighting based on such characteristics as current throughput, client data rates, SSID, PHY type, and other variables. Algorithms are used to process this information and determine the number of opportunities for each client's downstream transmissions. If implemented properly, airtime fairness makes better use of the medium by providing preferential access for higher data rate transmissions.

Summary

This chapter focused on 802.11 medium access. Every station has the right to communicate, and the management of access to the wireless medium is controlled through media access control. We discussed the difference between CSMA/CD and CSMA/CA as contention methods. CSMA/CA uses a pseudorandom contention method called Distributed Coordination Function. DCF uses four lines of defense to ensure that only one 802.11 radio is transmitting on the half-duplex medium.

We also discussed an optional contention-free method called Point Coordination Function. The 802.11e quality of service amendment added a new coordination function to 802.11 medium contention, known as Hybrid Coordination Function (HCF). The Wi-Fi Multimedia (WMM) certification was introduced by the Wi-Fi Alliance as a partial mirror of the 802.11e amendment. WMM is designed to meet the QoS requirements for time-sensitive applications such as audio, video, and voice over IEEE 802.11.

Airtime fairness was introduced as a way for vendors to provide faster devices with preferential access to the media when operating alongside devices that are transmitting at slower data rates.

Exam Essentials

Understand the similarities and differences between CSMA/CA and CSMA/CD.   Understand both access methods and know what makes them similar and what makes them different.

Define the four checks and balances of CSMA/CA and DCF.   Understand that virtual carrier sense, physical carrier sense, interframe spacing, and the random backoff timer all work together to ensure that only one 802.11 radio is transmitting on the half-duplex medium.

Define virtual and physical carrier senses.   Understand the purpose and basic mechanisms of the two carrier senses.

Explain DCF and PCF.   Define the basic operations of both Distributed Coordination Function and Point Coordination Function.

Define HCF quality of service mechanisms.   Hybrid Coordination Function defines the use of TXOPs and access categories in EDCA as well as the use of TXOPs and polling during HCCA.

Understand the Wi-Fi Multimedia (WMM) certification.   WMM is designed to provide quality of service capabilities to 802.11 wireless networks. WMM is a partial mirror of the 802.11e amendment. WMM currently provides for traffic priority via four access categories.

Understand the importance of airtime fairness and what it does.   Airtime fairness provides devices operating at faster data rates with preferential access to the medium. This preferential treatment provides all devices with equal access, resulting in all devices equally sharing the available transmission bandwidth.

Review Questions

1. DCF is also known as what? (Choose all that apply.)
   - **A.** Carrier Sense Multiple Access with Collision Detection (CSMA/CD)
   - **B.** Carrier Sense Multiple Access with Collision Avoidance (CSMA/CA)
   - **C.** Data Control Function
   - **D.** Distributed Coordination Function

2. 802.11 collision detection is handled using which technology?
   - **A.** Network allocation vector (NAV).
   - **B.** Clear channel assessment (CCA).
   - **C.** Duration/ID value.
   - **D.** Receiving an ACK from the destination station.
   - **E.** Positive collision detection cannot be determined.

3. ACK and CTS-to-self frames follow which interframe space?
   - **A.** EIFS
   - **B.** DIFS
   - **C.** PIFS
   - **D.** SIFS
   - **E.** LIFS

4. The carrier sense portion of CSMA/CA is performed by using which of the following methods? (Choose all that apply.)
   - **A.** Virtual carrier sense
   - **B.** Physical carrier sense
   - **C.** Channel sense window
   - **D.** Clear channel assessment

5. After the station has performed the carrier sense and determined that no other devices are transmitting for a period of a DIFS interval, what is the next step for the station?
   - **A.** Wait the necessary number of slot times before transmitting if a random backoff value has already been selected.
   - **B.** Begin transmitting.
   - **C.** Select a random backoff value.
   - **D.** Begin the random backoff timer.

6. If PCF is implemented, it can function in which of the following network environments? (Choose all that apply.)
   - **A.** Ad hoc mode
   - **B.** BSS

    C. IBSS

    D. Infrastructure mode

    E. BSA

7. Which of the following terms are affiliated with the virtual carrier sense mechanism? (Choose all that apply.)

    A. Contention window

    B. Network allocation vector

    C. Random backoff time

    D. Duration/ID field

8. The goal of allocating equal time as opposed to equal opportunity is known as what?

    A. Access fairness

    B. Opportunistic media access

    C. CSMA/CA

    D. Airtime fairness

9. CSMA/CA and DCF define which mechanisms that attempt to ensure that only one 802.11 radio can transmit on the half-duplex RF medium? (Choose all that apply.)

    A. Random backoff timer

    B. NAV

    C. CCMP

    D. CCA

    E. Interframe spacing

10. The Wi-Fi Alliance certification called Wi-Fi Multimedia (WMM) is based on which media access method defined by the 802.11-2012 standard?

    A. DCF

    B. PCF

    C. EDCA

    D. HCCA

    E. HSRP

11. Hybrid Coordination Function (HCF) defines what allotted period of time in which a station can transmit multiple frames?

    A. Block acknowledgment

    B. Polling

    C. Virtual carrier sense

    D. Physical carrier sense

    E. TXOP

12. WMM is based on EDCA and provides for traffic prioritization via which of the following access categories? (Choose all that apply.)

   A. WMM Voice priority

   B. WMM Video priority

   C. WMM Audio priority

   D. WMM Best Effort priority

   E. WMM Background priority

13. The 802.11e amendment (now part of the 802.11-2012 standard) defines which of the following medium access methods to support QoS requirements? (Choose all that apply.)

   A. Distributed Coordination Function (DCF)

   B. Enhanced Distributed Channel Access (EDCA)

   C. Hybrid Coordination Function (HCF)

   D. Point Coordination Function (PCF)

   E. Hybrid Coordination Function Controlled Access (HCCA)

14. What information that comes from the wired network is used to assign traffic into access categories on a WLAN controller?

   A. Duration/ID

   B. 802.1D priority tags

   C. Destination MAC address

   D. Source MAC address

15. What are the two reasons that 802.11 radios use physical carrier sense? (Choose all that apply.)

   A. To synchronize incoming transmissions

   B. To synchronize outgoing transmissions

   C. To reset the NAV

   D. To start the random backoff timer

   E. To assess the RF medium

16. What CSMA/CA mechanism is used for medium contention? (Choose all that apply.)

   A. NAV

   B. CCA

   C. Random backoff timer

   D. Contention window

17. Which field in the MAC header of an 802.11 frame resets the NAV timer for all listening 802.11 stations?

   A. NAV

   B. Frame control

C. Duration/ID

D. Sequence number

E. Strictly ordered bit

18. The EDCA medium access method provides for the prioritization of traffic via priority queues that are matched to eight 802.1D priority tags. What are the EDCA priority queues called?

A. TXOP

B. Access categories

C. Priority levels

D. Priority bits

E. PT

19. ACKs are required for which of the following frames?

A. Unicast

B. Broadcast

C. Multicast

D. Anycast

20. What QoS mechanism can be used to reduce medium contention overhead during a frame burst of low-latency traffic?

A. Delayed Block ACK

B. Contention period

C. Contention window

D. Contention-free period

E. Immediate Block ACK

Chapter

9

802.11 MAC Architecture

IN THIS CHAPTER, YOU WILL LEARN ABOUT THE FOLLOWING:

✓ **Packets, frames, and bits**

✓ **Data-Link layer**

    ▪ MAC Service Data Unit (MSDU)

    ▪ MAC Protocol Data Unit (MPDU)

✓ **Physical layer**

    ▪ PLCP Service Data Unit (PSDU)

    ▪ PLCP Protocol Data Unit (PPDU)

✓ **802.11 and 802.3 interoperability**

✓ **Three 802.11 frame types**

    ▪ Management frames

    ▪ Control frames

    ▪ Data frames

✓ **Beacon management frame (beacon)**

✓ **Passive scanning**

✓ **Active scanning**

✓ **Authentication**

    ▪ Open System authentication

    ▪ Shared Key authentication

✓ **Association**

✓ **Authentication and association states**

✓ **Basic and supported rates**

✓ **Roaming**

✓ **Reassociation**

✓ **Disassociation**

✓ **Deauthentication**

✓ **ACK frame**

✓ **Fragmentation**

✓ **Protection mechanism**

✓ **RTS/CTS**

✓ **CTS-to-Self**

✓ **Data frames**

✓ **Power management**

- Active mode
- Power Save mode
- Traffic indication map (TIM)
- Delivery traffic indication message (DTIM)
- Announcement traffic indication message (ATIM)
- WMM Power Save (WMM-PS) and U-APSD
- 802.11n power management

This chapter presents all of the components of the 802.11 MAC architecture. We discuss how upper-layer information is encapsulated within an 802.11 frame format. We cover the three major 802.11 frame types and a majority of the 802.11 frame subtypes. We examine many MAC layer tasks, such as active scanning, and the specific 802.11 frames that are used to accomplish these tasks. An often misunderstood capability of 802.11 is the ERP protection mechanism. We describe how 802.11b and 802.11g stations can coexist in the same BSS by using either the RTS/CTS or CTS-to-Self protection mechanism. This protection mechanism is also the foundation for coexistence between 802.11n devices and earlier legacy devices. Near the end of this chapter we discuss legacy 802.11 power management and enhanced WMM-PS power management, which are methods used to save battery life.

Packets, Frames, and Bits

When learning about any technology, at times you need to step back and focus on the basics. If you have ever flown an airplane, you know that it is important, when things get difficult, to refocus on the number one priority, the main objective—and that is to fly the airplane. Navigation and communications are secondary to flying the airplane. When dealing with any complex technology, it is easy to forget the main objective; this is as true with 802.11 communications as it is with flying. With 802.11 communications, the main objective is to transfer user data from one computing device to another.

As data is processed in a computer and prepared to be transferred from one computer to another, it starts at the upper layers of the OSI model and moves down until it reaches the Physical layer, where it is ultimately transferred to the other devices. Initially, a user may want to transfer a word processing document from their computer to a shared network disk on another computer. This document will start at the Application layer and work its way down to the Physical layer, get transmitted to the other computer, and then work its way back up the layers of the OSI model to the Application layer on the other computer.

As data travels down the OSI model for the purpose of being transmitted, each layer adds header information to that data. This enables the data to be reassembled when it is received by the other computer. At the Network layer, an IP header is added to the data that came from layers 4–7. A layer 3 IP *packet*, or datagram, encapsulates the data from the higher layers. At the Data-Link layer, a MAC header is added and the IP packet is encapsulated inside a *frame*. Ultimately, when the frame reaches the Physical layer, a PHY header with more information is added to the frame.

Data is eventually transmitted as individual bits at the Physical layer. A *bit* is a binary digit, taking a value of either 0 or 1. Binary digits are a basic unit of communication in digital computing. A byte of information consists of 8 bits.

In this chapter, we discuss how upper-layer information moves down the OSI model through the Data-Link and Physical layers from an 802.11 perspective.

Data-Link Layer

The 802.11 *Data-Link layer* is divided into two sublayers. The upper portion is the IEEE 802.2 *Logical Link Control (LLC)* sublayer, which is identical for all 802-based networks, although it is not used by all IEEE 802 networks. The bottom portion of the Data-Link layer is the *Media Access Control (MAC) sublayer*. The 802.11 standard defines operations at the MAC sublayer.

MAC Service Data Unit

When the Network layer (layer 3) sends data to the Data-Link layer, that data is handed off to the LLC and becomes known as the *MAC Service Data Unit (MSDU)*. The MSDU contains data from the LLC and layers 3–7. A simple definition of the MSDU is that it is the data payload that contains the IP packet plus some LLC data.

Later in this chapter, you will learn about the three major 802.11 frame types. 802.11 management and control frames do not carry upper-layer information. Only 802.11 data frames carry an MSDU payload in the frame body. The 802.11-2012 standard states that the maximum size of the MSDU is 2,304 bytes. The maximum frame body size is determined by the maximum MSDU size (2,304 octets) plus any overhead from encryption. With the ratification of the 802.11n-2009 amendment, aggregate MSDU (A-MSDU) was introduced. With A-MSDU, the maximum frame body size is determined by the maximum A-MSDU size of 3,839 or 7,935 octets, depending upon the STA's capability, plus any overhead from encryption. In Chapter 18, "802.11n," you will learn more about A-MSDUs.

MAC Protocol Data Unit

When the LLC sublayer sends the MSDU to the MAC sublayer, the MAC header information is added to the MSDU to identify it. The MSDU is now encapsulated in a *MAC Protocol Data Unit (MPDU)*. A simple definition of an 802.11 MPDU is that it is an 802.11 frame. As shown in Figure 9.1, an 802.11 MPDU consists of the following three basic components:

MAC Header   Frame control information, duration information, MAC addressing, and sequence control information are all found in the MAC header. Furthermore, QoS data frames contain specific QoS control information.

Frame Body   The frame body component can be variable in size and contains information that is different depending on the frame type and frame subtype. The MSDU upper layer payload is encapsulated in the frame body. The MSDU layer 3–7 payload is protected when using encryption.

Frame Check Sequence (FCS)   The FCS comprises a 32-bit *cyclic-redundancy check (CRC)* that is used to validate the integrity of received frames.

The 802.11 MAC header is discussed in more detail later in this chapter.

FIGURE 9.1   802.11 MPDU

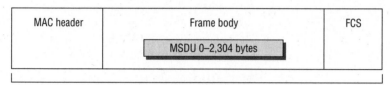

MPDU—802.11 data frame

At this point, the frame is ready to be passed onto the Physical layer, which will then further prepare the frame for transmission.

Physical Layer

Similar to the way the Data-Link layer is divided into two sublayers, the *Physical layer* is also divided into two sublayers. The upper portion of the Physical layer is known as the *Physical Layer Convergence Procedure (PLCP)* sublayer, and the lower portion is known as the *Physical Medium Dependent (PMD)* sublayer. The PLCP prepares the frame for transmission by taking the frame from the MAC sublayer and creating the PLCP Protocol Data Unit (PPDU). The PMD sublayer then modulates and transmits the data as bits.

PLCP Service Data Unit

The *PLCP Service Data Unit (PSDU)* is a view of the MPDU from the Physical layer. The MAC layer refers to the frame as the MPDU, while the Physical layer refers to this same frame as the PSDU. The only difference is from which layer of the OSI model you are looking at the frame.

PLCP Protocol Data Unit

When the PLCP receives the PSDU, it then prepares the PSDU to be transmitted and creates the *PLCP Protocol Data Unit (PPDU)*. The PLCP adds a preamble and PHY header to the PSDU. The preamble is used for synchronization between transmitting and receiving 802.11 radios. It is beyond the scope of this book and the CWNA exam to discuss all the details of the preamble and PHY header. When the PPDU is created, the PMD sublayer takes the PPDU and modulates the data bits and begins transmitting.

Figure 9.2 depicts a flowchart that shows the upper-layer information moving between the Data-Link and Physical layers.

FIGURE 9.2   Data-Link and Physical layers

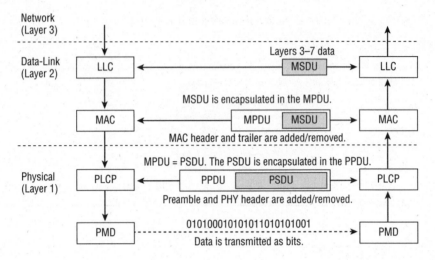

802.11 and 802.3 Interoperability

As you learned in Chapter 7, "Wireless LAN Topologies," the 802.11-2012 standard defines an *integration service (IS)* that enables delivery of MSDUs between the distribution system (DS) and a non-IEEE-802.11 local area network (LAN), via a portal. A simpler way of defining the integration service is to characterize it as a frame format transfer method. The portal is usually either an access point or a WLAN controller. As mentioned earlier, the payload of a wireless 802.11 data frame is the upper layer 3–7 information known as the MSDU. The eventual destination of this payload usually resides on a wired network infrastructure. Because the wired infrastructure is a different physical medium, an 802.11 data frame payload (MSDU) must be effectively transferred into an 802.3 Ethernet frame. For example, a VoWiFi phone transmits an 802.11 data frame to an access point. The MSDU payload of the frame is the VoIP packet with a final destination of a PBX server residing on the wired network. The job of the integration service is to first remove the 802.11 header and trailer and then encase the MSDU VoIP payload inside an 802.3 Ethernet frame. Normally, the integration service transfers frame payloads between an 802.11 and 802.3 medium. However, the IS could transfer an MSDU between the 802.11 medium and some sort of other medium, such as a cell phone data network. All of the IEEE 802 frame formats share similar characteristics, including the 802.11 frame format. Because the frames are similar, it makes it easier to translate the frames as they move from the 802.11 wireless network to the 802.3 wired network, and vice versa.

One of the differences between 802.3 Ethernet and 802.11 wireless frames is the frame size. 802.3 frames have a maximum size of 1,518 bytes with a maximum data payload of 1,500 bytes. If the 802.3 frames are 802.1Q tagged for VLANs and user priority, the maximum size of the 802.3 frame is 1,522 bytes with a data payload of 1,504 bytes. As you have just learned, 802.11 frames are capable of transporting frames with an MSDU payload of 2,304 bytes of *upper-layer* data. This means that as the data moves between the wireless and the wired network, the AP may receive a data frame that is too large for the wired network. This is rarely a problem thanks to the TCP/IP protocol suite. TCP/IP, the most common communications protocol used on networks, typically has an IP *maximum transmission unit (MTU)* size of 1,500 bytes. IP packets are usually 1,500 bytes based on the MTUs. When the IP packets are passed down to 802.11, even though the maximum size of the MSDU is 2,304 bytes, the size will be limited to the 1,500 bytes of the IP packets.

Much like in an 802.3 Ethernet frame, the header of an 802.11 frame contains MAC addresses. A MAC address is one of the following two types:

Individual Address   Individual addresses are assigned to unique stations on the network (also known as a *unicast address).*

Group Address   A multiple destination address (group address) could be used by one or more stations on a network. There are two kinds of group addresses:

Multicast-Group Address   An address used by an upper-layer entity to define a logical group of stations is known as a multicast-group address.

Broadcast Address   A group address that indicates all stations that belong to the network is known as a broadcast address. A broadcast address, all bits with a value of one, defines all stations on a local area network. In hexadecimal, the broadcast address would be FF:FF:FF:FF:FF:FF.

Although there are similarities, the MAC addressing used by 802.11 frames is much more complex than Ethernet frames. 802.3 frames have only a source address (SA) and destination address (DA) in the layer 2 header. As pictured in Figure 9.3, 802.11 frames have up to four address fields in the MAC header. 802.11 frames typically use only three of the MAC address fields. However, as we discussed in Chapter 7, an 802.11 frame sent within a wireless distribution system (WDS) requires all four MAC addresses.

Depending on whether the 802.11 traffic is upstream or downstream, the definition of each of the four MAC address fields in the layer 2 header will change. The five definitions are as follows:

Source Address (SA)   The MAC address of the original sending station is known as the SA. The source address can originate from either a wireless station or the wired network.

Destination Address (DA)   The MAC address that is the final destination of the layer 2 frame is known as the DA. The final destination may be a wireless station or could be a destination on the wired network such as a server or a router.

Transmitter Address (TA)   The MAC address of an 802.11 radio that is transmitting the frame onto the half-duplex 802.11 medium is known as the TA.

Receiver Address (RA)   The MAC address of the 802.11 radio that is intended to receive the incoming transmission from the transmitting station is known as the RA.

Basic Service Set Identifier (BSSID)   This is the MAC address that is the layer 2 identifier of the basic service set (BSS). The BSSID is the MAC address of the AP's radio or is derived from the MAC address of the AP's radio if multiple basic service sets exist.

Certain frames may not contain some of the address fields. Even though the number of address fields is different, both 802.3 and 802.11 identify a source address and a destination address and use the same MAC address format. The first three octets are known as the Organizationally Unique Identifier (OUI), and the last three octets are known as the extension identifier.

FIGURE 9.3   802.11 MAC header

Bytes	2	2	6	6	6	2	6	2
	Frame control	Duration/ID	Address 1	Address 2	Address 3	Sequence control	Address 4	QoS control

> For an in-depth look at 802.11 frame format, we suggest you read *CWAP Certified Wireless Analysis Professional Official Study Guide: Exam PW0-270* (Sybex, 2011). It is beyond the scope of the CWNA exam to explain the purpose of every field in the 802.11 MAC header. However, a very important field that was discussed earlier in the book is the Duration/ID field. As you learned in Chapter 8, "802.11 Medium Access," the duration value in the MAC header of a transmitting station is used to reset the NAV timer of other listening stations.

Three 802.11 Frame Types

Unlike many wired network standards, such as the IEEE 802.3 Std, which uses a single data frame type, the IEEE 802.11 standard defines three major frame types: management, control, and data. These frame types are further subdivided into multiple subtypes. In Chapter 8, you learned about the optional medium contention method of Point Coordination Function (PCF) and the quality-of-service (QoS) medium contention method called Hybrid Coordination Function (HCF). Some of the frame subtypes are defined to perform functions associated with PCF. PCF is optional and, to date, there are no known APs that support this technology. We have indicated any subtypes that are solely defined for PCF by placing *PCF only* next to these subtypes but will not address or describe them. It is also beyond the scope of this book to discuss all the frame subtypes used for QoS in HCF. We have placed *HCF* next to these subtypes but will not address or describe them.

Management Frames

802.11 *management frames* make up a majority of the frame types in a WLAN. Management frames are used by wireless stations to join and leave the basic service set (BSS). They are not necessary on wired networks, since physically connecting or disconnecting the network cable performs this function. However, because wireless networking is an unbounded medium, it is necessary for the wireless station to first find a compatible WLAN, then authenticate to the WLAN (assuming they are allowed to connect), and then associate with the WLAN (typically with an AP) to gain access to the wired network (the distribution system).

Another name for an 802.11 management frame is *Management MAC Protocol Data Unit (MMPDU)*. Management frames do not carry any upper-layer information. There is no MSDU encapsulated in the MMPDU frame body, which carries only layer 2 information fields and information elements. *Information fields* are fixed-length fields in the body of a management frame. *Information elements* are variable in length.

Following is a list of all 14 of the management frame subtypes as defined by the 802.11 standard and ratified amendments:

- Association request
- Association response
- Reassociation request
- Reassociation response
- Probe request
- Probe response
- Beacon
- Announcement traffic indication message (ATIM)
- Disassociation
- Authentication
- Deauthentication
- Action
- Action No ACK
- Timing advertisement

Control Frames

802.11 *control frames* assist with the delivery of the data frames and are transmitted at one of the basic rates. Control frames are also used to clear the channel, acquire the channel, and provide unicast frame acknowledgments. They contain only header information.

Following is a list of all nine of the control frame subtypes as defined by the 802.11 standard:

- Power Save Poll (PS-Poll)
- Request to send (RTS)

- Clear to send (CTS)
- Acknowledgment (ACK)
- Contention Free-End (CF-End) [PCF Only]
- CF-End + CF-ACK [PCF Only]
- Block ACK Request (BlockAckReq) [HCF Only]
- Block ACK (BlockAck) [HCF Only]
- Control wrapper

Data Frames

Most 802.11 *data frames* carry the actual data that is passed down from the higher-layer protocols. The layer 3 – 7 MSDU payload is normally encrypted for data privacy reasons. However, some 802.11 data frames carry no MSDU payload at all but do have a specific MAC control purpose within a BSS. Any data frames that do not carry an MSDU payload are not encrypted because a layer 3 – 7 data payload does not exist. There are a total of 15 data frame subtypes. The data subtype is usually referred to as the *simple data frame*. The simple data frame has MSDU upper-layer information encapsulated in the frame body. The integration service that resides in access points and WLAN controllers takes the MSDU payload of a simple data frame and transfers the MSDU into 802.3 Ethernet frames. Null function frames are sometimes used by client stations to inform the AP of changes in Power Save status.

The following is a list of all 15 of the data frame subtypes as defined by the 802.11 standard:

- Data (simple data frame)
- Null function (no data)
- Data + CF-ACK [PCF only]
- Data + CF-Poll [PCF only]
- Data + CF-ACK + CF-Poll [PCF only]
- CF-ACK (no data) [PCF only]
- CF-Poll (no data) [PCF only]
- CF-ACK + CF-Poll (no data) [PCF only]
- QoS Data [HCF]
- QoS Null (no data) [HCF]
- QoS Data + CF-ACK [HCF]
- QoS Data + CF-Poll [HCF]
- QoS Data + CF-ACK + CF-Poll [HCF]
- QoS CF-Poll (no data) [HCF]
- QoS CF-ACK + CF-Poll (no data) [HCF]

Beacon Management Frame

One of the most important frame types is the *beacon management frame*, commonly referred to as the beacon. Beacons are essentially the heartbeat of the wireless network. The AP of a basic service set sends the beacons while the clients listen for the beacon frames. Client stations only transmit beacons when participating in an independent basic service set (IBSS), also known as Ad Hoc mode. Each beacon contains a time stamp, which client stations use to keep their clocks synchronized with the AP. Because so much of successful wireless communications is based on timing, it is imperative that all stations be in sync with each other. By performing Exercise 9.1 , you will be able to inspect the contents of a beacon frame using a wireless packet analyzer. Some of the information that can be found inside the body of a beacon frame is listed in Table 9.1.

TABLE 9.1   Beacon frame contents

Information Type	Description
Time Stamp	Synchronization information
Spread Spectrum Parameter Sets	FHSS-, DSSS-, HR-DSSS-, ERP-, OFDM-, HT-, or VHT-specific information
Channel Information	Channel used by the AP or IBSS
Data Rates	Basic and supported rates
Service Set Capabilities	Extra BSS or IBSS parameters
SSID	Logical WLAN name
Traffic Indication Map (TIM)	A field used during the Power Save process
QoS Capabilities	Quality of service and Enhanced Distributed Channel Access (EDCA) information
Robust Security Network (RSN) Capabilities	TKIP or CCMP cipher information and authentication method
Vendor Proprietary Information	Vendor-unique or vendor-specific information

The beacon frame contains all the necessary information for a client station to learn about the parameters of the basic service set before joining the BSS. Beacons are transmitted about 10 times per second. This interval can be configured on some APs, but it cannot be disabled.

EXERCISE 9.1

Viewing Beacon Frames

1.   To perform this exercise, you need to first download the CWNA-CH9.PCAP file from the book's online resource area, which can be accessed at www.sybex.com/go/cwna4e.

2. After the file is downloaded, you will need packet analysis software to open the file. If you do not already have a packet analyzer installed on your computer, you can download Wireshark from www.wireshark.org.

3. Using the packet analyzer, open the CWNA-CH9.PCAP file. Most packet analyzers display a list of capture frames in the upper section of the screen, with each frame numbered sequentially in the first column.

4. Click on one of the first eight frames. All of these frames are beacon frames.

5. After selecting one of the beacon frames, in the lower section of the screen, browse through the information found inside the beacon frame body. You can expand a section by clicking on the plus sign next to the section.

Passive Scanning

In order for a station to be able to connect to an AP, it must first discover an AP. A station discovers an AP by either listening for an AP (passive scanning) or searching for an AP (active scanning). In *passive scanning*, the client station listens for the beacon frames that are continuously being sent by the APs, as seen in Figure 9.4.

FIGURE 9.4   Passive scanning

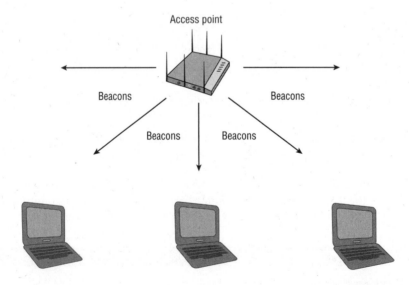

The client station will listen for the beacons that contain the same SSID that has been preconfigured in the client station's software utility. When the station hears one, it can then connect to that WLAN. If the client station hears beacons from multiple APs with the same SSID, it will determine which AP has the best signal, and it will attempt to connect to that AP.

It is important to understand that active and passive scanning can coexist on a network. Also, a station can use either or both methods of scanning to discover the network. Also, when an independent basic service set is deployed, all of the stations in Ad Hoc mode take turns transmitting the beacons since there is no AP. Passive scanning occurs in an ad hoc environment, just as it does in a basic service set.

Active Scanning

In addition to passively scanning for APs, client stations can actively scan for them. In *active scanning*, the client station transmits management frames known as *probe requests*. These probe requests either can contain the SSID of the specific WLAN that the client station is looking for or can look for any SSID. A client station that is looking for any SSID sends a probe request with the SSID field set to null. A probe request with the specific SSID information is known as a *directed probe request*. A probe request without the SSID information is known as a *null probe request*.

If a directed probe request is sent, all APs that support that specific SSID and hear the request should reply by sending a *probe response*. The information that is contained inside the body of a probe response frame is the same information that can be found in a beacon frame, with the exception of the traffic indication map (TIM). Just like the beacon frame, the probe response frame contains all of the necessary information for a client station to learn about the parameters of the basic service set before joining the BSS.

If a null probe request is sent, all APs that hear the request should reply by sending a probe response, as shown in Figure 9.5.

FIGURE 9.5   Active scanning

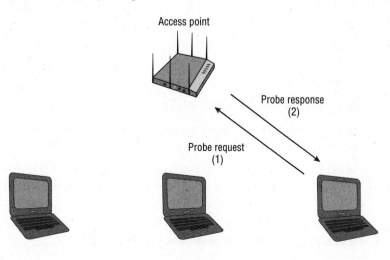

One drawback to passive scanning is that beacon management frames are broadcast only on the same channel as the AP. In contrast, active scanning uses probe request frames that are sent out across all available channels by the client station. If a client station receives probe responses from multiple APs, signal strength and quality characteristics are typically used by the client station to determine which AP has the best signal and thus which AP to connect to. The client station will sequentially send probe requests on each of the supported channels. In fact, it is common for a client station that is already associated to an AP and transmitting data to go off-channel and continue to send probe requests every few seconds across other channels. By continuing to actively scan, a client station can maintain and update a list of known APs, and if the client station needs to roam, it can typically do so faster and more efficiently.

How often a client station goes off-channel for active scanning purposes is proprietary. For example, an 802.11 radio in a mobile device such as a smartphone or tablet will probably send probe requests across all channels more frequently than an 802.11 radio in a laptop. By performing Exercise 9.2 , you will be able to look at probe request and probe response frames.

EXERCISE 9.2

Understanding Probe Requests and Probe Responses

1. To perform this exercise, you need to first download the CWNA-CH9.PCAP file from the book's online resource area, which can be accessed at www.sybex.com/go/cwna4e.

2. After the file is downloaded, you will need packet analysis software to open the file. If you do not already have a packet analyzer installed on your computer, you can download Wireshark from www.wireshark.org.

3. Using the packet analyzer, open the CWNA-CH9.PCAP file. Most packet analyzers display a list of capture frames in the upper section of the screen, with each frame numbered sequentially in the first column.

4. Scroll down the list of frames and click on frame #416, which is a probe request.

5. In the lower section of the screen, look at the SSID field in the frame body and notice that this is a directed probe request.

6. Click on frame #417, which is a probe response.

7. In the lower section of the screen, browse through the information found inside the frame body and notice that the information is similar to a beacon frame.

8. Click on frame #253, which is a probe request. Look at the SSID field in the frame body and notice that this is a null probe request, since it does not contain an SSID value.

9. Click on frames #254, #255, and #256. Notice that there are three probe responses to the null probe request. Each probe response has a different SSID.

Authentication

Authentication is the first of two steps required to connect to the 802.11 basic service set. Both authentication and association must occur, in that order, before an 802.11 client can pass traffic through the AP to another device on the network.

Authentication is a process that is often misunderstood. When many people think of authentication, they think of what is commonly referred to as network authentication— entering a username and password in order to get access to the network. In this chapter, we are referring to 802.11 authentication. When an 802.3 device needs to communicate with other devices, the first step is to plug the Ethernet cable into the wall jack. When this cable is plugged in, the client creates a physical link to the wired switch and is now able to start transmitting frames. When an 802.11 device needs to communicate, it must first authenticate with the AP or with the other stations if it is configured for Ad Hoc mode. This authentication is not much more of a task than plugging the Ethernet cable into the wall jack. The 802.11 authentication merely establishes an initial connection between the client and the AP. Think of this as authenticating that both of the devices are valid 802.11 devices.

The original 802.11 standard defined two different methods of authentication: Open System authentication and Shared Key authentication. Shared Key authentication is simply not used anymore; however, Open System authentication is still used for backward compatibility reasons. The following two sections describe these two original authentication methods.

Open System Authentication

Open System authentication is the simpler of the two authentication methods. It provides authentication without performing any type of client verification. It is essentially an exchange of hellos between the client and the AP. It is considered a null authentication because no exchange or verification of identity takes place between the devices. Open System authentication occurs with an exchange of frames between the client and the AP, as shown in Exercise 9.3.

Wired Equivalent Privacy (WEP) security can be used with Open System authentication; however, WEP is used only to encrypt the upper-layer information of data frames and only after the client station is 802.11 authenticated and associated. Because of its simplicity, Open System authentication is also used in conjunction with more advanced network security authentication methods such as PSK authentication and 802.1X/EAP.

EXERCISE 9.3

Using Open System Authentication

1.   To perform this exercise, you need to first download the CWNA-CH9.PCAP file from the book's online resource area, which can be accessed at www.sybex.com/ go/cwna4e.

2. After the file is downloaded, you will need packet analysis software to open the file. If you do not already have a packet analyzer installed on your computer, you can download Wireshark from www.wireshark.org.

3. Using the packet analyzer, open the CWNA-CH9.PCAP file. Most packet analyzers display a list of capture frames in the upper section of the screen, with each frame numbered sequentially in the first column.

4. Scroll down the list of frames and click on frame #418, which is an authentication request.

5. In the lower section of the screen, look at the 802.11 MAC header and note the source address and destination address.

6. Click on frame #419, which is an authentication response. Look at the 802.11 MAC header and note that the source address is the AP's BSSID and that the destination address is the MAC address of the client that sent the authentication request. Look at the frame body and note that authentication was successful.

Shared Key Authentication

Shared Key authentication uses WEP when authenticating client stations and requires that a static WEP key be configured on both the station and the AP. In addition to WEP being mandatory, authentication will not work if the static WEP keys do not match. The authentication process is similar to Open System authentication but includes a challenge and response between the AP and client station.

Shared Key authentication is a four-way authentication frame exchange:

1. The client station sends an authentication request to the AP.

2. The AP sends a cleartext challenge to the client station in an authentication response.

3. The client station then encrypts the cleartext challenge and sends it back to the AP in the body of another authentication request frame.

4. The AP then decrypts the station's response and compares it to the challenge text. If they match, the AP will respond by sending a fourth and final authentication frame the station, confirming the success. If they do not match, the AP will respond negatively. If the AP cannot decrypt the challenge, it will also respond negatively.

If Shared Key authentication is successful, the same static WEP key that was used during the Shared Key authentication process will also be used to encrypt the 802.11 data frames.

Although it might seem that Shared Key authentication is a more secure solution than Open System authentication, in reality Shared Key could be the bigger security risk. Anyone who captures the cleartext challenge phrase and then captures the encrypted challenge phrase in the response frame could potentially derive the static WEP key. If the static WEP key is compromised, a whole new can of worms has been opened because now all the data frames can be decrypted. Neither of the legacy authentication methods is considered strong enough for enterprise security and WEP is essentially a legacy encryption method that has been cracked. The more secure PSK and 802.1X/EAP authentication methods are discussed in Chapter 13, "802.11 Network Security Architecture."

Association

After the station has authenticated with the AP, the next step is for it to associate with the AP. When a client station associates, it becomes a member of a basic service set (BSS). *Association* means that the client station can send data through the AP and on to the distribution system medium. The client station sends an association request to the AP, seeking permission to join the BSS. The AP sends an association response to the client, either granting or denying permission to join the BSS. In the body of the association response frame is an association identifier (AID), a unique association number given to every associated client. You will learn later in this chapter that the AID is used during power management.

Association occurs after Shared Key or Open System authentication, as you will see in Exercise 9.4. After a client station becomes a member of the BSS by completing association, the client will begin communications at upper layers and establish IP connectivity.

EXERCISE 9.4

Understanding Association

1. To perform this exercise, you need to first download the CWNA-CH9.PCAP file from the book's online resource area, which can be accessed at www.sybex.com/go/cwna4e.

2. After the file is downloaded, you will need packet analysis software to open the file. If you do not already have a packet analyzer installed on your computer, you can download Wireshark from www.wireshark.org.

3. Using the packet analyzer, open the CWNA-CH9.PCAP file. Most packet analyzers display a list of capture frames in the upper section of the screen, with each frame numbered sequentially in the first column.

4. Scroll down the list of frames and click on frame #420, which is an association request. Look at the frame body.

5. Click on frame #421, which is the association response. Look at the frame body and note that the association was successful and that the client received an AID number.

Authentication and Association States

The 802.11 station keeps two variables for tracking the authentication state and the association state. The states that are tracked are as follows:

- Authentication state: unauthenticated or authenticated
- Association state: unassociated or associated

Together, these two variables create three possible states for the stations, as shown in Figure 9.6.

FIGURE 9.6   Authentication and association states

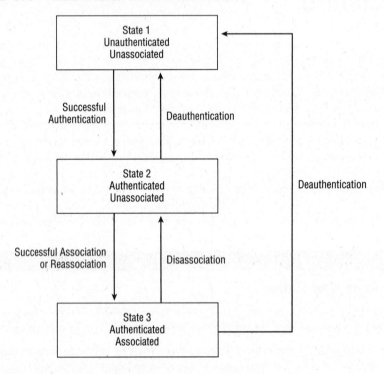

- State 1: initial start state, unauthenticated and unassociated
- State 2: authenticated and unassociated
- State 3: authenticated and associated (pending security mechanisms)

   Because a station must authenticate before it can associate, it can never be unauthenticated and associated. Since the introduction of 802.11i security mechanisms, the IEEE 802.11-2012 standard now considers there to a forth state in the connection state machine (State 4: authenticated and associated - PSK or 802.1X security mechanisms completed.)

Basic and Supported Rates

As you have learned in earlier chapters, the 802.11-2012 standard defines supported rates for various RF technologies. For example, HR-DSSS (802.11b) radios are capable of supporting data rates of 1, 2, 5.5, and 11 Mbps. ERP (802.11g) radios are capable of supporting the HR-DSSS data rates but are also capable of supporting ERP-OFDM rates of 6, 9, 12, 18, 24, 36, 48, and 54 Mbps.

Specific data rates can be configured for any AP as *required rates*. The 802.11-2012 standard defines required rates as *basic rates*. In order for a client station to successfully associate with an AP, the station must be capable of communicating by using the configured basic rates that the AP requires. If the client station is not capable of communicating with all of the basic rates, the client station will not be able to associate with the AP and will not be allowed to join the BSS.

In addition to the basic rates, the AP defines a set of supported rates. This set of supported rates is advertised by the AP in the beacon frame and is also in some of the other management frames. The supported rates are data rates that the AP offers to a client station, but the client station does not have to support all of them.

Roaming

As wireless LANs grew to multiple APs, the 802.11 standard provided the ability for the client stations to transition from one AP to another while maintaining network connectivity for the upper-layer applications. This ability is known as *roaming*, although the 802.11 standard does not specifically define what roaming is.

The decision to roam is currently made by the client station. What actually causes the client station to roam is a set of proprietary rules specified by the manufacturer of the wireless radio, usually determined by the signal strength, noise level, and bit-error rate. As the client station communicates on the network, it continues to look for other APs and will authenticate to those that are within range. Remember, a station can be authenticated to multiple APs but associated to only one AP. As the client station moves away from the AP that it is associated with and the signal drops below a predetermined threshold, the client station will attempt to connect to another AP and roam from its current BSS to a new BSS. Some WLAN vendors attempt to encourage or discourage roaming by manipulating the client station with the use of management frames. However, it should be understood that ultimately the roaming decision is made by the client station.

As the client station roams, the original AP and the new AP should communicate with each other across the distribution system medium and help provide a clean transition between the two. Many manufacturers provide this handoff, but it is not officially part of the 802.11 standard, so each vendor does it using its own method. In WLAN controller–based solutions, the roaming handoff mechanisms usually occur within the WLAN controller. The roaming handoff mechanisms occur at the edge of the network when the conversation is between cooperative APs that do not require a WLAN controller.

Reassociation

When a client station decides to roam to a new AP, it will send a *reassociation* request frame to the new AP. It is called a reassociation not because you are reassociating to the AP but because you are reassociating to the SSID of the wireless network.

Reassociation occurs after the client and the AP move through a serious of steps, as described here:

1. In the first step, the client station sends a reassociation request frame to the new AP.

    As shown in Figure 9.7, the reassociation request frame includes the BSSID (MAC address) of the AP it is currently connected to (we will refer to this as the original AP).

FIGURE 9.7   Reassociation process

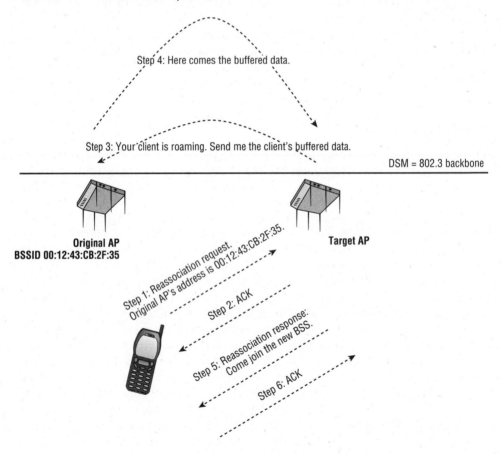

2. The new AP then replies to the station with an ACK.

3. The new AP attempts to communicate with the original AP by using the distribution system medium (DSM).

The new AP attempts to notify the original AP about the roaming client and requests that the original AP forward any buffered data. Please remember that any communications between APs via the DSM are not defined by the 802.11-2012 standard and are proprietary. In a controller-based WLAN solution, the inter-AP communications might occur within the controller. Cooperative APs which do not require a controller will communicate with each other at the edge of the network.

4. If this communication is successful, the original AP will use the distribution system medium to forward any buffered data to the new AP.

5. The new AP sends a reassociation response frame to the roaming client via the wireless medium.

6. The client sends an ACK to the new AP, confirming that it received the forwarded data.

If the reassociation is not successful, the client will retain its connection to the original AP and either continue to communicate with it or attempt to roam to another AP. In Exercise 9.5, you can look at the reassociation request and reassociation response frames.

Understanding Reassociation

1. To perform this exercise, you need to first download the CWNA-CH9.PCAP file from the book's online resource area, which can be accessed at www.sybex.com/go/cwna4e.

2. After the file is downloaded, you will need packet analysis software to open the file.If you do not already have a packet analyzer installed on your computer, you can download Wireshark from www.wireshark.org.

3. Using the packet analyzer, open the CWNA-CH9.PCAP file. Most packet analyzers display a list of capture frames in the upper section of the screen, with each frame numbered sequentially in the first column.

4. Scroll down the list of frames and click on frame #658, which is a reassociation request. Look at the frame body.

5. Click on frame #659, which is the reassociation response. Look at the frame body and note that the reassociation was successful and that the client received an AID number.

Disassociation

Disassociation is a notification, not a request. If a station wants to disassociate from an AP, or an AP wants to disassociate from stations, either device can send a disassociation frame.

This is a polite way of terminating the association. A client will do so when you shut down the operating system. An AP might do so if it is being disconnected from the network for maintenance. Disassociation cannot be refused by either party, except when management frame protection (defined in 802.11w) is negotiated and the message integrity check (MIC) fails. If the disassociation frame is not heard by the other party, MAC management is designed to accommodate loss of communications.

Deauthentication

Like disassociation, a *deauthentication* frame is a notification and not a request. If a station wants to deauthenticate from an AP, or an AP wants to deauthenticate from stations, either device can send a deauthentication frame. Because authentication is a prerequisite for association, a deauthentication frame will automatically cause a disassociation to occur. Deauthentication cannot be refused by either party, except when management frame protection (defined in 802.11w) is negotiated and the message integrity check (MIC) fails.

ACK Frame

The *ACK frame* is one of the nine control frames and one of the key components of the 802.11 CSMA/CA medium access control method. Since 802.11 is a wireless medium that cannot guarantee successful data transmission, the only way for a station to know that a frame it transmitted was properly received is for the receiving station to notify the transmitting station. This notification is performed using an ACK.

The ACK is a simple frame consisting of 14 octets of information, as depicted in Figure 9.8. When a station receives data, it waits for a short period of time known as a *short interframe space (SIFS)*. The receiving station copies the MAC address of the transmitting station from the data frame and places it in the Receiver Address (RA) field of the ACK frame. As you will see in Exercise 9.6, the receiving station then replies by transmitting the ACK. If all goes well, the station that sent the data frame receives the ACK with its MAC address in the RA field and now knows that the frame was received and was not corrupted. The delivery of every unicast frame must be verified, or a retransmission must take place. The ACK frame is used for delivery verification.

FIGURE 9.8   ACK control frame

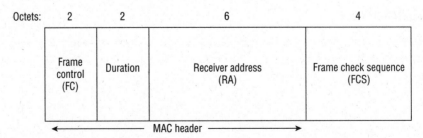

Every unicast frame must be followed by an ACK frame. If for any reason the unicast frame is corrupted, the 32-bit CRC known as the frame check sequence (FCS) fails and the receiving station will not send an ACK. If a unicast frame is not followed by an ACK, it is retransmitted. With a few rare exceptions, broadcast and multicast frames do not require acknowledgment.

EXERCISE 9.6

Understanding Acknowledgment

1. To perform this exercise, you need to first download the CWNA-CH9.PCAP file from the book's online resource area, which can be accessed at www.sybex.com/go/cwna4e.

2. After the file is downloaded, you will need packet analysis software to open the file. If you do not already have a packet analyzer installed on your computer, you can download Wireshark from www.wireshark.org.

3. Using the packet analyzer, open the CWNA-CH9.PCAP file. Most packet analyzers display a list of capture frames in the upper section of the screen, with each frame numbered sequentially in the first column.

4. Scroll down the list of frames and click on frame #1499, which is a data frame.

5. Observe the frame exchanges between frame #1500 and frame #11178. Notice that all the unicast frames are being acknowledged by the receiving station.

Fragmentation

The 802.11-2012 standard allows for fragmentation of frames. *Fragmentation* breaks an 802.11 frame into smaller pieces known as fragments, adds header information to each fragment, and transmits each fragment individually. Although the same amount of actual data is being transmitted, each fragment requires its own header, and the transmission of each fragment is followed by a SIFS and an ACK. In a properly functioning 802.11 network, smaller fragments will actually decrease data throughput because of the MAC sublayer overhead of the additional header, SIFS, and ACK of each fragment. On the other hand, if the network is experiencing a large amount of data corruption, lowering the 802.11 fragmentation setting may improve data throughput. Fragmentation was sometimes used in legacy 802.11b/g networks but is no longer needed with 802.11n/ac networks that support frame aggregation.

If an 802.11 frame is corrupted and needs to be retransmitted, the entire frame must be sent again. When the 802.11 frame is broken into multiple fragments, each fragment is smaller and transmits for a shorter period of time. If interference occurs, instead of an entire large frame becoming corrupted, it is likely that only one of the small fragments will become corrupted and only this one fragment will need to be retransmitted. Retransmitting the small fragment will take much less time than retransmitting the larger frame. If fragmentation is implemented, retransmission overhead may be reduced.

Figure 9.9 illustrates how smaller fragments reduce retransmission overhead. (Please note that this is a representation and not drawn to scale. Additionally, to simplify the illustration, ACKs were not included.) This illustration shows the transmission and retransmission of a large 1,500-byte frame above and the transmission and retransmission of smaller 500-byte fragments below. If there was no RF interference, only the solid-lined rectangles would need to be transmitted. Because of the additional headers (H) and the time between the fragments for each SIFS and ACK, the smaller fragments would take longer to transmit. However, if RF interference occurred, it would take less time to retransmit the smaller fragment than it would to retransmit the larger frame.

FIGURE 9.9 Frame fragmentation

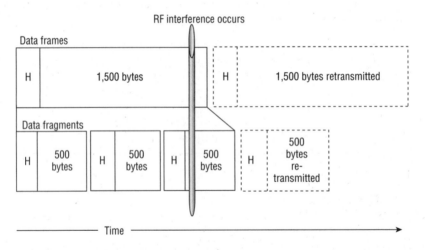

 The transmission of a fragment is treated the same way as the transmission of a frame. Therefore, every fragment must participate in the CSMA/CA medium access and must be followed by an ACK. If a fragment is not followed by an ACK, it will be retransmitted.

Not all wireless LAN adapters allow you to adjust the fragmentation settings. If you do set your wireless LAN adapter to use a smaller fragment size, you must realize that as you roam between APs and as you move between networks, all of your 802.11 frames will be fragmented using the setting you have configured. This means that if you roam to a location where there is no interference, your station will still be using the smaller frame fragments and will actually perform worse than if you had left the fragmentation value at its largest setting.

Protection Mechanism

The 802.11-2012 standard mandates support for both DSSS and OFDM technologies for ERP radios (802.11g). When HR-DSSS (802.11b) client stations need to communicate in a basic service set with an ERP (802.11g) AP and ERP (802.11g) client stations, the 802.11g devices have to provide compatibility for the slower 802.11b devices. ERP APs must also be backward compatible with legacy DSSS (802.11) client stations. This environment is often referred to as *mixed mode*. Contrary to what some people believe, the 802.11g devices do not simply switch to 802.11b mode and communicate using 802.11b data rates. In order for 802.11g, 802.11b, and legacy 802.11 stations to coexist within the same BSS, the 802.11g devices enable what is referred to as the protection mechanism, also known as 802.11g *Protected mode*. In Chapter 5, "IEEE 802.11 Standards," you learned that vendors often offer three configuration modes for 802.11g APs:

802.11b-Only Mode   When an 802.11g AP is running in this operational mode, support for DSSS and HR-DSSS technology is solely enabled. Effectively, the AP has been configured to be an 802.11b AP. Legacy 802.11 DSSS clients, 802.11b HR-DSSS clients, 802.11g clients using ERP-DSSS, and 802.11n clients using one of these three methods will all be able to communicate with the AP at data rates of 1, 2, 5.5, and 11 Mbps. Aggregate throughput will be the same as achieved in an 802.11b network.

802.11g-Only Mode   APs configured as g-only will communicate with only 802.11g client stations using ERP-OFDM technology. Support for 802.11 DSSS and 802.11b HR-DSSS is disabled; therefore, 802.11b HR-DSSS clients and legacy 802.11 DSSS clients will not be able to associate with the AP. Since 802.11n devices are backward compatible, they will be able to connect, but only using ERP-OFDM technology. Aggregate throughput will be equivalent to what can be achieved in an 802.11a network. For example, the aggregate throughput of an AP with a data rate of 54 Mbps might be about 19 Mbps to 20 Mbps. G-only wireless LANs are sometimes referred to as *Pure G* networks.

802.11b/g Mode   This is the default operational mode of most 802.11g APs and is often called mixed mode. Support for DSSS, HR-DSSS, and OFDM is enabled. Legacy 802.11 DSSS clients and 802.11b HR-DSSS clients will be able to communicate with the AP at data rates of 1, 2, 5.5, and 11 Mbps. The ERP (802.11g) clients will communicate with the AP by using the ERP-OFDM data rates of 6, 9, 12, 18, 24, 36, 48, and 54 Mbps. 802.11n clients will also be able to communicate with the AP, although they will have to use ERP also.

You need to understand that these vendor configurations are not part of the 802.11-2012 standard. Although most vendors do indeed support these configurations, the standard mandates support for 802.11 Clause 16 devices, 802.11b Clause 17 devices, and 802.11g Clause 19 devices within the ERP basic service set.

In Chapter 8, you learned that one of the ways of preventing collisions is for the stations to set a countdown timer known as the network allocation vector (NAV). This notification is known as NAV distribution. NAV distribution is done through the Duration/ID field that is part of the data frame. When a data frame is transmitted by a station, the Duration/ID field is used by the listening stations to set their NAV timers. Unfortunately, this is not inherently possible in a mixed-mode environment. If an 802.11g device were to transmit a data frame, 802.11b devices would not be able to interpret the data frame or the Duration/ID value because the 802.11b HR-DSSS devices are not capable of understanding 802.11g ERP-OFDM transmissions. The 802.11b devices would not set their NAV timers and could incorrectly believe that the medium is available. To prevent this from happening, the 802.11g ERP stations switch into what is known as Protected mode.

In a mixed-mode environment, when an 802.11g device wants to transmit data, it will first perform a NAV distribution by transmitting a *request to send/clear to send (RTS/CTS)* exchange with the AP or by transmitting a CTS-to-Self using a data rate and modulation method that the 802.11b HR-DSSS stations can understand. The RTS/CTS or CTS-to-Self will hopefully be heard and understood by all of the 802.11b and 802.11g stations. The RTS/CTS or CTS-to-Self will contain a Duration/ID value that will be used by all of the listening stations to set their NAV timers. To put it simply, using a slow transmission that all stations can understand, the ERP (802.11g) device notifies all the stations to reset their NAV values. After the RTS/CTS or CTS-to-Self has been used to reserve the medium, the 802.11g station can transmit a data frame by using OFDM modulation without worrying about collisions with 802.11b HR-DSSS or legacy 802.11 DSSS stations.

Within an ERP basic service set, the HR-DSSS (802.11b) and legacy 802.11 DSSS stations are known as non-ERP stations. The purpose of the protection mechanism is that ERP stations (802.11g) can coexist with non-ERP stations (802.11b and 802.11 legacy) within the same BSS. This allows the ERP stations to use the higher ERP-OFDM data rates to transmit and receive data yet still maintain backward compatibility with the older legacy non-ERP stations.

So what exactly triggers the protection mechanism? When an ERP (802.11g) AP decides to enable the use of a protection mechanism, it needs to notify all of the ERP (802.11g) stations in the BSS that protection is required. It accomplishes this by setting the NonERP Present bit, and the ERP stations will know that Protected mode is required. There are an assortment of reasons why Protected mode may be enabled. The following are three scenarios that can trigger protection in an ERP basic service set:

- If a non-ERP STA associates with an ERP AP, the ERP AP will enable the NonERP_ Present bit in its own beacons, enabling protection mechanisms in its BSS. In other words, an HR-DSSS (802.11b) client association will trigger protection.

- If an ERP AP hears a beacon from an AP where the supported data rates contain only 802.11b or 802.11 DSSS rates, it will enable the NonERP_Present bit in its own beacons, enabling protection mechanisms in its BSS. In simpler terms, if an 802.11g AP hears a beacon frame from an 802.11 or 802.11b AP or ad hoc client, the protection mechanism will be triggered.

- If an ERP AP hears a management frame (other than a probe request) where the supported rate includes only 802.11 or 802.11b rates, the NonERP_Present bit may be set to 1.

How Does 802.11b Affect 802.11g Throughput?

A common misconception is that 802.11g radios revert to 802.11b data rates when the protection mechanism is used. In reality, ERP (802.11g) radios still transmit data at the higher ERP-OFDM rates. However, when an HR-DSSS (802.11b) station causes an ERP (802.11g) BSS to enable the protection mechanism, a large amount of RTS/CTS or CTS-to-Self overhead is added prior to every ERP-OFDM data transmission. The aggregate data throughput loss is caused by the extra overhead and not by using slower 802.11b rates. A data rate of 54 Mbps usually will provide about 18 Mbps to 20 Mbps of aggregate throughput when protection is not enabled. After protection is enabled, the overhead will reduce the aggregate data throughput to below 13 Mbps—and possibly as low as 9 Mbps.

Because 802.11b/g networks are now considered legacy technology, the degradation of throughput caused by the ERP protection mechanism is usually no longer an issue because of the high data rates defined by 802.11n and 802.11ac. The 802.11n and 802.11ac amendments introduced additional transmission technologies that must also be backward compatible with 802.11a/b/g technology. Therefore, 802.11n and 802.11ac also use protection mechanisms. 802.11n/ac protection mechanisms also create MAC-layer overhead; however, the effective decrease in throughput is rarely noticed due to the higher data rates used by 802.11n and 802.11ac radios.

RTS/CTS

In order for a client station to participate in a BSS, it must be able to communicate with the AP. This is straightforward and logical; however, it is possible for the client station to be able to communicate with the AP but not be able to hear or be heard by any of the other client stations. This can be a problem because, as you may recall, a station performs collision avoidance by setting its NAV when it hears another station transmitting (virtual carrier sense) and by listening for RF (physical carrier sense). If a station cannot hear the other stations, or cannot be heard by the other stations, there is a greater likelihood that a collision can occur. *Request to send/clear to send (RTS/CTS)* is a mechanism that performs a NAV distribution and helps prevent collisions from occurring. This NAV distribution reserves the medium prior to the transmission of the data frame.

Now, let's look at the RTS/CTS from a slightly more technical perspective. This will be a basic explanation, because an in-depth explanation is beyond the scope of the exam. When RTS/CTS is enabled on a station, every time the station wants to transmit a frame it must perform an RTS/CTS exchange prior to the normal data transmissions. When the transmitting station goes to transmit data, it first sends an RTS frame. The duration value of the RTS frame resets the NAV timers of all listening stations so that they must wait until the CTS, DATA, and ACK have been transmitted. The receiving station, the AP, then sends a CTS, which is also used for NAV distribution. The duration value of the CTS frame resets the NAV timer of all listening stations so that they must wait until the DATA and ACK have been transmitted.

As you can see in Figure 9.10, the duration value of the RTS frame represents the time, in microseconds, that is required to transmit the CTS/DATA/ACK exchange plus three SIFS intervals. The duration value of the CTS frame represents the time, in microseconds, that is required to transmit the DATA/ACK exchange plus two SIFS intervals. If any station did not hear the RTS, it should hear the CTS. When a station hears either the RTS or the CTS, it will set its NAV to the value provided. At this point, all stations in the BSS should have their NAV set, and the stations should wait until the entire data exchange is complete. Figure 9.11 depicts an RTS/CTS exchange between a client station and an AP.

FIGURE 9.10 RTS/CTS duration values

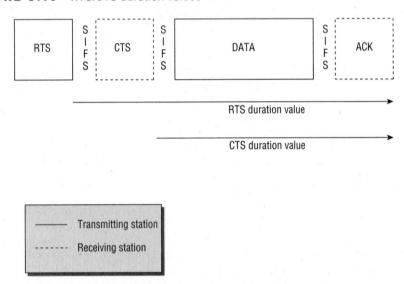

RTS/CTS is used primarily in two situations. It can be used when a hidden node exists (this is covered in Chapter 12), or it can be used automatically as a protection mechanism when different technologies such as 802.11b/g/n coexist in the same basic service set. Figure 9.11 depicts the RTS/CTS frame exchange.

CTS-to-Self

CTS-to-Self is used strictly as a protection mechanism for mixed-mode environments. One of the benefits of using CTS-to-Self over RTS/CTS as a protection mechanism is that the throughput will be higher because fewer frames are being sent.

When a station using CTS-to-Self wants to transmit data, it performs a NAV distribution by sending a CTS frame. This CTS notifies all other stations that they must wait until the DATA and ACK have been transmitted. Any station that hears the CTS will set their NAV to the value provided.

Since CTS-to-Self is used as a protection mechanism for mixed-mode environments, the ERP (802.11g) station will transmit the CTS by using DSSS technology that all stations can understand. Then the DATA and the ACK will be transmitted at a faster 802.11g speed by using ERP-OFDM data rates.

FIGURE 9.11   RTS/CTS frame exchange

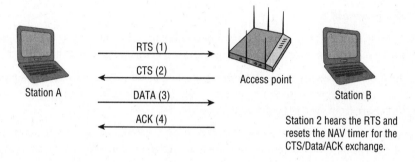

RTS duration = CTS/Data/ACK exchange
CTS duration = Data/ACK exchange
DATA duration = ACK
ACK duration = 0 (exchange is over)

Station C

Station 3 does not hear the RTS
but does hear the CTS and resets
the NAV timer for the Data/ACK
exchange.

RTS (1)
CTS (2)
Access point
DATA (3)
Station B
ACK (4)

Station A

Station 2 hears the RTS and
resets the NAV timer for the
CTS/Data/ACK exchange.

 NOTE   CTS-to-Self is better suited for use by an AP. It is important to make sure that all stations hear the CTS to reserve the medium, and this is most likely to occur if it is being sent by an AP. If a client station were to use CTS-to-Self, there is a chance that another client station on the opposite side of the BSS might be too far away from the CTS-to-Self and would not realize that the medium is busy. Even though this is true, from our experience, it appears that most use CTS-to-Self on client stations to reserve the medium instead of RTS/CTS. CTS-to-Self is used because of the decreased overhead when compared with RTS/CTS. Some vendors allow the user to select whether the client station uses RTS/CTS or CTS-to-Self when in Protected mode.

Data Frames

As mentioned earlier, there are 15 subtypes of data frames. The most common data frame is the *simple data frame*, which has MSDU upper-layer information encapsulated in the frame body. The integration service that resides in APs and WLAN controllers takes the MSDU payload of a simple data frame and transfers the MSDU into 802.3 Ethernet frames. For data privacy reasons, the MSDU data payload should usually be encrypted.

The *null function frame* is used by client stations to inform the AP of changes in Power Save status by changing the Power Management bit. When a client station decides to go off-channel for active scanning purposes, the client station will send a null function frame to the AP with the *Power Management bit* set to 1. As demonstrated in Exercise 9.7, when the Power Management bit is set to 1, the AP buffers all of that client's 802.11 frames. When the client station returns to the AP's channel, the station sends another null function frame with the Power Management bit set to 0. The AP then transmits the client's buffered frames. Some vendors also use the null function frame to implement proprietary power-management methods.

EXERCISE 9.7

Using Data Frames

1. To perform this exercise, you need to first download the CWNA-CH9.PCAP file from the book's online resource area, which can be accessed at www.sybex.com/go/cwna4e.

2. After the file is downloaded, you will need packet analysis software to open the file. If you do not already have a packet analyzer installed on your computer, you can download Wireshark from www.wireshark.org.

3. Using the packet analyzer, open the CWNA-CH9.PCAP file. Most packet analyzers display a list of capture frames in the upper section of the screen, with each frame numbered sequentially in the first column.

4. Scroll down the list of frames and click on frame #2001, which is an unencrypted simple data frame. Look at the frame body and notice the upper-layer information such as IP addresses and UDP port. This information is visible because no encryption is being used.

5. Click on frame #689, which is a null function frame. Look at the 802.11 MAC header. Look in the Frame Control field and note that the Power Management bit is set to 1. The AP will now buffer the client's traffic.

Power Management

One of the main uses of wireless networking is to provide mobility for the client station. Client mobility goes hand in hand with battery-operated client stations. When battery-operated devices are used, one of the biggest concerns is how long the battery will last until it needs to be recharged. To increase the battery time, a bigger, longer-lasting battery can be used or power consumption can be decreased. The 802.11 standard includes a power-management feature that can be enabled to help increase battery life. Battery life is extremely important for smartphones, tablets, handheld scanners, and VoWiFi phones. The battery life of mobile devices usually needs to last at least one 8-hour work shift. The two legacy power-management modes supported by the 802.11 standard are Active mode and Power Save mode. 802.11 power-management methods have also been enhanced by both the ratified 802.11e amendment and the ratified 802.11n-2009 amendment.

Active Mode

Active mode is a legacy power-management mode used by very old 802.11 stations. When a station is set for Active mode, the wireless station is always ready to transmit or receive data. Active mode is sometimes referred to as *Continuous Aware mode*, and it provides no battery conservation. In the MAC header of an 802.11 frame, the Power Management field is 1 bit in length and is used to indicate the power-management mode of the station. A value of 0 indicates that the station is in Active mode. Stations running in Active mode will achieve higher throughput than stations running in Power Save mode, but the battery life will typically be much shorter.

> Stations that are always connected to a power source should be configured to use Active mode.

Power Save Mode

Power Save mode is an optional mode for 802.11 stations. When a client station is set for Power Save mode, it will shut down some of the transceiver components for a period of time to conserve power. The wireless radio basically takes a short nap. The station indicates that it is using Power Save mode by changing the value of the Power Management bit to 1. When the Power Management bit is set to 1, the AP is informed that the client station is using power management, and the AP buffers all of that client's 802.11 frames.

Traffic Indication Map

If a station is part of a basic service set, it will notify the AP that it is enabling Power Save mode by changing the Power Management field to 1. When the AP receives a frame from a station with this bit set to 1, the AP knows that the station is in Power Save mode. If the AP then receives any data that is destined for the station in Power Save mode, the AP will store the information in a buffer. Any time a station associates to an AP, the station receives an *association identifier (AID)*. The AP uses this AID to keep track of the stations that are associated and the members of the BSS. If the AP is buffering data for a station in Power Save mode, when the AP transmits its next beacon, the AID of the station will be seen in a field of the beacon frame known as the *traffic indication map (TIM)*. The TIM field is a list of all stations that have undelivered data buffered on the AP, waiting to be delivered. Every beacon will include the AID of the station until the data is delivered.

After the station notifies the AP that it is in Power Save mode, the station shuts down part of its transceiver to conserve energy. A station can be in one of two states, either awake or doze:

- During the awake state, the client station can receive frames and transmit frames.

- During the doze state, the client station cannot receive or transmit any frames and operates in a very low power state to conserve power.

Because beacons are transmitted at a consistent predetermined interval known as the *target beacon transmission time (TBTT)*, all stations know when beacons will occur. The station will remain asleep for a short period of time and awaken in time to hear a beacon frame. The station does not have to awaken for every beacon. To conserve more power, the station can sleep for a longer period of time and then awaken in time to hear an upcoming beacon. How often the client station awakens is based on a client variable called the *listen interval* and is usually vendor specific.

When the station receives the beacon, it checks to see whether its AID is set in the TIM, indicating that a buffered unicast frame waits. If so, the station will remain awake and will send a PS-Poll frame to the AP. When the AP receives the PS-Poll frame, it will send the buffered unicast frame to the station. The station will stay awake while the AP transmits the buffered unicast frame. When the AP sends the data to the station, the station needs to know when all of the buffered unicast data has been received so that it can go back to sleep. Each unicast frame contains a 1-bit field called the More Data field. When the station receives a buffered unicast frame with the More Data field set to 1, the station knows that it cannot go back to sleep yet because there is some more buffered data that it has not yet received. When the More Data field is set to 1, the station knows that it needs to send another PS-Poll frame and wait to receive the next buffered unicast frame.

After all of the buffered unicast frames have been sent, the More Data field in the last buffered frame will be set to 0, indicating that there is currently no more buffered data, and the station will go back to sleep. The AP will set the value of the station's AID bit to 0, and when the next TBTT arrives, the AP will send a beacon. The station will remain asleep for a short period of time and again awaken in time to hear a beacon frame. When the station receives the beacon, it will again check to see whether its AID is set in the TIM. Assuming that there are no buffered unicast frames awaiting this station, the station's AID will not be set to 1 in the TIM and the station can simply go back to sleep until it is time to wake up and check again.

Delivery Traffic Indication Message

In addition to unicast traffic, network traffic includes multicast and broadcast traffic. Because multicast and broadcast traffic is directed to all stations, the BSS needs to provide a way to make sure that all stations are awake to receive these frames. A *delivery traffic indication map (DTIM)* is used to ensure that all stations using power management are awake when multicast or broadcast traffic is sent. DTIM is a special type of TIM. A TIM or DTIM is transmitted as part of every beacon.

A configurable setting on the AP called the *DTIM interval* determines how often a DTIM beacon is transmitted. A DTIM interval of 3 means that every third beacon is a DTIM beacon, whereas a DTIM interval of 1 means that every beacon is a DTIM beacon. Every beacon contains DTIM information that informs the stations when the next DTIM will occur. A DTIM value of 0 indicates that the current TIM is a DTIM. All stations will wake up in time to receive the beacon with the DTIM. If the AP has multicast or broadcast traffic to be sent, it will transmit the beacon with the DTIM and then immediately send the multicast or broadcast data.

After the multicast or broadcast data is transmitted, if a station's AID was in the DTIM, the station will remain awake and will send a PS-Poll frame and proceed with retrieving its buffered unicast traffic from the AP. If a station did not see its AID in the DTIM, or if its AID was set to 0, the station can go back to sleep.

The DTIM interval is important for any application that uses multicasting. For example, many VoWiFi vendors support *push-to-talk* capabilities that send VoIP traffic to a multicast address. A misconfigured DTIM interval would cause performance issues during a push-to-talk multicast.

Announcement Traffic Indication Message

If a station is part of an IBSS, there is no central AP to buffer data while the stations are in Power Save mode. A station will notify the other stations that it is enabling Power Save mode by changing the Power Management field to 1. When the station transmits a frame with this field set to 1, the other stations know to buffer any data that they may have for this station because this station is now in Power Save mode.

Periodically, all stations must wake up and notify each other if any station has buffered data that needs to be delivered to another station. This recurring period of time when all devices must be awake to exchange this information is known as the *announcement traffic indication message (ATIM) window*. During the ATIM window, if a station has buffered data for another station, it will send a unicast frame known as an *ATIM frame* to the other station. This unicast frame informs the station that it must stay awake until the next ATIM window so that it can receive the buffered data. Any station that either has buffered data for another station or has received an ATIM will stay awake so that the buffered data can be exchanged. All of the other stations can go to sleep and wait until the next ATIM window to go through this process again.

When the ATIM window expires, the nodes that have stayed awake go through the usual CSMA/CA process to exchange the unsent data. If a station is unable to transmit the data during this time, it will simply send another ATIM frame during the next ATIM window and then attempt to send the data during the following CSMA/CA period.

Do not confuse the ATIM frame with the TIM field. The ATIM is a frame used for power management by ad hoc clients not communicating through an AP. The TIM is a field in the beacon frame that tells client stations in Power Management mode that the AP has buffered unicast frames for the clients.

WMM Power Save and U-APSD

The main focus of the 802.11e amendment, which is now part of the 802.11-2012 standard, is quality of service. However, the IEEE 802.11e amendment also introduced an enhanced power-management method called *automatic power save delivery (APSD)*. The two APSD methods that are defined are *scheduled automatic power save delivery (S-APSD)* and *unscheduled automatic power save delivery (U-APSD)*. The S-APSD power-management method is beyond the scope of this book. The Wi-Fi Alliance's *WMM Power Save (WMM-PS)* certification is based on U-APSD. WMM-PS is an enhancement over the legacy power saving mechanisms already discussed. The goal of WMM-PS is to have client devices spend more time in a doze state and consume less power. WMM-PS is also designed to minimize latency for time-sensitive applications such as voice during the power-management process.

The legacy power-management methods have several limitations. As shown in Figure 9.12, a client using legacy power management must first wait for a beacon with a TIM before the client can request buffered unicast frames. The client must also send a unique PS-Poll frame to the AP to request every single buffered unicast frame. This ping-pong power-management method increases the latency of time-sensitive applications such as voice. The clients must also stay awake during the ping-pong process, which results in reduced battery life. In addition, the amount of time that the clients spend dozing is determined by the vendor's driver and not by the application traffic.

FIGURE 9.12   Legacy power management

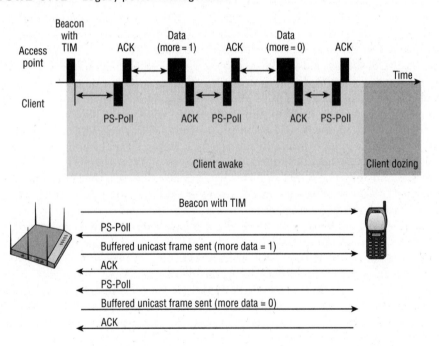

WMM-PS uses a trigger mechanism to receive buffered unicast traffic based on WMM access categories. You learned in Chapter 8 that 802.1D priority tags from the Ethernet side are used to direct traffic to four different WMM access-category priority queues.

The access-category queues are voice, video, best effort, and background. As shown in Figure 9.13, the client station sends a trigger frame related to a WMM access category to inform the AP that the client is awake and ready to download any frames that the AP may have buffered for that access category. The trigger frame can also be an 802.11 data frame, thus eliminating the need for a separate PS-Poll frame. The AP will then send an ACK to the client and proceed to send a frame burst of buffered application traffic during a transmit opportunity (TXOP).

FIGURE 9.13   WMM-PS

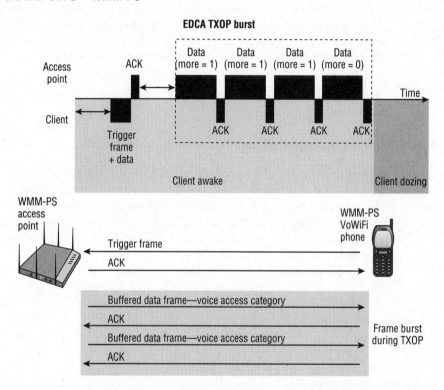

The advantages of this enhanced power-management method include the following:

- Applications now control the power-save behavior by setting doze periods and sending trigger frames. VoWiFi phones will obviously send triggers to the AP frequently during voice calls, whereas a laptop radio using a data application will have a longer doze period.

- The trigger and delivery method eliminates the need for PS-Poll frames.

- The client can request to download buffered traffic and does not have to wait for a beacon frame.

- All the downlink application traffic is sent in a faster frame burst during the AP's TXOP.

A couple of conditions have to be met for a Wi-Fi client to use the enhanced WMM-PS mechanisms:

- The client is Wi-Fi CERTIFIED for WMM-PS.

- The AP is Wi-Fi CERTIFIED for WMM-PS.

It should be noted that applications that do not support WMM-PS can still coexist with WMM Power Save–enabled applications. The data from the other applications will be delivered with legacy power-save methods.

> A white paper from the Wi-Fi Alliance called "Wi-Fi CERTIFIED for WMM®-Power Save: Support for Advanced Power Save for Mobile and Portable Devices in Wi-Fi® Networks (2005)" is available for download at www.wi-fi.org/discover-wi-fi/wi-fi-certified-wmm-programs.
>
> This white paper is highly recommended extra reading for the CWNA exam.

802.11n Power Management

The ratified 802.11n-2009 amendment also defines two new power-management methods. The first method is called *spatial multiplexing power save (SM power save)*. The purpose of SM power save is to enable a MIMO 802.11n device to power down all but one of its radio chains. The second new power-management method, *power save multi-poll (PSMP)*, has also been defined for use for HT (802.11n) radios. PSMP is an extension of automatic power save delivery (APSD), which was defined by the 802.11e amendment. A more detailed discussion about these two power-management methods is presented in Chapter 18.

Summary

This chapter covered key areas of the MAC architecture:

- 802.11 frame format

- Major 802.11 frame types

- 802.11 frame subtypes

- Fragmentation

- ERP protection mechanism

- Power management

It is important to understand the makeup of the three major 802.11 frame types and the purpose of each individual 802.11 frame and how they are used in scanning, authentication, association, and other MAC processes. You should understand the need for an ERP protection mechanism. Without one, mixed-mode networks would not be able to function. Both RTS/CTS and CTS-to-Self provide ERP (802.11g) protection mechanisms.

To help manage battery life, power management can be configured on a wireless station. Active mode provides no battery conservation of any kind, whereas Power Save mode can be invaluable for increasing the battery life of laptop and handheld computing devices. WMM and 802.11n have also enhanced power-management capabilities. We discussed the following power-management pieces in this chapter:

- Traffic indication map (TIM)
- Delivery traffic indication message (DTIM)
- Announcement traffic indication message (ATIM)
- WMM Power Save (WMM-PS)

Exam Essentials

Explain the differences between a PPDU, PSDU, MPDU, and MSDU.   Understand at which layer of the OSI model each data unit operates and what each data unit comprises.

Understand the similarities and differences of 802.11 frames and 802.3 frames.   The IEEE created both of these frame types. 802.11 and 802.3 frames share similar and different properties. Know how they compare to each other.

Know the three major 802.11 frame types.   Make sure you know the function of the management, control, and data frames. Know what makes the major frame types different. Data frames contain an MSDU, whereas management and control frames do not. Understand the purpose of each individual frame subtype.

Know the media access control (MAC) process and all of the frames that are used during this process.   Understand the function of each of the following: active scanning, passive scanning, beacon, probe request, probe response, authentication, association, reassociation, disassociation, and deauthentication.

Know the importance of the ACK frame for determining that a unicast frame was received and uncorrupted.   Understand that after a unicast frame is transmitted, there is a short interframe space (SIFS) and then the receiving station replies by transmitting an ACK. If this process is completed successfully, the transmitting station knows the frame was received and was not corrupted.

Know the benefits and detriments of fragmentation.   By default, fragmentation adds overhead, and fragmented frames are inherently slower than unfragmented frames. If RF interference exists, fragmentation can reduce the amount of retransmitted overhead, thus actually increasing the data throughput. If fragmentation does increase throughput, this is a clear indication of a transmission problem such as multipath.

Understand the importance of ERP protection mechanisms and how they function.   Protected mode allows ERP (802.11g), HR-DSSS (802.11b), and legacy DSSS devices to coexist within the same BSS. Protected mode can be provided by RTS/CTS or CTS-to-Self. CTS-to-Self is strictly a protection mechanism, but RTS/CTS can also be manually configured and used to identify or prevent hidden nodes.

Understand all of the technologies that make up power management.   Power management can be enabled to decrease power usage and increase battery life. Understand how buffered unicast traffic is received in a different way than buffered broadcast and multicast traffic. Understand the power-management enhancements defined by WMM-PS.

Review Questions

1. What is the difference between association frames and reassociation frames?

   A. Association frames are management frames, whereas reassociation frames are control frames.

   B. Association frames are used exclusively for roaming.

   C. Reassociation frames contain the BSSID of the original AP.

   D. Only association frames are used to join a BSS.

2. Which of the following contains only LLC data and the IP packet but does not include any 802.11 data?

   A. MPDU

   B. PPDU

   C. PSDU

   D. MSDU

   E. MMPDU

3. Which of the following are protection mechanisms? (Choose all that apply.)

   A. NAV back-off

   B. RTS/CTS

   C. RTS-to-Self

   D. CTS-to-Self

   E. WEP encryption

4. The presence of what type of transmissions can trigger the protection mechanism within an ERP basic service set? (Choose all that apply.)

   A. Association of an HR-DSSS client

   B. Association of an ERP-OFDM client

   C. HR-DSSS beacon frame

   D. ERP beacon frame with the NonERP_Present bit set to 1

   E. Association of an FHSS client

5. Which of the following information is included in a probe response frame? (Choose all that apply.)

   A. Time stamp

   B. Supported data rates

   C. Service set capabilities

   D. SSID

   E. Traffic indication map

6. Which of the following are true about beacon management frames? (Choose all that apply.)

   A. Beacons can be disabled to hide the network from intruders.

   B. Time-stamp information is used by the clients to synchronize their clocks.

   C. In a BSS, clients share the responsibility of transmitting the beacons.

   D. Beacons can contain vendor-proprietary information.

7. If WMM-PS is not supported, after a station sees its AID set to 1 in the TIM, what typically is the next frame that the station transmits?

   A. CTS

   B. PS-Poll

   C. ATIM

   D. ACK

8. When a station sends an RTS, the Duration/ID field notifies the other stations that they must set their NAV timers to which of the following values?

   A. 213 microseconds

   B. The time necessary to transmit the DATA and ACK frames

   C. The time necessary to transmit the CTS frame

   D. The time necessary to transmit the CTS, DATA, and ACK frames

9. How does a client station indicate that it is using Power Save mode?

   A. It transmits a frame to the AP with the Sleep field set to 1.

   B. It transmits a frame to the AP with the Power Management field set to 1.

   C. Using DTIM, the AP determines when the client station uses Power Save mode.

   D. It doesn't need to, because Power Save mode is the default.

10. What would cause an 802.11 station to retransmit a unicast frame? (Choose all that apply.)

   A. The transmitted unicast frame was corrupted.

   B. The ACK frame from the receiver was corrupted.

   C. The receiver's buffer was full.

   D. The transmitting station will never attempt to retransmit the data frame.

   E. The transmitting station will send a retransmit notification.

11. If a station is in Power Save mode, how does it know that the AP has buffered unicast frames waiting for it?

   A. By examining the PS-Poll frame

   B. By examining the TIM field

   C. When it receives an ATIM

   D. When the Power Management bit is set to 1

   E. From the DTIM interval

12. When is an ERP (802.11g) AP required by the IEEE 802.11-2012 standard to respond to probe request frames from nearby HR-DSSS (802.11b) stations? (Choose all that apply.)

   A. When the probe request frames contain a null SSID value

   B. When the AP supports only ERP-OFDM data rates

   C. When the AP supports only HR/DSSS data rates

   D. When the Power Management bit is set to 1

   E. When the probe request frames contain the correct SSID value

13. Which of the following are true about scanning? (Choose all that apply.)

   A. There are two types of scanning: passive and active.

   B. Stations must transmit probe requests in order to learn about local APs.

   C. The 802.11 standard allows APs to ignore probe requests for security reasons.

   D. It is common for stations to continue to send probe requests after being associated to an AP.

14. Given that an 802.11 MAC header can have as many as four MAC addresses, which type of addresses are not found in an 802.3 MAC header? (Choose all that apply.)

   A. SA

   B. BSSID

   C. DA

   D. RA

   E. TA

15. When a client station is first powered on, what is the order of frames generated by the client station and AP?

   A. Probe request/probe response, association request/response, authentication request/response

   B. Probe request/probe response, authentication request/response, association request/response

   C. Association request/response, authentication request/response, probe request/probe response

   D. Authentication request/response, association request/response, probe request/probe response

16. WLAN users have recently complained about gaps in audio and problems with the push-to-talk capabilities with the ACME Company's VoWiFi phones. What could be the cause of this problem?

   A. Misconfigured TIM setting

   B. Misconfigured DTIM setting

   C. Misconfigured ATIM setting

   D. Misconfigured BTIM setting

17. The WLAN help desk gets a call that all of the sudden, all of the HR-DSSS (802.11b) VoWiFi phones cannot connect to any of the ERP (802.11g) lightweight APs that are managed by a multiple-channel architecture WLAN controller. All the laptops with ERP (802.11g) radios can still connect. What are the possible causes of this problem? (Choose all that apply.)

    A. The WLAN admin disabled the 1, 2, 5.5, and 11 Mbps data rates on the controller.

    B. The WLAN admin disabled the 6 and 9 Mbps data rates on the controller.

    C. The WLAN admin enabled the 6 and 9 Mbps data rates on the controller as basic rates.

    D. The WLAN admin configured all the APs on channel 6.

18. In a multiple-channel architecture, roaming is controlled by the client station and occurs based on a set of proprietary rules determined by the manufacturer of the wireless radio. Which of the following parameters are often used when making the decision to roam? (Choose all that apply.)

    A. Received signal level

    B. Distance

    C. SNR

    D. WMM access categories

19. What are some of the advantages of using U-APSD and WMM-PS power management over legacy power-management methods? (Choose all that apply.)

    A. Applications control doze time and trigger frames.

    B. U-APSD APs transmit all voice and video data immediately.

    C. The client does not have to wait for a beacon to request data.

    D. Downlink traffic is sent in a frame burst.

    E. Data frames are used as trigger frames. PS-Poll frames are not used.

20. WMM-PS is based on which 802.11-2012 power-management method?

    A. S-APSD

    B. U-APSD

    C. PSMP

    D. SM Power Save

    E. PS-Poll

Chapter

10

WLAN Architecture

IN THIS CHAPTER, YOU WILL LEARN ABOUT THE FOLLOWING:

✓ **Wireless LAN client devices**

- 802.11 Radio form factors
- 802.11 Radio chipsets
- Client utilities
- Management, control and data planes

✓ **WLAN architecture**

- Autonomous WLAN architecture
- Centralized network management systems
- Cloud networking
- Centralized WLAN architecture
- Distributed WLAN architecture
- Unified WLAN architecture
- Hybrid architecture

✓ **Specialty WLAN infrastructure**

- Wireless workgroup bridge
- Wireless LAN bridges
- Enterprise WLAN router
- Wireless LAN mesh access points
- WLAN array
- Virtual AP system
- Real-time location systems
- VoWiFi

In Chapter 7, "Wireless LAN Topologies," we discussed the various 802.11 WLAN topologies. You learned that both client and access point stations can be arranged in 802.11 service sets to provide wireless access to another medium. In this chapter, we discuss the multiple devices that can be used in 802.11 topologies. Many choices exist for client station radio cards that can be used in desktops, laptops, smartphones, tablets, and so on.

We also discuss the three logical planes of network operation and where they apply in a WLAN. We explore the progression of WLAN infrastructure devices over the years and the various WLAN architectures that are available. We cover the purpose of many WLAN specialty devices that exist in today's Wi-Fi marketplace.

Finally, you will learn how special solutions, such as a real-time location system (RTLS) and VoWiFi, can be integrated with a WLAN.

Wireless LAN Client Devices

The main hardware in a Wi-Fi network interface card (NIC) is a half-duplex radio transceiver, which can exist in many hardware formats and chipsets. All Wi-Fi client NICs require a special driver to interface with the operating system, as well as software utilities to interface with the end user. Laptop Wi-Fi radios can work with Windows, Linux, and Macintosh, though they require a different driver and client software for each operating system. The drivers for many manufacturers' radios may already be included in the operating system, but often newer radios require or can benefit from an updated driver installation. Many vendors will provide an online automated method to update drivers; however, some may require that the driver be installed manually in the operating system. First generation Wi-Fi radio drivers are often buggy. An administrator or user should always ensure that the most current generation of drivers are installed.

With a software interface, the end user can configure a NIC to participate in a WLAN by using configuration settings that pertain to identification, security, and performance. These client utilities may be the manufacturer's own software utility or an incorporated software interface built into the operating system.

Next, we discuss the various radio NIC formats, the chipsets that are used, and software client utilities.

802.11 Radio Form Factors

802.11 radios are used in both client NICs and access points. The following sections focus mainly on how Wi-Fi radios can be used as client devices. 802.11 radios are manufactured in many *form factors*, meaning the NIC comes in different shapes and sizes. Many Wi-Fi radio card form factors, such as PCMCIA and USB, are meant to be used as add-on external devices, although the majority of Wi-Fi devices now use internal or integrated form factors.

External Wi-Fi radios

For many years, the only option you had when purchasing an 802.11 client NIC was a standard PC Card adapter, which was a peripheral for laptop computers. The PC Card form factor was developed by the Personal Computer Memory Card International Association (PCMCIA). Three *PCMCIA* adapters, also known as PC cards, are shown in Figure 10.1. The PCMCIA radio card can be used in any laptop or handheld device that has a PC card slot. Most PCMCIA cards have integrated antennas. Some PC cards have only internal integrated antennas, whereas others have both integrated antennas and external connectors. Very few laptops have PC card slots anymore, and PC cards have become obsolete in most environments.

FIGURE 10.1   PCMCIA adapter/PC card

Courtesy of Cisco Systems, Inc. Unauthorized use not permitted.

Figure 10.2 shows another peripheral 802.11 radio card form factor: the *ExpressCard* format. ExpressCard is a hardware standard that replaced PCMCIA cards. Most laptop manufacturers replaced PCMCIA slots with the smaller ExpressCard slots.

FIGURE 10.2   ExpressCard radio

Courtesy of Belkin

Secure Digital (SD) and *CompactFlash (CF)* are two peripheral radio card formats that were originally used with a handheld personal digital assistant (PDA). These cards typically require very low power and are smaller than the size of a matchbook. The use of the SD and CF formats with handheld devices has become less common because most handheld devices now have internal 802.11 radios using an embedded form factor.

We have discussed a few Wi-Fi radio form factors that can be used as external NICs with laptops and other mobile devices. However, the *Universal Serial Bus (USB)* 802.11 radio NIC remains the most popular choice for external Wi-Fi radio NICs because almost all computers have USB ports. USB technology provides simplicity of setup and does not require an external power source. 802.11 USB radio NICs exist either in the form of a small dongle device (see Figure 10.3) or as an external wired USB device with a separate USB cable connector. The dongle devices are compact and portable for use with a laptop computer, and the external devices can be connected to a desktop computer with a USB extension cable and placed on top of a desk for better reception.

FIGURE 10.3   802.11 USB NIC

 Real World Scenario

Can I Use the Same Radio in Different Laptops?

The answer to this question depends entirely on two things: the type of radio NIC you are using and whether there are device drivers for the operating system you are using. PCMCIA cards can be used in any laptop as long as the laptop has a PC Card slot. ExpressCards can be used in any laptop as long as the laptop has an ExpressCard slot. USB client adapters can be used by any laptop that has a USB port. Any laptop manufactured today will have a USB port and may have either a PC Card slot or more likely an ExpressCard slot. Using the same internal Mini PCI or Mini PCI Express Wi-Fi NIC in different laptops might be a different story.

Because Mini PCI radio NICs are typically installed in laptop computers, they should not be inserted and removed too many times. Another potential problem is that laptop manufacturers may support only a specific Mini PCI or Mini PCI Express radio chipset, which will limit your choice of laptops in which the NIC can be installed. Check with your laptop vendor before switching internal radios, and make sure that you have appropriate drivers for the specific device you are using. It should also be noted that not all Wi-Fi client device drivers are compatible with all operating systems and service packs.

Internal Wi-Fi Radios

For many years, external Wi-Fi radios were the norm because laptops did not have internal Wi-Fi radio capabilities. However, most laptops and other mobile devices now include an internal Wi-Fi radio. An internal radio format that was initially used is the *Mini PCI*. The Mini PCI is a variation of the Peripheral Component Interconnect (PCI) bus technology and was designed for use mainly in laptops. A Mini PCI radio was often used inside access points and is also the main type of radio used by manufacturers as the internal 802.11 wireless adapter inside laptops. The next generation bus technology form factor is the smaller *Mini PCI Express* and even smaller Half Mini PCI Express. It is almost impossible to buy a brand-new laptop today that does not have an internal Mini PCI or Mini PCI Express radio, as shown in Figure 10.4. A Mini PCI or Mini PCI Express radio card typically is installed from the bottom of the laptop and is connected to small antennas that are mounted along the edges of the laptop's monitor.

FIGURE 10.4   Mini PCI and Mini PCI Express radios

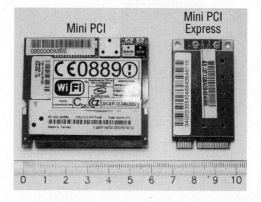

 Real World Scenario

Advantages of Using an External Wi-Fi Radio with a Laptop

Although Mini PCI, Mini PCI Express, and Half Mini PCI Express radios are removable from most laptops, there is no guarantee that any of these form factors will work in another vendor's laptop. One advantage of using ExpressCards, PCMCIA cards, or USB Wi-Fi adapters is that they can be moved and used in different laptops. Also, WLAN engineers usually use a PCMCIA, ExpressCard, or most commonly a USB when running 802.11 protocol analyzer software and/or site survey software applications. These applications often require a special driver for the 802.11 radio that will overwrite and/or conflict with the radio's original driver. Using an independent and external Wi-Fi radio for troubleshooting and site surveys is a common practice so that the driver of the internal Wi-Fi radio remains intact.

Mobile Devices

We have mainly discussed the various types of 802.11 radio NIC formats that are used with laptops. 802.11 radio cards are also used in many other types of handheld devices, such as smartphones, tablets, bar code scanners, and VoWiFi phones. Bar code scanners, such as the Honeywell mobile device pictured in Figure 10.5, have made use of 802.11 radios for many years.

FIGURE 10.5   Bar code scanner

Courtesy of Honeywell

Although older handheld devices did use some of the previously mentioned form factors, manufacturers of most handheld devices use an embedded form factor 802.11 radio (usually a single chip form factor that is embedded into the device's motherboard). Figure 10.6 shows a single chip Broadcom Wi-Fi radio that is found inside some models of the Apple iPhone. Almost all mobile devices use a single chip form factor that is embedded on the device's motherboard. The embedded radios often use a combo chipset for both Wi-Fi and Bluetooth radios.

For many years most people thought of only using their laptop for Wi-Fi connectivity. With the advent of smartphones and tablets, there has been a handheld client population explosion of mobile devices. In recent years, the number of mobile devices connecting to enterprise WLANs has exceeded the number of laptops connecting to the same enterprise WLANs. Technology research firm Gartner estimates that by 2020, the number of smartphones, tablets, and PCs in use will reach about 7.3 billion units worldwide.

Most users now expect Wi-Fi connectivity with numerous mobile devices in addition to their laptops. Because of the proliferation of personal mobile devices, a *bring your own device (BYOD)* policy is often needed to define how employees' personal devices may access the corporate WLAN. A *mobile device management (MDM)* solution might also be needed for onboarding both personal mobile devices and company issued devices onto the WLAN. BYOD strategies and MDM solutions are discussed in great detail in Chapter 20.

FIGURE 10.6 Embedded 802.11 radio

Wearables

One of the next big technology trends may well be wearable computers, also known as *wearables*. A wearable computing device is worn on a person's body and/or clothing. Wearables are meant to provide a constant interaction between a person and a computer, and the wearable becomes an extension of a user's body or mind. Although the concept of wearable computers is not new, wearables with embedded Wi-Fi radios have begun to find a way into the marketplace. Examples of wearable computers include smart watches, wristbands, exercise sensors, and glasses. Figure 10.7 is a picture of Wi-Fi aficionado and world-class blogger Blake Krone wearing a Google Glass headset. You can read Blake's blog at www.blakekrone.com. More information about Google Glass can be found at www.google.com/glass.

Much as with smartphones and tablets, users will soon want to connect to the company WLAN using their personal wearable computer devices. New challenges lie ahead for how IT administrators will manage the onboarding and access policies of wearables to the corporate WLAN. Additionally, wearables such as Google Glass have the potential for numerous applications in enterprise verticals such as healthcare and retail. UK-based Juniper Research projects that the number of wearable devices shipped will rise from about 13 million in 2013 to 130 million in 2018 and that the size of the market will jump from $1.4 billion in 2013 to $19 billion in 2018.

FIGURE 10.7   Google Glass

Internet of Things

When speaking about RFID devices, the phrase *Internet of Things (IoT)* is usually credited to Kevin Ashton:

www.rfidjournal.com/articles/view?4986

Over the years, most of the data generated on the Internet has been created by human beings. The theory of Internet of Things is that in the future, the bulk of the data generated on the Internet might be created by sensors, monitors, and machines. It should be noted that 802.11 radio NICs used as client devices have begun to show up in many types of machines and solutions. Wi-Fi radios already exist in gaming devices, stereo systems, and video cameras. Appliance manufacturers are putting Wi-Fi NICs in washing machines, refrigerators, and automobiles. The use of Wi-Fi radios in sensor and monitoring devices, as well as RFID, has many applications in numerous enterprise vertical markets.

Technology research firm Gartner estimates that by 2020, the number of IoT devices will be 26 billion units worldwide, which far exceeds the expected 7.3 billion PCs, tablets, and smartphones. Could this be the beginning of the self-aware Skynet predicted by the Terminator movies? All kidding aside, a large portion of IoT devices will most likely connect to the Internet with a Wi-Fi radio. Once again, new challenges lie ahead; IT administrators must manage the onboarding and access policies of IoT devices to the corporate WLAN.

802.11 Radio Chipsets

A group of integrated circuits designed to work together is often marketed as a *chipset*. Many 802.11 chipset manufacturers exist and sell their chipset technology to the various radio card manufacturers. Legacy chipsets will obviously not support all of the same features as newer chipset technologies. For example, a legacy chipset may support only 802.11a/b/g technology, whereas newer chipsets will support 802.11n/ac technology.

Some chipsets may only support the ability to transmit on the 2.4 GHz ISM band; other chipsets can transmit on either the 2.4 GHz or 5 GHz unlicensed frequencies. Chipsets that support both frequencies are used in 802.11a/b/g/n/ac client radios. The chipset manufacturers incorporate newer 802.11 technologies as they develop. Many proprietary technologies turn up in the individual chipsets, and some of these technologies will become part of the standard in future 802.11 amendments.

Detailed information about some of the most widely used Wi-Fi chipsets may be found at the following URLs: www.qca.qualcomm.com/, www.broadcom.com, and www.intel.com.

Client Utilities

An end user must have the ability to configure a wireless client NIC. Therefore, a software interface is needed in the form of *client utilities*. Much like a driver is the interface between a radio NIC and an operating system, the Wi-Fi client utility is effectively the software interface between the radio NIC and you. The software interface usually has the ability to create multiple connection profiles. One profile may be used to connect to the wireless network at work, another for connecting at home, and a third for connecting at a hotspot.

Configuration settings for a client utility typically include the service set identifier (SSID), transmit power, WPA/WPA2 security settings, WMM quality-of-service capabilities, and power-management settings. As mentioned in Chapter 7, some client NICs can also be configured for either Infrastructure or Ad Hoc mode. Most good client utilities have some sort of statistical information display, along with some sort of received signal strength measurement indicator tool.

Three major types, or categories, of client utilities exist:

- Integrated operating system client utilities
- Vendor-specific client utilities
- Third-party client utilities

The software interface that is most widely used to configure a Wi-Fi radio is usually the integrated operating system Wi-Fi client utilities. Laptop users will most likely use the Wi-Fi NIC configuration interface that is a part of the OS running on the laptop. The client software utilities are different depending on the OS of the laptop being used. The capabilities of the Wi-Fi client utilities also vary between different versions of operating systems. For example, the Wi-Fi client utility in Windows 7 is much improved and drastically different from the client utility found in Windows XP. The Windows 8 client utility is different than the Windows 7 client utility. The Mac OS X 10.6 (Snow Leopard) client utility is different from the Mac OS X 10.9 (Mavericks) client utility. Figure 10.8 shows the Windows 8 Wi-Fi client utility. Some OSs, such as the Mac OS X 10.9, offer Wi-Fi diagnostic tools, as shown in Figure 10.9.

FIGURE 10.8   Integrated OS client utility for Windows 8

The operating systems of handheld devices usually also include some sort of Wi-Fi client utility. Figure 10.10 shows the client interface found in the Apple iOS 7.0, which runs on iPads and iPhones.

FIGURE 10.9   Wireless diagnostic tool for Mac OS 10.8

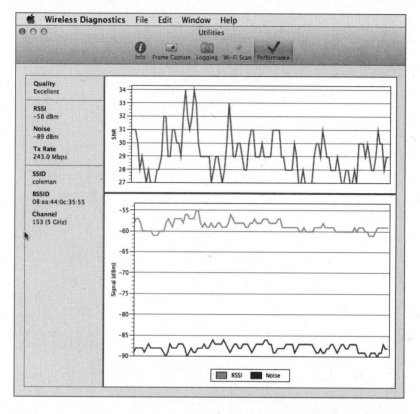

Vendor-specific software client utilities are sometimes available for use instead of an integrated operating system software interface. SOHO client utilities are usually simplistic in nature and are designed for ease of use for the average home user. The majority of vendor-specific software utilities are for peripheral device WLAN radios. The use of vendor-specific client utilities has decreased dramatically in recent years as the use of peripheral Wi-Fi radios has also declined. Enterprise-grade vendor client utilities provide the software interface for the more expensive enterprise-grade vendor cards. Typically, the enterprise-class utilities support more configuration features and have better statistical tools. Figure 10.11 shows the Intel PROSet wireless client interface that can be used on Windows-based laptops with an Intel Wi-Fi radio.

The last type of software interface for an 802.11 radio card is a third-party client utility, such as Juniper Networks Odyssey Access Client, pictured in Figure 10.12. Much like any integrated OS client software, a third-party utility will work with radio cards from different vendors, making administrative support much easier. In the past, third-party client utilities often brought the advantage of supporting many different EAP types, giving a WLAN administrator a wider range of security choices. The main disadvantage of third-party client utilities is that they cost extra money. Because integrated client utilities have improved over the years, the use of third-party Wi-Fi client utilities has declined.

FIGURE 10.10 Integrated OS client utility for iOS 7.0

FIGURE 10.11 Enterprise-class client utility

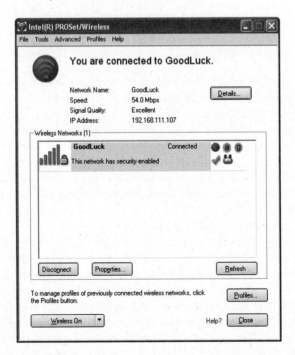

FIGURE 10.12   Third-party client utility

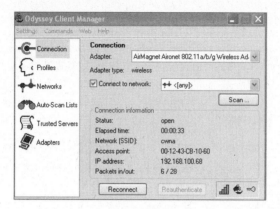

Management, Control, and Data Planes

Telecommunication networks are often defined as three logical planes of operation:

Management Plane   The *management plane* is defined by administrative network management, administration, and monitoring. An example of the management plane would be any network management solution that can be used to monitor routers and switches and other wired network infrastructure. A centralized network management server can be used to push both configuration settings and firmware upgrades to network devices.

Control Plane   The *control plane* consists of control or signaling information and is often defined as network intelligence or protocols. Dynamic layer 3 routing protocols, such as OSPF or BGP, used to forward data would be an example of control plane intelligence found in routers. Content addressable memory (CAM) tables and Spanning Tree Protocol (STP) are control plane mechanisms used by layer 2 switches for data forwarding.

Data Plane   The *data plane*, also known as the user plane, is the location in a network where user traffic is actually forwarded. An individual router where packets are forwarded is an example of the data plane. An individual switch forwarding an 802.3 Ethernet frame is an example of the data plane.

In an 802.11 environment, where these three logical planes of operation function is different depending on the type of WLAN architecture and the WLAN vendor. For example, in a legacy autonomous AP environment all three planes of operation exist in each standalone access point (although the control plane mechanisms were minimal). When WLAN controller solutions were first introduced in 2002, all three planes of operation were shifted into a centralized device. In modern-day deployments the planes of operation may be divided between access points, WLAN controllers, and/or a wireless network management server (WNMS).

Management Plane

The functions of the *management plane* within an 802.11 WLAN are as follows:

WLAN Configuration   Examples include the configurations of SSIDS, security, WMM, channel, and power settings.

WLAN Monitoring and Reporting   Monitoring of layer 2 statistics like ACKs, client associations, resassociations, and data rates occurs in the management plane. Examples of upper-layer monitoring and reporting include application visibility, IP connectivity, TCP throughput, latency statistics, and stateful firewall sessions.

WLAN Firmware Management   The ability to upgrade access points and other WLAN devices with the latest vendor operational code is included here.

Control Plane

The *control plane* is often defined by protocols that provide the intelligence and interaction between equipment in a network. Here are a few examples of control plane intelligence:

Dynamic RF   Coordinated channel and power settings for multiple access points are provided by the control plane. The majority of WLAN vendors implement some type of *dynamic RF* capability. Dynamic RF is also referred to by the more technical term *radio resource management (RRM)*.

Roaming Mechanisms   The control plane also provides support for roaming handoffs between access points. Capabilities may include L3 roaming, maintaining stateful firewall sessions of clients, and forwarding of buffered packets. Fast secure roaming mechanisms, such as opportunistic key caching (OKC), may also be used to forward client master encryption keys between access points.

Client Load Balancing   Collecting and sharing client load and performance metrics between access points to improve overall WLAN operations happens in the control plane.

Mesh Protocols   Routing user data between multiple access points requires some sort of mesh routing protocol. Most WLAN vendors use layer 2 routing methods to move user data between mesh access points. However, some vendors are using layer 3 mesh routing. The 802.11s amendment has defined standardized mesh routing mechanisms, but most WLAN vendors are currently using proprietary methods and metrics.

Data Plane

The *data plane* is where user data is forwarded. The two devices that usually participate in the data plane are the AP and a WLAN controller. A standalone AP handles all data forwarding operations locally. In a WLAN controller solution, data is normally forwarded from the centralized controller, but data can also be forwarded at the edge of the network by an AP. As with the management and control planes, each vendor has a unique method and recommendations for handling data forwarding. Data forwarding models will be discussed in greater detail later in this chapter.

WLAN Architecture

While the acceptance of 802.11 technologies in the enterprise continues to grow, the evolution of WLAN architecture has kept an equal pace. In most cases, the main purpose of 802.11 technologies is to provide a wireless portal into a wired infrastructure network. How an 802.11 wireless portal is integrated into a typical 802.3 Ethernet infrastructure continues to change drastically. WLAN vendors generally offer one of three primary WLAN architectures:

- Autonomous WLAN architecture
- Centralized WLAN architecture
- Distributed WLAN architecture

The following sections describe these three architectures in greater detail.

Autonomous WLAN Architecture

For many years, the conventional access point was a standalone WLAN portal device where all three planes of operation existed and operated on the edge of the network architecture. These APs are often referred to as *fat APs*, or *standalone APs*. However, the most common industry term for the traditional access point is *autonomous AP*.

All configuration settings exist in the autonomous access point itself, and therefore, the management plane resides individually in each autonomous AP. All encryption and decryption mechanisms and MAC layer mechanisms also operate within the autonomous AP. The distribution system service (DSS) and integration service (IS) that you learned about in Chapter 7 both function within an autonomous AP. The data plane also resides in each autonomous AP because all user traffic is forwarded locally by each individual access point. As shown in Figure 10.13, legacy autonomous APs have little shared control plane mechanisms.

An autonomous access point contains at least two physical interfaces: usually a radio frequency (RF) radio card and a 10/100/1000 Ethernet port. The majority of the time, these physical interfaces are bridged together by a virtual interface known as a *bridged virtual interface (BVI)*. The BVI is assigned an IP address that is shared by two or more physical interfaces. Access points operate as layer 2 devices; however, they still need a layer 3 address for connectivity to an IP network. The BVI is the management interface of an AP.

FIGURE 10.13   Simple wireless network using an autonomous architecture

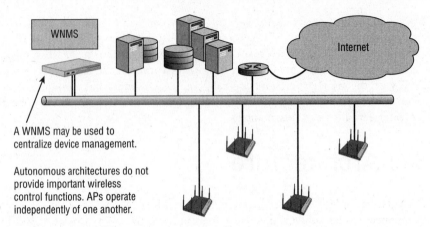

A WNMS may be used to
centralize device management.

Autonomous architectures do not
provide important wireless
control functions. APs operate
independently of one another.

An autonomous access point typically encompasses both the 802.11 protocol stack and the 802.3 protocol stack. These APs might have some of the following features:

- Multiple management interfaces, such as command line, web GUI, and SNMP
- WEP, WPA, and WPA2 security capabilities
- WMM quality-of-service capabilities
- Fixed or detachable antennas
- Filtering options, such as MAC and protocol
- Connectivity modes, such as root, repeater, bridge, and scanner
- Removable radio cards
- Multiple radio card and dual-frequency capability: 2.4 GHz and 5 GHz
- Adjustable or automated transmit power and channel settings
- 802.1Q VLAN support
- IEEE standards support
- 802.3af or 802.3at POE support

Autonomous APs might have some of the following advanced features:

- Built-in RADIUS and user databases
- VPN client and/or server support
- DHCP server
- Captive web portals

Autonomous APs are deployed at the access layer and typically are powered by a PoE-capable access layer switch. The integration service within an autonomous AP translates the 802.11 traffic into 802.3 traffic. The autonomous AP was the foundation that WLAN architects deployed for many years. However, most enterprise deployments of autonomous APs were replaced by a centralized architecture utilizing a WLAN controller, which is discussed later in this chapter.

Centralized Network Management Systems

One of the challenges for a WLAN administrator using a large WLAN autonomous architecture is management. As an administrator, would you want to configure 300 autonomous APs individually? One major disadvantage of using the traditional autonomous access point is that there is no central point of management. Any intelligent edge WLAN architecture with 25 or more autonomous access points is going to require some sort of *wireless network management system (WNMS)*.

A WNMS moves the management plane out of the autonomous access points. A WNMS provides a central point of management to configure and maintain thousands of autonomous access points. A WNMS can be a hardware appliance or a software solution. WNMS solutions can be vender specific or vender neutral.

In the past, the whole point of a WNMS server was to provide a central point of management for autonomous access points, which are now considered legacy devices. That definition has changed considerably over the years. Later in this chapter, you will learn about WLAN controllers, which are used as a central point of management for controller-based APs. WLAN controllers can effectively replace some of a WNMS server capabilities. A WLAN controller can function as a central point of management for access points in small-scale WLAN deployments. However, multiple WLAN controllers are needed in large-scale WLAN enterprise deployments. Currently, most WMNS servers are now used as a central point of management for multiple WLAN controllers in large-scale WLAN enterprises. WNMS servers that are used to manage multiple WLAN controllers from a single vendor may in some cases also be used to manage other vendors' WLAN infrastructure, including standalone access points.

The term WNMS is actually outdated because many of these centralized management solutions can also be used to manage other types of network devices, including switches, routers, firewalls, and VPN gateways. Therefore, *network management server (NMS)* is now used more often. NMS solutions are usually vendor specific; however, a few exist that can manage devices from a variety of networking vendors.

The main purpose of an NMS is to provide a central point of management and monitoring for network devices. Configuration settings and firmware upgrades can be pushed down to all the network devices. Although centralized management is the main goal, an NMS can have other capabilities, as well, such as RF spectrum planning and management of a WLAN. An NMS can also be used to monitor network architecture with alarms and notifications centralized and integrated into a management console. An NMS provides robust monitoring of network infrastructure as well as monitoring of wired and wireless clients connected to the network. As shown in Figure 10.14, NMS solutions usually have extensive diagnostic utilities that can be used for remote troubleshooting.

An NMS is a management plane solution; therefore, no control plane or data plane mechanisms exist within an NMS. For example, the only communications between an NMS and an access point are management protocols. Most NMS solutions use the *Simple Network Management Protocol (SNMP)* to manage and monitor the WLAN. Other NMS solutions also use CAPWAP as strictly a monitoring and management protocol.

Although user traffic is never forwarded by an access point to an NMS, the 802.11 client associations and traffic can be still be monitored. Figure 10.15 shows an NMS display of multiple client associations across multiple APs.

FIGURE 10.14 NMS diagnostic utilities

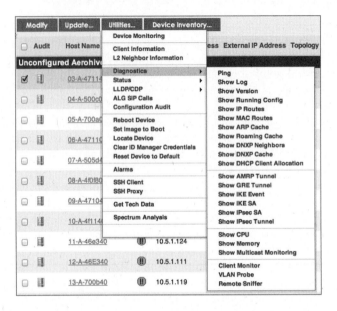

FIGURE 10.15 NMS client monitoring

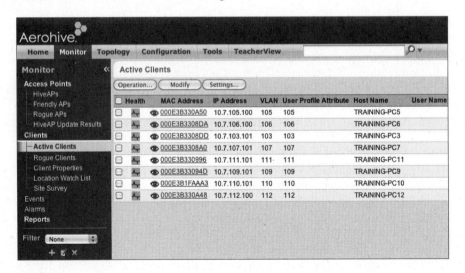

NMS solutions can be deployed at a company data center in the form of a hardware appliance or as a virtual appliance that runs on VMware or some other virtualization platform. A network management server that resides in a company's own data center is often referred to as an on-premise NMS. NMS solutions are also available in the cloud as a software subscription service.

Cloud Networking

Cloud computing and *cloud networking* are catchphrases used to describe the advantages of computer networking functionality when provided under a *software as a service (SaaS)* model. The idea behind cloud networking is that applications and network management, monitoring, functionality, and control are provided as a software service. Amazon is a good example of a company that provides an elastic cloud-based IT infrastructure so other companies can offer pay-as-you-go subscription pricing for enterprise applications and network services.

The two most common cloud networking models are as follows:

Cloud-Enabled Networking   With *cloud-enabled networking (CEN)*, the management plane resides in the cloud, but data plane mechanisms such as switching and routing remain on the local network and usually in hardware. Several WLAN vendors offer cloud-enabled NMS solutions as a subscription service that manages and monitors WLAN infrastructure and clients. Some control plane mechanisms can also be provided with a CEN model. For example, WLAN vendors have begun to also offer subscription-based application services along with their cloud-enabled management solutions. Some examples of these subscriptions services include cloud-enabled guest management, NAC, and MDM solutions.

Cloud-Based Networking   With cloud-based networking (CBN), the data plane is also moved to the cloud with the intent of eliminating hardware other than that used to access the Internet at the local network.

Centralized WLAN Architecture

The next progression in the development of WLAN integration is the centralized WLAN architecture. This model uses a central WLAN controller that resides in the core of the network. In the centralized WLAN architecture, autonomous APs have been replaced with *controller-based access points*, also known as *lightweight APs* or *thin APs*. Beginning in 2002, many WLAN vendors decided to move to a WLAN controller model where all three planes of operation would reside inside the controller. Effectively, all planes were moved out of access points and into a WLAN controller:

Management Plane   Access points are configured and managed from the WLAN controller using a subset of NMS capabilities.

Control Plane   Dynamic RF, load balancing, roaming handoffs, and other mechanisms exist in the WLAN controller.

Data Plane   The WLAN controller exists as a data distribution point for user traffic. Access points tunnel all user traffic to a central controller.

The encryption and decryption capabilities might reside in the centralized WLAN controller or may still be handled by the controller-based APs, depending on the vendor. The distribution system services (DSS) and integration service (IS) that you learned about in Chapter 7 both now typically function within the WLAN controller. Some time-sensitive operations are still handled by the AP.

WLAN Controller

At the heart of the centralized WLAN architecture model is the *WLAN controller* (see Figure 10.16). WLAN controllers are often referred to as *wireless switches* because they are indeed an Ethernet-managed switch that can process and forward data at the Data-Link layer (layer 2) of the OSI model. Many of the WLAN controllers are multilayer switches that can also route traffic at the Network layer (layer 3). However, *wireless switch* has become an outdated term and does not adequately describe the many capabilities of a WLAN controller.

AP Management   As mentioned earlier, the majority of the access point functions such as power, channels, and supported data rates are configured on the WLAN controller. This allows for centralized management and configuration of APs. Some vendors use proprietary protocols for communications between the WLAN controller and their controller-based APs. These proprietary protocols can transfer configuration settings, update firmware, and maintain keep-alive traffic. A WLAN management protocol has gained acceptance. Many WLAN vendors use the Control and Provisioning of Wireless Access Points (CAPWAP) protocol for managing and monitoring access points.

FIGURE 10.16   Centralized WLAN architecture: WLAN controller

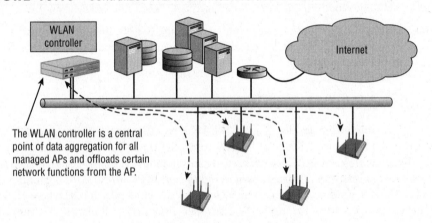

The WLAN controller is a central point of data aggregation for all managed APs and offloads certain network functions from the AP.

A WLAN controller may have some of these many features:

802.11 Traffic Tunneling   A key feature of most WLAN controllers is that the integration service (IS) and distribution system services (DSS) operate within the WLAN controller. In other words, all 802.11 traffic that is destined for wired-side network resources must first pass through the controller and be translated into 802.3 traffic by the integration service before being sent to the final wired destination. Therefore, controller-based access points send their 802.11 frames to the WLAN controller over an 802.3 wired connection.

As you learned in Chapter 9, "802.11 MAC Architecture," the 802.11 frame format is complex and is designed for a wireless medium and not a wired medium. An 802.11 frame cannot travel through an Ethernet 802.3 network by itself. So, how can an 802.11 frame traverse between a lightweight AP and a WLAN controller? The answer is inside an IP-encapsulated tunnel. Each 802.11 frame is encapsulated entirely within the body of an IP packet. Many

WLAN vendors use *Generic Routing Encapsulation (GRE)*, which is a commonly used network tunneling protocol. Although GRE is often used to encapsulate IP packets, GRE can also be used to encapsulate an 802.11 frame inside an IP tunnel. The GRE tunnel creates a virtual point-to-point link between the controller-based AP and the WLAN controller. WLAN vendors that do not use GRE use other proprietary protocols for the IP tunneling. The CAPWAP management protocol can also be used to tunnel user traffic.

As pictured in Figure 10.17, the WLAN controller is usually deployed close to network resources at the core layer. The controller-based access points are connected to access layer switches that provide PoE. The controller-based APs tunnel their 802.11 frames all the way back to the WLAN controller, from the access layer all the way back to the core layer. The distribution system service inside the controller directs the traffic, while the integration service translates an 802.11 data MSDU into an 802.3 frame. After 802.11 data frames have been translated into 802.3 frames, they are then sent to their final wired destination.

FIGURE 10.17   WLAN controller and IP tunneling—core layer

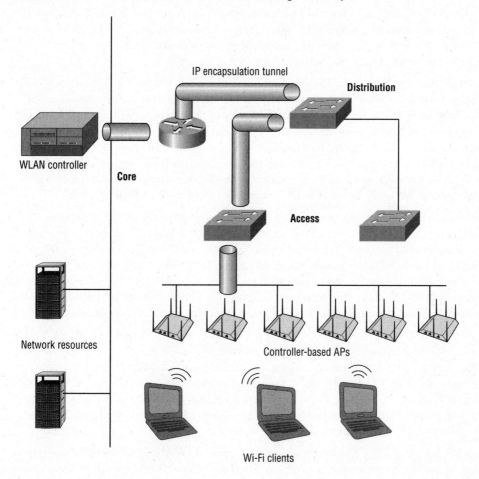

Most WLAN controllers are deployed at the core layer; however, they may also be deployed at either the distribution layer or even the access layer. Exactly where a WLAN controller is deployed depends on the WLAN vendor's solution, and the intended wireless integration into the preexisting wired topology. Multiple WLAN controllers that communicate with each other may be deployed at different network layers, providing they can communicate with each other.

AP Group Profiles   An AP group profile defines the configuration settings for a single AP or group of access points. Settings such as channel, transmit power, and supported data rates are examples of settings configured in an AP group profile. An AP can belong to only one AP group profile but may support multiple WLAN profiles.

WLAN Profiles   WLAN controllers are capable of supporting multiple WLANs, which are often called *WLAN profiles*. Different groups of 802.11 clients can connect to a different SSID which is unique to each profile. The WLAN profile is a set of configuration parameters that are configured on the WLAN controller. The profile parameters can include the WLAN logical name (SSID), WLAN security settings, VLAN assignment, and quality-of-service (QoS) parameters.

WLAN profiles often work together with *role-based access control (RBAC)* mechanisms. When users connect to a WLAN, users are assigned to specific roles. Do not confuse the WLAN profile with an AP group profile. Multiple WLAN profiles can be supported by a single AP; however, an AP can only belong to one AP group.

Multiple BSSIDs   You learned in Chapter 7 that every WLAN has a logical name (SSID) and that each WLAN BSS has a unique layer 2 identifier, the *basic service set identifier (BSSID)*. The BSSID is typically the MAC address of the access point's radio. WLAN controllers have the capability of creating multiple BSSIDs. As you just learned, the WLAN controller allows for the creation of multiple WLANs, each with a unique logical identifier (SSID) that is also assigned to a specific VLAN. Because the BSSID is the MAC address of the WLAN, and because the WLAN controller can support many virtual WLANs on the same physical AP, each virtual WLAN is typically linked with a unique BSSID.

As shown in Figure 10.18, the multiple BSSIDs are usually increments of the original MAC address of the AP's radio. As depicted in Figure 10.16, within each AP's coverage area, multiple WLANs can exist. Each WLAN has a logical name (SSID) and a unique layer 2 identifier (BSSID), and each WLAN is usually mapped to a unique virtual local area network (VLAN) that is mapped to a unique subnet (layer 3). In other words, multiple layer 2/3 domains can exist within one layer 1 domain. Try to envision multiple basic service sets (BSSs) that are linked to multiple VLANs, yet they all exist within the same coverage area of a single access point.

VLANs   WLAN controllers fully support the creation of VLANs and 802.1Q VLAN tagging. Multiple wireless user VLANs can be created on the WLAN controller so that user traffic can be segmented. VLANs may be assigned statically to WLAN profiles or may be assigned using a RADIUS attribute. A more detailed discussion of wireless VLANs can be found in Chapter 13, "802.11 Network Security Architecture." User VLANs are directly attached to the WLAN controller, and users access those VLANs through the IP tunnel between the AP and the controller.

User Management   WLAN controllers usually provide the ability to control the who, when, and where in terms of using role-based access control (RBAC) mechanisms. A more detailed discussion of RBAC can be found in Chapter 13.

Layer 2 Security Support   WLAN controllers fully support layer 2 WEP, WPA, and WPA2 encryption. Authentication capabilities include internal databases, as well as full integration with RADIUS and LDAP servers.

Layer 3 and 7 VPN Concentrators   Some WLAN controller vendors also offer VPN server capabilities within the controller. The controller can act as a VPN concentrator or endpoint for PPTP, IPsec, or SSL VPN tunnels.

Captive Portal   WLAN controllers have captive portal features that can be used with guest WLANs and guest WLAN profiles. Because the captive portal authenticates users but has very limited encryption capabilities, it is rarely used for anything other than guest access.

FIGURE 10.18   WLANs, multiple BSSIDs, and VLANs

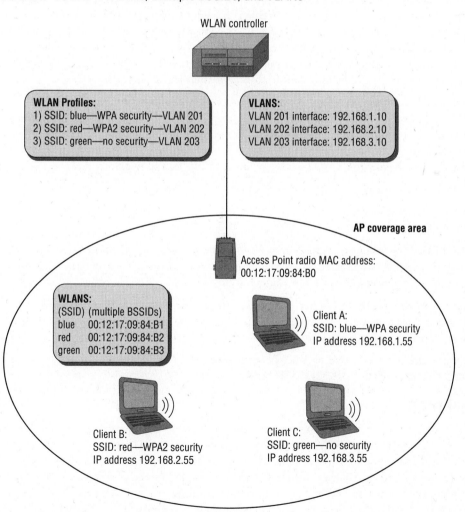

Automatic Failover and Load Balancing WLAN controllers usually provide support for Virtual Router Redundancy Protocol (VRRP) for redundancy purposes. Most vendors also offer proprietary capabilities to load-balance wireless clients between multiple controller-based APs.

Internal Wireless Intrusion Detection Systems Some WLAN controllers have integrated WIDS capabilities for security monitoring. A more detailed discussion on WIDS can be found in Chapter 14, "Wireless Attacks, Intrusion Monitoring, and Policy."

Dynamic RF Spectrum Management The majority of WLAN controllers implement some type of *dynamic RF* capability. A WLAN controller is a centralized device that can dynamically change the configuration of the controller-based access points based on accumulated RF information gathered from the access points' radios. In a WLAN controller environment, the access points will monitor their respective channels as well as use off-channel scanning capabilities to monitor other frequencies. Any RF information heard by any of the access points is reported back to the WLAN controller. Based on all of the RF monitoring from multiple access points, the WLAN controller will make dynamic changes to the RF settings of the lightweight APs. Some access points may be told to change to a different channel, whereas other APs may be told to change their transmit power settings.

Dynamic RF is sometimes referred to as *radio resource management (RRM)*. Standards-based RRM mechanisms have been defined; however, the WLAN controller vendors all implement proprietary dynamic RF functionality. When implemented, dynamic RF provides automatic cell sizing, automatic monitoring, troubleshooting, and optimization of the RF environment— which can best be described as a self-organizing and self-healing wireless LAN.

Bandwidth Management Bandwidth pipes can be restricted upstream or downstream.

Firewall Capabilities Stateful packet inspection is available with an internal firewall in some WLAN controllers.

Layer 3 Roaming Support Capabilities to allow seamless roaming across layer 3 routed boundaries are fully supported. A more detailed discussion on layer 3 roaming and the Mobile IP standard can be found in Chapter 12, "WLAN Troubleshooting and Design."

Power over Ethernet (PoE) When deployed at the access layer, WLAN controllers can provide direct power to controller-based APs via PoE. However, most controller-based APs are powered by third-party edge switches.

Management Interfaces Many WLAN controllers offer full support for common management interfaces such as GUI, CLI, SSH, and so forth.

Split MAC

The majority of WLAN controller vendors implement what is known as a *split MAC architecture*. With this type of WLAN architecture, some of the MAC services are handled by the WLAN controller, and some are handled by the access point. For example, the integration service and distribution system service are handled by the controller. WMM QoS methods are usually handled by the controller. Depending on the vendor, encryption and decryption of 802.11 data frames might be handled by the controller or by the AP.

You have already learned that 802.11 frames are tunneled between the controller-based APs and the WLAN controller. 802.11 data frames are usually tunneled to the controller because the controller's integration service transfers the layer 3–7 MSDU payload of the 802.11 data frames into 802.3 frames that are sent off to network resources. Effectively, the WLAN controller is needed to provide a centralized gateway to network resources for the payload of 802.11 data frames. 802.11 management and control frames do not have an upper-layer payload and therefore are never translated into 802.3 frames. 802.11 management and control frames do not necessarily need to be tunneled to the WLAN controller because the controller does not have to provide a gateway to network resources for these types of 802.11 frames.

In a split MAC architecture, many of the 802.11 management and control frame exchanges occur only between the client station and the controller-based access point and are not tunneled back to the WLAN controller. For example, beacons, probe responses, and ACKs may be generated by the controller-based AP instead of the controller. It should be noted that most WLAN controller vendors implement split MAC architectures differently. The Internet Engineering Task Force (IETF) has proposed a set of standards for WLAN controller protocols called *Control and Provisioning of Wireless Access Points (CAPWAP)*. CAPWAP does define split MAC standards.

> More information about the proposed Control and Provisioning of Wireless Access Points (CAPWAP) standards can be found on IETF's website, at www.ietf.org/html.charters/capwap-charter.html.

Controller Data Forwarding Models

As mentioned earlier, the centralized WLAN architecture usually means that the data plane exists in the WLAN controller because all user traffic is sent from the access points to the WLAN controller using IP encapsulation. However, there are two types of data forwarding methods when using WLAN controllers:

Centralized Data Forwarding   Where all data is forwarded from the AP to the WLAN controller for processing, it may be used in many cases, especially when the WLAN controller manages encryption and decryption or applies security and QoS policies.

Distributed Data Forwarding   Where the AP performs data forwarding locally, it may be used in situations where it is advantageous to perform forwarding at the edge and to avoid a central location in the network for all data, which may require significant processor and memory capacity at the controller. Distributed local data forwarding is also used to avoid high-latency WAN links and to provide traffic with the most efficient forwarding path when communications do not involve centralized resources.

As shown in Figure 10.19, centralized data forwarding relies on the WLAN controller to forward data. The AP and WLAN controller form an IP encapsulation tunnel, and all user data traffic is passed to the controller for forwarding (or comes from the controller). In essence, the AP plays a passive role in user data handling.

As shown in Figure 10.20, with distributed forwarding scenarios, the AP is solely responsible for determining how and where to forward user data traffic. The controller is not an active participant in these processes. This includes the application of QoS or security policies to data. Generally speaking, the device that handles the majority of MAC functions is also likely to handle data forwarding. The decision to use distributed or centralized forwarding is based on a number of factors such as security, VLANs, and throughput. One major disadvantage of distributed data forwarding is that some control plane mechanisms may be unavailable because they exist only in the WLAN controller. Control plane mechanisms that may be lost include dynamic RF, layer 3 roaming, firewall policy enforcement, and fast secure roaming. However, as the controller architecture has matured, some WLAN vendors have also pushed some of the control plane mechanisms back to the APs at the edge of the network.

FIGURE 10.19   Centralized data forwarding

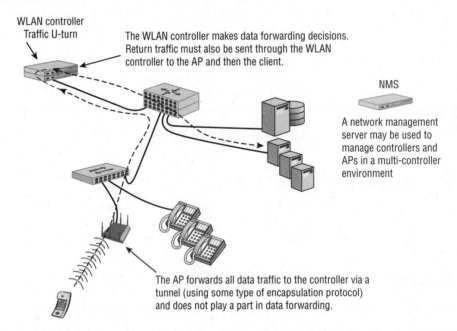

As 802.11ac technology and bandwidth becomes increasingly prevalent in large, enterprise networks, *centralized data forwarding* may become more difficult and expensive due to the traffic loads that can now be generated on the WLAN. Larger controllers with 10 Gbps links will become more commonplace. Additionally, WLAN controller manufacturers are now beginning to embrace *distributed data forwarding* in different ways.

Remote Office WLAN Controller

Although WLAN controllers typically reside on the core of the network, they can also be deployed at the access layer, usually in the form of a remote office WLAN controller. A remote office WLAN controller typically has much less processing power than a core WLAN controller and is also less expensive. The purpose of a remote office WLAN controller is to allow remote and branch offices to be managed from a single location. Remote WLAN controllers typically communicate with a central WLAN controller across a WAN link. Secure VPN tunneling capabilities are usually available between controllers across the WAN connection. Through the VPN tunnel, the central controller will download the network configuration settings to the remote WLAN controller, which will then control and manage the local APs. These remote controllers will allow for only a limited number of controller-based APs. Features typically include Power over Ethernet, internal firewalling, and an integrated router using NAT and DHCP for segmentation.

FIGURE 10.20   Distributed data forwarding

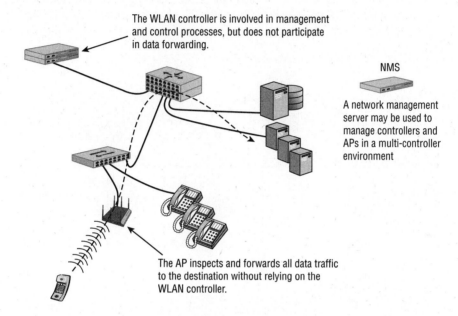

The WLAN controller is involved in management and control processes, but does not participate in data forwarding.

NMS

A network management server may be used to manage controllers and APs in a multi-controller environment

The AP inspects and forwards all data traffic to the destination without relying on the WLAN controller.

Distributed WLAN Architecture

A recent trend has been to move away from the centralized WLAN controller architecture toward a distributed architecture. Some WLAN vendors, such as Aerohive Networks, have designed their entire WLAN system around a distributed architecture. Some of the WLAN controller vendors now also offer a distributed WLAN architecture solution, in addition to their controller-based solution. In these systems, cooperative access points are used, and control plane mechanisms are enabled in the system with inter-AP communication via cooperative protocols. A distributed WLAN architecture combines multiple access points with a suite of cooperative protocols, without requiring a WLAN controller. Distributed WLAN architectures are modeled after traditional routing and switching design models, in that the network nodes provide independent distributed intelligence but work together as a system to cooperatively provide control mechanisms.

As shown in Figure 10.21, the protocols enable multiple APs to be organized into groups that share control plane information between the APs to provide functions such as layer 2 roaming, layer 3 roaming, firewall policy enforcement, cooperative RF management, security, and mesh networking. The best way to describe a distributed architecture is to think of it as a group of access points with most of the WLAN controller intelligence and capabilities mentioned earlier in this chapter. The control plane information is shared between the APs using proprietary protocols.

In a distributed architecture, each individual access point is responsible for local forwarding of user traffic. As mentioned earlier, since the advent of 802.11n, WLAN controller vendors have begun to offer distributed data forwarding solutions to handle traffic load. Because a distributed WLAN architecture entirely eliminates a centralized WLAN controller, all user traffic is forwarded locally by each independent AP. In a distributed architecture, the data plane resides in the access points at the edge on the network. No WLAN controller exists; therefore the data does not need to be tunneled to the core of the network.

FIGURE 10.21 Distributed WLAN architecture

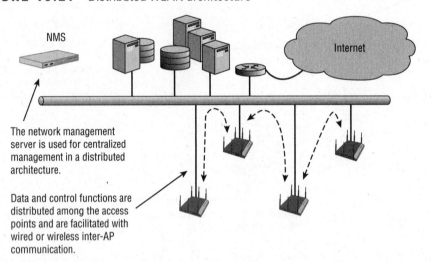

The network management server is used for centralized management in a distributed architecture.

Data and control functions are distributed among the access points and are facilitated with wired or wireless inter-AP communication.

Although the control plane and data planes have moved back to the APs in a distributed WLAN architecture, the management plane remains centralized. Configuration and monitoring of all access points in the distributed model is still handled by an NMS server. The NMS server might be an on-premise server or might be offered as a cloud-based service.

Most of the features mentioned in the earlier section about WLAN controllers can also be found in a distributed WLAN architecture even though there is no WLAN controller. For example, a captive web portal that normally resides in a WLAN controller instead resides inside the individual APs. The stateful firewall and RBAC capabilities found in a centralized WLAN controller now exist cooperatively in the APs. Back-end roaming mechanisms and dynamic RF are also cooperative. As mentioned earlier, all control plane mechanisms reside in the access points at the edge of the network in a distributed WLAN architecture. The APs implement control plane mechanisms cooperatively using proprietary protocols.

How VLANs are deployed in a WLAN environment depends on the design of the network, as well as the type of WLAN architecture that is in place. One very big difference between using a controller-based model vs. a distributed model is how VLANs are implemented in the network design. In the WLAN controller model, most user traffic is centrally forwarded to the controller from the APs. Because all the user traffic is encapsulated, a controller-based AP typically is connected to an access port on an Ethernet switch that is tied to a single VLAN.

With a WLAN controller architecture, the user VLANs usually reside in the core of the network. The user VLANs are not available at the access layer switch. The controller-based APs are connected to an access port of the edge switch. The user VLANs are still available to the wireless users because all of the user VLANs are encapsulated in an IP tunnel between the controller-based APs at the edge and the WLAN controller in the core.

The distributed model, however, requires support for multiple user VLANs at the edge. Each access point is therefore connected to an 802.1Q trunk port on an edge switch that supports VLAN tagging. All of the users VLANs are configured in the access layer switch. The access points are connected to an 802.1Q trunk port of the edge switch. The user VLANS are tagged in the 802.1Q trunk and all wireless user traffic is forwarded at the edge of the network.

Although the whole point of a cooperative and distributed WLAN model is to avoid centrally forwarding user traffic to the core, the access points may also have IP-tunneling capabilities. Some WLAN customers require that guest VLAN traffic not cross internal networks. In that scenario, a standalone AP might forward only the guest user VLAN traffic in an IP tunnel that terminates at a tunnel concentrator that is deployed in a DMZ. Individual APs can also function as a VPN client or VPN server using IPsec encrypted tunnels across a WAN link.

Another advantage of the distributed WLAN architecture is scalability. As a company grows at one location or multiple locations, more APs will obviously have to be deployed. When a WLAN controller solution is in place, more controllers might also have to be purchased and deployed as the AP count grows. With the controller-less distributed WLAN architecture, only new APs are deployed as the company grows. Many vertical markets such as K–12 education and retail have schools or stores at numerous locations. A distributed WLAN architecture can be the better choice as opposed to deploying a WLAN controller at each location.

Unified WLAN Architecture

WLAN architecture could very well take another direction by fully integrating WLAN controller capabilities into wired network infrastructure devices. Wired switches and routers at both the core and the edge would also have WLAN controller capabilities, thereby allowing for the combined management of the wireless and wired networks. This unified architecture has already begun to be deployed by some vendors and will likely grow in acceptance as WLAN deployments become more commonplace and the need for fuller seamless integration continues to rise.

Hybrid Architecture

It is important to understand that none of the WLAN architectures described in this chapter are written in stone. Many hybrids of these WLAN architectures exist among the WLAN vendors. As was already mentioned, some of the WLAN controller vendors are pushing some of the control plane intelligence back into the access points. One WLAN controller vendor has a cloud-based controller where much of the control plane intelligence exists in the cloud.

Typically, the data plane is centralized when using WLAN controllers, but distributed data forwarding is also available. With a controller-less distributed WLAN architecture, all data is forwarded locally, but the ability to centralize the data plane is a capability of a distributed WLAN architecture.

In a distributed WLAN architecture, the management plane resides in an on-premise or cloud-based network management server. With the WLAN controller model, a subset of the management plane normally exists in the WLAN controller. However, the management plane might also be pushed into an NMS that not only manages the controller-based APs but also manages the WLAN controllers.

Specialty WLAN Infrastructure

In the previous sections, we discussed the progression of WLAN network infrastructure devices that are used to integrate an 802.11 wireless network into a wired network architecture. The Wi-Fi marketplace has also produced many specialty WLAN devices in addition to APs and WLAN controllers. Many of these devices, such as bridges and mesh networks, have become extremely popular, although they operate outside of the defined 802.11 standards. You will look at these devices in the following sections.

Wireless Workgroup Bridge

A *workgroup bridge (WGB)* is a wireless device that provides wireless connectivity for wired infrastructure devices that do not have radio cards. The radio card inside the WGB associates with an access point and joins the basic service set (BSS) as a client station. As depicted in Figure 10.22, multiple Ethernet devices are connected behind the wired side of the WGB. This provides fast wireless connectivity for wired devices through the association the WGB has with the access point. Because the WGB is an associated client of the access point, the WGB does not provide connectivity for other wireless clients. It is also important to understand that only the radio card inside the WGB can contend for the 802.11 wireless medium, and the wired cards behind the WGB cannot contend for the half-duplex RF medium.

Most wireless workgroup bridges can provide connectivity for as many as eight wired devices, but it depends on the vendor. Some WGBs provide connectivity for only one wired device and are sometimes referred to as a *universal client*. The workgroup bridge can be very useful in providing wireless connectivity for small desktop workgroups, cash registers, network printers, and any other devices with Ethernet ports. The need for WGBs has greatly diminished because 802.11 radios are replacing Ethernet cards in many client devices.

Wireless LAN Bridges

A common specialty deployment of 802.11 technology is the *wireless LAN bridge*. The purpose of bridging is to provide wireless connectivity between two or more wired networks. A bridge generally supports all the same features that an autonomous access point possesses, but the purpose is to connect wired networks and not to provide wireless connectivity to client stations. Although bridge links are sometimes used indoors, generally they are used outdoors to connect the wired networks inside two buildings. An outdoor bridge link is often used as a redundant backup to T1 or fiber connections between buildings. Outdoor wireless bridge links are even more commonly used as replacements to T1 or fiber connections between buildings because of their substantial cost savings.

FIGURE 10.22   Wireless workgroup bridge

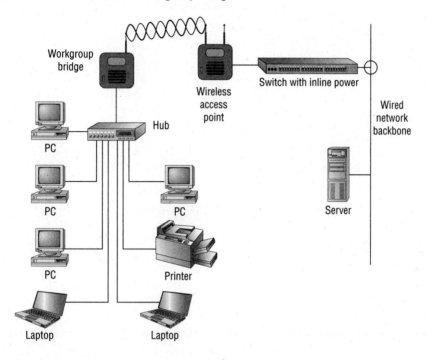

Wireless bridges support two major configuration settings: *root* and *nonroot*. Bridges work in a parent/child-type relationship, so think of the root bridge as the parent and the nonroot bridge as the child.

A bridge link that connects only two wired networks is known as a *point-to-point (PtP)* bridge. Figure 10.23 shows a PtP connection between two wired networks using two 802.11 bridges and directional antennas. Note that one of the bridges must be configured as the parent root bridge and the other bridge is configured as the child nonroot bridge.

FIGURE 10.23   Point-to-point WLAN bridging

A *point-to-multipoint (PtMP)* bridge link connects multiple wired networks. The root bridge is the central bridge, and multiple nonroot bridges connect back to the root bridge. Figure 10.24 shows a PtMP bridge link between four buildings. Please note that the root bridge is using a high-gain omnidirectional antenna, whereas the nonroot bridges are all using unidirectional antennas pointing back to the antenna of the root bridge. Also notice that there is only one root bridge in a PtMP connection. There can never be more than one root bridge.

FIGURE 10.24   Point-to-multipoint WLAN bridging

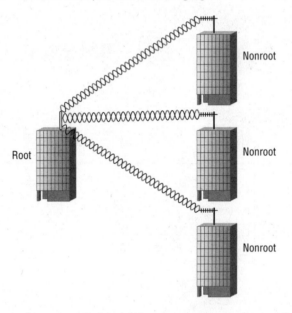

Besides the root and nonroot modes, bridges have other vendor configuration modes, as described in Table 10.1.

TABLE 10.1   Vendor bridge configuration modes

Configuration Mode	Description
WGB mode	Converts a bridge into a workgroup bridge
Root with Clients	Root bridge that also allows clients to associate
Nonroot with Clients	Nonroot bridge that also allows clients to associate
Root without Clients	Root bridge that does not allow clients to associate
Nonroot without Clients	Nonroot bridge that does not allows clients to associate

Clients can affect the throughput of the bridge link because the clients add medium contention overhead. Also, because of performance issues, the repeater mode is not a recommended mode for wireless bridging. If at all possible, a better bridge deployment practice is to use two separate bridge links, as opposed to repeating the link of a root bridge to a nonroot bridge.

Considerations when deploying outdoor bridge links are numerous, including the Fresnel zone, earth bulge, free space path loss, link budget, and fade margin. There may be other considerations as well, including the IR and EIRP power regulations as defined by the regulatory body of your country.

Point-to-point links in the 2.4 GHz band can be as long as a few miles. A problem that might occur over a long-distance link is an ACK timeout. Because of the half-duplex nature of the medium, every unicast frame must be acknowledged. Therefore, a unicast frame sent across a long-distance PtP link by one bridge must immediately receive an ACK frame from the opposite bridge, sent back across the same long-distance link. Even though RF travels at the speed of light, the ACK may not be received quickly enough. The original bridge will time out after not receiving the ACK frame for a certain period of microseconds and will assume that a collision has occurred. The original bridge will then retransmit the unicast frame even though the ACK frame is on the way. Retransmitting unicast traffic that does not need to be resent can cause throughput degradation of as much as 50 percent. To resolve this problem, most bridges have an ACK timeout setting that can be adjusted to allow a longer period of time for a bridge to receive the ACK frame across the long-distance link.

A common problem with point-to-multipoint bridging is mounting the high-gain omnidirectional antenna of the root bridge too high, as pictured in Figure 10.25. The result is that the vertical line of sight with the directional antennas of the nonroot bridges is not adequate. The solution for this problem is to use a high-gain omnidirectional antenna that provides a certain amount of electrical downtilt or to use directional sector antennas aligned to provide omnidirectional coverage.

FIGURE 10.25   Common bridging challenge

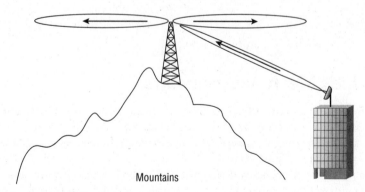

Mountains

Enterprise WLAN Routers

In addition to the main corporate office, companies often have branch offices in remote locations. A company might have branch offices across a region or an entire country, or they may even be spread globally. The challenge for IT personnel is how to provide a seamless enterprise wired and wireless solution across all locations. A distributed solution using enterprise-grade WLAN routers at each branch office is a common choice.

Keep in mind that WLAN routers are very different from access points. Unlike access points, which use a bridged virtual interface, wireless routers have separate routed interfaces. The radio card exists on one subnet while the WAN Ethernet port exists on a different subnet.

Branch WLAN routers have the ability to connect back to corporate headquarters with VPN tunnels. Employees at the branch offices can access corporate resources across the WAN through the VPN tunnel. Even more important is the fact that the corporate VLANs, SSIDs, and WLAN security can all be extended to the remote branch offices. An employee at a branch office connects to the same SSID that they would connect to at corporate headquarters. The wired and wireless network access policies are therefore seamless across the entire organization. These seamless policies can be extended to the WLAN routers at each branch location.

The enterprise-grade WLAN routers are very similar to the consumer-grade Wi-Fi routers that most of us use at home. However, enterprise WLAN routers are manufactured with better-quality hardware and offer a wider array of features.

The following features are often supported by enterprise WLAN routers:

- Configurable 802.11 radios
- Multiport Ethernet switch for connecting wired clients
- PoE-enabled Ethernet ports
- Network Address Translation (NAT)
- Port Address Translation (PAT)
- Port forwarding
- Firewall
- VPN client
- DHCP server
- USB support for 3G/4G cellular backhaul

Wireless LAN Mesh Access Points

Almost all WLAN vendors now offer *WLAN mesh access point* capabilities. Wireless mesh APs communicate with each other by using proprietary layer 2 routing protocols and create a self-forming and self-healing wireless infrastructure (a mesh) over which edge devices can communicate, as shown in Figure 10.26.

A self-forming WLAN mesh network automatically connects access points upon installation and dynamically updates routes as more clients are added. Because interference may occur, a self-healing WLAN mesh network will automatically reroute data traffic in a Wi-Fi mesh cell. Proprietary layer 2 intelligent routing protocols determine the dynamic routes based on measurement of traffic, signal strength, data rates, hops, and other parameters. Although a WLAN mesh network can be a mesh of repeater-like access points that all operate on one frequency, dual-band mesh APs are now much more common. With dual-band

WLAN mesh APs, typically the 5 GHz radios are used for the mesh infrastructure and to provide backhaul whereas the 2.4 GHz radios are used to provide access to the client stations.

FIGURE 10.26   Wireless LAN mesh network

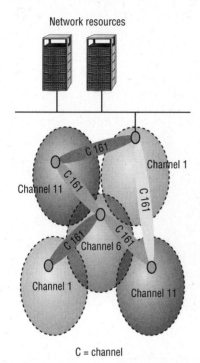

Network resources

2.4 GHz channels 1, 6, and 11 used for access coverage

5 GHz channel 161 used for backhaul

Channel 11

Channel 1

Channel 6

Channel 1

Channel 11

C = channel

WLAN Array

A company called Xirrus offers a proprietary solution that combines a WLAN controller and multiple access points in a single hardware device known as a Wi-Fi array. The CWNP program uses the generic term *WLAN array* to describe this technology. As shown in Figure 10.27, up to 16 access-point radios using sector antennas and an embedded WLAN controller all reside in one device. The WLAN controller is obviously deployed at the access layer because the device is mounted on the ceiling. The embedded WLAN controller offers many of the same features and capabilities found in more traditional WLAN controllers.

One of the key points of a WLAN array is that each AP has a sector antenna providing directional coverage. Each AP therefore provides a sector of coverage. The WLAN array is simply an indoor sectorized array solution that provides 360 degrees of horizontal coverage by combining the directional coverage of all the sector APs. The directional coverage of each AP increases the range much like an outdoor sectorized array. The number of radios that are in a WLAN array often depends on the model and configuration. A WLAN array may have four

AP radios, eight AP radios, or even as many as sixteen AP radios. A 16 access-point WLAN array would consist of four 2.4 GHz radios and twelve 5 GHz radios. One of the radios can be used as a full-time sensor device for the WIDS that is embedded with the controller.

FIGURE 10.27 WLAN array

Courtesy of Xirrus

One major advantage of the WLAN array solution is that much less physical equipment needs to be deployed; therefore, the number of devices that have to be installed and managed is drastically reduced. WLAN arrays are also useful in high user density environments and can also be used to reduce cable runs.

Virtual AP System

Several WLAN vendors offer solutions known as *virtual APs*. A virtual access point solution uses multiple access points that all share a single basic service set identifier (BSSID). Because the multiple access points advertise only a single virtual MAC address (BSSID), client stations believe they are connected to only a single access point, although they may be roaming across multiple physical APs. The main advantage is that clients experience a *zero handoff* time and many of the latency issues associated with roaming are resolved. All the handoff and management is handled by a central WLAN controller. A virtual AP solution also uses a unique WLAN topology called *single-channel architecture (SCA)*. All of the access points in an SCA transmit on the same channel but contend for the airtime in a coordinated manner handled by the WLAN controller. WLAN vendors such as Meru Networks and Extricom use creative proprietary methods outside the constraints of the 802.11-2012 standard to provide virtual AP and SCA topologies.

A more detailed discussion about single-channel architecture (SCA) and multiple-channel architecture (MCA) can be found in Chapter 12.

Real-Time Location Systems

Network management servers (NMSs), WLAN controllers and WIDS solutions have some integrated capabilities to track 802.11 clients by using the access points as sensors. However, the tracking capabilities are not necessarily real-time and may be accurate to within only about 25 feet. The tracking capabilities in WLAN controllers and WIDS solutions provide a *near-time* solution and cannot track Wi-Fi RFID tags. Several companies, such as AeroScout and Ekahau, provide a WLAN *real-time location system (RTLS)*, which can track the location of any 802.11 radio device as well as active Wi-Fi RFID tags with much greater accuracy. The components of an overlay WLAN RTLS solution include the preexisting WLAN infrastructure, preexisting WLAN clients, Wi-Fi RFID tags, and an RTLS server. Additional RTLS WLAN sensors can also be added to supplement the preexisting WLAN APs.

Active RFID tags and/or standard Wi-Fi devices transmit a brief signal at a regular interval, adding status or sensor data if appropriate. Figure 10.28 shows an active RFID tag attached to a hospital IV pump. The signal is received by standard wireless APs (or RTLS sensors), without any infrastructure changes needed, and is sent to a processing engine that resides in the RTLS server at the core of the network. The RTLS server uses signal strength and/or time-of-arrival algorithms to determine location coordinates.

FIGURE 10.28   Active 802.11 RFID tag

Courtesy of AeroScout

As Figure 10.29 shows, a software application interface is then used to see location and status data on a display map of the building's floor plan. The RTLS application can display maps, enable searches, automate alerts, manage assets, and interact with third-party applications.

FIGURE 10.29 RTLS application

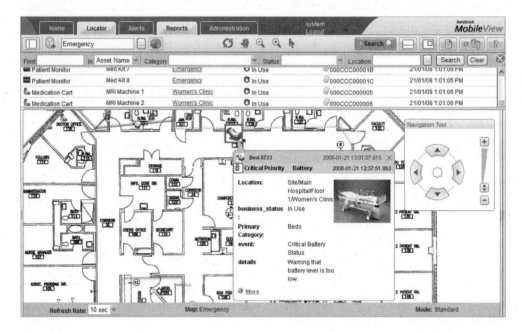

Courtesy of AeroScout

VoWiFi

VoIP communications have been around for many years on wired networks. However, using VoIP on an 802.11 wireless LAN presents many challenges due to the RF environment and QoS considerations. In recent years, the demand for *Voice over Wi-Fi (VoWiFi)* solutions has grown considerably. The WLAN can be used to provide communications for all data applications while at the same time providing for voice communications using the same WLAN infrastructure. The components needed to deploy a VoWiFi solution include the following:

VoWiFi Telephones A VoWiFi phone is similar to a cell phone except the radio is an 802.11 radio instead of a cellular radio. VoWiFi phones are 802.11 client stations that communicate through an access point. They fully support WEP, WPA, and WPA2 encryption and WMM quality-of-service capabilities. Figure 10.30 shows SpectraLink's 8030 VoWiFi phone, which has an 802.11a/b/g radio and can operate in either the 2.4 GHz or the 5 GHz band. VoWiFi technology can also reside in form factors other than a telephone.

As pictured in Figure 10.31, VoWiFi vendor Vocera sells an 802.11 communications badge that is a wearable device that weighs less than two ounces. The Vocera badge is a fully functional VoWiFi phone that also uses speech recognition and voiceprint verification software. Currently most VoWiFi solutions use the *Session Initiation Protocol (SIP)* as the signaling protocol for voice communications over an IP network.

FIGURE 10.30   VoWiFi phone (SpectraLink 8030)

FIGURE 10.31   Vocera communications badge

Courtesy of Vocera

802.11 Infrastructure (APs and Controllers)   An existing WLAN infrastructure is used for 802.11 communications between the VoWiFi and access points. Standalone APs and/or WLAN controller solutions can both be used.

PBX   A *private branch exchange (PBX)* is a telephone exchange that serves a particular business or office. PBXs make connections among the internal telephones of a private company and also connect them to the *public switched telephone network (PSTN)* via trunk lines. The PBX provides dial tone and may provide other features such as voicemail.

WMM Support   As discussed in earlier chapters, WMM mechanisms are needed to properly support QoS.

Summary

In this chapter, we discussed the various types of radio card formats, their chipsets, and the software interfaces needed for client station configuration. We also showed you the logical progression that WLAN devices have made, starting from autonomous access points, moving to WLAN controllers, and then moving along a path toward a distributed architecture. In addition, we covered specialty WLAN infrastructure devices that often meet needs that may not be met by more traditional WLAN architecture.

The authors of this book recommend that before you take the CWNA exam, you get some hands-on experience with some WLAN infrastructure devices. We understand that most individuals cannot afford a $10,000 WLAN controller; however, we do recommend that you purchase at least one 802.11a/b/g/n client adapter and either an access point or a SOHO wireless router. Many enterprise WLAN vendors also offer "free access point" programs to potential customers. Hands-on experience will solidify much of what you have learned in this chapter as well as in many of the other chapters in this book.

Exam Essentials

Know the major radio card formats.   The 802.11 standard does not mandate what type of format can be used by an 802.11 radio. 802.11 radios exist in multiple formats.

Understand the need for client adapters to have an operating system interface and a user interface.   A client adapter requires a special driver to communicate with the operating system and a software client utility for user configuration.

Identify the three major types of client utilities.   The three types of client utilities are enterprise, integrated, and third party.

Define the three logical network planes of operation.   Understand the differences between the management, control, and data plane. Be able to explain where they are used within different WLAN architectures.

Explain the progression of WLAN architecture.   Be able to explain the differences and similarities of autonomous, centralized, and distributed WLAN architectures.

Identify the capabilities of all WLAN legacy infrastructure devices.   Understand the capabilities of autonomous APs. Explain the differences between autonomous APs and controller-based APs.

Identify the capabilities of a WLAN controller solution.   Understand all the features and functionality that a WLAN controller solution provides. Be able to explain IP tunneling, split MAC architecture, virtual BSSIDs, WLAN profiles, and dynamic RF.

Identify the capabilities of a distributed WLAN architecture.   Understand that all the control plane mechanisms reside in cooperative protocols at the edge of the network and that user traffic is forwarded locally. The management plane is centralized in the form of an NMS.

Explain the role and configuration of WLAN bridges and workgroup bridges.   The CWNA test covers bridging quite extensively. Know all of the different types of bridges and the difference between root and nonroot bridges. Be able to explain the differences between point-to-point and point-to-multipoint bridging. Understand bridging problems such as ACK timeout, and study other bridging considerations that are covered in other chapters, such as the Fresnel zone and system operating margin.

Explain WLAN specialty infrastructure.   Be able to explain how RTLS and VoWiFi solutions can all be integrated with a WLAN. Explain other nontraditional WLAN solutions such as WLAN arrays.

Review Questions

1. What type of 802.11 radio form factor is normally used in mobile devices?

    A. Integrated single chip

    B. PCMCIA

    C. Express Mini PCI

    D. Mini PCI

    E. Secure Digital

2. How many root bridges exist in a point-to-multipoint bridge link?

    A. None

    B. One

    C. Two

    D. Multiple

    E. All of the above

3. Which radio formats can be used by 802.11 technology?

    A. CF

    B. Secure Digital

    C. PCMCIA

    D. Mini PCI

    E. ExpressCard

    F. Proprietary

    G. All of the above

4. Which type of access points normally use centralized data forwarding?

    A. Autonomous AP

    B. Controller-based AP

    C. Cooperative AP within a distributed WLAN architecture

    D. None of the above

5. What capabilities can be found on a WLAN controller? (Choose all that apply.)

    A. VRRP

    B. Captive portal

    C. HSRP

    D. RBAC

    E. Wireless intrusion detection system

6. Which protocols are used to transport 802.11 frames between a controller-based AP and a WLAN controller? (Choose all that apply.)

   A. GRE

   B. CCMP

   C. Mobile IP

   D. CAPWAP

   E. Proprietary IP tunneling protocols

   F. All of the above

7. Which of these WLAN architectures may require the use of an NMS server to manage and monitor the WLAN?

   A. Autonomous WLAN architecture

   B. Centralized WLAN architecture

   C. Distributed WLAN architecture

   D. All of the above

8. What are some of the common capabilities of a WLAN controller architecture?

   A. Dynamic RF

   B. AP management

   C. Layer 3 roaming support

   D. Bandwidth throttling

   E. Firewall

   F. All of the above

9. Which logical plane of network operation is typically defined by protocols and intelligence?

   A. User plane

   B. Data plane

   C. Network plane

   D. Control plane

   E. Management plane

10. Which option best describes a device used to provide wireless connectivity for a small number of wired clients?

   A. VPN router

   B. Wireless workgroup bridge

   C. Wireless mesh router

   D. Wireless Ethernet repeater

   E. Wireless bridge

11. What are the two main components of a centralized WLAN architecture? (Choose all that apply.)

    A. WLAN controller

    B. Wireless network management system

    C. Enterprise wireless gateway

    D. Cooperative control AP

    E. Controller-based AP

12. What planes of operation reside in the access points of a distributed WLAN architecture? (Choose all that apply.)

    A. Radio plane

    B. Data plane

    C. Network plane

    D. Control plane

    E. Management plane

13. A network administrator is having a hard time getting two WLAN bridges to associate with one another in a PtP link. The bridge in building A is on the 172.16.1.0/24 network, and the bridge in building B resides on the 172.16.2.0/24 network. What is the most likely cause?

    A. The bridges are on different subnets.

    B. The bridges are both configured as nonroot.

    C. The gateway address is incorrect.

    D. The ACK timeout setting is short.

    E. There is impedance overflow.

14. Billy must connect building A via a WLAN bridge link to building C, which is 30 miles away. He cannot make a direct connection of that distance because of regulatory power restrictions in his country. Building B sits between the two remote buildings. What is the best way for Billy to link the two buildings together using WLAN bridges?

    A. Place a root bridge on building A with a highly directional antenna, a nonroot bridge on building B with an omnidirectional antenna, and a root bridge on building C with a highly directional antenna.

    B. Place a root bridge on building A with a highly directional antenna, a repeater bridge on building B with an omnidirectional antenna, and a root bridge on building C with a highly directional antenna.

    C. Place a nonroot bridge on building A with a highly directional antenna, a root bridge on building B with an omnidirectional antenna, and a nonroot bridge on building C with a highly directional antenna.

D. Place a root bridge on building A with a highly directional antenna and a nonroot bridge on building B with a highly directional antenna. Set up another root bridge on building B with a highly directional antenna and a nonroot bridge on building C with a highly directional antenna. Connect the two bridges on building B via a switch or router.

E. None of the above.

15. Which WLAN architectural models typically require support for 802.1Q tagging at the edge on the network when multiple user VLANs are required? (Choose all that apply.)

A. Autonomous WLAN architecture

B. Centralized WLAN architecture

C. Distributed WLAN architecture

D. None of the above

16. What term best describes a WLAN centralized architecture where the integration service (IS) and distribution system services (DSS) are handled by a WLAN controller while generation of certain 802.11 management and control frames are handled by a controller-based AP?

A. Cooperative control

B. Distributed data forwarding

C. Distributed hybrid architecture

D. Distributed WLAN architecture

E. Split MAC

17. Where is redundancy needed if user traffic is being tunneled in a centralized WLAN architecture?

A. Redundant radios

B. Redundant controllers

C. Redundant access switches

D. Redundant access points

E. None of the above

18. What would be needed for multiple basic service sets (BSSs) to exist within the same coverage area of a single access point and in that coverage area, all the client stations would be segmented in separate layer 2 and 3 domains but all communicate within a single layer 1 RF domain? (Choose all that apply.)

A. Virtual BSSIDs

B. SSIDs

C. VLANs

D. Autonomous APs

E. None of the above

19. What are some of the parameters of a WLAN profile that can be configured on a WLAN controller? (Choose all that apply.)

A. SSID

B. Channel

C. VLAN

D. WMM

E. WPA-2

20. What are some of the necessary components of a VoWiFi architecture? (Choose all that apply.)

A. VoWiFi phone

B. SIP

C. WMM support

D. Proxy server

E. PBX

Chapter

11

WLAN Deployment and Vertical Markets

IN THIS CHAPTER, YOU WILL LEARN ABOUT THE FOLLOWING:

✓ Deployment considerations for commonly supported WLAN applications and devices

- ▪ Data
- ▪ Voice
- ▪ Video
- ▪ Real-Time Location Services (RTLS)
- ▪ Mobile devices (tablets and smartphones)

✓ Corporate data access and end-user mobility

✓ Network extension to remote areas

✓ Bridging—building-to-building connectivity

✓ Wireless ISP (WISP)—last-mile data delivery

✓ Small office/home office (SOHO)

✓ Mobile office networking

✓ Branch offices

✓ Educational/classroom use

✓ Industrial—warehousing and manufacturing

✓ Retail

✓ Healthcare—hospitals and offices

✓ Municipal networks

✓ Hotspots—public network access

✓ Stadium networks

✓ Transportation networks

✓ Law enforcement networks

✓ First-responder networks

✓ Fixed mobile convergence

✓ WLAN and health

✓ WLAN vendors

In this chapter, you will learn about environments where wireless networks are commonly deployed. We will consider the pros and cons of wireless in various environments along with areas of concern. Finally, we will discuss the major commercial WLAN vendors and provide links to their websites.

Deployment Considerations for Commonly Supported WLAN Applications and Devices

As wireless networking has expanded, numerous applications and devices have benefited, and along the way these applications and devices have helped to expand the growth of wireless networking. Although applications such as data and video have benefited due to the flexibility and mobility that wireless affords them, they are not wireless-intrinsic applications. Voice, real-time location services (RTLSs), and network access using mobile devices are three uses that are inherently dependent on a WLAN and will continue to expand the use of WLANs. No matter which of these applications or devices you are implementing on your network, you will need to consider certain factors when planning, designing, and supporting your WLAN. The following sections focus on considerations for commonly supported WLAN applications and devices.

To delve even deeper into deployment considerations, check out *CWDP: Certified Wireless Design Professional Official Study Guide: Exam PW0-250* by Shawn M. Jackman, Marcus Burton, Matt Swartz, and Thomas W. Head (Sybex, 2011).

Data

When data-oriented applications are discussed, email and web browsing are two of the most common applications that come to mind. When planning for network traffic over any type of network, wireless or wired, you need to first look at the protocols that are being implemented. Protocols are communications methods or techniques used to communicate between devices on a network. Protocols can be well designed, based on documented standards, or they can be proprietary, using unique communications methods. Data-oriented applications are often based on well-known protocols and are therefore usually easy to work with because a great deal of knowledge already exists about how they communicate.

One of the most important aspects of designing a network to handle data-oriented applications is to ensure that the network design is capable of handling the amount of data that will be transferred. Most data applications are forgiving of slight network delays, but problems can arise if there is not enough available data bandwidth. When designing your wireless network, analyze the data requirements of your users and make sure that the data rates at which the users will connect are capable of handling the amount of data that they will be transmitting.

Voice

When designing a WLAN to support voice communications, keep in mind that, unlike data communications, voice communications are not tolerant of network delays, dropped packets, or sporadic connections. Designing a WLAN to support voice communications can also be a challenge because there are so many differences in how vendors implement their voice products. Each vendor has unique guidelines for designing voice applications. This is true not only for vendors of voice handsets or software applications, but also for infrastructure vendors. So, it is important to understand the best practice methods for installing your voice system.

Voice devices are typically handheld devices that do not transmit with as much power as laptops. Since a wireless device requires more battery power to transmit a strong signal, the transmit power of VoWiFi phones is typically less than other devices in order to increase battery longevity. This reduced power level will decrease the distance that a VoWiFi phone can operate from an access point, thus requiring smaller cell sizes, and more APs will be necessary to ensure adequate coverage.

Video

The transmission of video is typically more complex than voice. In addition to multiple streams of data for video and voice, video often includes streams for setting up and tearing down the connection. Unless you are using the WLAN for a real-time videoconference, video can likely take a backseat to audio. In most cases, video has a higher loss tolerance than voice. Choppy audio during a videoconference would likely be highly disruptive, causing participants to ask the speaker to repeat what was said, whereas if the audio is clear and the video choppy, the speaker would likely be understood the first time.

In regard to video transmission, it is important to identify the type of video that is being transmitted and the function or purpose of that transmission. If you ask an average computer user about video transmission, they will likely think of streaming video—a movie, TV show, or funny video clip downloaded by a user, who may be either stationary or mobile. If you were to ask an executive about video transmission, they will likely think of video as part of a videoconference or a webinar, and the user will most likely be stationary. If you were to ask a facilities or security person about video transmission, they will likely think of streaming video generated by a wireless surveillance camera, most likely permanently mounted to the building. Your WLAN might have any or all of these types of video traffic.

Once you have identified the type of video that will be used on your WLAN, you can plan your network. You need to evaluate the system or software that is transmitting the wireless video traffic to determine the type of traffic and protocols along with the network load. As part of the protocol evaluation, you will need to research whether the video transmissions are using multicast transmissions or quality of service (QoS).

Real-Time Location Services

Location-based technology has garnered a lot of attention in WLAN designs. Most manufacturers of enterprise WLAN systems tout some sort of location capability with their products. Some have features that are built in, whereas others offer integration hooks to third-party vendors who specialize in location technology and have sophisticated software applications related to specific industry vertical markets. Figure 11.1 shows an RTLS system, displaying the location of a wireless device.

FIGURE 11.1   Ekahau Vision RTLS software

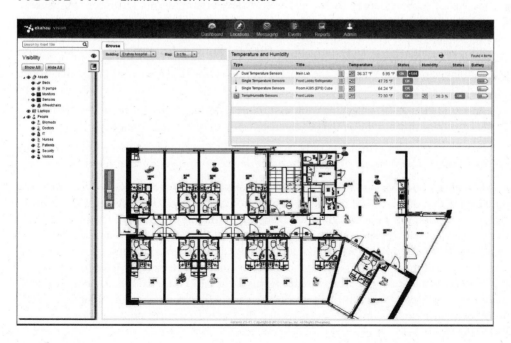

Location tracking is expanding incredibly quickly as more and more uses are identified. RTLSs can be used to locate or track people or devices on a WLAN. Healthcare is one of the biggest users of location-based technology. Because healthcare providers, such as hospitals, have to run 24/7 shifts, and since many of the assets are shared, RTLSs can be extremely useful for tracking equipment that may be necessary in an emergency or for identifying the closest doctor or specialist.

RTLSs can be used to track any 802.11 radio, or a specialized 802.11 RFID tag can be affixed to a non-802.11 asset so that it can be managed and tracked. Tags can be affixed to any device to provide tracking and help deter theft. Tags can also be worn by employees, children at amusement parks, hospital staff or patients, to name a few. Each RTLS vendor is unique and will be able to provide you with recommendations and best practice documents for deploying your RTLS equipment.

Mobile Devices

We are currently seeing one of the most amazing transitions in networking as employees—from receptionists to CEOs—are bringing their own 802.11-capable devices, such as laptops, tablets, and smartphones, to work and expect—and in many cases demand—that these devices be supported on the corporate network. The primary devices that people are requesting access for are cell phones and tablets that are also capable of communicating using 802.11 radios. Unlike changes in enterprise technology, which is planned and controlled by the IT department, the push for support of mobile devices is being made by the end user. Many organizations see access for these devices as a benefit for employees and are pressuring the IT department to provide access and support.

Multiple concerns arise with integrating these devices into the network:

- Making sure that the devices are capable of connecting to the network using the proper authentication

- Ensuring the use of encryption protocols along with the ability for these devices to be able to smoothly roam throughout the network without losing connectivity

- Providing network access, not only based upon the identity of the user of the device but also based upon the type of device or other device or connection characteristics

Many 802.11 networks that have been in use for a few years were designed to communicate with more powerful devices such as laptop computers. The coverage area of any 802.11 network needs to be designed small enough so that any device can respond back to the access point with a strong enough signal. Handheld devices often transmit at a lower signal level than laptop computers. If a network was designed to communicate with more powerful transmitters, it is possible that a tablet or smartphone may not have sufficient power to transmit back to an access point. If this is the case, these mobile devices are likely to experience RF dead spots throughout the network. Many companies are designing their WLANs to have smaller coverage areas so that these mobile devices do not experience intermittent service.

The introduction of these mobile devices has become a huge trend in the industry, typically known as bring your own device (BYOD), and it has become such a concern that we have dedicated an entire chapter to this topic, Chapter 20, "Bring Your Own Device (BYOD)."

Corporate Data Access and End-User Mobility

With the increased throughput provided by 802.11n and now 802.11ac technology, many organizations have been transitioning to these higher-speed wireless networks while reducing the number of devices connecting to the network via wired connections—in many cases retiring some of the unused or underused wired switches. As mentioned earlier, another major influence pressing organizations to expand their wireless networks is the proliferation of Wi-Fi-enabled personal mobile devices.

The installation of wired network jacks is expensive, often costing as much as—or even more than—$200 (in U.S. dollars) per jack. As companies reorganize workers and departments, network infrastructure typically needs to be changed as well. Other areas, such as warehouses, conference rooms, manufacturing lines, research labs, and cafeterias, are often difficult places to effectively install wired network connections. In these and other environments, the installation of wireless networks can save the company money and provide consistent network access to all users.

Providing continuous access and availability throughout the facility has become paramount in the past few years. With computer access and data becoming critical components of many people's jobs, it is important for networks to be continuously available and to be able to provide the up-to-the-moment information that is being demanded. By installing a wireless network throughout the building or campus, the company makes it easy for employees to meet and discuss or brainstorm while maintaining access to corporate data, email, and the Internet from their laptops and mobile devices, no matter where they are in the building or on the campus.

A big trend in the consumer electronics marketplace has been the addition of wireless radios in devices. Wireless adapters are extremely small and can easily be integrated in these portable devices. Connectivity to the Internet also allows devices to be easily updated, along with providing more capabilities. In addition to the trend of connecting personal electronics, devices keep getting smaller, lighter, and leaner. With this push toward leaner devices, Ethernet adapters have either given way to wireless radios or been bypassed all together in favor of wireless.

Whatever the reason for installing wireless networking, companies must remember its benefits and its flaws. Wireless provides mobility, accessibility, and convenience, but if not designed and implemented properly, it can lack in performance, availability, and throughput. Wireless is an access technology, providing connectivity to end-user stations. Wireless should rarely be considered for distribution or core roles, except for building-to-building bridging or mesh backhaul. Even in these scenarios, make sure that the wireless bridge will be capable of handling the traffic load and throughput needs.

Network Extension to Remote Areas

If you think about it carefully, network extension to remote areas was one of the driving forces of home wireless networking, which also helped drive the demand for wireless in the corporate environment. As households connected to the Internet and as more households purchased additional computers, there was a need to connect all the computers in the house to the Internet. Although many people installed Ethernet cabling to connect their computers, this was typically too costly, impractical because of accessibility, or beyond the technical capabilities of the average homeowner.

At the same time, 802.11 wireless devices were becoming more affordable. The same reasons for installing wireless networking in a home are also valid for installing wireless in offices, warehouses, and just about any other environment. The cost of installing network cabling for each computer is expensive, and in many environments, running cable or fiber is difficult because of building design or aesthetic restrictions. When wireless networking equipment is installed, far fewer cables are required, and equipment placement can often be performed without affecting the aesthetics of a building.

Bridging: Building-to-Building Connectivity

To provide network connectivity between two buildings, you can install an underground cable or fiber between the two buildings, you can pay for a high-speed leased data circuit, or you can use a building-to-building wireless bridge. All three are viable solutions, each with its benefits and disadvantages.

Although a copper or fiber connection between two buildings will potentially provide you with the highest throughput, installing copper or fiber between two buildings can be expensive. If the buildings are separated by a long distance or by someone else's property, this may not even be an option. After the cable is installed, there are no monthly service fees since you own the cable.

Leasing a high-speed data circuit can provide flexibility and convenience, but because you do not own the connection, you will pay monthly service fees. Depending on the type of service that you are paying for, you may or may not be able to easily increase the speed of the link.

A wireless building-to-building bridge requires that the two buildings have a clear RF line of sight between them. After this has been determined, or created, a point-to-point (PTP) or point-to-multipoint (PTMP) transceiver and antenna can be installed. The installation is typically easy for trained professionals to perform, and there are no monthly service fees after installation, because you own the equipment.

In addition to connecting two buildings via a PTP bridge, three or more buildings can be networked together by using a PTMP solution. In a PTMP installation, the building that is most centrally located will be the central communication point, with the other devices communicating directly to the central building. This is known as a *hub and spoke* or star configuration.

WARNING A potential problem with the PTMP solution is that the central communication point becomes a single point of failure for all the buildings. To prevent a single point of failure and to provide higher data throughput, it is not uncommon to install multiple point-to-point bridges.

Wireless ISP: Last-Mile Data Delivery

The term *last mile* is often used by phone and cable companies to refer to the last segment of their service that connects a home subscriber to their network. The last mile of service can often be the most difficult and costly to run because at this point a cable must be run individually to every subscriber. This is particularly true in rural areas where there are very few subscribers and they are separated by large distances. In many instances, even if a subscriber is connected, the subscriber may not be able to receive some services such as high-speed Internet because services such as xDSL have a maximum distance limitation of 18,000 feet (5.7 km) from the central office.

Wireless Internet service providers (WISPs) deliver Internet services via wireless networking. Instead of directly cabling each subscriber, a WISP can provide services via RF communications from central transmitters. WISPs often use wireless technology other than 802.11, enabling them to provide wireless coverage to much greater areas. Some small towns have had success using 802.11 mesh networks as the infrastructure for a WISP. However, 802.11 technology generally is not intended to scale to the size needed for city-wide WISP deployments.

Service from WISPs is not without its own problems. As with any RF technology, the signal can be degraded or corrupted by obstacles such as roofs, mountains, trees, and other buildings. Proper designs and professional installations can ensure a properly working system.

Small Office/Home Office

One common theme of a *small office/home office (SOHO)* is that your job description spans janitor to IT staff and includes everything in between. Small-business owners and home-office employees are typically required to be self-sufficient because there are usually few, if any, other people around to help them. Wireless networking has helped to make it easy for a SOHO employee to connect the office computers and peripheral devices together, as well as to the Internet. The main purpose of a SOHO 802.11 network is typically to provide wireless access to an Internet gateway. As depicted in Figure 11.2, many wireless SOHO devices also have multiple Ethernet ports, providing both wireless and wired access to the Internet.

FIGURE 11.2 D-Link wireless SOHO router

Most SOHO wireless routers provide fairly easy-to-follow installation instructions and offer reasonable performance and security, though less than what their corporate counter-parts provide. They are generally not as flexible or feature rich as comparable corporate products, but most SOHO environments do not need all the additional capabilities. What the SOHO person gets is a capable device at a quarter of the price paid by their corporate counterparts. Dozens of devices are available to provide the SOHO worker with the ability to install and configure their own secure Internet-connected network without spending a fortune. Many SOHO wireless routers even have the ability to provide guest access, allow-ing visitors Internet access while preventing them from accessing the local network.

Mobile Office Networking

Mobile homes or trailer offices are used for many purposes: as temporary offices during construction or after a disaster or as temporary classrooms to accommodate unplanned changes in student population, for example. Mobile offices are simply an extension of the office environment. These structures are usually buildings on wheels that can be easily deployed for short- or long-term use on an as-needed basis. Since these structures are not permanent, it is usually easy to extend the corporate or school network to these offices by using wireless networking.

A wireless bridge can be used to distribute wireless networking to the mobile office. If needed, an AP can then be used to provide wireless network access to multiple occupants of the office. By providing networking via wireless communications, you can alleviate the cost of run-ning wired cables and installing jacks. Additional users can connect and disconnect from the network without the need for any changes to the networking infrastructure. When the mobile office is no longer needed, the wireless equipment can simply be unplugged and removed.

Moveable wireless networks are used in many environments, including military maneuvers, disaster relief, concerts, flea markets, and construction sites. Because of the ease of installation and removal, mobile wireless networking can be an ideal networking solution.

Branch Offices

In addition to the main corporate office, companies often have branch offices in remote locations. A company might have branch offices across a region, an entire country, or even around the world. The challenge for IT personnel is how to provide a seamless enterprise wired and wireless solution across all locations. A distributed solution using enterprise-grade WLAN routers at each branch office is a common choice. Branch routers have the ability to connect back to corporate headquarters with VPN tunnels. Employees at the branch offices can access corporate resources across the WAN through the VPN tunnel. Even more important is the fact that the corporate VLANs, SSIDs, and WLAN security can all be extended to the remote branch offices. An employee at a branch office connects to the same SSID that they would connect to at corporate headquarters. The wired and wireless network access policies are therefore seamless across the entire organization. These seamless policies can be extended to WLAN routers, access points, and switches at each branch location.

Most companies do not have the luxury or need to have an IT employee at each branch office. Therefore, a network management server (NMS) at a central location is used to manage and monitor the entire enterprise network.

Educational/Classroom Use

Wireless networking can be used to provide a safe and easy way of connecting students to a school network. Because the layout of most classrooms is flexible (with no permanently installed furniture), installing a wired network jack for each student is not possible. Because students would be constantly connecting to and disconnecting from the network at the beginning and end of class, the jacks would not last long even if they were installed. Prior to wireless networking, in classrooms that were wired with Ethernet, usually all the computers were placed on tables along the classroom walls, with the students typically facing away from the instructor. Wireless networking enables any classroom seating arrangement to be used, without the safety risk of networking cables being strung across the floor.

A wireless network also enables students to connect to the network and work on schoolwork anywhere in the building without having to worry about whether a wired network jack is nearby or whether someone else is already using it. In addition to the flexibility the wireless network is able to provide in a classroom environment, in many schools wireless networking has become a necessity: Computer tablets are quickly becoming commonplace devices in all levels of education. These tablets rely solely on wireless networking to provide Internet and local area networking access.

Schools typically require more access points for coverage because of the wall materials between classrooms. Most classroom walls are made of cinderblock to attenuate noise between classrooms. The cinderblock also attenuates the 2.4 and 5 GHz RF signals dramatically. In order to provide −70 dBm or greater coverage, an access point is often needed in at least every other classroom.

The use of wireless bridging is also prevalent in campus environments. Many universities and colleges use many types of wireless bridge links, including 802.11, to connect buildings campuswide.

Network access control (NAC) has become an integral part of many school networks. NAC can be used to "fingerprint," or identify authentication and authorization information about devices connecting to the network. This information is then used to regulate or control the access that the user has on the network. Access can be regulated or restricted based upon many different criteria, such as time, location, access method, device type, and user identity along with many other properties. NAC is discussed in more detail in Chapter 20.

Industrial: Warehousing and Manufacturing

Warehouses and manufacturing facilities are two environments in which wireless networking has been used for years, even before the 802.11 standard was created. Because of the vast space and the mobile nature of the employees in these environments, companies saw the need to provide mobile network access to their employees so they could more effectively perform their jobs. Warehouse and manufacturing environments often deploy wireless handheld devices, such as bar code scanners, which are used for inventory control.

Most 802.11 networks deployed in either a warehouse or manufacturing environment are designed for coverage rather than capacity. Handheld devices typically do not require much bandwidth, but large coverage areas are needed to provide true mobility. Most early deployments of 802.11 frequency hopping technology were in manufacturing and warehouse environments. Wireless networks are able to provide the coverage and mobility required in a warehouse environment—and provide it cost-effectively.

Retail

There are four key uses of wireless in retail locations. The first is the wireless network that provides support relating to the operations of the store and the retail transactions. The second is a newer and growing use, which is tracking analytics of the retail customer. The third is location-based mapping and tracking services. The fourth is supplemental Internet access, often necessitated by poor cellular coverage inside the retail establishment.

The retail environment is similar to many other business environments. Cash registers, time clocks, inventory control scanners, and just about every electronic device used to run a retail location is becoming networked with a WLAN radio. Connectivity of these devices provides faster and more accurate information and enhances the retail environment for the customer.

To further support and understand customers and their behaviors, retail analytic products are being installed to monitor customer movement and behavior. Strategically placed access points or sensor devices listen for probe frames from Wi-Fi-enabled smart phones. MAC addresses are used to identify each unique device, and signal strength is used to monitor and track the location of the shopper. Figure 11.3 shows a retail analytics dashboard. Analytics can identify the path the shopper took while walking through the store as well as the time spent in different areas of the store. This information can be used to identify shopping patterns along with analysis of the effectiveness of in-store displays and advertisements. One such company that is partnering with multiple WLAN vendors is Euclid Analytics.

FIGURE 11.3   Retail analytics

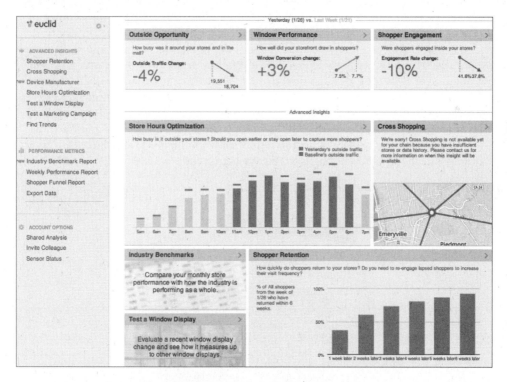

In addition to retail location and trend analysis, indoor location and mapping applications are beginning to provide new services to shoppers and visitors. Retail centers, hospitals, hotels, subways, and museums (and many other types of organizations) can provide turn-by-turn directions to visitors, along with promotions, and other location-based services. As an example, navigating through a large hospital can be confusing. A mobile app can provide turn-by-turn directions for family and friends to locate a patient's room. Conference centers and hotels can use this technology to direct visitors to meeting and event rooms. Special events, advertisements, or services can be offered as the visitor is navigating through the building.

Another key reason to implement wireless in a retail location is to provide supplemental connectivity in lieu of cellular coverage. Retail locations cannot depend upon customers having Internet access through their cellular phone network. Due to the scale and often product density, cellular phone access may not exist or be dependable. Providing wireless access for shoppers may make for a more pleasant and satisfied shopping experience and will likely result in more sales.

Healthcare: Hospitals and Offices

Although healthcare facilities such as hospitals, clinics, and doctors' offices may seem very different from other businesses, they have many of the same networking needs as other companies: data access and end-user mobility. Healthcare providers need quick, secure, and accurate access to patient and hospital or clinic data, so they can react and make decisions. Wireless networks can provide mobility, giving healthcare providers faster access to important data by delivering the data directly to a handheld device that the doctor or nurse carries with them. Medical carts used to enter and monitor patient information often have wireless connections back to the nursing station. Some companies have even integrated 802.11 wireless adapters directly into the equipment that is used to monitor and track the patient's vital signs, such as the monitoring system shown in Figure 11.4, which uses Wi-Fi to transmit patient EKG and vital signs to the nursing station.

FIGURE 11.4   Welch Allyn Propaq

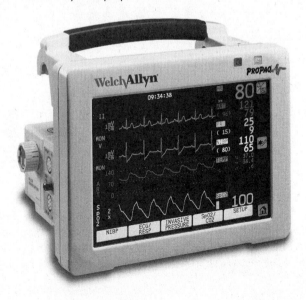

VoWiFi is another common use of 802.11 technology in a medical environment, providing immediate access to personnel no matter where they are in the hospital. RTLS solutions using 802.11 Wi-Fi tags for inventory control are also commonplace.

Hospitals rely on many forms of proprietary and industry-standard wireless communications that may have the potential of causing RF interference with 802.11 wireless networks. Many hospitals have designated a person or department to help avoid RF conflicts by keeping track of the frequencies and biomedical equipment used within the hospital.

Distributed healthcare is also an emerging trend. Hospitals often have many remote locations. Urgent care facilities are widespread and very often a WLAN branch office solution is required.

Municipal Networks

Over the past few years, municipal networks have received much attention. Cities and towns announced their intentions of providing wireless networking access to their citizens throughout the area. Many municipalities viewed this as a way of providing service to some of their residents who could not necessarily afford Internet access. Although this is a well-intentioned idea, communities often underestimated the scale and cost of these projects, and many taxpayers did not want their taxes spent on what they considered to be an unnecessary service. Although most of these earlier plans for citywide municipal 802.11 networks have been scrapped, there has been an increased interest and success in deploying 802.11 in many downtown and high-density areas. Some of these are provided by the municipality, and others are provided by individuals or business groups.

Hotspots: Public Network Access

The term *hotspot* typically refers to a free or pay-for-use wireless network that is provided as a service by a business. When people think of hotspots, they typically associate them with cafes, bookstores, or a hospitality-type businesses, such as a hotel or convention center. Hotspots can be used effectively by businesses to attract customers or as an extension of a business's services, in the case of Internet service providers offering these services in heavily travelled areas. Business travelers and students often frequent restaurants or cafes that are known to provide free Internet access. Many of these establishments benefit from the increased business generated by offering a hotspot. Free hotspots have drawn much attention to the 802.11 wireless industry, helping to make more people aware of the benefits of the technology.

Other hotspot providers have had difficulty convincing people to pay upward of $40 per month for a subscription. Many airports and hotel chains have installed pay-for-use hotspots; however, there are many providers, each one offering a separate subscription, which is often not practical for the consumer.

Most hotspot providers perform network authentication by using a special type of web page known as a *captive portal*. When a user connects to the hotspot, the user must open up a web browser. No matter what web page the user attempts to go to, a logon web page will be displayed instead, as shown in Figure 11.5. This is the captive portal page. If the hotspot provider is a paid service, the user must enter either their subscription information if they are a subscriber to the service or their credit card information if they are paying for hourly or daily usage. Many free hotspots also use captive portals as a method for requiring users to agree to a usage policy before they are allowed access to the Internet. If the user agrees to the terms of the policy, they are required to either enter some basic information or click a button, validating their agreement with the usage policy. Many corporations also use captive portals to authenticate guest users onto their corporate networks.

FIGURE 11.5 Example of a captive portal

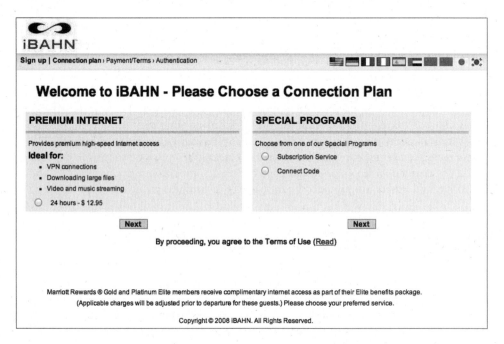

Do Hotspots Provide Data Security?

It is important to remember that hotspot providers (free or pay-for-use) do not care about the security of your data. The free provider typically offers you Internet access as a way of encouraging you to visit their location, such as a cafe, and buy some of whatever it is they sell. The pay-for-use hotspot provider performs authentication to make sure you are a paid subscriber, and after you have proven that, they will provide you with access to the Internet.

Except for rare occasions, neither of these hotspot providers performs any data encryption. Because of this, business users often use VPN client software to provide a secure encrypted tunnel back to their corporate network whenever they are using a hotspot. Many companies require employees to use a VPN during any connection to a public network. Further discussion of security issues related to hotspot use is found in Chapter 14, "Wireless Attacks, Intrusion Monitoring, and Policy."

Stadium Networks

Technology-savvy fans are driving sport, concert, and event stadiums and arenas to expand the services that they are providing. Fans expect and demand a complete multimedia experience when attending events, including access to replays and real-time statistics. Through apps or websites, in-seat food and beverage ordering and delivery enhances the experience by allowing the fan to enjoy the action instead of standing in line for refreshments. Through texting and social media, fans expect to be able to share their sporting or concert experience with friends or interact with other attendees.

A well-designed stadium network can allow the venue to target sections or groups of people with directed advertisements, special offers, or customized services. Offers or services for fans in the bleacher seats would likely be different than those targeting the fans in the skyboxes. In addition to providing wireless services to the fans, it is important to remember that the stadium is a business and needs to support its own infrastructure and services at an event. A wireless network is needed to provide event operations with services such as reliable high-speed Internet access in the press box, ticketing and point-of-sale transaction processing, and video surveillance.

Transportation Networks

In discussing Wi-Fi transportation networks, the three main modes of transportation—trains, planes, and automobiles—are typically mentioned. In addition to these three primary methods of transportation, two others need to be mentioned. The first is boats, both cruise ships and commuter ferries, and the second is buses, similar to but different from automobiles.

Providing Wi-Fi service to any of the transportation methods is easy. Simply install one or more access points in the vehicle. Except for the cruise ship and large ferries, most of these methods of transportation would require only a few access points to provide Wi-Fi coverage. The primary use of these networks is to provide hotspot services for end users so that they can gain access to the Internet. The difference between a transportation network and a typical hotspot is that the network is continually moving, making it necessary for the transportation network to use some type of mobile uplink services.

To provide an uplink for a train, which is bound to the same path of travel for every trip, a metropolitan wireless networking technology such as WiMAX could be used along the path of the tracks. With the other transportation networks, for which the path of travel is less bounded, the more likely uplink method would be via some type of cellular or satellite network connection. However, if WiMAX begins to be deployed in larger areas, either could be an acceptable uplink method for trains, buses, or automobiles.

Commuter ferries are likely to provide uplink services via cellular or WiMAX, because they are likely within range of these services. For ferries that travel farther distances away from shore and cruise ships, a satellite link is typically used.

Many airlines either have installed or are in the process of installing Wi-Fi on their planes. The Wi-Fi service in the plane consists of one or more access points connected either to a cellular router that communicates with a skyward facing network of cellular towers on the ground or to a satellite router that uplinks that data to a satellite and then to a terrestrial station. The cellular-based system requires a network of terrestrial-based cellular receivers; therefore, it is not used for transoceanic flights. This in-flight service is typically offered for a nominal fee and is available only while the airplane is flying and when the airplane is at cruising altitude. Bandwidth metering is used to prevent any one user from monopolizing the connection.

Law Enforcement Networks

Although Wi-Fi networks cannot provide the wide area coverage necessary to provide continuous wireless communications needed by law enforcement personnel, they can still play a major role in fighting crime. Many law enforcement agencies are using Wi-Fi as a supplement to their public safety wireless networks.

In addition to the obvious mobility benefits of using Wi-Fi inside police stations, many municipalities have installed Wi-Fi in the parking lots outside the police station and other municipal buildings as a supplement to their wireless metropolitan networks. These outdoor networks are sometimes viewed as secured hotspots. Unlike public hotspots, these networks provide both authentication and high levels of encryption. In addition to municipalities incorporating wireless technology into law enforcement, many are adding non-Wi-Fi-based automation to utilities through the use of supervisory control and data acquisition (SCADA) equipment. Because of this growth in the use of different wireless technologies, we are starting to see municipalities designate a person or department to keep track of the frequencies and technologies that are being used.

Municipal Wi-Fi hotspots typically provide high-speed communications between networking equipment in the police cars and the police department's internal network. An interesting example of a good use of this network is the uploading of vehicle video files. With many police cars being equipped with video surveillance, and with these surveillance videos often being used as evidence, it is important to not only transfer these video files to a central server for cataloging and storage, but to also do it with the least amount of interaction by the police officer to preserve the chain of evidence.

When a police car arrives at one of these municipal Wi-Fi hotspots, the computer in the car automatically uploads the video files from the data storage in the car to the central video library. Automating this process minimizes the risk of data corruption and frees up the officer to do other, more important tasks.

Special Use of 4.9 GHz Band

In some countries, a 4.9 GHz band has been set aside for use by public safety and emergency response organizations. This band typically requires a license to use, but the licensing process is usually more of a formality to ensure that the band is being used properly. This frequency is more commonly implemented and used with outdoor equipment, and since it has limited use, performance degradation from RF interference is less likely.

First-Responder Networks

When medical and fire rescue personnel arrive at the scene of an emergency, it is important for them to have fast and easy access to the necessary resources to handle the emergency at hand. Many rescue vehicles are being equipped with either permanently mounted Wi-Fi access points or easily deployed, self-contained portable access points that can quickly and easily blanket a rescue scene with a Wi-Fi bridge to the emergency personnel's data network. In a disaster, when public service communications systems such as cellular phone networks may not be working because of system overload or outages, a Wi-Fi first-responder network may be able to provide communications between local personnel and possibly shared access to central resources.

During a disaster, assessing the scene and triaging the victims (grouping victims based on the severity of their injuries) is one of the first tasks. Historically, the task of triage included paper tags that listed the medical information and status of the victim. Some companies have created electronic triage tags that can hold patient information electronically and transmit it via Wi-Fi communications.

Fixed Mobile Convergence

One of the hot topics relating to Wi-Fi is known as *fixed mobile convergence (FMC)*. The goal of FMC systems is to provide a single device, with a single phone number that is capable of switching between networks and always using the lowest-cost network. Figure 11.6 illustrates an FMC phone network.

FIGURE 11.6   FMC network design

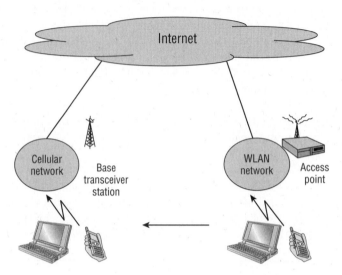

With the flexibility and mobility of cellular phones, it is common for people to use them even in environments (home or work) where they are stationary and have access to other phone systems that are frequently less costly. FMC devices typically are capable of communicating via either a cellular phone network or a VoWiFi network. If you had an FMC phone and were at your office or home, where a Wi-Fi network is available, the phone would use the Wi-Fi network for any incoming or outgoing phone calls. If you were outside either of these locations and did not have access to a Wi-Fi network, the phone would use the cellular network for any incoming or outgoing phone calls.

FMC devices also allow you to roam across networks, so you could initiate a phone call from within your company by using the Wi-Fi network. As you walk outside, the FMC phone would roam from the Wi-Fi network to the cellular network and seamlessly transition between the two networks. With fixed mobile convergence, you would be able to have one device and one phone number that would work wherever you were, using the least costly network that was available at the time.

WLAN and Health

Over the years, there has been a concern about adverse health effects from the exposure of humans and animals to radio waves. The World Health Organization and government agencies set standards that establish exposure limits to radio waves, to which RF products must comply. Tests performed on WLANs have shown that they operate substantially below the required safety limits set by these organizations. Also, Wi-Fi signals, as compared to other RF signals, are much lower in power. The World Health Organization has also concluded that there is no convincing scientific evidence that weak radio-frequency signals, such as those found in 802.11 communications, cause adverse health effects.

You can read more about some of these findings at the following websites:

- U.S. Federal Communications Commission: `transition.fcc.gov/oet/rfsafety/rf-faqs.html`
- World Health Organization: `www.who.int/peh-emf`
- Wi-Fi Alliance: `www.wi-fi.org`

WLAN Vendors

There are many vendors in the 802.11 WLAN marketplace. The following is a list of some of the major WLAN vendors. Please note that each vendor is listed in only one category, even if they offer products and services that cover multiple categories. This is most notable with the infrastructure vendors, who often offer additional capabilities as features of their products, such as security and troubleshooting.

WLAN Infrastructure   These 802.11 enterprise equipment vendors manufacture and sell controllers and access points:

Aerohive Networks: `www.aerohive.com`

AirTight Networks: `www.airtightnetworks.com`

Aruba Networks: `www.arubanetworks.com`

Cisco Systems: `www.cisco.com`

Extreme Networks: `www.extremenetworks.com`

Extricom: `www.extricom.com`

Hewlett-Packard: `www.hp.com`

Juniper Networks: `www.juniper.net`

Meru Networks: `www.merunetworks.com`

Motorola: `www.motorolasolutions.com`

Proxim Wireless Corporation: `www.proxim.com`

Ruckus Wireless: `www.ruckuswireless.com`

Ubiquiti Networks: `www.ubnt.com`

Xirrus: `www.xirrus.com`

WLAN Mesh Infrastructure   These WLAN vendors specialize in 802.11 mesh networking:

Ericsson: `www.ericsson.com`

Firetide: `www.firetide.com`

General Dynamics C4 Systems: `www.gdc4s.com/wireless`

MeshDynamics: www.meshdynamics.com

Strix Systems: www.strixsystems.com

Tropos Networks: www.tropos.com

WLAN Troubleshooting and Design Solutions   These are some companies that make and/
or sell 802.11 protocol analyzers, spectrum analyzers, site survey software, RTLS software,
and other WLAN analysis solutions:

AeroScout: www.aeroscout.com

Berkeley Varitronics Systems: www.bvsystems.com

Ekahau: www.ekahau.com

Euclid Analytics: www.euclidanalytics.com

Fluke Networks: www.flukenetworks.com

MetaGeek: www.metageek.net

Riverbed Technology: www.riverbed.com

TamoSoft: www.tamos.com

WildPackets: www.wildpackets.com

Wireshark: www.wireshark.org

7signal: www.7signal.com

WLAN Security Solutions   These WLAN companies offer client onboarding solutions or
802.1X/EAP supplicant/server solutions:

Cloudessa: cloudessa.com

Cloudpath Networks: www.cloudpath.net

VoWiFi Solutions   Manufacturers of 802.11 VoWiFi phones and VoIP gateway solutions
include the following:

Ascom: www.ascom.com

ShoreTel Networks: www.shoretel.com

Spectralink: www.spectralink.com

Vocera: www.vocera.com

Mobile Device Management Vendors   These are some of the WLAN vendors selling
mobile device management (MDM) solutions:

Airwatch: www.air-watch.com

JAMF Software: www.jamfsoftware.com

Mobile Iron: www.mobileiron.com

WLAN SOHO Vendors These are some of the many WLAN vendors selling SOHO solutions that can provide Wi-Fi for the average home user:

Apple: www.apple.com

Belkin International: www.belkin.com

Buffalo Technology: www.buffalotech.com

D-Link: www.dlink.com

Hawking Technology: www.hawkingtech.com

Netgear: www.netgear.com

SMC Networks: www.smc.com

Summary

This chapter covered some of the design, implementation, and management environments in which wireless networking is used. Although many of these environments are similar, each has unique characteristics. It is important to understand these similarities and differences and how wireless networking is commonly deployed.

Exam Essentials

Know the different WLAN vertical markets. Wireless networking can be used in many environments, with each vertical market having a different primary reason or focus for installing the wireless network. Know these environments and their main reasons for deploying 802.11 wireless networking.

Know fixed mobile convergence. With cellular networking and Wi-Fi networking so common, phone vendors are beginning to provide phones that are capable of communicating over both networks and provide roaming between them. Know what FMC is and the reasons and benefits of deploying it.

Review Questions

1. Which of the following are objectives of fixed mobile convergence? (Choose all that apply.)
    A. Have a single phone number.
    B. Have a single device.
    C. Always use the best-performing network.
    D. Use the lowest-cost network.

2. Which of the following is another form of a public hotspot network? (Choose all that apply.)
    A. Law enforcement network
    B. First-responder network
    C. Transportation network
    D. Municipal network

3. Which type of organization often has a person responsible for keeping track of frequency usage inside the organization?
    A. Law enforcement
    B. Hotspot
    C. Hospital
    D. Cruise ship

4. On which of these transportation networks is satellite a functional solution for providing uplink to the Internet?
    A. Bus
    B. Automobile
    C. Train
    D. Cruise ship

5. Fixed mobile convergence provides roaming across which of the following wireless technologies? (Choose all that apply.)
    A. Bluetooth
    B. Wi-Fi
    C. WiMAX
    D. Cellular phone

6. Which of the following is typically the most important design goal when designing a warehouse WLAN?
    A. Capacity
    B. Throughput

C. RF interference

D. Coverage

7. Corporations often install wireless networks to provide which of the following capabilities? (Choose all that apply.)

A. Easy mobility for the wireless user within the corporate building or campus environment

B. Highest-speed network access when compared with wired networking

C. Internet access for visitors and guests

D. The ability to easily add network access in areas where installation of wired connections is difficult or expensive

8. Last-mile Internet service is provided by which of the following? (Choose all that apply.)

A. Telephone company

B. Long-distance carrier

C. Cable provider

D. WISPs

9. Which of the following is the main purpose of a SOHO 802.11 network?

A. Shared networking

B. Internet gateway

C. Network security

D. Print sharing

10. Which of the following are examples of mobile office networking? (Choose all that apply.)

A. Construction-site offices

B. Temporary disaster-assistance office

C. Remote sales office

D. Temporary classrooms

11. Warehousing and manufacturing environments typically have which of the following requirements? (Choose all that apply.)

A. Mobility

B. High-speed access

C. High capacity

D. High coverage

12. Which of the following is least likely to be offered by a hotspot provider?

A. Free access

B. Paid access

    C. Network authentication

    D. Data encryption

13. Which of the following are good uses for portable networks? (Choose all that apply.)

    A. Military maneuvers

    B. Disaster relief

    C. Construction sites

    D. Manufacturing plants

14. Which of the following terms refer to a PTMP network design? (Choose all that apply.)

    A. PTP

    B. Mesh

    C. Hub and spoke

    D. Star

15. Most early deployments of 802.11 FHSS were used in which type of environment?

    A. Mobile office networking

    B. Educational/classroom use

    C. Industrial (warehousing and manufacturing)

    D. Healthcare (hospitals and offices)

16. When using a hotspot, you should do which of the following to ensure security back to your corporate network?

    A. Enable WEP.

    B. Enable 802.1X/EAP.

    C. Use an IPsec VPN.

    D. Security cannot be provided because you do not control the access point.

17. What are some popular 802.11 applications used in the healthcare industry? (Choose all that apply.)

    A. VoWiFi

    B. Bridging

    C. RTLS

    D. Patient monitoring

18. Multiple point-to-point bridges between the same locations are often installed for which of the following reasons? (Choose all that apply.)

    A. To provide higher throughput

    B. To prevent channel overlap

    C. To prevent single point of failure

    D. To enable support for VLANs

19. What are some of the key concerns of healthcare providers when installing a wireless network? (Choose all that apply.)

A. RF interference

B. Faster access to patient data

C. Secure and accurate access

D. Faster speed

20. Public hotspots typically provide clients with which of the following security features?

A. Server authentication.

B. Encryption.

C. TKIP.

D. No client security is available.

Chapter

12

WLAN Troubleshooting and Design

IN THIS CHAPTER, YOU WILL LEARN ABOUT THE FOLLOWING:

✓ **Layer 2 retransmissions**

- RF interference
- Multipath
- Adjacent channel interference
- Low SNR
- Mismatched power settings
- Near/far
- Hidden node

✓ **802.11 coverage considerations**

- Dynamic rate switching
- Roaming
- Layer 3 roaming
- Co-channel interference
- Channel reuse/multiple channel architecture
- Channel reuse/channel bonding
- Single channel architecture
- Capacity vs. coverage
- Band steering
- Load balancing

- High Density WLANs
- Oversized coverage cells
- Physical environment

✓ **Voice vs. data**

✓ **Performance**

✓ **Weather**

✓ **Upper layer troubleshooting**

Diagnostic methods that are used to troubleshoot wired 802.3 networks should also be applied when troubleshooting a wireless local area network (WLAN). A bottoms-up approach to analyzing the OSI reference model layers also applies to wireless networking. A wireless networking administrator should always try to first determine whether problems exist at layer 1 and layer 2.

As with most networking technologies, most problems usually exist at the Physical layer. Simple layer 1 problems, such as nonpowered access points or client radio driver problems, are often the root cause of connectivity or performance issues. Because WLANs use radio frequencies to deliver data, troubleshooting a WLAN offers many unique layer 1 challenges not found in a typical wired environment. The bulk of this chapter discusses the numerous potential problems that can occur at layer 1 and the solutions that might be implemented to prevent or rectify the layer 1 problems. A spectrum analyzer is often a useful tool when diagnosing layer 1 RF interference issues.

After eliminating layer 1 as a source of possible troubles, a WLAN administrator should try to determine whether the problem exists at the Data-Link layer. Authentication and association problems often occur because of improperly configured security and administrative settings on access points, WLAN controllers, and client utility software. A WLAN protocol analyzer is often an invaluable tool for troubleshooting layer 2 problems.

In this chapter, we discuss many coverage considerations and troubleshooting issues that may develop when deploying an 802.11 wireless network. RF propagation behaviors and RF interference will affect both the performance and coverage of your WLAN. Because mobility is usually required in a WLAN environment, many roaming problems often occur and must be addressed. The half-duplex nature of the medium also brings unique challenges typically not seen in a full-duplex environment. Different considerations also need to be given to outdoor 802.11 deployments. In this chapter, we discuss how to identify, troubleshoot, prevent, and fix instances of potential WLAN problems. Throughout this chapter we will also discuss WLAN design basics, such as channel reuse patterns, channel bonding, and band steering. A properly designed WLAN will help to prevent many of the common problems, such as co-channel interference and adjacent cell interference.

Layer 2 Retransmissions

The mortal enemy of WLAN performance is layer 2 retransmissions that occur at the MAC sublayer. As you have learned, unicast 802.11 frames must be acknowledged. If a collision occurs or any portion of a unicast frame is corrupted, the *cyclic redundancy check (CRC)* will fail and the receiving 802.11 radio will not return an ACK frame to the transmitting 802.11 radio. If an ACK frame is not received by the original transmitting radio, the unicast frame is not acknowledged and will have to be retransmitted. Additionally, aggregate frames are acknowledged with a Block ACK, and if one of the aggregated frames is corrupted, it will also have to be retransmitted.

Excessive layer 2 retransmissions adversely affect the WLAN in two ways. First, layer 2 retransmissions increase overhead and therefore decrease throughput. Many different factors can affect throughput, including a WLAN environment with abundant layer 2 retransmissions.

Second, if application data has to be retransmitted at layer 2, the delivery of application traffic becomes delayed or inconsistent. Applications such as VoIP depend on the timely and consistent delivery of the IP packet. Excessive layer 2 retransmissions usually result in latency and jitter problems for time-sensitive applications such as voice and video. When discussing VoIP, people are often confused about the difference between latency and jitter.

Latency *Latency* is the time it takes to deliver a packet from the source device to the destination device. A delay in the delivery (increased latency) of a VoIP packet due to layer 2 retransmissions can result in echo problems.

Jitter *Jitter* is a variation of latency. Jitter measures how much the latency of each packet varies from the average. If all packets travel at exactly the same speed through the network, jitter will be zero. A high variance in the latency (jitter) is a common result of 802.11 layer 2 retransmissions. Jitter will result in choppy audio communications, and constant retransmissions will result in reduced battery life for VoWiFi phones.

Most data applications in a Wi-Fi network can handle a layer 2 retransmission rate of up to 10 percent without any noticeable degradation in performance. However, time-sensitive applications such as VoIP require that higher-layer IP packet loss be no greater than 2 percent. Therefore, Voice over Wi-Fi (VoWiFi) networks need to limit layer 2 retransmissions to 5 percent or less to ensure the timely and consistent delivery of VoIP packets.

How can you measure layer 2 retransmissions? As shown in Figure 12.1, any good 802.11 protocol analyzer can track layer 2 retry statistics for the entire WLAN. 802.11 protocol analyzers can also track retry statistics for each individual WLAN access point and client station. Layer 2 retry statistics can also usually be centrally monitored across an entire WLAN enterprise from a WLAN controller or from a network management server (NMS).

Unfortunately, layer 2 retransmissions are a result of many possible problems. Multipath, RF interference, and low signal-to-noise ration (SNR) are problems that exist at layer 1 yet result in layer 2 retransmissions. Other causes of layer 2 retransmissions include hidden nodes, near/far problems, mismatched power settings, and adjacent channel interference, which are all usually a symptom of improper WLAN design.

FIGURE 12.1 Layer 2 retransmission statistics

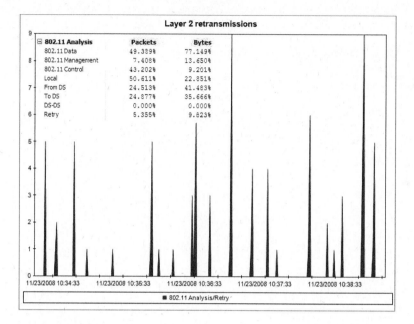

RF Interference

Various types of RF interference can greatly affect the performance of an 802.11 WLAN. Interfering devices may prevent an 802.11 radio from transmitting, thereby causing a denial of service. If another RF source is transmitting with strong amplitude, 802.11 radios can sense the energy during the clear channel assessment (CCA) and defer transmission entirely. The other typical result of RF interference is that 802.11 frame transmissions become corrupted. If frames are corrupted due to RF interference, excessive retransmissions will occur and therefore throughput will be reduced significantly. There are several different types of interference, as described in the following sections.

Narrowband Interference

A narrowband RF signal occupies a smaller and finite frequency space and will not cause a denial of service (DoS) for an entire band, such as the 2.4 GHz ISM band. A narrowband signal is usually very high amplitude and will absolutely disrupt communications in the frequency space in which it is being transmitted. Narrowband signals can disrupt one or several 802.11 channels.

Narrowband RF interference can also result in corrupted frames and layer 2 retransmissions. The only way to eliminate narrowband interference is to locate the source of the interfering device with a spectrum analyzer. To work around interference, use a spectrum analyzer to determine the affected channels and then design the channel reuse plan around the interfering narrowband signal. Figure 12.2 shows a spectrum analyzer capture of a narrowband signal close to channel 11 in the 2.4 GHz ISM band.

FIGURE 12.2   Narrowband RF interference

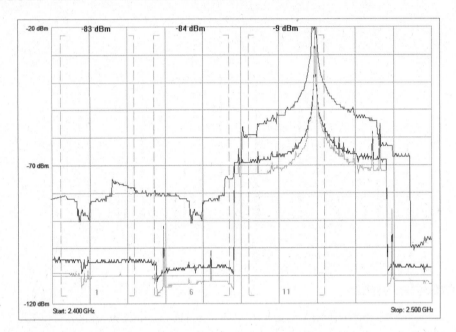

Wideband Interference

A source of interference is typically considered wideband if the transmitting signal has the capability to disrupt the communications of an entire frequency band. Wideband jammers exist that can create a complete DoS for the 2.4 GHz ISM band. The only way to eliminate wideband interference is to locate the source of the interfering device with a spectrum analyzer and remove the interfering device. Figure 12.3 shows a spectrum analyzer capture of a wideband signal in the 2.4 GHz ISM band with average amplitude of –60 dBm.

All-Band Interference

The term *all-band interference* is typically associated with frequency hopping spread spectrum (FHSS) communications that usually disrupt the 802.11 communications at 2.4 GHz. As you learned in earlier chapters, FHSS constantly hops across an entire band, intermittingly transmitting on very small subcarriers of frequency space. A legacy 802.11 FHSS radio, for example, transmits on hops that are 1 MHz wide in the 2.4 GHz band. 802.11b radios transmit in a stationary 22 MHz of frequency space and 802.11g/n radios transmit on fixed channels of 20 MHz of spectrum. While hopping and dwelling, an FHSS device will transmit in sections of the frequency space occupied by an 802.11b/g/n channel.

Although an FHSS device will not typically cause a denial of service, the frame transmissions from the 802.11b/g/n devices can be corrupted from the all-band transmissions of a legacy 802.11 FHSS interfering radio.

FIGURE 12.3   Wideband RF interference

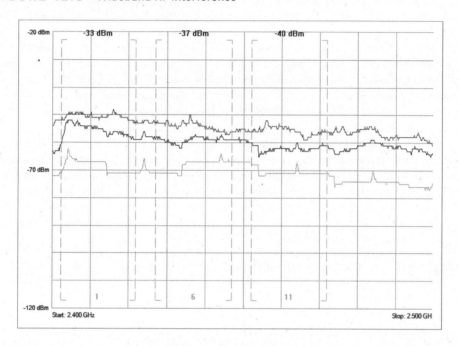

 Real World Scenario

What Devices Cause RF Interference?

Numerous devices, including cordless phones, microwave ovens, and video cameras, can cause RF interference and degrade the performance of an 802.11 WLAN. The 2.4 GHz ISM band is extremely crowded, with many known interfering devices. Interfering devices also transmit in the 5 GHz U-NII bands, but the 2.4 GHz frequency space is much more crowded. If RF interference cannot be eliminated at 2.4 GHz, special consideration should be given to deploying the WLAN in the less-crowded 5 GHz frequency bands. The tool that is necessary to locate sources of interference is a spectrum analyzer.

In Chapter 16, "Site Survey System and Devices," we discuss proper spectrum analysis techniques that should be part of every wireless site survey. Chapter 16 also lists the many interfering devices that can cause problems in both the 2.4 GHz and 5 GHz frequency ranges.

Bluetooth (BT) is a short-distance RF technology used in WPANs. Bluetooth uses FHSS and hops across the 2.4 GHz ISM band at 1,600 hops per second. Older Bluetooth devices were known to cause severe all-band interference. Newer Bluetooth devices utilize adaptive mechanisms to avoid interfering with 802.11 WLANs. Bluetooth adaptive frequency hopping is most effective at avoiding interference with a single AP transmitting on one 2.4 GHz channel. If multiple 2.4 GHz APs are transmitting on channels 1, 6 and 11 in the same physical area, it is impossible for the Bluetooth transmitters to avoid interfering with the WLAN. Digital Enhanced Cordless Telecommunications (DECT) cordless telephones also use frequency hopping transmissions. A now-defunct WLAN technology known as HomeRF also used FHSS; therefore, HomeRF devices can potentially cause all-band interference. Other frequency hopping devices that you may run across include various types of medical telemetry units. Although all the FHSS interferers mentioned so far transmit in the 2.4 GHz ISM band, 5 GHz frequency hopping transmitters that can cause interference also exist.

Frequency hopping transmitters do not usually result in as much data corruption as fixed-channel transmitters; however, the existence of a high number of frequency hopping transmitters in a finite space can result in a high amount of 802.11 data corruption and is especially devastating to VoWiFi communications. The only way to eliminate all-band interference is to locate the interfering device with a spectrum analyzer and remove the interfering device. Figure 12.4 shows a spectrum analyzer capture of a frequency hopping transmission in the 2.4 GHz ISM band.

FIGURE 12.4 All-band RF interference

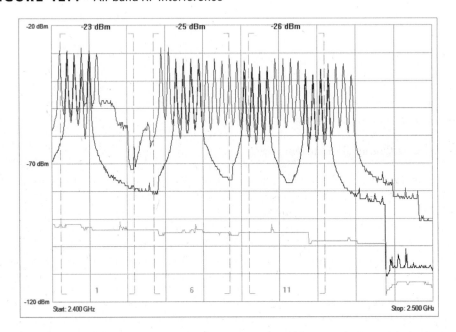

Multipath

As discussed in Chapter 2, "Radio Frequency Fundamentals," *multipath* can cause *intersymbol interference (ISI)*, which causes data corruption. Because of the difference in time between the primary signal and the reflected signals, known as the *delay spread*, the receiver can have problems demodulating the RF signal's information. The delay spread time differential results in corrupted data. If the data is corrupted because of multipath, layer 2 retransmissions will result.

Multipath can be a serious problem when working with legacy 802.11a/b/g equipment. The use of directional antennas will often reduce the number of reflections, and antenna diversity can also be used to compensate for the negative effects of multipath. Multipath is an RF phenomenon that for many years caused destructive effects when older 802.11a/b/g technology was deployed. However, because most WLAN deployments have upgraded to 802.11n or 802.11ac technology, multipath is no longer our enemy. Multipath has a constructive effect with 802.11n/ac transmissions that utilize *multiple-input, multiple-output (MIMO)* antennas and *maximum ratio combining (MRC)* signal processing techniques.

In Chapter 16, we discuss active and passive site survey techniques. The main purpose of the active site survey is to look at the percentage of layer 2 retries. If it is determined during the spectrum analysis portion of the site survey that no RF interference occurred, the most likely cause of the layer 2 retransmissions will be multipath. WLAN vendor Berkeley Varitronics Systems makes a line of WLAN troubleshooting tools that can detect and then visualize occurrences of multipath and the delay spread into a useful graphical display, shown in Figure 12.5.

FIGURE 12.5   Multipath analysis troubleshooting tool

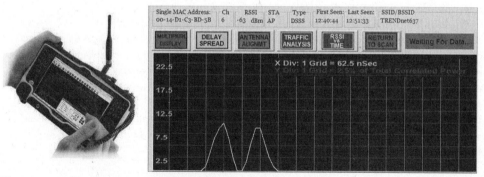

Photo courtesy of Berkeley Varitronics Systems

There is no way to fix multipath indoors because some reflection will always occur, and thus there will always be multiple paths of the same signal. However, many of the negative effects of multipath, including intersymbol interference, can be compensated for with the use of antenna diversity, which is covered in Chapter 4, "Radio Frequency Signal and Antenna Concepts." High-multipath environments exist indoors in areas such as long corridors and anywhere metal is located (for example, warehouses with metal shelving or metal racks). Before the advent of 802.11 MIMO radios, patch and panel antennas were used indoors with legacy 802.11a/b/g radios to help reduce reflections and hopefully reduce the negative effects of multipath. Semidirectional indoor antennas were often deployed in high multipath environments, such as a warehouse or retail store with a lot of metal racks or shelving. The use of indoor standard diversity patch antennas is highly recommended in high-multipath environments if legacy 802.11a/b/g networks are still deployed. Using a semidirectional antenna will cut down on reflections and thereby decrease data corruption and layer 2 retransmissions.

Now that MIMO technology is prevalent, patch and panel antennas are no longer needed because multipath is constructive. 802.11n and 802.11ac MIMO patch antennas are still used indoors but for a much different reason. The most common use case for using a MIMO patch antenna indoors is a high-density environment. A high-density environment can be described as an area where numerous Wi-Fi client devices exist in a very small area. An example might be a gymnasium at a school or a meeting hall packed with people using multiple Wi-Fi radios. In a high-density scenario, an omnidirectional antenna might not be the best solution for coverage. MIMO patch and panel antennas are often mounted from the ceiling downward to provide tight "sectors" of coverage. The most common use of indoor MIMO patch antennas is for high-density environments. 802.11n/ac radios use MIMO technology, which actually takes advantage of multipath. It should be noted that 802.11n/ac radios are required to be backward compatible with older 802.11a/b/g radios. 802.11n/ac access points will not solve the problems that multipath creates for legacy devices because older 802.11a/b/g client devices are still negatively affected by multipath.

 Real World Scenario

Is Multipath Really a Problem?

The short answer is that multipath can be a problem if legacy 802.11a/b/g access points and clients are still the deployed solution in high-multipath indoor environments, such as long corridors and anywhere metal is located. However, 802.11n/ac is the present-day Wi-Fi technology, and therefore, businesses continue to upgrade enterprise WLAN infrastructure with 802.11n/ac access points. The majority of client devices sold today also utilize 802.11n/ac chipsets. As legacy 802.11a/b/g technology is replaced, troubleshooting destructive multipath in most cases has become an afterthought, because 802.11n/ac MIMO technology thrives on multipath.

Adjacent Channel Interference

Most Wi-Fi vendors use the term *adjacent channel interference* to refer to degradation of performance resulting from overlapping frequency space that occurs due to an improper channel reuse design. In the WLAN industry, an adjacent channel is considered to be the next or previous numbered channel. For example, channel 3 is adjacent to channel 2.

As you learned in Chapter 6, "Wireless Networks and Spread Spectrum Technologies," the 802.11-2012 standard requires 25 MHz of separation between the center frequencies of 802.11b/g channels in order for them to be considered nonoverlapping. As pictured in

Figure 12.6, only channels 1, 6, and 11 can meet these IEEE requirements in the 2.4 GHz ISM band in the United States if three channels are needed. Channels 2 and 7 are nonoverlapping, as well as 3 and 8, 4 and 9, and 5 and 10. The important thing to remember is that there must be five channels of separation in adjacent coverage cells. Some countries allow the use of all 14 IEEE 802.11-defined channels in the 2.4 GHz ISM band, but because of the positioning of the center frequencies, no more than 3 channels can be used while avoiding frequency overlap. Even if all 14 channels are available, most vendors and end users still choose to use channels 1, 6, and 11.

FIGURE 12.6   2.4 GHz nonoverlapping channels

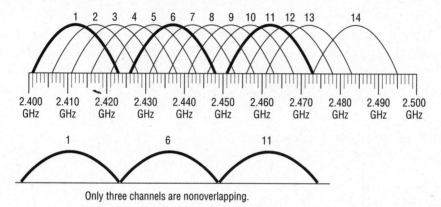

Only three channels are nonoverlapping.

When designing a wireless LAN, you need overlapping coverage cells in order to provide for roaming. However, the overlapping cells should not have overlapping frequencies, and in the United States only channels 1, 6, and 11 should be used in the 2.4 GHz ISM band to get the most available, nonoverlapping channels. Overlapping coverage cells with overlapping frequencies cause what is known as adjacent channel interference. If overlapping coverage cells also have frequency overlap from adjacent channels, the transmitted frames will become corrupted, the receivers will not send ACKs, and layer 2 retransmissions will significantly increase. Later in this chapter, we discuss channel reuse patterns that are used to mitigate adjacent channel interference.

Twenty-five channels are currently available in the 5 GHz U-NII bands, as shown in Figure 12.7. These 25 channels are technically considered nonoverlapping channels because there is 20 MHz of separation between the center frequencies. In reality, there will be some frequency overlap of the sidebands of each OFDM channel. The good news is that you are not limited to only three channels and many more channels can be used in a 5 GHz channel reuse pattern, which is discussed later in this chapter.

Low SNR

The *signal-to-noise ratio (SNR)* is an important value because if the background noise is too close to the received signal or the received signal level is too low, data can be corrupted and retransmissions will increase. The SNR is not actually a ratio. It is simply the difference in decibels between the received signal and the background noise (noise floor), as shown in Figure 12.8. If an 802.11 radio receives a signal of –70 dBm and the noise floor is measured at –95 dBm, the difference between the received signal and the background noise is 25 dB. The SNR is therefore 25 dB.

FIGURE 12.7   5 GHz nonoverlapping channels

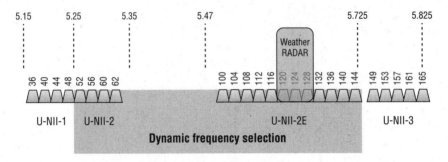

FIGURE 12.8   Signal-to-noise ratio

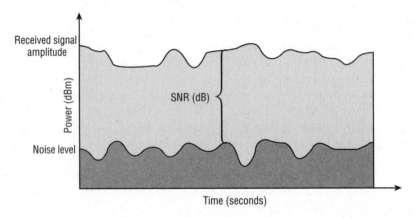

Data transmissions can become corrupted with a very low SNR. If the amplitude of the noise floor is too close to the amplitude of the received signal, data corruption will occur and result in layer 2 retransmissions. An SNR of 25 dB or greater is considered good signal quality, and an SNR of 10 dB or lower is considered poor signal quality. To ensure that frames are not corrupted, many vendors recommend a minimum SNR of 20 dB for data WLANs and a minimum SNR of 25 dB for voice WLANs.

When designing for coverage during a site survey, the normal recommended best practice is to provide for a –70 dBm or stronger received signal that is well above the noise floor. When designing for WLANs with VoWiFi clients, a –67 dBm or stronger signal that is even higher above the noise is recommended. Figure 12.9 shows a noise floor of –95 dBm. When a client station receives a –70 dBm signal from an access point, the SNR is 25 dBm and, therefore, no data corruption results. However, another client receives a weaker −88 dBm signal and a very low SNR of 7 dB. Because the received signal is so close to the noise floor, data corruption will occur and result in layer 2 retransmissions.

FIGURE 12.9   High and low signal-to-noise ratio

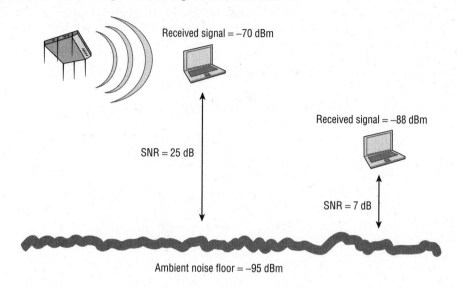

Received signal = −70 dBm

Received signal = −88 dBm

SNR = 25 dB

SNR = 7 dB

Ambient noise floor = −95 dBm

Measuring SNR

Keep in mind that measuring the SNR requires a device that can measure the raw ambient RF energy of the noise floor. Although many WLAN vendors have access points with spectrum analysis capabilities, most 802.11 client radios are not functional as spectrum analyzers. Although 802.11 client radios can transmit and receive data at a prodigious rate, they generally cannot interpret raw ambient RF signals. Wi-Fi radios can decode the modulated data bits sent from other Wi-Fi radios but generally are not the best tool to measure the noise floor. The best device that can truly measure non-encoded RF energy is a spectrum analyzer, and that is your best tool to measure SNR.

Mismatched Power Settings

Another potential cause of layer 2 retransmissions is mismatched transmit power settings between an access point and a client radio. Communications can break down if a client station's transmit power level is less than the transmit power level of the access point. As a client moves to the outer edges of the coverage cell, the client can "hear" the AP; however, the AP cannot "hear" the client.

As you can see in Figure 12.10, if an access point has a transmit power of 100 mW and a client has a transmit power of 20 mW, the client will hear a unicast frame from the AP because the received signal is within the client station's receive sensitivity capabilities. However, when the client sends an ACK frame back to the AP, the amplitude of the client's transmitted signal has dropped well below the receive sensitivity threshold of the AP's radio. The ACK frame is not "heard" by the AP, which then must retransmit the unicast frame. All of the client's transmissions are effectively seen as noise by the AP, and layer 2 retransmissions are the result.

FIGURE 12.10   Mismatched AP and client power

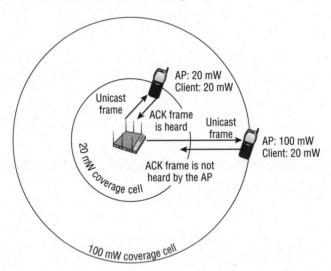

How do you prevent layer 2 retries that are caused by mismatched power settings between the AP and clients? The best solution is to ensure that all of the client transmit power settings match the access point's transmit power. A best practice for legacy APs was that the AP power never be set to more than the lowest-powered client station. However, significant improvements in AP receive sensitivity have essentially fixed many issues with client and AP mismatch power settings. With that in mind, configuring an access point to transmit at full power is not a good idea and may cause this problem. Although an AP can usually be configured to transmit to as much as 100 mW, many clients such as smartphones and tablets may only have transmitters capable of 25 mW.

One way to test whether the mismatched AP/client power problem exists is to listen with a protocol analyzer. An AP/client power problem exists if the frame transmissions of the client station are corrupted when you listen near the access point but are not corrupted when you listen near the client station.

AP/client power problems usually occur because APs are often deployed at full power to increase range. Increasing the power of an access point is the wrong way to increase range. If you want to increase the range for the clients, the best solution is to increase the antenna gain of the access point. Most people do not understand the simple concept of *antenna reciprocity*, which means that antennas amplify received signals just as they amplify transmitted signals. A high-gain antenna on an access point will amplify the AP's transmitted signal and extend the range at which the client is capable of hearing the signal. The AP's high-gain antenna will also amplify the received signal from a distant client station.

It should be noted that dynamic RF capabilities used by many WLAN vendors are notorious for causing mismatched power settings between the APs and client stations. An access point might dynamically increase its transmit power to a level above the client's transmit power. Dynamic changes of AP transmit power are well known to cause problems with VoWiFi phones. If the AP cannot hear the phone because of mismatched power, choppy audio may occur or phone conversations may drop entirely. The ratified 802.11k amendment does make it possible for an AP to inform clients to use transmit power control (TPC) capabilities to change their transmit amplitude dynamically to match the AP's power. However, most clients do not yet support 802.11k mechanisms.

As stated earlier, in recent years there has been significant improvements to access point hardware. Improved receive sensitivity of AP radios has essentially fixed many issues with client and AP mismatched power settings in indoor environments. Problems that occur because of mismatched power settings are more likely to occur outdoors. In this chapter, you will learn that there are many problems that can occur if an AP is transmitting at full power. Mismatched power settings is one potential problem, but problems such as co-channel interference, improper capacity, and hidden nodes are more common.

Near/Far

Disproportionate transmit power settings between multiple clients may also cause communication problems within a basic service set (BSS). A low-powered client station that is at a great distance from the access point could become an unheard client if other high-powered stations are very close to that access point. The transmissions of the high-powered stations could raise the noise floor near the AP to a higher level. The higher noise floor would corrupt the far station's incoming frame transmissions and prevent this lower-powered station from being heard, as shown in Figure 12.11. Near/far is not just caused by raising the noise floor. The problem is more often caused by an AP radio's inability to perform automatic gain control on a very loud signal and then a very quiet signal subsequently. It is a bit like going to a concert and then trying to hear a whisper when you leave. It is the rapid adjustment to highly different amplitudes that causes most near/far issues. This scenario is referred to as the near/far problem.

The half-duplex nature of the medium usually prevents most near/far occurrences. You can troubleshoot near/far problems with a protocol analyzer the same way you would troubleshoot the mismatched AP/client power problem.

Please understand that the medium access methods employed by Carrier Sense Multiple Access with Collision Avoidance (CSMA/CA) usually averts the near/far problem. A well-planned WLAN that provides for −70 dBm or stronger coverage should also negate any worries about near/far issues.

FIGURE 12.11 The near/far problem

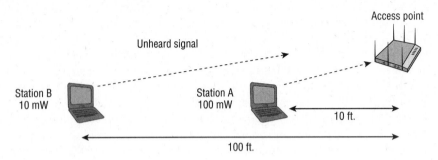

Hidden Node

In Chapter 8, "802.11 Medium Access," you learned about physical carrier sense and clear channel assessment (CCA). CCA involves listening for 802.11 RF transmissions at the Physical layer; the medium must be clear before a station can transmit. The problem with physical carrier sense is that all stations may not be able to hear each other. Remember that the medium is half-duplex and, at any given time, only one radio can be transmitting. What would happen, however, if one client station that was about to transmit performed a CCA but did not hear another station that was already transmitting? If the station that was about to transmit did not detect any RF energy during its CCA, it would transmit. The problem is that you then have two stations transmitting at the same time. The end result is a collision, and the frames will become corrupted. The frames will have to be retransmitted.

The *hidden node* problem occurs when one client station's transmissions are heard by the access point but are not heard by any or all of the other client stations in the basic service set (BSS). The clients would not hear each other and therefore could transmit at the same time. Although the access point would hear both transmissions, because two client radios are transmitting at the same time on the same frequency, the incoming client transmissions would be corrupted.

Figure 12.12 shows the coverage area of an access point. Note that a thick block wall resides between one client station and all of the other client stations that are associated to the access point. The RF transmissions of the lone station on the other side of the wall cannot be heard by all of the other 802.11 client stations, even though all the stations can hear the AP. That unheard station is the hidden node. What keeps occurring is that every time the hidden node transmits, another station is also transmitting and a collision occurs. The hidden node continues to have collisions with the transmissions from all the other stations that cannot hear it during the clear channel assessment. The collisions continue on a regular basis and so do the layer 2 retransmissions, with the final result being a decrease in throughput. A hidden node can drive retransmission rates above 15 to 20 percent or even higher. Retransmissions, of course, will affect throughput, latency, and jitter.

FIGURE 12.12   Hidden node—obstruction

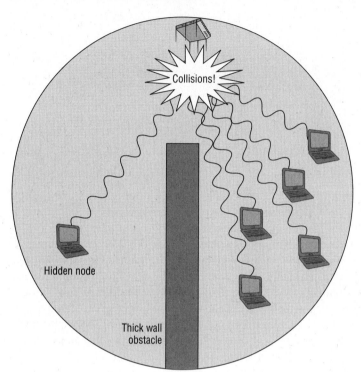

The hidden node problem may exist for several reasons—for example, poor WLAN design or obstructions such as a newly constructed wall or a newly installed bookcase. A user moving behind some sort of obstruction can cause a hidden node problem. VoWiFi phones and other mobile Wi-Fi devices often become hidden nodes because users take the mobile device into quiet corners or areas where the RF signal of the phone cannot be heard by other client stations. Users with wireless desktops often place their device underneath a metal desk and effectively transform the desktop radio into an unheard hidden node.

The hidden node problem can also occur when two client stations are at opposite ends of an RF coverage cell and they cannot hear each other, as shown in Figure 12.13. This often happens when coverage cells are too large as a result of the access point's radio transmitting at too much power. Later in this chapter, you will learn that an often recommended practice is to disable the data rates of 1 and 2 Mbps on the 2.4 GHz radio of an access point for capacity purposes. Another reason for disabling those data rates is that a 1 and 2 Mbps coverage cell at 2.4 GHz can be quite large and often results in hidden nodes. If hidden node problems occur in a network planned for coverage, then RTS/CTS may be needed. This is discussed in detail later in this section.

FIGURE 12.13 Hidden node—large coverage cell

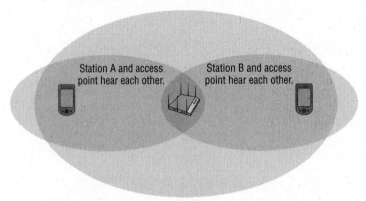

Station A and Station B cannot hear each other.

Another cause of the hidden node problem is distributed antenna systems. Some manufacturers design distributed systems, which are basically made up of a long coaxial cable with multiple antenna elements. Each antenna in the distributed system has its own coverage area. Many companies purchase a *distributed antenna system (DAS)* for cost-saving purposes. Distributed antenna systems and leaky cable systems are specialty solutions that are sometimes deployed because they can also provide coverage for cellular phone frequencies. The hidden node problem, as shown in Figure 12.14, will almost always occur if only a single access point is connected to the DAS. If a DAS solution is deployed, multiple APs will still be needed.

FIGURE 12.14 Hidden node—distributed antenna system

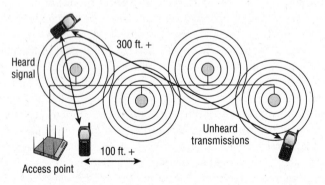

So how do you troubleshoot a hidden node problem? If your end users complain of a degradation of throughput, one possible cause is a hidden node. A protocol analyzer is a useful tool in determining hidden node issues. If the protocol analyzer indicates a higher retransmission rate for the MAC address of one station when compared to the other client stations, chances are a hidden node has been found. Some protocol analyzers even have hidden node alarms based on retransmission thresholds.

Another way is to use request to send/clear to send (RTS/CTS) to diagnose the problem. If a client device can be configured for RTS/CTS, try lowering the RTS/CTS threshold on a suspected hidden node to about 500 bytes. This level may need to be adjusted depending on the type of traffic being used. For instance, let's say you have deployed a terminal emulation application in a warehouse environment and a hidden node problem exists. In this case, the RTS/CTS threshold should be set for a much lower size, such as 50 bytes. Use a protocol analyzer to determine the appropriate size. As you learned in Chapter 9, "802.11 MAC Architecture," RTS/CTS is a method in which client stations can reserve the medium. In Figure 12.15, you see a hidden node initiating an RTS/CTS exchange.

FIGURE 12.15   Hidden node and RTS/CTS

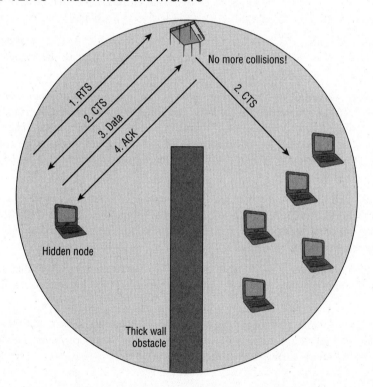

The stations on the other side of the obstacle may not hear the RTS frame from the hidden node, but they will hear the CTS frame sent by the access point. The stations that hear the CTS frame will reset their NAV for the period of time necessary for the hidden node to transmit the data frame and receive its ACK frame. Implementing RTS/CTS on a hidden node will reserve the medium and force all other stations to pause; thus, the collisions and retransmissions will decrease.

Collisions and retransmissions as a result of a hidden node will cause throughput to decrease. RTS/CTS usually decreases throughput as well. However, if RTS/CTS is implemented on a suspected hidden node, throughput will probably *increase* due to the stoppage of the collisions and retransmissions. If you implement RTS/CTS on a suspected hidden node and throughput increases, you have confirmed the existence of a hidden node.

RTS/CTS typically should not be viewed as a mechanism to fix the hidden node problem. Many legacy 802.11 client devices had the ability to adjust RTS/CTS thresholds. In reality, most current client devices cannot be manually configured for RTS/CTS. If available, RTS/CTS can be a temporary fix for the hidden node problem but should usually be used for only diagnostic purposes. One exception to that rule is point-to-multipoint (PtMP) bridging. The nonroot bridges in a PtMP scenario will not be able to hear each other because they are miles apart. RTS/CTS should be implemented on nonroot PtMP bridges to eliminate collisions caused by hidden node bridges that cannot hear each other.

The following methods can be used to fix a hidden node problem:

Use RTS/CTS to diagnose. Use either a protocol analyzer or RTS/CTS to diagnose the hidden node problem. RTS/CTS can also be used as a temporary fix to the hidden node problem.

Increase power to all stations Most client stations have a fixed transmission power output. However, if power output is adjustable on the client side, increasing the transmission power of client stations will increase the transmission range of each station. If the transmission range of all stations is increased, the likelihood of the stations hearing each other also increases. This is not a recommended fix because increasing client power can increase cochannel interference.

Remove the obstacles. If it is determined that some sort of obstacle is preventing client stations from hearing each other, simply removing the obstacle will solve the problem. Obviously, you cannot remove a wall, but if a metal desk or file cabinet is the obstacle, it can be moved to resolve the problem.

Move the hidden node station. If one or two stations are in an area where they become unheard, simply moving them within transmission range of the other stations will solve the problem.

Add another access point. If moving the hidden nodes is not an option, adding another access point in the hidden area to provide coverage will rectify the problem. The best fix for a continuous hidden node problem is to add another AP.

802.11 Coverage Considerations

Providing for both coverage and capacity in a WLAN design solves many problems. Roaming problems and interference issues will often be mitigated in advance if proper

WLAN design techniques are performed and a thorough site survey is conducted. In the following sections, we discuss many considerations that should be addressed to provide proper coverage, capacity, and performance within an 802.11 coverage zone.

Dynamic Rate Switching

As client station radios move away from an access point, they will shift down to lower-bandwidth capabilities by using a process known as *dynamic rate switching (DRS)*. Access points can support multiple data rates depending on the spread spectrum technology used by the AP radio. For example, a legacy 802.11b radio supports data rates of 11, 5.5, 2, and 1 Mbps. Data rate transmissions between the access point and the client stations will shift down or up depending on the quality of the signal between the two radios, as pictured in Figure 12.16. There is a correlation between signal quality and distance from the AP. As mobile client stations move further away from an access point, both the AP and the client will shift down to lower rates that require a less complex modulation coding scheme (MCS). For example, transmissions between two 802.11b radios may be at 11 Mbps at 30 feet but 2 Mbps at 100 feet.

FIGURE 12.16   Dynamic rate switching

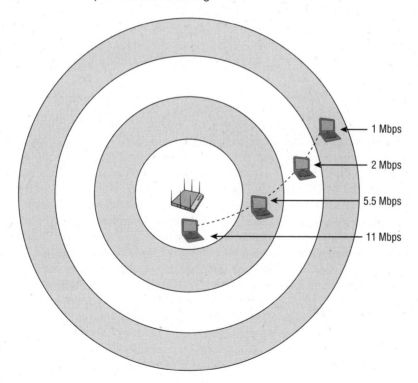

DRS is also referred to as *dynamic rate shifting, adaptive rate selection,* and *automatic rate selection.* All these terms refer to a method of speed fallback on a Wi-Fi radio receiver (Rx) as the incoming signal strength and quality from the transmitting Wi-Fi radio decreases. The objective of DRS is upshifting and downshifting for rate optimization and improved performance. Effectively, the lower data rates will have larger concentric zones of coverage than the higher data rates, as Figure 12.17 shows.

FIGURE 12.17 Data rate coverage zones

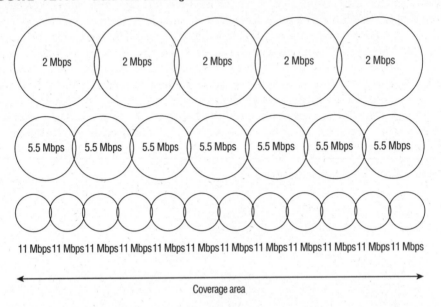

11 Mbps 11 Mbps 11 Mbps 11 Mbps 11 Mbps 11 Mbps 11 Mbps 11 Mbps 11 Mbps 11 Mbps 11 Mbps

Coverage area

The thresholds used for dynamic rate switching are proprietary and are defined by 802.11 radio manufacturers. Most vendors base DRS on receive signal strength indicator (RSSI) thresholds, packet error rates, and retransmissions. RSSI metrics are usually based on signal strength and signal quality. In other words, a station might shift up or down between data rates based on received signal strength in dBm and possibly on a signal-to-noise ratio (SNR) value. Because vendors implement DRS differently, you may have two different vendor client radios at the same location, while one is communicating with the access point at 5.5 Mbps and the other is communicating at 1 Mbps. For example, one vendor might shift down from data rate 11 Mbps to 5 Mbps at –75 dBm, whereas another vendor might shift between the same two rates at –78 dBm. Keep in mind that DRS works with all 802.11 physical layers (PHYs). For example, the same shifting of rates will also occur with 802/11a/g radios shifting between 54, 48, 36, 24, 18, 12, 9, and 6 Mbps data rates. As a result, there is a correlation between signal quality and distance from the AP.

Please understand that all WLAN radios use dynamic rate switching. As already mentioned, client radios shift down to lower data rates if there is a weaker received signal from the AP. The radio within an access point also uses dynamic rate switching. Based on the incoming received signal strength from a client, an access point radio will shift data rates for the downstream transmission back to the client radio.

It is often a recommend practice to turn off the two lowest data rates of 1 and 2 Mbps when designing a 2.4 GHz 802.11b/g/n network. A WLAN network administrator might want to consider disabling the two lowest rates on a 2.4 GHz access point for three reasons: sticky client roaming problems, medium contention, and the hidden node problem. In Figure 12.18, you will see that multiple client stations are in the 1 Mbps zone and only one lone client is in the 11 Mbps zone. Remember that wireless is a half-duplex medium and only one radio can transmit on the medium at a time.

FIGURE 12.18   Frame transmission time

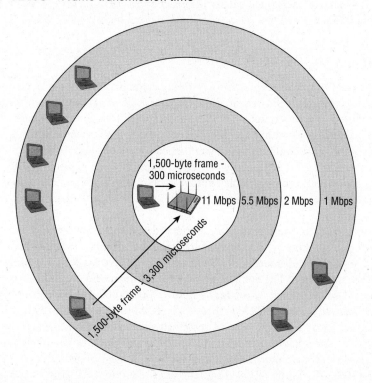

When 802.11 radios transmit at very low data rates such as 1 Mbps and 2 Mbps, effectively they cause medium-contention overhead for higher data rate transmitters due to the long wait time. All radios access the medium in a pseudorandom fashion, as defined by CSMA/CA. A radio transmitting a 1,500-byte data frame at 11 Mbps might occupy the medium for 300 microseconds. Another radio transmitting at 1 Mbps per second may take 3,300 microseconds to deliver that same 1,500 bytes. Radios transmitting at slower data rates will occupy the medium much longer, whereas faster radios have to wait. If multiple radios get on the outer cell edges and transmit at slower rates consistently, the perceived

throughput for the radios transmitting at higher rates is much slower because of having to wait for slower transmissions to finish. For this reason, too many radios on outer 1 and 2 Mbps cells can adversely affect throughput.

In Chapter 8, you learned about *airtime fairness*. Most vendors use proprietary airtime fairness mechanisms only for downstream transmissions from an AP to an associated client. Airtime fairness mechanisms are normally used for prioritizing the higher data rate downstream transmissions from an access point over the lower data rate downstream transmissions from an access point to client stations. If airtime fairness mechanisms are implemented properly, disabling the lower data rates on a 2.4 GHz access point may not be required. However, another reason to consider turning off the lower data rates is the hidden node problem, which was explained earlier in this chapter. Turning off the lower data rates is also a common practice to limit cell size when designing high-density WLANs.

Roaming

As you have learned throughout this book, *roaming* is the method by which client stations move between RF coverage cells in a seamless manner. Client stations switch communications through different access points. Seamless communications for client stations moving between the coverage zones within an extended service set (ESS) is vital for uninterrupted mobility. One of the most common issues you'll need to troubleshoot is problems with roaming. Roaming problems are usually caused by poor network design or faulty client device drivers. Because of the proprietary nature of roaming, problems can also occur when radios from multiple vendors are deployed. Changes in the WLAN environment can also cause roaming hiccups.

Client stations, and not the access point, make the decision on whether or not to roam between access points. Some vendors may involve the access point or WLAN controller in the roaming decision, but ultimately, the client station initiates the roaming process with a reassociation request frame. The method by which a client station decides to roam is a set of proprietary rules determined by the manufacturer of the 802.11 radio, usually defined by *receive signal strength indicator (RSSI)* thresholds. RSSI thresholds usually involve signal strength, noise level, and bit-error rate. As the client station communicates on the network, it continues to look for other access points via probing and listening on other channels and will hear received signals from other APs. The variable of most importance will always be received signal strength: As the received signal from the original AP grows weaker and a station hears a stronger signal from another known access point, the station will initiate the roaming process. However, other variables such as SNR, error rates, and retransmissions may also have a part in the roaming decision.

As shown in Figure 12.19, as the client station moves away from the original access point with which it is associated and the signal drops below a predetermined threshold, the client station will attempt to connect to a new target access point that has a stronger signal. The client sends a frame, called the reassociation request frame, to start the roaming procedure.

FIGURE 12.19   Roaming

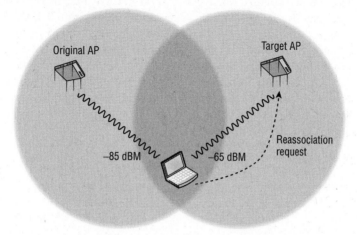

Because roaming is proprietary, a specific vendor client station may roam sooner than a second vendor client station as they move through various coverage cells. Some vendors like to encourage roaming, whereas others trigger roaming at lower received signal thresholds. In an environment where a WLAN administrator must support multiple vendor radios, different roaming behaviors will most assuredly be seen. For the time being, a WLAN administrator will always face unique challenges because of the proprietary nature of roaming. As discussed in Chapter 5, "IEEE 802.11 Standards," the ratified 802.11k amendment defined the use of *radio resource measurement (RRM)* and *neighbor reports* to enhance roaming performance. The ratified 802.11r amendment also defines faster secure handoffs when roaming occurs between cells in a wireless LAN using the strong security defined in a robust security network (RSN).

Client-Side Support of 802.11k and 802.11r Mechanisms

Most WLAN infrastructure vendors already support 802.11k and 802.11r technology in their APs and controllers, but most client devices do not. Some aspects of the 802.11r (secure roaming) and 802.11k (resource management) amendments are tested by the Wi-Fi Alliance with a certification called Voice Enterprise. Although the Voice Enterprise certification is a reality, the majority of clients still do not support 802.11k and 802.11r mechanisms. Over time, we can expect more support for 802.11k and 802.11r technology on the client side.

The best way to ensure that seamless roaming will commence is proper design and a thorough site survey. When you're designing an 802.11 WLAN, most vendors recommend 15 percent to 30 percent overlap of –70 dBm coverage cells. For years, WLAN design guides and white papers from various WLAN vendors referenced the 15 percent to 30 percent coverage cell overlap, as shown in Figure 12.20. The problem is: How do you calculate and measure cell overlap? Should the cell overlap area be measured by circumference, diameter, or radius? Additionally, WLAN vendor white papers (and even this book) use illustrations to depict the coverage cells as perfectly round and circular. In reality, coverage cells are oddly shaped, like an amoeba or a starburst. How can you measure coverage cell overlap if every coverage cell has a different shape?

FIGURE 12.20   Cell overlap

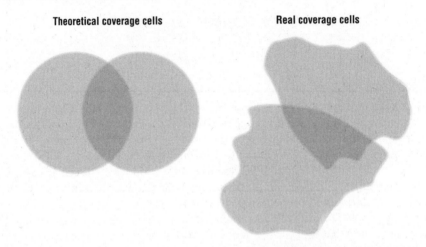

Wi-Fi site survey expert Keith Parsons has for years preached about the fallacy of measuring access point coverage overlap. Coverage overlap is really duplicate coverage from the perspective of a Wi-Fi client station. A proper site survey should be conducted to make sure that a client always has adequate duplicate coverage from multiple access points. In other words, each Wi-Fi client station (STA) needs to hear at least one access point at a specific RSSI and a backup or secondary access point at a different RSSI. Typically, most vendor RSSI thresholds require a received signal of –70 dBm for the higher data rate communications. Therefore, the client station needs to hear a second AP with a signal of -70 dBm or greater when the coverage of the first AP drops to -70 dBm or lower. The only way to determine whether proper duplicate coverage is available for clients is by conducting a coverage analysis site survey. Proper site survey procedures are discussed in detail in Chapter 16.

Roaming problems will occur if there is not enough duplicate cell coverage. Too little duplicate coverage will effectively create a roaming dead zone, and connectivity might even temporarily be lost. On the flip side, too much duplicate coverage will also cause roaming problems. For example, a client station may stay associated with its original AP and not connect to a second access point even though the station is directly underneath the second access point. This can also create a situation in which the client device is constantly switching back and forth between the two or more APs on different channels. If a client station can also hear dozens of APs on the same channel with very strong signals, a degradation in performance will occur due to medium contention overhead.

Another design issue of great importance is latency. The 802.11-2012 standard suggests the use of an 802.1X/EAP security solution in an enterprise. The average time involved during the authentication process can be 700 milliseconds or longer. Every time a client station roams to a new access point, reauthentication is required when an 802.1X/EAP security solution has been deployed. The time delay that is a result of the authentication process can cause serious interruptions with time-sensitive applications. VoWiFi requires a roaming handoff of 150 milliseconds or much less when roaming. A *fast secure roaming (FSR)* solution is needed if 802.1X/EAP security and time-sensitive applications are used together in a wireless network. Currently, most WLAN vendors implement a nonstandard method of FSR called opportunistic key caching (OKC) that has grown over the years in terms of client-side support. The IEEE has defined *fast basic service set transition (FT)* mechanisms as a standard for fast and secure roaming; however, widespread support on the client side for FT mechanisms has yet to become a reality. As stated earlier, now that the Wi-Fi Alliance has implemented the Voice Enterprise certification, standardized FT mechanisms are slowly becoming a reality.

Neither nonstandard fast secure roaming mechanisms, such as opportunistic key caching (OKC), nor standard fast BSS transition (FT) roaming mechanisms are tested on the CWNA exam. Fast secure roaming mechanisms is a heavily tested subject in the Certified Wireless Security Professional (CWSP) exam.

Changes in the WLAN environment can also cause roaming headaches. RF interference will always affect the performance of a wireless network and can make roaming problematic as well. Very often new construction in a building will affect the coverage of a WLAN and create new dead zones. If the physical environment where the WLAN is deployed changes, the coverage design might have to change as well. It is always a good idea to periodically conduct a coverage survey to monitor changes in coverage patterns.

Troubleshooting roaming by using a protocol analyzer is tricky because the reassociation roaming exchanges occur on multiple channels. To troubleshoot a client roaming between channels 1, 6, and 11, you would need three separate protocol analyzers on three separate laptops that would produce three separate frame captures. CACE Technologies offers a product called AirPcap that is a USB 802.11 radio. As shown in Figure 12.21, three AirPcap USB radios can be configured to capture frames on channels 1, 6, and 11 simultaneously. All three radios are connected to a USB hub and save the frame captures of all three channels into a single time-stamped capture file. The AirPcap solution allows for multichannel monitoring with a single protocol analyzer. Other WLAN analyzer vendors also offer multichannel monitoring capabilities.

FIGURE 12.21   AirPcap provides multichannel monitoring and roaming analysis.

Layer 3 Roaming

One major consideration when designing a WLAN is what happens when client stations roam across layer 3 boundaries. Wi-Fi operates at layer 2 and roaming is essentially a layer 2 process. As pictured in Figure 12.22, the client station is roaming between two access points. The roam is seamless at layer 2, but a router sits between the two access points, and each access point resides in a separate subnet. In other words, the client station will lose layer 3 connectivity and must acquire a new IP address. Any connection-oriented applications that are running when the client reestablishes layer 3 connectivity will have to be restarted. For example, a VoIP phone conversation would disconnect in this scenario, and the call would have to be reestablished.

Because 802.11 wireless networks are usually integrated into preexisting wired topologies, crossing layer 3 boundaries is often a necessity, especially in large deployments. The only way to maintain upper-layer communications when crossing layer 3 subnets is to provide a *layer 3 roaming* solution that is based on the Mobile IP standard. *Mobile IP* is an Internet Engineering Task Force (IETF) standard protocol that allows mobile device users to move from one layer 3 network to another while maintaining their original IP address. Mobile IP is defined in IETF request for comment (RFC) 3344. Layer 3 roaming solutions based on Mobile IP use some type of tunneling method and IP header encapsulation to allow packets to traverse between separate layer 3 domains with the goal of maintaining upper-layer communications. Most WLAN vendors now support some type of layer 3 roaming solution, as shown in Figure 12.23.

As shown in the WLAN architecture example in Figure 12.23, a mobile client receives an IP address, also known as a home address, on a home network. The mobile client's IP address is known to a device on the network called the *home agent (HA)*. The original WLAN controller on the client's home network serves as the home agent. The home agent is a single point of contact for a client when it roams across layer 3 boundaries. The HA shares client MAC/IP database information in a table called a *home agent table (HAT)* with another device called a *foreign agent (FA).*

FIGURE 12.22   Layer 3 roaming boundaries

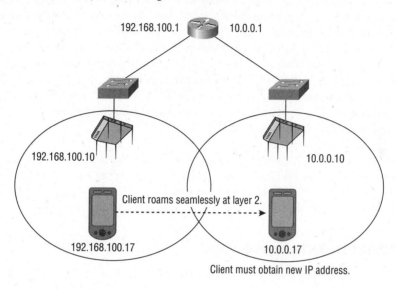

FIGURE 12.23   Mobile IP

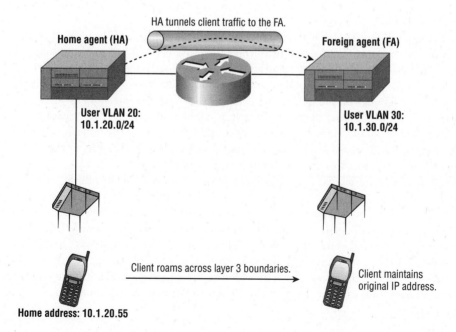

In this example, the foreign agent is another WLAN controller that handles all Mobile IP communications with the home agent on behalf of the client. The foreign agent's IP address is known as the *care-of address*. When the client roams across layer 3 boundaries, the client is roaming to a foreign network where the FA resides. The FA uses the HAT tables to locate the HA of the mobile client station. The FA contacts the HA and sets up a Mobile IP tunnel. Any traffic that is sent to the client's home address is intercepted by the HA and sent through the Mobile IP tunnel to the FA. The FA then delivers the tunneled traffic to the client and the client is able to maintain connectivity using the original home address. In our example, the Mobile IP tunnel is between WLAN controllers. Mobile IP tunnels are established between access points if the WLAN vendor does not use controllers. In a WLAN architecture where there is no controller, tunneling of user traffic occurs between access points that assume the roles of HA and FA.

Although maintaining upper-layer connectivity is possible with these layer 3 roaming solutions, increased latency is sometimes an issue. Additionally, layer 3 roaming may not be a requirement for your network. Less complex infrastructure often uses a simpler, flat layer 2 design. Larger enterprise networks often have multiple user and management VLANs linked to multiple subnets; therefore, a layer 3 roaming solution will be required.

Co-channel Interference

One of the most common mistakes many businesses make when first deploying a WLAN is to configure multiple access points all on the same channel. If all of the APs are on the same channel, unnecessary medium contention overhead occurs. As you have learned, CSMA/CA dictates half-duplex communications, and only one radio can transmit on the same channel at any given time.

As shown in Figure 12.24, if an AP on channel 1 is transmitting, all nearby access points and clients on the same channel will defer transmissions. The result is that throughput is adversely affected: Nearby APs and clients have to wait much longer to transmit because they have to take their turn. The unnecessary medium contention overhead that occurs because all the APs are on the same channel is called *co-channel interference (CCI)*. In reality, the 802.11 radios are operating exactly as defined by the CSMA/CA mechanisms, and this behavior should really be called *co-channel cooperation*. The unnecessary medium contention overhead caused by co-channel interference is a result of improper channel reuse design, which is discussed in the next section of this chapter.

Please do not confuse adjacent channel interference with co-channel interference. However, adjacent channel interference is also a result of improper channel reuse design. As Figure 12.25 shows, overlapping coverage cells that also have overlapping frequency space from adjacent cells will result in corrupted data and layer 2 retransmissions. Please refer back to Figure 12.6 and you will see that channels 1 and 4, channels 4 and 7, and channels 7 and 11 all have overlapping frequency space. Adjacent channel interference is a much more serious problem than co-channel interference because of the corrupted data and layer 2 retries. Proper channel reuse design is the answer to both co-channel and adjacent channel interference.

FIGURE 12.24 Co-channel interference

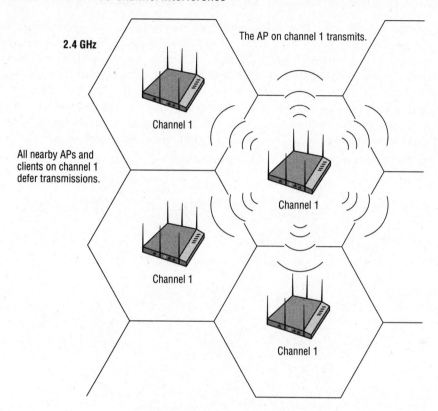

FIGURE 12.25 Adjacent channel interference

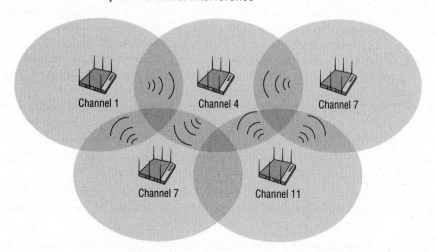

Channel Reuse/Multiple-Channel Architecture

To avoid co-channel and adjacent channel interference, a channel reuse design is necessary. Once again, overlapping RF coverage cells are needed for roaming, but overlapping frequencies must be avoided. The only three channels that meet these criteria in the 2.4 GHz ISM band are channels 1, 6, and 11 in the United States. Overlapping coverage cells, therefore, should be placed in a *channel reuse* pattern similar to the one pictured in Figure 12.26. A WLAN channel reuse pattern also goes by the name of *multiple-channel architecture (MCA)*. WLAN architecture with overlapping coverage cells that utilizes three channels at 2.4 GHz, or numerous channels at 5 GHz, would be considered a multiple-channel architecture.

FIGURE 12.26   2.4 GHz multiple-channel architecture

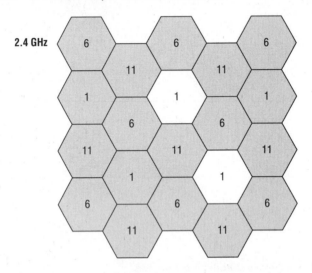

It should be noted that it is impossible to avoid all instances of co-channel interference when using a three-channel reuse pattern at 2.4 GHz, because there is always a certain amount of bleed-over between coverage cells transmitting on the same channel. If only three channels are available for a channel reuse pattern, it is pretty much a given that there will be access points on the same channel within hearing distance of each other. In Europe and other regions of the world, more channels are legally available for license-free communications in the 2.4 GHz ISM band. In Europe, a WLAN four-channel reuse pattern of channels 1, 5, 9 and 13 is sometimes deployed. Although there is a small amount of frequency overlap between those four channels, the performance might in some cases be better if the medium contention overhead of co-channel cooperation can be reduced because there is less bleed-over. The four-channel plan still has disadvantages:

- If a nearby business has APs deployed on the traditional 1-6-11 plan, the neighboring business's APs will cause severe adjacent channel interference with your APs deployed with a 1-5-9-13 plan.

- Also, all North American Wi-Fi radios are restricted by firmware and cannot transmit on channel 13. Any visiting customer or employee with a laptop, iPad, or other mobile device that was purchased in North America will not be able to connect to a European access point transmitting on channel 13.

For these reasons, the more traditional three-channel plan is usually deployed in Europe. A four-channel plan should never be used in the United States or Canada.

Please understand that client station transmissions also result in the medium contention performance downgrade known as co-channel interference. As shown in Figure 12.27, if a client is at the outer edges of a coverage cell, the client's transmissions may propagate into another cell using the same channel. All of the radios in the other cell will defer if they hear the original client's transmissions.

FIGURE 12.27   Clients and co-channel interference

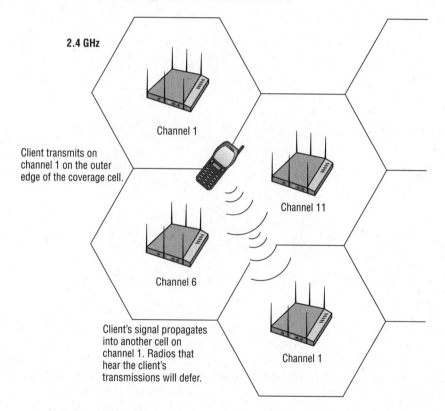

Channel reuse patterns should also be used in the 5 GHz frequency bands. If all the 5 GHz channels are legally available for transmissions, a total of 25 channels may be available for a channel reuse pattern at 5 GHz. Only 22 of the 25 channels are available for a 5 GHz channel reuse pattern in the United States. Channels 120–128 are reserved for Terminal Doppler Weather Radar (TDWR) in the United States; therefore, the FCC defines dynamic frequency selection (DFS) regulations that restrict use of the 5600 MHz–5650 MHz frequency band. In Europe, fewer channels are available for a 5 GHz reuse pattern because the four U-NII-3 channels and channel 165 are not usually available without a license. With the advent of 802.11ac technology, a new channel 144 has been added to the U-NII-2E band. Currently, the majority of 5 GHz radios do not yet transmit on channel 144.

Depending on the region, and other considerations, 8 channels, 12 channels, 17 channels, 22 channels, or other combinations may be used for 5 GHz channel reuse patterns. For example, Figure 12.28 depicts a 5 GHz channel reuse pattern using the 12 channels available in U-NII-1, U-NII-2, and U-NII-3. Although by the IEEE's definition, all 5 GHz channels are considered nonoverlapping, in reality there is some frequency sideband overlap from adjacent channels. It is a recommended practice that any adjacent coverage cells use a frequency that is at least two channels apart and not use an adjacent frequency. Following this simple rule will prevent adjacent channel interference from the sideband overlap.

FIGURE 12.28   5 GHz multiple-channel architecture

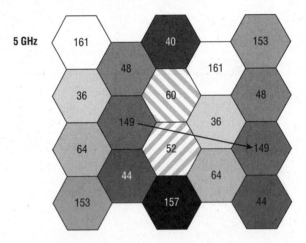

Distance to cell with same channel is at least two cells.

Figure 12.28 also shows that the second recommended practice for 5 GHz channel reuse design is that there should be at least two cells of coverage space distance between any two access points transmitting on the same channel. Following this rule will prevent co-channel interference from APs and most likely also from clients. The client's signal will have to propagate a greater distance and should attenuate to an amplitude level below the noise floor before the signal reaches another coverage cell using the same channel.

Real World Scenario

How Many Channels Should I Use in a 5 GHz Channel Reuse Pattern?

Several factors should be considered when planning a 5 GHz channel reuse pattern:

- The first factor is what channels are available legally in your country or region.

  In Europe, a pattern utilizing most of the channels in the U-NII-1, U-NII-2, and U-NII-2E bands is quite common. The U-NII-3 channels are rarely used in the pattern because of regulatory domain restrictions.

- The second factor to consider is what channels the client population supports.

  In the United States, 22 channels are available for a reuse pattern; however, it might be a good idea to use only an 8-channel pattern consisting of the non-DFS U-NII-1/U-NII-3 bands, as shown in the following illustration.

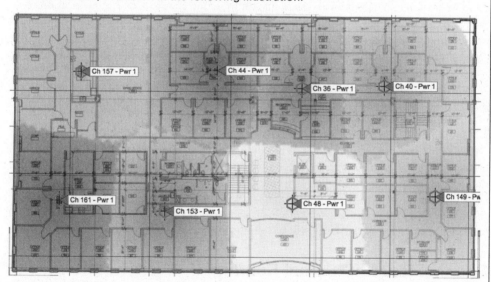

Wi-Fi radios must be certified to transmit in the dynamic frequency selection (DFS) channels to avoid interference with radar. A high likelihood exists that the client population may not be certified for dynamic frequency selection (DFS) channels in the U-NII-2 and U-NII-2e bands. Even though the access points have been certified to transmit in the DFS channels, the clients cannot and therefore the clients are limited to eight channels of U-NII-1 and U-NII-3 bands. Non-DFS clients will not be able to connect to access points transmitting in U-NII-2 and U-NII-2E.

Unless all of your 5 GHz–capable clients support DFS channels, your network will likely be designed around U-NII-1/U-NII-3, which limits it to eight nonoverlapping channels in most countries. The good news is that most current-day client devices are being certified to transmit on the DFS channels and the inclusion of DFS channels in channel reuse patterns is becoming more commonplace.

It is necessary to always think three-dimensionally when designing a multiple-channel architecture reuse pattern. If access points are deployed on multiple floors in the same building, a reuse pattern will be necessary, such as the one pictured in Figure 12.29. A common mistake is to deploy a cookie-cutter design by performing a site survey on only one floor and then placing the access points on the same channels and same locations on each floor. A site survey must be performed on all floors, and the access points often need to be staggered to allow for a three-dimensional reuse pattern. Also, the coverage cells of each access point should not extend beyond more than one floor above and below the floor where the access point is mounted. It is inappropriate to always assume that the coverage bleed-over to other floors will provide sufficient signal strength and quality. In some cases, the floors are concrete or steel and allow very little, if any, signal coverage through. As a result, a survey is absolutely required.

Most enterprise access points have dual-frequency capabilities, allowing for both 2.4 GHz and 5 GHz wireless networks to be deployed in the same area. The 802.11a/n/ac radio in an access point transmits at 5 GHz, and the signal will attenuate faster than the signal that is being transmitted at 2.4 GHz from the 802.11b/g/n radio. Therefore, when performing a site survey for deploying dual-frequency WLANs, you should perform the 5 GHz site survey first and determine the placement of the access points. After those locations are identified, channel reuse patterns will have to be used for each respective frequency.

Channel Reuse/Channel Bonding

802.11n technology introduced the capability of bonding two 20 MHz channels to create a larger 40 MHz channel. Channel bonding effectively doubles the frequency bandwidth, meaning double the data rates that can be available to 802.11n radios. 40 MHz channels will be discussed in greater detail in Chapter 18, "802.11n." Channel bonding is typically used only in the 5 GHz bands.

As shown in Figure 12.30, a total of twelve 40 MHz channels are available to be used in a reuse pattern when deploying an enterprise WLAN. However, two of the twelve 40 MHz channels currently cannot be used in the United States because they fall within the TDWR band. Two of the 40 MHz channels often are not used in Europe because they fall within the U-NII-3 band that requires light licensing in many countries.

FIGURE 12.29 Three-dimensional channel reuse

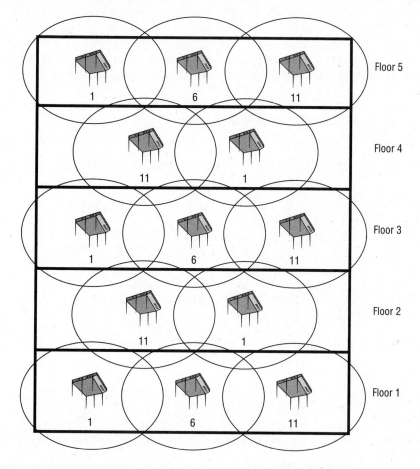

FIGURE 12.30 40 MHz channels

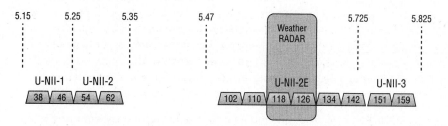

802.11n radios that have 40 MHz channel bonding enabled are backward compatible with legacy 80211a radios that only support 20 MHz radios. The number of 40 MHz channels that can be used in a channel reuse pattern by 802.11n radios depends on the number of 20 MHz channels that are being used in a 20 MHz reuse pattern. For example, many

WLAN deployments in the United States do not use the DFS channels because many legacy clients do not support DFS. Therefore, the available eight channels in only the U-NII-1 and U-NII-3 bands are used in a 20 MHz reuse pattern.

However, 802.11n client radios with channel bonding capability will have a total of four 40 MHz channels available for transmissions. As depicted in Figure 12.31, effectively a four-channel 40 MHz channel reuse pattern is used by the 802.11n AP and client radios that have enabled channel bonding.

FIGURE 12.31   40 MHz channel reuse

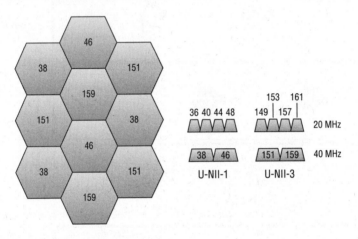

🌐 **Real World Scenario**

Why Is Channel Bonding Optional and Are There Any Disadvantages?

At first glance, you would think that channel bonding should always be enabled because of the higher data rates that are available to 802.11n radios. For example, the highest potential data rate for a 3×3:3 MIMO radio transmitting on a 20 MHz channel is 217 Mbps. The highest potential data rate for a 3×3:3 MIMO radio transmitting on a 40 MHz channel is 450 Mbps. After looking at these numbers, most administrators assume that channel bonding would be enabled by default. However, many WLAN access point vendors require that channel bonding be manually enabled because there is the potential for channel bonding to negatively impact the performance of the WLAN.

Let's go back to 20 MHz design for one moment. One of the advantages of using 5 GHz over 2.4 GHz is that there are many more 5 GHz 20 MHz channels that can be used in a reuse pattern. Only three 20 MHz channels can be used in 2.4 GHz. The problem with only using three 20 MHz channels is that there will always be some amount of co-channel interference even though these channels are nonoverlapping. Therefore, a certain amount of medium contention overhead always exists at 2.4 GHz simply because there are not enough channels and frequency spaces. Medium contention overhead due to APs on the same 20 MHz channel can almost be completely avoided in 5 GHz because there are more channels. A 5 GHz eight or twelve 20 MHz channel reuse design will greatly decrease co-channel interference and medium contention overhead.

Now, consider a 40 MHz reuse pattern. If eight 20 MHz channels are being used, a four channel 40 MHz channel reuse pattern then exists. Although the bandwidth is doubled for the 802.11n radios, there will be an increase of medium contention overhead because there are only four channels and access points on the same channel will likely hear each other. The medium contention overhead may have a negative impact and offset any gains in performance that the extra bandwidth might provide.

So, should you use channel bonding or not? If four or fewer 40 MHz channels are available, you might not want to turn on channel bonding, especially if the 5 GHz radios are transmitting at a higher power level. If the majority of the WLAN clients do not support channel bonding, there is no reason to enable the capability. For example, earlier versions of 802.11n smartphones and tablets did not support bonding. Even if all the 802.11n clients support 40 MHz channel bonding, performance testing would be highly recommended if only four 40 MHz channels are deployed.

However, if the DFS bands are enabled, as many as ten 40 MHz channels are available, and therefore a much better reuse pattern that cuts down on medium contention will be available. The key is that the client radios must support DFS and should support channel bonding.

As 802.11ac technology becomes more commonplace, the need for the extra 5 GHz frequency space is even more important. 802.11ac introduces the use of 80 MHz and 160 MHz channels. 802.11ac channels will be discussed in greater detail in Chapter 19, "Very-High Throughput (VHT) and 802.11ac."

Single-Channel Architecture

As of this writing, two WLAN vendors, Meru Networks and Extricom, promote an alternative WLAN channel design solution known as the *single-channel architecture (SCA)*. Another WLAN vendor, Ubiquiti Networks, offers SCA as an optional feature. Imagine a WLAN network with multiple access points all transmitting on the same channel and all sharing the same BSSID. A single-channel architecture is exactly what you have just imagined. The client stations see transmissions on only a single channel with one SSID (logical WLAN identifier) and one BSSID (layer 2 identifier). From the perspective of the client station, only one access point exists. In this type of WLAN architecture, all access points in the network can be deployed on one channel in 2.4 GHz or 5 GHz frequency bands. Uplink and downlink transmissions are coordinated by a WLAN controller on a single 802.11 channel in such a manner that the effects of co-channel interference are minimized.

Let's first discuss the single BSSID. Single-channel architecture consists of a WLAN controller and multiple lightweight access points. As shown in Figure 12.32, each AP has its own radio with its own MAC address; however, they all share a *virtual BSSID* that is broadcast from all the access points.

FIGURE 12.32 Single-channel architecture

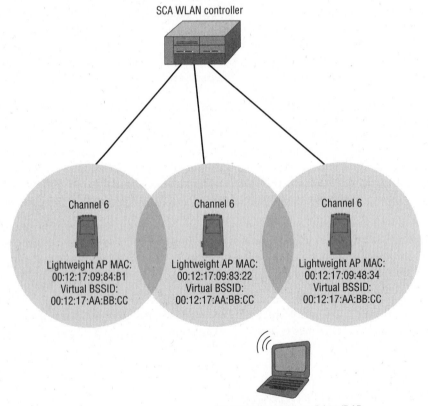

Because the multiple access points advertise only one single virtual MAC address (BSSID), client stations believe they are connected to only a single access point, although they may be roaming across multiple physical APs. You have learned that clients make the roaming decisions. In a single-channel architecture (SCA) system, the clients think they are associated to only one AP, so they never initiate a layer 2 roaming exchange. All of the roaming handoffs are handled by a central WLAN controller.

As Figure 12.33 shows, the main advantage is that clients experience a *zero handoff* time, and the latency issues associated with roaming times are resolved. The *virtual AP* used by SCA solutions is potentially an excellent marriage for VoWiFi phones and 802.1X/ EAP solutions. As we discussed earlier, the average time involved during the EAP authentication process can be 700 milliseconds or longer. Every time a client station roams to a new access point, reauthentication is required when an 802.1X/EAP security solution has been deployed. VoWiFi requires a roaming handoff of 150 ms or less. The virtual BSSID eliminates the need for reauthentication while physically roaming within a single channel architecture and thus a zero handoff time.

FIGURE 12.33   Zero handoff time

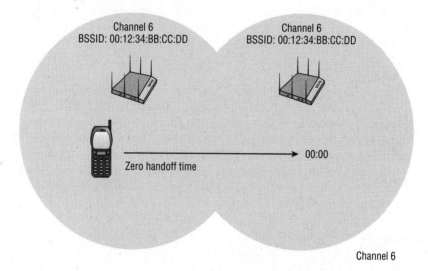

You have learned that client stations make the roaming decision in an MCA environment. However, client stations do not know that they roam in an SCA environment. The clients must still be mobile and transfer layer 2 communications between physical access points. All the client-roaming mechanisms are now handled back on the WLAN controller, and client-side roaming decisions have been eliminated. All station associations are maintained at the SCA WLAN controller, and the SCA controller manages all the lightweight APs. The SCA controller assigns to a unique access point the responsibility of handling downlink transmissions for an individual client station. When the controller receives the incoming transmissions of a client, the SCA controller evaluates the RSSI values of the client's transmissions. Based on incoming RSSI measurements, the SCA controller can allocate a specific AP for downlink transmissions. The client believes that it is associated to a single AP. However, the client moves between different physical APs based on RSSI measurements evaluated by the controller.

One big advantage of the single-channel architecture is that adjacent channel interference is no longer an issue. If all the access points are on the same channel, there can be no frequency overlap and, thus, no adjacent channel interference. However, a legitimate question about an SCA WLAN solution is: Why doesn't co-channel interference occur if all of the channels are on the same channel? The answer is that co-channel interference does occur, it is just centrally managed by the WLAN controller by scheduling transmissions for APs within range of one another. If all of the APs are on the same channel in an MCA wireless network, unnecessary medium contention overhead occurs. In a typical MCA environment, each access point has a unique BSSID and a separate channel, and each AP's coverage cell is a single-collision domain. In an SCA wireless environment, the collision domains are managed dynamically by the SCA controller based on RSSI algorithms. The controller ensures that nearby devices on the same channel are not transmitting at the same time. Most of the mechanisms used by SCA vendors are proprietary and beyond the scope of this book.

For many years, the procedures just described were a competitive advantage for the SCA companies selling into verticals where VoWiFi was needed. However, opportunistic key caching (OKC) and other fast secure roaming mechanisms have become more commonplace and VoWiFi is deployed extensively within the more traditional MCA architecture. One of the major SCA companies also offers the capability to disable SCA and use multiple channels like all the other vendors.

A major disadvantage of the single-channel architecture is the capacity issue because only one channel is available. In a 2.4 GHz SCA deployment, multiple APs can be co-located by using three channels and three virtual BSSIDs. Co-location design in single-channel architecture is often referred to as *channel stacking*. Each layer of multiple APs on a single channel and using the same virtual BSSID is known as a *channel blanket* or *channel span*. Although this might sound like a good idea in theory, most customers are not willing to pay for three co-located access points everywhere coverage is needed. Another possible disadvantage with an SCA architecture is that the contention domain is very large. Although AP transmissions are coordinated by an SCA controller to minimize collisions with other APs, SCA technology is highly proprietary and there is no guarantee that client transmissions can be controlled to perfection.

Capacity vs. Coverage

When a wireless network is designed, two concepts that typically compete with each other are *capacity* and *coverage*. In the early days of wireless networks, it was common to install an access point with the power set to the maximum level to provide the largest coverage area possible. This was typically acceptable because there were very few wireless devices. Also, access points were very expensive, so companies tried to provide the most coverage while using the fewest access points. Figure 12.34 shows the outline of a building along with the coverage area that is provided by three APs in a multiple-channel architecture. If there are just a few client stations, this type of wireless design is quite acceptable.

With the proliferation of wireless devices, network design has changed drastically from the early days. Proper network design now entails providing necessary coverage while trying to limit the number of devices connected to any single access point at the same time. This is what is meant by *capacity vs. coverage*. As you know, all of the client stations that connect to a single access point share the throughput capabilities of that access point. Therefore, it is important to design the network to try to limit the number of stations that are simultaneously connected to a single access point. This is performed by first determining the maximum number of stations that you want connected to an access point at the same time (this will vary from company to company depending on network usage). In an MCA environment, you need to determine how big the cell size needs to be to provide the proper capacity, and then you need to adjust the power level of the access point in order to create a cell of the desired size.

FIGURE 12.34 RF coverage of a building using three APs with few wireless stations

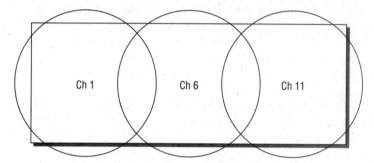

Figure 12.35 shows the outline of the same building, but because there are many more wireless stations, the cell sizes have been decreased while the number of cells has been increased. Adjusting the transmit power to limit the coverage area is known as *cell sizing* and is the most common method of meeting capacity needs in an MCA environment.

FIGURE 12.35 Cell sizing—multiple-channel architecture

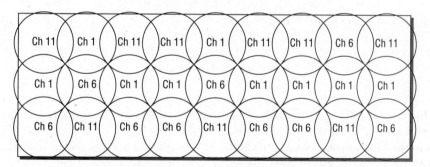

WLANs with high user density are becoming a greater concern due to the client population explosion that has occurred. Wi-Fi networks are no longer just about wireless laptop connectivity. Most users now want to connect to the enterprise WLAN with multiple devices, including tablets and smartphones with Wi-Fi radios. Luckily, 802.11n/ac technology has provided greater bandwidth to handle more clients; however, even 802.11n/ac access points can become overwhelmed. Most WLAN vendors implement proprietary load balancing, band steering, and other MAC layer mechanisms to further assist capacity needs in a high-density user environment.

Band Steering

The unlicensed 5 GHz frequency spectrum offers many advantages over the unlicensed 2.4 GHz frequency spectrum for Wi-Fi communications. The 5 GHZ U-NII bands offer a wider range of frequency space and many more channels. A proper 5 GHz channel reuse pattern using multiple channels will greatly decrease medium contention overhead caused by co-channel interference. In the 2.4 GHz band, there is always a certain amount of medium contention overhead due to CCI simply because there are only three channels.

Another major detrimental trait of the 2.4 GHz band is that, in addition to this band being used for WLAN networking, it is heavily used by many other types of devices, including microwave ovens, baby monitors, cordless telephones, and video cameras. With all of these different devices operating in the same frequency range, there is much more interference and a much higher noise floor than in the 5 GHz bands.

So, if the use of the 5 GHz bands will provide better throughput and performance, how can we encourage the clients to use this band? To start, it is the client that decides which AP and which band to connect to, typically based on the strongest signal that it hears for the SSID that it wants to connect to. Most access points have both 2.4 GHz and 5 GHz radios in them, with both of them advertising the same SSIDs. Since the 5 GHz signals naturally attenuate more than the 2.4 GHz signals, it is likely that the client radio will identify the 2.4 GHz radio as having a stronger signal and connect to it by default. In many environments, the client would be capable of making a strong and fast connection with either of the AP's radios but will choose the 2.4 GHz signal because it is the strongest. A technology known as band steering has been developed to try to encourage dual-band client radios to connect to a 5 GHz AP radio instead of to a 2.4 GHz AP radio.

Band steering is not an IEEE 802.11–developed technology. As of this writing, all implementations of band steering are proprietary. Although band steering implementations are proprietary, most vendors implement this technology using similar techniques by manipulating the MAC sublayer. When a dual-frequency client first starts up, it will transmit probe requests on both the 2.4 and 5 GHz bands looking for an AP. When a dual-frequency AP hears probe requests on both bands originating from the same client radio, the AP knows that the client is capable of operating in the 5 GHz band. As depicted in Figure 12.36, the AP will then try to steer the client to the 5 GHz band by responding to the client using only 5 GHz transmissions. Although the client is steered to the 5 GHz AP, there may be reasons for the client to connect to the AP using the 2.4 GHz radio. If the client radio continues to try to connect to the AP using the 2.4 GHz radio, the AP will ultimately allow the connection.

Clients usually have a much better connection and better performance when connected to the 5 GHz band, and therefore AP vendors offer band steering capabilities. It should be noted that some client device vendors may also implement proprietary client-side band steering. Mac OS and iOS client devices typically prefer to connect to 5 GHz AP radios before they associate with 2.4 GHz AP radios. Some client vendors also offer the capability to configure client-side band steering with software client utilities.

Although band steering is normally used to encourage clients to connect to 5 GHz access points, clients can also be steered to the 2.4 band. As shown in Figure 12.37, many WLAN vendors can define a percentage of clients to be directed to the 5 GHz band, with the remainder directed to the 2.4 GHz band. In environments where a high density of client devices exists, band steering to both frequencies can be used to balance an almost equal number of clients to both of the radios in the AP. For example, 55 clients connect to the 2.4 GHz radio and 60 clients connect to the 5 GHz radio. Effectively, band steering can be used to load balance clients between the frequencies. Please do not confuse this type of single AP frequency balancing with load balancing clients between multiple access points. Load balancing between multiple access points is described in the next section of this chapter.

FIGURE 12.36   Band steering to 5 GHz

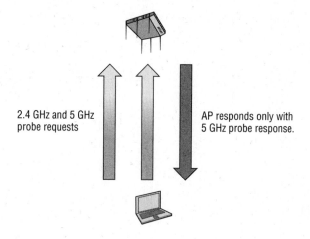

2.4 GHz and 5 GHz
probe requests

AP responds only with
5 GHz probe response.

FIGURE 12.37   Band steering for frequency balancing

Band Steering

Note: The following band steering settings will be applied to both the 2.4 and 5 GHz radios.

☑ Enable the steering of clients from the 2.4 to 5 GHz bands

Band steering mode	Balance band use ⬍
Ratio of 5 GHz to 2.4 GHz clients	50 (1-100%)

Load Balancing

WLAN vendors also use methods to manipulate the MAC sublayer to balance clients between multiple access points. As illustrated in Figure 12.38, load balancing clients between access points ensures that a single AP is not overloaded with too many clients and that the total client population can be served by numerous APs with the final result being better performance. When a client wants to connect to an AP, the client will send an association request frame to the AP. If an AP is already overloaded with too many clients, the AP will defer the association response to the client. The hope is that the client will then send another association request to another nearby AP with a lesser amount of client load. Over time, the client associations will be fairly balanced across multiple APs. The client load information will obviously have to be shared among the access points. Load balancing is a control plane mechanism that can exist either in a distributed architecture where all the APs communicate or within a centralized architecture that utilizes a WLAN controller.

Load balancing between access points is typically implemented in areas where there is a high density of clients and roaming is not necessarily the priority. In areas where roaming is needed, load balancing is usually not a good idea because the mechanisms may cause clients to become sticky and stay associated to the AP too long. Please understand that load balancing between APs can be detrimental to the roaming process.

FIGURE 12.38   Load balancing between APs

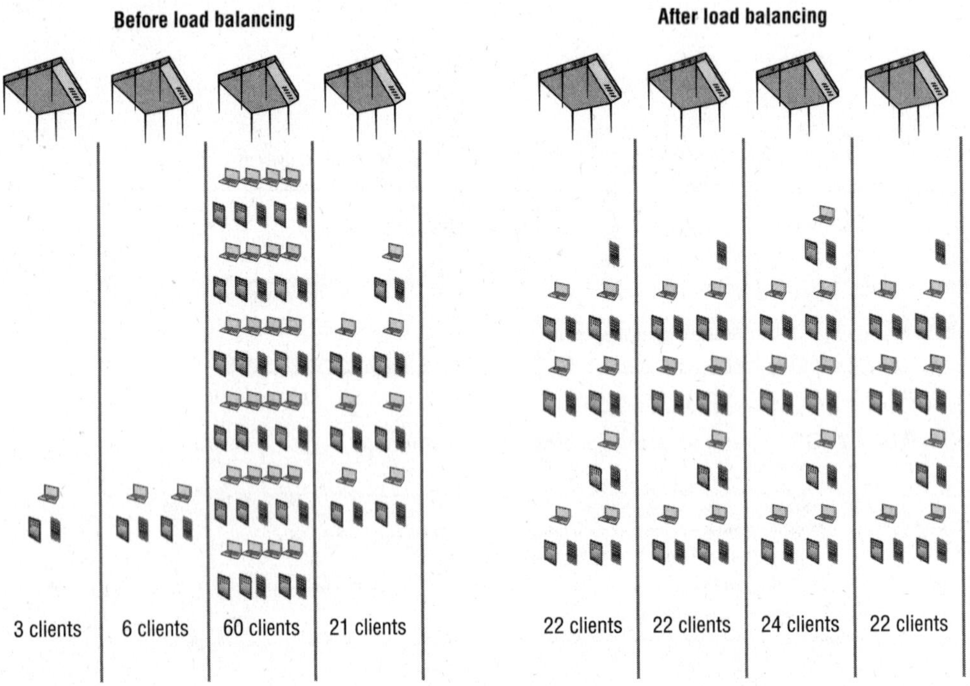

High-Density WLANs

As we have discussed, designing for device and user capacity is very different from designing for coverage. First and foremost, careful planning is needed based on the type of applications being used, the types of devices, and the number of client devices.

The question that is always asked is: How many client devices can connect to an AP radio? The correct answer is: It depends. If the access point is using 802.11n radios with 20 MHz channels, a good rule of thumb is that each radio could support 35 to 50 active devices for average use, such as web browsing and checking email. However, the numbers can vary greatly based on the capabilities of the client devices and the applications that are being used. An 802.11n tablet with a 1×1:1 MIMO radio transmitting on a 20 MHz channel can achieve a data rate of 65 Mbps with TCP throughput of 30 Mbps to 40 Mbps. An 802.11n laptop with a 2×2:2 radio transmitting on a 20 MHz channel might achieve a data rate of 130 Mbps with TCP throughput of 70 Mbps to 80 Mbps. Additionally, different applications require different amounts of TCP throughput, as shown in Table 12.1.

TABLE 12.1 Applications and TCP throughput consumption

Application	Required throughput
Email/web browsing	500 Kbps 1 Mbps
Printing	1 Mbps
SD video streaming	1 Mbps to 1.5 Mbps
HD video streaming	2 Mbps to 5 Mbps

Once you have determined the types of devices that are being used and the types of applications, you can then calculate the amount of airtime consumption. For example, an Apple iPad transmitting on a 20 MHz channel can connect at a data rate of 65 Mbps and might achieve a maximum amount of 30 Mbps of TCP throughput. A 2 Mbps video application running on an iPad will consume 6.67 percent of the airtime consumption on a 20 MHz channel (2 ÷ 30 = 6.67). A 2×2:2 laptop transmitting on a 20 MHz channel might connect with a data rate of 130 Mbps with TCP throughput of close to 70 Mbps. The same 2 Mbps HD video application running on the laptop will consume about 2.86 percent of airtime consumption (2 ÷ 70 = 2.86).

Once you have determined amount of airtime consumption, you can then calculate the number of active devices that an AP radio can support. Wi-Fi expert Andrew von Nagy, one of the technical editors of this book, recommends several good formulas for these calculations. An 802.11 access point is considered to be fully burdened at about 80 percent of airtime utilization. To estimate the number of devices supported on a single AP radio, divide the individual airtime required per device into 80 percent.

80 ÷ single device airtime consumption = # devices per AP radio

For example, the 2 Mbps HD video application running on the iPads consumes 6.67 percent of airtime per device. Therefore, 80 ÷ 6.67 = 12 iPads that could run the application concurrently on a 20 MHz channel through a single 802.11n AP radio. The AP most likely has a 2.4 GHz and a 5 GHz radio, therefore 24 iPads could run the same HD video application through a single AP if the devices were balanced between the two frequencies. The same 2 Mbps HD video application running on the laptops consumed 2.86 percent of airtime per device. Therefore, 80 ÷ 2.86 = 28 laptops that could conceivably run the application concurrently on a 20 MHz channel through a single 802.11n AP radio.

To calculate the number of AP radios needed, multiple the number of client devices by the amount of airtime consumption and divide by 80 percent.

(# of devices × single device airtime consumption) ÷ 80% = number of AP radios

For example, (150 iPads × 6.67) ÷ 80% = 12.5 AP radios. Therefore, seven dual-band APs could adequately handle 150 iPads concurrently using a very high bandwidth application. What if you also needed 150 laptops using the same streaming application in the same area with the iPads? Calculate (150 laptops × 2.86) ÷ 80% = 5.36 AP radios. Therefore, you would probably need three more dual-band access points. A total of ten dual-band 802.11n APs transmitting with 20 MHz channels would be able to handle concurrent 1 Mbps HD video streams to 150 iPads and 150 laptops.

Keep in mind that these numbers are estimates and extensive testing post-deployment is always a good idea. A free predictive WLAN capacity planning spreadsheet is available for download at www.revolutionwifi.net.

A high-density WLAN usually requires numerous access points in a single designated area—for example, multiple APs deployed in an auditorium filled with many users with multiple Wi-Fi devices. Most WLAN vendors have their own high-density WLAN design guides; however, some general rules remain consistent when designing a high-capacity WLAN:

- 802.11n or 802.11ac access points should always be deployed as opposed to legacy 802.11a/b/g APs.
- Disable the 802.11b data rates to cut down on medium contention overhead and protection mechanism overhead. Keep in mind that 802.11b clients will not be allowed to associate.
- If possible, deploy only 802.11n or 802.11ac client devices and select a high minimum data rate, such as 18 Mbps.
- Lower the AP transmit power for cell sizing purposes and to limit co-channel inference.
- For stability, use static channel and power settings instead of dynamic RF mechanisms.
- Implement band steering ratios to load balance the client between the 2.4 GHz and 5 GHz radios on individual APs.
- Enable load balancing mechanisms between multiple APs.
- In the 5 GHz band, use 20 MHz channels to cut down on medium contention if DFS channels are not supported. If the client devices support DFS channels as well as channel bonding, use 40 MHz channels.
- Consider using semidirectional MIMO patch antennas for the APs to provide sectorized coverage.
- Consider disabling some of the 2.4 GHz radios in the access points to cut down on 2.4 GHz co-channel interference.

We highly recommend that you also read your WLAN vendor's specific high-density design guide for tips and configuration settings that may be unique to a WLAN vendor.

Oversized Coverage Cells

As we've mentioned several times, a mistake often made when deploying access points is to have the APs transmit at full power. Although most indoor APs may have full transmit power settings as high as 100 mW, they should rarely be deployed at full power. Effectively, this extends the range of the access point, but it causes many of the problems that have been discussed throughout this chapter. Oversized coverage usually will not meet your capacity needs. Oversized coverage cells can cause hidden node problems. Access points at full power will most likely also increase the odds of co-channel interference due to bleed-over transmissions. In some cases, APs at full power may not be able to hear the transmissions of client stations with lower transmit power. For all of these reasons, typical indoor WLAN deployments are designed with the APs set at about one-fourth to one-third transmit power. Higher user density environments will require that the AP transmit power be set at the lowest setting of 1 mW. If the access point coverage and range is a concern, the best method of extending range is to increase the AP antenna gain instead of increasing transmit power.

Physical Environment

Although physical environment does not cause RF interference, physical obstructions can indeed disrupt and corrupt an 802.11 signal. An example of this is the scattering effect caused by a chain-link fence or safety glass with wire mesh. The signal is scattered and rendered useless. The only ways to eliminate physical interference is to remove the obstruction or add more APs. Keep in mind that the physical environment of every building and floor is different and the shape and size of coverage cells will vary widely. The best method of dealing with the physical environment is to perform a proper site survey, as described in detail in Chapter 16.

Voice vs. Data

As you have already learned, most data applications in a Wi-Fi network can handle a layer 2 retransmission rate of up to 10 percent without any noticeable degradation in performance. However, time-sensitive applications such as VoIP require that higher-layer IP packet loss be no greater than 2 percent. Therefore, Voice over Wi-Fi (VoWiFi) networks need to limit layer 2 retransmissions to 5 percent or less to guarantee the timely and consistent delivery of VoIP packets. When layer 2 retransmissions exceed 5 percent, latency problems may develop and jitter problems will most likely surface.

Of Canaries and Cockroaches

The canary-and-coal-mine analogy is often used to describe the difference between voice traffic and other data application traffic within a WLAN environment. Early coal mines did not have ventilation systems, so miners would bring a caged canary into new coal shafts. Canaries are more sensitive to methane and carbon monoxide than humans, which made them ideal for detecting dangerous gas buildups. As long as the canary (voice traffic) was singing, the miners knew their air supply in the mine (WLAN) was safe. A dead canary signaled the presence of deadly gases, and the miners would evacuate or put on respirator masks. However, some species, such as a cockroach (data traffic), can still survive within the coal mine despite the existence of the deadly gases but probably would have a better life if the poor conditions did not exist.

All too often, WLANs are deployed in an enterprise without any type of site survey. Also, many WLANs are initially designed to provide coverage only for data applications and not for voice. Most enterprise data applications will operate within a poorly designed WLAN but will not run optimally. (The lack of a site survey or an improper survey often result in a poor design.) Many companies that decide to add a VoWiFi solution to their WLAN at a later date quickly discover that the WLAN has many problems. The VoWiFi phones may have choppy audio or echo problems. The VoWiFi phones may disconnect or die like a canary. Adding voice to the WLAN often exposes existing problems: Because data applications can withstand a much higher layer 2 retransmission rate, problems that existed within the WLAN may have gone unnoticed. As shown in Table 12.2, IP voice traffic is more susceptible to late or inconsistent packet delivery due to layer 2 retransmissions.

TABLE 12.2   IP voice and IP data comparison

IP voice	IP data
Small, uniform-size packets	Variable-size packets
Even, predictable delivery	Bursty delivery
Highly affected by late or inconsistent packet delivery	Minimally affected by late or inconsistent packet delivery
"Better never than late"	"Better late than never"

Optimizing the WLAN to support voice traffic will optimize the network for all wireless clients, including the clients running data applications other than voice. A proper site survey will reduce lower layer 2 retransmissions and provide an environment with the seamless coverage that is required for VoWiFi networks.

Performance

When designing and deploying a WLAN, you will always be concerned about both coverage and capacity. Various factors can affect the coverage range of a wireless cell, and just as many factors can affect the aggregate throughput in an 802.11 WLAN. The following variables can affect the *range* of a WLAN:

Transmission Power Rates   The original transmission amplitude (power) will have an impact on the range of an RF cell. An access point transmitting at 30 mW will have a larger coverage zone than an access point transmitting at 1 mW if the same antenna is used. APs with too much transmission amplitude can cause many problems, as already discussed in this chapter.

Antenna Gain   Antennas are passive-gain devices that focus the original signal. An access point transmitting at 30 mW with a 6 dBi antenna will have greater range than it would if it used only a 3 dBi antenna. If you want to increase the range for the clients, the best solution is to increase the antenna gain of the access point.

Antenna Type   Antennas have different coverage patterns. Using the right antenna will give the proper coverage and reduce multipath and nearby interference.

Wavelength   Higher frequency signals have a smaller wavelength property and will attenuate faster than a lower-frequency signal with a larger wavelength. All things being equal, 2.4 GHz access points have a greater range than 5 GHz access points due to the difference in the length of their waves.

Free Space Path Loss   In any RF environment, free space path loss (FSPL) attenuates the signal as a function of distance and frequency.

Physical Environment   Walls and other obstacles will attenuate an RF signal because of absorption and other RF propagation behaviors. A building with concrete walls will require more access points than a building with drywall because concrete is denser and attenuates the signal faster than drywall.

As you have learned in earlier chapters, proper WLAN design must take into account both coverage and capacity. The variables just mentioned all affect coverage and range. Capacity performance considerations are equally as important as range considerations. Please remember that 802.11 data rates are considered data bandwidth and not throughput. The following are among the many variables that can affect the *throughput* of a WLAN:

Carrier Sense Multiple Access with Collision Avoidance (CSMA/CA) The medium access method that uses interframe spacing, physical carrier sense, virtual carrier sense, and the random back-off timer creates overhead and consumes bandwidth. The overhead due to medium contention usually is 50 percent or greater in legacy 802.11a/b/g networks. Medium contention overhead is usually 35 percent to 40 percent in 802.11n/ac networks.

Encryption Extra overhead is added to the body of an 802.11 data frame whenever encryption is implemented. WEP/RC4 encryption adds an extra 8 bytes of overhead per frame, TKIP/RC4 encryption adds an extra 20 bytes of overhead per frame, and CCMP/AES encryption adds an extra 16 bytes of overhead per frame. Layer 3 VPNs often use DES or 3DES encryption, both of which also consume significant bandwidth. Recent gains in processing capabilities and 802.11n/ac data rates have made encryption overhead much less of an issue in recent years.

Application Use Different types of applications have variable affects on bandwidth consumption. VoWiFi and data collection scanning typically do not require a lot of bandwidth. Other applications that require file transfers or database access are often more bandwidth intensive. High definition video streaming is also bandwidth intensive.

Number of Clients Remember that the WLAN is a shared medium. All throughput is aggregate, and all available bandwidth is shared.

Layer 2 Retransmissions As we have discussed throughout this chapter, various problems can cause frames to become corrupted. If frames are corrupted, they will need to be retransmitted and throughput will be affected.

Weather

When deploying a wireless mesh network outdoors or perhaps an outdoor bridge link, a WLAN administrator must take into account the adverse affect of weather conditions. The following weather conditions must be considered:

Lightning Direct and indirect lightning strikes can damage WLAN equipment. Lightning arrestors should be used for protection against transient currents. Solutions such as lightning rods or copper/fiber transceivers may offer protection against lightning strikes.

Wind Because of the long distances and narrow beamwidths, highly directional antennas are susceptible to movement or shifting caused by wind. Even slight movement of a highly directional antenna can cause the RF beam to be aimed away from the receiving antenna, interrupting the communications. In high-wind environments, a grid antenna will typically remain more stable than a parabolic dish. Other mounting options may be necessary to stabilize the antenna from movement.

Water   Conditions such as rain, snow, and fog present two unique challenges. First, all outdoor equipment must be protected from damage caused by exposure to water. Water damage is often a serious problem with cabling and connectors. Connectors should be protected with drip loops and coax seals to prevent water damage. Cables and connectors should be checked on a regular basis for damage. A radome (weatherproof protective cover) should be used to protect antennas from water damage.

Outdoor bridges, access points, and mesh routers should be protected from the weather elements by using appropriate National Electrical Manufacturers Association (NEMA) enclosure units. Precipitation can also cause an RF signal to attenuate. A torrential downpour can attenuate a signal as much as 0.08 dB per mile (0.05 dB per kilometer) in both the 2.4 GHz and 5 GHz frequency ranges. Over long-distance bridge links, a system operating margin (SOM) of 20 dB is usually recommended to compensate for attenuation due to rain, fog, or snow.

Air Stratification   A change in air temperature at high altitudes is known as *air stratification* (layering). Changes in air temperature can cause refraction. Bending of RF signals over long-distance point-to-point links can cause misalignment and performance issues. K-factor calculations may be necessary to compensate for refraction over long-distance links.

UV/Sun   UV rays and ambient heat from rooftops can damage cables over time if proper cable types are not used.

Upper-Layer Troubleshooting

Although this chapter has focused on troubleshooting the WLAN at layers 1 and 2 of the OSI model, upper-layer troubleshooting may still be a necessity. WLANs very often get blamed for causing problems that actually exist in the wired network at higher layers. If an employee cannot connect to the corporate WLAN, the employee will blame the WLAN even though the actual problem is somewhere else on the corporate network. If it can be determined that the problem is not a layer 1 or layer 2 problem, then the problem is usually a networking issue or problems with an application.

The good news is that many WLAN vendors offer upper-layer troubleshooting tools that are available in network management servers and WLAN controllers or from the command line of APs. As shown in Figure 12.39, a diagnostic tool can be used to send DHCP requests across a range of VLANs to verify the availability of a VLAN and IP subnet. If a VLAN was to fail, the various points of failure include a misconfigured switch, incorrect IP helper address, and DHCP scope with no remaining leases. Many vendors also have tools to test the connection between a RADIUS server and an AP or WLAN controller for 802.1X diagnostics. Remember that an access point is a wireless portal to complete network infrastructure. If the Wi-Fi network is not the problem, troubleshooting layers 3–7 will be necessary.

FIGURE 12.39   Upper-layer networking diagnostic tools

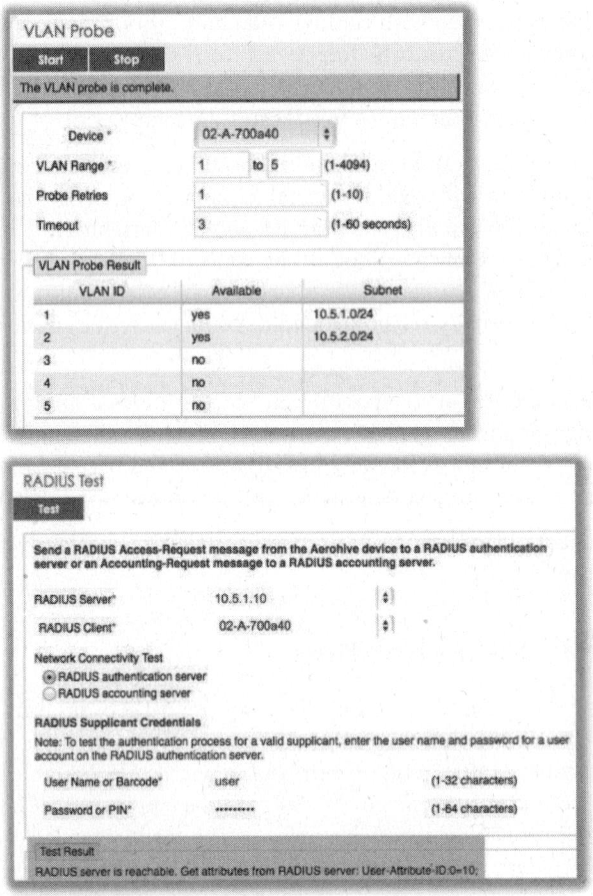

Summary

In this chapter, we discussed numerous 802.11 coverage considerations. Troubleshooting for coverage, capacity, and performance problems can quite often be avoided with proper network design and comprehensive site surveys. We discussed the many causes of layer 2 retransmissions and the negative effects on the WLAN because of retries. Because wireless should always be considered an ever-changing environment, problems such as roaming, hidden nodes, and interference are bound to surface.

Tools such as protocol analyzers and spectrum analyzers are invaluable when troubleshooting both layer 2 and layer 1 problems. We discussed and compared the differences between multiple- and single-channel architecture. We also discussed the many performance variables that can affect both range and throughput. We covered many design basics such a channel reuse patterns and guidelines for high-density WLAN environments. We discussed the challenges that are unique to both voice and data WLAN deployments. Finally, we discussed weather conditions that can impact outdoor RF communications and the steps that might be necessary for protection against Mother Nature.

Exam Essentials

Explain the causes and effect of layer 2 retransmissions.   Understand that layer 2 retransmissions can be caused by multipath, hidden nodes, mismatched power settings, RF interference, low SNR, near/far problems, and adjacent channel interference. Layer 2 retransmissions affect throughput, latency, and jitter.

Define dynamic rate switching.   Understand the process of stations shifting between data rates. Know that dynamic rate switching is also referred to as dynamic rate shifting, adaptive rate selection, and automatic rate selection. Explain why disabling the two lower 802.11b/g data rates is often recommended.

Explain the various aspects of roaming.   Understand that roaming is proprietary in nature. Know the variables that client stations may use when initiating the roaming process. Understand the importance of proper coverage cell overlap. Describe latency issues that can occur with roaming. Understand why crossing layer 3 boundaries can cause problems and what solutions might exist.

Define the differences between adjacent channel interference and co-channel interference.   Understand the negative effects of both adjacent channel interference and co-channel interference. Explain why channel reuse patterns minimize the problems. Know what to consider when designing channel reuse patterns at both 2.4 GHz and 5 GHz in a multiple channel architecture.

Explain the differences between MCA and SCA wireless LAN design.   Understand that MCA uses cell sizing to meet capacity needs whereas SCA uses channel stacking to meet capacity needs. Explain the virtual BSSID and other aspects of an SCA design.

Identify the various types of interference.   Know the differences between all-band, narrowband, wideband, physical, and intersymbol interference. Understand that a spectrum analyzer is your best interference-troubleshooting tool.

Explain the hidden node problem.   Identify all the potential causes of the hidden node problem. Explain how to troubleshoot hidden nodes as well as how to fix the hidden node problem.

Understand the importance of channel reuse.   Explain why channel reuse patterns are necessary to prevent co-channel and adjacent channel interference

Define the aspects of band steering, load balancing, and high-density WLANs   Explain the benefits of these design capabilities and when they should be used.

Understand the consequences of weather conditions.   Explain the problems that might arise due to water conditions, wind, lightning, and air stratification. Explain how these problems might be solved.

Review Questions

1. What are some recommended best practices when deploying a high-density WLAN? (Choose all that apply.)

   A. Deploying unidirectional MIMO patch antennas

   B. Band steering of all clients to 5 GHz

   C. Load balancing

   D. Low AP transmit power

   E. Layer 3 roaming

2. If the access points transmit on the same frequency channel in an MCA architecture, what type of interference is caused by overlapping coverage cells?

   A. Intersymbol interference

   B. Adjacent channel interference

   C. All-band interference

   D. Narrowband interference

   E. Co-channel interference

3. What variables might affect range in an 802.11 WLAN? (Choose all that apply.)

   A. Transmission power

   B. CSMA/CA

   C. Encryption

   D. Antenna gain

   E. Physical environment

4. What can be done to fix the hidden node problem? (Choose all that apply.)

   A. Increase the power on the access point.

   B. Move the hidden node station.

   C. Increase power on all client stations.

   D. Remove the obstacle.

   E. Decrease power on the hidden node station.

5. Layer 2 retransmissions occur when frames become corrupted. What are some of the causes of layer 2 retries? (Choose all that apply.)

   A. High SNR

   B. Low SNR

   C. Co-channel interference

   D. RF interference

   E. Adjacent channel interference

6. What scenarios might result in a hidden node problem? (Choose all that apply.)

   A. Distributed antenna system

   B. Coverage cells that are too large

   C. Coverage cells that are too small

   D. Physical obstruction

   E. Co-channel interference

7. What are some of the negative effects of layer 2 retransmissions? (Choose all that apply.)

   A. Decreased range

   B. Excessive MAC sublayer overhead

   C. Decreased latency

   D. Increased latency

   E. Jitter

8. Several users are complaining that their VoWiFi phones keep losing connectivity. The WLAN administrator notices that the frame transmissions of the VoWiFi phones are corrupted when listened to with a protocol analyzer near the access point but are not corrupted when listened to with the protocol analyzer near the VoWiFi phone. What is the most likely cause of this problem?

   A. RF interference

   B. Multipath

   C. Hidden node

   D. Adjacent channel interference

   E. Mismatched power settings

9. A single user is complaining that her VoWiFi phone has choppy audio. The WLAN administrator notices that the user's MAC address has a retry rate of 25 percent when observed with a protocol analyzer. However, all the other users have a retry rate of about 5 percent when also observed with the protocol analyzer. What is the most likely cause of this problem?

   A. Near/far

   B. Multipath

   C. Co-channel interference

   D. Hidden node

   E. Low SNR

10. What type of interference is caused by overlapping coverage cells with overlapping frequencies?

    A. Intersymbol interference

    B. Adjacent channel interference

    C. All-band interference

    D. Narrowband interference

    E. Co-channel interference

11. Based on RSSI metrics, concentric zones of variable data rate coverage exist around an access point due to the upshifting and downshifting of client stations between data rates. What is the correct name of this process, according to the IEEE 802.11-2012 standard?

    A. Dynamic rate shifting

    B. Dynamic rate switching

    C. Automatic rate selection

    D. Adaptive rate selection

    E. All of the above

12. Which of these weather conditions is a concern when deploying a long-distance point-to-point bridge link?

    A. Wind

    B. Rain

    C. Fog

    D. Changes in air temperature

    E. All of the above

13. What variables might affect range in an 802.11 WLAN?

    A. Wavelength

    B. Free space path loss

    C. Brick walls

    D. Trees

    E. All of the above

14. Given: Wi-Fi clients can roam seamlessly at layer 2 if all the APs are configured with the same SSID and same security settings. However, if clients cross layer 3 boundaries, a layer 3 roaming solution will be needed. Which device functions as the home agent if a Mobile IP solution has been implemented in an enterprise WLAN environment where no WLAN controller is deployed?

    A. Wireless network management server (WNMS)

    B. Access layer switch

    C. Layer 3 switch

    D. Access point on the original subnet

    E. Access point on the new subnet

15. Which of the following can cause roaming problems? (Choose all that apply.)

    A. Too little cell coverage overlap

    B. Too much cell coverage overlap

   C. Free space path loss

   D. CSMA/CA

   E. Hidden node

16. What are some problems that can occur when an access point is transmitting at full power? (Choose all that apply.)

   A. Hidden node

   B. Co-channel interference

   C. Mismatched power between the AP and the clients

   D. Intersymbol interference

17. Why would a WLAN network administrator consider disabling the two lowest rates on an 802.11b/g/n access point? (Choose all that apply.)

   A. Medium contention

   B. Adjacent channel interference

   C. Hidden node

   D. Intersymbol interference

   E. All of the above

18. Which type of interference is caused by destructive multipath?

   A. Intersymbol interference

   B. All-band interference

   C. Narrowband interference

   D. Wideband interference

   E. Physical interference

19. In a multiple-channel architecture (MCA) design, what is the greatest number of nonoverlapping channels that can be deployed in the 2.4 GHz ISM band?

   A. 3

   B. 12

   C. 11

   D. 14

   E. 4

20. What factors should be taken into consideration when designing a channel reuse plan for 5 GHz access points? (Choose all that apply.)

   A. Regulatory channels permitted

   B. Number of VLANs permitted

   C. Encryption

   D. DFS support for the clients

   E. DFS support for the APs

Chapter 13

802.11 Network Security Architecture

IN THIS CHAPTER, YOU WILL LEARN ABOUT THE FOLLOWING:

✓ **802.11 security basics**

- Data privacy and integrity
- Authentication, authorization, and accounting (AAA)
- Segmentation
- Monitoring and policy

✓ **Legacy 802.11 security**

- Legacy authentication
- Static WEP encryption
- MAC filters
- SSID cloaking

✓ **Robust security**

- Robust security network (RSN)
- Authentication and authorization
- PSK authentication
- Proprietary PSK authentication
- 802.1X/EAP framework
- EAP types
- Dynamic encryption-key generation
- 4-Way Handshake
- WPA/WPA2-Personal
- TKIP encryption
- CCMP encryption

✓ **Traffic segmentation**

- VLANs
- RBAC

✓ **Infrastructure security**

- Physical security
- Interface security

✓ **VPN wireless security**

- Layer 3 VPNs
- SSL VPN
- VPN deployment
- Guest WLAN security
- Captive portal

In this chapter and the next, you will learn about one of the most often discussed topics relating to 802.11 wireless networks: security. In this chapter, we discuss legacy 802.11 security solutions, as well as more robust solutions that are now defined by the 802.11-2012 standard. WLAN security had a bad reputation in its early years—and deservedly so. The legacy security mechanisms originally defined by the IEEE did not provide the adequate authentication and data privacy that are needed in a mobility environment. Although there is no such thing as 100 percent security, properly installed and managed solutions do exist that can fortify and protect your wireless network.

Numerous wireless security risks exist, and in Chapter 14, "Wireless Attacks, Intrusion Monitoring, and Policy," you will learn about many of the potential attacks that can be attempted against an 802.11 wireless network and how these attacks can be monitored.

Many of the attacks against an 802.11 network can be defended with proper implementation of the security architectures that are discussed in this chapter. However, many attacks cannot be mitigated and can merely be monitored and hopefully responded to.

Although 8 percent of the CWNA exam covers 802.11 security, the CWNP program offers another certification, Certified Wireless Security Professional (CWSP), which focuses on just the topic of wireless security. The CWSP certification exam requires a more in-depth understanding of 802.11 security. However, this chapter and the next will give you a foundation of wireless security that should help you pass the security portions of the CWNA exam as well as give you a head start in the knowledge you will need to implement proper wireless security.

802.11 Security Basics

When you are securing a wireless 802.11 network, five major components are typically required:

- Data privacy and integrity
- Authentication, authorization, and accounting (AAA)
- Segmentation
- Monitoring
- Policy

Because data is transmitted freely and openly in the air, proper protection is needed to ensure data privacy, so strong encryption is needed. The function of most wireless networks is to provide a portal into some other network infrastructure, such as an 802.3

Ethernet backbone. The wireless portal must be protected, and therefore an authentication solution is needed to ensure that only authorized devices and users can pass through the portal via a wireless access point (AP). After users have been authorized to pass through the wireless portal, VLANs and identity-based mechanisms are needed to further restrict access to network resources. 802.11 wireless networks can be further protected with continuous monitoring by a wireless intrusion detection system. All of these security components should also be cemented together with policy enforcement.

For wired or wireless networks, never take network security lightly. Unfortunately, WLAN security still has a bad reputation with some people because of the weak legacy 802.11 security mechanisms that were originally deployed. However, in 2004, the 802.11i amendment was ratified and defined strong encryption and better authentication methods. The 802.11i amendment is now part of the 802.11-2012 standard and fully defines a robust security network (RSN), which is discussed later in this chapter. If proper encryption and authentication solutions are deployed, a wireless network can be just as secure, if not more secure, than the wired segments of a network. When properly implemented, the five components of 802.11 security discussed in this chapter and the next will lay a solid foundation for protecting your WLAN.

Data Privacy and Integrity

802.11 wireless networks operate in license-free frequency bands, and all data transmissions travel in the open air. Protecting data privacy in a wired network is much easier because physical access to the wired medium is more restricted, whereas access to wireless transmissions is available to anyone in listening range. Therefore, using cipher encryption technologies to obscure information is mandatory to provide proper data privacy. A *cipher* is an algorithm used to perform encryption.

The two most common algorithms used to protect data are the *RC4 algorithm* (RC stands for Ron's Code or Rivest Cipher) and the *Advanced Encryption Standard (AES)* algorithm. Some ciphers encrypt data in a continuous stream, whereas others encrypt data in groupings known as blocks.

RC4 Algorithm   The RC4 algorithm is a streaming cipher used in technologies that are often used to protect Internet traffic, such as Secure Sockets Layer (SSL). The RC4 algorithm is used to protect 802.11 wireless data and is incorporated into two legacy encryption methods known as WEP and TKIP, both of which are discussed later in this chapter.

Advanced Encryption Standard Algorithm   The AES algorithm, originally named the Rijndael algorithm, is a block cipher that offers much stronger protection than the RC4 streaming cipher. AES is used to encrypt 802.11 wireless data by using an encryption method known as *Counter Mode with Cipher Block Chaining Message Authentication Code Protocol (CCMP)*, which will also be discussed later in this chapter. The AES algorithm encrypts data in fixed data blocks with choices in encryption key strength of 128, 192, or 256 bits. The AES cipher is the mandated algorithm of the U.S. government for protecting both sensitive and classified information.

In Chapter 9, "802.11 MAC Architecture," you learned about the three major types of 802.11 wireless frames. Inside the body of a management frame is layer 2 information necessary for the basic operation of the BSS, and historically, 802.11 management frames have not been encrypted. However, the need to protect some critical network functions such as authentication and association was introduced with the 802.11w amendment, which provides protection for certain types of management frames. Control frames have no body and also are not encrypted. The information that needs to be protected is the upper-layer information inside the body of 802.11 data frames. If data encryption is enabled, the *MAC Service Data Unit (MSDU)* inside the body of any 802.11 data frame is protected by layer 2 encryption. Most of the encryption methods discussed in this chapter use layer 2 encryption, which is used to protect the layer 3–7 information found inside the body of an 802.11 data frame. In Exercise 13.1, you will use an 802.11 protocol analyzer to view the MSDU payload of an 802.11 data frame.

EXERCISE 13.1

Using Unencrypted and Encrypted Data Frames

1. To perform this exercise, you need to first download the CWNA_CHAPTER13.PCAP file from the book's web page at www.sybex.com/go/cwna4e.

2. After the file is downloaded, you will need packet analysis software to open the file. If you do not already have a packet analyzer installed on your computer, you can download Wireshark from www.wireshark.org.

3. Using the packet analyzer, open the CWNA_CHAPTER13.PCAP file. Most packet analyzers display a list of capture frames in the upper section of the screen, with each frame numbered sequentially in the first column.

4. Scroll down the list of frames and click on frame #8, which is an unencrypted simple data frame. Look at the frame body and notice the upper-layer information such as IP addresses and TCP ports.

5. Click on frame #136, which is an encrypted simple data frame. Look at the frame body and notice that WEP encryption is being used and that the upper-layer information cannot be seen.

WEP, TKIP and CCMP all use a data integrity check to ensure that the data has not been maliciously altered. WEP uses an integrity check value (ICV) and TKIP uses a message integrity check (MIC). CCMP also uses a message integrity check (MIC) that is much stronger than the data integrity methods used in TKIP or WEP.

Authentication, Authorization, and Accounting

Authentication, authorization, and accounting (AAA) is a key computer security concept that defines the protection of network resources:

Authentication   Authentication is the verification of identity and credentials. Users or devices must identify themselves and present credentials, such as usernames and passwords or digital certificates. More secure authentication systems use multifactor authentication, which requires at least two sets of different types of credentials to be presented.

Authorization   Authorization determines if the device or user is authorized to have access to network resources. This can include identifying whether you can have access based upon the type of device you are using (laptop, tablet, or phone), time of day restrictions, or location. Before authorization can be determined, proper authentication must occur.

Accounting   Accounting is tracking the use of network resources by users and devices. It is an important aspect of network security, used to keep a historical trail of who used what resource, when, and where. A record is kept of user identity, which resource was accessed, and at what time. Keeping an accounting trail is often a requirement of many industry regulations, such as the payment card industry (PCI).

Remember that the usual purpose of an 802.11 wireless network is to act as a portal into an 802.3 wired network. It is therefore necessary to protect that portal with strong authentication methods so that only legitimate users with the proper credentials will be authorized onto network resources.

Segmentation

Although it is of the utmost importance to secure an enterprise wireless network by utilizing both strong encryption and an AAA solution, an equally important aspect of wireless security is segmentation. Segmentation is the chosen method of separating user traffic within a network. Prior to the introduction of stronger authentication and encryption techniques, wireless was viewed as an untrusted network segment. Therefore, before the ratification of the 802.11i security amendment, the entire wireless segment of a network was commonly treated as an untrusted segment and the wired 802.3 network was considered the trusted segment.

Now that better security solutions exist, properly secured WLANs are more seamlessly and securely integrated into the wired infrastructure. It is still important to separate users into proper groups, much like what is done on any traditional network. Once authorized onto network resources, users can be further restricted as to what resources may be accessed and where they can go. Segmentation can be achieved through a variety of means, including firewalls, routers, VPNs, and VLANs. The most common wireless segmentation strategy used in 802.11 enterprise WLANs is segmentation using virtual LANs (VLANs). Segmentation is also intertwined with role-based access control (RBAC), which is discussed later in this chapter.

Monitoring and Policy

Encryption, AAA, and segmentation security components will provide data privacy and secure network resources. However, a full-time monitoring solution is also needed to protect against possible attacks that target the WLAN. Numerous layer 1 and layer 2 attacks are possible, and in Chapter 14, you will learn about many of the potential attacks that can be attempted against an 802.11 wireless network and how these attacks can be monitored by a wireless intrusion detection system (WIDS). Chapter 14 also discusses some of the fundamental components of a wireless security policy that are needed to cement a foundation of Wi-Fi security. Depending on the level of risk assessment, not all businesses require a monitoring solution; however, if the budget permits, a WLAN monitoring solution is highly recommended.

Legacy 802.11 Security

The original 802.11 standard defined very little in terms of security. The authentication methods first outlined in 1997 basically provided an open door into the network infrastructure. The encryption method defined in the original 802.11 standard has long been cracked and is considered inadequate for data privacy. In the following sections, you will learn about the legacy authentication and encryption methods that were the only defined standards for 802.11 wireless security from 1997 until 2004. Later in this chapter, you will learn about the more robust security that was defined in the *802.11i* security amendment that is now part of the current 802.11-2012 standard.

Legacy Authentication

You already learned about legacy authentication in Chapter 9. The original 802.11 standard specified two methods of authentication: *Open System authentication* and *Shared Key authentication*. When discussing authentication, we often think of validating the identity of a user when they are connecting or logging onto a network. 802.11 authentication is very different from this. These legacy authentication methods were not so much an authentication of user identity, but more of an authentication of capability. Think of these authentication methods as verification between the two devices that they are both valid 802.11 devices.

Open System authentication provides authentication without performing any type of user verification. It is essentially a two-way exchange between the client radio and the access point:

1. The client sends an authentication request.

2. The access point then sends an authentication response.

Because Open System authentication does not require the use of any credentials, every client gets authenticated and therefore authorized onto network resources after they have been associated. Static WEP encryption is optional with Open System authentication and may be used to encrypt the data frames after Open System authentication and association occur.

As you learned in Chapter 9, Shared Key authentication used Wired Equivalent Privacy (WEP) to authenticate client stations and required that a static WEP key be configured on both the station and the access point. In addition to WEP being mandatory, authentication would not work if the static WEP keys did not match. The authentication process was similar to Open System authentication but included a challenge and response between the radio cards. Shared Key authentication was a four-way authentication frame handshake:

1. The client station sent an authentication request to the access point.

2. The access point sent a cleartext challenge to the client station in an authentication response.

3. The client station encrypted the cleartext challenge and sent it back to the access point in the body of another authentication request frame.

4. The access point decrypted the station's response and compared it to the challenge text:

    ▪ If they matched, the access point would respond by sending a fourth and final authentication frame to the station confirming the success.

    ▪ If they did not match, the access point would respond negatively. If the access point could not decrypt the challenge, it would also respond negatively.

If Shared Key authentication was successful, the same static WEP key that was used during the Shared Key authentication process would also be used to encrypt the 802.11 data frames.

Open System vs. Shared Key

Although it might seem that Shared Key authentication is a more secure solution than Open System authentication, in reality Shared Key could be the bigger security risk. During the Shared Key authentication process, anyone who captures the cleartext challenge phrase and then captures the encrypted challenge phrase in the response frame could potentially derive the static WEP key. If the static WEP key is compromised, a whole new can of worms has been opened because now all the data frames can be decrypted, and the attacker can gain direct access to the network. Neither of the legacy authentication methods is considered strong enough for enterprise security. Shared Key authentication has been deprecated and is no longer recommended. More secure 802.1X/EAP authentication methods are discussed later in this chapter.

Static WEP Encryption

Wired Equivalent Privacy (WEP) is a layer 2 encryption method that uses the RC4 streaming cipher. The original 802.11 standard initially only defined 64-bit WEP as a supported encryption method. Shortly thereafter, 128-bit WEP was also defined as a supported encryption process. The three main goals of WEP encryption are as follows:

Confidentiality   The primary goal of confidentiality was to provide data privacy by encrypting the data before transmission.

Access Control   WEP also provides access control, which is basically a crude form of authorization. Client stations that do not have the same matching static WEP key as an access point are refused access to network resources.

Data Integrity   A data integrity checksum known as the *integrity check value (ICV)* is computed on data before encryption and used to prevent data from being modified.

Although 128-bit WEP was feasible, initially the U.S. government allowed the export of only 64-bit technology. After the U.S. government loosened export restrictions on key size, WLAN radio manufacturers began to produce equipment that supported 128-bit WEP encryption. As you can see in Figure 13.1, 64-bit WEP uses a secret 40-bit static key, which is combined with a 24-bit number selected by the radio's device drivers. This 24-bit number, known as the *initialization vector (IV)*, is sent in cleartext and is different on every frame. Although the IV is said to be different on every frame, there are only 16,777,216 different IV combinations; therefore, you are forced to reuse the IV values. The effective key strength of combining the IV with the 40-bit static key is 64-bit encryption. 128-bit WEP encryption uses a 104-bit secret static key that is also combined with a 24-bit IV.

FIGURE 13.1   Static WEP encryption key and initialization vector

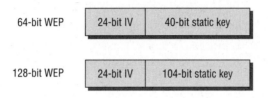

A static WEP key can usually be entered either as hexadecimal (hex) characters (0–9 and A–F) or as ASCII characters. The static key must match on both the access point and the client device. A 40-bit static key consists of 10 hex characters or 5 ASCII characters, whereas a 104-bit static key consists of 26 hex characters or 13 ASCII characters. Not all client stations or access points support both hex and ASCII. Many clients and access points support the use of up to four separate static WEP keys from which a user can choose one as the default transmission key (Figure 13.2 shows an example). The transmission key is the static key that is used to encrypt data by the transmitting radio. A client or access point may use one key to encrypt outbound traffic and a different key to decrypt received traffic. However, each of the four key must match exactly on both sides of a link for encryption/decryption to work properly.

FIGURE 13.2   Transmission key

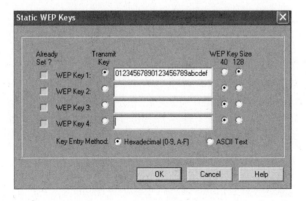

How does WEP work?

1. WEP runs a cyclic redundancy check (CRC) on the plaintext data that is to be encrypted and then appends the integrity check value (ICV) to the end of the plaintext data.

2. A 24-bit cleartext initialization vector (IV) is then generated and combined with the static secret key.

3. WEP then uses both the static key and the IV as seeding material through a pseudorandom algorithm that generates random bits of data known as a keystream.

    These pseudorandom bits are equal in length to the plaintext data that is to be encrypted.

4. The pseudorandom bits in the keystream are then combined with the plaintext data bits by using a Boolean XOR process.

    The end result is the WEP ciphertext, which is the encrypted data.

5. The encrypted data is then prefixed with the cleartext IV.

    Figure 13.3 illustrates this process.

FIGURE 13.3   WEP encryption process

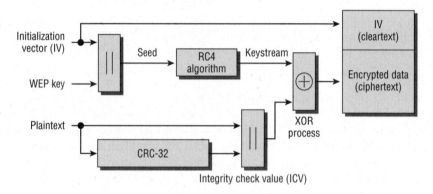

Unfortunately, WEP has quite a few weaknesses, including the following four main attacks:

IV Collisions Attack   Because the 24-bit initialization vector is in cleartext and is different in every frame, all 16 million IVs will eventually repeat themselves in a busy WEP encrypted network. Because of the limited size of the IV space, IV collisions occur, and an attacker can recover the secret key much easier when IV collisions occur in wireless networks.

Weak Key Attack   Because of the RC4 key-scheduling algorithm, weak IV keys are generated. An attacker can recover the secret key much easier by recovering the known weak IV keys.

Reinjection Attack   Hacker tools exist that implement a packet reinjection attack to accelerate the collection of weak IVs on a network with little traffic.

Bit-Flipping Attack   The ICV data integrity check is considered weak. WEP encrypted packets can be tampered with.

WEP cracking tools have been available for many years. These cracking tools may use a combination of the first three mentioned attacks and can crack WEP in less than 5 minutes.

After an attacker has compromised the static WEP key, any data frame can be decrypted with the newly discovered key. Later in this chapter, we discuss TKIP, which is an enhancement of WEP and has not been cracked although there are some vulnerabilities. CCMP encryption uses the AES algorithm and is an even stronger encryption method. As defined by the original 802.11 standard, WEP encryption is considered optional. WEP has been cracked and has been an unacceptable encryption method for the enterprise for over 10 years. If legacy devices that only support WEP encryption are still being deployed, these devices should be replaced immediately.

MAC Filters

Every network card has a physical address known as a MAC address. This address is a 12-digit hexadecimal number. Every 802.11 radio has a unique MAC address. Most vendors provide MAC filtering capabilities on their access points. MAC filters can be configured to either allow or deny traffic from specific client MAC addresses to associate and connect to an AP.

The 802.11 standard does not define MAC filtering, and any implementation of MAC filtering is vendor specific. Most vendors use MAC filters to deny client associations to an AP. Other vendors use MAC firewall filters to apply restrictions that will allow traffic only from specific client stations to pass through based on their unique MAC addresses. Any other client stations whose MAC addresses are not on the allowed list will not be able to pass traffic through the virtual port of the access point and on to the distribution system medium. It should be noted that MAC addresses can be *spoofed*, or impersonated, and any amateur hacker can easily bypass any MAC filter by spoofing an allowed client MAC address. Because of spoofing and because of all the administrative work involved with setting up MAC filters, MAC filtering is not considered a reliable means of security for wireless enterprise networks. MAC filters can be used as a security measure to protect legacy radios that do not support stronger security. For example, older handheld bar code scanners may use 802.11 radios that support only static WEP. Best practices dictate an extra layer of security by segmenting the handheld devices in a separate VLAN with a MAC filter based on the manufacturer's OUI address (the first three octets of the MAC address that are manufacturer specific).

SSID Cloaking

Remember in *Star Trek* when the Romulans cloaked their spaceship, but somehow Captain Kirk always found the ship anyway? Well, there is a way to "cloak" your service set identifier (SSID). Access points typically have a setting called *Closed Network* or *Broadcast SSID*. By either enabling a closed network or disabling the broadcast SSID feature, you can hide, or cloak, your wireless network name.

When you implement a closed network, the SSID field in the beacon frame is null (empty), and therefore passive scanning will not reveal the SSID to client stations that are listening to beacons. The SSID, which is also often called the ESSID, is the logical identifier of a WLAN. The idea behind cloaking the SSID is that any client station that does not know the SSID of the WLAN will not be able to discover the WLAN and therefore will not associate.

Many wireless client software utilities transmit probe requests with null SSID fields when actively scanning for access points. Additionally, there are many popular and freely available WLAN scanning software programs such as inSSIDer, NetStumbler, and iStumbler that can be used by individuals to discover wireless networks. Most of these discovery programs also send out null probe requests actively scanning for access points. When you implement a closed network, the access point responds to null probe requests with probe responses; however, as in the beacon frame, the SSID field is null, and therefore the SSID is hidden to client stations that are using active scanning. Implementing a closed network varies between WLAN vendors; some vendor access points may simply ignore null probe requests when a closed network has been configured. Effectively, your wireless network is temporarily invisible, or cloaked. Note that an access point in a closed network will respond to any configured client station that transmits directed probe requests with the properly configured SSID. This ensures that legitimate end users will be able to authenticate and associate to the AP. However, any client stations that are not configured with the correct SSID will not be able to authenticate or associate.

Although implementing a closed network may hide your SSID from some of these WLAN discovery tools, anyone with a layer 2 wireless protocol analyzer can capture the frames transmitted by any legitimate end user and discover the SSID, which is transmitted in cleartext. In other words, a hidden SSID can be found usually in seconds with the proper tools. Many wireless professionals will argue that hiding the SSID is a waste of time, whereas others view a closed network as just another layer of security.

Although you can hide your SSID to cloak the identity of your wireless network from novice hackers (often referred to as *script kiddies*) and nonhackers, it should be clearly understood that SSID cloaking is by no means an end-all wireless security solution. The 802.11 standard does not define SSID cloaking, and therefore, all implementations of a closed network are vendor specific. As a result, incompatibility can potentially cause connectivity problems with older legacy cards or when using cards from different vendors on your own network. Be sure to know the capabilities of your devices before implementing a closed network. Cloaking the SSID can also become an administration and support issue. Requiring end users to configure the SSID in the radio software interface often results in more calls to the help desk because of misconfigured SSIDs.

Robust Security

In 2004, the 802.11i security amendment was ratified and is now part of the 802.11-2012 standard. The 802.11-2012 standard defines an enterprise authentication method as well as a method of authentication for home use. The current standard defines the use of an 802.1X/EAP authentication and also the use of a preshared key (PSK) or a passphrase.

802.1X/EAP is a strong authentication method most often deployed in the enterprise. The less complex PSK authentication is normally used in small office, home office (SOHO) environments but can be deployed in the enterprise as well. The 802.11-2012 standard also requires the use of strong, dynamic encryption-key generation methods. CCMP/AES encryption is the default encryption method, and TKIP/RC4 is an optional encryption method.

Prior to the ratification of the 802.11i amendment, the Wi-Fi Alliance introduced the *Wi-Fi Protected Access (WPA)* certification as a snapshot of the not-yet-released 802.11i amendment, supporting only TKIP/RC4 dynamic encryption-key generation. 802.1X/EAP authentication was intended for the enterprise, and passphrase authentication was suggested in a SOHO environment.

After 802.11i was ratified, the Wi-Fi Alliance introduced the WPA2 certification. *WPA2* is a more complete implementation of the 802.11i amendment and supports both CCMP/ AES and TKIP/RC4 dynamic encryption-key generation. 802.1X/EAP authentication is more complex and meant for the enterprise, whereas passphrase authentication is simpler and meant for a SOHO environment. Any 802.11 radios manufactured after 2005 are most likely WPA2 compliant. If a radio is WPA compliant, it most likely only supports TKIP/ RC4 encryption. If the radio is WPA2 compliant, it supports the stronger CCMP/AES dynamic encryption. Table 13.1 offers a valuable comparison of the various security standards and certifications.

TABLE 13.1   Security standards and certifications comparison

802.11 standard	Wi-Fi Alliance certification	Authentication method	Encryption method	Cipher	Key generation
802.11 legacy		Open System or Shared Key	WEP	RC4	Static
	WPA-Personal	WPA Passphrase (also known as WPA PSK and WPA Preshared Key)	TKIP	RC4	Dynamic
	WPA-Enterprise	802.1X/EAP	TKIP	RC4	Dynamic
802.11-2012 (RSN)	WPA2-Personal	WPA2 Passphrase (also known as WPA2 PSK and WPA2 Preshared Key)	CCMP (mandatory) TKIP (optional)	AES (mandatory) RC4 (optional)	Dynamic
802.11-2012 (RSN)	WPA2-Enterprise	802.1X/EAP	CCMP (mandatory) TKIP (optional)	AES (mandatory) RC4 (optional)	Dynamic

Robust Security Network (RSN)

The 802.11-2012 standard defines what are known as a *robust security network (RSN)* and *robust security network associations (RSNAs)*. Two stations (STAs) must authenticate and associate with each other, as well as create dynamic encryption keys through a process known as the 4-Way Handshake. This association between two stations is referred to as an RSNA. In other words, any two radios must share dynamic encryption keys that are unique between those two radios. CCMP/AES encryption is the mandated encryption method, and TKIP/RC4 is an optional encryption method.

A robust security network (RSN) is a network that allows for the creation of only robust security network associations (RSNAs). An RSN can be identified by a field found in beacons, probe response frames, association request frames, and reassociation request frames. This field is known as the *RSN Information Element (IE)*. This field may identify the cipher suite capabilities of each station. The 802.11-2012 standard does allow for the creation of pre–robust security network associations (pre-RSNAs) as well as RSNAs. In other words, legacy security measures can be supported in the same basic service set (BSS) along with RSN-security-defined mechanisms. A *transition security network (TSN)* supports RSN-defined security, as well as legacy security such as WEP, within the same BSS, although most vendors do not support a TSN.

Authentication and Authorization

As you learned earlier in this chapter, authentication is the verification of user identity and credentials. Users must identify themselves and present credentials such as passwords or digital certificates. Authorization involves whether a device or user is granted access to network resources and services. Before authorization to network resources can be granted, proper authentication must occur.

The following sections detail more advanced authentication and authorization defenses. You will also learn that dynamic encryption capabilities are also possible as a by-product of these stronger authentication solutions.

PSK Authentication

The 802.11-2012 standard defines authentication and key management (AKM) services. AKM services require both authentication processes and the generation and management of encryption keys. An *authentication and key management protocol (AKMP)* can be either a preshared (PSK) or an EAP protocol used during 802.1X authentication. 802.1X/EAP requires a RADIUS server and advanced skills to configure and support it. The average home or small business Wi-Fi user has no knowledge of 802.1X/EAP and does not have a RADIUS server in their living room. PSK authentication is meant to be used in SOHO environments because the stronger enterprise 802.1X authentication solutions are not available. Therefore, the security used in SOHO environments is *PSK authentication*. WPA/WPA2-Personal utilizes PSK authentication. On the other hand, WPA/WPA2-Enterprise refers to the 802.1X/EAP authentication solution.

Most SOHO wireless networks are secured with WPA/WPA2-Personal mechanisms. Prior to the IEEE ratification of the 802.11i amendment, the Wi-Fi Alliance introduced the Wi-Fi Protected Access (WPA) certification as a snapshot of the not-yet-released 802.11i amendment, but it supported only TKIP/RC4 dynamic encryption-key generation. 802.1X/EAP authentication was suggested for the enterprise, while a passphrase authentication method called WPA-Personal was the suggested security mechanism in a SOHO environment.

The intended goal of WPA-Personal was to move away from static encryption keys to dynamically generated keys using a simple passphrase as a seed. WPA/WPA2-Personal allows an end user to enter a simple ASCII character string, dubbed a passphrase, anywhere from 8 to 63 characters in size. Behind the scenes, a passphrase-to-PSK-mapping function takes care of the rest. Therefore, all the user has to know is a single, secret passphrase to gain access to the WLAN, as shown in Figure 13.4.

FIGURE 13.4   Client configured with static passphrase

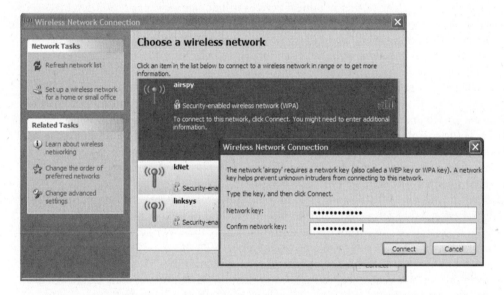

In June 2004, the IEEE 802.11 TGi working group formally ratified 802.11i, which added support for CCMP/AES encryption. The Wi-Fi Alliance revised the previous WPA specification to WPA2 and incorporated the CCMP/AES cipher. Therefore, the only practical difference between WPA and WPA2 has to do with the encryption cipher. WPA-Personal and WPA2-Personal both use the PSK authentication method; however, WPA-Personal specifies TKIP/RC4 encryption and WPA2-Personal specifies CCMP/AES. TKIP encryption has slowly been phased out over the years and is not supported for any of the 802.11n and 802.11ac data rates. In other words, older 802.11a/b/g radios that support only WPA-Personal and TKIP might still be deployed. Any 802.11 radios manufactured after 2006 will be certified for WPA2-Personal and use CCMP/AES encryption. If PSK authentication is the chosen security method, WPA2-Personal should always be used.

The Wi-Fi Alliance name for PSK authentication is WPA-Personal or WPA2-Personal. However, WLAN vendors have many marketing names for PSK authentication, including WPA/WPA2-Passphrase, WPA/WPA2-PSK, and WPA/WPA2-Preshared Key.

Proprietary PSK Authentication

Keep in mind that the simple PSK authentication method defined by WPA/WPA2 Personal can be a weak authentication method that is vulnerable to brute-force offline dictionary attacks. Because the passphrase is static, PSK authentication is also susceptible to social engineering attacks.

Although passphrases and PSK authentication are intended for use in a SOHO environment, in reality WPA/WPA2-Personal is often still used in the enterprise. For example, even though fast secure roaming (FSR) mechanisms have been possible for a while, some older VoWiFi phones and other handheld devices still do not yet support 802.1X/EAP. As a result, the strongest level of security used with these devices is PSK authentication. Cost issues may also drive a small business to use the simpler WPA/WPA2-Personal solution as opposed to installing, configuring, and supporting a RADIUS server for 802.1X/EAP.

The biggest problem with using PSK authentication in the enterprise is social engineering. The PSK is the same on all WLAN devices. If an end user accidentally gives the PSK to a hacker, WLAN security is compromised. If an employee leaves the company, to maintain a secure environment all of the devices have to be reconfigured with a new 256-bit PSK. Because the passphrase or PSK is shared by everyone, a strict policy should be mandated stating that only the WLAN security administrator is aware of the passphrase or PSK. That, of course, creates another administrative problem because of the work involved in manually configuring each device.

Several enterprise WLAN vendors have come up with a creative solution to using WPA/WPA2-Personal that solves some of the biggest problems of using a single passphrase for WLAN access. Each computing device or user will have their own unique PSK for the WLAN. Individual users can be mapped to a unique WPA/WPA2-Personal passphrase. A database of unique PSKs mapped to usernames or client stations must be stored on all access points or on a centralized WLAN controller. Individual users are then assigned a unique PSK that is created either dynamically or manually. As shown in Figure 13.5, the authenticator maintains a database of each individual PSK for each individual client. The PSKs that are generated can also have an expiration date. Unique time-based PSKs can also be used in a guest WLAN environment as a replacement for more traditional username/password credentials.

Currently, two WLAN vendors offer proprietary PSK solutions, which provide the capability of unique PSKs for each user: Aerohive Networks' Private PSK and Ruckus Wireless Dynamic PSK. Proprietary PSK solutions provide a way to implement unique credentials without the burden of deploying a more complex 802.1X/EAP solution. Social engineering and brute-force dictionary attacks are still possible, but they are harder to accomplish if strong and lengthy passphrase credentials are implemented. If a unique PSK is compromised, an administrator only has to revoke the single PSK credential and no longer has to reconfigure all access points and end user devices. Unfortunately, some WLAN client devices have limited support for 802.1X/EAP. In situations such as these, proprietary PSK solutions may be of benefit for those classes of devices and a vast improvement over standard WPA/WPA2-Personal. A proprietary PSK solution provides unique user credentials that standard PSK cannot provide. Additionally, proprietary PSK solutions with unique credentials do not require anywhere near the complex configuration needed for 802.1X/EAP.

FIGURE 13.5   Proprietary PSK

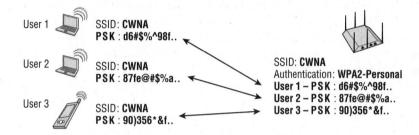

802.1X/EAP Framework

The IEEE *802.1X* standard is not specifically a wireless standard and is often mistakenly referred to as 802.11x. The 802.1X standard is a *port-based access control* standard. 802.1X-2001 was originally developed for 802.3 Ethernet networks. Later, 802.1X-2004 provided additional support for 802.11 wireless networks and Fiber Distributed Data Interface (FDDI) networks and has been further modified to support other technologies in later revisions. 802.1X provides an authorization framework that allows or disallows traffic to pass through a port and thereby access network resources. An 802.1X framework may be implemented in either a wireless or wired environment. The 802.1X framework consists of three main components:

Supplicant   A host with software that requests authentication and access to network resources is known as a supplicant. Each supplicant has unique authentication credentials that are verified by the authentication server.

Authenticator   An authenticator device blocks traffic or allows traffic to pass through its port entity. Authentication traffic is normally allowed to pass through the authenticator, whereas all other traffic is blocked until the identity of the supplicant has been verified. The authenticator maintains two virtual ports: an uncontrolled port and a controlled port. The uncontrolled port allows EAP authentication traffic to pass through, and the controlled port blocks all other traffic until the supplicant has been authenticated.

Authentication Server (AS)   The authentication server validates the credentials of the supplicant that is requesting access and notifies the authenticator that the supplicant has been authorized. The authentication server (AS) maintains a user database or may proxy with an external database, such as an LDAP database, to authenticate user credentials.

Within an 802.3 Ethernet network, the supplicant would be a desktop host, the authenticator would be a managed switch, and the authentication server would typically be a *Remote Authentication Dial-In User Service (RADIUS)* server. In an 802.11 wireless environment, the supplicant would be a client station requesting access to network resources. As seen in Figure 13.6, a standalone access point would be the authenticator, blocking access via virtual ports, and the AS is typically an external RADIUS server. Figure 13.6 also shows that when an 802.1X security solution is used with a WLAN controller solution, the WLAN controller is typically the authenticator—and not the controller-based access points. In either case, directory services are often provided by a Lightweight Directory Access Protocol (LDAP) database that the RADIUS server communicates with directly. Active Directory would be an example of an LDAP database that is queried by a RADIUS server. Note that some WLAN vendors offer solutions where either a standalone AP or a WLAN controller can dual-function as a RADIUS server and perform direct LDAP queries, thus eliminating the need for an external RADIUS server.

FIGURE 13.6   802.1X comparison—standalone vs. controller-based access points

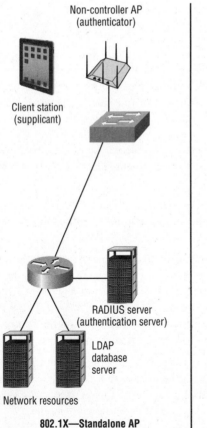
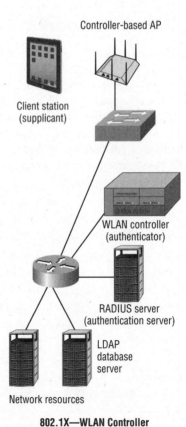

As you can see in Figure 13.7, the root bridge would be the authenticator and the nonroot bridge would be the supplicant if 802.1X security is used in a WLAN bridged network.

FIGURE 13.7   WLAN bridging and 802.1X

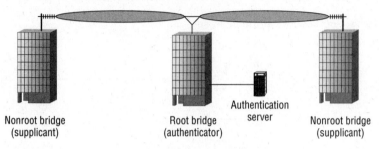

Nonroot bridge
(supplicant)

Root bridge
(authenticator)

Authentication
server

Nonroot bridge
(supplicant)

Point-to-multipoint WLAN bridging

Although the *supplicant*, *authenticator*, and *authentication server* work together to provide the framework for 802.1X port-based access control, an authentication protocol is needed to perform the authentication process. *Extensible Authentication Protocol (EAP)* is used to provide user authentication. EAP is a flexible layer 2 authentication protocol used by the supplicant and the authentication server to communicate. The authenticator allows the EAP traffic to pass through its virtual uncontrolled port. After the authentication server has verified the credentials of the supplicant, the server sends a message to the authenticator that the supplicant has been authenticated; the authenticator is then authorized to open the virtual controlled port and allow all other traffic to pass through. Figure 13.8 depicts the generic 802.1X/EAP frame exchanges.

The 802.1X/EAP framework, when used with wireless networks, provides the necessary means of validating user identity as well as authorizing client stations onto the wired network infrastructure.

EAP Types

As noted earlier, *EAP* stands for *Extensible Authentication Protocol*. The key word in EAP is *extensible*. EAP is a layer 2 protocol that is very flexible, and many different flavors of EAP exist. Some, such as Cisco's Lightweight Extensible Authentication Protocol (LEAP), are proprietary, whereas others, such as Protected Extensible Authentication Protocol (PEAP), are considered standards based. Some provide for only one-way authentication; others provide two-way authentication. Mutual authentication not only requires that the authentication server validate the client credentials, but the supplicant must also authenticate the validity of the authentication server. By validating the authentication server, the supplicant can ensure that the username and password are not inadvertently given to a rogue authentication server. Most types of EAP that require mutual authentication use a server-side digital certificate to validate the authentication server. A server-side certificate is installed on the RADIUS server, while the *certificate authority (CA)* root certificate resides on the supplicant. During the EAP exchange the supplicant's root certificate is used to verify the server-side certificate. The certificate exchange also creates an encrypted *Secure Sockets Layer (SSL) / Transport Layer Security (TSL)* tunnel in which the supplicant's username/password credentials or client certificate can be exchanged. Many of the secure forms of EAP use *tunneled authentication.* The SSL/TLS tunnel is used to encrypt and protect the user credentials during the EAP exchange.

FIGURE 13.8 802.1X/EAP authentication

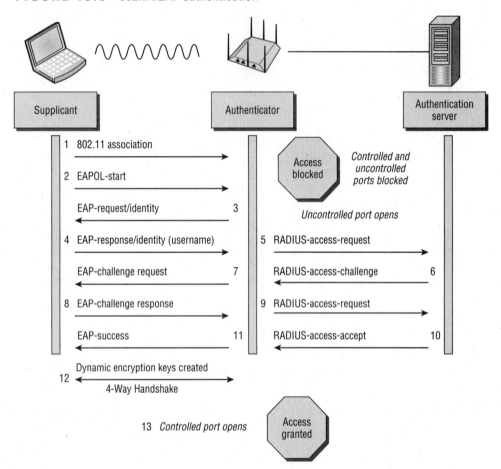

Table 13.2 provides a comparison chart of many of the various types of EAP. It is beyond the scope of this book to discuss in detail all the authentication mechanisms and differences between the various flavors of EAP. The CWSP exam will test you heavily on the operations of the various types of EAP authentication. The CWNA exam will not test you on the specific EAP functions.

Dynamic Encryption-Key Generation

Although the 802.1X/EAP framework does not require encryption, the use of encryption is recommended. You have already learned that the purpose of 802.1X/EAP is authentication

TABLE 13.2 EAP comparison table

	EAP-MD5	EAP-LEAP	EAP-TLS	EAP-TTLS	PEAPv0 (EAP-MSCHAPv2)	PEAPv0 (EAP-TLS)	PEAPv1 (EAP-GTC)	EAP-FAST
Security Solution	RFC-3748	Cisco proprietary	RFC-5216	RFC-5281	IETF draft	IETF draft	IETF draft	RFC-4851
Digital Certificates—Client	No	No	Yes	Optional	No	Yes	Optional	No
Digital Certificates—Server	No	No	Yes	Yes	Yes	Yes	Yes	No
Client Password Authentication	Yes	Yes	N/A	Yes	Yes	No	Yes	Yes
PACs—Client	No	No	No	No	No	No	No	Yes
PACs—Server	No	No	No	No	No	No	No	Yes
Credential Security	Weak	Weak (depends on password strength)	Strong	Strong	Strong	Strong	Strong	Strong (if Phase 0 is secure)
Encryption Key Management	No	Yes	Yes	Yes	Yes	Yes	Yes	Yes
Mutual Authentication	No	Debatable	Yes	Yes	Yes	Yes	Yes	Yes
Tunneled Authentication	No	No	Optional	Yes	Yes	Yes	Yes	Yes
Wi-Fi Alliance Supported	No	No	Yes	Yes	Yes	No	Yes	Yes

and authorization. However, a by-product of 802.1X/EAP is the generation and distribution of dynamic encryption keys. EAP protocols that utilize mutual authentication provide "seeding material" that can be used to generate encryption keys dynamically. Until now, you have learned about only static WEP keys. The use of static keys is typically an administrative nightmare, and when the same static key is shared among multiple users, the secret is easy to compromise via social engineering. The advantage of dynamic keys is that every user has a different and unique key that cannot be compromised by social engineering attacks.

After an EAP frame exchange where mutual authentication is required, both the AS and the supplicant know information about each other because of the exchange of credentials. This newfound information is used as seeding material or keying material to generate a matching dynamic encryption key for both the supplicant and the authentication server. These dynamic keys are generated *per session per user*, meaning that every time a client station authenticates, a new key is generated and every user has a unique and separate key.

Dynamic WEP Encryption

Prior to 2004, many vendors implemented solutions that generated dynamic WEP encryption keys as a result of 802.1X/EAP authentication. Dynamic WEP was never standardized but was used by vendors until TKIP and CCMP became available to the marketplace.

Dynamic WEP was a short-lived encryption-key management solution that was often implemented prior to the release of WPA-certified WLAN products. The generation and distribution of dynamic WEP keys as a by-product of the EAP authentication process had many benefits and was preferable to the use of static WEP keys. Static keys were no longer used and did not have to be entered manually. Also, every user had a separate and independent key. If a user's dynamic WEP key was compromised, only that one user's traffic could be decrypted. However, a dynamic WEP key could still be cracked, and if compromised, it could indeed be used to decrypt data frames. Dynamic WEP still had risks.

Please understand that a dynamic WEP key is not the same as TKIP or CCMP encryption keys that are also generated dynamically. WPA/WPA2 security defines the creation of stronger and safer dynamic TKIP/RC4 or CCMP/AES encryption keys that are also generated as a by-product of the EAP authentication process.

4-Way Handshake

As we explained earlier, the 802.11-2012 standard defines what is known as a robust security network (RSN) and robust security network associations (RSNAs). Two stations (STAs) must establish a procedure to authenticate and associate with each other as well as create dynamic encryption keys through a process known as the *4-Way Handshake*.

RSNAs utilize a dynamic encryption-key management method that involves the creation of five separate keys. It is beyond the scope of this book to fully explain this entire process, but a brief explanation is appropriate. Part of the RSNA process involves the creation of two master keys known as the *Group Master Key (GMK)* and the *Pairwise Master Key (PMK)*.

The PMK is created as a result of the 802.1X/EAP authentication. A PMK can also be created from *PSK* authentication instead of the 802.1X/EAP authentication. These master keys are the seeding material used to create the final dynamic keys that are used for encryption and decryption. The final encryption keys are known as the *Pairwise Transient Key (PTK)* and the *Group Temporal Key (GTK)*. The PTK is used to encrypt/decrypt unicast traffic, and the GTK is used to encrypt/decrypt broadcast and multicast traffic.

These final keys are created during a four-way EAP frame exchange that is known as the 4-Way Handshake. The 4-Way Handshake will always be the final four frames exchanged during either an 802.1X/EAP authentication or a PSK authentication. Whenever TKIP/RC4 or CCMP/AES dynamic keys are created, the 4-Way Handshake must occur. Also, every time a client radio roams from one AP to another, a new 4-Way Handshake must occur so that new unique dynamic keys can be generated. An example of the 4-Way Handshake can be seen in Exercise 13.2.

The CWNA exam currently does not test on the mechanics of the dynamic encryption-key creation process, which was originally defined by the 802.11i amendment. The process is heavily tested in the CWSP exam.

WPA/WPA2-Personal

Do you have a RADIUS server in your home or small business? The answer to that question will almost always be no. If you do not own a RADIUS server, 802.1X/EAP authentication will not be possible. WPA/WPA2-Enterprise solutions require 802.1X for mutual authentication using some form of EAP. Additionally, an authentication server will be needed. Because most of us do not have a RADIUS server in our basement, the 802.11-2012 standard offers a simpler method of authentication using a PSK. This method involves manually typing matching passphrases on both the access point and all client stations that will need to be able to associate to the wireless network. A formula is run that converts the passphrase to a Pairwise Master Key (PMK) used with the 4-Way Handshake to create the final dynamic encryption keys.

This simple method of authentication and encryption key generation is known as WPA/WPA2-Personal. Other names include WPA/WPA2 Preshared Key and WPA/WPA2 PSK. Although this is certainly better than static WEP and Open System authentication, WPA/WPA2-Personal still requires significant administrative overhead and has potential social engineering issues in a corporate or enterprise environment. In Chapter 14, you will learn that WPA/WPA2-Personal is susceptible to offline brute-force dictionary attacks and may not be the best security solution in the enterprise. An 802.1X/EAP solution as defined by WPA/WPA2-Enterprise is the preferred method of security in a corporate and workplace environment.

TKIP Encryption

The optional encryption method defined for a robust security network is *Temporal Key Integrity Protocol (TKIP)*. This method uses the RC4 cipher just as WEP encryption does. As a matter of fact, TKIP is an enhancement of WEP encryption that addresses many of the known weaknesses of WEP. The problem with WEP was not the RC4 cipher but how the encryption key was created. TKIP was developed to rectify the problems that were inherent in WEP.

TKIP starts with a 128-bit temporal key that is combined with a 48-bit initialization vector (IV) and source and destination MAC addresses in a complicated process known as per-packet key mixing. This key-mixing process mitigates the known IV collision and weak key attacks used against WEP. TKIP also uses a sequencing method to mitigate the rein-jection attacks used against WEP. Additionally, TKIP uses a stronger data integrity check known as the *message integrity check (MIC)* to mitigate known bit-flipping attacks against WEP. The MIC is sometimes referred to by the nickname *Michael*. All TKIP encryption keys are dynamically generated as a final result of the 4-Way Handshake.

WEP encryption adds an extra 8 bytes of overhead to the body of an 802.11 data frame. When TKIP is implemented, because of the extra overhead from the extended IV and the MIC, a total of 20 bytes of overhead is added to the body of an 802.11 data frame. Because TKIP uses the RC4 algorithm and is simply WEP that has been enhanced, most vendors released a WPA firmware upgrade that gave legacy WEP-only cards the capability of using TKIP encryption. The 802.11n and higher amendments do not permit the use of WEP encryption or TKIP encryption for the *High Throughput (HT)* and *Very High Throughput (VHT)* data rates. The Wi-Fi Alliance will only certify 802.11n radios that use CCMP encryption for the higher data rates. For backward compatibility, newer radios will still support TKIP and WEP for the slower data rates defined for legacy 802.11a/b/g radios.

CCMP Encryption

The default encryption method defined under the 802.11i amendment is known as *Counter Mode with Cipher Block Chaining Message Authentication Code Protocol (CCMP)*. This method uses the Advanced Encryption Standard (AES) algorithm (Rijndael algorithm). CCMP/AES uses a 128-bit encryption-key size and encrypts in 128-bit fixed-length blocks. An 8-byte message integrity check (MIC) is used that is considered much stronger than the one used in TKIP. Also, because of the strength of the AES cipher, per-packet key mixing is unnecessary. All CCMP encryption keys are dynamically generated as a final result of the 4-Way Handshake.

CCMP/AES encryption will add an extra 16 bytes of overhead to the body of an 802.11 data frame. Because the AES cipher is processor intensive, older legacy 802.11 devices do not have the processing power necessary to perform AES calculations. Older 802.11 devices cannot be firmware upgraded, and a hardware upgrade is needed to support WPA2.

EXERCISE 13.2

802.1X/EAP and 4-Way Handshake Process

1. To perform this exercise, you need to first download the CWNA_CHAPTER13.PCAP file from the book's web page at www.sybex.com/go/cwna4e.

2. After the file is downloaded, you will need packet analysis software to open the file. If you do not already have a packet analyzer installed on your computer, you can down-load Wireshark from www.wireshark.org.

3. Using the packet analyzer, open the CWNA_CHAPTER13.PCAP file. Most packet analyzers display a list of capture frames in the upper section of the screen, with each frame numbered sequentially in the first column.

4. Scroll down the list of frames and observe the EAP frame exchange from frame #209 to frame #246.

5. Scroll down the list of frames and observe the 4-Way Handshake from frame #247 to frame #254.

Real World Scenario

How Should Authentication and Encryption Be Deployed in the Enterprise?

As you have learned, the goal of authentication is to validate user credentials, whereas the goal of encryption is to ensure data privacy. However, you have also learned that the two processes are dependent on each other because dynamic TKIP or CCMP encryption keys are generated as a by-product of either 802.1X/EAP or PSK authentication. As shown in the following graphic, when deploying a WPA/WPA2-Enterprise solution, the supplicant and the authentication server must support the same EAP protocol. Furthermore, the supplicant and the authenticator must support the same dynamic encryption method.

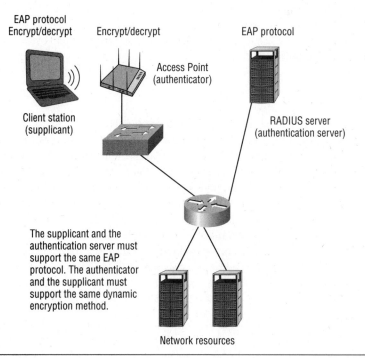

PSK authentication (WPA/WPA2-Personal) should be avoided in the enterprise due to the risk of social engineering and offline dictionary attacks. One advantage of using PSK authentication is that it does not have the latency issues of 802.1X/EAP. Legacy devices may not support fast, secure roaming mechanisms such as opportunistic key caching (OKC) or Wi-Fi Voice Enterprise. PSK authentication is often still used in the enterprise with legacy VoWiFi phones that require authentication exchanges during roaming hand-offs to occur in less than 150 milliseconds. PSK authentication is often used in the enter-prise for iPads and iPhones using iOS 5.0 or older, which do not support OKC. Otherwise, 802.1X/EAP (WPA/WPA2-Enterprise) solutions should be used for authentication when-ever possible.

TKIP has slowly been phased out and is not supported for 802.11n or 802.11ac data rates. CCMP encryption uses the stronger AES cipher and is the preferred method of providing for data privacy.

Traffic Segmentation

As discussed earlier in this chapter, segmentation is a key part of a network design. Once authorized onto network resources, user traffic can be further restricted as to what resources may be accessed and where user traffic is destined. Segmentation can be achieved through a variety of means, including firewalls, routers, VPNs, and VLANs. A common wireless segmentation strategy used in 802.11 enterprise WLANs is layer 3 segmentation that employs VLANs mapped to different subnets. Segmentation is also often intertwined with role-based access control (RBAC).

VLANs

Virtual local area networks (VLANs) are used to create separate broadcast domains in a layer 2 network and are often used to restrict access to network resources without regard to physical topology of the network. VLANs are a layer 2 concept and are used extensively in switched 802.3 networks for both security and segmentation purposes. VLANs are mapped to unique layer 3 subnets, although it is possible to match a VLAN to multiple sub-nets. VLANs are used to support multiple layer 3 networks on the same layer 2 switch.

In a WLAN environment, individual SSIDs can be mapped to individual VLANs, and users can be segmented by the SSID/VLAN pair, all while communicating through a single access point. Each SSID can also be configured with separate security settings. Most enter-prise access points have the ability to broadcast as many as 16 SSIDs and each SSID can be mapped to a unique VLAN. A common strategy is to create a guest, voice, and employee SSID/VLAN pair as shown in Figure 13.9. Managment access to the WLAN controllers or APs should also be isolated on a separate VLAN.

FIGURE 13.9   Wireless VLANs

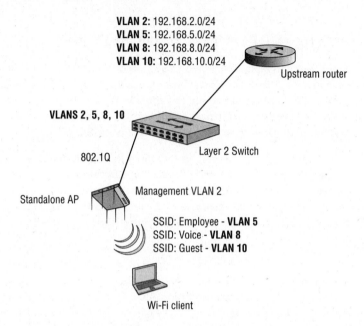

Guest SSID/VLAN   The SSID mapped to the guest VLAN often is an open SSID, although all guest users should be restricted via a firewall policy. Guest users are denied access to local network resources and routed off to an Internet gateway.

Voice SSID/VLAN   The voice SSID might be using a security solution, such as a WPA2 Passphrase, and the VoWiFi client traffic is typically routed to a VoIP server or private branch exchange (PBX).

Employee SSID/VLAN   The employee SSID uses a stronger security solution, such as WPA2-Enterprise, and access control lists (ACLs) or firewall policies allow the employees to access full network resources once authenticated.

The way VLANs are deployed in a WLAN environment depends on the design of the network as well as the type of WLAN architecture that is in place. With a WLAN controller architecture, the user VLANs usually reside in the core of the network. The user VLANs are not available at the access layer switch. The controller-based APs are connected to an access port of the edge switch. The user VLANs are still available to the wireless users because all of the user VLANs are encapsulated in an IP tunnel between the controller-based APs at the edge and the WLAN controller in the core.

When cooperative APs or autonomous APs are deployed, all of the user VLANs are configured in the access layer switch. The standalone access points are connected to an 802.1Q trunk port of the edge switch. The user VLANS are tagged in the 802.1Q trunk and all wireless user traffic is forwarded at the edge of the network.

> ### 🌐 Real World Scenario
>
> #### Can a Single Employee SSID Be Mapped to Multiple VLANs?
>
> Very often each user VLAN can be tied to a unique SSID. Most WLAN vendors allow a radio to broadcast as many as 16 SSIDs. However, broadcasting out 16 SSIDs is a bad practice because of the layer 2 overhead created by the 802.11 management and control frames for each SSID. A 40 percent performance reduction could be the result of using 16 SSIDs. The best practice is to never broadcast more than 3 or 4 SSIDs.
>
> What if you want your employees segmented into multiple VLANs? Can a single employee SSID be mapped to multiple VLANs? RADIUS attributes can be leveraged for VLAN assignment when using 802.1X authentication on the employee SSID. When a RADIUS server provides a successful response to an authentication request, the ACCESS-ACCEPT response can contain a series of *attribute-value pairs (AVPs)*.
>
> One of the most popular uses of RADIUS AVPs is assigning users to VLANs dynamically, based on the identity of the authenticating user. Instead of segmenting users to different SSIDs that are each mapped to a unique user VLAN, all the users can be associated to a single SSID and dynamically assigned to different VLANs. The main benefit of this solution is that existing ACLs or firewalls between VLANs can be extended to the WLAN clients. Assuming the AP (or WLAN controller) has access to the VLAN that is assigned, the WLAN client will be placed on that unique VLAN after authenticating.

RBAC

Role-based access control (RBAC) is another approach to restricting system access to authorized users. Many of the WLAN vendors provide RBAC capabilities. The three main components of an RBAC approach are users, roles, and permissions.

Separate roles can be created, such as a sales role or a marketing role. Individuals or groups of users are assigned to one of these roles. Permissions can be defined as layer 2 permissions (VLANS or MAC filters), layer 3 permissions (access control lists), layers 4–7 permissions (stateful firewall rules), and bandwidth permissions. All of these permissions can also be time or location based. The permissions are mapped to the roles. When wireless users authenticate via the WLAN, they inherit the permissions of whatever roles they have been assigned. For example, users who associate with a "Guest" SSID are placed in a unique guest VLAN. The users then authenticate via a captive portal and are assigned a guest role. The guest role may have bandwidth permissions that restrict them to 100 kbps of bandwidth and allow them to use only ports 80 (HTTP), 443 (HTTPS), 25 (SMTP), and 110 (POP) during working hours. This scenario would restrict guest users who are accessing the Internet from hogging bandwidth and only allow them to view web pages and check email between 9 a.m. and 5 p.m. When used in a WLAN environment, role-based access control can provide granular wireless user management.

Infrastructure Security

An often-overlooked aspect of wireless security is protecting the infrastructure equipment. In addition to protecting Wi-Fi hardware from theft, you must secure the management interfaces so that only authorized administrators have access. Protecting hardware and interfaces should never be ignored in an 802.11 enterprise. Only encrypted administer logins using SSH should be permitted and Telnet should always be disabled.

Physical Security

Access points and other WLAN hardware can be quite expensive. Enterprise access points can cost as much as $2,000 (in U.S. dollars). Although access points are usually mounted in or near the ceiling, theft can be a problem. Enclosure units with locks can be mounted in the ceiling or to the wall. Access points locked inside the enclosure units are safeguarded against theft. The enclosure units also prevent unwanted individuals from using a serial cable or console cable to try to gain access to the AP. Secure enclosure units may also meet aesthetic demands by keeping the access point out of plain sight.

Interface Security

All wireless infrastructure devices must be able to be accessed by administrators through a management interface. Enterprise equipment usually can be configured either through a command-line interface or a web interface or via *Simple Network Management Protocol (SNMP)*. Any interface that is not used should be turned off. For example, if the administrator configures the access points only via a command-line interface (CLI), turn off the web interface capabilities on the access points. At a minimum, all the passwords for these configuration options should be changed from the factory defaults. Keep in mind that some management interfaces have multiple default user levels. The default levels can include administrator, guest, and management. The passwords for all of these levels should be changed.

Most infrastructure devices should also support some type of encrypted management capabilities. Newer Wi-Fi hardware should support SSH, HTTPS, or SNMPv3. Older legacy equipment may not support encrypted login capabilities. It is also a highly recommended practice to configure your infrastructure devices from only the wired side and never configure them wirelessly, although with more organizations replacing their wired networks in favor of wireless networks, this may not be feasible. If devices are configured from the wireless side, an intruder might be able to capture your wireless packets and be able to watch what you are doing. If wireless management is allowed, it should be restricted to secured SSIDs only.

When performing administration through a wireless connection, there is also a chance that you will accidentally lock yourself out of the device while configuring Wi-Fi hardware that you are connecting through. It should be noted that some vendors offer a wireless backdoor to troubleshoot problems via the CLI interface of an AP while connected to a secure SSID.

An access point will broadcast an emergency WPA2-Personal SSID that is triggered by the loss of IP connectivity between the AP and the default gateway. An administrator can then securely connect to the emergency SSID and create a wireless console connection to the CLI of the AP. This provides a method for the admin to identify why layer 3 connectivity was lost without having to climb a ladder to connect to the console port of the AP.

VPN Wireless Security

Although the 802.11-2012 standard clearly defines layer 2 security solutions, the use of upper-layer *virtual private network (VPN)* solutions can also be deployed with WLANs. VPNs are typically not recommended to provide wireless security in the enterprise due to the overhead and because faster, more secure layer 2 solutions are now available. Although not usually a recommended practice, VPNs were often used for WLAN security because the VPN solution was already in place inside the wired infrastructure. VPNs do have their place in Wi-Fi security and should definitely be used for remote access. They are also sometimes used in wireless bridging environments. The two major types of VPN topologies are router-to-router or client-server based.

Use of VPN technology is mandatory for remote access. Your end users will take their laptops off site and will most likely use public access Wi-Fi hotspots. Because there is no security at most hotspots, a VPN solution is needed. The VPN user will need to bring the security to the hotspot in order to provide a secure, encrypted connection. It is imperative that users implement a VPN solution coupled with a personal firewall whenever accessing any public access Wi-Fi networks.

Layer 3 VPNs

VPNs have several major characteristics. They provide encryption, encapsulation, authentication, and data integrity. VPNs use secure tunneling, which is the process of encapsulating one IP packet within another IP packet. The first packet is encapsulated inside the second or outer packet. The original destination and source IP address of the first packet is encrypted along with the data payload of the first packet. VPN tunneling, therefore, protects your original private layer 3 addresses and also protects the data payload of the original packet. Layer 3 VPNs use layer 3 encryption; therefore, the payload that is being encrypted is the layer 4–7 information. The IP addresses of the second or outer packet are seen in cleartext and are used for communications between the tunnel endpoints. The destination and source IP addresses of the second or outer packet will point to the public IP address of the VPN server and VPN client software.

The most commonly used layer 3 VPN technology is *Internet Protocol Security (IPsec)*. IPsec VPNs use stronger encryption methods and more secure methods of authentication and are the most commonly deployed VPN solution. IPsec supports multiple ciphers, including DES, 3DES, and AES. Device authentication is achieved by using either a server-side certificate or a preshared key. IPsec VPNs require client software to be installed on the remote devices that connect to a VPN server. Most IPsec VPNS are NAT-transversal, but any firewalls at a remote site require (at a minimum) that UDP ports 4500 and 500 be open. A full explanation of IPsec technology is beyond the scope of this book, but IPsec is usually the choice for VPN technology in the enterprise.

SSL VPN

VPN technologies do exist that operate at other layers of the OSI model, including SSL tunneling. Unlike an IPsec VPN, an SSL VPN does not require the installation and configuration of client software on the end user's computer. A user connects to a *Secure Sockets Layer (SSL)* VPN server via a web browser. The traffic between the web browser and the SSL VPN server is encrypted with the SSL protocol or Transport Layer Security (TLS). TLS and SSL encrypt data connections above the Transport layer, using asymmetric cryptography for privacy and a keyed message authentication code for message reliability.

Although most IPsec VPN solutions are NAT-transversal, SSL VPNs are often chosen because of issues with NAT or restrictive firewall policies at remote locations.

VPN Deployment

VPNs are most often used for client-based security when connected to public access WLANs and hotspots that do not provide security. Because most hotspots do not provide layer 2 security, it is imperative that end users provide their own security. VPN technology can provide the necessary level of security for remote access when end users connect to public access WLANs. Since no encryption is used at public access WLANs, a VPN solution is usually needed to provide for data privacy, as shown in Figure 13.10.

FIGURE 13.10   VPN established from a public hotspot

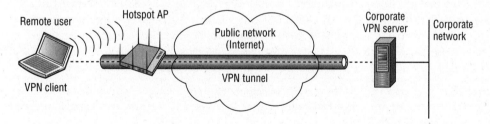

Another common use of VPN technology is to provide site-to-site connectively between a remote office and a corporate office. Most WLAN vendors now offer VPN client-server capabilities in either their APs or WLAN controllers. As shown in Figure 13.11, a branch office WLAN controller with VPN capabilities can tunnel WLAN client traffic and bridged wired-side traffic back to the corporate network. Other WLAN vendors can also tunnel user traffic from a remote AP to a VPN server gateway.

FIGURE 13.11   Site-to-site VPN

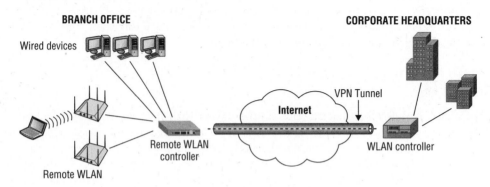

Guest WLAN Security

Most businesses like to provide Wi-Fi guest access as a convenience to visitors. Guest wireless networks allow Internet access to visitors, such as contractors, students, or salespeople. Many organizations understand the need for their visitors to be able to access the Internet, especially to access email. Therefore, many organizations provide WLAN guest access with a unique SSID and guest VLAN. Firewalls are also often used to further restrict the guest user capabilities and even the bandwidth that is available to guests. The security for guest WLAN users is much different than security provided for the corporate WLAN users. The main security goal of a guest WLAN is to provide guests with an easily accessible wireless portal to the Internet, while at the same time restricting guest user access from the rest of the company network. The security components of a guest WLAN normally consist of the following:

Guest SSID   Multiple corporate SSIDs are broadcasted by the company APs along with a guest SSID that can be easily discovered by any guest user. The guest SSID is normally an open network that has no WPA/WPA2 encryption security. Although encryption is not usually provided for guest users, some WLAN vendors have begun to offer secure guest access that does provide data privacy using dynamic PSK credentials. Encrypted guest access can also be provided with 802.1X with Hotspot 2.0 using Wi-Fi CERTIFIED Passport client devices.

Guest VLAN   Guest user traffic should be segmented into a unique VLAN tied to an IP subnet that does not mix with the employee user VLANs. Guest traffic is often also routed to a demilitarized zone (DMZ).

Firewall Policy   Guest WLAN firewall policies tend to be very restrictive. Guest firewall policies typically allow for DHCP and DNS but restrict access to private networks 10.0.0.0/8, 172.16.0.0/12, and 192.168.0.0/16. Guest users are not allowed on these private networks because corporate network servers and resources usually reside on the private IP space. The guest firewall policy normally routes all user traffic straight to an Internet gateway and away from corporate network infrastructure.

Captive Web Portal   Guest users must normally log in through a captive web portal page before they can proceed to the Internet. One of the most important aspects of the captive web portal page is the legal disclaimer. A good legal disclaimer informs the guest users about acceptable behavior while using the guest WLAN. Businesses are also legally protected if something bad should happen to a guest user's WLAN device, such as being infected by a computer virus. A *captive portal* solution effectively turns a web browser into an authentication service. To authenticate, the user must launch a web browser. After the browser is launched and the user attempts to go to a website, no matter what web page the user attempts to browse, the user is redirected to a logon prompt, which is the captive portal logon web page. Captive portals can redirect unauthenticated users to a login page using an IP redirect, DNS redirection, or redirection by HTTP.

Guest Management Solution   Most guest WLANS require a guest user to authenticate with credentials via a captive web portal. Therefore, a database of user credentials must be created. Unlike a preexisting Active Directory database, a guest user database is created on the fly. Guest user information is usually collected when the guests arrive at company offices. Someone has to be in charge of managing the database and creating the guest user database entries. IT administrators are typically too busy to manage a guest database; therefore, the individual who manages the database is usually a receptionist or the person who greets guests at the front door. Many WLAN vendors offer guest management solutions, which are simple admin accounts to a RADIUS server or some other type of database server. The guest management administrators have the access rights to create guest user accounts on the database server. Other WLAN vendors use cloud-based servers to distribute secure guest credentials in the form of unique dynamic PSKs. A guest management solution that utilizes unique PSKs as credentials also provides data privacy for guest users with WPA2 encryption.

Over the past few years, there has also been a greater push for the guest user to create their own account, what is commonly referred to as self-registration. When the guest is redirected to the captive web portal, if they do not already have a guest account, a link on the login web page redirects the guest to a self-registration page. Simple self-registration pages allow the guest to simply fill out a form, and their guest account is created and displayed or printed for them. More advanced self-registration pages require the guest to enter an email or SMS address, which is then used by the registration system to send the user their logon credentials. Guest users can also be required to enter the email address of an employee, who must approve and sponsor the guest prior to allowing the guest access on the network. The sponsor typically receives an email requesting access for the guest, with a link in the email that allows the sponsor to easily accept or reject the request. Once the user has registered or been sponsored, they can log on using their newly created credentials.

Captive Portal

Most hotspots and guest networks are secured by a captive portal. A captive portal is essentially the integration of a firewall with an authentication web page. Although captive portals are often associated with hotspots and wireless guest networks, the technology is not specifically affiliated with wireless networks. When a user connects to the guest network, whether wired or wireless, any packets that the user transmits are intercepted and blocked from accessing a gateway to the network resources until the user has authenticated through the captive portal. Figure 13.12 shows the logon section of a captive portal web.

FIGURE 13.12   Logon section of a captive web portal

Captive portals are available as standalone software solutions, but most WLAN vendors offer integrated captive portal solutions. The captive portal may exist within a WLAN controller, or it may be deployed at the edge within an access point. As shown in Figure 13.13, WLAN vendors that support captive portals provide the ability to customize the captive portal page. You can typically personalize the page by adding graphics, such as a company logo, inserting an acceptable use policy, or configuring the logon requirements.

FIGURE 13.13   You can customize the captive web portal.

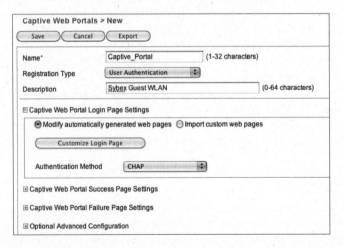

Authenticating to a captive portal typically requires the user to enter a username and password. This username and password are verified against a RADIUS database. If the username and password are valid, the user is then allowed to access other resources, such as the

Internet. A firewall policy normally restricts the guest users from any corporate resources but gives the users access to an Internet gateway.

Not all captive portal pages require a username and password for authentication. Some vendors have begun to use unique dynamic PSKs as user credentials. A guest management solution that utilizes unique PSKs as credentials also provides data privacy for guest users with WPA2 encryption.

Some organizations deploy a guest WLAN where the captive web portal does not require any credentials whatsoever. Captive web portals that do not require credentials still provide an acceptable use policy, which functions as a legal disclaimer for the guest network

 A more detailed discussion about WLAN guest access and management can be found in Chapter 20.

Summary

In this chapter, you learned that five major facets are needed for wireless security. A strong encryption solution is needed to protect the data frames. A mutual authentication solution is needed to ensure that only legitimate users are authorized to use network resources. A segmentation solution is necessary to further restrict users as to what resources they may access and where they can go. 802.11 wireless networks can be further protected with continuous monitoring and enforcement of WLAN security policy.

We discussed legacy 802.11 authentication and encryption solutions and why they are weak. We covered the stronger 802.1X/EAP authentication solutions and the benefits of dynamic encryption-key generation, as well as what is defined by the 802.11-2012 standard and the related WPA/WPA2 certifications. The 802.11-2012 standard defines a layer 2 robust security network using either 802.1X/EAP or PSK authentication and defines CCMP/AES or TKIP/RC4 dynamic encryption. Finally, we explored proper infrastructure and interface security as well as VPN technology in a WLAN environment.

It is important to understand the capabilities and limitations of the devices that will be deployed within your 802.11 wireless networks. Ideally, devices will be segmented into separate VLANs by using 802.1X/EAP authentication and CCMP/AES encryption. VoIP phones, mobile scanners, tablets, handheld devices, and so on are often not equipped with the ability to handle more advanced security capabilities. Proper designs must take into account all of these components to ensure the most dynamic and secure network.

Exam Essentials

Define the concept of AAA.   Be able to explain the differences between authentication, authorization, and accounting and why each is needed for a WLAN network.

Explain why data privacy and segmentation are needed.   Be able to discuss why data frames must be protected with encryption. Know the differences between the various encryption ciphers. Understand how VLANs and RBAC mechanisms are used to further restrict network resources.

Understand legacy 802.11 security.   Identify and understand Open System authentication and Shared Key authentication. Understand how WEP encryption works and know all of its weaknesses.

Explain the 802.1X/EAP framework.   Be able to explain all of the components of an 802.1X solution and the EAP authentication protocol. Understand that dynamic encryption-key generation is a by-product of mutual authentication.

Define the requirements of a robust security network (RSN).   Understand what the 802.11-2012 standard specifically defines for robust security and be able to contrast what is defined by both the WPA and WPA2 certifications.

Understand TKIP/RC4 and CCMP/AES.   Be able to explain the basics of both dynamic encryption types and why they are the end result of an RSN solution.

Explain VLANs and VPNs.   Understand that VLANs are typically used for wireless segmentation solutions. Define the basics of VPN technology and when it might be used in a WLAN environment.

Understand Guest WLAN security.   Be able to explain the purpose the security mechanisms implemented for wireless guest access. Understand captive portals, firewall restrictions, and guest management.

Review Questions

1. Which WLAN security mechanism requires that each WLAN user have unique authentication credentials?

   A. WPA-Personal

   B. 802.1X/EAP

   C. Open System

   D. WPA2-Personal

   E. WPA-PSK

2. Which wireless security standards and certifications call for the use of CCMP/AES encryption? (Choose all that apply.)

   A. WPA

   B. 802.11-2012

   C. 802.1X

   D. WPA2

   E. 802.11 legacy

3. 128-bit WEP encryption uses a user-provided static key of what size?

   A. 104 bytes

   B. 64 bits

   C. 124 bits

   D. 128 bits

   E. 104 bits

4. What three main components constitute an 802.1X/EAP framework? (Choose all that apply.)

   A. Supplicant

   B. Authorizer

   C. Authentication server

   D. Intentional radiator

   E. Authenticator

5. The 802.11 legacy standard defines which wireless security solution?

   A. Dynamic WEP

   B. 802.1X/EAP

   C. 64-bit static WEP

   D. Temporal Key Integrity Protocol

   E. CCMP/AES

6. Paul has been hired as a consultant to secure the Levasseur Corporation's WLAN infrastructure. He has been asked to choose a solution that will both protect the company's equipment from theft and hopefully protect the access point's configuration interfaces from outside attackers. What recommendations would be appropriate? (Choose all that apply.)

   A. Mounting all access points in lockable enclosure units

   B. Using an IPsec VPN

   C. Configuring all access points via Telnet

   D. Configuring access points from the wired side using HTTPS or SSH

   E. Implementing 802.1X/EAP

7. Which security solutions may be used to segment a wireless LAN? (Choose all that apply.)

   A. VLAN

   B. WEP

   C. RBAC

   D. CCMP/AES

   E. TKIP/RC4

8. What wireless security solutions are defined by Wi-Fi Protected Access? (Choose all that apply.)

   A. Passphrase authentication

   B. LEAP

   C. TKIP/RC4

   D. Dynamic WEP

   E. CCMP/AES

9. Name the three main components of a role-based access control solution.

   A. EAP

   B. Roles

   C. Encryption

   D. Permissions

   E. Users

10. What does 802.1X/EAP provide when implemented for WLAN security? (Choose all that apply.)

   A. Access to network resources

   B. Verification of access point credentials

   C. Dynamic authentication

   D. Dynamic encryption-key generation

   E. Verification of user credentials

11. Which technologies use the RC4 cipher? (Choose all that apply.)

    A. Static WEP

    B. Dynamic WEP

    C. CCMP

    D. TKIP

    E. MPPE

12. What must occur to generate dynamic TKIP/RC4 or CCMP/AES encryption keys? (Choose all that apply.)

    A. Shared Key authentication and 4-Way Handshake

    B. 802.1X/EAP authentication and 4-Way Handshake

    C. Static WEP and 4-Way Handshake

    D. PSK authentication and 4-Way Handshake

13. For an 802.1X/EAP solution to work properly, which two components must both support the same type of EAP? (Choose all that apply.)

    A. Supplicant

    B. Authorizer

    C. Authenticator

    D. Authentication server

14. When you're using an 802.11 wireless controller solution, which device would be usually function as the authenticator?

    A. Access point

    B. LDAP server

    C. WLAN controller

    D. RADIUS server

15. Identify some aspects of the Temporal Key Integrity Protocol. (Choose all that apply.)

    A. 128-bit temporal key

    B. 24-bit initialization vector

    C. Message integrity check

    D. 48-bit IV

    E. Diffie-Hellman Exchange

16. In a point-to-point bridge environment where 802.1X/EAP is used for bridge authentication, what device in the network acts as the 802.1X supplicant?

    A. Nonroot bridge

    B. Controller

    C. Root bridge

    D.   RADIUS server

    E.   Layer 3 core switch

17. CCMP encryption uses which AES key size?

    A.   192 bits

    B.   64 bits

    C.   256 bits

    D.   128 bits

18. Identify the security solutions that are defined by WPA2. (Choose all that apply.)

    A.   802.1X/EAP authentication

    B.   Dynamic WEP encryption

    C.   Optional CCMP/AES encryption

    D.   Passphrase authentication

    E.   DES encryption

19. What encryption method does the IEEE 802.11-2012 standard mandate for robust security network associations and what method is optional?

    A.   WEP, AES

    B.   IPsec, AES

    C.   MPPE, TKIP

    D.   TKIP, WEP

    E.   CCMP, TKIP

20. Which layer 2 protocol is used for authentication in an 802.1X framework?

    A.   Extensible Authorization Protocol

    B.   Extended Authentication Protocol

    C.   Extensible Authentication Protocol

    D.   CHAP/PPP

    E.   Open System

Chapter

14

Wireless Attacks, Intrusion Monitoring, and Policy

IN THIS CHAPTER, YOU WILL LEARN ABOUT THE FOLLOWING:

✓ **Wireless attacks**

- Rogue wireless devices
- Peer-to-peer attacks
- Eavesdropping
- Encryption cracking
- Authentication attacks
- MAC spoofing
- Management interface exploits
- Wireless hijacking
- Denial of service (DoS)
- Vendor-specific attacks
- Social engineering

✓ **Intrusion monitoring**

- Wireless intrusion detection system (WIDS)
- Wireless intrusion prevention system (WIPS)
- Mobile WIDS
- Spectrum analyzer

✓ **Wireless security policy**

- General security policy
- Functional security policy
- Legislative compliance
- PCI compliance
- 802.11 wireless policy recommendations

In Chapter 13, "802.11 Network Security Architecture," we discussed legacy 802.11 security solutions, as well as the more robust security that is defined in the 802.11-2012 standard. In this chapter, we cover the wide variety of attacks that can be launched against 802.11 wireless networks. Some of these attacks can be mitigated by using the strong encryption and mutual authentication solutions that we discussed in Chapter 13. However, others cannot be prevented and can only be detected. Therefore, we also discuss the wireless intrusion detection systems that can be implemented to expose both layer 1 and layer 2 attacks. The most important component for a secure wireless network is a properly planned and implemented corporate security policy. This chapter also discusses some of the fundamental components of a wireless security policy that are needed to cement a foundation of Wi-Fi security.

Wireless Attacks

As you have learned throughout this book, the main function of an 802.11 WLAN is to provide a portal into a wired network infrastructure. The portal must be protected with strong authentication methods so that only legitimate users and devices with the proper credentials will be authorized to have access to network resources. If the portal is not properly protected, unauthorized users can gain access to these resources. The potential risks of exposing these resources are endless. An intruder could gain access to financial databases, corporate trade secrets, or personal health information. Network resources can be damaged.

What would be the financial cost to an organization if an intruder used the wireless network as a portal to disrupt or shut down a SQL server or email server? If the Wi-Fi portal is not protected, any individual wishing to cause harm could upload data such as viruses, Trojan horse applications, keystroke loggers, or remote control applications. Spammers have already figured out that they can use open wireless gateways to the Internet to commence spamming activities. Other illegal activities, such as software theft and remote hacking, may also occur through an unsecured gateway.

While an intruder can use the wireless network to attack wired resources, equally at risk are all of the wireless network resources. Any information that passes through the air can be captured and possibly compromised. If not properly secured, the management interfaces of Wi-Fi equipment can be accessed. Many wireless users are fully exposed for peer-to-peer attacks. Finally, the possibility of denial-of-service attacks against a wireless network always exists. With the proper tools, any individual with ill intent can temporarily disable a Wi-Fi network, thus denying legitimate users access to the network resources.

In the following sections, you will learn about many of the potential attacks that can be launched against 802.11 wireless networks.

Rogue Wireless Devices

The big buzz-phrase in Wi-Fi security has always been the *rogue access point*: a potential open and unsecured gateway straight into the wired infrastructure that the company wants to protect. In Chapter 13, you learned about 802.1X/EAP authentication solutions that can be put in place to prevent unauthorized access. However, what is there to prevent an individual from installing their own wireless portal onto the network backbone? A rogue access point is any unauthorized Wi-Fi device that is not under the management of the proper network administrators. The most worrisome type of unauthorized rogue Wi-Fi device is one that is connected to the wired network infrastructure, as depicted in Figure 14.1. The skull and crossbones icon in Figure 14.1 is a common symbol used to represent rogue APs, as well as pirates. Any $50 SOHO Wi-Fi access point or router can be plugged into a live data port. The rogue device will just as easily act as a portal into the wired network infrastructure. Because the rogue device will likely be configured with no authorization and authentication security in place, any intruder could use this open portal to gain access to network resources.

The individuals most responsible for installing rogue access points are typically not hackers; they are employees not realizing the consequences of their actions. Wi-Fi networking has become ingrained in our society, and the average employee has become accustomed to the convenience and mobility that Wi-Fi offers. As a result, it is not uncommon for an employee to install their own wireless devices in the workplace because the employee believes installing their own wireless device is easier or more reliable than using the corporate WLAN. The problem is, although these self-installed access points might provide the wireless access that the employees desire, they are often unsecured. Only a single open portal is needed to expose network resources, and many large companies have discovered literally dozens of rogue access points that have been installed by employees.

Ad hoc wireless connections also have the potential of providing rogue access into the corporate network. Very often an employee will have a laptop or desktop plugged into the wired network via an Ethernet network card. On that same computer, the employee has a Wi-Fi radio and has set up an ad hoc Wi-Fi connection with another employee. This connection may be set up on purpose or may be accidental and occur as an unwitting result of the manufacturer's default configurations. As shown in Figure 14.2, the Ethernet connection and the Wi-Fi network interface controller (NIC) can be bridged together—an intruder might access the ad hoc wireless network and then potentially route their way to the Ethernet connection and get onto the wired network.

FIGURE 14.1 Rogue access point

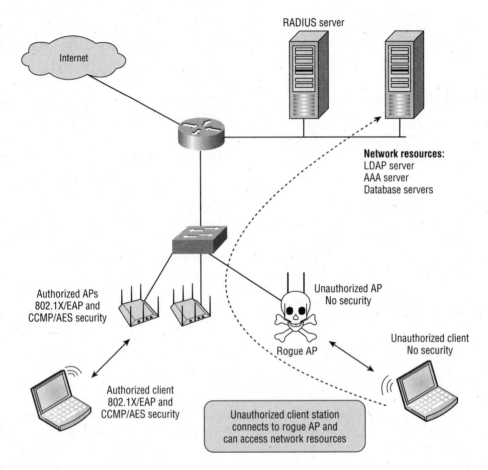

Many government agencies and corporations ban the use of ad hoc networks for this very reason. The ability to configure an ad hoc network can and should be disabled on most enterprise client devices. On some computers, it is possible to limit the use of multiple NICs simultaneously. This is a great feature that can prevent bridged networks from occurring while allowing flexibility for the user. When the user plugs an Ethernet cable into the computer, the wireless adapter is automatically disabled, eliminating the risk of an intentional or unintentional bridged network.

As stated earlier, most rogue APs are installed by employees not realizing the consequences of their actions, but any malicious intruder can use these open portals to gain access. Furthermore, besides physical security, there is nothing to prevent an intruder from also connecting their own rogue access point via an Ethernet cable into any live data port provided in a wall plate. Later in this chapter, we discuss intrusion prevention systems that can both detect and disable rogue access points as well as ad hoc clients.

FIGURE 14.2   Bridged ad hoc WLAN

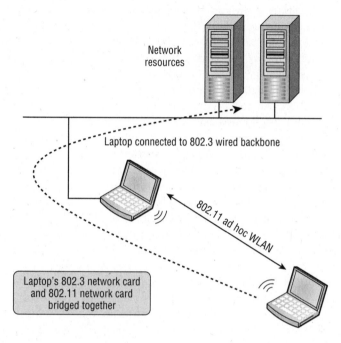

If an 802.1X solution is deployed for the wireless network, it can also be used to secure the network ports on the wired network. Some WLAN vendors have also begun to support MACsec for wired-side port control. The IEEE 802.1AE Media Access Control Security standard, often referred to as MACsec, specifies a set of protocols to meet the security requirements for protecting data traversing Ethernet LANs. In that case, any new device, including APs, would need to be authenticated to the network prior to being given access. This is a good way to not only utilize existing resources but also provide better security for your wired network by protecting against rogue APs.

Most businesses do not use an 802.1X/EAP solution for wired port control. Therefore, a WLAN monitoring solution known as a wireless intrusion detection system (WIDS) is usually recommended to detect potential rogue devices. Most WIDS vendors prefer to call their products a wireless intrusion prevention system (WIPS). The reason that they refer to their products as prevention systems is that they are all now capable of mitigating attacks from rogue APs and rogue clients.

Peer-to-Peer Attacks

As mentioned earlier, wireless resources may also be attacked. A commonly overlooked risk is the *peer-to-peer attack*. As you learned in earlier chapters, an 802.11 client station can be configured in either Infrastructure mode or Ad Hoc mode. When configured in Ad Hoc mode, the wireless network is known as an independent basic service set (IBSS), and all communications are peer-to-peer without the need for an access point. Because an IBSS is by nature a peer-to-peer connection, any user who can connect wirelessly with another user can potentially gain access to any resource available on either computer. A common use of ad hoc networks is to share files on the fly. If shared access is provided, files and other assets can accidentally be exposed. A personal firewall is often used to mitigate peer-to peer attacks. Some client devices can also disable this feature so that the device will connect to only certain networks and will not associate to a peer-to-peer without approval.

Users that are associated to the same access point are potentially just as vulnerable to peer-to-peer attacks as IBSS users. Properly securing your wireless network often involves protecting authorized users from each other, because hacking at companies is often performed internally by employees. Any users associated to the same AP that are members of the same basic service set (BSS) and are in the same VLAN are susceptible to peer-to-peer attacks because they reside in the same layer 2 and layer 3 domains. In most WLAN deployments, Wi-Fi clients communicate only with devices on the wired network, such as email or web servers, and peer-to-peer communications are not needed. Therefore, most enterprise AP vendors provide some proprietary method of preventing users from inadvertently sharing files with other users or bridging traffic between the devices. If connections are required to other wireless peers, the traffic is routed through a layer 3 switch or other network device before passing to the desired destination station.

Client isolation is a feature that can often be enabled on WLAN access points or controllers to block wireless clients from communicating with other wireless clients on the same wireless VLAN. Client isolation, or the various other terms used to describe this feature, usually means that packets arriving at the AP's wireless interface are not forwarded back out of the wireless interface to other clients. This isolates each user on the wireless network to ensure that a wireless station cannot be used to gain layer 3 or higher access to another wireless station. The client isolation feature is usually a configurable setting per SSID linked to a unique VLAN. With client isolation enabled, client devices cannot communicate directly with other client devices on the wireless network, as shown in Figure 14.3.

Although *client isolation* is the most commonly used term, some vendors instead use the term *peer-to-peer blocking* or *public secure packet forwarding (PSPF)*. Not all vendors implement client isolation in the same fashion. Some WLAN vendors can only implement client isolation on an SSID/ VLAN pair on a single access point, whereas others can enforce the peer-blocking capabilities across multiple APs.

Some applications require peer-to-peer connectivity. Many VoWiFi phones offer push-to-talk capabilities that use multicasting. VoWiFi phones are typically segmented in a separate wireless VLAN from the rest of wireless data clients. Client isolation should not be enabled in the VoWiFi VLAN if push-to-talk multicasting is required because it can prevent these devices from functioning properly.

FIGURE 14.3   Client isolation

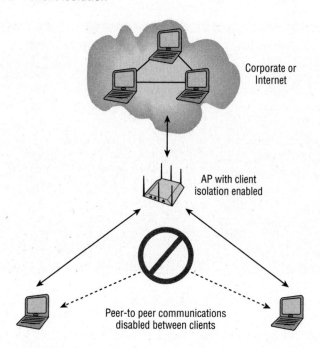

Corporate or
Internet

AP with client
isolation enabled

Peer-to peer communications
disabled between clients

Eavesdropping

As we've mentioned throughout this book, 802.11 wireless networks operate in license-free frequency bands, and all data transmissions travel in the open air. Access to wireless transmissions is available to anyone within listening range, and therefore strong encryption is mandatory. Wireless communications can be monitored via two eavesdropping methods: casual eavesdropping and malicious eavesdropping.

Casual eavesdropping is sometimes referred to as *WLAN discovery*. Casual eavesdropping is accomplished by simply exploiting the 802.11 frame exchange methods that are clearly defined by the 802.11-2012 standard. Software utilities known as WLAN discovery tools exist for the purpose of finding open WLAN networks.

Many wireless client software utilities instruct the radio to transmit probe requests with null SSID fields when actively scanning for APs. Additionally, there are many popular and freely available WLAN discovery software programs, such as inSSIDer, WiFiFoFum, and iStumbler, that can be used by individuals to discover wireless networks. WLAN discovery tools send out null probe requests across all license-free 802.11 channels with the hope of receiving probe response frames containing wireless network information, such as SSID, channel, encryption, and so on. Some WLAN discovery tools may also use passive scanning methods. Shown in Figure 14.4, a very popular WLAN discovery tool is inSSIDer, which is available from www.metageek.net.

FIGURE 14.4 MetaGeek inSSIDer

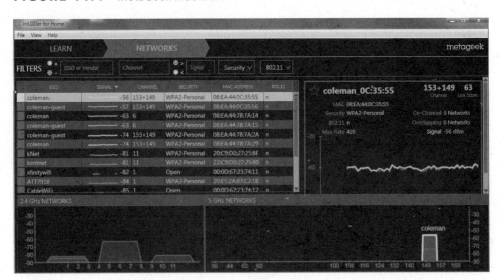

WLAN discovery is typically considered harmless and in the past was referred to as *wardriving*. Wardriving was strictly the act of looking for wireless networks, usually while in a moving vehicle. The term *wardriving* was derived from wardialing from the 1983 film *WarGames*. Wardialing was an old technique employed by hackers using computer modems to scan thousands of telephone numbers automatically to search for other computers with which they could connect. In the early days of Wi-Fi, the original wardriving software tool was a freeware program called NetStumbler. Although still available as a free download, NetStumbler was not been updated in many years. However, many newer WLAN discovery tools exist that operate on a variety of operating systems. Figure 14.5 depicts the WLAN discovery tool WiFiFoFum. Multiple WLAN discovery tools are available for Android mobile devices, but currently there are not many tools for iOS mobile devices.

By technical design, the very nature of 802.11 passive and active scanning is to provide the identifying network information that is accessible to anyone with an 802.11 radio. Because this is an inherent necessary function of 802.11 communications, wardriving is not a crime. However, the goal of many wardrivers is to find open 802.11 wireless networks that can provide free gateway access to the Internet. Although the legality of using an open wireless gateway to the Internet remains unclear in many countries, the majority of wardrivers are not hackers intending harm but rather simply wireless users wanting temporary, free Internet access. The legality of using someone else's wireless network without permission is often unclear, but be warned that people have been arrested and prosecuted as a result of these actions.

Wardiving is now considered an outdated term and concept. In the very early days of Wi-Fi, wardriving was a hobby and sport for techno-geeks and hackers looking to find WLANs. Wardriving competitions were often held at hacker conventions to see who could find the most WLANs. While the sport of wardriving has faded into the past, millions of individuals now use WLAN discovery tools to still find available Wi-Fi networks.

FIGURE 14.5   WiFiFoFum WLAN discovery tool

 We do not encourage or support the efforts of using wireless networks
that you are not authorized to use. We recommend that you connect only
to wireless networks that you are authorized to access.

What Tools Are Needed for WLAN Discovery?

To start finding WLANs, you will need an 802.11 client NIC and a WLAN discovery application. Numerous freeware-based discovery tools exist, including inSSIDer for Windows,
WiFi Scanner for the Mac OS, and WiFiFoFum for Android. You can download inSSIDer
from www.metageek.net, WiFi Scanner from www.wlanbook.com, and WiFiFoFum from
www.wififofum.net.

Global positioning system (GPS) devices in conjunction with WLAN discovery tools can
be used to pinpoint longitude and latitude coordinates of the signal from APs that are

discovered. WLAN discovery capture files with GPS coordinates can be uploaded to large dynamic mapping databases on the Internet. The Wireless Geographic Logging Engine (WIGLE), maintains a searchable database of more than 120 million Wi-Fi networks. Go to www.wigle.net and type in your address to see whether any wireless access points have already been discovered in your neighborhood.

While casual eavesdropping is considered harmless, *malicious eavesdropping*, the unauthorized use of 802.11 protocol analyzers to capture wireless communications, is typically considered illegal. Most countries have some type of wiretapping law that makes it a crime to listen in on someone else's phone conversation. Additionally, most countries have laws making it illegal to listen in on any type of electromagnetic communications, including 802.11 wireless transmissions.

Many commercial and freeware 802.11 protocol analyzers exist that allow wireless network administrators to capture 802.11 traffic for the purpose of analyzing and troubleshooting their own wireless networks. Protocol analyzers are passive devices working in an RF monitoring mode that captures any transmissions within range. The problem is that anyone with malicious intent can also capture 802.11 traffic from any Wi-Fi network. Because protocol analyzers capture 802.11 frames passively, a wireless intrusion detection system (WIDS) cannot detect malicious eavesdropping. For this reason, a strong, dynamic encryption solution such as TKIP/RC4—or even better, CCMP/AES—is mandatory. Any cleartext communications, such as email, FTP, and Telnet passwords, can be captured if no encryption is provided. Furthermore, any unencrypted 802.11 frame transmissions can be reassembled at the upper layers of the OSI model. Email messages can be reassembled and, therefore, read by an eavesdropper. Web pages and instant messages can also be reassembled. VoIP packets can be reassembled and saved as a WAV sound file. Malicious eavesdropping of this nature is highly illegal. Because of the passive and undetectable nature of this attack, encryption must always be implemented to provide data privacy.

The most common targets of malicious eavesdropping attacks are public access hotspots. Public hotspots rarely offer security and usually transfer data without encryption, making hotspot users prime targets. As a result, it is imperative that a VPN security solution be implemented for all mobile users who connect outside of your company's network.

Encryption Cracking

In Chapter 13, you learned that Wired Equivalent Privacy (WEP) encryption has been cracked. The current WEP-cracking tools that are freely available on the Internet can crack WEP encryption in as little as 5 minutes. There are several methods used to crack WEP encryption. However, an attacker usually needs only to capture several hundred thousand encrypted packets with a protocol analyzer and then run the captured data through a WEP-cracking software program, as shown in Figure 14.6. The software utility will usually then be able to derive the secret 40-bit or 104-bit key in a matter of seconds. After the secret key has been revealed, the attacker can decrypt any and all encrypted traffic. In other words, an attacker can then eavesdrop on the WEP-encrypted network. Because the attacker can decrypt the traffic, they can reassemble the data and read it as if there was no encryption whatsoever.

FIGURE 14.6   WEP-cracking utility

```
 * Got   286716! unique IVs | fudge factor = 2
 * Elapsed time [00:00:03] | tried 1 keys at 20 k/m

KB     depth    votes
 0      0/  1    DA(   60) 70(   23) 55(   15) A2(    5) CD(    5) 3E(    4)
 1      0/  2    BD(   57) 2A(   32) 29(   22) 1D(   13) F9(   13) 9F(   12)
 2      0/  1    8C(   51) 67(   23) 48(   15) DD(   15) D6(   13) FA(   12)
 3      0/  3    1D(   30) A5(   17) 07(   15) 7B(   12) 4B(   10) 63(   10)
 4      0/  1    43(   66) B1(   15) D2(    6) 1A(    5) 20(    5) 21(    5)
 5      0/  5    92(   27) 23(   25) 02(   18) 2F(   17) C1(   16) 36(   12)
 6      0/  1    C6(   51) 54(   17) 50(   15) 66(   15) 01(   13) 4A(   13)
 7      0/  2    84(   29) C0(   17) EE(   13) 80(   12) 49(   11) F6(   11)
 8      0/  1    81(1808) 09( 119) 99( 116) 32(   75) 49(   75) 9D(   65)
 9      0/  1    C4(1947) E1( 125) FC( 123) BD( 105) 8C(   98) 2F(   85)
10      0/  1    8A( 580) 41( 120) 18(   93) ED(   85) B0(   65) 97(   60)
11      0/  1    08(   97) FF(   29) 5D(   20) 1E(   17) 18(   15) 5E(   15)
12      0/  1    1B( 145) DD(   21) 46(   20) 1C(   15) 76(   15) 07(   13)

       KEY FOUND! [ DABD8C1D4392C68481C48A081B ]
```

Authentication Attacks

As you have already learned, authorization to network resources can be achieved by either an 802.1X/EAP authentication solution or the use of PSK authentication. The 802.11-2012 standard does not define which type of EAP authentication method to use, and all flavors of EAP are not created equal. Some types of EAP authentication are more secure than others. As a matter of fact, *Lightweight Extensible Authentication Protocol (LEAP)*, once one of the most commonly deployed 802.1X/EAP solutions, is susceptible to offline dictionary attacks. The hashed password response during the LEAP authentication process is crackable.

An attacker merely has to capture a frame exchange when a LEAP user authenticates and then run the capture file through an offline dictionary attack tool, as shown in Figure 14.7. The password can be derived in a matter of seconds. The username is also seen in cleartext during the LEAP authentication process. After the attacker gets the username and password, they are free to impersonate the user by authenticating onto the WLAN and then accessing any network resources that are available to that user. Stronger EAP authentication protocols that use tunneled authentication are not susceptible to offline dictionary attacks.

FIGURE 14.7   Offline dictionary attack

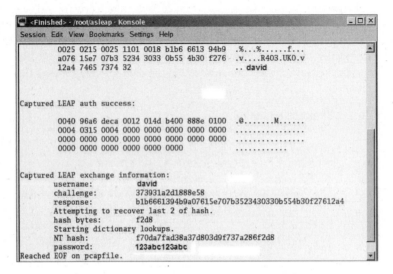

The biggest risk with any authentication attack is that all network resources become vulnerable if the authentication credentials are compromised. The risks of authentication attacks are similar to rogue access points. If an authorized WLAN portal can be compromised and the authentication credentials can be obtained, network resources are exposed. Because of these severe risks, it is therefore necessary to secure the corporate WLAN infrastructure properly with an 802.1X/EAP solution that uses a RADIUS server and the tunneled authentication EAP protocols discussed in Chapter 13.

Because most home users do not have a RADIUS server in their house, weaker WPA/WPA2-Personal authentication methods are normally used at home. WPA/WPA2-Personal, also known as PSK authentication, is a weak authentication method that is vulnerable to an offline brute-force dictionary attack. Hacking utilities are available that can derive the WPA/WPA2 passphrase by using an offline dictionary attack. An attacker who obtains the passphrase can associate to the WPA/WPA2 access point. Even worse is that after obtaining the passphrase, the hacker can also begin to decrypt the dynamically generated TKIP/RC4 or CCMP/AES encryption key. In Chapter 13, you learned that a function is run to convert the passphrase to a Pairwise Master Key (PMK), which is used with the 4-Way Handshake to create the final dynamic encryption keys. If a hacker has the passphrase and captures the 4-Way Handshake, they can re-create the dynamic encryption keys and decrypt traffic. If the passphrase is compromised, the attacker can access network resources and decrypt traffic. In situations where there is no AAA server or the client devices do not support 802.1X authentication, a proprietary PSK authentication solution implementing unique PSKs is recommended.

A policy mandating very strong passphrases of 20 characters or more should always be in place whenever a WPA/WPA2-Personal solution is deployed. Furthermore, because passphrases are static, they are susceptible to social engineering attacks. To prevent social engineering attacks, policy must dictate that only the administrator has knowledge of any static passphrases and that the passphrases never be shared with end users. Several enterprise WLAN vendors now offer proprietary PSK solutions that provide the capability of unique PSKs for each user.

MAC Spoofing

All 802.11 radios have a physical address known as a *MAC address*. This address is a 12-digit hexadecimal number that is seen in cleartext in the layer 2 header of 802.11 frames. Wi-Fi vendors often provide MAC filtering capabilities on their APs. Usually, MAC filters are configured to apply restrictions that will allow traffic only from specific client stations to pass through. These restrictions are based on their unique MAC addresses. All other client stations whose MAC addresses are not on the allowed list will not be able to pass traffic through the virtual port of the access point and onto the distribution system medium. MAC filtering is often used as a security mechanism for legacy client devices, such as mobile handheld scanners, that do not support the stronger authentication and encryption techniques.

Unfortunately, MAC addresses can be *spoofed*, or impersonated, and any amateur hacker can easily bypass any MAC filter by spoofing an allowed client station's address. MAC spoofing can often be achieved in the Windows operating system by simply editing the Wi-Fi radio's MAC address in Device Manager or by performing a simple edit in the Registry. Third-party software utilities such as the one shown in Figure 14.8 can also be used to assist in MAC spoofing.

FIGURE 14.8   MAC spoofing software utility

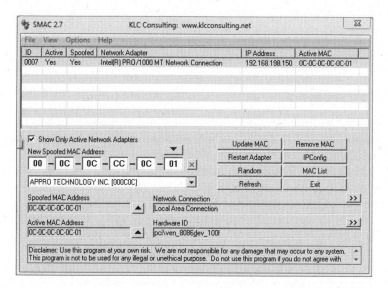

Because of spoofing and because of all of the administrative work involved with setting up MAC filters, MAC filtering is not considered a reliable means of security for wireless enterprise networks and should be implemented only as a last resort. As mentioned earlier, MAC filtering is used as part of a layered security architecture to better secure legacy client devices that are not capable of 802.1X/EAP protection.

Management Interface Exploits

Wireless infrastructure hardware, such as autonomous APs and WLAN controllers, can be managed by administrators via a variety of interfaces, much like managing wired infrastructure hardware. Devices can typically be accessed via a web interface, a command-line interface, a serial port, a console connection, and/or Simple Network Management Protocol (SNMP).

As we discussed, it is imperative that these interfaces be protected. Interfaces that are not used should be disabled. Strong passwords should be used, and encrypted login capabilities using SSH (Secure Shell) or Hypertext Transfer Protocol Secure (HTTPS) should always be utilized.

Lists of all the default settings of every major manufacturer's access points exist on the Internet and are often used for security exploits by hackers. It is not uncommon for attackers to use security holes left in management interfaces to reconfigure APs. Legitimate users and administrators can find themselves locked out of their own Wi-Fi equipment. After gaining access via a management interface, an attacker might even be able to initiate a firmware upgrade of the wireless hardware and, while the upgrade is being performed, power off the equipment. This attack could likely render the hardware useless, requiring it to be returned to the manufacturer for repair.

Policy often dictates that all WLAN infrastructure devices be configured from only the wired side of the network. If an administrator attempts to configure a WLAN device while connected wirelessly, the administrator could lose connectivity due to configuration changes being made. Some WLAN vendors offer secure wireless console connectivity capabilities for troubleshooting and configuration.

Wireless Hijacking

An attack that often generates a lot of press is *wireless hijacking*, also known as the *evil twin attack*. The attacker configures access point software on a laptop, effectively turning a Wi-Fi client radio into an access point. Some small Wi-Fi USB devices also have the ability to operate as an AP. The access point software is configured with the same SSID that is used by a public hotspot access point. The attacker then sends spoofed disassociation or deauthentication frames, forcing users associated with the hotspot AP to roam to the evil twin AP. At this point, the attacker has effectively hijacked wireless clients at layer 2 from the original AP. Although deauthentication frames are usually used as one way to start a hijacking attack, an RF jammer can also be used to force any clients to roam to an evil twin AP.

The evil twin will typically be configured with a Dynamic Host Configuration Protocol (DHCP) server available to issue IP addresses to the clients. At this point, the attacker will have hijacked the users at layer 3 and will now have a private wireless network and be free to perform peer-to-peer attacks on any of the hijacked clients. The user's computer could, during the process of connecting to the evil twin, fall victim to a DHCP attack, an attack that exploits the DHCP process to dump root kits or other malware onto the victim's computer in addition to giving them an IP address as expected.

The attacker may also be using a second wireless NIC with their laptop to execute what is known as a *man-in-the-middle attack*, as you can see in Figure 14.9. The second WLAN radio is associated to the hotspot access point as a client. In operating systems, networking interfaces can be bridged together to provide routing. The attacker has bridged together their second wireless NIC with the Wi-Fi radio that is being used as the evil twin access point. After the attacker hijacks the users from the original AP, the traffic is then routed from the evil twin AP through the second Wi-Fi radio, right back to the original AP from which the users have just been hijacked. The result is that the users remain hijacked; however, they still have a route back through the gateway to their original network, so they never know they have been hijacked. The attacker can therefore sit in the middle and execute peer-to-peer attacks indefinitely while remaining completely unnoticed.

FIGURE 14.9   Wireless hijacking/man-in-the-middle attack

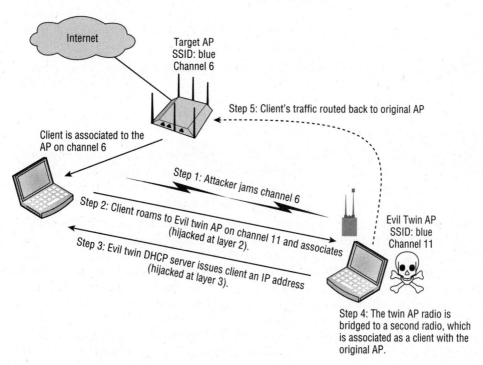

These attacks can take another form in what is known as a *Wi-Fi phishing attack*. The attacker may also have web server software and captive portal software. After the users have been hijacked to the evil twin access point, they will be redirected to a login web page

that looks exactly like the hotspot's login page. Then the attacker's fake login page may request a credit card number from the hijacked user. Phishing attacks are common on the Internet and are now appearing at your local hotspot.

The only way to prevent a hijacking, man-in-the-middle, or Wi-Fi phishing attack is to use a mutual authentication solution. Mutual authentication solutions not only validate the user connecting to the network, they also validate the network to which the user is connecting. 802.1X/EAP authentication solutions require that mutual authentication credentials be exchanged before a user can be authorized. A user cannot get an IP address unless authorized; therefore, users cannot be hijacked.

Denial of Service (DoS)

The attack on wireless networks that seems to receive the least amount of attention is the *denial of service (DoS)*. With the proper tools, any individual with ill intent can temporarily disable a Wi-Fi network by preventing legitimate users from accessing network resources. The good news is that monitoring systems exist that can detect and identify DoS attacks immediately. The bad news is that usually nothing can be done to prevent DoS attacks other than locating and removing the source of the attack.

DoS attacks can occur at either layer 1 or layer 2 of the OSI model. Layer 1 attacks are known as *RF jamming attacks*. The two most common types of RF jamming attacks are intentional jamming and unintentional jamming:

Intentional Jamming   Intentional jamming attacks occur when an attacker uses some type of signal generator to cause interference in the unlicensed frequency space. Both narrowband and wideband jammers exist that will interfere with 802.11 transmissions, either causing all data to become corrupted or causing the 802.11 radios to continuously defer when performing a clear channel assessment (CCA).

Unintentional Jamming   Whereas an intentional jamming attack is malicious, unintentional jamming is more common. Unintentional interference from microwave ovens, cordless phones, and other devices can also cause denial of service. Although unintentional jamming is not necessarily an attack, it can cause as much harm as an intentional jamming attack.

The best tool to detect any type of layer 1 interference, whether intentional or unintentional, is a spectrum analyzer. A good example of a standalone spectrum analyzer is the Wi-Spy USB spectrum analyzer, which is available from www.metageek.net.

The more common type of denial-of-service attacks that originate from hackers are layer 2 DoS attacks. A wide variety of layer 2 DoS attacks exist that are a result of manipulating 802.11 frames. The most common involves spoofing disassociation or deauthentication frames. The attacker can edit the 802.11 header and spoof the MAC address of an access point or a client in either the transmitter address (TA) field or the receiver address (RA) field. The attacker then retransmits the spoofed deauthentication frame repeatedly. The station that receives the spoofed deauthentication frame thinks the spoofed frame is coming from a legitimate station and disconnects at layer 2.

Many more types of layer 2 DoS attacks exist, including association floods, authentication floods, PS-Poll floods, and virtual carrier attacks. Luckily, any good wireless intrusion detection system will be able to alert an administrator immediately to a layer 2 DoS attack. The 802.11w-2009 amendment defines *management frame protection (MFP)* mechanisms for the prevention of spoofing certain types of 802.11 management frames. These 802.11w frames are referred to as *robust management frames*. Robust management frames can be protected by the management frame protection service and include disassociation, deauthentication, and robust action frames. Action frames are used to request a station to take action on behalf of another station, and not all action frames are robust.

It should be noted that the 802.11w amendment did not put an end to all layer 2 DoS attacks. Numerous layer 2 DoS attacks exist that cannot be prevented. Furthermore, 802.11w MFP mechanisms are not yet widely supported on the client side. However, enterprise WLAN vendors have begun to implement 802.11w mechanisms on access points; therefore, some of the more common layer 2 DoS attacks can be prevented.

A spectrum analyzer is your best tool to detect a layer 1 DoS attack, and a protocol analyzer or wireless IDS is your best tool to detect a layer 2 DoS attack. The best way to prevent any type of denial-of-service attack is physical security. The authors of this book recommend guard dogs and barbed wire. If that is not an option, there are several vendor solutions that provide intrusion detection at layers 1 and 2.

Where Can You Learn More about WLAN Security Risk Assessment?

This chapter covers the basics of Wi-Fi security attacks and intrusion monitoring. Although numerous books have been written about wireless hacking, a good starting point is *CWSP Certified Wireless Security Professional Official Study Guide: Exam PW0-204* (Sybex, 2010). Many WLAN security auditing tools are also available for Wi-Fi penetration testing.

One of the more popular Wi-Fi penetration testing tools is the Wi-Fi Pineapple. The Wi-Fi Pineapple is a WLAN auditing tool from Hak5 that uses custom hardware and software with a web interface. More information about the Wi-Fi Pineapple can be found at www.wifipineapple.com.

Another good website with information about WLAN auditing software tools is Wirelessdefence.org, which provides a collection of "top tips" for the auditing of 802.11 networks and is an attempt to provide a one-stop shop for common tasks encountered by WLAN security auditors. Many WLAN auditing tools are available for download at http://wirelessdefence.org.

Vendor-Specific Attacks

Hackers often find holes in the firmware code used by specific WLAN access point and WLAN controller vendors. Most of these vendor-specific exploits are in the form of buffer overflow attacks. When these vendor-specific attacks become known, the WLAN vendor usually makes a firmware fix available in a timely manner. These attacks can be best avoided by staying informed through your WLAN vendor's support services.

Social Engineering

Hackers do not compromise most wired or wireless networks with the use of hacking software or tools. The majority of breaches in computer security occur due to social engineering attacks. *Social engineering* is a technique used to manipulate people into divulging confidential information, such as computer passwords. The best defense against social engineering attacks are strictly enforced policies to prevent confidential information from being shared.

Any information that is static is extremely susceptible to social engineering attacks. WEP encryption uses a static key, and WPA/WPA2-Personal requires the use of a static PSK or passphrase. You should avoid both of these security methods because of their static nature.

Intrusion Monitoring

When most people think of wireless networking, they think only in terms of access and mobility, not in terms of attacks or intrusions. However, it has become increasingly necessary to constantly monitor for the many types of attacks mentioned in this chapter because of the potential damage they can cause. Businesses of all sizes have begun to deploy 802.11 wireless networks for mobility, and at the same time are running a wireless intrusion detection system (WIDS) to monitor for attacks. Many companies are concerned about the potential damage that would result from rogue APs. It is not unusual for a company to deploy a WIDS before deploying the wireless network that is meant to provide access.

Wireless intrusion monitoring has evolved, and most current systems have methods to prevent and mitigate some of the known wireless attacks. While most systems are distributed for scalability across a large enterprise, single laptop versions of intrusion monitoring systems also exist. Most wireless intrusion monitoring exists at layer 2, but layer 1 wireless intrusion monitoring systems are now also available to scan for potential layer 1 attacks.

Wireless Intrusion Detection System

In today's world, a *wireless intrusion detection system (WIDS)* might be necessary even if there is no authorized 802.11 Wi-Fi network on site. Wireless can be an intrusive technology, and if wired data ports at a business are not controlled, any individual (including employees) can install a rogue access point. Because of this risk, many companies such as banks and other financial institutions, as well as hospitals, choose to install a WIDS before deploying a Wi-Fi network for employee access. After an 802.11 network is installed for access, it has become almost mandatory to also have a WIDS because of the other numerous attacks against Wi-Fi, such as DoS, hijacking, and so on. The typical WIDS is a client-server model that consists of three components:

WIDS Server   A WIDS server is a software server or hardware server appliance acting as a central point of monitoring security and performance data collection. The server uses signature analysis, behavior analysis, protocol analysis, and RF spectrum analysis to detect potential threats. Signature analysis looks for patterns associated with common WLAN attacks. Behavior analysis looks for 802.11 anomalies. Protocol analysis dissects the MAC layer information from 802.11 frames. Protocol analysis may also look at the layer 3–7 information of 802.11 data frames that are not encrypted. Spectrum analysis monitors RF statistics, such as signal strength and signal-to-noise ratio (SNR). Performance analysis can be used to gauge WLAN health statistics, such as capacity and coverage.

Management Consoles   A software-based management console is used to communicate back to a WIDS server from a desktop station. The management console is the software interface used for administration and configuration of the server and sensors. The management console can also be used for 24/7 monitoring of 802.11 wireless networks.

Sensors   Hardware- or software-based sensors may be placed strategically to listen to and capture all 802.11 communications. Sensors are the eyes and ears of a WIDS monitoring solution. Sensors use 802.11 radios to collect information used in securing and analyzing WLAN traffic. Figure 14.10 depicts the client-server model used by most wireless intrusion detection systems.

FIGURE 14.10   Wireless intrusion detection system (WIDS)

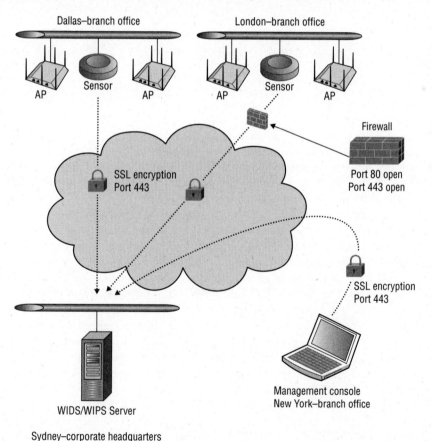

Sensors are basically radio devices that are in a constant listening mode as passive devices. The sensor devices are usually hardware based and resemble an access point. The sensors have some intelligence but must communicate with the centralized WIDS server. The centralized server can collect data from literally thousands of sensors from many remote locations and thus meet the scalability needs of large corporations. Management consoles can also be installed at remote locations, and while they talk back to the centralized server, they can also monitor all remote WLANs where sensors are installed. Figure 14.11 shows a WIDS management console from AirTight Networks.

FIGURE 14.11 WIDS management console

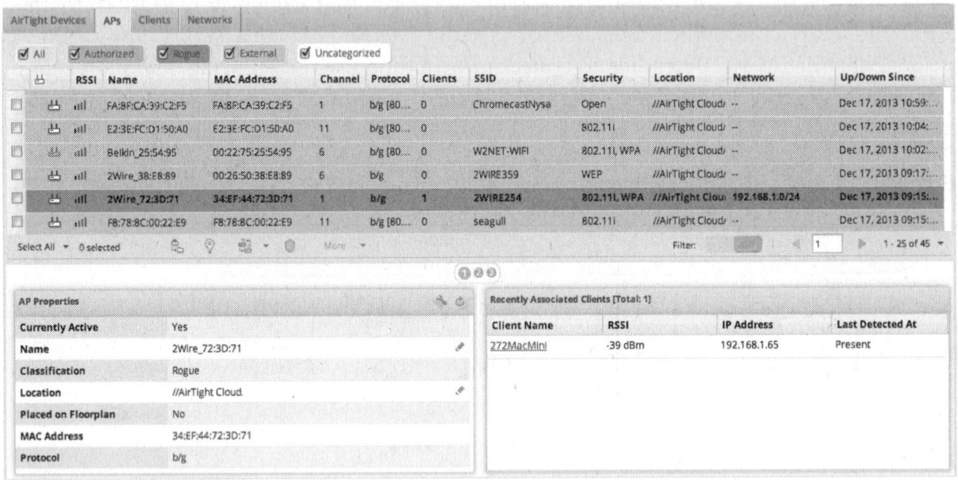

Standalone sensors do not provide access to WLAN clients because they are configured in a listen-only mode. The sensors constantly scan all 14 channels in the 2.4 GHz ISM band, as well as all of the channels in the 5 GHz U-NII bands. On rare occasions, the sensors can also be configured to listen on only one channel or a select group of channels. Access points can also be used as part-time sensors. An AP can use off-channel scanning methods to monitor other channels while still spending the majority of time on the AP's home channel to provide client access.

WIDS are best at monitoring layer 2 attacks, such as MAC spoofing, disassociation attacks, and deauthentication attacks. Most WIDS have alarms for as many as 100 potential security risks. An important part of deploying a WIDS is setting the policies and alarms. False positives are often a problem with intrusion detection systems, but they can be less of a problem if proper policies and thresholds are defined. Policies can be created to define the severity of various alerts as well as provide for alarm notifications. For example, an alert for broadcasting the SSID might not be considered severe and might even be disabled. However, a policy might be configured that classifies a deauthentication spoofing attack as severe, and an email message or SMS test message might be sent automatically to the network administrator.

Although most of the scrutiny that is performed by a WIDS is for security purposes, many WIDS also have performance-monitoring capabilities. For example, performance alerts might be in the form of excessive bandwidth utilization or excessive reassociation and roaming of VoWiFi phones.

Currently, three WIDS design models exist:

Overlay   The most secure model is an overlay WIDS that is deployed on top of the existing wireless network. This model uses an independent vendor's WIDS and can be deployed to monitor any existing or planned WLAN. The overlay systems typically have more extensive features, but they are usually more expensive. The overlay solution consists of a WIDS server and sensors that are not part of the WLAN solution that provides access to clients. Dedicated overlay systems are not as common as they used to be; many of the WIDS capabilities have been integrated into most enterprise WLAN products.

Integrated   Most WLAN vendors have fully integrated WIDS capabilities. A centralized WLAN controller or a centralized *network management server (NMS)* functions as the IDS server. Access points can be configured in a full-time sensor-only mode or can act as part-time sensors when not transmitting as access points. In WLAN controller deployments, the APs use off-channel scanning procedures for dynamic RF spectrum management purposes. The APs are also effectively part-time sensors for the integrated IDS server when listening off channel. A recommended practice would be to also deploy some APs as full-time sensors. The integrated solution is a less expensive solution but may not have all the capabilities that are offered in an overlay WIDS.

Integration Enabled   Wi-Fi vendors often integrate their APs and management systems with the major WIDS vendors. The Wi-Fi vendor's APs integrate software code that can be used to turn the APs into sensors that will communicate with the third-party WIDS server. Standalone or controller-based APs can be converted into full-time sensors that gather security monitoring information for a separate third-party WIDS server.

Although all three of these WIDS architectures exist, the integrated WIDS is by far the most widely deployed. Overlay WIDS are usually cost prohibitive for most WLAN customers. The more robust overlay WIDS solutions are usually deployed in defense, finance, and retail vertical markets where the budget for an overlay solution may be available.

Wireless Intrusion Prevention System (WIPS)

Most WIDS vendors prefer to call their product a *wireless intrusion prevention system (WIPS)*. The reason that they prefer the term *prevention systems* is that they are all now capable of mitigating attacks from rogue APs and rogue clients. A WIPS characterizes access points and client radios in four or more classifications. Although various WIPS vendors use different terminology, some examples of classifications include the following:

Infrastructure Device   This classification refers to any client station or AP that is an authorized member of the company's wireless network. A network administrator can manually label each radio as an infrastructure device after detection from the WIPS or can import a list of all the company's WLAN radio MAC addresses into the system.

Unknown Device   The unknown device classification is assigned automatically to any new 802.11 radios that have been detected but not classified as a rogue or infrastructure device yet. Unknown devices are considered interfering devices and are usually investigated further to determine whether they are a valid infrastructure device, a neighbor's devices, or a potential future threat.

Known Device   This classification refers to any client station or AP that is detected by the WIPS and whose identity is known. A known device is initially considered an interfering device. The known device label is typically manually assigned by an administrator to radio devices of neighboring businesses that are not considered a threat.

Rogue Device   The rogue classification refers to any client station or AP that is considered an interfering device and a potential threat. Most WIPS define rogue APs as devices that are actually plugged into the network backbone and are not known or managed by the organization. Most of the WIPS vendors use a variety of proprietary methods of determining whether a rogue AP is actually plugged into the wired infrastructure.

Most WIPS vendors use different terminology when classifying devices. For example, some WIPSs classify all unauthorized devices as rogue devices, whereas other WIPS solutions only assign the rogue classification to APs or WLAN devices that have been detected with a connection to the wired network. After a client station or AP has been classified as a rogue device, the WIPS can effectively mitigate an attack. WIPS vendors have several ways of accomplishing this. One of the most common methods is to use spoofed deauthentication frames. As shown in Figure 14.12, the WIPS will have the sensors go active and begin transmitting deauthentication frames that spoof the MAC addresses of the rogue APs and rogue clients. The WIPS uses a known layer 2 denial-of-service attack as a countermeasure. The effect is that communications between the rogue AP and clients are rendered useless. This countermeasure can be used to disable rogue APs, individual client stations, and rogue ad hoc networks.

FIGURE 14.12   Wireless rogue containment

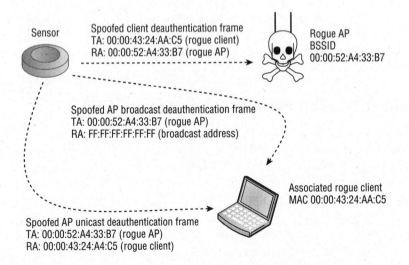

Many WIPS also use a wired-side termination process to effectively mitigate rogue devices. The wired-side termination method of rogue mitigation uses the Simple Network Management Protocol (SNMP) for *port suppression*. Many WIPSs can determine that the rogue AP is connected to the wired infrastructure and may be able to use SNMP to disable the managed switch port that is connected to the rogue AP. If the switch port is closed, the attacker cannot access network resources that are behind the rogue AP.

The WIPS vendors have other proprietary methods of disabling rogue APs and client stations, and often their methods are not published. Currently, the main purpose of a WIPS is to contain and disable rogue devices. In the future, other wireless attacks might be mitigated as well.

 Real World Scenario

Will a WIPS Protect against All Known Rogue Devices?

The simple answer is no. Although wireless intrusion prevention systems are outstanding products that can mitigate most rogue attacks, some rogue devices will go undetected. The radios inside the WIPS sensors typically monitor the 2.4 GHz ISM band and the 5 GHz U-NII frequencies. Channel 165 of the 5 GHz ISM band is also often monitored as well as some channels in the 4.9 GHz range, which is reserved for public safety in the United States but is a common channel band in Japan. Older legacy wireless networking equipment exists that transmits in the 900 MHz ISM band, and these devices will not be detected.

The radios inside the WIPS sensors also use only direct sequencing spread spectrum (DSSS) and Orthogonal Frequency Division Multiplexing (OFDM) technologies. Wireless networking equipment exists that uses frequency hopping spread spectrum (FHSS) transmissions in the 2.4 GHz ISM band and will also go undetected. The only tool that will 100 percent detect either a 900 MHz or frequency hopping rogue access point is a spectrum analyzer capable of operating in those frequencies.

Not all WIPS have spectrum analysis capabilities, although distributed spectrum analysis is becoming more common. Even if a WIPS has spectrum analysis capabilities, it can only perform spectrum analysis within a range of supported frequencies—typically the same frequencies that it monitors as a WIPS device. The WIPS should also monitor all the available channels and not just the ones permitted in your resident country.

Mobile WIDS

Several of the wireless intrusion detection/prevention vendors also sell laptop versions of their distributed products. The software program is a protocol analyzer capable of decoding frames with some layer 1 analysis capabilities as well. The mobile WIDS software uses a standard Wi-Fi client radio as the sensor. Most 802.11 protocol analyzer software offers standalone mobile security and performance analysis tools. The mobile WIDS will have many of the same policy, alarm, and detection capabilities as the vendor's distributed solution.

Think of a mobile WIDS as a single sensor, server, and console built into one unit. The mobile WIDS will be able to detect only attacks within its listening range, but the advantage is that the device is mobile. One useful feature of a mobile WIDS is that it can detect a rogue AP and client and then be used to track them down. The mobile WIDS locks onto the RF signal of the rogue device, and then an administrator can locate the transmitting rogue by using a directional antenna. Figure 14.13 shows a location feature, common in a mobile WIDS.

FIGURE 14.13   Mobile WIDS locator tool

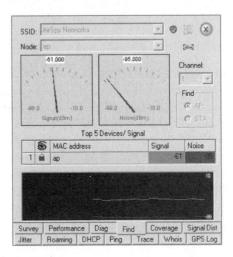

Spectrum Analyzer

In Chapter 15, "Radio Frequency Site Survey Fundamentals," and Chapter 16, "Site Survey Systems and Devices," we discuss the benefits of using a spectrum analyzer during a wireless site survey. WLAN administrators have also begun to realize the benefit of using spectrum analyzers for security purposes. The layer 2 WIDS vendors have long made claims that their products could detect layer 1 DoS attacks, namely, RF jamming. The truth of the matter is that the WIDS vendors are excellent at detecting all of the numerous layer 2 attacks but have limited success with layer 1 detection because the sensor radios are not spectrum analyzers.

A *spectrum analyzer* is a frequency domain tool that can detect any RF signal in the frequency range that is being scanned. A spectrum analyzer that monitors the 2.4 GHz ISM band will be able to detect both intentional jamming and unintentional jamming devices. Some spectrum analyzers can look at the RF signature of the interfering signal and classify the device. For example, the spectrum analyzer might identify the signal as a microwave oven, a Bluetooth transmitter, or an 802.11 FHSS radio. A spectrum analyzer might also be used to locate rogue 900 MHz or frequency hopping APs.

Two forms of spectrum analysis systems are available: mobile and distributed. Most spectrum analyzers are standalone mobile solutions; however, some WIPS vendors have begun to offer distributed spectrum analysis systems that use a centralized server and remote hardware spectrum analyzer cardbus sensors. Other WIPS vendors are providing distributed spectrum analysis by using the RF capabilities of the 802.11 radios already available in access points that function as sensors. A *distributed spectrum analysis system (DSAS)* is effectively a layer 1 wireless intrusion detection system that can detect and classify RF interference. The DSAS has the ability to categorize interference types based on frequency signatures. This can be useful to help classify and locate interfering devices. Most DSAS solutions use access points for the distributed spectrum analysis. Some vendor APs use an integrated spectrum analyzer card that operates independently from the 802.11 radio. Other vendor APs use the 802.11 radio to accomplish a lower grade of spectrum analysis.

Wireless Security Policy

In Chapter 13, you learned about the various authentication, encryption, and RBAC methods that can be used to secure an 802.11 wireless network. In this chapter, you have learned about wireless intrusion detection systems that can be used to monitor for possible threats. Securing a wireless network and monitoring for threats are absolute necessities, but both are worthless unless proper security policies are in place. What good is an 802.1X/EAP solution if the end users share their passwords? Why purchase an intrusion detection system if a policy has not been established on how to deal with rogue APs?

More and more businesses have started to amend their network usage policies to include a wireless policy section. If you have not done so already, a WLAN section should absolutely be added to the corporate security policy. Two good resources for learning about best practices and computer security policies are the SANS Institute and the National Institute of Standards and Technology (NIST).

Security policy templates from the SANS Institute can be downloaded from www.sans.org/resources/policies. You can download the NIST special publication document 800-48 regarding wireless security from http://csrc.nist.gov/publications/nistpubs.

General Security Policy

When establishing a wireless security policy, you must first define a *general policy*. A general wireless security policy establishes why a wireless security policy is needed for an organization. Even if a company has no plans for deploying a wireless network, there should be at a minimum a policy for how to deal with rogue wireless devices. A general wireless security policy defines the following items:

Statement of Authority   The statement of authority defines who put the wireless policy in place and the executive management that backs the policy.

Applicable Audience   The applicable audience is the audience to whom the policy applies, such as employees, visitors, and contractors.

Violation Reporting Procedures   Violation reporting procedures define how the wireless security policy will be enforced, including what actions should be taken and who is in charge of enforcement.

Risk Assessment and Threat Analysis   The risk assessment and threat analysis defines the potential wireless security risks and threats and what the financial impact will be on the company if a successful attack occurs.

Security Auditing   Internal auditing procedures, as well as the need for independent outside audits, should also be defined.

Functional Security Policy

A *functional policy* is also needed to define the technical aspects of wireless security. The functional security policy establishes how to secure the wireless network in terms of what solutions and actions are needed. A functional wireless security policy will define the following items:

Policy Essentials   Basic security procedures, such as password policies, training, and proper usage of the wireless network, are policy essentials and should be defined.

Baseline Practices   Baseline practices define minimum wireless security practices such as configuration checklists, staging and testing procedures, and so on.

Design and Implementation   The actual authentication, encryption, and segmentation solutions that are to be put in place are defined.

Monitoring and Response   All wireless intrusion detection procedures and the appropriate response to alarms are defined.

Legislative Compliance

In most countries, there are mandated regulations on how to protect and secure data communications within all government agencies. In the United States, NIST maintains the Federal Information Processing Standards (FIPS). Of special interest to wireless security is the FIPS 140-2 standard, which defines security requirements for cryptography modules. The use of validated cryptographic modules is required by the U.S. government for all unclassified communications. Other countries also recognize the FIPS 140-2 standard or have similar regulations.

In the United States, other legislation exists for protecting information and communications in certain industries. These include the following:

HIPAA   The Health Insurance Portability and Accountability Act (HIPAA) establishes national standards for electronic healthcare transactions and national standards for providers, health insurance plans, and employers. The goal is to protect patient information and maintain privacy.

Sarbanes-Oxley   The Sarbanes-Oxley Act of 2002 defines stringent controls on corporate accounting and auditing procedures with a goal of corporate responsibility and enhanced financial disclosure.

GLBA   The Gramm-Leach-Bliley Act (GLBA) requires banks and financial institutions to notify customers of policies and practices disclosing customer information. The goal is to protect personal information such as credit card numbers, Social Security numbers, names, addresses, and so forth.

Information about the FIPS regulations can be found at http://csrc.nist.gov/publications/fips. Learn more about HIPAA at www.hhs.gov/ocr/hipaa. You can find general information about Sarbanes-Oxley at www.sarbanes-oxley-101.com and about GLBA at www.ftc.gov.

PCI Compliance

As more of us rely on credit cards as our primary method of payment, more of us risk losing our card numbers to attackers and identity thieves through unsecure processing and/or storing of our cardholder information. The Payment Card Industry (PCI) realizes that in order to sustain continued business growth, measures must be taken to protect customer data and card numbers. The PCI Security Standards Council (SSC) has implemented regulations for organizations processing and storing cardholder information. This is commonly referred to as the PCI Standard. Within this standard are components governing the use of wireless devices. Visit these websites to learn more about the PCI standard:

www.pcisecuritystandards.org

www.pcisecuritystandards.org/pdfs/PCI_DSS_Wireless_Guidelines.pdf

802.11 Wireless Policy Recommendations

Although a detailed and thorough policy document should be created, we highly recommend these six wireless security policies:

BYOD Policy   Employees like to bring their personal Wi-Fi devices, such as tablets and smartphones, to the workplace. Employees usually expect to be able to use their personal Wi-Fi devices on the secure corporate WLAN. Each employer needs to define a *bring your own device (BYOD)* policy that clearly states how personal devices will be onboarded onto the secure corporate WLAN. The BYOD policy should also state how the personal devices can be used while connected to the company WLAN and which corporate network resources are accessible. BYOD is discussed in great detail in Chapter 20, "Bring Your Own Device."

Remote-Access WLAN Policy   End users take their laptops and handheld devices off site and away from company grounds. Most users likely use wireless networks at home and at wireless hotspots to access the Internet. By design, many of these remote wireless networks have absolutely no security in place, and it is imperative that a remote access WLAN policy be strictly enforced. This policy should include the required use of an IPsec or SSL VPN solution to provide device authentication, user authentication, and strong encryption of all wireless data traffic. Hotspots are prime targets for malicious eavesdropping attacks. Personal firewalls should also be installed on all remote computers to prevent peer-to-peer attacks. Personal firewalls will not prevent hijacking attacks or peer-to-peer attacks, but they will prevent attackers from accessing your most critical information. Endpoint WLAN policy-enforcement software solutions exist that force end users to use VPN and firewall security when accessing any wireless network other than the corporate WLAN. The remote access policy is mandatory because the most likely and vulnerable location for an attack to occur is at a public-access hotspot.

Rogue AP Policy   No end users should ever be permitted to install their own wireless devices on the corporate network. This includes APs, wireless routers, wireless hardware USB clients, and other WLAN NICs. Any users installing their own wireless equipment could open unsecured portals into the main infrastructure network. This policy should be strictly enforced.

Ad Hoc Policy   End users should not be permitted to set up ad hoc or peer-to-peer networks. Peer-to-peer networks are susceptible to peer attacks, and can serve as unsecured portals to the infrastructure network if the computer's Ethernet port is also in use.

Wireless LAN Proper Use Policy   A thorough policy should outline the proper use and implementation of the main corporate wireless network. This policy should include proper installation procedures, proper security implementations, and allowed application use on the wireless LAN.

IDS Policy   Policies should be written defining how to properly respond to alerts generated by the wireless intrusion detection system. An example would be how to deal with the discovery of rogue APs and all the necessary actions that should take place.

These six policies are simple but are a good starting point in writing a wireless security policy document.

Summary

In this chapter, we discussed all the potential wireless attacks and threats. The rogue access point has always been the biggest concern in terms of wireless threats, followed immediately by social engineering. We discussed many other serious threats, such as peer-to-peer attacks and eavesdropping, that can have consequences that are just as serious. We also discussed denial-of-service attacks that cannot be mitigated and can only be monitored. We covered the various solutions that are available for intrusion monitoring. Most intrusion detection solutions use a distributed client-server model, and some offer rogue prevention capabilities. Finally, we discussed the need for sound wireless security policies that will act as a foundation for the wireless security solutions that you implement.

Exam Essentials

Understand the risk of the rogue access point.   Be able to explain why the rogue AP provides a portal into network resources. Understand that employees are often the source of rogue APs.

Define peer-to-peer attacks.   Understand that peer-to-peer attacks can happen via an access point or through an ad hoc network. Explain how to defend against this type of attack.

Know the risks of eavesdropping.   Explain the difference between casual and malicious eavesdropping. Explain why encryption is needed for protection.

Define authentication and hijacking attacks.   Explain the risks behind these types of attacks. Understand that a strong 802.1X/EAP solution is needed to mitigate them.

Explain wireless denial-of-service attacks.   Know the difference between layer 1 and layer 2 DoS attacks. Explain why these attacks cannot be mitigated and can only be monitored.

Understand the types of wireless intrusion solutions.   Explain the difference between a WIDS and a WIPS. Understand that most solutions are distributed client-server models. Know the various components of an intrusion monitoring solution as well as the various models. Understand which attacks can be monitored and which can be prevented.

Understand the need for a wireless security policy.   Explain the difference between general and functional policies.

Review Questions

1. Which of these attacks are considered denial-of-service attacks? (Choose all that apply.)

   A. Man-in-the-middle

   B. Jamming

   C. Deauthentication spoofing

   D. MAC spoofing

   E. Peer-to-peer

2. Which of these attacks would be considered malicious eavesdropping? (Choose all that apply.)

   A. NetStumbler

   B. Peer-to-peer

   C. Protocol analyzer capture

   D. Packet reconstruction

   E. PS polling attack

3. Which of these attacks will not be detected by a wireless intrusion detection system (WIDS)?

   A. Deauthentication spoofing

   B. MAC spoofing

   C. Rogue access point

   D. Eavesdropping with a protocol analyzer

   E. Association flood

4. Which of these attacks can be mitigated with a mutual authentication solution? (Choose all that apply.)

   A. Malicious eavesdropping

   B. Deauthentication

   C. Man-in-the-middle

   D. Wireless hijacking

   E. Authentication flood

5. Select two types of rogue devices that cannot be detected by a layer 2 wireless intrusion prevention system (WIPS):

   A. 900 MHz radio

   B. 802.11h-compliant device

   C. FHSS radio

   D. 802.11b routers

   E. 802.11g mixed-mode device

6. When you're designing a wireless policy document, what two major areas of policy should be addressed?

   A. General policy

   B. Functional policy

   C. Rogue AP policy

   D. Authentication policy

   E. Physical security

7. What can happen when an intruder compromises the PSK or passphrase used during WPA/WPA2-Personal authentication? (Choose all that apply.)

   A. Decryption

   B. ASLEAP attack

   C. Spoofing

   D. Encryption cracking

   E. Access to network resources

8. Which of these attacks are considered layer 2 denial-of-service attacks? (Choose all that apply.)

   A. Deauthentication spoofing

   B. Jamming

   C. Virtual carrier attacks

   D. PS-Poll floods

   E. Authentication floods

9. Which of these can cause unintentional RF jamming attacks against an 802.11 wireless network? (Choose all that apply.)

   A. Microwave oven

   B. Signal generator

   C. 2.4 GHz cordless phones

   D. 900 MHz cordless phones

   E. Deauthentication transmitter

10. Which of these tools will best detect frequency hopping rogue devices? (Choose all that apply.)

   A. Standalone spectrum analyzer

   B. Distributed spectrum analyzer

   C. Distributed layer 2 WIDS

   D. Mobile layer 2 WIDS

   E. Layer 2 WIPS

11. Select two solutions that can help mitigate peer-to-peer attacks from other clients associated to the same 802.11 access point.

A. Personal firewall

B. Client isolation

C. OSPF

D. MAC filter

12. What type of solution can be used to perform countermeasures against a rogue access point?

A. WIDS

B. 802.1X/EAP

C. WIPS

D. TKIP/RC4

E. WINS

13. Select the four labels that a WIPS uses to classify an 802.11 device.

A. Infrastructure

B. Known

C. Enabled

D. Disabled

E. Rogue

F. Unknown

14. Scott is an administrator at the Williams Lumber Company, and his WIPS has detected a rogue access point. What actions should he take after the WIPS detects the rogue AP? (Choose the best two answers.)

A. Enable the layer 2 rogue containment feature that his WIPS provides.

B. Unplug the rogue AP from the electrical outlet upon discovery.

C. Call the police.

D. Call his mother.

E. Unplug the rogue AP from the data port upon discovery.

15. Which of these attacks are wireless users susceptible to at a public-access hotspot? (Choose all that apply.)

A. Wi-Fi phishing

B. Happy AP attack

C. Peer-to-peer attack

D. Malicious eavesdropping

E. 802.11 sky monkey attack

F. Man-in-the-middle

G. Wireless hijacking

16. Select two components that should be mandatory in every remote access wireless security policy.

A. Encrypted VPN

B. 802.1X/EAP

C. Personal firewall

D. Captive portal

E. Wireless stun gun

17. MAC filters are typically considered to be a weak security implementation because of what type of attack?

A. Spamming

B. Spoofing

C. Phishing

D. Cracking

E. Eavesdropping

18. Which WIDS architecture is the most commonly deployed?

A. Integrated

B. Overlay

C. Access distribution

D. Edge distribution

E. Overlay enabled

19. Which of these encryption technologies have been cracked? (Choose all that apply.)

A. 64-bit WEP

B. TKIP/RC4

C. CCMP/AES

D. 128-bit WEP

E. Wired Equivalent Privacy

20. What is another name for a wireless hijacking attack?

A. Wi-Fi phishing

B. Man-in-the-middle

C. Fake AP

D. Evil twin

E. AirSpy

Chapter 15

Radio Frequency Site Survey Fundamentals

IN THIS CHAPTER, YOU WILL LEARN ABOUT THE FOLLOWING:

✓ **WLAN site survey interview**

- Customer briefing
- Business requirements
- Capacity and coverage requirements
- Existing wireless network
- Infrastructure connectivity
- Security expectations
- Guest access

✓ **Documentation and reports**

- Forms and customer documentation
- Deliverables
- Additional reports

✓ **Vertical market considerations**

- Outdoor surveys
- Aesthetics
- Government
- Education
- Healthcare
- Hotspots
- Retail
- Warehouses
- Manufacturing
- Multitenant buildings

Chapter 16, "Site Survey Systems and Devices," discusses wireless site surveys from a technical perspective. You will learn about all the procedures and tools required for proper coverage, spectrum, and capacity planning. In this chapter, however, we discuss the wireless site survey from an administrative perspective. Much preparation must take place before the WLAN site survey is conducted. The needs of the WLAN must be predetermined and the proper questions must be asked.

In this chapter, we cover all the necessary preparations for the site survey and the documentation that must be assembled prior to it. We also discuss all the final reports that are delivered upon completion of the WLAN site survey. Finally, we outline unique wireless site survey considerations that should be given to different vertical markets.

WLAN Site Survey Interview

Is a site survey even needed? The answer to that question is almost always a resounding *yes*. If an owner of a small retail flower shop desires a wireless network, the site survey that is conducted may be as simple as placing a small office, home office (SOHO) Wi-Fi router in the middle of the shop, turning the transmit power to a lower setting, and making sure you have connectivity. Performing a site survey in a medium or large business entails much more physical work and time. Before the actual survey is conducted, a proper *site survey interview* should occur to both educate the customer and properly determine their needs.

Asking the correct questions during a site survey interview not only ensures that the proper tools are used during the survey, it also makes the survey more productive. Most important, the end result of a thorough interview and thorough survey will be a WLAN that meets all the intended mobility, coverage, and capacity needs. The following sections cover the questions that should be thoughtfully considered during the site survey interview.

Customer Briefing

Even though 802.11 technologies have been around since 1997, much misunderstanding and misinformation about wireless networking still exists. Because many businesses and individuals are familiar with Ethernet networks, a "just plug it in and turn it on" mentality is prevalent. If a wireless network is being planned for your company or for a prospective client, it is highly recommended that you sit management down, give them an overview of 802.11 wireless networking, and talk with them about how and why site surveys are conducted.

You do not need to explain the inner workings of orthogonal frequency division multiplexing or the Distributed Coordination Function; however, a conversation about the advantages of Wi-Fi, as well as the limitations of a WLAN, is a good idea.

There is a good chance that the company already has a WLAN and the customer briefing is about an upgrade to the existing WLAN. However, a brief explanation about the advantages of mobility would be an excellent start for a customer that is looking to deploy Wi-Fi for the very first time. Chances are that a wireless network is already being considered because the company's end users have requested wireless access to the company network using their own personal devices such as smartphones and tablets.

Just as important is a discussion about the bandwidth and throughput capabilities of 802.11a/b/g/n/ac technology. Enterprise users are accustomed to 100 Mbps full-duplex or better speeds on the wired network. Because of vendor hype, people often believe that a Wi-Fi network will automatically provide them with similar bandwidth and throughput. Management will need to be educated that because of overhead, the aggregate throughput of a WLAN is 50 percent to 70 percent of the advertised data rate.

It should also be explained that the medium is a half-duplex shared medium and not full-duplex. The average customer usually has many misconceptions in regard to WLAN bandwidth versus actual throughput. The advent of 802.11n and now 802.11ac WLAN equipment has addressed greater throughput needs, thus making the bandwidth/throughput conversation less painful.

Another appropriate discussion is why a site survey is needed. A very brief explanation on how RF signals propagate and attenuate will provide management with a better understanding of why an RF site survey is needed to ensure the proper coverage and enhance performance. A discussion and comparison of a 2.4 GHz vs. a 5 GHz WLAN might also be necessary. If management is properly briefed on the basics of Wi-Fi as well as the importance of a site survey, the forthcoming technical questions will be answered in a more suitable fashion.

Business Requirements

The first question that should be posed is, What is the purpose of the WLAN? If you have a complete understanding of the intended use of a wireless network, the result will be a better-designed WLAN. For example, a VoWiFi network has very different requirements than a heavily used data network. If the purpose of the WLAN is only to provide users a gateway to the Internet, security and integration recommendations will be different. A warehouse environment with 200 handheld scanners is very different from an office environment. A hospital's wireless network will have different business requirements than an airport's wireless network. Here are some of the business requirement questions that should be asked:

What applications will be used over the WLAN?   This question could have both capacity and quality of service (QoS) implications. A wireless network for graphic designers moving huge graphics files across the WLAN would obviously need more bandwidth than a wireless network for nothing but wireless bar code scanners. If time-sensitive applications such as voice or video are required, legacy proprietary QoS needs might have to be addressed, and standardized 802.11e/WMM solutions will need to be deployed to meet these QoS needs.

Who will be using the WLAN?   Different types of users have different capacity and performance needs. Users may also need to be separated for organizational purposes. Groups of users might be segmented into separate SSIDs and VLANs or even segmented by different frequencies. This is also an important consideration for security roles.

What types of devices will be connecting to the WLAN?   Will employees be allowed to connect their personal devices to the network? Does the company have a *bring your own device (BYOD)* strategy and is a *mobile device management (MDM)* solution needed? Handheld wireless barcode scanners may also be segmented into separate VLANs or by frequency. VoWiFi phones are always put in a separate VLAN than data users with laptops. Many handheld devices use older 802.11b or 802.11g radios and can transmit in only the 2.4 GHz ISM band. The capabilities of the devices may also force decisions in security, frequency, technology, and data rates.

We discuss the varying business requirements of different vertical markets later in this chapter. Defining the purpose of the WLAN in advance will lead to a more productive site survey and is imperative to the eventual design of the WLAN.

Capacity and Coverage Requirements

After the purpose of the WLAN has been clearly defined, the next step is to begin asking all the necessary questions for planning the site survey and designing the wireless network. Although the final design of a WLAN is completed after the site survey is conducted, some preliminary design based on the *capacity* and *coverage* needs of the customer is recommended. You will need to sit down with a copy of the building's floor plan and ask the customer where they want RF coverage. The answer will almost always be everywhere. If a VoWiFi deployment is planned, that answer is probably legitimate because VoWiFi phones will need mobility and connectivity throughout the building. Furthermore, because of the proliferation of mobile devices such as smartphones and tablets, broad coverage is usually a necessity.

However, the need for blanket coverage might not be necessary. Do laptop data users need access in a storage area? Do they need connectivity in the outdoor courtyard? Do handheld bar code scanners used in a warehouse area need access in the front office? The answer to these questions will often vary depending on the earlier questions that were asked regarding the purpose of the WLAN. However, if you can determine that certain areas of the facility do not require coverage, you will save the customer money and yourself time when conducting the physical survey.

Considering the Proliferation of Wireless Devices

The recent Wi-Fi client population explosion usually dictates that RF coverage be wide-ranging throughout most buildings and locations. In the past, Wi-Fi networks were mostly used to provide access to laptop users. In recent years, an unbridled growth in mobile devices with Wi-Fi radios has occurred. Consider all the mobile devices, such as iPhones, iPads, and Android phones and tablets. Wi-Fi radios are now a common component in most smartphones, tablets, scanners, and many other mobile devices. Although mobile devices initially were intended for personal use, most employees now use them in the corporate workplace as well. Employees now have expectations of being able to connect to a corporate WLAN with multiple personal mobile devices. Because of the proliferation of personal mobile devices, a bring your own device (BYOD) policy is needed to define how employees' personal devices may access the corporate WLAN. A mobile device management (MDM) solution might also be needed for onboarding both personal mobile devices and company issued devices (CIDs) onto the WLAN. BYOD strategies and MDM solutions are discussed in great detail in Chapter 20, "Bring Your Own Device."

Depending on the layout and the materials used inside the building, some preplanning might need to be done as to what type of antennas to use in certain areas of the facility. A high-density area may require semidirectional patch antennas for sectorized coverage as opposed to using omnidirectional antennas. When the survey is performed, this will be confirmed or adjusted accordingly.

The most often neglected aspect prior to the site survey is determining capacity needs of the WLAN. As mentioned in Chapter 11, "WLAN Deployment and Vertical Markets," you must not just consider coverage; you must also plan for capacity. Cell sizing for a high-density WLAN design might be necessary to properly address your capacity requirements. In order for the wireless end user to experience acceptable performance, a ratio of average number of users per access point must be established. The answer to the capacity question depends on a host of variables, including answers to earlier questions about the purpose of the WLAN. Capacity will not be as big of a concern in a warehouse environment using mostly handheld data scanners. However, if the WLAN has average to heavy data requirements, capacity will absolutely be a concern. The following are among the many factors that need to be considered when planning for capacity:

Data Applications   The applications that are used will have a direct impact on the number of Wi-Fi devices that should be communicating on average through an access point. So the next question is, what is a good average number of connected devices per access point? Once again, it depends entirely on the purpose of the WLAN and the applications being used. However, in an 802.11a/b/g/n network, 35–50 data WLAN devices per radio is an often-quoted figure for typical WLAN applications such as web browsing and email. Many WLAN vendors' marketing material states that 100 or 200 devices can connect to an 802.11n access point at the same time. Although more than a hundred devices might be able to connect to an AP radio, these numbers are not realistic for active devices due to the nature of the half-duplex shared medium. 35 to 50 active Wi-Fi devices per radio on a dual-frequency 802.11n access point is realistic with average application use, such as web browsing. 802.11ac access points can provide for a greater number of active connections and might be a viable solution in areas with a high density of users and devices.

User and Device Density   Three important questions need to be asked with regard to users. First, how many users currently need wireless access and how many Wi-Fi devices will they be using? Second, how many users and devices may need wireless access in the future? These first two questions will help you to begin adequately planning for a good ratio of devices per access point while allowing for future growth. The third question of great significance is, Where are the users? Sit down with network management and indicate on the floor plan of the building any areas of high user density. For example, one company might have offices with only 1 or 2 people per room, whereas another company might have 30 or more people in a common area separated by cubicle walls. Other examples of areas with high user density are call centers, classrooms, and lecture halls. Plan to conduct the physical survey when the users are present and not during off-hours. A high concentration of human bodies can attenuate the RF signal because of absorption.

Peak On/Off Use   Be sure to ask what the peak times are—that is, when access to the WLAN is heaviest. For example, a conference room might be used only once a day or once a month. Certain applications might be heavily accessed through the WLAN at specified times. Another peak period could be when one shift leaves and another arrives.

Existing Transmitters   This does not refer just to previously installed 802.11 networks. Rather, it refers to interfering devices such as microwaves, cordless headsets, cordless phones, wireless machinery, and so on. Often, this is severely overlooked. If a large open area will house the help desk after the wireless is installed, you may be thinking of capacity. However, if you don't know that the employees are using 2.4 GHz cordless headsets or Bluetooth keyboards and mice, you may be designing a network destined for failure.

Portability vs. Mobility   There are two types of mobility. The first is related to being portable and the other is true mobility. To help explain this, think of a marketing manager working on a presentation and saving it on a network share. He later wants to give that presentation in the boardroom. If he picks up his laptop, closes the lid, and walks to the conference room, where he opens the laptop, connects to the wireless network, and gives his presentation, that is being portable. He may have disconnected in between access points, and that is okay.

However, having true mobility means that a user remains connected 100 percent of the time while traveling through the facility. This would be indicative of VoWiFi or warehouse scanning applications. As mentioned earlier, most users now carry some sort of personal mobile device, such as a smartphone; therefore, true mobility is almost always an understood requirement.

Determining which type of connectivity is necessary can be key for not only troubleshooting an existing network but also for designing a new one.

Backward Compatibility for Legacy Devices It should be understood in advance that if there is any requirement for backward compatibility with legacy clients, the 802.11 protection mechanisms will always adversely affect throughput. The impact of protection mechanisms is not as severe on an 802.11n network, but it can be significant on a legacy 802.11b/g network. Enterprise deployments will almost always require some level of backward compatibility to provide access for older 802.11a/b/g radios found in handhelds, VoWiFi phones, or older laptops. Many handheld mobile devices, such as older barcode scanners, still do not have 802.11n radios and backward compatibility will be required.

Carefully planning coverage and capacity needs prior to the site survey will help you determine some of the design scenarios you might need, including AP power settings, types of antennas, and cell sizes. The physical site survey will still have to be conducted to validate and further determine coverage and capacity requirements.

 Real World Scenario

How Many Simultaneous VoWiFi Telephone Calls Can an Access Point Support?

Several factors come into play, including cell bandwidth, average use, and vendor specifics. When deploying over 5 GHz, WLAN vendor, Cisco, recommends a maximum of 27 simultaneous bidirectional voice calls when connected at 24 Mbps or higher. Because of medium contention, that number drops to a recommended maximum of 20 calls when connected at 12 Mbps. Different vendor-specific access point characteristics can also affect the number of concurrent calls, and extensive testing is recommended. Probability models also exist for predicting VoWiFi traffic. Not every Wi-Fi phone user will be making a call at the same time. Probabilistic traffic formulas use a telecommunications unit of measurement known as an *Erlang*. An Erlang is equal to 1 hour of telephone traffic in 1 hour of time. Some online VoWiFi Erlang traffic calculators can be found at www.erlang.com

---

Existing Wireless Network

Quite often the reason you are conducting a WLAN site survey is that you have been called in as a consultant to fix an existing deployment. Professional site survey companies have reported that as much as 40 percent of their business is troubleshooting existing WLANs, which often requires conducting a second site survey or discovering that one was never conducted to begin with.

As more corporations and individuals become educated in 802.11 technologies, the percentage will obviously drop. Sadly, many untrained integrators or customers just install the access points wherever they can mount them and leave the default power and channel settings on every AP. Usually, site surveys must be conducted either because of performance problems or difficulty roaming. Performance problems are often caused by RF interference, low SNR, adjacent cell interference, or cochannel cooperation. Roaming problems may also be interference related or caused by a lack of adequate coverage and/or by a lack of proper duplicate cell coverage for roaming. Here are some of the questions that should be asked prior to the reparative site survey:

What are the current problems with the existing WLAN?   Ask the customer to clarify the problems. Are they throughput related? Are there frequent disconnects? Is there any difficulty roaming? In what part of the building do the problems occur most often? Is the problem happening with one WLAN device or multiple devices? How often do the problems occur, and have any steps been taken to duplicate the troubles?

Are there any known sources of RF interference?   More than likely the customer will have no idea, but it does not hurt to ask. Are there any microwave ovens? Do people use cordless phones or headsets? Does anyone use Bluetooth for keyboards or mice? After asking these interference questions, you should always perform a spectrum analysis, which is the *only* way to determine whether there is any RF interference in the area that may inhibit future transmissions.

Are there any known coverage dead zones?   This is related to the roaming questions, and areas probably exist where proper coverage is not being provided. Remember, this could be too little or too much coverage. Both create roaming and connectivity problems.

Does prior site survey data exist?   Chances are that an original site survey was not even conducted. However, if old site survey documentation exists, it may be helpful when troubleshooting existing problems. It is important to note that unless quantifiable data was collected that shows dBm strengths, the survey report should be viewed with extreme caution.

What equipment is currently installed?   Ask what type of equipment is being used, such as 802.11a (5 GHz) or 802.11b/g (2.4 GHz), and which vendor has been used. Is the customer looking to upgrade to an 802.11n or 802.11ac network? Once again, the customer might have no idea, and it will be your job to determine what has been installed and why it is not working properly. Also check the configurations of the devices, including service set identifiers (SSIDs), WEP or WPA keys, channels, power levels, and firmware versions. Often issues can be as simple as all the access points are transmitting on the same channel or there is a buffer issue that can be resolved with the latest firmware update.

Depending on the level of troubleshooting that is required on the existing wireless network, a second site survey consisting of coverage and spectrum analysis will often be necessary. After the new site survey has been conducted, adjustments to the existing WLAN equipment typically are adequate. However, the worst-case scenario would involve a complete redesign of the WLAN. Keep in mind that whenever a second site survey is necessary, all the same questions that are asked as part of a survey for a new installation (Greenfield survey) should also be asked prior to the second site survey. If wireless usage requirements have changed, a redesign might be the best course of action.

Infrastructure Connectivity

You have already learned that the usual purposes of a WLAN are to provide client mobility and to provide access via an AP into a preexisting wired network infrastructure. Part of the interview process includes asking the correct questions so that the WLAN will integrate properly into the existing wired architecture. Asking for a copy of the wired network topology map is highly recommended.

For security reasons, the customer may not want to disclose the wired topology, and you may need to sign a nondisclosure agreement. It is a good idea to request that an agreement be signed to protect you legally as the integrator. Be sure that someone in your organization with the authority to sign finalizes the agreement.

Understanding the existing topology will also be of help when planning WLAN segmentation and security proposals and recommendations. With or without a topology map, the following topics are important to ensure the desired infrastructure connectivity:

Roaming   Is roaming required? In most cases, the answer will be *yes*, because mobility is a key advantage of wireless networking. Any devices that run connection-oriented applications will need seamless roaming. Seamless roaming is mandatory if handheld devices and/or VoWiFi phones are deployed. With the advent of smartphones and tablets, most end users expect mobility. Providing for secure seamless roaming is pretty much an afterthought.

It should also be understood that there might be certain areas where the WLAN was designed so that roaming is a very low priority, such as areas with a high density of users. For example, a gymnasium filled with 800 people might have APs on the ceiling with MIMO patch antennas to provide for unidirectional sectorized coverage. This is a WLAN design with high density as the priority, as opposed to mobility and roaming.

Another important roaming consideration is whether users will need to roam across layer 3 boundaries. A Mobile IP solution or a proprietary layer 3 roaming solution will be needed if client stations need to roam across subnets. Special consideration has to be given to roaming with VoWiFi devices because of the issues that can arise from network latency. With regard to the existing network, it is imperative that you determine whether the wired network infrastructure will support all the new wireless features. For instance, if you want to roll out three SSIDs with different VLANs but haven't checked to see if the customer's network switches can be configured with VLANs, you may have a serious problem.

Wiring Closets   Where are the wiring closets located? Will the locations that are being considered for AP installation be within a 100-meter (328-foot) cable drop from the wiring closets?

Antenna Structure   If an outdoor network or point-to-point bridging application is requested, some additional structure might have to be built to mount the antennas. Asking for building diagrams of the roof to locate structural beams and existing roof penetrations is a good idea. Depending on the weight of the installation, you may also need to consult a structural engineer.

Switches   Will the access points be connected by category 5 (CAT5) cabling to unmanaged switches or managed switches? CAT5e or higher grade cabling is usually needed to maximize 802.3af PoE. An unmanaged switch will only support a single VLAN. A managed switch will be needed if multiple VLANs are required. Are there enough switch ports? What is the power budget of the switch? Who will be responsible for configuring the VLANs?

PoE   How will the access points be powered? Because APs are often mounted in the ceiling, Power over Ethernet (PoE) will likely be required to remotely power the access points. Very often the customer will not yet have a PoE solution in place, and further investment will be needed. If the customer already does have a PoE solution installed, it must be determined whether the PoE solution is compliant with 802.3af or 802.3at (PoE Plus). Also, is the solution an endpoint or midspan solution? If the customer is migrating toward a future 802.11ac deployment of access points, more power will be needed and 802.3at power sourcing equipment will be necessary.

Regardless of what the customer has, it is important to make sure that it is compatible with the system you are proposing to install. If PoE injectors need to be installed, you will need to make sure there are sufficient power outlets. If not you, who will be responsible for installing those? If you are installing 802.11ac access points, they may require an 802.3at PoE Plus solution to properly power all MIMO radios.

Segmentation   How will the WLAN and/or users of the WLAN be segmented from the wired network? Will the entire wireless network be on a separate IP subnet tied to unique VLANs? Will VLANs be used, and is a guest VLAN necessary? Will firewalls or VPNs be used for segmentation? Or will the wireless network be a natural extension to the wired network and follow the same wiring, VLAN numbering, and design schemes as the wired infrastructure? All these questions are also directly related to security expectations.

Naming Convention   Does the customer already have a naming convention for cabling and network infrastructure equipment, and will one need to be created for the WLAN?

User Management   Considerations regarding RBAC, bandwidth throttling, and load balancing should be discussed. Do they have an existing RADIUS server or does one need to be installed? What type of LDAP user database is being used? Where will usernames and passwords be stored? Will usernames and passwords be used for authentication, or will they be using client certificates? Will guest user access be provided?

Device Management   Will employees be allowed to access the WLAN with their own personal devices? How will personal and company-issued mobile devices be managed? Do they want to provide different levels of access based upon device type, such as, for example, smartphone, tablet, personal laptop, or corporate laptop? A BYOD strategy may be needed, as well as an MDM solution.

Infrastructure Management   How will the WLAN remote access points be managed? Is a central management solution a requirement? Will devices be managed using SSH2, SNMP, or HTTP/HTTPS? Do they have standard credentials that they would like to use to access these management interfaces?

A comprehensive site interview that provides detailed feedback about infrastructure connectivity requirements will result in a more thorough site survey and a well-designed wireless network. Seventy-five percent of the work for a good wireless network is in the pre-engineering. It creates the road map for all the other pieces.

Security Expectations

Network management personnel should absolutely be interviewed about security expectations. All data privacy and encryption needs should be discussed. All AAA requirements must be documented. It should be determined whether the customer plans to implement a wireless intrusion detection or prevention system (WIDS or WIPS) for protection against rogue APs and the many other types of wireless attacks. Older devices may not support fast secure roaming mechanisms, and 802.1X/EAP might not be an option for those devices.

A comprehensive interview regarding security expectations will provide the necessary information to make competent security recommendations after the site survey has been conducted and prior to deployment. Industry-specific regulations such as the Health Insurance Portability and Accountability Act (HIPAA), Gramm-Leach-Bliley, and Payment Card Industry (PCI) may have to be taken into account when making security recommendations. U.S. government installations may have to abide by the strict Federal Information Processing Standards (FIPS) 140-2 regulations, and all security solutions may need to be FIPS compliant.

All of these answers should also assist in determining whether the necessary hardware and software exists to perform these functions. If not, it will be your job to consider the requirements and recommendations that may be necessary.

Guest Access

Because of the widespread acceptance of Wi-Fi in business environments, most companies offer some sort of wireless guest access to the Internet. Guest users access the WLAN via the same access points. However, they usually connect via a guest SSID that redirects the guest users to a captive portal. The guest captive portal serves two purposes:

- The login screen forces guest users to accept the corporate legal disclaimer.
- After logging in, the guest users are provided with a gateway to the Internet.

It should be noted that all users who connect with the guest SSID should be allowed to go only to the Internet gateway and should be properly segmented from all other network resources in a separate guest VLAN. Firewall restrictions and bandwidth throttling are also common when deploying guest WLANs. Another topic of conversation is who will manage the guest network. Guest user management is discussed in great detail in Chapter 20.

Documents and Reports

During the site survey interview (and prior to the site survey), proper documentation about the facility and network must be obtained. Additionally, site survey checklists should be created and adhered to during the physical survey. After the physical survey is performed, you will deliver to the customer a professional and comprehensive final report. Additional reports and customer recommendations may also be included with the final report. This report should provide detailed instructions on how to install and configure the proposed network so that anyone could read the report and understand your intent.

Forms and Customer Documentation

Before the site survey interview, you must obtain some critical documentation from the customer:

Blueprints You need a floor plan layout in order to discuss coverage and capacity needs with network administration personnel. As discussed earlier in this chapter, while reviewing floor plan layouts, keep in mind that capacity and coverage requirements will be preplanned. Photocopies of the floor plan will also need to be created and used to record the RF measurements that are taken during the physical site survey, as well as to record the locations of hardware placement. Some software survey tools allow you to import floor plans, and the software will record the survey results on the floor plan for you. Figure 15.1 is an example of a typical floor plan. These are highly recommended and make the final report much easier to compile.

What if the customer does not have a set of blueprints? Blueprints can be located via a variety of sources. The original architect of the building will probably still have a copy of the blueprints. Many public and private buildings' floor plans might also be located at a public government resource such as city hall or the fire department. Businesses are usually required to post a fire escape plan. Many site surveys have been conducted using a simple fire escape plan that has been drawn to scale if blueprints cannot be located. In a worst-case scenario, you may have to use some graph paper and map out the floor plan manually. In Chapter 16, "Site Survey Systems and Devices," we discuss RF modeling software that can be used to create predictive capacity and coverage simulations. Predictive analysis tools require detailed information about building materials that may be found in blueprints. Blueprints may already be in a vector graphic format (with the filename extensions .dwg and .dwf) for importing into a predictive analysis application, or they may have to be scanned.

FIGURE 15.1   Typical Floor Plan

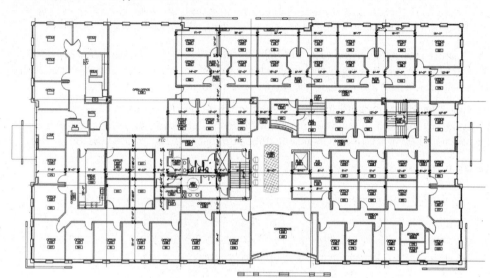

Topographic Map   If an outdoor site survey is planned, a topographic map, also called a *contour map*, will be needed. Contour maps display terrain information, such as elevations, forest cover, and the locations of streams and other bodies of water. Figure 15.2 depicts a typical topographic map. A topographic map will be a necessity when performing bridging calculations, such as Fresnel zone clearance.

Network Topology Map   Understanding the layout of the customer's current wired network infrastructure will speed up the site survey process and allow for better planning of the WLAN during the design phase. A computer network topology map will provide necessary information such as the location of the wiring closets and layer 3 boundaries. The WLAN topology will be integrated as seamlessly as possible into the wired infrastructure. VLANs will normally be used for segmentation for both the wired and wireless networks.

Acquiring a network topology map from the customer is a highly recommended practice that will result in a well-designed and properly integrated WLAN. Some organizations may not wish to reveal their wired network topology for security reasons. It may be necessary to obtain security clearance and/or sign nondisclosure agreements to gain access to these documents.

Security Credentials   You might need proper security authorization to access facilities when conducting the site survey. Hospitals, government facilities, and many businesses require badges, passes, and maybe even an escort for entrance into certain areas. A meeting with security personnel and/or the facilities manager in advance of the survey will be necessary in order to meet all physical security requirements. You do not want to show up at the customer site and be asked to return at another time because somebody forgot to schedule a security escort. Regardless of the security requirements, it is always a good idea to have the network administrator alert everyone that you will be in the area.

As a site survey professional, you will have created your own documentation or necessary checklists that will be used during the site survey interview as well as during the actual physical survey. There are several types of survey checklists:

Interview Checklist A detailed checklist containing all the questions to be asked during the site survey interview should be created in advance. The many detailed interview questions discussed earlier in this chapter will all be outlined in the interview checklist.

FIGURE 15.2 Topographic map

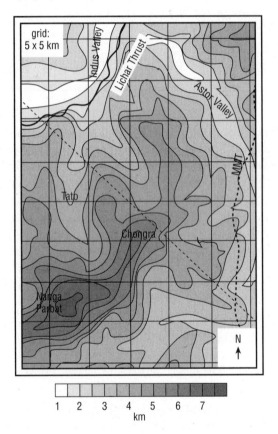

Installation Checklist Many site survey professionals prefer to record all installation details on the floor plan documents. An installation checklist detailing hardware placement and mounting for each individual access point is also an option. Information about AP location, antenna type, antenna orientation, mounting devices, and power sources may be logged.

Equipment Checklist   For organizational purposes, a checklist of all the hardware and software tools used during the survey might also be a good idea. All the necessary tools needed for both indoor and outdoor site surveys are covered in Chapter 16.

Deliverables

After the interview process has been completed and the survey has been conducted, a final report must be delivered to the customer. Information gathered during the site survey will be organized and formatted into a professional technical report for the customer's review. Compiled information contained in the *deliverables* will include the following:

Purpose Statement   The final report should begin with a WLAN purpose statement that stipulates the customer requirements and business justification for the WLAN.

Spectrum Analysis   Be sure to identify potential sources of interference.

RF Coverage Analysis   Define RF cell boundaries.

Hardware Placement and Configuration   Recommend AP placement, antenna orientation, channel reuse pattern, power settings, and any other AP-specific information such as installation techniques and cable routing.

Capacity and Performance Analysis   Include results from application throughput testing, which is sometimes an optional analysis report included with the final survey report.

Chapter 16 covers in detail the methods and tools used to compile all the necessary analytical information that belongs in the final report. A detailed site survey report may be hundreds of pages, depending on the size of the facility. Site survey reports often include pictures that were taken with a digital camera during the survey. Pictures can be used to record AP placement, as well as to identify problems such as interfering RF devices or potential installation problems such as a solid ceiling or concrete walls. Professional site survey software applications exist that also generate professional-quality reports using pre-formatted forms.

An example of a professional site survey report is included at the book's online resource area, which can be accessed at www.sybex.com/go/cwna4e. The site survey report was provided by Netrepid, a professional wireless services company. This Adobe PDF file is called sitesurvey.pdf.

Additional Reports

Along with the site survey report, other recommendations will be made to the customer so that appropriate equipment and security are deployed. Usually, the individuals and/or company that performed the site survey are also hired for the installation of the wireless network. The customer, however, might use the information from the site survey report to conduct their own deployment. Regardless of who handles the installation work, other recommendations and reports will be provided along with the site survey report:

Vendor Recommendations   Many enterprise wireless vendors exist in the marketplace. It is a highly recommended practice to conduct the site survey using equipment from the same vendor who will supply the equipment that will later be deployed on site. Although the IEEE has set standards in place to ensure interoperability, every Wi-Fi vendor's equipment operates in some sort of proprietary fashion. You have already learned that many aspects of roaming are proprietary. The mere fact that every vendor's radios use proprietary RSSI thresholds is reason enough to stick with the same vendor during surveying and installation. Many site survey professionals have different vendor kits for the survey work. It is not unheard of for a survey company to conduct two surveys with equipment from two different vendors and present the customer with two separate options. However, the interview process will usually determine in advance the vendor recommendations that will be made to the customer.

Implementation Diagrams   Based on information collected during the site survey, a final design diagram will be presented to the customer. The implementation diagram is basically a wireless topology map that illustrates where the access points will be installed and how the wireless network will be integrated into the existing wired infrastructure. AP placement, VLANs, and layer 3 boundaries will all be clearly defined.

Bill of Materials   Along with the implementation diagrams will be a detailed *bill of materials (BOM)* that itemizes every hardware and software component necessary for the final installation of the wireless network. The model number and quantity of each piece of equipment will be necessary. This includes access points, bridges, wireless switches, antennas, cabling, connectors, and lightning arrestors.

Project Schedule and Costs   A detailed deployment schedule should be drafted that outlines all timelines, equipment costs, and labor costs. Particular attention should be paid to the schedule dependencies, such as delivery times and licensing, if applicable.

Security Solution Recommendations   As mentioned earlier in this chapter, security expectations should be discussed during the site survey interview. Based on these discussions, the surveying company will make comprehensive wireless security recommendations. All aspects of authentication, authorization, accounting, encryption, and segmentation should be included in the security recommendations documentation.

Wireless Policy Recommendations   An addendum to the security recommendations might be corporate wireless policy recommendations. You might need to assist the customer in drafting a wireless network security policy if they do not already have one.

Training Recommendations   One of the most overlooked areas when deploying new solutions is proper training. It is highly recommended that wireless administration and security training sessions be scheduled with the customer's network personnel. Additionally, condensed training sessions should be scheduled with all end users.

Vertical Market Considerations

No two site surveys will ever be exactly alike. Every business has its own needs, issues, and considerations when conducting a survey. Some businesses may require an outdoor site survey instead of an indoor survey. A vertical market is a particular industry or group of businesses in which similar products or services are developed and marketed. The following sections outline the distinctive subjects that must be examined when a WLAN is being considered in specialized vertical markets.

Outdoor Surveys

Some of the focus of this book and the CWNA exam is on outdoor site surveys for establishing bridge links. Calculations necessary for outdoor bridging surveys are numerous, including the Fresnel zone, earth bulge, free space path loss, link budget, and fade margin. However, outdoor site surveys for the purpose of providing general outdoor wireless access for users are becoming more commonplace. As the popularity of wireless mesh networking continues to grow, outdoor wireless access has become more commonplace. Outdoor site survey kits using outdoor mesh APs will be needed.

Weather conditions, such as lightning, snow and ice, heat, and wind, must also be contemplated. Most important is the apparatus that the antennas will be mounted to. Unless the hardware is designed for outdoor use, the outdoor equipment must ultimately be protected from the weather elements by using NEMA-rated enclosure units (*NEMA* stands for National Electrical Manufacturers Association) like the one pictured in Figure 15.3. NEMA weatherproof enclosures are available with a wide range of options, including heating, cooling, and PoE interfaces.

Safety is also a big concern for outdoor deployments. Consideration should be given to hiring professional installers. Certified tower climbing courses and tower safety and rescue training courses are available.

> Information about RF health and safety classes can be found at www.sitesafe .com. Also, tower climbing can be dangerous work. Information about tower climbing and safety training can be found at www.comtrainusa.com.

All RF power regulations, as defined by the regulatory body of your country, will need to be considered. If towers are to be used, you may have to contact several government agencies. Local and state municipalities may have construction regulations, and a permit is almost always required. In the United States, if any tower exceeds a height of 200 feet above ground level (AGL) or is within a certain proximity to an airport, both the FCC and Federal Aviation Administration (FAA) must be contacted. If a roof mount is to be installed that is greater than 20 feet above the highest roof level, the FCC and FAA may have to be consulted as well. Other countries have similar types of height restrictions, and you must contact the proper RF regulatory authority and aviation authority to find out the details.

FIGURE 15.3   NEMA enclosure

Photo courtesy of Netrepid, Inc.

Aesthetics

An important aspect of the installation of wireless equipment is the "pretty factor." Many businesses prefer that all wireless hardware remain completely out of sight. Aesthetics is extremely important in retail environments and in the hospitality industry (restaurants and hotels). Any business that deals with the public will require that the Wi-Fi hardware be hidden or at least secured. WLAN vendors continue to design more aesthetic-looking access points and antennas. Some vendors have even camouflaged access points to resemble smoke detectors. Indoor enclosures, like the one pictured in Figure 15.4, can also be used to conceal access points from sight. Most enclosure units can be locked to help prevent theft of expensive Wi-Fi hardware.

Government

The key concern during government wireless site surveys is security. When security expectations are addressed during the interview process, careful consideration should be given to all aspects of planned security. Many U.S. government agencies, including the military, require that all wireless solutions be FIPS 140-2 compliant. Other government agencies may require that the wireless network be completely shielded or shut off during certain times of the day. Be sure to check export restrictions before traveling to other countries with certain equipment. The United States forbids the export of AES encryption technology to some countries. Other countries have their own regulations and customs requirements.

FIGURE 15.4 Indoor enclosure

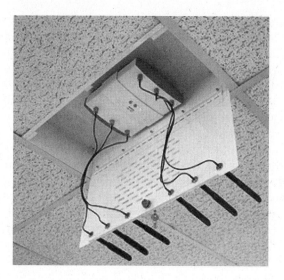

Photo courtesy of Netrepid, Inc.

Obtaining the proper security credentials will most likely be a requirement before conducting the government survey. An identification badge or pass often is required. In some government facilities, an escort is needed in certain sensitive areas.

Education

As with government facilities, obtaining the proper security credentials in an education environment usually is necessary. Properly securing access points in lockable enclosure units is also necessary to prevent theft or tampering. Because of the high concentration of students, user density should be accounted for during capacity and coverage planning. K–12 schools across the United States are implementing 1:1 iPad deployments, where every student in every classroom has access to an iPad tablet. Because of these 1:1 programs, it is not uncommon to deploy an access point in every classroom to meet the device density needs. More information about Apple and the education vertical market can be found at www.apple.com/education.

In campus environments, wireless access is required in most buildings, and very often bridging solutions are needed between buildings across the campus. Some older educational facilities were constructed in such a manner as to serve as disaster shelters. That means that propagation in these areas is limited. Most school buildings use dense wall materials such as cinderblock or brick to attenuate the sound between classrooms. These materials also heavily attenuate RF signals.

Healthcare

One of the biggest concerns in a healthcare environment is sources of interference from the biomedical equipment that exists on site. Many biomedical devices operate in the ISM bands. For example, cauterizing devices in operating rooms have been known to cause problems with wireless networks. There is also a concern with 802.11 radios possibly interfering with biomedical equipment.

A meeting will be necessary with the biomedical department that maintains and services all biomedical equipment. Some hospitals have a person responsible for tracking and monitoring all RF devices in the facility.

A thorough spectrum analysis survey using a spectrum analyzer is extremely important. We recommend that you conduct several sweeps of these areas and compare them to ensure the greatest probability of capturing all the possible interferers. Because of the many potential sources of interference in the 2.4 GHz ISM band, it is likely that 5 GHz hardware will be deployed in many areas. Often, the dense environments require 5 GHz simply because you will need more channel options to prevent co-channel interference. Hospitals are usually large in scale, and a site survey may take many weeks; a predictive site survey can save a lot of time. Long hallways, multiple floors, fire safety doors, reflective materials, concrete construction, lead-lined X-ray rooms, and wire mesh safety glass are some of the physical conditions that you will encounter during the survey.

The applications used in the medical environment should all be considered during the interview and the survey. Numerous healthcare applications now exist for handheld iOS and Android devices. Tablets and smartphones are being used by doctors and nurses to access these mobile applications. Mobile devices are also used to transfer large files, such as X-ray graphics. Medical carts use radios to transfer patient data back to the nursing stations. VoWiFi phone deployments are commonplace in hospitals because of the communication mobility that they provide to nurses. Wi-Fi real-time location systems (RTLSs) using active 802.11 RFID tags are commonplace in hospitals for asset management tracking. Because of the presence of medical patients, proper security credentials and/or an escort will often be necessary. Many applications are connection oriented, and drops in connectivity can be detrimental to the operation of these applications.

Hotspots

Hotspots continue to grow in popularity, and many businesses are looking to provide wireless Internet access for their customers. Many hotspots are small, and care should be taken to limit the RF coverage area by using a single access point at a lower power setting. However, some large facilities, such as airports and convention centers, have begun offering wireless access, and obviously multiple access points and wider coverage will be needed. Security solutions at hotspots are usually limited to a captive portal solution for user authentication against a customer database.

Retail

A retail environment often has many potential sources of 2.4 GHz interference. Store demonstration models of cordless phones, baby monitors, and other ISM band devices can cause problems. The inventory storage racks and bins and the inventory itself are all potential sources of multipath problems. Heavy user density should also be considered, and a retail site survey should be done in the height of the shopping season as opposed to late January when the malls are empty.

Wireless applications that are used in retail stores include handheld scanners used for data collection and inventory control. Retail stores may also be looking for a retail analytics solution to monitor customer behavior and trends over the WLAN. Point-of-sale devices, such as cash registers, may also have Wi-Fi radios. You may still run into older frequency hopping equipment that may cause all-band interference with an 802.11b/g/n (2.4 GHz) network. Steps may be necessary to upgrade the older equipment. Coverage is usually a greater concern than capacity because wireless data-collection devices require very little bandwidth, and the number used in a particular area is typically limited.

Warehouses

Some of the earliest deployments of 802.11 technology were in warehouses for the purpose of inventory control and data collection. A 2.4 GHz WLAN will likely be deployed because most handheld devices currently use 2.4 GHz radios. Coverage, not capacity, is usually the main objective when designing a wireless network in a warehouse. Warehouses are filled with metal racks and all sorts of inventory that can cause reflections and multipath. The use of directional antennas in a warehouse environment may be a requirement if legacy 802.11a/b/g access points are still being used. High ceilings often cause mounting problems as well as coverage issues. Indoor chain-link fences that are often used to secure certain areas will scatter and block a 2.4 GHz RF signal. Seamless roaming is also mandatory because the handheld devices will be mobile. Forklifts that can move swiftly through the warehouse often have computing devices with Wi-Fi radios. Legacy deployments of 802.11 FHSS hardware and/or legacy 900 MHz radios still exist in some warehouse environments. Handheld WLAN barcode scanners are now often being replaced with smart phones that use barcode scanning applications.

Manufacturing

A manufacturing environment is often similar to a warehouse environment in terms of multipath interference and coverage design. However, a manufacturing plant presents many unique site survey challenges, including safety and the presence of employee unions. Heavy machinery and robotics may present safety concerns to the surveyor, and special care should be taken so as not to mount access points where they might be damaged by other machines. Many manufacturing plants also work with hazardous chemicals and materials. Proper protection gear may need to be worn, and ruggedized access points or enclosures may have to be installed. Technology manufacturing plants often have clean rooms, and the surveyor will have to wear a clean suit and follow clean room procedures if they are even allowed in the room.

Many manufacturing plants are union shops with union employees. A meeting with the plant's union representative may be necessary to make sure that no union policies will be violated by the site surveyor team.

Multitenant Buildings

By far the biggest issue when conducting a survey in a multitenant building is the presence of other WLAN equipment used by nearby businesses. Office building environments are extremely cluttered with 802.11b/g/n wireless networks that operate at 2.4 GHz. Almost assuredly all of the other tenants' WLANs will be powered to full strength, and some equipment will be on nonstandard channels such as 2 and 8, which will likely interfere with your WLAN equipment. If at all possible, strong consideration should be given to deploying a WLAN using the 5 GHz U-NII bands.

Summary

In this chapter, you have learned about all the preparations and questions that must be asked prior to conducting a wireless site survey. The site survey interview is an important process necessary to both educate the customer and determine the customer's wireless needs. Defining the business purpose of the wireless network leads to a more productive survey. Capacity and coverage planning, as well as planning for infrastructure connectivity, is all part of the site survey interview. Before the site survey interview, you should obtain critical documentation such as blueprints or topographical maps from the customer. Interview and installation checklists are used during the site survey interview and during the actual physical survey. Different survey considerations are required for different vertical markets. After the site survey is completed, you will deliver to the customer a final site survey report, as well as additional reports and recommendations.

Exam Essentials

Define the site survey interview. Be able to explain the importance of the interview process prior to the wireless site survey. Understand that the interview is for educating the customer and clearly defining all their wireless needs.

Identify the questions necessary to determine capacity and coverage needs. Understand the importance of proper capacity and coverage planning. Define all the numerous considerations when planning for RF cell coverage, bandwidth, and throughput.

Explain existing wireless network troubleshooting concerns. Be able to explain the questions necessary to troubleshoot an existing WLAN installation prior to conducting a secondary site survey.

Define infrastructure connectivity issues. Understand all the necessary questions that must be asked in order to guarantee proper integration of the WLAN into the existing wired infrastructure.

Identify site survey documentation and forms. Correctly identify all the documentation that must be assembled and created prior to the site survey. Be familiar with all the information and documentation that is needed in the final deliverables.

Explain vertical market considerations. Understand the business requirements of different vertical markets and how these requirements will alter the site survey and final deployment.

Review Questions

1. You have been hired by the XYZ Company for a wireless site survey. Which statements best describe site survey best practices when choosing vendor equipment to be used during the survey? (Choose two answers.)

    A. When conducting a wireless site survey with a WLAN switch, you should use both standalone and contoller-based access points.

    B. When conducting a wireless site survey with standalone access points, you should use different vendors' APs together.

    C. When conducting a wireless site survey with a WLAN controller, you should use the controller-based access points from the same vendor.

    D. When conducting a wireless site survey with standalone access points, you should use standalone access points from the same vendor.

    E. When a wireless site survey is conducted, proprietary security solutions are often implemented.

2. Name a unique consideration when deploying a wireless network in a hotel or other hospitality business. (Choose the best answer.)

    A. Equipment theft

    B. Aesthetics

    C. Segmentation

    D. Roaming

    E. User management

3. Which of the following statements best describe security considerations during a wireless site survey? (Choose all that apply.)

    A. Questions will be asked to define the customer's security expectations.

    B. Wireless security recommendations will be made after the survey.

    C. Recommendations about wireless security policies may also be made.

    D. During the survey, both mutual authentication and encryption should be implemented.

4. The ACME Corporation has hired you to design a wireless network that will have data clients, VoWiFi phones, and access for guest users. The company wants the strongest security solution possible for the data clients and phones. Which design best fits the customer's requirements?

    A. Create one wireless VLAN. Segment the data clients, VoWiFi phones, and guest users from the wired network. Use an 802.1X/EAP authentication and CCMP/AES encryption for a wireless security solution.

    B. Create three separate VLANs. Segment the data clients, VoWiFi phones, and guest users into three distinct VLANs. Use an 802.1X/EAP authentication and TKIP encryption for security in the data VLAN. Use WPA2-Personal in the voice VLAN. The guest VLAN will have no security other than possibly a captive portal.

C. Create three separate VLANs. Segment the data clients, VoWiFi phones, and guest users into three distinct VLANs. Use an 802.1X/EAP authentication with CCMP/AES encryption for security in the data VLAN. Use WPA2-Personal in the voice VLAN. The guest VLAN traffic will require a captive web portal and guest firewall policy for security.

D. Create two separate VLANs. The data and voice clients will share one VLAN while the guest users will reside in another. Use an 802.1X/EAP authentication and CCMP/AES encryption for security in the data/voice VLAN. The guest VLAN will have no security other than possibly a captive portal.

5. What are some additional recommendations that can be made along with the final site survey report? (Choose all that apply.)

A. Training recommendations

B. Security recommendations

C. Coverage recommendations

D. Capacity recommendations

E. Roaming recommendations

6. What documents might be needed prior to performing an indoor site survey for a new wireless LAN? (Choose all that apply.)

A. Blueprints

B. Network topography map

C. Network topology map

D. Coverage map

E. Frequency map

7. What roaming issues should be discussed during an interview for a future VoWiFi network? (Choose all that apply.)

A. Layer 2 boundaries

B. Layer 3 boundaries

C. Layer 4 boundaries

D. Latency

E. Throughput

8. You have been hired by the Barry Corporation to conduct an indoor site survey. What information will be in the final site survey report that is delivered? (Choose all that apply.)

A. AP placement

B. Firewall settings

C. Router access control lists

D. Access point transmit power settings

E. Antenna orientation

9. The Kellum Corporation has hired you to troubleshoot an existing WLAN. The end users are reporting having difficulties when roaming. What are some of the possible causes? (Choose all that apply.)

A. Clients stations can only hear a –70 dBm signal from one access point.

B. Clients stations hear a –70 dBm signal from 30 access points.

C. The RF coverage cells are co-located.

D. There is interference from the cellular network.

E. There is interference from 2.4 GHz portable phones.

10. After conducting a simple site survey in the office building where your company is located on the fifth floor, you have discovered that other businesses are also operating access points on nearby floors on channels 2 and 8. What is the best recommendation you will make to management about deploying a new WLAN for your company?

A. Install a 2.4 GHz access point on channel 6 and use the highest available transmit power setting to overpower the WLANs of the other businesses.

B. Speak with the other businesses. Suggest that they use channels 1 and 6 at lower power settings. Install a 2.4 GHz access point using channel 9.

C. Speak with the other businesses. Suggest that they use channels 1 and 11 at lower power settings. Install a 2.4 GHz access point using channel 6.

D. Recommend installing a 5 GHz access point.

E. Install a wireless intrusion prevention system (WIPS). Classify the other businesses' access points as interfering and implement deauthentication countermeasures.

11. The Harkins Corporation has hired you to make recommendations about a future wireless deployment that will require more than 300 access points to meet all coverage require-ments. What is the most cost-efficient and practical recommendation in regard to providing electrical power to the access points?

A. Recommend that the customer replace older edge switches with new switches that have inline PoE.

B. Recommend that the customer replace the core switch with a new core switch that has inline PoE.

C. Recommend that the customer use single-port power injectors.

D. Recommend that the customer hire an electrician to install new electrical outlets.

12. The Chang Company has hired you to troubleshoot an existing legacy 802.11a/b/g WLAN. The end users are reporting having difficulties with throughput performance. What are some of the possible causes of the difficulties? (Choose all that apply.)

A. Multipath interference

B. Co-channel interference

C. Co-location interference

D. Inadequate capacity planning

E. Low client device transmit power

13. What factors need to be considered when planning for capacity and coverage in a 5 GHz WLAN? (Choose all that apply.)

A. Data applications

B. User density

C. Peak usage level

D. DFS channels

14. During the interview process, which topics will be discussed so that the WLAN will integrate properly into the existing wired architecture?

A. PoE

B. Segmentation

C. User management

D. Infrastructure management

E. All of the above

15. The Jackson County Regional Hospital has hired you for a wireless site survey. Prior to the site survey, employees from which departments at the hospital should be consulted? (Choose all that apply.)

A. Network management

B. Biomedical department

C. Hospital security

D. Custodial department

E. Marketing department

16. Typically what are the biggest concerns when planning for a WLAN in a warehouse environment? (Choose all that apply.)

A. Capacity

B. Coverage

C. Security

D. Roaming

17. What type of hardware may be necessary when installing APs to be used for outdoor wireless coverage? (Choose all that apply.)

A. NEMA enclosure

B. Parabolic dish antennas

C. Patch antennas

D. Outdoor ruggedized core switch

18. What is a telecommunications unit of measurement of traffic equal to 1 hour of telephone traffic in 1 hour of time?

    A. Ohm

    B. dBm

    C. Erlang

    D. Call hour

    E. Voltage Standing Wave Ratio

19. What additional documentation is usually provided along with the final site survey deliverable? (Choose all that apply.)

    A. Bill of materials

    B. Implementation diagrams

    C. Network topology map

    D. Project schedule and costs

    E. Access point user manuals

20. The WonderPuppy Coffee Company has hired you to make recommendations about deploying wireless hotspots inside 500 coffee shops across the country. What solutions might you recommend? (Choose all that apply.)

    A. WPA2-Personal security solution

    B. 802.11 a/b/g/n access points at 100 mW transmit power

    C. 802.11a/b/g/n access points at 1 to 5 mW transmit power

    D. NEMA enclosures

    E. Captive portal authentication

    F. 802.1X/EAP security solution

Chapter

16

Site Survey Systems and Devices

IN THIS CHAPTER, YOU WILL LEARN ABOUT THE FOLLOWING:

✓ **Site survey defined**

- Protocol and spectrum analysis

- Standalone

- Integrated

- Spectrum analysis

- Coverage analysis

- AP placement and configuration

- Application analysis

✓ **Site survey tools**

- Indoor site survey tools

- Outdoor site survey tools

✓ **Coverage analysis**

- Manual

- Predictive

- Dynamic RF

- Wireless network validation

In Chapter 15, "Radio Frequency Site Survey Fundamentals," we discussed wireless site surveys from an administrative perspective. You learned what information to gather and what to plan for prior to the actual Wi-Fi site survey. In this chapter, we present the wireless site survey from a technical perspective. A proper site survey should include spectrum analysis as well as coverage analysis so that optimum 802.11 communications are realized. Determining the proper placement and configuration of the 802.11 equipment during the site survey is essential to reaching your expected performance goals for the wireless network. RF signal propagation studies are needed to determine existing and new RF coverage patterns. Many variables—such as walls, floors, doors, plumbing, windows, elevators, buildings, trees, and mountains—can have a direct effect on the coverage of an access point or wireless bridge.

In the past 10 years, the use of 802.11 networking has increased astronomically. People have become dependent upon it and entrust it with critical and sometimes lifesaving applications. Therefore, it is necessary to verify the network after it has been installed. In this chapter, you will learn about site survey validation and different site survey validation techniques and tools.

We also discuss how to perform a site survey, the types of site surveys, and the tools that can be used during a site survey. Site survey professionals often have their own unique technical approach for executing a site survey. We like to think of it as almost an art form, and in this chapter, we will help you take the first steps in becoming a wireless site survey Picasso.

Site Survey Defined

When most individuals are asked to define a wireless site survey, the usual response is that a site survey is for determining RF coverage. In the early days of wireless networking when there were far fewer wireless client stations connecting to the wireless network, that definition was absolutely correct. However, not only do present-day wireless networks need to provide the coverage that was sought when early site surveys were performed, but they often also need to provide higher throughput for denser deployments of stations. To achieve these goals, the site survey must encompass so much more than just determining coverage, including looking for potential sources of interference as well as the proper placement, installation, and configuration of 802.11 hardware and related components. In the following sections, we cover the often overlooked, yet necessary, spectrum analysis requirement of the site survey and the often misunderstood coverage analysis requirement. During the coverage analysis process, a determination will be made for the proper placement of access points, the transmission power of the access point radios, and the proper use of antennas.

Nowadays, capacity performance and application testing are key components of a proper sight survey. Depending on the purpose of the wireless network, different tools can be used to assist with the site survey, which is why the site survey interview and planning process is so important. Throughout the remainder of this chapter, we also cover the variety of tools that may be used as part of your site survey arsenal.

Protocol and Spectrum Analysis

Ten years ago, if you wanted to plan and design a wireless network, the likelihood of interference from other networks or wireless devices was much less than it is now. With most homes and businesses having wireless networks deployed, along with many other wireless devices in the work and home environment, a proper site survey requires that you perform both a protocol analysis of your environment and a spectrum analysis.

As WLAN technology has advanced, the complexity and knowledge required to use PC-based spectrum analyzers has become far less than what is needed to use traditional analyzers. Additionally, costs have drastically decreased, putting spectrum analyzers well into reach for even moderately sized jobs and companies. A spectrum analyzer will help identify whether there is any type of RF interference from 802.11 devices or other devices that could interfere with your WLAN. If the interference is from 802.11-based equipment, it is important to use a protocol analyzer to further investigate the signal.

Wi-Fi-based protocol analyzers can examine 802.11 frames and identify SSID and BSSID information along with packet and security information. Signal strength measurements along with channel information can be monitored and documented, provide an overview, and at times, provide an RF map of the existing 802.11 environment. Even if encryption is used, protocol analyzers can extract many pieces of information from the 802.11 management frames. Some Wi-Fi protocol analyzers are specifically designed for performing site surveys. They can integrate maps or floor plans with this wireless data from test APs to perform site surveys, overlay the AP signals on a floor plan, and indicate the expected coverage based on sample readings.

Wi-Fi-oriented spectrum and protocol analyzers fall into two categories: standalone and integrated. Next, you will learn about the differences between these two types of systems.

Standalone

Wi-Fi cards and spectrum analyzer cards go about seeing the RF world in slightly different ways. The Wi-Fi card can see frames and modulated bits going across the RF medium. Protocol analyzers take the data received by the Wi-Fi cards and provide packet analysis of that data. Spectrum analyzers monitor the RF signal itself.

Whether a spectrum analyzer is an expensive piece of test equipment or software running on a PC with a USB spectrum adapter connected to it, these devices are designed to sense and monitor strictly the RF signal that is received within a specific frequency range. Because the Wi-Fi receiver and the spectrum analyzer receiver are separate devices that monitor different pieces of information, historically they have been standalone devices, each performing a dedicated task.

Integrated

It is one thing for a spectrum analyzer to know and recognize a variety of RF interferers' signatures but still another to speculate what the effect of that interferer will be on the wireless LAN. Enter Wi-Fi integration; this is the holy grail of 802.11 analysis. This may be the secret sauce that puts one vendor in a unique space compared with the competitors. By correlating the raw RF with the data from the Wi-Fi card, you can better understand the effects of various scenarios on your wireless network. As you can imagine, this capability will not be found in the less expensive products.

Look to spectrum and protocol analyzer vendors to be adding more integration between both the spectrum analysis cards and Wi-Fi cards. Try to get an appropriate level of Wi-Fi integration to meet your needs. The less you understand about RF fundamentals and 802.11 basics, the more you will need and benefit from the expert analysis software that is built into some of these integrated products.

Spectrum Analysis

Before conducting the coverage analysis survey, locating sources of potential interference is a must. Some companies and consultants still ignore *spectrum analysis* because of the cost generally associated with purchasing the necessary spectrum analyzer hardware; however, with the prices of PC-based analyzers decreasing over recent years, spectrum analysis has become more of the norm with site surveys.

Spectrum analyzers are frequency domain measurement devices that can measure the amplitude and frequency space of electromagnetic signals. Dedicated benchtop spectrum analyzer hardware can cost upward of $100,000 (in US dollars), thereby making them cost prohibitive for many businesses. The good news is that several companies have solutions, both hardware and software based, that are designed specifically for 802.11 site survey spectrum analysis and are drastically less expensive. Figure 16.1 depicts a PC-based spectrum analyzer that uses a USB-based adapter that is capable of monitoring both the 2.4 GHz and 5 GHz spectrums.

To conduct a proper 802.11 spectrum analysis survey, the *spectrum analyzer* needs to be capable of scanning both the 2.4 GHz ISM band and the 5 GHz U-NII bands. Several companies sell software-based solutions that work with special cards or USB adapters. These software-based spectrum analyzers are designed specifically for 802.11 site surveys and can correctly identify specific energy pulses, such as those from a microwave oven or cordless phone. Be judicious in your research of these software tools. Some might measure only other 802.11 devices and are not true spectrum analyzers. A true spectrum analyzer picks up RF energy regardless of the source.

So, why is spectrum analysis even necessary? If the background noise level exceeds −85 dBm in either the 2.4 GHz ISM band or the 5 GHz U-NII bands, the performance of the wireless network can be severely degraded. A noisy environment can cause the data in 802.11 transmissions to become corrupted. Consider the following:

- If the data is corrupted, the cyclic redundancy check (CRC) will fail and the receiving 802.11 radio will not send an ACK frame to the transmitting 802.11 radio.

- If an ACK frame is not received by the original transmitting radio, the unicast frame is not acknowledged and will have to be retransmitted.

- If an interfering device, such as a microwave oven, causes retransmissions above 10 percent, the performance or throughput of the wireless LAN will suffer significantly.

FIGURE 16.1   Wi-Spy DBx 2.4 GHz and 5 GHz PC-based spectrum analyzer

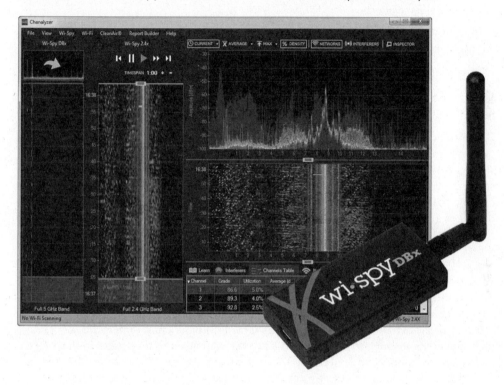

Most data applications in a Wi-Fi network can handle a layer 2 retransmission rate of up to 10 percent without any noticeable degradation in performance. However, time-sensitive applications such as VoIP require that higher-layer IP packet loss be no greater than 1 percent. Therefore, Voice over Wi-Fi (VoWiFi) networks need to limit retransmissions at layer 2 to about 10 percent or less to guarantee the timely delivery of VoIP packets.

Interfering devices might also prevent an 802.11 radio from transmitting. If another RF source is transmitting with strong amplitude, an 802.11 radio can sense the energy during the clear channel assessment (CCA) and defer transmission. If the source of the interference is a constant signal, an 802.11 radio will continuously defer transmissions until the medium is clear. In other words, a strong source of RF interference could actually prevent your 802.11 client stations and access point radios from transmitting at all.

It is a recommended practice to conduct spectrum analysis of all frequency ranges, especially in the 2.4 GHz ISM band. The 2.4 to 2.5 GHz ISM band is an extremely crowded frequency space. The following are potential sources of interference in the 2.4 GHz ISM band:

- Microwave ovens
- 2.4 GHz cordless phones, DSSS and FHSS
- Fluorescent bulbs
- 2.4 GHz video cameras
- Elevator motors
- Cauterizing devices
- Plasma cutters
- Bluetooth radios
- Nearby 802.11, 802.11b, 802.11g, or 802.11n (2.4 GHz) WLANs

A common everyday interfering item that should be documented during the site survey interview is the location of any microwave ovens. Microwave ovens typically operate at 800 to 1,000 watts. Although microwave ovens are shielded, they can become leaky over time. Commercial-grade microwave ovens will be shielded better than a discount microwave oven that you can buy at many retail outlets. A received signal of −40 dBm is about 1/10,000 of a milliwatt (mW) and is considered a strong signal for 802.11 communications. If a 1,000 watt microwave oven is as little as 0.0000001 percent leaky, the oven will interfere with the 802.11 radio.

Figure 16.2 shows a spectrum view of a microwave oven. Note that this microwave operates dead center in the 2.4 GHz ISM band. Some microwave ovens can congest the entire frequency band. You should also check whether the call centers, receptionist, or other employees use a Bluetooth mouse, keyboard, or headset. These can also cause interference.

Because of the extreme crowding of the 2.4 GHz ISM band, many enterprise deployments are switching to 802.11n and 802.11ac equipment that operates in the 5 GHz U-NII bands. Switching to a 5 GHz WLAN is often a wise choice in the enterprise because the 5 GHz U-NII bands are currently not very crowded and there are more choices for channel reuse patterns. Not nearly as many interfering devices exist, and there are not as many neighboring 5 GHz networks that can potentially cause interference. Although there is much less interference present at 5 GHz as compared to 2.4 GHz, this may change over time. Just as everyone moved from 900 MHz to 2.4 GHz to avoid interference, the band-jumping effect may also catch up with 5 GHz.

It is also important to note that the evolution of Wi-Fi technology is transitioning away from the 2.4 GHz spectrum. Very High Throughput (VHT) technology defined by the 802.11ac amendment operates only in the 5 GHz U-NII bands. Since most enterprises deploy dual-frequency access points that have multiple radios (effectively installing both a 2.4 GHz and a 5 GHz network simultaneously), the 2.4 GHz radio will continue to support 802.11b/g/n communications, while the 5 GHz radio will support 802.11a/n/ac communications. These dual-frequency APs are important, since many of the current Wi-Fi-capable phones and tablets only support 2.4 GHz.

Newer 802.11ac-capable devices along with 5 GHz 802.11n–capable devices benefit from connecting to the less congested 5 GHz U-NII bands, while compatibility is still provided for 2.4 GHz–only devices. Current potential sources of interference in 5 GHz U-NII bands include the following:

- 5 GHz cordless phones
- Radar
- Perimeter sensors
- Digital satellite
- Nearby 5 GHz WLANs
- Outdoor wireless 5 GHz bridges

FIGURE 16.2   Microwave oven spectrum use

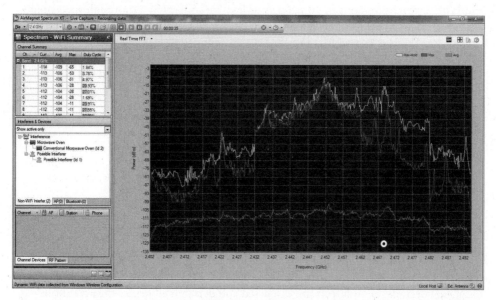

The 802.11-2012 standard defines *dynamic frequency selection (DFS)* and *transmit power control (TPC)* mechanisms to satisfy regulatory requirements for operation in the 5 GHz band to avoid interference with 5 GHz radar systems. As you learned in earlier chapters, 802.11h-compliant radios are required to detect radar at 5 GHz and not transmit to avoid interfering with the radar systems. Using a 5 GHz spectrum analyzer during a site survey may help determine in advance whether radar transmissions exist in the area where the WLAN deployment is planned.

Although many devices can cause problems in both frequencies, one of the most common causes of interference is other wireless LANs. Strong signals from other nearby WLANs can be a huge problem, especially in a multitenant building environment. You may need to cooperate with neighboring businesses to ensure that their access points are not powered too high and that they are on channels that will not interfere with your access points. Once again, because of the proliferation of 2.4 GHz WLAN equipment, many businesses are now choosing to switch to 5 GHz WLAN solutions.

After locating the sources of interference, the best and simplest solution is to eliminate them entirely. If a microwave oven is causing problems, consider purchasing a more expensive commercial-grade oven that is less likely to be a nuisance. Other devices, such as 2.4 GHz cordless phones, should be removed and a policy that bans them should be strictly enforced. 5.8 GHz cordless phones operate in the 5.8 GHz ISM band, which overlaps with the upper U-NII band (5.725 GHz to 5.850 GHz). Indoor use of 5.8 GHz phones will cause interference with 5 GHz radios transmitting in the upper U-NII band.

If interfering devices cannot be eradicated in the 2.4 GHz bands, consider moving to the less crowded 5 GHz U-NII bands. As stated earlier in this chapter, a VoWiFi network needs to limit layer 2 retransmissions to 10 percent or less, meaning that a thorough spectrum analysis of the 2.4 GHz ISM band is a necessity. In the past, VoWiFi phones operated only in the very crowded 2.4 GHz ISM band. 5 GHz VoWiFi phones are now widely available and are the better choice for VoIP transmissions. If your WLAN is being used for either data or voice or for both, a proper and thorough spectrum analysis is mandatory in an enterprise environment.

It is important to make sure you know what your client devices are capable of before determining the spectrum to use. If all or some of your client devices are restricted to using 2.4 GHz, that may be your only option and you will need to be able to plan and engineer around the environment.

Coverage Analysis

After you conduct a spectrum analysis site survey, your next step is the all-important determination of proper 802.11 RF coverage inside your facility. During the site survey interview, capacity and coverage requirements are discussed and determined before the actual site survey is performed. In certain areas of your facility, smaller cells or co-location may be required because of a high density of users or heavy application bandwidth requirements.

After all the capacity and coverage needs have been determined, RF measurements must be taken to guarantee that these needs are met and to determine the proper placement and configuration of the access points and antennas. Proper *coverage analysis* must be performed using some type of *received signal strength* measurement tool or planning tool. This tool could be something as simple as the received signal strength meter in your wireless card's client utility, or it could be a more expensive and complex site survey software package. The capabilities of built-in utilities are typically limited, and they should only be used for small deployments or for spot checking. All of these measurement tools are discussed in more detail later in this chapter.

So, how do you conduct proper coverage analysis? That question is often debated by industry professionals. Many site survey professionals have their own techniques; however, we will try to describe a basic procedure for coverage analysis.

One mistake that many people make during the site survey is leaving the access point radio at the default full-power setting. A 2.4 GHz radio transmitting at 100 mW will often cause interference with other access point coverage cells simply because it is generating too much power. APs set to full power can cause a hidden node problem. A good starting point for a 2.4 GHz access point is 25 mW transmit power. After the site survey is performed, the power can be increased if needed to meet unexpected coverage needs, or it can be decreased to meet capacity needs.

When you are designing for coverage during a site survey, the normal recommended best practice is to provide for a –70 dBm or stronger received signal, which is well above the noise floor. When you are designing for WLANs with VoWiFi clients, a –67 dBm or stronger signal that is even higher above the noise is recommended.

The hardest part of physically performing a coverage analysis site survey is often finding where to place the first access point and determining the boundaries of the first RF cell. The procedure outlined next explains how this can be achieved and is further illustrated in Figure 16.3:

FIGURE 16.3   Starting coverage cell

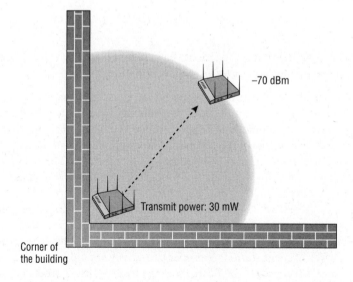

1. Place an access point with a power setting of 30 mW (or the power level that you determine is ideal for your environment) in the corner of the building.

2. Walk diagonally away from the access point toward the center of the building until the received signal drops to –70 dBm, or the signal strength that you are planning for. This is the location where you place your first access point. (–70 dBm will be used as the desired signal level throughout the rest of this example. If you are using a different desired signal level, use it in place of this.)

3. Temporarily mount the access point in the first location and begin walking throughout the facility to find the –70 dBm endpoints, also known as *cell boundaries* or *cell edges*.

4. Depending on the shape and size of the first coverage cell, you may want to change the power settings and/or move the initial access point.

After the first coverage cell and boundaries have been determined, the next question is where to place the next access point. The placement of the next access point is performed by using a technique that is similar to the one you used to place the first access point.

Think of the cell boundary of the first access point, where the signal is –70 dBm, as the initial starting point, similar to the way you used the corner of the building as your initial starting point, and do the following:

1. From the first access point, walk parallel to the edge of the building, and place a temporary access point at the location where the received signal is –70 dBm, as pictured in Figure 16.4.

2. Now walk away from this access point, parallel to the edge of the building, until the received signal drops to –70 dBm.

3. Move to that location and temporarily mount the access point. The AP mounted at this location will provide for the first coverage cell.

4. Begin walking throughout the facility to find the –70 dBm endpoints, or cell boundaries.

5. Again, depending on the shape and size of the first coverage cell, you may want to change the power settings and/or move this access point.

It is important to avoid excessive overlap because it can cause frequent roaming and performance degradation. The shape and size of the building and the attenuation caused by the various materials of walls and obstacles will require you to change the distances between access points to ensure proper cell overlap. After finding the proper placement of the second access point and all of its cell boundaries, repeat the procedure all over again. The rest of a manual site survey like this one is basically repeating this procedure over and over again, effectively daisy-chaining throughout the building until all coverage needs are determined.

WLAN design guides and white papers from various WLAN vendors often reference 15 percent to 30 percent coverage cell overlap for roaming purposes. However, there is no way to measure coverage cell overlap. Coverage overlap is really duplicate coverage from the perspective of a Wi-Fi client station. A proper site survey should be conducted to make sure that a client always has proper duplicate coverage from multiple access points. In other words, each Wi-Fi client station needs to hear at least one access point at a specific received signal strength indicator (RSSI) and a backup or secondary access point at a different RSSI. Typically, vendor RSSI thresholds require a received signal of greater than −70 dBm for the higher data rate communications. Therefore, a client station needs to see at least two access points at the desired signal level so that the client can roam if necessary.

The following cell edge measurements are taken during the site survey:

- Received signal strength (dBm), also known as received signal level (RSL)
- Noise level (dBm)
- Signal-to-noise ratio, or SNR (dB)

FIGURE 16.4   Second AP location

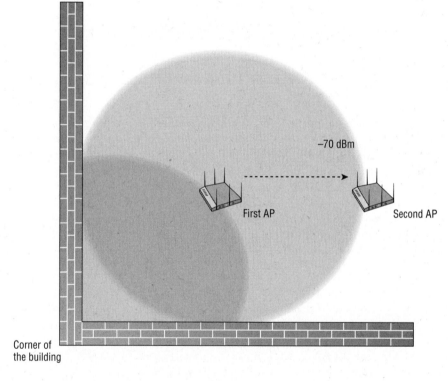

The received signal strength measurements that are recorded during a site survey typically depend on the intended use of the WLAN. If the intent of the WLAN is primarily to provide low density data service versus capacity, a lower received signal of −73 dBm might be used as the boundary for your overlapping cells. When throughput and capacity are a higher priority, using a received signal of −70 dBm or higher is recommended. When you are designing for WLANs with VoWiFi clients, a −67 dBm or stronger signal that is even higher above the noise is recommended. The SNR is an important value because, if the background noise is too close to the received signal, data can be corrupted and retransmissions will increase. The SNR is simply the difference in decibels between the received signal and the background noise, as shown in Figure 16.5. Many vendors recommend a minimum SNR of 18 dB for data networks and a minimum of 25 dB for voice networks.

FIGURE 16.5   Signal-to-noise ratio

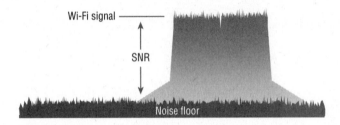

SNR Measuring Requirements

Keep in mind that measuring the SNR requires a device that can measure the raw ambient RF energy of the noise floor. It should be understood that an 802.11 wireless network interface card (NIC) is not a spectrum analyzer, and though it can transmit and receive data at a prodigious rate, it cannot see raw ambient RF signals. A Wi-Fi radio can decode the modulated data bits sent from another Wi-Fi radio but cannot truthfully measure the noise floor. A Wi-Fi NIC can be used to measure the received signal; however, the best device that can truly measure non-encoded RF energy is a spectrum analyzer and therefore it's your best tool to measure SNR.

Some site survey professionals prefer to use data rate measurements (as opposed to received signal strength measurements) when determining their cell boundaries. The problem with using the data rate is that vendors have different received signal strength indicator (RSSI) thresholds and different vendor cards will shift between data rates at different dBm levels. Cell design can be performed using one vendor's RSSI threshold values if the company deploying the WLAN intends to use just that one vendor's radios. If measurements are based on received signal levels (RSLs), the WLAN surveyor can always go back and map different client cards and data rates without having to resurvey. A site survey using just data rates or a proprietary signal strength measurement threshold does not allow for any flexibility between vendors. Table 16.1 depicts the recommended minimum received signal and minimum SNR for a WLAN data network using one vendor's highly sensitive radio card.

Most VoWiFi manufacturers require a minimum received signal of –67 dBm. Therefore, overlapping cells of –67 dBm is a good idea for VoWiFi wireless networks in order to provide a fade margin buffer. The recommended SNR ratio for a VoWiFi network is 25 dB or higher. Figure 16.6 depicts the recommended coverage for a 2.4 GHz VoWiFi network.

TABLE 16.1   WLAN data cell—vendor recommendations

Data rate	Minimum received signal	Minimum signal-to-noise ratio
54 Mbps	–71 dBm	25 dB
36 Mbps	–73 dBm	18 dB
24 Mbps	–77 dBm	12 dB
12/11 Mbps	–82 dBm	10 dB
6/5.5 Mbps	–89 dBm	8 dB
2 Mbps	–91 dBm	6 dB
1 Mbps	–94 dBm	4 dB

FIGURE 16.6   VoWiFi cell recommendations

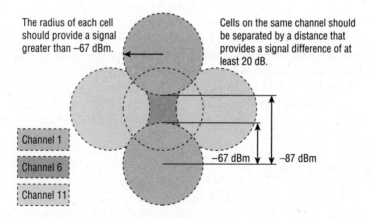

The radius of each cell should provide a signal greater than –67 dBm.

Cells on the same channel should be separated by a distance that provides a signal difference of at least 20 dB.

Channel 1

Channel 6

Channel 11

–67 dBm   –87 dBm

The radius of each cell should provide a signal greater than –67 dBm. Cells on the same channel should be separated by a distance that provides a signal difference of at least 20 dB.

Although figures and drawings often depict the RF coverage as nice round symmetrical cells, the reality is that cell boundaries usually have an erratic shape that might resemble a starfish or elements in a Pablo Picasso painting.

AP Placement and Configuration

As you have just read, coverage analysis also determines the proper placement of access points and power settings. When the site survey is conducted, all the cell edge measurements will be recorded and written on a copy of the floor plan of the building. An entry with the exact location of each access point must also be recorded. Next to the entry of each access point should be the transmission power level of the AP's radio when the survey was conducted. The location of all the wiring closets will also be noted on the floor plan, and care should be taken to ensure that the placement of any access point is within a 100-meter (328-foot) cable run back to the wiring closet because of copper Ethernet cabling distance limitations. Be sure to account for vertical cabling distances as well as horizontal runs.

Another often overlooked component in WLAN design during coverage analysis is the use of semidirectional antennas. Many deployments of WLANs use only the manufacturer's default low-gain omnidirectional antenna, which typically has about 2.14 dBi of gain. Buildings come in many shapes and sizes and often have long corridors or hallways where the coverage of an indoor semidirectional antenna may be much more advantageous. Many warehouse devices still use legacy non-802.11n technology, which is more susceptible to problems caused by multipath. Using a unidirectional antenna in areas where there are metal racks, file cabinets, and metal lockers can be advantageous at times because you can cut down on reflections. Figure 16.7 depicts the use of semidirectional antennas in a warehouse with long corridors and metal racks that line the corridors.

With 802.11n and 802.11ac technology, semidirectional MIMO patch antennas are often pointed down from the ceiling to provide for sectors of coverage in areas where there is a high density of users and devices. A good site survey kit should have a variety of antennas, both omnidirectional and semidirectional. Do not be afraid to provide coverage in a building by using a combination of both low-gain omnidirectional antennas and indoor semidirectional antennas, as shown in Figure 16.8.

When a semidirectional antenna is used, recording the received signal strength, SNR, and noise level measurements is still necessary to find the coverage edges. Simply record the signal measurements along the directional path and the edges of the directional path where the antenna is providing coverage.

Application Analysis

Whereas spectrum analysis and coverage analysis are considered mandatory during 802.11 wireless site surveys, *application analysis* has not always been. With the proliferation of Wi-Fi networks along with the importance of these networks in the enterprise, capacity planning has become an integral part of the site survey process. This takes into account not only the user capacity but the bandwidth capacity as well. Cell sizing or co-location can be planned and surveyed during the coverage analysis portion of the survey.

Software tools exist that can perform application stress testing of a WLAN. These tools will typically be used at the tail end of a site survey, during a post-install survey. Several companies offer 802.11a/b/g/n/ac multistation emulation hardware that can simulate multiple concurrent virtual wireless client stations. The virtual client stations can have individual security settings. Roaming performance can also be tested. The 802.11a/b/g/n/ac multistation emulator works in conjunction with another component that can emulate hundreds of protocols and generate traffic bidirectionally through the virtual client stations. A great use of such a device could be to test the performance of a simulated wireless data network along with simulated wireless VoIP traffic.

FIGURE 16.7   Legacy use of semidirectional antennas

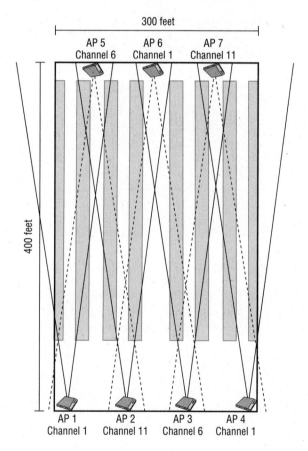

Site Survey Tools

Anyone who is serious about deploying wireless networks will put together a site survey toolbox with a multitude of products that can aid the site survey process. The main tool will be some sort of signal measurement software utility that interfaces with your wireless client card and is used for signal analysis. Prepackaged site survey kits can be found for sale on the Internet, but most site survey professionals prefer to put together their own kit. Indoor and outdoor site surveys are very different in nature, and in the following sections we discuss the various tools that are used in both types of surveys.

FIGURE 16.8   Omnidirectional and semidirectional antenna combination

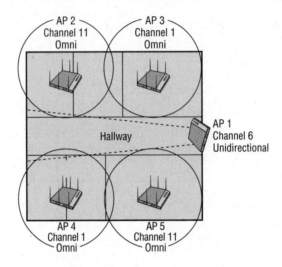

Indoor Site Survey Tools

As stated earlier, a spectrum analyzer will be needed for locating potential sources of interference. Your main weapon in your coverage analysis arsenal will be a received signal strength measurement tool. If you are performing a simple site survey, this tool could be something as basic as the received signal strength meter in your wireless card's client utility. For most site surveys, however, it is recommended that you use a more expensive and complex site survey software package. There are many other tools, though, that can assist you when you are conducting the physical site survey. Here are some of the tools that you might use for an indoor site survey:

Spectrum Analyzer   This analyzer is needed for frequency spectrum analysis.

Blueprints   Blueprints or floor plans of the facility are needed to map coverage and mark RF measurements. CAD software may be needed to view and edit digital copies of the blueprints.

Signal Strength Measurement Software   You will need this software for RF coverage analysis.

802.11 Client Card   This card is used with the signal measurement software.

Access Point   At least one AP is needed, preferably two. Autonomous access points can be used as standalone devices during the site survey. Controller-based lightweight APs require a controller, but some can be configured to operate without the use of a controller for this purpose. Some lightweight APs function as cooperative devices, so for the purpose of a site survey, they can operate as a standalone AP or as part of a cluster.

WLAN Controller   Most WLAN controller vendors manufacture small controllers that are designed for use in branch and remote offices. When you are performing a site survey and a controller is required, a small remote office WLAN controller that weighs 2 pounds will be easier and cheaper to work with than a core WLAN controller that weighs 30 pounds.

Battery Pack   A battery pack is a necessity because the site survey engineer does not want to have to run electrical extension cords to power the access point while it is temporarily mounted for the site survey. Not only does the battery pack provide power to the access point, it also provides a safer environment because you do not have to run a loose power cord across the floor, and it makes it easier and quicker to move the access point to a new location.

Binoculars   It may seem strange to have binoculars for an indoor sight survey, but they can be very useful in tall warehouses and convention centers. They can also be handy for looking at things in the plenum space above the ceiling.

Flashlight   A powerful, directional flashlight can come in handy in a dark corner or in a ceiling.

Walkie-Talkies or Cell Phones   When performing a site survey in an office environment, it is often necessary to be as quiet and unobtrusive as possible. Walkie-talkies or cell phones are typically preferred over yelling across the room. You must also remember that RF is three-dimensional and it is common for one person to be on one floor with the access point while the other person is on another floor checking the received signal.

Antennas   A variety of both indoor omnidirectional and indoor directional antennas historically has been common in indoor Wi-Fi site survey kits. Although external antennas are still used, their use is not as common as in the past. Most enterprise AP vendors integrate antennas directly into their APs, with the placement and antenna radiation pattern designed for the AP to be ceiling mounted. If the internal antennas do not meet your design needs, most enterprise AP vendors also have AP models that support external antennas.

Temporary Mounting Gear   During the site survey, you will be temporarily mounting the access point—often high up, just below the ceiling. Some sort of solution is needed to temporarily mount the AP. Bungee cords and plastic ties are often used, as well as good old-fashioned duct tape. Figure 16.9 shows a professional site survey cart with a mast that can expand up to 22 feet tall for site surveys in office or warehouse environments. Tripods can also be used to temporarily mount and move APs during a site survey. The mast or tripod can be moved within the building, bypassing the need to temporarily mount the access point to a wall or ceiling.

Digital Camera   A digital camera should be used to record the exact location of the access point placement. Recording this information visually will assist whoever does the final installation at a later date. Setting the date/time on the pictures may also come in handy when viewing the pictures later. With the incredible optical zoom capabilities available on moderately priced consumer cameras, a digital camera can also be used in lieu of binoculars.

FIGURE 16.9 WLAN mobile site survey mast

Wi-Fi Surveyor Warehouse Model, courtesy of Caster Tray

Measuring Wheel or Laser Measuring Meter A tool is needed to make sure the access point will in fact be close enough for a 100-meter cable run back to the wiring closet. Keep in mind that a 100-meter cable run includes running the CAT5 or CAT6 cabling through the plenum. A measuring wheel or a laser distance measuring tool could be used to help easily measure the distance back to the wiring closet or for documenting the distance from walls for mounting an AP in a large room.

Colored Electrical Tape Everyone remembers the fable of Hansel and Gretel and how they used breadcrumbs to leave a trail to find their way home. The colored tape can be used to leave a trail back to where you want to mount the access points. Leave a small piece of colored electrical tape at the location where the access point was temporarily mounted during the site survey. This will assist whoever does the final AP installation at a later date.

Ladder or Forklift Ladders and/or forklifts may be needed to temporarily mount the access point to the ceiling.

When conducting a site survey, you should use the same 802.11 access point hardware that you plan on deploying. Keep in mind that every vendor is different and implements RSSI differently. It is not advisable to conduct a coverage analysis survey using one vendor's access point and then deploy a completely different vendor's hardware. Many established site survey companies have put together vendor site survey kits so that they can offer their customers several options.

Outdoor Site Survey Tools

As mentioned in Chapter 15, much of the focus of this book and the CWNA exam is on outdoor site surveys that are for establishing bridge links. However, outdoor site surveys for the purpose of providing general outdoor wireless access for users are becoming more commonplace. Outdoor site surveys are conducted using either outdoor access points or mesh routers, which are the devices typically used to provide access for client stations in an outdoor environment. These outdoor Wi-Fi surveys will use most of the same tools as an indoor site survey but may also use a global positioning system (GPS) device to record latitude and longitude coordinates. Although outdoor 802.11 deployments can be used to provide access, usually a discussion of outdoor site surveys is about wireless bridging or wireless backhaul for surveillance cameras or electronic monitoring equipment. Wi-Fi bridging exists at the distribution layer and is used to provide a wireless link between two or more wired networks.

An entirely different set of tools is needed for an outdoor bridging site survey, and many more calculations are required to guarantee the stability of the bridge link. In earlier chapters, you learned that the calculations necessary when deploying outdoor bridge links are numerous, including the Fresnel zone, earth bulge, free space path loss, link budget, and fade margin. Other considerations may include the intentional radiator (IR) and equivalent isotropically radiated power (EIRP) limits as defined by the regulatory body of your country. Weather conditions are another major consideration in any outdoor site survey, and proper protection against lightning and wind will need to be deployed. An outdoor wireless bridging site survey usually requires the cooperative skills of two individuals. The following list includes some of the tools that you might use for an outdoor bridging site survey:

Topographic Map   Instead of a building floor plan, a topographic map that outlines elevations and positions will be needed.

Link Analysis Software   Point-to-point link analysis software can be used with topographic maps to generate a bridge link profile and also perform many of the necessary calculations, such as Fresnel zone and EIRP. The bridge link analysis software is a predictive modeling tool.

Calculators   Software calculators and spreadsheets can be used to provide necessary calculations for link budget, Fresnel zone, free space path loss, and fade margin. Other calculators can provide information about cable attenuation and voltage standing wave ratio (VSWR). In Exercise 16.1, you will use a calculator to determine cable attenuation.

Maximum Tree Growth Data   Trees are a potential source of obstruction of the Fresnel zone, and unless a tree is fully mature, it will likely grow taller. A chainsaw is not always the answer, and planning antenna height based on potential tree growth might be necessary. The regional or local agricultural government agency should be able to provide you with the necessary information regarding the local foliage and what type of growth you can expect.

Binoculars   Visual line of sight can be established with the aid of binoculars. However, please remember that determining RF line of sight means calculating and ensuring Fresnel zone clearance. For links longer than 5 miles or so, this will be almost impossible. A solid understanding of topography and earth bulge is necessary to plan a bridge link.

Walkie-Talkies or Cell Phones   802.11 bridge links may span up to (or at times exceed) a mile. Two site survey engineers working as a team will need some type of device for communicating during the survey.

Signal Generator and Wattmeter   A signal generator can be used together with a wattmeter, also known as a Bird meter, to test cabling, connectors, and accessories for signal loss and VSWR. This testing gear can be used for testing cabling and connectors before deployment. The testing gear can also be used after deployment to check that water and other environmental conditions have not damaged the cabling and connectors. Figure 16.10 depicts a signal generator and a wattmeter.

FIGURE 16.10   Signal generator and wattmeter

Variable-Loss Attenuator   A variable-loss attenuator has a dial that enables you to adjust the amount of energy that is absorbed. It can be used during an outdoor site survey to simulate different cable lengths or cable losses.

Inclinometer   This device is used to determine the height of obstructions. Doing so is crucial when you need to ensure that a link path is clear of obstructions.

GPS   Recording the latitude and longitude of the transmit sites and any obstructions or points of interest along the path is important for planning. A GPS can easily provide this information.

Digital Camera   You will want to take pictures of outdoor mounting locations, cable paths, grounding locations, obstructions, and so on. You will likely need a camera with a good optical zoom lens. If you have a strong enough zoom lens on your camera, you may also be able to use it to identify and document the visual line of sight of your link.

Spectrum Analyzer   This device should be used to test ambient RF levels at transmit sites.

High-Power Spotlight or Sunlight Reflector   In the case of a wireless bridge, you will need to make sure you are surveying in the right direction. As the path gets farther away, the ability to identify a specific rooftop or tower becomes harder and harder. To aid in this task, a high-power (3 million candle or greater) spotlight or a sunlight reflector may be used. Because light travels so well, it can be used to narrow in on the actual remote site and ensure that the survey is conducted in the right direction.

Antennas and access points are not typically used during the bridging site survey. Bridging hardware is rarely installed during the survey because most times a mast or some other type of structure has to be built. If all the bridging measurements and calculations are accurate, the bridge link will most likely work. An outdoor site survey for a mesh network will require mesh APs and antennas.

EXERCISE 16.1

Cable Loss Calculations

To perform this exercise, you need to go to the Times Microwave website (www.timesmicrowave.com). On the website, look for the link to the free online calculator.

1.   In the Product text box, choose a grade of cable called LMR-1700-DB.

2.   In the Frequency text box, enter **2500**, and in the Run Length text box, enter **200** feet.

3.   Click the Calculate button.

Note the amount of dB loss per 100 feet for this specific cable.

4.   Under the Product text box, choose a lower grade of cable called LMR-400.

5.   In the Frequency window, enter **2500**, and in the Length window, enter **200** feet.

6.   Click the Calculate button.

Note that this grade of cabling is rated at a much higher dB loss per 100 feet.

Coverage Analysis

We have already discussed the many considerations of coverage analysis in an earlier section of this chapter. In the following sections, we discuss the two major types of coverage analysis site surveys: manual and predictive. We also explore the software tools that can be used to assist you with these types of coverage analysis surveys. Finally, we examine dynamic and adaptive WLAN technology.

Manual

Manual coverage analysis involves the techniques described earlier, which are used to find the cell boundaries. There are two major types of manual coverage analysis surveys:

Passive   During a *passive manual survey*, the radio collects RF measurements, including received signal strength (dBm), noise level (dBm), and signal-to-noise ratio (dB). Although the client adapter is not associated to the access point during the survey, information is received from radio signals that exist at layer 1 and layer 2.

Active   During an *active manual survey*, the radio is associated to the access point and has layer 2 connectivity, allowing for low-level frame transmissions. If layer 3 connectivity is also established, low-level data traffic such as Internet Control Message Protocol (ICMP) pings are sent in 802.11 data frame transmissions. Layer 1 RF measurements can also be recorded during the active survey. However, upper-layer information such as packet loss and layer 2 retransmission percentages can be measured because the client card is associated to a single access point.

Most vendors recommend that both passive and active manual site surveys be conducted. The information from both manual surveys can then be compared, contrasted, and/or merged into one final coverage analysis report. So, what measurement software tools can be used to collect the data required for both passive and active manual surveys? There are numerous free site survey utilities that can be downloaded from the Internet, including inSSIDer for Windows-based computers and iStumbler for Macintosh computers. Both of these tools can be used for a passive coverage analysis survey.

Most Wi-Fi vendors' client card utility software comes at the very least with a passive survey tool that can be used to measure received signal strength and SNR. Some vendors' software client utilities also include active survey capabilities. On a Macintosh computer, if you hold the Option key down while clicking the Airport Status icon on the menu bar, you will see additional information about your wireless network connection, including PHY mode, BSSID, channel, security, RSSI, and transmit rate, as shown in Figure 16.11. If the connection is using 802.11n or 802.11ac technology, it will even display the MCS index.

Some handheld devices such as VoWiFi phones or Wi-Fi bar code scanners may have site survey capabilities built into the internal software that runs on the handheld device. A common mistake that surveyors make is to hold the VoWiFi phone in a horizontal position when measuring RF signals during a manual site survey.

The internal antenna of the VoWiFi phone is typically vertically polarized, and holding the phone in a horizontal position results in misleading signal measurements. We suggest holding the phone as it will be used, not holding it in a way that creates the best signal readings. Commercial RF site survey applications like the one shown in Figure 16.12 have gained wide acceptance and generally provide better results.

FIGURE 16.11   Macintosh detailed Wi-Fi information

FIGURE 16.12   Commercial coverage analysis application

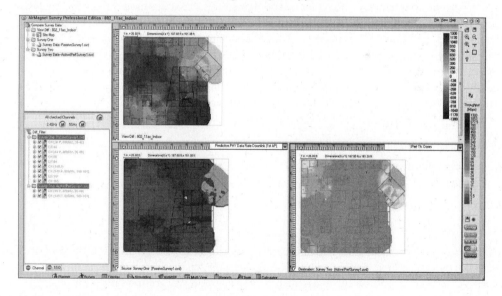

AirMagnet Survey Professional, courtesy of Fluke Networks

These commercial packages allow the site survey engineer to import a graphic of the building's floor plans into the application. A variety of graphic formats are usually supported, and the floor plan typically must be to scale. The commercial application works with an 802.11 client radio and takes measurements in either a passive manual mode or an active manual mode. The site survey engineer walks through the building capturing the RF information while also recording the location on the graphic of the floor plan that is displayed in the software. The information collected during both active and passive modes can then be merged, and a visual representation of the RF footprints or coverage cells is displayed over the graphic floor plan.

These commercial packages can also retain the information, which can then be used for offline modeling, so the WLAN design engineer can create some what-if scenarios by changing channel and power settings. Commercial site survey applications can also assist in capacity planning in regard to data rates per cell. Floor plans for multiple floors can be loaded into the applications, and 3D coverage analysis is often possible. For outdoor site surveys, GPS capabilities are included to log latitude and longitude coordinates.

Predictive

The last method of RF coverage analysis uses applications that provide RF simulations and modeling design capabilities. *Predictive coverage analysis* is accomplished using an application that creates visual models of RF coverage cells, bypassing the need for actually capturing RF measurements. Projected cell coverage zones are created using modeling algorithms and attenuation values.

Blueprints and floor plans often use vector graphic formats (.dwg, .dwf) and can contain layer information, including the type of building materials that are used. Predictive analysis software often supports both vector and raster graphics (.bmp, .jpg, .tif) and allows for the import of building floor plans. The WLAN design engineer will indicate in the software what materials are used in the floor plan. The predictive application already has attenuation values for various materials, such as drywall, concrete, and glass, programmed into the software. The software creates forecast models using the predictive algorithms and the attenuation information. The modeling forecast can include the following:

- Channel reuse patterns
- Coverage cell boundaries
- Access point placement
- Access point power settings
- Number of access points
- Data rates

Virtual access points are created and overlaid on the floor plan graphic. Multiple what-if scenarios can be created by changing the power settings, channel settings, or antenna type of the virtual access points, which can also be moved to any location on the floor plan. Predictive applications are an excellent tool to use with blueprints of buildings that have yet to be built.

Many of the enterprise wireless vendors provide predictive site survey tools for their customers or partners to use to design and plan a wireless network. Some of these tools allow the designer to identify types of walls and assign attenuation values, while others allow the designer to identify an area along with the type of expected attenuation: open space, cubicles, or offices. This allows the designer to specify the expected attenuation without having to identify and enter every object that attenuates signal. As networks are being designed with more APs to provide denser coverage, this type of predictive coverage analysis is becoming more commonplace.

Which Type of Coverage Survey Is Better? Manual or Predictive?

Nothing beats an old-fashioned onsite manual coverage survey if you have the time and the money, although entering the initial data for a predictive survey can also be time-consuming. Most site survey engineers have begun using predictive modeling software to cut down on the time and costs needed for the manual site survey. A forecast model is first created with the predictive application, and then the site survey engineer conducts a manual site survey to validate the projected design.

Predictive coverage analysis software can be a valuable tool, but some sort of manual site survey is still necessary to confirm the coverage simulations. Predictive analysis surveys have become much more commonplace in recent years. Manual site surveys are now often considered to be a quick validation survey that verifies the coverage of a predictive analysis.

Dynamic RF

Could the need for manual site surveys ever be eliminated? Most site survey professionals would argue that a manual coverage analysis of some type will always be needed. However, many WLAN vendors argue that dynamic RF technologies exist that eliminate or drastically reduce the need for manual coverage analysis.

Currently, software and hardware solutions already exist that provide *radio resource management (RRM)*, where access points can dynamically change their configuration based on accumulated RF information. gathered from the access points radios. Based on the accumulated RF information, the access points adjust their power and channel settings, dynamically changing the RF coverage cells. Radio resources management is also referred to as dynamic RF.

RRM can address isolated WLAN capacity needs by utilizing dynamic load balancing of clients between the access points. When implemented, RRM provides automatic cell sizing, automatic monitoring, troubleshooting, and optimization of the RF environment, which can best be described as a self-organizing wireless LAN. RRM cannot make up for a poorly planned network, but it can help adjust and adapt to periodic or isolated surges in network usage and demand.

🌐 **Real World Scenario**

Is a Site Survey Even Needed If the WLAN Vendor Supports Dynamic RF Capabilities?

In recent years, RRM technology has gained wide acceptance because almost all WLAN vendors offer some sort of dynamic RF solution. Many of the vendors' customers have had excellent success with dynamic RF deployments. Very often, sales representatives of the various WLAN controller vendors claim that a site survey is no longer necessary because of the dynamic and self-organizing nature of their RRM solution. Although dynamic RF technology has come a long way in recent years, allowing the APs to adapt to the environment, RRM does not provide for AP placement. A manual and/or predictive model survey should be the first order of business *pre-deployment*. Installation and validation of the network design should then be performed. Dynamic RF capabilities are used *post-deployment* to automatically make necessary channel and power changes in a live operational environment.

In a WLAN controller environment, the thin access points monitor their respective channels as well as use off-channel scanning capabilities to monitor other frequencies. Any RF information heard by the access points is reported back to the WLAN controller. Based on all the RF monitoring from multiple access points, the WLAN controller will make dynamic changes. Some lightweight access points may be told to change to a different channel while other APs may be told to change their transmit power settings.

Wireless Network Validation

Immediately after a wireless network has been installed, it is important to audit or validate the installation. This validation allows you to verify the RF coverage and data rates that are being provided by the installed network; you can then compare the actual values with expected values from your network design plans. Hopefully, these numbers meet or exceed your expectations. If they do not, you will need to further analyze why and then determine whether the actual coverage and data rates are acceptable or whether you will need to modify your installation to improve your network. If you hired a company to design and install your network for you, this network validation is important to ensure that they delivered what was promised and expected.

Unfortunately, a wireless network does not always behave as expected. Over time or even overnight, the performance of the network could degrade. This degradation could be caused by a change in how the network is used, hardware or software problems, failure with access points or the WLAN controller, or a change in the physical operating environment of the network. Any or all of these can affect the RF coverage. In this situation, a wireless network validation may be able to help you with identifying the cause of your problem.

A wireless network validation is typically performed by systematically walking through the building or coverage area of the wireless network and taking RF and network measurements. These measurements are then documented on the floor plan or map. This information should help you to identify where and why your problem exists.

There are many products on the market that can help you perform a wireless network validation. Many of the site survey planning tools can be used to perform wireless network validation, allow you to take network measurements, and provide you with visual RF heatmaps of your environment. This often involves an extensive and tedious process of walking through your building while carrying a laptop. In lieu of walking around with a laptop, or as an additional resource, you may use a handheld tool, like the one shown in Figure 16.13.

Handheld Wi-Fi testers are typically ruggedized to protect them from accidents and misuse. Handheld RF scanners can identify both access points and client devices. They can provide extensive information about the access points, SSIDs, RF signals, security, and network traffic, along with many other pieces of information. A good handheld tool can provide you with an extensive array of information and allow you to understand what a client device sees on the network, hopefully helping you to understand if the network is operating correctly and, if not, why.

FIGURE 16.13   Fluke AirCheck Wi-Fi Tester

Fluke AirCheck Wi-Fi Tester, courtesy of Fluke Networks

Summary

In this chapter, you learned the mandatory and optional aspects of a wireless site survey. In the past, spectrum and coverage analysis surveys have always been mandatory. With the increase in the demand for and dependency that is being placed on wireless LANs, application and throughput testing are also now advisable. We discussed the importance of locating potential sources of interference by using a spectrum analyzer, and we defined all the steps necessary to conduct both a manual and passive coverage analysis site survey.

This chapter also provided a discourse of all the tools necessary for either an indoor or outdoor site survey. We covered the three major types of coverage analysis as well as self-organizing WLAN technology. Conducting a well-defined and thorough wireless site survey will lay the foundation for proper WLAN design and WLAN management. A site survey validation will ensure that your planned design is operating as expected.

Exam Essentials

Define spectrum, coverage, and application analysis.   Understand why both spectrum and coverage analysis are considered mandatory and application analysis, although optional, is also typically needed.

Identify sources of WLAN interference.   Describe all of the various devices that are potential sources of interference in both the 2.4 GHz ISM and the 5 GHz U-NII bands.

Explain RF measurements.   Be able to explain the procedure used while conducting coverage analysis and the different types of RF measurements recorded, including received signal strength and signal-to-noise ratio.

Understand AP placement and configuration.   Explain how AP placement, power, and channel settings are part of coverage analysis.

Identify all site survey tools.   Understand the difference between an outdoor and indoor site survey, and identify all the necessary tools.

Explain the two types of coverage analysis.   Describe the differences between manual and predictive site surveys, and explain self-organizing WLAN technology.

Understand the importance of performing a wireless network validation.   Explain the importance of a wireless network validation to verify a newly installed network or to help troubleshoot a network that is not operating as expected.

Review Questions

1. The Crocker company has generated a visual model of RF coverage for its corporate headquarters by using predictive modeling site survey software. The next step requires validation with a manual site survey. What modeling parameters should be validated during the manual site survey? (Choose all that apply.)

   A. AP placement and power settings

   B. Throughput

   C. Coverage boundaries

   D. Encryption settings

   E. Roaming parameters

2. Which potential regional weather conditions can adversely affect an outdoor wireless bridge link and should be noted during an outdoor site survey? (Choose all that apply.)

   A. Lightning

   B. Dew point

   C. Wind

   D. Cloud cover

   E. Thunder

3. Name the major types of coverage analysis site surveys. (Choose all that apply.)

   A. Assisted

   B. Self-organizing

   C. Manual

   D. Capacity

   E. Predictive

4. ACME Hospital uses a connection-oriented telemetry monitoring system in the cardiac care unit. Management wants the application available over a WLAN. Uptime is very important because of the critical nature of the monitoring system. What should the site survey engineer be looking for that might cause a loss of communication over the WLAN? (Choose all that apply.)

   A. Medical equipment interference

   B. Safety glass containing metal mesh wire

   C. Patients

   D. Bedpans

   E. Elevator shafts

5. Which type of coverage analysis requires a radio card to be associated to an access point?

   A. Associated

   B. Passive

   C. Predictive

   D. Assisted

   E. Active

6. Which of the following tools can be used in an indoor site survey? (Choose all that apply.)

   A. Measuring wheel

   B. GPS

   C. Ladder

   D. Battery pack

   E. Microwave oven

7. Which of the following tools might be used in an outdoor site survey used to provide outdoor coverage? (Choose all that apply.)

   A. Spectrum analyzer

   B. Outdoor blueprints or topography map

   C. Mesh routers

   D. GPS

8. Name potential sources of interference in the 5 GHz U-NII band. (Choose all that apply.)

   A. Microwave oven

   B. Cordless phones

   C. FM radios

   D. Radar

   E. Nearby 802.11b/g WLAN

9. Which of these measurements are taken during a passive manual site survey? (Choose all that apply.)

   A. SNR

   B. dBi

   C. dBm signal strength

   D. dBd

10. Which of the following tools is not necessary for an outdoor bridging site survey?

   A. Inclinometer

   B. Digital camera

   C. Blueprints

D. Spectrum analyzer

E. GPS

11. Name the necessary calculations for an outdoor bridging survey under 5 miles. (Choose all that apply.)

A. Link budget

B. Free space path loss

C. Fresnel zone

D. Fade margin adjustment

E. Height of the antenna beamwidth

12. Name potential sources of interference that might be found during a 2.4 GHz site survey. (Choose all that apply.)

A. Toaster oven

B. Nearby 802.11 FHSS access point

C. Plasma cutter

D. Bluetooth headset

E. 2.4 GHz video camera

13. Which of the following tools can be used in an indoor 802.11 site survey? (Choose all that apply.)

A. Multiple antennas

B. 902 to 928 MHz spectrum analyzer

C. Client adapter

D. Access point

E. Floor plan map

14. Brandon Burmeister is a site survey engineer who is planning to deploy a wireless controller solution with dual-radio, dual-frequency lightweight access points. The employees will be assigned to the 5 GHz network, and the guest users will be assigned to the 2.4 GHz network. CCMP/AES encryption will be required for the employees, while the guest users will use only static WPA-PSK. Name the best possible choice that Brandon has for coverage analysis. (Choose the best answer.)

A. Conduct a predictive site survey for the 5 GHz network and an assisted site survey for the 2.4 GHz network.

B. Conduct manual coverage analysis for the 2.4 GHz network first and then conduct manual coverage analysis for the 5 GHz network.

C. Conduct a predictive site survey for the 2.4 GHz network and an assisted site survey for the 5 GHz network.

D. Conduct manual coverage analysis for the 5 GHz network first and then conduct manual coverage analysis for the 2.4 GHz network based on the AP placement of the 5 GHz APs.

15. Savannah has to perform a site survey for a WLAN by using a multiple-channel architecture (MCA) system in a 20-story building with multiple tenants. What should Savannah consider during the planning and implementation stages of the site survey? (Choose all that apply.)

- **A.** Other tenants' WLANs should be considered.
- **B.** Only WLAN controller solutions with lightweight APs should be deployed and not autonomous access points.
- **C.** Access points should use high-gain omnidirectional antennas to provide coverage across multiple floors.
- **D.** Access points should be at full transmit power to provide coverage across multiple floors.
- **E.** The cell coverage of each access point should extend to only one floor above and one floor below to create a three-dimensional channel reuse pattern.

16. Which of the following tools may be found within an indoor site survey kit? (Choose all that apply.)

- **A.** Digital camera
- **B.** Colored electrical tape
- **C.** Grid antenna
- **D.** Access point enclosure unit
- **E.** Temporary mounting gear

17. Jane Barrett is installing a controller-based wireless network that uses both software and hardware to monitor and dynamically change the power and channel settings of the APs. This technology is known as what? (Choose all that apply.)

- **A.** Dynamic rate selection (DRS)
- **B.** Radio resource management (RRM)
- **C.** Adaptive radio configuration (ARC)
- **D.** Self-organizing wireless LAN

18. What access point settings should be recorded during manual coverage analysis? (Choose all that apply.)

- **A.** Power settings
- **B.** Encryption settings
- **C.** Authentication settings
- **D.** Channel setting
- **E.** IP address

19. Which type of manual coverage analysis does not require a radio card to be associated to an access point?

    A. Associated

    B. Passive

    C. Predictive

    D. Assisted

    E. Active

20. Which type of site survey uses modeling algorithms and attenuation values to create visual models of RF coverage cells?

    A. Associated

    B. Passive

    C. Predictive

    D. Assisted

    E. Active

Chapter

17

Power over Ethernet (PoE)

IN THIS CHAPTER, YOU WILL LEARN ABOUT THE FOLLOWING:

✓ **History of PoE**

    ▪ Nonstandard PoE

    ▪ IEEE 802.3af

    ▪ IEEE Std 802.3-2005, Clause 33

    ▪ IEEE 802.3at-2009

    ▪ IEEE Std 802.3-2012, Clause 33

✓ **PoE devices (overview)**

    ▪ Powered device (PD)

    ▪ Power-sourcing equipment (PSE)

    ▪ Endpoint PSE

    ▪ Midspan PSE

    ▪ Power-sourcing equipment pin assignments

✓ **Planning and deploying PoE**

    ▪ Power planning

    ▪ Redundancy

    ▪ 802.11n or 802.11ac and PoE

In this chapter, you will learn about the various ways that an Ethernet cable can be used to provide power to networking devices. *Power over Ethernet (PoE)* is not a Wi-Fi technology, nor is it used specifically for Wi-Fi devices. However, it has become the predominant method for powering enterprise-class access points, thus making it a necessary and important topic when discussing wireless networking.

History of PoE

Before we begin this chapter, we need to explain what PoE is. Over the years, computer networking typically entailed connecting a stationary, electrically powered computer system to a wired network. The computers were anything from desktop PCs to servers and mainframes. As is typical with technology, larger computers gave way to smaller computers, and laptop and portable devices began to appear. Eventually, some of the networking devices became small enough, both physically and electronically, that it became possible and practical not only to use the Ethernet cable to transmit data to the device, but also to send the electricity necessary to power the device.

The concept of providing power from the network dates back to the birth of the telephone, which to this day still receives power from the telephone network. Computer networking devices that are often powered with PoE are desktop Voice over IP (VoIP) phones, cameras, and access points. Ethernet cables consist of four pairs of wires. With 10 Mbps and 100 Mbps Ethernet, two pairs are used for transmitting and receiving data and the other two pairs are unused. Gigabit Ethernet uses all four pairs of wires to transmit and receive data. As you will see later in this chapter, this is not a problem, since PoE can provide power on the unused wires or on the same wires that are used to transmit and receive data.

When you are providing power to devices via the same Ethernet cable that provides the data, a single low-voltage Ethernet cable is all you need to install a networked PoE device. The use of PoE devices alleviates the need to run electrical cables and outlets to every location that needs to be connected to the network. Not only does this greatly reduce the cost of installing network devices, it also increases flexibility in terms of where these devices can be installed and mounted. Moving devices is also easier, because all that is required at the new location is a PoE-powered Ethernet cable.

Nonstandard PoE

As with most new technologies, the initial PoE products were proprietary solutions created by individual companies that recognized the need for the technology. The IEEE process to create a PoE standard began in 1999; however, it would take about four years before the standard became a reality. In the meantime, vendor-proprietary PoE continued to proliferate. Proprietary PoE solutions often used different voltages, and mixing proprietary solutions could result in damaged equipment.

IEEE 802.3af

The *IEEE 802.3af* Power over Ethernet committee created the PoE amendment to the 802.3 standard. It was officially referred to as IEEE 802.3 "Amendment: Data Terminal Equipment (DTE) Power via Media Dependent Interface." This amendment to the IEEE 802.3 standard was approved on June 12, 2003, and defined how to provide PoE to 10BaseT (Ethernet), 100BaseT (Fast Ethernet), and 1000BaseT (Gigabit Ethernet) devices.

IEEE Std 802.3-2005, Clause 33

In June 2005, the IEEE revised the 802.3 standard, creating IEEE Std 802.3-2005. The 802.3af amendment was one of four amendments that were incorporated into this revised standard. In the 2005 revision of the 802.3 standard, and in the more recent revisions (it was revised in 2008, and again in 2012), *Clause 33* is the section that defines PoE.

IEEE 802.3at-2009

The IEEE 802.3at amendment was ratified in 2009. 802.3at is also known as PoE+ or PoE plus, since it extends the capabilities of PoE as originally defined in the 802.3af amendment. Two of the main objectives of the 802.3at Task Group were to be able to provide more power to powered devices and to maintain backward compatibility with Clause 33 devices. As APs become faster and incorporate newer technologies, such as multiple input, multiple output (MIMO), they require more power to operate. Switches and controllers that incorporate 802.3at technology are able to provide power to legacy APs as well as newer APs that require more power. The IEEE 802.3at amendment is able to provide up to 30 watts of power using two pairs of wires in an Ethernet cable. The 802.3at amendment defines PoE devices as either Type 1 or Type 2. Devices capable of supporting the higher power defined in the 802.3at amendment are defined as Type 2 devices, and devices not capable of supporting the higher power are defined as Type 1 devices.

Typically, when an 802 amendment is created and ratified, the amendment document is essentially a series of additions, deletions, and edits that modify and update the base standard. With 802.3at, the PoE section (Clause 33) of the 802.3-2008 standard was entirely replaced by the 802.3at amendment.

IEEE Std 802.3-2012, Clause 33

In December 2012, the IEEE revised the 802.3 standard again and created IEEE Std 802.3-2012. Just as the 802.3af amendment had been incorporated into the 802.3

standard in 2005, with the release of the 802.3-2012 revised standard, the 802.3at amendment was officially incorporated into this new revision. Clause 33 of the IEEE Std 802.3-2012 now included the higher power capabilities defined by the 802.3at amendment.

An Overview of PoE Devices

The PoE standard defines two types of PoE devices: powered devices (PDs) and power-sourcing equipment (PSE). These devices communicate with each other and provide the PoE infrastructure.

Powered Device

The *powered device (PD)* either requests or draws power from the power-sourcing equipment. PDs must be capable of accepting up to 57 volts from either the data lines or the unused pairs of the Ethernet cable. The PD must also be able to accept power with either polarity from the power supply in what is known as mode A or mode B, as described in Table 17.1.

TABLE 17.1 PD pinout

Conductor	Mode A	Mode B
1	Positive voltage, negative voltage	
2	Positive voltage, negative voltage	
3	Negative voltage, positive voltage	
4		Positive voltage, negative voltage
5		Positive voltage, negative voltage
6	Negative voltage, positive voltage	
7		Negative voltage, positive voltage
8		Negative voltage, positive voltage

The PD must reply to the power-sourcing equipment with a *detection signature* and notify the power-sourcing equipment whether it is in a state in which it will accept power or will not accept power. The detection signature is also used to indicate that the PD is compliant with 802.3-2012, Clause 33. If the device is determined not to be compliant, power to the device will be withheld. If the device is in a state in which it will accept power, the PD can optionally provide a *classification signature*. This classification signature lets the power-sourcing equipment know how much power the device will need.

Type 2 devices perform a two-event Physical layer classification or Data-Link layer classification, which allows a Type 2 PD to identify whether it is connected to a Type 1 or a Type 2 PSE. If mutual identification cannot be completed, the device can only operate as a Type 1 device.

Table 17.2 lists the current values used to identify the various classification signatures. If none of these current values are measured, the device is considered to be a Class 0 device. If the device is not identified, the PSE does not know how much power the device needs; therefore, it allocates the maximum power. If the device is classified, the PSE has to allocate only the amount of power needed by the PD, thus providing better power management. Proper classification of the devices can lead to a managed reduction in power usage and can also enable you to connect more devices to a single PoE-capable switch.

TABLE 17.2 PD classification signature measured electrical current values

Parameter	Conditions	Minimum	Maximum	Unit
Class 0	14.5 V to 20.5 V	0	4	milliampere (mA)
Class 1	14.5 V to 20.5 V	9	12	mA
Class 2	14.5 V to 20.5 V	17	20	mA
Class 3	14.5 V to 20.5 V	26	30	mA
Class 4	14.5 V to 20.5 V	36	44	mA

In the past, some vendors used proprietary layer 2 discovery protocols to perform classification. Although these techniques are good from the power-management and consumption perspective, they are proprietary and will not work with other manufacturers' products. *Link Layer Discovery Protocol (LLDP)* is a standards-based layer 2 neighbor discovery protocol that can also be used for more detailed power classification. Table 17.3 lists the classes of PoE devices and the range of maximum power that they use. Power classes 0 to 3 are for Type 1 devices that will work with 802.3af power sourcing equipment. Power class 4 is meant for Type 2 devices that work with 802.3at (PoE+) power sourcing equipment. The maximum power draw of an 802.3af-compliant device is 12.95 watts, and the maximum power draw of an 802.3at-compliant device is 25.5 watts.

TABLE 17.3   PD power classification and usage

Class	Usage	Range of maximum power used	Class description
0	Default	0.44 W to 12.95 W	Class unimplemented
1	Optional	0.44 W to 3.84 W	Very low power
2	Optional	3.84 W to 6.49 W	Low power
3	Optional	6.49 W to 12.95 W	Mid power
4	Type 2 devices	12.95 W to 25.5 W	High power

Can 802.3af-Compliant Access Points Use More Power?

Although a PSE port might offer 15.4 watts of power, the maximum draw of an 802.3af-compliant PD is 12.95 W. For example, an access point might use as much as 12.95 W on CAT3 cabling or higher. The power draw is always lower than the original power source because of insertion loss from the cable. In reality, a PD might be able to draw more power if higher grade cabling is used. For example, a 3x3:3 MIMO access point might actually need 14.95 W to operate with full functionality. Most WLAN vendors will recommend the use of CAT5e cabling or better so that 802.11n access points can draw more than 12.95 W and fully power all the MIMO radios.

Power-Sourcing Equipment

The *power-sourcing equipment (PSE)* provides power to the PD. The power supplied is at a nominal 48 volts (44 volts to 57 volts). The PSE searches for powered devices by using a direct current (DC) detection signal. After a PoE-compliant device is identified, the PSE will provide power to that device. If a device does not respond to the detection signature, the PSE will withhold power. This prevents noncompliant PD equipment from becoming damaged.

As you can see in Table 17.4, the amount of power provided by the PSE is greater than what is used by the PD (Table 17.3). This is because the PSE needs to account for the worst-case scenario, in which there may be power loss due to the cables and connectors between the PSE and the PD. The maximum draw of any powered device is 25.5 watts. The PSE can also classify the PD if the PD provided a classification signature. Once connected, the PSE continuously checks the connection status of the PD along with monitoring for other electrical conditions, such as short circuits. When power is no longer required, the PSE will stop providing it. Power-sourcing equipment is divided into two types of equipment: endpoint and midspan.

TABLE 17.4   PSE power

Class	Minimum power from the PSE
0	15.4 W
1	4.0 W
2	7.0 W
3	15.4 W
4	30.0 W

Endpoint PSE

An *endpoint PSE* provides power and Ethernet data signals from the same device. Endpoint devices are typically PoE-enabled Ethernet switches, such as the 48-port switch shown in Figure 17.1. Because the PoE-enabled switches are used to power access layer devices (such as APs and phones), the switches are typically access layer switches, as opposed to distribution or core switches. Some specialty devices, such as WLAN controllers (as shown in Figure 17.2), may also function as endpoint PSE equipment. Most controller-based APs are powered by an access layer switch; however, some of the smaller model or branch WLAN controllers might also be used to power access points.

FIGURE 17.1   Aerohive SR2048P: 48-port Gigabit Ethernet access switch with PoE

FIGURE 17.2   An Aruba 7010 wireless controller with PoE

Endpoint equipment can provide power using two methods referred to as Alternative A and Alternative B:

Alternative A   With *Alternative A*, the PSE places power on the data pair. Figure 17.3 shows how a 10BaseT/100BaseTX endpoint PSE provides power using Alternative A, and Figure 17.4 shows how a 1000BaseT endpoint PSE provides power using Alternative A.

Alternative B   Originally, *Alternative B* was designed to provide power on the spare unused pair of wires in a 10BaseT/100BaseTX cable, as shown in Figure 17.5. A 1000BaseT endpoint PSE can also use Alternative B to provide power to a PD by placing the power on two of the data 1000BaseT data pairs, as depicted in Figure 17.6. Endpoint PSE is compatible with 10BaseT (Ethernet), 100BaseTX (Fast Ethernet), and 1000BaseT (Gigabit Ethernet). When 802.3af was initially ratified, 1000BaseT (Gigabit Ethernet) devices could receive PoE from only endpoint devices.

In the next section of this chapter, you will see that that is no longer true. With the ratification of 802.3at, 1000BaseT devices could also be powered using either endpoint PoE or midspan PoE.

FIGURE 17.3   10BaseT/100BaseTX endpoint PSE, Alternative A

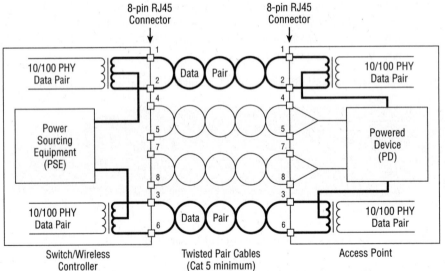

Midspan PSE

A *midspan PSE* acts as a pass-through device, adding power to an Ethernet segment. Midspan equipment enables you to provide PoE to existing networks without having to replace the existing Ethernet switches. A midspan PSE is placed between an Ethernet source (such as an Ethernet switch) and a PD. The midspan PSE acts as an Ethernet repeater while adding power to the Ethernet cable. Originally with 802.3af, midspan devices were only capable of using Alternative B—and only with 10BaseT and 100BaseTX PDs. With the ratification of 802.3at, midspan devices were able to use either Alternative A or Alternative B and they could provide support for 1000BaseT devices.

FIGURE 17.4   1000BaseT endpoint PSE, Alternative A

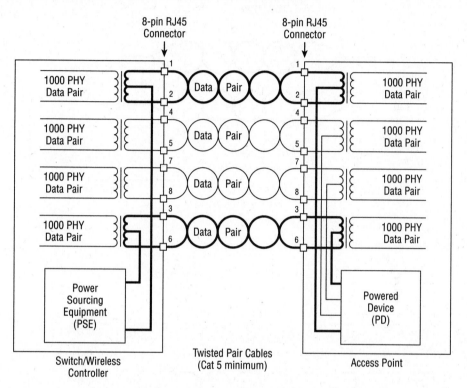

Figure 17.7 shows how a 10BaseT/100BaseTX midspan PSE provides power using Alternative A, and Figure 17.8 shows how a 1000BaseT midspan PSE provides power using Alternative A. Figure 17.9 shows a 10BaseT/100BaseTX midspan PSE providing power using Alternative B, and Figure 17.10 shows how a 1000BaseT midspan PSE provides power using Alternative B.

Figure 17.11 shows a single-port midspan device, along with three multiport devices. The midspan PSE is commonly known as a *power injector* (single-port device) or a PoE hub (multiport device).

Figure 17.12 shows three typical ways of providing power to a PD. Option 1 illustrates an endpoint PoE-enabled switch with inline power. This switch provides both Ethernet and power to the AP. Option 2 and Option 3 illustrate two methods of providing midspan power. Option 2 shows a multiport midspan PSE commonly referred to as an *inline power patch panel*, and Option 3 shows a single-port midspan PSE commonly referred to as a *single-port power injector*.

FIGURE 17.5   10BaseT/100BaseTX endpoint PSE, Alternative B

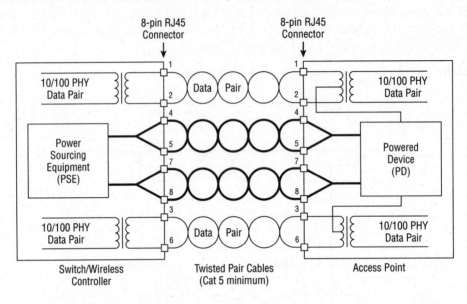

FIGURE 17.6   1000BaseT endpoint PSE, Alternative B

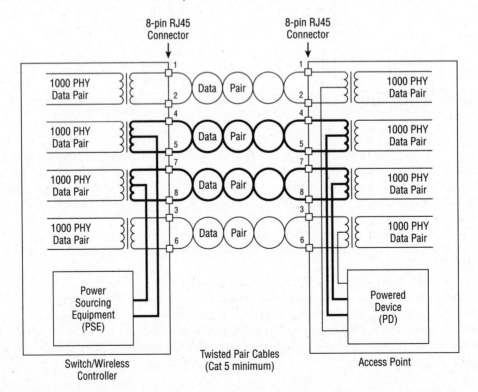

FIGURE 17.7   10BaseT/100BaseTX midspan PSE, Alternative A

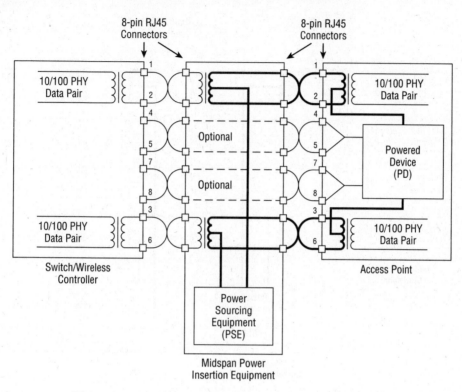

Power-Sourcing Equipment Pin Assignments

The power-sourcing equipment (PSE) must have a *medium dependent interface (MDI)* to carry the current to the powered device (PD). *MDI* is essentially the technical term for the Ethernet cabling connector. Keep in mind that the Ethernet maximum distance limitations of 100 meters (328 feet) still apply when PoE mechanisms are utilized.

There are two valid four-wire pin connections used to provide PoE. In each of these configurations, the two pairs of conductors carry the same nominal current in both magnitude and polarity. When you power a device using Alternative A, the positive voltage is matched to the transmit pair of the PSE. The input pairs of an Ethernet cable must connect to the output pairs of the device it is connected to. This is known as medium dependent interface crossover (MDIX or MDI-X). Many devices are capable of automatically identifying and providing the crossover connection if needed. If a PSE is configured to automatically configure MDI/MDI-X (also called Auto MDI-X, or automatic crossover), the port may choose either Alternative A polarity choice, as described in Table 17.5.

FIGURE 17.8 1000BaseT midspan PSE, Alternative A

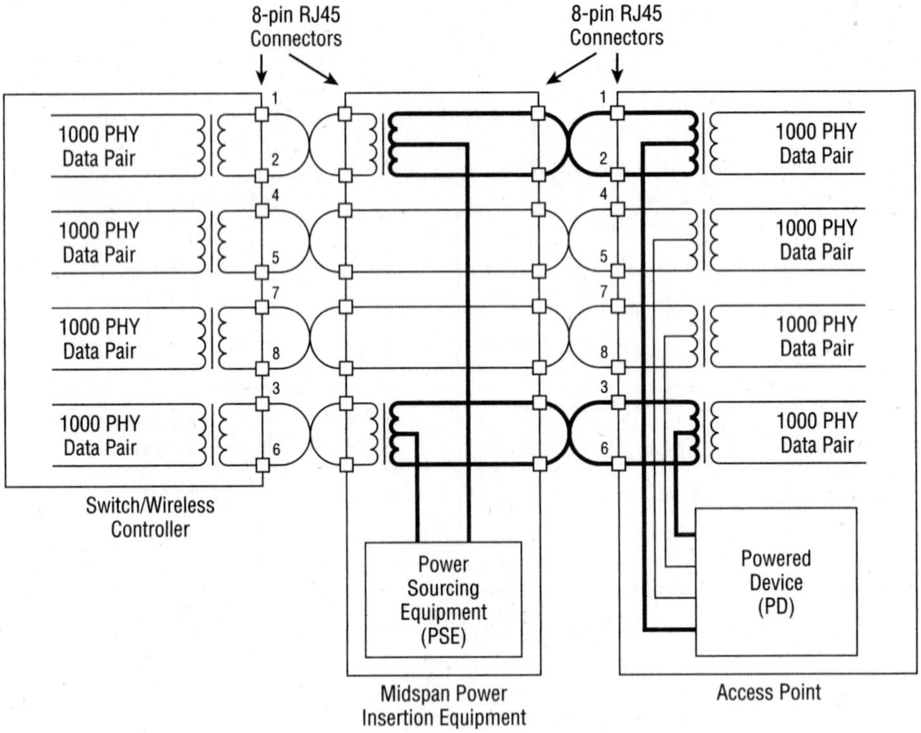

FIGURE 17.9 10BaseT/100BaseTX midspan PSE, Alternative B

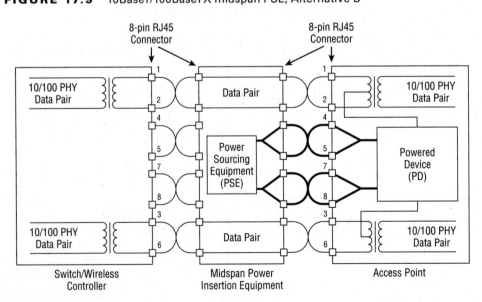

FIGURE 17.10   1000BaseT midspan PSE, Alternative B

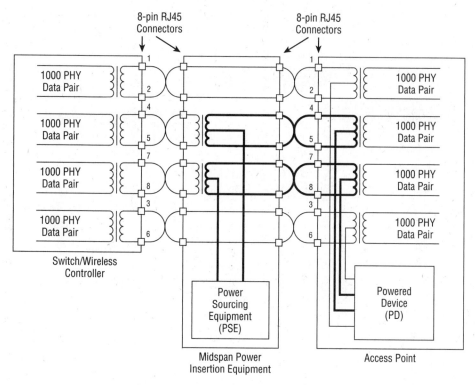

FIGURE 17.11   PowerDsine power injector and PoE hubs

FIGURE 17.12 Three PSE solutions

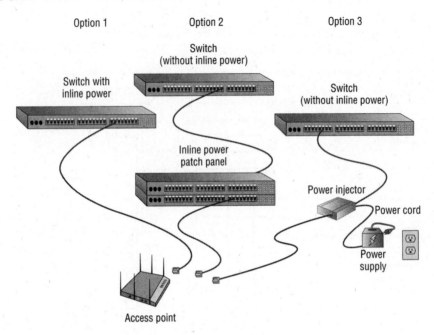

TABLE 17.5 PSE pinout alternatives

Conductor	Alternative A (MDI-X)	Alternative A (MDI)	Alternative B (all)
1	Negative voltage	Positive voltage	
2	Negative voltage	Positive voltage	
3	Positive voltage	Negative voltage	
4			Positive voltage
5			Positive voltage
6	Positive voltage	Negative voltage	
7			Negative voltage
8			Negative voltage

Planning and Deploying PoE

In the past, when non-PoE desktop VoIP telephones and APs were connected to the network, each device had to be individually plugged into a power outlet. These outlets were spread around the building or campus, distributing the power needs. PoE now consolidates the power source to the wiring closet or data center, requiring that only an Ethernet cable be connected to the PoE-powered device.

Power Planning

Instead of the power being distributed for hundreds or thousands of devices, the power for these devices is now being sourced from either a single or a limited number of locations. At maximum power for a PD, the PSE must be capable of providing 15.4 W or 30 W of power to each PoE device, depending on whether your devices require PoE+. Assuming that your PDs do not require PoE+, this means that a typical PoE-enabled 24-port Ethernet switch must be able to provide about 370 watts of power to provide PoE to all 24 ports (15.4 watts × 24 ports = 369.6 watts). This does not include the amount of power necessary for the switch to perform its networking duties. A simple way of determining whether the power supply of the switch is powerful enough is to determine the size of the power supply for the equivalent non-PoE switch and add 15.4 watts for each PoE device that you will be connecting to the switch, or 30 watts for each PoE+ device you will be connecting to the switch.

The maximum power a 110-volt power supply is capable of providing is 3,300 watts (110 volts × 30 amperes). Let's assume that a wiring closet is supplied with a 110 volt, 15 amp circuit (1,650 watts), which is not uncommon. Enterprise-grade PoE-enabled switches often consist of multiple 48-port line cards housed in a chassis. The chassis itself may require 1,000 to 2,000 watts. If the 48-port line cards draw 15.4 watts per port, a total power draw of 740 watts would be required. Depending on the power requirements of the chassis, 3,300 watts would be able to power only the chassis and two to three fully populated 48-port line cards.

Because many devices such as 802.11 APs, video cameras, and desktop VoIP phones may require power, situations often arise where there simply is not enough available wattage to power all the PoE ports. Network engineers have begun to realize the need and importance for a *power budget*. Careful planning is needed to ensure that enough power is available for all the PDs. Powered devices that are capable of classification can greatly assist in conserving energy and subtracting less power from the power budget. A device that needs to draw 3 watts and is not capable of providing a classification signature would be classified as Class 0 by default and subtract 15.4 watts from the power budget. Effectively, 12 watts of power would be wasted. If that same device was capable of providing a classification signature and was classified as a Class 1 device, only 4 watts would be subtracted from the power budget. Classification of PDs will grow in importance as the need for 802.11 deployments grows.

Enterprise switch vendors will list the PoE power budget within the switch specification sheet. The PoE power budget listed in a spec sheet is indeed the amount of power that is available to the ports and is not earmarked for other switch functions. When reading the power budget specifications of a switch, be sure to determine how many ports are PoE-capable. For example, Vendor-A might have a 24-port gigabit switch with a PoE power budget of 195 watts, but the budget is only available to 8 of the 24 ports. Vendor-B might also offer a 24-port gigabit switch with a PoE power budget of 195 watts, but the budget can be available to any of the 24 ports. Vendor-C might sell a 24-port switch with a much larger PoE power budget of 408 watts available to all 24 ports. Keep in mind: The larger the power budget, the cost of the PoE-enabled switch rises significantly.

As shown in Figure 17.13, most switches have the ability to designate whether the port is a standard 802.3af port or 802.3at (PoE+) port. An 802.11a/b/g/n access point will normally need the full 15.4 watts provided by an 802.3af port; however, a VoIP desktop phone might only need 7 watts from the port. The 802.3af port for the phone could be manually configured for only 7 watts and, therefore, save 8.4 watts, which does not need to be subtracted from the overall PoE power budget. PoE ports can often also be configured with a priority level. Higher priority PoE ports take precedence for receiving power in the event that the PoE budget is exceeded. Proper planning of the PoE budget to ensure that the budget is never exceeded is best practice. PoE port priority is also important if there is hardware failure on the switch. PoE switches often require multiple power supplies. If one of the power supplies fail, the switch may not be able to provide power to all of the devices connected to it. PoE port priority allows the network administrator to identify which devices are more critical than others.

FIGURE 17.13 Port level PoE budgeting

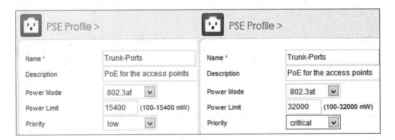

The power budget of a switch or multiple switches should be monitored to make sure that all devices can maintain power. PSE active budget information can usually be seen from the command line of a switch or the GUI interface or monitored by a centralized *network management server (NMS)*. In the example shown in Figure 17.14, a switch has an overall budget of 194.3 watts. An access point is plugged into port 1 and is currently using 5.5 watts, which means 188.8 watts can still be used by other devices. In this example, the AP has been classified as a Class 0 device, which means it can draw as much as 12.95 watts. If an AP is not very busy, it may only need 5 or 6 watts, but if the AP has many clients connected with heavy traffic, the full 12.95 watts might be needed. Therefore, always plan your power budget based on the maximum draw that devices such as access points might use.

FIGURE 17.14   Power budget monitoring

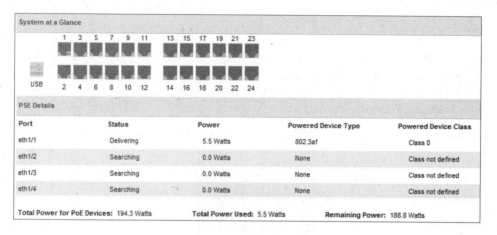

Port	Status	Power	Powered Device Type	Powered Device Class
eth1/1	Delivering	5.5 Watts	802.3af	Class 0
eth1/2	Searching	0.0 Watts	None	Class not defined
eth1/3	Searching	0.0 Watts	None	Class not defined
eth1/4	Searching	0.0 Watts	None	Class not defined

Total Power for PoE Devices: 194.3 Watts   Total Power Used: 5.5 Watts   Remaining Power: 188.8 Watts

---

Why Are My Access Points Randomly Rebooting?

WLAN vendors commonly receive support calls from customers complaining that all of a sudden access points randomly begin to reboot. In most cases, the root cause of random rebooting of APs is that the switch power budget has been eclipsed. Very often, if an AP cannot get the power that it needs, the AP will reboot and try again. Remember that other devices, such as desktop VoIP phones, also use PoE. An extra PoE-powered device might have been plugged into a switch port and the power budget has been exceeded. Proper power budgeting for access points and any other PoE-capable devices is paramount.

Because of the demand for PoE-enabled devices, some switch manufacturers have replaced their 110 volt/30 amp power supplies with 220 volt/20 amp power supplies. The manufacturers are also putting larger power supplies in their switches to handle the additional requirements of PoE. Some PoE switches support power supplies as large as 9,000 watts. As the demand for PoE devices increases, the need to manage and troubleshoot PoE problems will also increase. Test equipment, like that shown in Figure 17.15, can be placed between the PSE and the PD to troubleshoot PoE link issues.

The more PoE devices that you add to the network, the more you concentrate the power requirements in the data center or wiring closet. As your power needs increase, electrical circuits supplying power to the PoE switches might have to be increased. Also, as the power increases, you increase the amount of heat that is generated in the wiring closets, often requiring more climate-control equipment. When you are using high-wattage power supplies, we recommend that you also use redundant power supplies.

Redundancy

As children, we knew that even when there was an electrical failure, the telephone still worked and provided the ability to call someone. This is a level of service that we have come to expect. As VoIP and VoWiFi telephones replace traditional telephone systems, it is important to still provide this same level of continuous service. To achieve this, you should make sure that all of your PoE PSE equipment is connected to uninterruptible power sources. Additionally, it may be important enough to provide dual Ethernet connections to your PoE PD equipment.

FIGURE 17.15 Fluke NetTool Series II inline network tester

Be Careful with PoE

With the increase in popularity of PoE and the requirement to provide power to devices like APs and VoIP telephones, more PoE jacks are being deployed in the office space. One of the nice and necessary features of PoE is that when a device is plugged in, the

PSE can determine whether the device is PoE capable and, if so, will provide power to that device. If the device is not PoE capable, then Ethernet without power will be provided to the device.

Depending on the brand and model of your PoE switch, when a PoE-enabled device is unplugged from the switch, it is possible for the port of the switch to maintain its PoE status for a few seconds, even though there is nothing plugged into the switch. If you were to quickly plug another device into the same port, it is possible for the PoE switch to provide power to that device, even if it is not a PoE-capable device. This introduces a risk of damage to the device.

To prevent this risk from occurring, after unplugging any Ethernet device, you should get into the habit of waiting 5 to 10 seconds before plugging another device into that port or jack. This 5- to10-second delay should be long enough for the PoE port to disable itself. Then when another device is plugged into that port, PoE will identify whether the new device is PoE capable.

802.11n or 802.11ac and PoE

In Chapter 18, "802.11n," you will learn that most current enterprise 802.11n APs use 2x2:2 or 3x3:3 MIMO radios and are dual-frequency capable. In other words, a 3x3:3 dual-frequency 802.11n AP has a total of six radio chains, or transmitters that require power. Power is needed for the three 2.4 GHz transmit chains as well as for the three 5 GHz transmit chains. When the first-generation of 802.11n access points debuted, in many cases, 12.95 watts was insufficient to power a dual-frequency MIMO AP with six transmit radio chains. Some of these multi-radio APs might have needed as much as 20 watts of power.

The first generation of 802.11n APs could be powered sufficiently with 802.3at switches, but most customers still owned 802.3af switches that were only capable of 15.4 watts of power per port. Therefore, many of the WLAN vendors devised various techniques so that the first generation of 802.11n APs could operate using the lower 802.3af power. However, the trade-off was downgraded performance of the first-generation 802.11n APs that operated with 802.3af PSE equipment. The most common method was to downgrade the MIMO capability of the 802.11n access points so that 802.3af power could be used. 802.11n APs with 3x3:3 transmitter capability might only use a single transmitter when using 802.3af PoE and therefore conserve power. The downside was that not all of the MIMO transmitter capabilities were being used by the APs.

The good news is that almost all of the current generation of 3x3:3 dual-frequency 802.11n APs are indeed capable of running with full transmitter capabilities using 802.3af PoE. The 802.11n AP power consumption is lighter and better controlled with the newer hardware that is now available. However, the six transmit radio chains still require more than the 12.95 watts maximum draw that is defined by the 802.3af standard. The MIMO

APs may draw as much as 15 watts from PSE that is capable of 15.4 watts. The WLAN vendors are squeezing a little extra power draw from the PSE. Category 5e or higher cabling is required for an AP to get the extra power draw. Category 3 cabling will not work.

In Chapter 19, "Very High Throughput (VHT) and 802.11ac," you will learn that the 802.11ac radios operate on the 5 GHz band; however, the 2.4 GHz radios still use 802.11n technology. The 802.11ac radios use more complex modulation and can provide for the use of 80 MHz or larger channels at 5 GHz. These new 802.11ac mechanisms require more processing resources and therefore require more power. So, the first generation of 802.11ac 3x3:3 APs require more power than 802.3af can provide and 802.3at power is needed for some of the 802.11ac radios to be fully operational. Some WLAN vendors have released their first-generation 802.11ac access points and 802.3af is fully supported. History has repeated itself, and many of the WLAN vendors have devised various techniques so that the first generation of 802.11ac APs can operate using the lower 802.3af power. However, the trade-off is downgraded performance of the first-generation 802.11ac APs that operate in an 802.3af mode. Once again, the most common method is to downgrade the MIMO capability of the 802.11ac access points so that 802.3af power can be used. 802.11ac APs with 3x3:3 transmitter capability might only use one or two transmitters when using 802.3af PoE and therefore conserve power. The downside is that not all of the MIMO transmitter capabilities are being used by the APs. Other vendors have chosen to disable processor-intensive 802.11ac functions, such as 80 MHz channel capability and the use of more complex modulation. In other words, the 802.11ac 3x3:3 MIMO radio can still use all three transmitters, but effectively the radio functions as an 802.11n radio when using the lower 802.3af power. The good news is that several WLAN vendors now offer 3x3:3 802.11ac access points that are fully functional with 802.3af power.

A second wave of 802.11ac access points is appearing. The next generation of 802.11ac hardware will use a new chipset that enables beamforming capabilities, which will require more processing resources and therefore more power. Most likely the second wave of 802.11ac access points will also use 4x4:4 MIMO radios, which also will require more power. As we move toward the next generation of MIMO access points, the use of 802.3at power will most likely be a requirement.

There is no reason you cannot use an available power outlet to provide electrical current to an AP. The downside is that most APs are deployed in areas where a power outlet is not conveniently accessible. The best way to power 802.11n and 802.11ac APs is to deploy a PoE+ (802.3at) PSE that is capable of providing 30 watts via an Ethernet cable. With the fast growth of wireless, if you are purchasing PoE switches, you should only consider switches that are 802.3at (PoE+) capable.

Summary

This chapter focused on Power over Ethernet and the equipment and techniques necessary to provide service to PDs. Power over Ethernet can be provided in two general ways: through proprietary PoE or through standards-based PoE (802.3af or 802.3at, integrated into the IEEE Std 802.3 in Clause 33).

Standards-based PoE consists of a few key components:

- Powered device (PD)
- Power-sourcing equipment (PSE)
- Endpoint PSE
- Midspan PSE

These components work together to provide a functioning PoE environment.

The final section of this chapter covered considerations that need to be made when planning and deploying PoE:

- Power planning
- Redundancy

Exam Essentials

Know the history of PoE.   Make sure you know the history of PoE, the original 802.3af amendment, the 802.3at amendment, and current references to IEEE Std 802.3, Clause 33.

Be familiar with the various PoE devices and how they interoperate.   Make sure you know about the various PoE devices and their roles in providing PoE. Understand how the following devices work: powered device (PD), power-sourcing equipment (PSE), endpoint PSE, and midspan PSE.

Know the different device classes and the classification process.   Make sure you know the five device classes and how the classification process works to determine the class of a PD. Know how much current each class of devices uses along with how much power the PSE generates for each class of devices.

Review Questions

1. The IEEE 802.3af and 802.3at amendments have been incorporated into the IEEE Std 802.3 revised standard and are defined in which clause?

   A. Clause 15

   B. Clause 17

   C. Clause 19

   D. Clause 33

   E. Clause 43

2. If a classification signature is not provided, the device is considered to be in what class?

   A. 0

   B. 1

   C. 2

   D. 3

   E. 4

3. Which types of PoE devices are defined by the standard? (Choose all that apply.)

   A. PSE

   B. PPE

   C. PD

   D. PT

4. A powered device (PD) must be capable of accepting up to how many volts from either the data lines or the unused pairs of the Ethernet cable?

   A. 14.5 volts

   B. 20.5 volts

   C. 48 volts

   D. 57 volts

5. To qualify as compliant with the 802.3at amendment (now part of the 802.3 standard), a powered device (PD) must do which of the following? (Choose all that apply.)

   A. Be able to accept power over the unused data pairs.

   B. Reply to the PSE with a detection signature.

   C. Accept power with either polarity from the PSE.

   D. Reply to the PSE with a classification signature.

6. A VoIP telephone is connected to a 24-port PoE midspan PSE. If the telephone does not provide a classification signature, how much power will the PSE provide to the telephone?

   A. 12.95 watts

   B. 4.0 watts

    C. 7.0 watts

    D. 15.4 watts

7. An endpoint PSE that provides power by using Alternative B is capable of providing power to devices by using which of the following Ethernet technologies? (Choose all that apply.)

    A. 10BaseT

    B. 100BaseTX

    C. 1000BaseT

    D. 100BaseFX

8. What is the range of maximum power used by a class 4 PD?

    A. 0.44 to 12.95 watts

    B. 3.84 to 6.49 watts

    C. 6.49 to 12.95 watts

    D. 12.95 to 25.5 watts

    E. 15 to 30 watts

9. At maximum power requirements, a 24-port 802.3at-compliant PoE Ethernet switch must be able to provide about how many total watts of power to PoE devices on all ports?

    A. 15.4 watts

    B. 370 watts

    C. 720 watts

    D. 1,000 watts

    E. Not enough information is provided to answer the question.

10. If an 802.3at-compliant AP is equipped with two radios and requires 7.5 watts of power, how much power will the PSE provide to it?

    A. 7.5 watts

    B. 10.1 watts

    C. 15 watts

    D. 15.4 watts

    E. 30.0 watts

11. The PSE provides power within a range of _____ volts, with a nominal value of _____ volts.

    A. 14.5 to 20.5, 18

    B. 6.49 to 12.95, 10.1

    C. 12 to 19, 15.4

    D. 44 to 57, 48

12. Tim has installed an Ethernet switch that is compliant with 802.3at. He is having problems with his APs randomly rebooting. Which of the following could be causing his problems?

    A. Many PoE VoIP telephones are connected to the same Ethernet switch.

    B. Most of the Ethernet cables running from the switch to the APs are 90 meters long.

C. The Ethernet cables are only Cat 5e.

D. The switch is capable of 1000BaseT, which is not compatible with VoIP telephones.

13. You are designing an 802.3at-compliant network and are installing a 24-port Ethernet switch to support 10 Class 1 VoIP phones and 10 Class 0 APs. The switch requires 500 watts to perform its basic switching functions. How much total power will be needed?

   A. 500 watts

   B. 694 watts

   C. 808 watts

   D. 1,000 watts

14. You are designing an 802.3at-capable network and are installing a 24-port Ethernet switch to support 10 Class 2 cameras and 10 Class 3 APs. The switch requires 1,000 watts to perform its basic switching functions. How much total power will be needed?

   A. 1,080 watts

   B. 1,224 watts

   C. 1,308 watts

   D. 1,500 watts

15. When a PoE network is installed, what is the maximum distance from the PSE to the PD, as defined in the standards? (Choose all that apply.)

   A. 90 meters

   B. 100 meters

   C. 300 feet

   D. 328 feet

   E. 328 meters

16. What is the maximum power draw of an 802.3at PD?

   A. 12.95 watts

   B. 15 watts

   C. 7.4 watts

   D. 25.5 watts

   E. 30 watts

17. What is the maximum power used by a PD Class 0 device?

   A. 3.84 W

   B. 6.49 W

   C. 12.95 W

   D. 15.4 W

18. The PSE will apply a voltage of between 14.5 and 20.5 and measure the resulting current to determine the class of the device. Which current range represents Class 2 devices?

    A. 0 to 4 mA

    B. 5 to 8 mA

    C. 9 to 12 mA

    D. 13 to 16 mA

    E. 17 to 20 mA

19. A PD must be capable of accepting power with either polarity from the power supply. In mode A, on which conductors/wires does the PD accept power?

    A. 1, 2, 3, 4

    B. 5, 6, 7, 8

    C. 1, 2, 3, 6

    D. 4, 5, 7, 8

20. A Type 2 PSE will perform a two-event Physical layer classification or Data-Link layer classification. If mutual identification cannot be completed, what does the Type 2 device do?

    A. Defaults as a Category 0 device.

    B. PoE cannot be enabled.

    C. Operates as a Type 1 device.

    D. Provides 15.4 watts of power using Alternative A.

Chapter

18

802.11n

IN THIS CHAPTER, YOU WILL LEARN ABOUT THE FOLLOWING:

✓ **802.11n-2009 amendment**

✓ **Wi-Fi Alliance certification**

✓ **MIMO**

- Radio chains
- Spatial multiplexing (SM)
- MIMO diversity
- Space-time block coding (STBC)
- Cyclic shift diversity (CSD)
- Transmit beamforming (TxBF)

✓ **HT channels**

- 20 MHz non-HT and HT channels
- 40 MHz channels
- 40 MHz Intolerant
- Guard interval (GI)
- Modulation and coding scheme (MCS)
- HT PHY
- Non-HT legacy
- HT Mixed
- HT Greenfield

✓ **HT MAC**

- A-MSDU
- A-MPDU
- Block Acknowledgment

- RIFS
- HT power management

✓ **HT operation**

- 20/40 channel operation
- HT protection modes (0–3)
- RTS/CTS and CTS-to-self

✓ **802.11n migration and deployment**

In this chapter, we discuss the Wi-Fi technology that is defined under the 802.11n-2009 amendment. The original main objective of the 802.11n amendment was to increase the data rates and the throughput in both the 2.4 GHz and 5 GHz frequency bands. The 802.11n amendment defines an operation known as *High Throughput (HT)*, which provides PHY and MAC enhancements to provide for data rates potentially as high as 600 Mbps.

802.11n requires a whole new approach to the Physical layer, using a technology called *multiple-input, multiple-output (MIMO)* that requires the use of multiple radios and antennas. As you learned in earlier chapters, multipath is an RF behavior that can cause performance degradation in legacy 802.11a/b/g WLANs. 802.11n radios use MIMO technology, which takes advantage of multipath to increase throughput as well as range.

Besides the use of MIMO technology, HT mechanisms defined by the 802.11n amendment provide for enhanced throughput using other methods. We will discuss the use of 40 MHz channels that provide greater frequency bandwidth. Enhancements to the MAC sublayer also provide for greater throughput with the use of frame aggregation. Although the 802.11e amendment originally defined enhancements to power management, the 802.11n amendment also provides for new power management techniques.

Finally, we discuss the various modes of operation for an HT network and how HT radio transmissions can coexist in the same WLAN environment with radios that use the other legacy technologies we have discussed throughout this book.

802.11n and HT technology are so complex that an entire book dedicated to the topic would probably not be able to fully cover every aspect of HT. However, in this chapter we cover all the key components of HT and the topics needed to properly prepare you for the CWNA exam.

802.11n-2009 Amendment

The 802.11n-2009 amendment defines High Throughput (HT) Clause 20 radios that use multiple-input, multiple-output (MIMO) technology in unison with *Orthogonal Frequency Division Multiplexing (OFDM)* technology. The benefits of using MIMO are increased throughput and even greater range. Enhancements to the MAC sublayer of the Data-Link layer for greater throughput are also defined in the 802.11n amendment.

Many of the mechanisms defined by the 802.11n amendment are vastly different from legacy 802.11a/b/g technologies. However, Clause 20 radios (HT) are required to be backward compatible with older Clause 17 radios (HR-DSSS), Clause 18 radios (OFDM), and Clause 19 radios (ERP). In simpler words, 802.11n radios are backward compatible with legacy 802.11a/b/g radios. A dual-frequency 802.11n Wi-Fi radio is usually referred to as an 802.11a/b/g/n radio.

As you have learned, 802.11b and 802.11g radios can transmit in only the 2.4 GHz ISM band, whereas 802.11a radios transmit in the 5 GHz U-NII bands. It should be noted that the technology defined for use by 802.11n radios is not frequency dependent. HT technology can be used in both the 2.4 GHz ISM band and the 5 GHz U-NII bands. Since the ratification of the 802.11n amendment in 2009, the bulk of the Wi-Fi radio chipsets sold have been 802.11n capable.

After the 802.11n amendment was ratified in 2009, a significant growth in WLAN deployments developed over the next several years. Many businesses upgraded from their legacy 802.11a/b/g infrastructures as 802.11n clients became more commonplace. 802.11n is now the most widely deployed current Wi-Fi technology. The recently ratified 802.11ac-2013 *Very High Throughput (VHT)* amendment builds upon 802.11n technology to achieve gigabit and higher data rates. WLAN vendors have begun to offer 802.11ac access points, and client radios with 802.11ac chipsets have begun to enter the marketplace. The enhancements defined by the 802.11ac-2013 amendment will be discussed in great detail in Chapter 19, "Very High Throughput (VHT) and 802.11ac."

Wi-Fi Alliance Certification

The Wi-Fi Alliance maintains a vendor certification program for 802.11n called Wi-Fi CERTIFIED n. 802.11n products are tested for both mandatory and optional baseline capabilities, as described in Table 18.1. All certified products must also support both Wi-Fi Multimedia (WMM) quality of service (QoS) mechanisms and WPA/WPA2 security mechanisms. Wi-Fi CERTIFIED n devices can operate in both the 2.4 GHz and 5 GHz frequency bands and are also backward compatible with 802.11a/b/g certified devices. Some of the capabilities tested are for access points only.

TABLE 18.1   Wi-Fi CERTIFIED n baseline requirements

Feature	Explanation	Type
Support for two spatial streams	Access points are required to transmit and receive at least two spatial streams. Client stations are required to transmit and receive at least one spatial stream.	Mandatory
Support for three spatial streams	Access points and client stations capable of transmitting and receiving three spatial streams.	Optional (tested if implemented)

Feature	Explanation	Type
Support for A-MPDU and A-MSDU in receive mode. Support for A-MPDU in transmit mode.	Required for all devices. Reduces MAC layer overhead.	Mandatory
Support for Block ACK	Required for all devices. Sends a single Block ACK frame to acknowledge multiple received frames.	Mandatory
2.4 GHz operation	Devices can be 2.4 GHz only, 5 GHz only, or dual-band. For this reason, both frequency bands are listed as optional.	Optional (tested if implemented)
5 GHz operation	Devices can be 2.4 GHz only, 5 GHz only, or dual-band. For this reason, both frequency bands are listed as optional.	Optional (tested if implemented)
Concurrent operation in 2.4 GHz and 5 GHz bands	This mode is tested for APs only. APs capable of operating in both bands are certified as "concurrent dual-band."	Optional (tested if implemented)
40 MHz channels in the 5 GHz band	Bonding of two adjacent 20 MHz channels to create a single 40 MHz channel. Provides twice the frequency bandwidth.	Optional (tested if implemented)
20/40 MHz coexistence mechanisms in the 2.4 GHz band	If an AP supports 40 MHz channels in the 2.4 GHz band, coexistence mechanisms are required. Default 2.4 GHz channel size is 20 GHz.	Optional (tested if implemented)
Greenfield preamble	Greenfield preamble cannot be interpreted by legacy stations. The Greenfield preamble improves efficiency of the 802.11n networks with no legacy devices.	Optional (tested if implemented)
Short guard interval (short GI), 20 and 40 MHz	Short GI is 400 nanoseconds; the traditional GI is 800 nanoseconds. Improves data rates by 10%.	Optional (tested if implemented)
Space-time block coding (STBC)	Improves reception by encoding data streams in blocks across multiple antennas. Access points can be certified for STBC.	Optional (tested if implemented)
HT Duplicate mode	Allows an AP to send the same data simultaneously on each 20 MHz channel within a bonded 40 MHz channel.	Optional (tested if implemented)

The Wi-Fi Alliance actually began certifying 802.11n products before the 802.11n-2009 amendment was ratified. However, prior to the Wi-Fi CERTIFIED n certification program, many WLAN vendors offered *pre-802.11n* products in the SOHO marketplace. Many of these products were not interoperable with other vendors' products and are not compatible with certified Wi-Fi Alliance products. The pre-802.11n products were never meant for deployment in the enterprise.

A white paper from the Wi-Fi Alliance titled "Wi-Fi CERTIFIED n: Longer-Range, Faster-Throughput, Multimedia-Grade Wi-Fi Networks" can be downloaded from the Wi-Fi Alliance website at www.wi-fi.org/discover-wi-fi/wi-fi-certified-n.

MIMO

The heart and soul of the 802.11n amendment exists at the Physical (PHY) layer with the use of a technology known as multiple-input, multiple-output (MIMO). MIMO requires the use of multiple radios and antennas, called radio chains, which are defined later in this chapter. MIMO radios transmit multiple radio signals at the same time to take advantage of multipath.

In traditional 802.11 environments, the phenomenon of multipath has long caused problems. *Multipath* is a propagation phenomenon that results in two or more paths of the same signal arriving at a receiving antenna at the same time or within nanoseconds of each other. Due to the natural broadening of the waves, the propagation behaviors of reflection, scattering, diffraction, and refraction will occur. A signal may reflect off an object or may scatter, refract, or diffract. These propagation behaviors can each result in multiple paths of the same signal. As you learned in Chapter 2, "Radio Frequency Fundamentals," the negative effects of multipath can include loss of amplitude and data corruption. 802.11n MIMO systems, however, take advantage of multipath and, believe it or not, multipath then becomes your friend.

In a typical indoor environment, multiple RF signals sent by a MIMO radio will take multiple paths to reach the MIMO receivers. For example, as shown in Figure 18.1, multiple copies of the three original signals will be received by multiple antennas. The MIMO receiver will then use advanced *digital signal processing (DSP)* techniques to sort out the originally transmitted signals. A high multipath environment actually helps a MIMO receiver differentiate between the unique data streams carried on the multiple RF signals. As a matter of fact, if multiple signals sent by a MIMO transmitter all arrive simultaneously at the receiver, the signals will cancel each other and the performance is basically the same as a non-MIMO system.

Transmitting multiple streams of data with a method called *spatial multiplexing (SM)* provides for greater throughput and takes advantage of the old enemy known as multipath. MIMO systems can also use multiple antennas to provide for better transmit and receive diversity, which can increase range and reliability. There are various transmit and receive diversity techniques. Space-time block coding (STBC) and cyclic shift diversity (CSD) are transmit diversity techniques where the same transmit data is sent out of multiple antennas. STBC communication is possible only between 802.11n devices. CSD diversity signals can be received by either 802.11n or legacy devices. Transmit beamforming (TxBF) is a technique where the same signal is transmitted over multiple antennas and the antennas act like a phased array. Maximal ratio combining (MRC) is a type of receive diversity technique where multiple received signals are combined, thus improving sensitivity. Spatial multiplexing and diversity techniques are explained in greater detail in the following sections.

FIGURE 18.1   MIMO operation and multipath

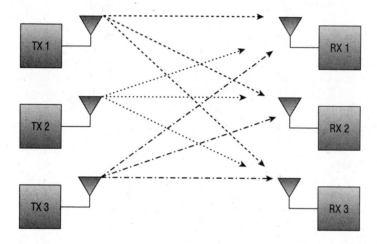

Radio Chains

Conventional 802.11 radios transmit and receive RF signals by using a *single-input single-output (SISO)* system. SISO systems use a single radio chain. A *radio chain* is defined as a single radio and all of its supporting architecture, including mixers, amplifiers, and analog/digital converters.

A MIMO system consists of multiple radio chains, with each radio chain having its own antenna. A MIMO system is characterized by the number of transmitters and receivers used by the multiple radio chains. For example, a 2×3 MIMO system would consist of three radio chains with two transmitters and three receivers. A 3×3 MIMO system would use three radio chains with three transmitters and three receivers. In a MIMO system, the first number always references the transmitters (TX), and the second number references the receivers (RX).

Figure 18.2 illustrates both 2×3 and 3×3 MIMO systems. Please note that both systems utilize three radio chains; however, the 3×3 system has three transmitters, whereas the 2×3 system has only two transmitters.

FIGURE 18.2 2×3 and 3×3 MIMO

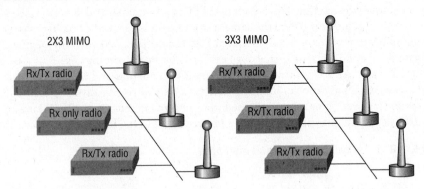

The use of multiple transmitters in a MIMO system provides for the transmission of more data via spatial multiplexing. The use of multiple receivers increases signal-to-noise ratio (SNR) because of advanced MIMO antenna diversity. Both of these benefits are discussed in greater detail in the following sections. The 802.11n standard allows for MIMO systems up to 4×4 using four radio chains. Each radio chain requires power. A 2×2 MIMO system would require much less of a power draw than a 4×4 MIMO system.

Spatial Multiplexing (SM)

You have already learned that MIMO radios will transmit multiple signals. A MIMO radio also has the ability to send independent unique data streams. Each independent data stream is known as a *spatial stream*, and each unique stream can contain data that is different from the other streams transmitted by one or more of the other radio chains. Each stream will also travel a different path, because there is at least a half-wavelength of space between the multiple transmitting antennas. The fact that the multiple streams follow different paths to the receiver because of the space between the transmitting antennas is known as *spatial diversity*. Sending multiple independent streams of unique data using spatial diversity is often also referred to as *spatial multiplexing (SM)* or *spatial diversity multiplexing (SDM)*.

The benefit of sending multiple unique data streams is that throughput is drastically increased. If a MIMO access point sends two unique data streams to a MIMO client station that receives both streams, the throughput is effectively doubled. If a MIMO access point sends three unique data streams to a MIMO client station that receives all three streams, the throughput is effectively tripled.

Do not confuse the independent unique streams of data with the number of transmitters. In fact, when referring to MIMO radios it is important to also reference how many unique streams of data are sent and received by MIMO radios. Most Wi-Fi vendors use a three-number syntax when describing MIMO radio capabilities. In a MIMO system, the first number always references the transmitters (TX), and the second number references the receivers (RX). The third number represents how many unique streams of data can be sent or received.

For example, a 3×3:2 MIMO system would use three transmitters and three receivers, but only two unique data streams are utilized. A 3×3:3 MIMO system would use three transmitters and three receivers with three unique data streams.

Figure 18.3 depicts a 3×3:3 MIMO AP transmitting three independent streams of unique data to a 3×3:3 MIMO client.

FIGURE 18.3   Multiple spatial streams

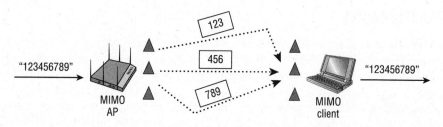

It is important to understand that not all 802.11n radios have the same MIMO capabilities. Many earlier 802.11n access points deployed 3×3:2 instead of 3×3:3 MIMO radios. Many WLAN vendors also offer less expensive 802.11n access points using 2×2:2 MIMO radios. On the client side, a variety of combinations have existed, with many laptops using 3×3:2 or 3×3:3 MIMO radios. Some handheld devices still only use the legacy SISO capabilities found in 802.11a/b/g. However, many handheld devices, such as smartphones and tablets, deploy 802.11n radios with 1×1:1 capabilities that effectively function as a SISO radio with some 802.11n capabilities. A 1×1:1 802.11n radio will not offer the full advantages of using multiple spatial streams; however, some of the 802.11n MAC enhancements can still be employed.

If good RF conditions exist, when a 3×3:3 access point and a 3×3:3 client device are communicating with each other, three spatial streams can be used for unicast transmissions. However, when a 3×3:3 access point and a 2×2:2 client device are communicating with each other, only two spatial streams will be used for unicast transmissions. When a client radio joins a basic service set (BSS), the access point is advised about the client radio MIMO capabilities.

The 802.11n amendment does allow for the use of up to a 4×4:4 MIMO system. The majority of enterprise 802.1n access points are either 2×2:2 or 3×3:3. However, there is a wide variety of MIMO capabilities among 802.11n client devices. 802.11n laptops usually have either 2×2:2 or 3×3:3 radios, while most 802.11n mobile devices, such as smartphones and tablets, only have a 1×1:1 MIMO radio because the addition of more radio chains would drain the battery life of the mobile devices. Additionally, the majority of 802.11n mobile devices originally only transmitted on the 2.4 GHz band. Smartphone and tablet vendors now typically offer dual-frequency 802.11n radios that transmit on both the 2.4 and 5 GHz frequency bands.

Multiple spatial streams can be sent with the same (equal) modulation or they can be sent using different (unequal) modulation. For example, a 3×3:3 MIMO radio can transmit three data streams using the same 64-quadrature amplitude modulation (QAM) technique.

Another example is a 3×3:3 MIMO radio transmitting two streams by using 64-QAM and the third stream using quadrature phase-shift keying (QPSK) modulation because of a higher noise floor. A 3×3:3 MIMO system using *equal modulation* would accomplish greater throughput than a 3×3:3 MIMO system using *unequal modulation*. Although unequal modulation is theoretically and technically possible, WLAN vendors have never implemented unequal modulation with 802.11n radios.

MIMO Diversity

If you cover one of your ears with your hand, will you hear better or worse with a single ear? Obviously, you will hear better with two ears. Do you think you would be able to hear more clearly if you had three or four ears instead of just two? Do you think you would be able to hear sounds from greater distances if you had three or four ears instead of just two? Yes, a human being would hear more clearly and with greater range if equipped with more than two ears. MIMO systems employ advanced antenna diversity capabilities that are analogous to having multiple ears.

Antenna diversity often is mistaken for the spatial multiplexing capabilities that are utilized by MIMO. Antenna diversity (both receive and transmit) is a method of using multiple antennas to survive the negative effects of multipath. As you just learned, MIMO takes advantage of multipath with spatial multiplexing to increase data capacity. Simple *antenna diversity* is a method of compensating for multipath as opposed to utilizing multipath. Multipath produces multiple copies of the same signal that arrive at the receiver with different amplitudes.

In Chapter 4, "Radio Frequency Signal and Antenna Concepts," you learned about traditional antenna diversity, which consists of one radio with two antennas. Most pre-802.11n radios use *switched diversity*. When receiving RF signals, switched diversity systems listen with multiple antennas. Multiple copies of the same signal arrive at the receiver antennas with different amplitudes. The signal with the best amplitude is chosen, and the other signals are ignored. Switched diversity is also used when transmitting, but only one antenna is used. The transmitter will transmit out of the diversity antenna where the best amplitude signal was last heard.

As the distance between a transmitter and receiver increases, the received signal amplitude decreases to levels closer to the noise floor. As the signal-to-noise ratio (SNR) diminishes, the odds of data corruption grow. Listening with two antennas increases the odds of hearing at least one signal without corrupted data. Now, imagine if you had three or four antennas listening for the best received signal by using switched diversity. The probabilistic odds of hearing signals with stronger amplitudes and uncorrupted data have increased even more. The increased probability of hearing at least one uncorrupted signal in a switched diversity system using three or four antennas often results in increased range.

When receive diversity is used, the signals may also be linearly combined by using a signal processing technique called *maximal ratio combining (MRC)*. MRC algorithms are used to combine multiple received signals by looking at each unique signal and optimally combining the signals in a method that is additive as opposed to destructive. MIMO systems using MRC will effectively raise the SNR level of the received signal. As shown in Figure 18.4, maximal ratio combining is useful when a non-MIMO radio transmits to a MIMO receiver and multipath occurs. The MRC algorithm focuses on the signal with the highest SNR level; however, it may still combine information from the noisier signals. The end result is that less data corruption occurs because a better estimate of the original data has been reconstructed.

FIGURE 18.4   Maximal ratio combining (MRC)

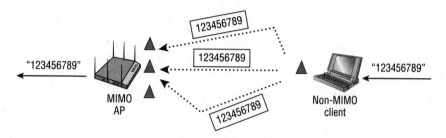

MRC uses a receive-combining function that assesses the phase and SNR of each incoming signal. Each received signal is phase-shifted so that they can be combined. The amplitude of the incoming signals is also modified to focus on the signal with the best SNR.

Space-Time Block Coding (STBC)

Space-time block coding (STBC) is a method where the same information is transmitted on two or more antennas. It is a type of transmit diversity. STBC can be used when the number of radio chains exceeds the number of spatial streams. By sending copies of the same information on multiple antennas, the actual rate of the data transmitted does not increase as transmit antennas are added. STBC does, however, increase the receiver's ability to detect signals at a lower SNR than would be otherwise possible. The receive sensitivity of the radio system improves. STBC and cyclic shift diversity (CSD) are transmit diversity techniques where the same transmit data is sent out of multiple antennas. STBC communication is possible only between 802.11n devices. CSD diversity signals can be received by either 802.11n or legacy devices.

Cyclic Shift Diversity (CSD)

Cyclic shift diversity (CSD) is another transmit diversity technique specified in the 802.11n standard. Unlike STBC, a signal from a transmitter that uses CSD can be received by legacy 802.11g and 802.11a devices. For mixed mode deployments, where 802.11n coexists with 802.11g and 802.11a devices, there is a need to have a way of transmitting the symbols in the legacy OFDM preamble over multiple transmit antennas. CSD is used and a cyclic delay is applied to each of the transmitted signals. The delays are calculated to minimize the correlation between the multiple signals. A conventional legacy system would treat the multiple received signals as multipath versions of the same signal. The cyclic delay is chosen to be within the limits of the guard interval (GI) so that it does not cause excessive intersymbol interference (ISI). An 802.11n system has no problem using the multiple signals to improve the overall SNR of the preamble. The details of how CSD works will not be part of the CWNA exam. CSD is one of the finer and least discussed features of 802.11n but nonetheless still important to equipment vendor radio designers.

Transmit Beamforming (TxBF)

The 802.11n amendment also proposes an optional PHY capability called *transmit beamforming (TxBF)*, which uses phase adjustments. Transmit beamforming can be used when there are more transmitting antennas than there are spatial data streams.

Transmit beamforming is a method that allows a MIMO transmitter using multiple antennas to adjust the phase and amplitude of the outgoing transmissions in a coordinated method. When multiple copies of the same signal are sent to a receiver, the signals will usually arrive out of phase with each other. If the transmitter (TX) knows about the RF characteristic of the receiver's location, the phase of the multiple signals sent by a MIMO transmitter can be adjusted. When the multiple signals arrive at the receiver, they are in phase, resulting in constructive multipath instead of the destructive multipath caused by out-of-phase signals. Carefully controlling the phase of the signals transmitted from multiple antennas has the effect of emulating a directional antenna.

Because transmit beamforming results in constructive multipath communication, the result is a higher signal-to-noise ratio and greater received amplitude. Therefore, transmit beamforming will result in greater range for individual clients communicating with an access point. Transmit beamforming will also result in higher throughput because of the higher SNR that allows for the use of more complex modulation methods that can encode more data bits. The higher SNR also results in fewer layer 2 retransmissions.

Transmit beamforming could be used together with spatial multiplexing (SM); however, the number of spatial streams is constrained by the number of receiving antennas. For example, a 4×4:4 MIMO radio might be transmitting to a 2×2:2 MIMO radio, which can only receive two spatial streams. The 4×4:4 MIMO radio will send only two spatial streams but might also use the other antennas to form beams that are more focused to the receiving 2×2:2 MIMO receiver. In practice, transmit beamforming will probably be used when spatial multiplexing is not the best option. As pictured in Figure 18.5, when utilizing transmit beamforming the transmitter will not be sending multiple unique spatial streams but will instead be sending multiple streams of the same data with the phase adjusted for each RF signal.

Transmitters that use beamforming will try to adjust the phase of the signals based on feedback from the receiver by using *sounding frames*. The transmitter is considered the *beamformer*, while the receiver is considered the *beamformee*. The beamformer and the beamformee work together to educate each other about the characteristics of the MIMO channel. This exchange of sounding frames is used to measure the RF channel and create a computative assessment on how to better steer RF energy to a receiver. The assessment is known as a *steering matrix*.

FIGURE 18.5   Transmit beamforming data

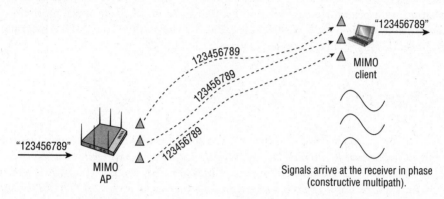

Transmit beamforming relies on *implicit feedback* or *explicit feedback* from both the transmitter and receiver. Any frame can be used as a sounding frame. Null function data frames can be used if another frame is not used. When using implicit feedback, the beam-former sends a sounding frame and then receives long training symbols transmitted by the beamformee, which allows the MIMO channel between the beamformee and beamformer to be estimated by the beamformer. In other words, there is no direct feedback from the beamformee and thus the beamformer creates the steering matrix. A good analogy for implicit feedback is sonar. Sonar is a method in which submarines use sound propagation underwater to detect other vessels. A submarine sends out a sound wave, and based on the characteristics of the returning sound wave, the crew can determine the type of vessel that might be in the path of the submarine. However, there is no direct explicit feedback from the vessel to the submarine.

Much more information can be exchanged between two HT radios if they are both capable of explicit feedback. When using explicit feedback, the beamforcee makes a direct estimate of the channel from training symbols sent to the beamformee by the beamformer. The beamformee takes that information and sends additional feedback back to the beam-former. In other words, the beamformee creates the steering matrix. The beamformer then transmits based on the feedback from the beamformee. It should be noted that explicit beamforming has never really been used with 802.11n radios. However, the 802.11ac amendment defines only explicit beamforming.

The first several generations of 802.11n chipsets did not incorporate transmit beamform-ing capabilities, and the Wi-Fi Alliance does not test the technology for 802.11n radios. Variations of transmit beamforming capabilities are available in some enterprise WLAN vendor access points, but support for transmit beamforming with 802.11n clients simply has not happened. With some vendor-specific exceptions, 802.11n transmit beamforming has not been utilized due to the lack of client-side support for the technology.

So are you wondering why this chapter has so much information about transmit beamforming? Even though transmit beamforming never really caught on with 802.11n radios, it is widely believed that 802.11ac will make use of the technology in the near future. 802.11ac defines a technology called *multi-user MIMO (MU-MIMO)* that is dependent on explicit transmit beamforming. Transmit beamforming may become much more commonplace when the second wave of 802.11ac radios hit the marketplace. MU-MIMO with transmit beamforming will be discussed in greater detail in Chapter 19.

HT Channels

In previous chapters, you learned that the 802.11a amendment defined the capabilities of radios using *Orthogonal Frequency Division Multiplexing (OFDM)* technology in the 5 GHz U-NII bands. 802.11g defined the capabilities of radios using ERP-OFDM, which is effectively the same technology except that transmissions occur in the 2.4 GHz ISM band. The 802.11n amendment also defines the use of OFDM channels. However, key differences exist for 802.11n (HT) radios. As mentioned earlier in this chapter, 802.11n (HT) radios can operate in either frequency.

You have already learned that 802.11n radios use spatial multiplexing to send multiple independent streams of unique data. Spatial multiplexing is one method of increasing the throughput. The OFDM channels used by 802.11n radios use more subcarriers and there is also an option to bond channels together. The greater frequency bandwidth provided by the OFDM channels used by 802.11n (HT) radios also provides for greater eventual throughput.

20 MHz Non-HT and HT Channels

As you learned in Chapter 6, "Wireless Networks and Spread Spectrum Technologies," 802.11a and 802.11g radios use 20 MHz OFDM channels. As pictured in Figure 18.6, each channel consists of 64 subcarriers. Forty-eight of the subcarriers transmit data, while four of the subcarriers are used as pilot tones for dynamic calibration between the transmitter and receiver. The remaining subcarriers are not used. OFDM technology also employs the use of convolutional coding and forward error correction.

802.11n (HT) radios also use the same OFDM technology and have the capability of using either 20 MHz channels or 40 MHz channels. The 20 MHz channels used by HT radios have four extra subcarriers and can carry a little more data than a non-HT OFDM channel. As a result, the HT 20 MHz channel with a single spatial stream can provide greater aggregate throughput for the same frequency space. As pictured in Figure 18.7, an HT 20 MHz OFDM channel also has 64 subcarriers. However, 52 of the subcarriers transmit data, while 4 of the subcarriers are used as pilot tones for dynamic calibration between the transmitter and receiver. In other words, although some unused subcarriers still exist, an 802.11n radio makes use of four additional subcarriers for data transmissions. Using these four additional subcarriers is a more efficient use of the available frequency space in the 20 MHz channels.

FIGURE 18.6   20 MHz non-HT (802.11a/g) channel

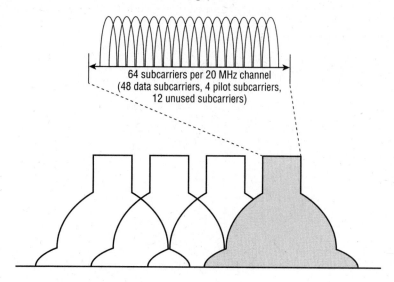

FIGURE 18.7   20 MHz HT (802.11n) channel

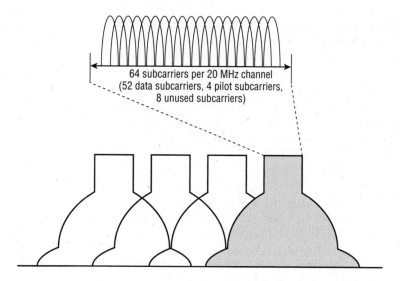

40 MHz Channels

802.11n (HT) radios also have the capability of using 40 MHz OFDM channels. As pictured in Figure 18.8, the 40 MHz HT channels use 128 OFDM subcarriers; 108 of the subcarriers transmit data, whereas 6 of the subcarriers are used as pilot tones for dynamic calibration between the transmitter and receiver. The remaining subcarriers are not used. A 40 MHz channel effectively doubles the frequency bandwidth available for data transmissions.

FIGURE 18.8   40 MHz HT (802.11n) channel

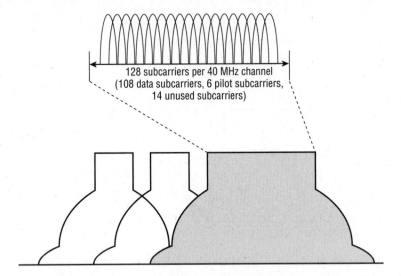

128 subcarriers per 40 MHz channel
(108 data subcarriers, 6 pilot subcarriers,
14 unused subcarriers)

The 40 MHz channels used by HT radios are essentially two 20 MHz OFDM channels that are bonded together. Each 40 MHz channel consists of a primary and secondary 20 MHz channel. The primary and secondary 20 MHz channels must be adjacent 20 MHz channels in the frequency in which they operate. As pictured in Figure 18.9, the two 20 MHz channels used to form a 40 MHz channel are designated as primary and secondary and are indicated by two fields in the body of certain 802.11 management frames. The primary field indicates the number of the primary channel. A positive or negative offset indicates whether the secondary channel is one channel above or one channel below the primary channel.

A standard 20 MHz HT channel reserves some frequency bandwidth at the top and bottom of the channel to avoid interference with adjacent 20 MHz HT channels. When two 20 MHz HT channels are bonded together, some of the formerly unused subcarriers at the bottom of the higher channel and at the top end of the lower channel can used to transmit data. Therefore, an HT (802.11n) 40 MHz channel uses a total of 114 subcarriers instead of 112 subcarriers.

As you learned in Chapter 12, "WLAN Troubleshooting and Design," channel reuse patterns are needed in multiple channel architecture (MCA). Channel reuse patterns using

40 MHz channels at 5 GHz are also feasible because of all the frequency bandwidth available in the 5 GHz bands. The use of 40 MHz HT channels in the 5 GHz frequency bands makes perfect sense because there are many more 20 MHz channels that can be bonded together in various pairs, as pictured in Figure 18.10. As mentioned in Chapter 6, in the near future, the FCC may allot even more 5 GHz frequency space, which could be used for 20 MHz and larger channels.

FIGURE 18.9   Channel bonding

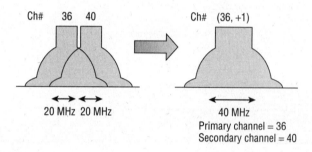

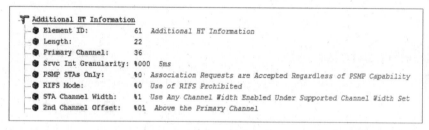

FIGURE 18.10   Channel bonding—5 GHz U-NII bands

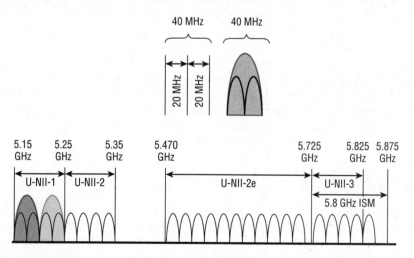

Deploying 40 MHz HT channels at 2.4 GHz unfortunately does not scale well in multiple channel architecture. As you learned in earlier chapters, although fourteen channels are available at 2.4 GHz, there are only three nonoverlapping 20 MHz channels available in the 2.4 GHz ISM band. When the smaller channels are bonded together to form 40 MHz channels in the 2.4 GHz ISM band, any two 40 MHz channels will overlap, as shown in Figure 18.11. In other words, only one 40 MHz channel can be used at 2.4 GHz, and the possibility of a channel reuse pattern is essentially impossible.

FIGURE 18.11   Channel bonding—2.4 GHz ISM band

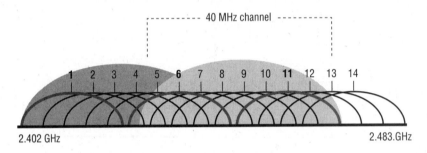

Forty MHz Intolerant

As you just learned, only one nonoverlapping 40 MHz channel can be deployed in the 2.4 GHz band, and therefore, a channel reuse pattern using multiple 40 MHz channels in 2.4 GHz is impossible. However, it is still possible to turn on channel bonding in the 2.4 GHz band. A 2.4 GHz access point transmitting on a 40 MHz channel will interfere with other nearby APs that have been deployed using a standard 20 MHz channel reuse pattern of 1, 6, and 11. By default, 802.11n clients and APs will use 20 MHz channels when transmitting in the 2.4 GHz band. They can also advertise that they are *Forty MHz Intolerant* using various 802.11n management frames. Any 802.11n AP using a 40 MHz channel will be forced to switch back to using only 20 MHz channels if they receive the frames from nearby 802.11n 2.4 GHz stations that are intolerant.

Effectively, Forty MHz Intolerant operations are a protection against your next-door neighbor who might deploy a 40 MHz channel and interfere with your 2.4 GHz 20 MHz channels. Enterprise WLAN access points will always have 20 MHz channels as the default setting at 2.4 GHz. It should be noted that the Forty MHz Intolerant operations are meant for 2.4 GHz only and are not permitted in 5 GHz.

Guard Interval (GI)

For digital signals, data is modulated onto the carrier signal in bits or collections of bits called *symbols*. When 802.11a/g radios transmit at 54 Mbps, each OFDM symbol contains 288 bits; 216 of these bits are data, and 72 of the bits are error-correction bits. All the data bits of an OFDM symbol are transmitted across the 48 data subcarriers of a 20 MHz non-HT channel.

802.11a/g radios use an 800-nanosecond *guard interval (GI)* between OFDM symbols. The guard interval is a period of time between symbols that accommodates the late arrival of symbols over long paths. In a multipath environment, symbols travel different paths, and therefore some symbols arrive later. A "new" symbol may arrive at a receiver before a "late" symbol has been completely received. This is known as *intersymbol interference (ISI)* and often results in data corruption.

In earlier chapters, we discussed ISI and delay spread. The delay spread is the time differential between multiple paths of the same signal. Normal delay spread is 50 nanoseconds to 100 nanoseconds, and a maximum delay spread is about 200 nanoseconds. The guard interval should be two to four times the length of the delay spread. Think of the guard interval as a buffer for the delay spread. The normal guard interval is an 800-nanosecond buffer between symbol transmissions. As pictured in Figure 18.12, a guard interval will compensate for the delay spread and help prevent intersymbol interference. If the guard interval is too short, intersymbol interference can still occur.

FIGURE 18.12 Guard interval

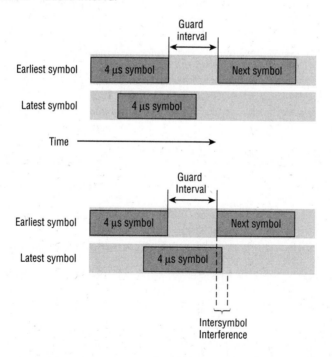

802.11n also uses an 800-nanosecond guard interval; however, a shorter 400-nanosecond guard interval is optional. A shorter guard interval results in a shorter symbol time, which has the effect of increasing data rates by about 10 percent. If the optional, shorter 400-nanosecond guard interval is used with an 802.11n radio, throughput will increase; however, the odds of an intersymbol interference occurrence increases. If intersymbol interference does indeed occur because of the shorter GI, the result is data corruption. If data corruption occurs, layer 2 retransmissions will increase and the throughput will be adversely affected. Therefore, a 400-nanosecond guard interval should be used in RF environments without excessive multipath which could cause late symbols to overlap with new symbols. If throughput goes down because of a shorter GI setting, the default guard interval setting of 800 nanoseconds should be used instead.

Modulation and Coding Scheme (MCS)

802.11n data rates are defined with a *modulation and coding scheme (MCS)* matrix. Non-HT radios that used OFDM technology (802.11a/g) defined data rates of 6 Mbps to 54 Mbps, based on the modulation and coding method that was used. HT radios, however, define data rates based on numerous factors, including modulation, coding method, the number of spatial streams, channel size, and guard interval. Each modulation coding scheme is a variation of these multiple factors. Seventy-seven modulation coding schemes exist for both 20 MHz HT channels and 40 MHz HT channels. There are eight mandatory modulation and coding schemes for 20 MHz HT channels, as shown in Table 18.2. The eight mandatory MCSs for 20 MHz channels are comparable to basic (required) rates.

TABLE 18.2   Mandatory modulation and coding schemes—20 MHz channel

MCS index	Modulation	Spatial streams	Data rates	
			800 ns GI	**400 ns GI**
0	BPSK	1	6.5 Mbps	7.2 Mbps
1	QPSK	1	13.0 Mbps	14.4 Mbps
2	QPSK	1	19.5 Mbps	21.7 Mbps
3	16-QAM	1	26.0 Mbps	28.9 Mbps
4	16-QAM	1	39.0 Mbps	43.3 Mbps
5	64-QAM	1	52.0 Mbps	57.8 Mbps
6	64-QAM	1	58.5 Mbps	65.0 Mbps
7	64-QAM	1	65.0 Mbps	72.2 Mbps

As you can see in Table 18.2, the modulation type, the guard interval, and the number of spatial streams all determine the eventual data rate. Table 18.3 describes the modulation and coding schemes for a 20 MHz channel using four spatial streams.

TABLE 18.3 MCS—20 MHz channel, four spatial streams

MCS index	Modulation	Spatial streams	Data rates	
			800 ns GI	**400 ns GI**
24	BPSK	4	26.0 Mbps	28.9 Mbps
25	QPSK	4	52.0 Mbps	57.8 Mbps
26	QPSK	4	78.0 Mbps	86.7 Mbps
27	16-QAM	4	104.0 Mbps	115.6 Mbps
28	16-QAM	4	156.0 Mbps	173.3 Mbps
29	64-QAM	4	208.0 Mbps	231.1 Mbps
30	64-QAM	4	234.0 Mbps	260.0 Mbps
31	64-QAM	4	260.0 Mbps	288.9 Mbps

Table 18.4 describes the modulation and coding schemes for a 40 MHz channel using one spatial stream.

TABLE 18.4 MCS—40 MHz channel, one spatial stream

MCS index	Modulation	Spatial streams	Data rates	
			800 ns GI	**400 ns GI**
0	BPSK	1	13.5 Mbps	15.0 Mbps
1	QPSK	1	27.0 Mbps	30.0 Mbps
2	QPSK	1	40.5 Mbps	45.0 Mbps

TABLE 18.4 MCS—40 MHz channel, one spatial stream *(continued)*

MCS index	Modulation	Spatial streams	Data rates	
3	16-QAM	1	54.0 Mbps	60.0 Mbps
4	16-QAM	1	81.0 Mbps	90.0 Mbps
5	64-QAM	1	108.0 Mbps	120.0 Mbps
6	64-QAM	1	121.5 Mbps	135.0 Mbps
7	64-QAM	1	135.0 Mbps	150.0 Mbps

Table 18.5 depicts the modulation and coding schemes for a 40 MHz channel using four spatial streams.

TABLE 18.5 MCS—40 MHz channel, four spatial streams

MCS index	Modulation	Spatial streams	Data rates	
			800 ns GI	**400 ns GI**
24	BPSK	4	54.0 Mbps	60.0 Mbps
25	QPSK	4	108.0 Mbps	120.0 Mbps
26	QPSK	4	162.0 Mbps	180.0 Mbps
27	16-QAM	4	216.0 Mbps	240.0 Mbps
28	16-QAM	4	324.0 Mbps	360.0 Mbps
29	64-QAM	4	432.0 Mbps	480.0 Mbps
30	64-QAM	4	486.0 Mbps	540.0 Mbps
31	64-QAM	4	540.0 Mbps	600.0 Mbps

Other factors, such as the use of unequal modulation, can also determine the final data rate. As depicted in Table 18.6, different spatial streams might use different modulation methods.

TABLE 18.6   MCS—40 MHz channel, four spatial streams, unequal modulation

MCS index	Modulation				Data rates	
	Stream 1	Stream 2	Stream 3	Stream 4	800 ns GI	400 ns GI
67	16-QAM	16-QAM	16-QAM	QPSK	283.4 Mbps	315.0 Mbps
68	64-QAM	QPSK	QPSK	QPSK	243.0 Mbps	270.0 Mbps

HT PHY

In earlier chapters, you learned that a MAC Service Data Unit (MSDU) is the layer 3–7 payload of an 802.11 data frame. You also learned that a MAC Protocol Data Unit (MPDU) is a technical name for an entire 802.11 frame. An MPDU consists of a layer 2 header, body, and trailer.

When an MPDU (802.11 frame) is sent down from layer 2 to the Physical layer, a preamble and PHY header are added to the MPDU. This creates what is called a *Physical Layer Convergence Procedure Protocol Data Unit (PPDU)*. Describing all the details of the PHY preamble and header is well beyond the scope of the CWNA exam. The main purpose of the preamble is to use bits to synchronize transmissions at the Physical layer between two 802.11 radios. The main purpose of the PHY header is to use a signal field to indicate how long it will take to transmit the 802.11 frame (MPDU) and to notify the receiver of the MCS (data rate) that is being used to transmit the MPDU. The 802.11n amendment defines the use of three PPDU structures that use three different preambles. One of the preambles is a legacy format, and two are newly defined HT preamble formats.

Non-HT Legacy

The first PPDU format is called *non-HT* and is often also referred to as a legacy format because it was originally defined by Clause 18 of the 802.11-2012 standard for OFDM transmissions. As shown in Figure 18.13, the non-HT PPDU consists of a preamble that uses legacy short and long training symbols, which are used for synchronization. An OFDM symbol consists of 12 bits. The header contains the signal field, which indicates the time needed to transmit the payload of the non-HT PPDU, which of course is the MPDU (802.11 frame).

FIGURE 18.13   802.11n PPDU formats

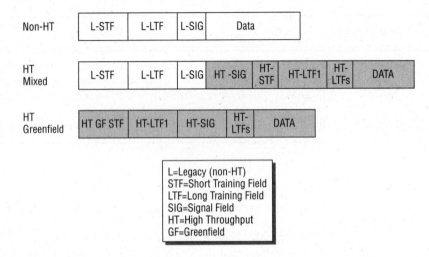

L=Legacy (non-HT)
STF=Short Training Field
LTF=Long Training Field
SIG=Signal Field
HT=High Throughput
GF=Greenfield

Support for the non-HT legacy format is mandatory for 802.11n radios, and transmissions can occur in only 20 MHz channels. The non-HT format effectively is the same format used by legacy 802.11a and 802.11g radios. The 802.11n radio will use multiple antennas for incoming transmissions from a legacy 802.11a/b/g device. The 802.11n receive diversity will improve the incoming transmissions from legacy 802.11a/b/g radios.

HT Mixed

The first of the two new PPDU formats defined in the 802.11n amendment is the *HT Mixed* format. As shown in Figure 18.13, the beginning of the preamble contains the non-HT training symbols and legacy signal field that can be decoded by legacy 802.11a and 802.11g radios. The rest of the HT Mixed preamble and header cannot be decoded by legacy 802.11a/g devices. HT information includes the HT-SIG and HT training symbols.

The HT Signal (HT-SIG) contains information about the MCS, frame length, 20 MHz or 40 MHz channel size, frame aggregation, guard interval, and STBC. The HT Short Training Field (HT-STF) and HT Long Training Field (HT-LTF) are used for synchronization between MIMO radios.

Non-802.11n receivers will not be able to read the frame, but the length field in the legacy section of the header will allow them to know how long the medium is going to be busy, and they will therefore stay silent without having to do an energy detect at each cycle. The HT Mixed format is the most commonly used format because it supports both HT and legacy 802.11a/g OFDM radios. The HT Mixed format is also considered mandatory, and transmissions can occur in both 20 MHz and 40 MHz channels. When a 40 MHz channel is used, all broadcast traffic must be sent on a legacy 20 MHz channel so as to maintain interoperability with the 802.11a/g non-HT clients. Also, any transmissions to and from the non-HT clients will have to use a legacy 20 MHz channel.

HT Greenfield

The second of the two new PPDU formats defined by the 802.11n amendment is the *HT Greenfield* format. An 802.11n radio in HT Greenfield mode can receive frames from legacy devices; however, legacy devices cannot understand the HT Greenfield preamble. Therefore, any legacy device will interpret an HT Greenfield transmission as noise. Greenfield mode is almost never used because there are almost always legacy 802.11a/b/g client radios present in the environment.

Greenfield format is optional, and the HT radios can transmit by using both 20 MHz and 40 MHz channels. This mode does not require the use of the HT protection methods (discussed later in this chapter) and therefore overall throughput is better because RTS/CTS frames are not needed to signal legacy devices.

HT MAC

So far, we have discussed all the enhancements to the Physical layer that 802.11n radios use to achieve greater bandwidth and throughput. The 802.11n amendment also addresses new enhancements to the MAC sublayer of the Data-Link layer to increase throughput and improve power management. Medium contention overhead is addressed by using two new methods of frame aggregation. New methods are also addressed using interframe spacing and block acknowledgments to limit the amount of fixed MAC overhead. Finally, two new methods of power management are defined for HT Clause 20 radios.

A-MSDU

As you can see in Figure 18.14, every time a unicast 802.11 frame is transmitted, a certain amount of fixed overhead exists as a result of the PHY header, MAC header, MAC trailer, interframe spacing, and acknowledgment frame. Medium contention overhead also exists because of the time required when each frame must contend for the medium.

FIGURE 18.14   802.11 unicast frame overhead

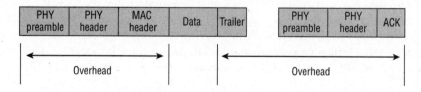

The 802.11n amendment introduced two new methods of frame aggregation to help reduce the overhead. *Frame aggregation* is a method of combining multiple frames into a single frame transmission. The fixed MAC layer overhead is reduced, and overhead caused by the random backoff timer during medium contention is also minimized.

The first method of frame aggregation is known as *Aggregate MAC Service Data Unit (A-MSDU)*. As you learned in earlier chapters, the MSDU is the layer 3–7 payload of a data frame. As Figure 18.15 shows, multiple MSDUs can be aggregated into a single frame transmission.

FIGURE 18.15 A-MSDU

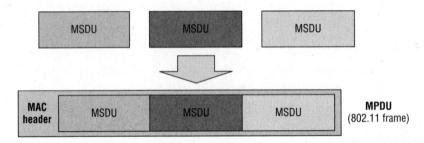

An 802.11n access point using A-MSDU aggregation would receive multiple 802.3 frames, remove the 802.3 headers and trailers, and then wrap the multiple MSDU payloads into a single 802.11 frame for transmission. The aggregated MSDUs will have a single wireless receiver when wrapped together in a single frame.

The entire aggregated frame is encrypted with the Counter Mode with Cipher Block Chaining Message Authentication Code Protocol (CCMP) cipher. It should be noted, however, that the individual MSDUs must all be of the same 802.11e QoS access category. Voice MSDUs cannot be mixed with Best Effort or Video MSDUs inside the same aggregated frame.

A-MPDU

The second method of frame aggregation is known as *Aggregate MAC Protocol Data Unit (A-MPDU)*. As you learned in earlier chapters, the MPDU is an entire 802.11 frame including the MAC header, body, and trailer. As pictured in Figure 18.16, multiple MPDUs can be aggregated into a single frame transmission.

The individual MPDUs within an A-MPDU must all have the same receiver address. Also, the data payload of each MPDU is encrypted separately using the CCMP cipher. Much like MSDU aggregation, individual MPDUs must all be of the same 802.11e QoS access category. Voice MPDUs cannot be mixed with Best Effort or Video MPDUs inside the same aggregated frame. Please note that MPDU aggregation has more overhead than MSDU aggregation because each MPDU has an individual MAC header and trailer.

802.11n radios still support a basic Power Save mode, which is based on the original 802.11 power-management mechanisms. Access points buffer frames for stations in basic Power Save mode. The stations wake up when delivery traffic indication message (DTIM) beacons are broadcast and the stations download their buffered frames.

The first new power-management method is called *spatial multiplexing power save (SM power save)*. The purpose of SM power save is to allow a MIMO 802.11n device to power down all but one of its radios. For example, a 4×4 MIMO device with four radio chains would power down three of the four radios, thus conserving power. SM power save defines two methods of operation: static and dynamic.

When static SM power save is utilized, a MIMO client station powers down all the client's radios except for one single radio. Effectively, the MIMO client station is now the equivalent of a SISO radio that is capable of sending and receiving only one spatial stream. The client uses an SM power save action frame to inform the access point that the MIMO client is using only one radio and is capable of receiving only one spatial stream from the AP. The SM power save action frame is also used to tell the AP that the client station has powered up all of its radios and now is capable of transmitting and receiving multiple spatial streams once again.

When dynamic SM power save is utilized, the MIMO client can also power down all but one of the client's radios but can power up the radios again much more rapidly. The client station disables all but one of the radios after a frame exchange. An access point can trigger the client to wake up the sleeping radios by sending a request-to-send (RTS) frame. The client station receives the RTS frame, powers up the sleeping radios, and sends a clear-to-send (CTS) frame back to the access point. The client can now once again transmit and receive multiple spatial streams. The client uses an SM power save action frame to inform the AP of the client's dynamic power save state.

The second new power-management method, *Power Save Multi Poll (PSMP)*, has also been defined for use by 802.11n (HT) radios. PSMP is an extension of automatic power save delivery (APSD) that was defined by the 802.11e amendment. Unscheduled PSMP is similar to U-APSD and uses the same delivery-enabled and trigger-enabled mechanisms. Scheduled PSMP is also similar to S-APSD and is an effective method for streaming data and other scheduled transmissions.

HT Operation

802.11n access points can operate in several modes of channel operation. An access point could be manually configured to only transmit on legacy 20 MHz channels, although most 802.11n APs are configured to operate as a 20/40 basic service set. A 20/40 BSS allows 20 MHz 802.11a/g client stations and 20/40 MHz–capable 802.11n stations to operate within the same cell at the same time. In earlier chapters, you learned about the protection mechanisms used in an ERP (802.11g) network. RTS/CTS and CTS-to-Self mechanisms are used to ensure that 802.11b HR-DSSS clients do not transmit when ERP-OFDM transmissions are occurring. The 802.11n amendment requires backward compatibility with 802.11a and 802.1b/g radios. Therefore, the 802.11n amendment defines *HT protection modes* that enable HT Clause 20 radios to be backward compatible with older Clause 17 radios (HR-DSSS), Clause 18 radios (OFDM), and Clause 19 radios (ERP).

20/40 Channel Operation

20 MHz 802.11a/g stations and 20/40 MHz–capable 802.11n stations can operate within the same cell at the same time when they are associated to an 802.11n (HT) access point. Older legacy 802.11a/g stations will obviously use 20 MHz transmissions. 802.11n radios can operate in either a 20 MHz–only channel mode or a 20/40 MHz channel operation mode. The HT radios that are 20/40 capable can use 40 MHz transmissions when communicating with each other; however, they would need to use 20 MHz transmissions when communicating with the legacy stations. Several rules apply for the operation of 20 MHz and 40 MHz stations within the same HT 20/40 basic service set:

- The 802.11n access point must declare 20-only or 20/40 support in the beacon management frame.
- 802.11n client stations must declare 20-only or 20/40 in the association or reassociation frames.
- Client stations must reassociate when switching between 20-only and 20/40 modes.
- If 20/40-capable stations transmit by using a single 20 MHz channel, they must transmit on the primary channel and not the secondary channel.

HT Protection Modes (0–3)

To ensure backward compatibility with older 802.11a/b/g radios, 802.11n (HT) access points may signal to other 802.11n stations when to use one of four HT protection modes. A field in the beacon frame called the HT Protection field has four possible settings of 0–3. Much like an ERP (802.11g) access point, the protection modes may change dynamically depending on devices that are nearby or associated to the HT (802.11n) access point. The protection mechanisms that are used are RTS/CTS, CTS-to-Self, Dual-CTS, or other protection methods. The four modes are as follows:

Mode 0—Greenfield (No Protection) Mode   This mode is referred to as *Greenfield* because only HT radios are in use. All the HT client stations must also have the same operational capabilities. If the HT basic service set is a 20 MHz BSS, all the stations must be 20 MHz capable. If the HT basic service set is a 20/40 MHz BSS, all the stations must be 20/40 capable. If these conditions are met, there is no need for protection.

Mode 1—HT Nonmember Protection Mode   In this mode, all the stations in the BSS must be HT stations. Protection mechanisms kick in when a non-HT client station or non-HT access point is heard that is not a member of the BSS. For example, an HT AP and stations may be transmitting on a 40 MHz HT channel. A non-HT 802.11a access point or client station is detected to be transmitting in a 20 MHz space that interferes with either the primary or secondary channel of the 40 MHz HT channel.

Mode 2—HT 20 MHz Protection Mode   In this mode, all the stations in the BSS must be HT stations and are associated to a 20/40 MHz access point. If a 20 MHz–only HT station associates to the 20/40 MHz AP, protection must be used. In other words, the 20/40-capable HT stations must use protection when transmitting on a 40 MHz channel in order to prevent the 20 MHz–only HT stations from transmitting at the same time.

Mode 3—Non-HT Mixed Mode   This protection mode is used when one or more non-HT stations are associated to the HT access point. The HT basic service set can be either 20 MHz or 20/40 MHz capable. If any 802.11a/b/g radios associate to the BSS, protection will be used. Mode 3 will probably be the most commonly used protection mode because most basic service sets will most likely have legacy 802.11a/b/g devices as members.

RTS/CTS and CTS-to-Self

When HT protection is enabled within an HT BSS, an HT STA will precede HT transmissions with either an RTS/CTS control frame exchange or a CTS-to-Self control frame using modulation and coding understandable to the STAs that are being protected against. The Duration ID within these control frames causes STAs to update their network allocation vector (NAV). When protecting the transmission of 40 MHz HT frames against legacy 802.11a radios and legacy 802.11g radios, protection mechanism control frames can be sent over the 40 MHz channel using non-HT duplicate transmissions. Non-HT duplicate transmissions allow the two identical 20 MHz non-HT control frames to be transferred simultaneously on both the primary and secondary channels, as pictured in Figure 18.18.

FIGURE 18.18   Non-HT duplicate format

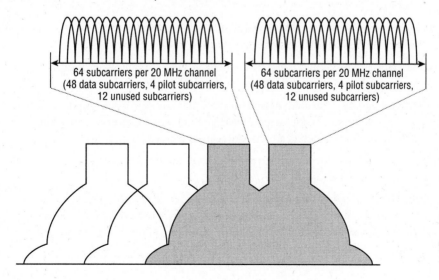

Non-HT duplicate transmissions will be sent using 802.11a data rates in the 5 GHz band or 802.11g data rates in the 2.4 GHz band. In Figure 18.18, you can see that non-HT duplicate transmissions are just sending the same data on two adjacent 20 MHz OFDM channels at the same time. These 20 MHz channels consist of 64 subcarriers, 48 of which transmit data, and 4 that are used as pilot tones. This will cause STAs operating in either the primary or secondary channel to update their NAVs and defer their transmissions. Non-HT duplicate mode improves error rate performance but is not widely implemented by WLAN vendors.

Summary

In this chapter, you learned the history of the 802.11n amendment and how the Wi-Fi Alliance has already begun to certify 802.11n equipment for interoperability. We also discussed all the methods used by 802.11n (HT) radios to increase throughput and range at the Physical layer. In addition to PHY enhancements, HT radios utilize MAC layer mechanisms to enhance throughput and power management. Finally, we discussed HT modes of operation that are used for protection mechanisms and co-existence with older legacy 802.11a/b/g technologies. 802.11n technology is "next generation" technology because of the promise of greater throughput as well as greater range. 802.11n has become the de facto standard technology, replacing most 802.11a/b/g networks. Since the 802.11ac standard is designed to only operate in the 5 GHz frequency range, dual-radio 802.11ac access points will continue to support 802.11n in the 2.4 GHz frequency range for some time to come.

Exam Essentials

Define the differences between MIMO and SISO.   Understand that SISO devices use only one radio chain, whereas MIMO systems use multiple radio chains.

Understand spatial multiplexing.   Describe how SM takes advantage of multipath and sends multiple spatial streams, resulting in increased throughput.

Explain MIMO diversity.   Be able to explain the differences between simple switched diversity and the advanced diversity used by MIMO antenna systems. Explain the use of maximal ratio combining, which is a form of receive diversity.

Understand transmit beamforming.   Explain how optional transmit beamforming can use multiple antennas for phase adjustments.

Understand 20 MHz and 40 MHz channels.   Understand legacy 20 MHz channels, 20 MHz HT channels, and 40 MHz channels and how they use OFDM. Explain why 40 MHz channels work best in the 5 GHz U-NII bands. Explain primary and secondary channels.

Explain the guard interval.   Describe how the guard interval compensates for intersymbol interference. Discuss the use of both 800- and 400-nanosecond GIs.

Understand modulation coding schemes.   Explain how modulation coding schemes are used to define data rates and all the variables that can affect the data rates.

Explain the three HT PPDU formats.   Describe the differences between non-HT legacy, HT Mixed, and HT Greenfield.

Understand HT MAC enhancements.   Explain how the use of A-MSDU, A-MPDU, block ACKs, and RIFS are used to increase throughput at the MAC sublayer. Define the two new power-management methods used by HT radios.

Explain the HT protection modes.   Describe the differences between protection modes 0–3. Explain the use of Dual-CTS.

Review Questions

1. Thirty 2×2:2 access points have been deployed at a school where all the client devices are 1×1:1 802.11n tablets. The access points are transmitting on 20 MHz channels with the standard guard interval of 800 ns. What is the highest 802.11n data rate that can be used for communications between the APs and tablets?

   A. 54 Mbps

   B. 65 Mbps

   C. 72 Mbps

   D. 150 Mbps

   E. 300 Mbps

2. How can a MIMO system increase throughput at the Physical layer? (Choose all that apply.)

   A. Spatial multiplexing

   B. A-MPDU

   C. Transmit beamforming

   D. 40 MHz channels

   E. Dual-CTS protection

3. Which new power-management method defined by the 802.11n amendment conserves power by powering down all but one radio?

   A. A-MPDU

   B. Power Save protection

   C. PSMP

   D. SM power save

   E. PS mode

4. The guard interval is used as a buffer to compensate for what type of interference?

   A. Co-channel interference

   B. Adjacent cell interference

   C. RF interference

   D. HT interference

   E. Intersymbol interference

5. Name some of the factors that a modulation and coding scheme (MCS) uses to define data rates for an HT radio. (Choose all that apply.)

   A. Modulation method

   B. Equal/unequal modulation

C. Number of spatial streams

D. GI

E. Channel size

6. How can an HT radio increase throughput at the MAC sublayer of the Data-Link layer? (Choose all that apply.)

A. A-MSDU

B. RIFS

C. A-MPDU

D. Guard interval

E. MTBA

7. Transmit beamforming uses what type of frames to analyze the MIMO channel before transmitting directed paths of data?

A. Trigger frames

B. Beaming frames

C. Sounding frames

D. SM power save action frames

8. A 3×3:2 MIMO radio can transmit and receive how many unique streams of data?

A. Two.

B. Three.

C. Four.

D. Three equal and four unequal streams.

E. None—the streams are not unique data.

9. Name a capability not defined for A-MPDU.

A. Multiple QoS access categories

B. Independent data payload encryption

C. Individual MPDUs having the same receiver address

D. MPDU aggregation

10. Which HT protection modes allow only for the association of HT stations in the HT basic service set? (Choose all that apply.)

A. Mode 0—Greenfield mode

B. Mode 1—HT nonmember protection mode

C. Mode 2—HT 20 MHz protection mode

D. Mode 3—HT Mixed mode

11. Which of these capabilities are considered mandatory for an 802.11n access point as defined by the Wi-Fi Alliance's vendor certification program called Wi-Fi CERTIFIED n? (Choose all that apply.)

    A. Three spatial streams in receive mode

    B. WPA/WPA2

    C. WMM

    D. Two spatial streams in transmit mode

    E. 2.4 GHz–40 MHz channels

12. MIMO radios use which mechanisms for transmit diversity? (Choose all that apply.)

    A. Maximum ratio combining (MRC)

    B. Spatial multiplexing (SM)

    C. Space-time block coding (STBC)

    D. Cyclic shift diversity (CSD)

    E. Multiple traffic ID block acknowledgment (MTBA)

13. 802.11n (HT) radios are backward compatible with which of the following types of 802.11 radios? (Choose all that apply.)

    A. 802.11b radios (HR-DSSS)

    B. 802.11a radios (OFDM)

    C. 802.11 legacy radios (FHSS)

    D. 802.11g radios (ERP)

14. How does transmit beamforming (TxBF) use multiple MIMO antennas to increase range?

    A. Beamsteering

    B. Phase shifting

    C. Dynamic beamforming

    D. Spatial multiplexing

15. Which HT PPDU formats support both 20 MHz and 40 MHz channels? (Choose all that apply.)

    A. Non-HT legacy format

    B. PCO mode

    C. HT Mixed format

    D. HT Greenfield format

16. A WLAN consultant has recommend that a new 802.11n HT network be deployed by using channels in the 5 GHz U-NII bands. Why would he recommend 5 GHz over 2.4 GHz?

    A. HT radios do not require DFS and TPC in the 5 GHz bands.

    B. HT radios get better range using TxBF in the 5 GHz bands.

C. 40 MHz channels do not scale in the 2.4 GHz ISM band.

D. 5 GHz HT radios are less expensive than 2.4 GHz HT radios.

17. What 802.11n mode of operation sends the same data on two adjacent 20 MHz channels?

A. Greenfield mode

B. HT Mixed mode

C. Non-HT duplicate mode

D. LDPC mode

18. What frequencies are defined for 802.11n (HT) radio transmissions? (Choose all that apply.)

A. 902–928 MHz

B. 2.4–2.4835 GHz

C. 5.15–5.25 GHz

D. 5.25–5.35 MHz

19. What PHY layer mechanism might be used to increase throughput for an HT radio in a clean RF environment with minimal reflections and low multipath?

A. Maximum ratio combining

B. 400-nanosecond guard interval

C. Switched diversity

D. Spatial multiplexing

E. Spatial diversity

20. What PHY layer mechanisms might be used to increase the range for an 802.11n radio using a MIMO system? (Choose all that apply.)

A. Maximum ratio combining

B. Guard interval

C. Transmit beamforming

D. Spatial multiplexing

Chapter

19

Very High Throughput (VHT) and 802.11ac

IN THIS CHAPTER, YOU WILL LEARN ABOUT THE FOLLOWING:

✓ **802.11ac-2013 amendment**

✓ **5 GHz only**

✓ **20, 40, 80, and 160 MHz channels**

✓ **256-QAM modulation**

✓ **Modulation and coding schemes**

✓ **Single-user MIMO**

✓ **802.11ac data rates**

✓ **VHT MAC**

  ▪ A-MPDU

  ▪ RTS/CTS

✓ **Beamforming**

  ▪ Explicit beamforming

  ▪ Multiuser MIMO

  ▪ Multiuser beamforming

  ▪ Quality of service

✓ **Infrastructure requirements**

  ▪ Ethernet

  ▪ Power

✓ **802.11ac in a SOHO or home**

- Device radios

- Data flow/usage

- Spatial streams

- Wider 802.11ac channels

- MU-MIMO

✓ **Wi-Fi Alliance certification**

 In 2009, the IEEE ratified the 802.11n amendment and High Throughput (HT). The introduction of 802.11n was a milestone and game changer for Wi-Fi networks. The increased data rates offered by 802.11n provided organizations with the technology necessary to scale down or even replace their end-user wired network with wireless. Although the faster data rates of 802.11n allowed companies to unplug their users, the demand for faster networks is continuous. In response to end users' thirst for faster networks, 802.11ac was developed and was ratified in December 2013.

Compared with the other 802.11 PHYs that preceded it, the introduction of 802.11n was revolutionary. It did not just update and enhance the existing 802.11 standard. With technologies such as MIMO, spatial streams, bonded channels, aggregate MSDU, and aggregate MPDU, 802.11n required us to sit down and spend time learning about how Wi-Fi had changed. So four years later, once again a new PHY has been introduced—the latest 802.11 PHY, 802.11ac. The goal of this chapter is to introduce you to the technologies covered by this amendment.

The 802.11ac-2013 amendment defines a new operation known as Very High Throughput (VHT), which provides PHY and MAC enhancements and allows data rates potentially as high as 6.933 Gbps. Although the amendment specifies data rates up to 6.933 Gbps, 802.11ac products will be implemented in multiple phases, with two key initial phases. The first phase supports rates up to 1.3 Gbps, and the second phase is expected to support rates up to 3.5 Gbps.

With 802.11ac, many of the technologies that were introduced with 802.11n are being enhanced to achieve faster data rates. Increased channel bandwidth, more radio chains and spatial streams, and an enhanced modulation and coding scheme are the three technologies that help the first deployments of 802.11ac provide data rates of up to 1.3 Gbps. These enhancements are more evolutionary than revolutionary and enhance and improve technologies that we are already familiar with.

The second-phase rollout of 802.11ac will further enhance these technologies by increasing the number of radio chains and spatial streams to achieve even higher data rates. In addition to achieving faster speeds, 802.11ac products will introduce a technology that will be revolutionary, drastically changing how Wi-Fi behaves. This second-phase rollout will change Wi-Fi from a single transmission at a time technology to a multiuser technology. This change is comparable to the changes that occurred when Ethernet networks transitioned from repeater-based, single collision domain networks to switch-based broadcast domain environments. This revolutionary new technology is known as multiuser MIMO, or MU-MIMO. In order to make MU-MIMO successful, 802.11ac uses beamforming, technology that was initially introduced with 802.11n. This chapter will introduce you to 802.11ac and how it achieves its faster data rates and provide information about how MU-MIMO works.

802.11ac-2013 Amendment

The 802.11ac-2013 amendment was ratified on December 11, 2013. The amendment is officially known as "Amendment 4: Enhancements for Very High Throughput for Operation in Bands below 6 GHz." Although the amendment title states bands below 6 GHz, 802.11ac technology does not operate in the 2.4 GHz ISM band, only the 5 GHz U-NII bands. 802.11ac introduces Very High Throughput (VHT) technology with maximum transmission speed of 6.933 Gbps.

Table 19.1 provides a summary of the differences between 802.11n and 802.11ac. This chapter will discuss all of the new features and capabilities of 802.11ac, along with highlighting the similarities and the differences between the two technologies. Remember that 802.11ac will be implemented in multiple phases, so some of the features or capabilities listed in the table may not exist yet in live product.

TABLE 19.1   Comparison of 802.11n and 802.11ac

Technology	802.11n	802.11ac
Frequency	2.4 GHz and 5 GHz	5 GHz only
Modulation	BPSK, QPSK, 16-QAM, 64-QAM	BPSK, QPSK, 16-QAM, 64-QAM, 256-QAM
Channel widths	20 MHz, 40 MHz	20 MHz, 40 MHz, 80 MHz, 160 MHz
Spatial streams	Up to four	Up to eight on APs, up to four on clients
Short Guard Interval Support	Yes	Yes
Beamforming	Multiple types, both implicit and explicit, not typically implemented	Explicit beamforming with null data packets (NDPs)
Number of modulation and coding schemes (MCSs)	77	10
Support for A-MSDU and A-MPDU	Yes	Yes, all frames transmitted as A-MPDU
MIMO support	Single-user MIMO	Single-user MIMO and multiuser MIMO (MU-MIMO)
Maximum # of simultaneous user transmissions	One	Four
Maximum data rate	600 Mbps	6.933 Gbps

5 GHz Only

Over the years, it has become common practice for enterprises to install dual-band access points throughout their networks. This practice has allowed organizations to migrate to the 5 GHz band while still providing support for older 802.11b/g clients and other single-radio 2.4 GHz clients. Many organizations also use the dual-band APs to provide guest access solely on the slower and more limited 2.4 GHz band. Employee access is provided on the 2.4 GHz band for older devices and on the less congested 5 GHz band for better performance.

With the introduction of 40 MHz channels in 802.11n and the limit of 3 nonoverlapping channels in the 2.4 GHz band, enterprises cannot effectively implement 40 MHz channels with their 2.4 GHz radios. Therefore, in order to benefit from the faster data rates of 802.11n, companies have migrated to 5 GHz radios. However, support for 2.4 GHz radios in older devices is still needed. This is accomplished with dual-radio access points.

802.11ac expands channel widths even further than 802.11n, with channel widths of 80 MHz and 160 MHz. Due to the limited frequency space in the 2.4 GHz band, 802.11ac is designed to operate only in the 5 GHz band where much more frequency space is available.

Dual-Band APs and 802.11ac

Dual-band APs will continue to be manufactured and installed. The 2.4 GHz radios will support 802.11b/g/n, although they will still be limited by only three available channels. The 5 GHz radios will support 802.11ac and be backward compatible with 802.11a and 5 GHz 802.11n and will support channels that are 20, 40, 80, and ultimately 160 MHz wide.

20, 40, 80, and 160 MHz Channels

802.11ac channels are a further evolution of the enhancements that were introduced with the 802.11n amendment. When Orthogonal Frequency Division Multiplexing (OFDM) was introduced with 802.11a, the channels were 20 MHz wide. The 20 MHz channels consisted of 64 subcarriers, each one 312.5 KHz wide, as pictured in Figure 19.1. Of these, 52 subcarriers are used by 802.11a OFDM, 48 to transmit data and 4 as pilot carriers.

802.11n introduced an enhanced 20 MHz channel and increased the number of subcarriers that could be used to 56, as pictured in Figure 19.2. Of these 56 subcarriers, 52 are used to transmit data and the other 4 are used as pilot carriers.

802.11n also introduced a 40 MHz channel, which combined two 20 MHz channels, as pictured in Figure 19.3. The 40 MHz channel consists of 128 subcarriers; 108 transmit data, 6 act as pilot carriers, and the other 14 are unused.

FIGURE 19.1   20 MHz non-HT (802.11a) channel

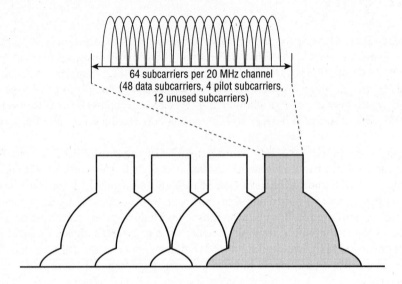

FIGURE 19.2   20 MHz HT (802.11n) channel

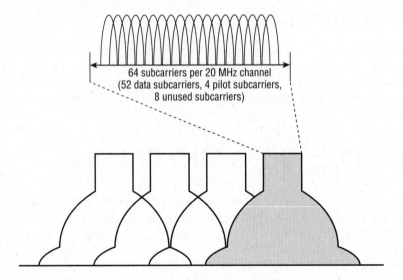

When two 20 MHz HT channels are bonded together, some of the formerly unused subcarriers at the bottom of the higher channel and at the top end of the lower channel are able to be used to transmit data. That is why the number of subcarriers is slightly more than two times the 56 subcarriers in a 20 MHz channel.

Each bonded channel consists of a primary and secondary 20 MHz channel. The channels must be adjacent. A positive or negative offset indicates whether the secondary channel is the channel above or the channel below the primary channel. This is pictured in Figure 19.4.

FIGURE 19.3   40 MHz HT (802.11n) channel

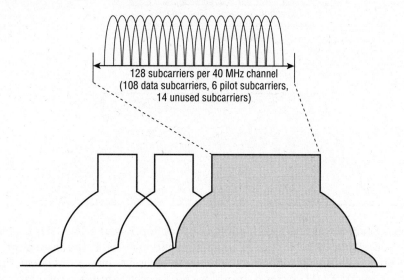

128 subcarriers per 40 MHz channel
(108 data subcarriers, 6 pilot subcarriers,
14 unused subcarriers)

FIGURE 19.4   Channel bonding

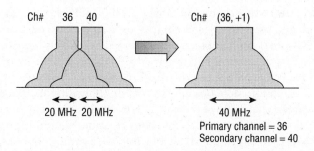

Ch#   36   40

Ch#   (36, +1)

20 MHz 20 MHz

40 MHz
Primary channel = 36
Secondary channel = 40

802.11ac introduced two new channel widths: 80 MHz and 160 MHz. Just as a 40 MHz channel is created by combining two 20 MHz channels, an 80 MHz channel combines two 40 MHz channels. The two 40 MHz channels that make up the 80 MHz channel must be adjacent. (An 80 MHz channel is pictured in Figure 19.5.) Some of the formerly unused subcarriers between the adjacent channels are now able to be used. Therefore, the number of 80 MHz subcarriers used is slightly more than two times the 114 subcarriers in a 40 MHz channel. The new 80 MHz channel consists of 256 subcarriers, of which 234 are used to transmit data, 8 are used as pilot carriers, and the remaining 14 are unused.

FIGURE 19.5   80 MHz VHT (802.11ac) channel

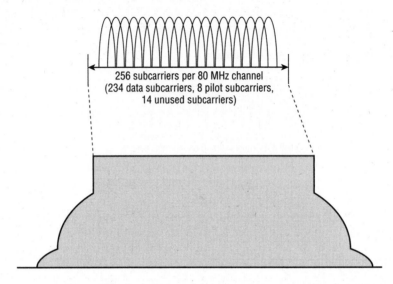

256 subcarriers per 80 MHz channel
(234 data subcarriers, 8 pilot subcarriers,
14 unused subcarriers)

The second channel width that was introduced with 802.11ac is a 160 MHz channel. As you might deduce, the 160 MHz channel is made up of two 80 MHz channels; however, the two 80 MHz channels do not have to be adjacent. If the channels are adjacent, then it is referred to as a 160 MHz channel. If they are not adjacent, then it is referred to as an 80+80 MHz channel. Since these channels can be adjacent or separated, they are treated as two individual 80 MHz channels, and you do not gain any unused subcarriers between the channels. Therefore, a 160 MHz channel is simply two 80 MHz channels and consists of 512 subcarriers, with 468 used to transmit data, 16 used as pilot carriers, and the remaining 28 are unused. Now that you have seen all of the channel widths individually, Figure 19.6 displays them across the current and proposed U-NII bands. This figure includes the channels defined in the FCC "Notice of Proposed Rulemaking," document #13-22. We realize that different regulatory domains may restrict or allow different frequency ranges, and there is even a chance that some of the new U-NII-2B channels may not get approved by the FCC. Taking both of these variables into consideration, we still believe it is worthwhile to see the 20 MHz, 40 MHz, 80 MHz, and 160 MHz channel options in the 5 GHz U-NII bands.

With 802.11n, an access point (AP) could be configured to use either 20 MHz channels or 40 MHz channels. When an AP was configured for a 40 MHz channel, it could not transmit until both the primary and secondary 20 MHz channels were available. A neighboring 20 MHz AP could be transmitting on either of the 20 MHz channels and force the 40 MHz AP to wait before it could transmit, reducing the performance capabilities of the 802.11n AP.

With 802.11ac, a new feature has been added that allows the AP to choose the channel width on a per-frame basis. This feature is known as *dynamic bandwidth operation*. As an example, when an 802.11ac AP, operating at 80 MHz on channels 36, 40, 44, and 48, wants to transmit, it must first check to see if all four channels are available.

If one of the channels, such as 36, is currently being using by another AP, instead of waiting for all four channels to be available to perform an 80 MHz transmission, the AP can transmit using a 40 MHz transmission on channels 44 and 48. This capability allows 802.11ac devices to adapt to the environment while transmitting on the widest available channel.

FIGURE 19.6   20, 40, 80, and 160 MHz channels

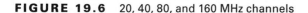
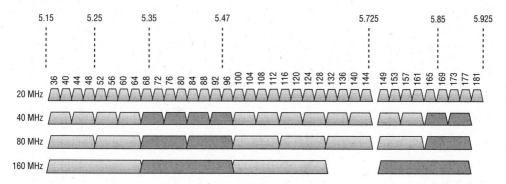

The ability to switch bandwidth dynamically adds complexity to the channel selection process for the person, or more likely the wireless networking software, that is configuring the AP. Prior to 802.11ac, channel selection simply meant choosing a single channel for the radio. With an 802.11ac radio, channel selection for a single radio can require the selection of up to four channel groupings. In the example shown in Figure 19.7, channels 36 through 64 are chosen for the 160 MHz channel. From this grouping of channels, 36 through 48 are chosen as the primary 80 MHz channel. Then channels 36 through 40 are chosen as the primary 40 MHz channel, and finally, channel 36 is chosen as the primary 20 MHz channel.

FIGURE 19.7   Single AP 160 MHz channel plan

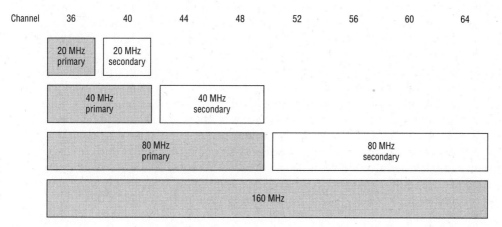

Choosing four channel groupings for an AP may not seem that difficult, but it becomes much more difficult and important when choosing channels for multiple APs. Figure 19.8 illustrates the channel plans for two APs that are using the same channels, 36 through 64 for 160 MHz transmissions. In this example, either AP can transmit at 160 MHz, providing that channels 36 through 64 are not currently being used by the other AP. Since the primary channels of these APs are different, both could transmit at the same time using 80 MHz wide transmissions. AP1 could transmit on its primary 80 MHz channel, channels 36 through 48, while AP2 transmitted on its primary 80 MHz channel, channels 52 through 64. If a third and fourth AP were configured for the same 160 MHz channels, they would not be able to choose an 80 MHz channel range that was not already chosen by AP1 or AP2; however, APs 3 and 4 would be able to choose 40 MHz primary channels that are not already used, either channels 44 and 48 or channels 52 and 56. Now you understand how primary channel selection becomes more complex as more APs join the network.

FIGURE 19.8   Two APs, 160 MHz channel plan

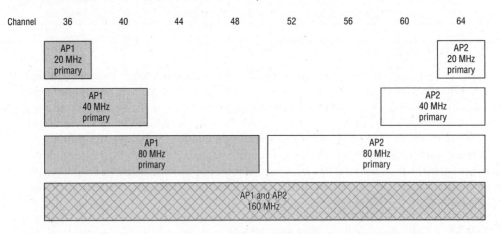

Just as more lanes on a highway allow more cars to travel down a road, wider channels allow more data to be transmitted. In its initial phase, 802.11ac supports channels that are 20 MHz, 40 MHz, and 80 MHz wide. The wider 40 MHz and 80 MHz channels are a key component to delivering the faster transmission speeds offered by 802.11ac. The second phase of 802.11ac will provide support for the maximum channel width of 160 MHz. The extreme size of the 160 MHz channels limits the number of available 160 MHz channels. Therefore, 160 MHz channels will most likely be deployed less often and used to address specific low-density, high-throughput requirements. Remember that in order to transmit using a 160 MHz channel, the access point must do a clear channel assessment across the entire 160 MHz frequency range, and all eight 20 MHz channels must be available before the transmission can begin. Fortunately, as we explained in this section, if the 160 MHz channel is not available, 802.11ac allows the AP to step down and transmit on a narrower channel if that primary channel is available.

256-QAM Modulation

In Chapter 1, "Overview of Wireless Standards, Organizations, and Fundamentals," we explained how waves are manipulated, or modulated, in order to carry data. The chapter described how amplitude, frequency, or phase could be varied to represent a single bit of data, or even multiple bits of data. Over the years, newer and faster modulation methods have been incorporated into 802.11 physical layer (PHY) technologies. With the introduction of each new and faster PHY, a newer modulation method, capable of encoding more bits, was also introduced and thus increased the effective speed and performance of the network. It is important to remember that even as new transmission and modulation methods are introduced, the older and slower methods are still supported and used.

As a client moves away from an access point and the signal level decreases, dynamic rate switching causes the client to shift to a slower data rate to maintain a connection. Even though we tend to highlight the latest and greatest technologies that are introduced with the most recent standard or amendment, the older and slower technologies are still key and necessary components of any infrastructure. This section describes 256-QAM, which was introduced with the 802.11ac amendment. (QAM is the acronym for quadrature amplitude modulation and is pronounced "kwam," which rhymes with "Tom.") The following is a list of modulation methods that are used with 802.11 networks:

DBPSK—Differential binary phase shift keying

DQPSK—Differential quadrature phase shift keying

BPSK—Binary phase shift keying

QPSK—Quadrature phase shift keying

16-QAM—16 quadrature amplitude modulation

64-QAM—64 quadrature amplitude modulation

256-QAM—256 quadrature amplitude modulation

256-QAM is an evolutionary upgrade that was introduced with 802.11ac. The 802.11a amendment introduced 64-QAM modulation. 64-QAM identifies 64 unique values. 64-QAM essentially performs a phase shift that can differentiate eight different levels and also performs an amplitude shift, which can also differentiate eight different levels. Combine the two of them and the system has the ability to identify the 64 unique values. Having 64 distinct values provide the ability for each value to represent 6 bits ($2^6 = 64$). QAM is often represented by symbols displayed in a constellation chart, as shown in Figure 19.9. Each dot represents a unique symbol—a different grouping of 6 bits.

With 802.11ac, a new modulation method was introduced, 256-QAM. 256-QAM identifies 256 unique values, using 16 different levels of phase shift and 16 different levels of amplitude shift. Because there are 256 distinct values, each value is able to represent 8 bits. ($2^8 = 256$). The constellation chart for 256-QAM is displayed in Figure 19.10.

FIGURE 19.9   64-QAM constellation chart

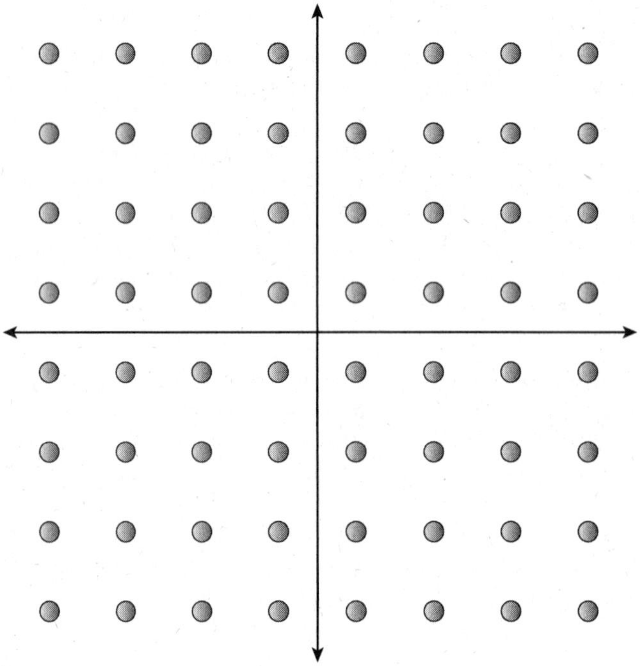

Now that we have provided a basic explanation of 64-QAM and 256-QAM, we need to delve a little deeper so that you understand what is happening and how the two differ. When a 64-QAM radio transmits data, it modifies the amplitude and phase of the wave and then transmits it. The receiving radio must then take the signal and identify the amplitude and phase modifications that were made to identify which of the 64 symbols was transmitted. This is not always easy because noise and interference can make it difficult to identify the values of the transmitted signal.

As an analogy, consider an archer shooting arrows at a target. Suppose that the target is a 2-meter-square board with evenly spaced 1-inch dots in rows and columns of eight that stands on the roof of a building, which we will call the target roof. Ten meters away from the target roof is another roof where an Olympic archer is standing. We will call this the shooting roof. In perfect conditions, our Olympic archer never misses. However, the space between these two buildings is unpredictably windy, not only from side to side, but also with updrafts and downdrafts. From the shooting roof, we ask the archer to shoot an arrow at a specific dot on the target. Since the winds are so unpredictable, the archer does not make any adjustments or corrections, only aims for the chosen dot and hopes that the winds do not push the arrow too far off target.

When the arrow hits the target, a person on the target roof looks at the location of the arrow and, using a ruler, measures the distance of the arrow from the nearest dots and attempts to identify which dot the archer was shooting at. As an example, Figure 9.11

shows four dots and the location where the arrow hit. In this figure, the person would identify the upper-right dot as the one that the archer was aiming for. At this short distance, unless the wind was incredibly strong, the archer should be able to accurately shoot the arrow on or near the correct dot, and the person at the target should be able to properly identify which dot the archer was aiming for.

FIGURE 19.10   256-QAM constellation chart

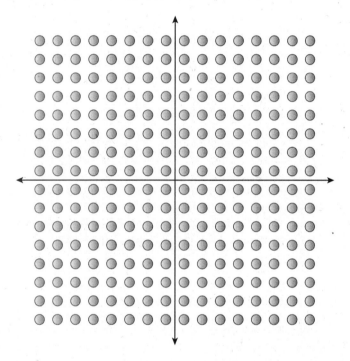

If we incrementally move the archer farther away from the target, the wind will interfere more with the flight of the arrow, possibly making it drift farther from the dot that the archer was aiming for. The farther away from the target, the less successful the archer will be. 64-QAM behaves similarly. The transmitting radio modulates the signal and transmits it. The amplitude and phase adjustments are exact and a perfectly modulated signal is generated by the radio. Noise, interference, and signal attenuation alter the signal so that when it is received it has been modified. The receiver takes the signal and maps it on the constellation diagram and calculates the error vector to identify the constellation point, which equates to the data that was transmitted.

So, now that you have a general idea of how 64-QAM behaves, how does it relate to 256-QAM? That is fairly straightforward. In our archer analogy, instead of having 64 dots on the target, we use the same size target but place 256 dots on it. This means that there is less room for error, and the effect of the wind on the arrow is much more critical. In the same way, 256-QAM is more sensitive to noise and interference. Because of this, 802.11ac receiver performance requires about 5 dB of additional gain as compared to 64-QAM.

FIGURE 19.11 Example target

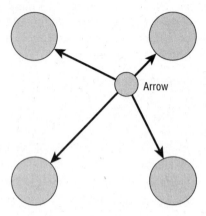

256-QAM is used for the highest modulation coding sets. To achieve these higher data rates, higher signal-to-noise ratios are needed. This also means that the clients need to be close to the AP in order to achieve these data rates. Since a 256-QAM signal can transmit 8 bits per subcarrier compared with the 6 bits that were transmitted with 64-QAM, a speed increase of 33 percent is achieved solely by deploying this feature.

As mentioned earlier, 802.11ac is only supported in the 5 GHz bands, leaving 802.11n as the fastest technology supported in 2.4 GHz. The fastest modulation officially supported by the 802.11n amendment is 64-QAM. With 802.11ac dual-band radios, even though 256-QAM is not part of the 802.11n standard, the technology is already integrated into the 802.11ac radio chipsets. Therefore, many vendors are enabling this technology on the 2.4 GHz radios, unofficially increasing the fastest 2.4 GHz data rates by about 33 percent.

 Some of the chipset vendors have introduced this capability, sometimes known as *Turbo-QAM* when implemented on the 2.4 GHz radios. *Turbo-QAM* is a Broadcom marketing term for 256-QAM deployed on a 2.4 GHz radio and does not imply the implementation of any other 802.11ac technologies in the 2.4 GHz band.

Modulation and Coding Schemes

802.11n (HT) defined 77 different modulation and coding schemes (MCSs). HT radios defined MCSs based on numerous factors, including modulation, coding method, the number of spatial streams, channel size, and guard interval. 802.11n also defined MCSs that allowed unequal modulation, which is the use of different modulation and coding schemes at the same time on different spatial streams. 802.11ac simplified this by defining only 10 MCS options, as shown in Table 19.2.

2.4 GHz 802.11n radios. That still leaves it to deal with coexisting on the 5 GHz band with 802.11a and 802.11n radios. Fortunately, all three PHYs use the OFDM preamble. When a transmission is performed using any of these PHYs, the other radios hear the preamble and can calculate how long to wait before they can transmit.

A-MPDU

All 802.11ac frames are transmitted using the Aggregate MAC Protocol Data Unit (A-MPDU) frame format, even if only a single frame is being transmitted. A-MPDU reduces some of the overhead involved with transmitting multiple frames. Aggregation also shifts some of the frame information from the Physical Layer Convergence Protocol (PLCP) header to the MPDU header. Since PLCP information is transmitted at the lowest supported data rate, and the MPDU information is transmitted at the higher data rates, this will improve performance.

The higher transmission speeds of 802.11ac make Reduced Interframe Space (RIFS) obsolete. 802.11n allowed the use of RIFS (2 µs) instead of SIFS (10 µs), which decreased the amount of time needed to transmit multiple frames. By transmitting A-MPDU frames, 802.11ac removes the need for multiple transmissions of individual frames with individual headers and individual ACKs. An A-MPDU frame reduces the per-frame overhead and only requires a single block ACK. Because of this, the 802.11ac amendment states that the use of RIFS is not supported and is obsolete.

RTS/CTS

In Chapter 12, "WLAN Troubleshooting and Design," we explained how request to send/ clear to send (RTS/CTS) is used to address the problems that can arise from a hidden node. 802.11ac can also use RTS/CTS to perform dynamic bandwidth operations. Figure 19.12 shows a basic service set (BSS) with AP1 and Station1 communicating using an 80 MHz wide channel made up of channels 36, 40, 44, and 48, with channel 36 configured as the primary channel. AP2 and Station2 form another BSS, using a 40 MHz channel made up of channels 44 and 48, with channel 44 configured as the primary channel. The basic service area (BSA) of AP1 and AP2 are only large enough so that they can communicate and hear RF from their respective stations. However, the stations are close enough to each other that they can hear each other's transmissions.

Each of the APs uses its primary channel to transmit beacon frames and to perform media access control tasks. However, if AP1 wants to transmit a frame to Station1 using an 80 MHz wide channel, it needs to make sure that the entire channel is available and it needs to reserve the channel, otherwise the transmission will be corrupted. So AP1 sends an RTS frame using a method known as a *non-HT duplicate frame*. Using an 802.11a frame format, AP1 attempts to send an RTS frame across each of the four channels that make up AP1's 80 MHz channel. If all four channels are available, and if Station1 receives the RTS frames, it will transmit four CTS frames. The top half of Figure 19.13 illustrates the four RTS and CTS frame transmissions. As neighboring nodes hear the RTS or CTS, they set their network allocation vector (NAV) to the RTS duration value or the CTS duration value and defer any transmissions until their NAV timer counts down to zero.

FIGURE 19.12   Interfering laptops

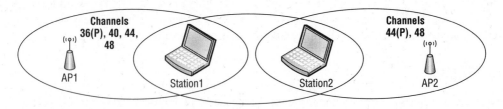

FIGURE 19.13   Dynamic bandwidth operation using RTS/CTS

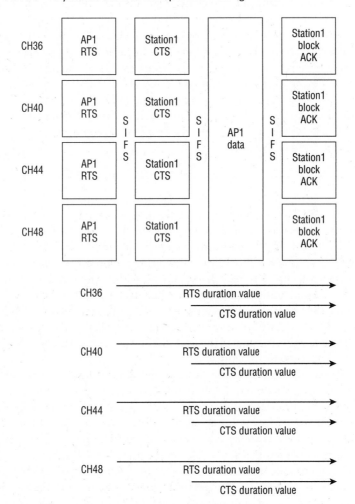

When AP1 receives all four CTS frames, it knows that all four channels are available and reserved and it can perform an 80 MHz data transmission. After the data is transmitted and the data frame is received correctly, Station1 will send four block ACK frames.

So, what happens if all four channels are not available? Figure 19.14 shows this process. AP1 begins by sending RTS frames across the four channels that make up its 80 MHz channel. In this example, let us assume that Station2 was also transmitting a frame when AP1 was transmitting the RTS frames. Because Station2 is transmitting, Station1 does not receive the RTS frames on channels 44 and 48 but does receive them on channels 36 and 40. Station1 proceeds to reply to AP1 with CTS frames on channels 36 and 40. When AP1 receives the CTS frames, it performs a 40 MHz data transmission on channels 36 and 40. Station1 then responds with two block ACK frames.

FIGURE 19.14   Dynamic bandwidth operation using RTS/CTS

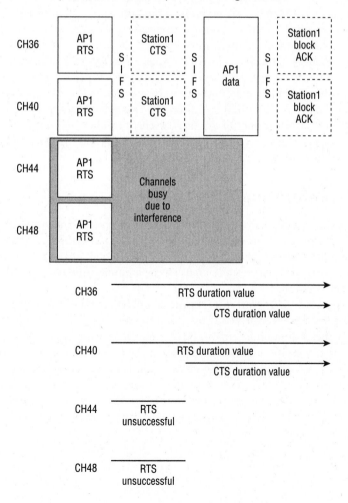

Beamforming

It is time for the revolutionary part of this chapter, and beamforming is the first piece of it. We have to admit, this is a really cool technology. To begin, beamforming can occur from the AP to the client, or vice versa. However, for our initial explanation, let us use an example of beamforming from an AP to a client.

Access points and clients typically have omnidirectional antennas that radiate the RF signal fairly equally and consistently as the signal travels horizontally away from the antenna. Instead of equally radiating the RF signal, beamforming allows an 802.11 transmitter to focus or direct the RF energy toward a specific client.

To perform beamforming, the multiple radio chains in the AP transmit the same information through different antennas. The APs time their transmissions so that the waves of all of the antennas arrive at the receiving radio at the same time and in phase with each other. This should result in a signal increase of approximately 3 decibels. This increase in signal strength can move the communications between the radios to a higher data rate. The increase will not likely be sufficient to affect the higher 256-QAM data rates (or the lower data rates), but it will affect communications in the middle data rate ranges.

802.11ac calls the transmitting radio the beamformer and the receiving radio the beamformee. Beamforming can be adjusted on a frame-by-frame basis, so for one transmission the AP can be the beamformer and for another the client can be the beamformer. An AP can send a beamformed transmission to a station, and if a station supports multiple radio chains, it can send beamformed frames to the AP.

Explicit Beamforming

The 802.11n amendment defined multiple beamforming methods. However, 802.11ac only uses explicit beamforming and requires support by both the transmitter and receiver in order for beamforming to be used. Explicit beamforming uses an interactive calibration process to identify how to perform the transmission using the multiple radio chains. This process is known as channel sounding.

To begin the process, the beamformer transmits a null data packet (NDP) announcement frame, which notifies the beamformee of the intent to send a beamformed transmission. The beamformer then follows this with an NDP frame. The beamformee processes each OFDM subcarrier and creates feedback information. The feedback contains information regarding power and the phase shift between each pair of transmit and receive antennas. This information is used to create a feedback matrix that is then compressed and sent back to the beamformer. This exchange of frames is shown in Figure 19.15. The beamformer uses the feedback matrix to calculate a steering matrix that is used to direct the data transmission to the beamformee.

FIGURE 19.15   Single-user beamform sounding process

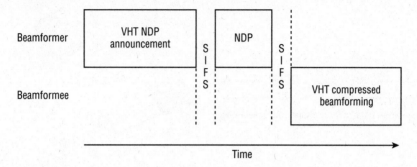

Although this section explained the beamforming process, it really explained what is known as single-user beamforming. The next section will introduce you to the most revolutionary part of 802.11ac, known as multiuser MIMO. After explaining multiuser MIMO, we will continue to further explain beamforming, specifically multiuser beamforming.

Multiuser MIMO

So here it is, the 802.11ac technology that changes one of the fundamental concepts of wireless networks, multiuser MIMO (MU-MIMO). Up until now, an 802.11 AP was only able to communicate with one device at a time. When an AP made a transmission, it was addressed to a single client device. With 802.11ac, it is possible to communicate with up to four devices simultaneously. This is being compared with the transition that Ethernet made when layer 1 hubs were replaced by layer 2 switches.

802.11n and 802.11ac APs are capable of transmitting multiple streams of data. However, due to technology costs and battery consumption, many of the most common and popular client devices that are used on wireless networks are only capable of transmitting a single stream of data. This means that when an access point is communicating with a wireless tablet or other handheld device, much of the potential of the technology is not being utilized. 802.11ac provides a solution to this by allowing an AP to communicate with up to four clients simultaneously.

The goal of MU-MIMO is to use as many spatial streams as possible, whether the transmission is with one client using four spatial streams or with four clients using one spatial stream each. Due to the advanced signal processing that is required, MU-MIMO is only supported for downstream transmission from an AP to multiple clients. Figure 19.16 shows an AP that is capable of transmitting four spatial streams. In this illustration, it is using two spatial streams to transmit to a laptop while using a third stream to transmit to a tablet, and a fourth stream is transmitting to an 802.11ac-capable smartphone.

FIGURE 19.16 Multiuser MIMO

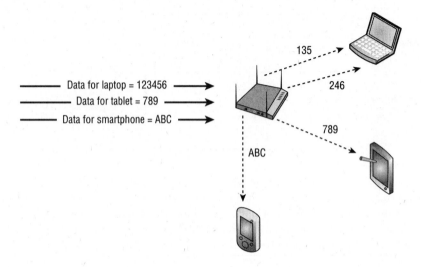

Beamforming is a critical part of MU-MIMO. In a previous section of this chapter, explicit beamforming was explained. In the next section, we will explain how multiuser beamforming is necessary for MU-MIMO to be successful.

Multiuser Beamforming

Earlier in this chapter we explained how 802.11ac performs explicit beamforming, and we also explained the principles of MU-MIMO. It is now time to discuss these two technologies together and the importance of beamforming to the success of MU-MIMO.

With single-user MIMO, beamforming is used to focus a signal to a client. This focused transmission should increase the level of the signal that the client receives—and hopefully allow the AP and client to communicate using a higher data rate than would be possible without beamforming. With MU-MIMO, the task of beamforming is not just performed for transmitting to a single client, it's performed for transmitting to up to four clients at a time.

To begin the MU-MIMO beamforming process, the AP performs a channel sounding procedure, similar but more complex than with SU-MIMO. To begin the process, the AP transmits a null data packet (NDP) announcement frame, notifying multiple beamformees of the intent to send a beamformed transmission. The AP then follows this with an NDP frame. As with beamforming to a single user, each beamformee processes each OFDM subcarrier and creates feedback information, creating a compressed *feedback matrix*. The first beamformee responds to the AP with its compressed feedback matrix. The AP then polls each additional beamformee sequentially using Beamforming Report Poll frames. Figure 19.17 illustrates this process.

FIGURE 19.17   Multiuser beamform sounding process

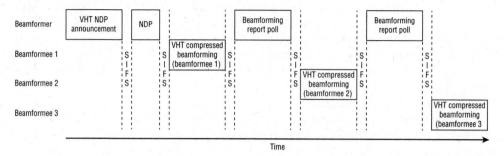

The AP then uses the feedback matrix from each of the beamformees to create a single *steering matrix*. The steering matrix defines transmit parameters for communications between each of the antennas on the AP and each of the antennas on each of the client devices, as illustrated in Figure 19.18.

FIGURE 19.18   Beamformed transmissions in a MU-MIMO environment

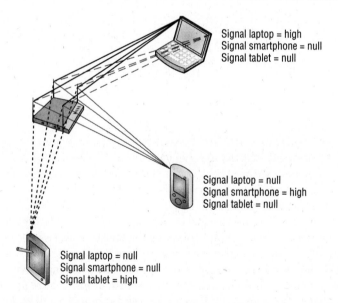

It is important to remember that in Figure 19.18, the AP is sending 16 transmissions, 4 from each antenna. Of those 16 transmissions, the receiving antenna needs to be able to distinguish and interpret the signal that is directed toward it while trying to ignore the other 12 transmissions. Beamformees that are too close to each other could experience inter-user interference from signals directed toward other users. Ideally, the users are physically separated enough from each other and the beamformed signal for the intended user device is strong while that signal received by the other users is low or null. Figure 19.18 illustrates how the different signals should be recognized by the user. If the user devices are separated enough, then the beamformed signal to the intended user should be strong and the signals received by the other users should be null or weak.

After the AP transmits the multiuser frame, the client stations must each acknowledge its frame. As stated earlier, MU-MIMO is only performed from the AP to the client, so the acknowledgments must be single-user transmissions. Since every 802.11ac frame is an A-MPDU frame, all acknowledgments are performed as block acknowledgments. When a block acknowledgment is required, the originator of the frame, in this case the AP, sends a *Block Acknowledgment Request (BAR)* frame to the receiver, who replies with a block acknowledgment. Since this is a MU-MIMO frame, the AP sends a BAR frame to a user, waits for the block acknowledgment from that user, and then sequentially repeats the process with the other users. This sequence is illustrated in Figure 19.19.

FIGURE 19.19   MU-MIMO block acknowledgments

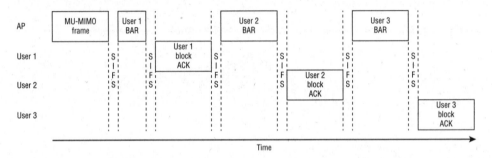

Now that you understand how MU-MIMO works in a simplified communications process example with an AP using MU-MIMO to communicate with three client stations (a two spatial stream laptop, a tablet, and a smart phone), it is important for you to realize that an 802.11ac AP could be easily supporting 20 or 30 clients at the same time. Each client is capable of one or more spatial streams. Using Carrier Sense Multiple Access with Collision Avoidance (CSMA/CA), the AP and clients gain access to the media in order to transmit frames between each other. The AP keeps track of the capabilities of each client and goes through the beamforming and block acknowledgment processes for each transmission that it performs. From one transmission to the next, the AP may be sending frames to a different grouping of stations, which would require different matrix information. The AP will periodically need to update its steering matrix in order to redirect or refocus the signal to the new location of a moving beamformee.

Quality of Service

The core concepts and procedures of quality of service (QoS) remain the same with 802.11ac. With the implementation of MU-MIMO, the implementation of the queuing and transmission of QoS frames is handled differently than in single-user wireless environments.

As defined previously in the standard, there are four access categories, which are listed here in order of highest to lowest priority:

AC_VO (access category voice)

AC_VI (access category video)

AC_BE (access category best effort)

AC_BK (access category background)

To explain how QoS and MU-MIMO work, we will be referencing Figure 19.20. To begin, as shown at the top of the illustration, the MSDU data is separated into the four access categories. In this example, the AP gains access to the channel to transmit voice data to Station 1. Since the AP gained control to transmit voice data, the AC_VO access category is considered the primary access category, while the other access categories are known as the secondary access categories.

The AP takes the first AC_VO frame for Station 1 and begins to construct a multiuser frame. The AP takes frames for the other stations and adds them to the multiuser frame, providing that the stations are spatially distinct and the frames are shorter than the primary frame. These other frames can be from the primary or secondary access category. Any shorter frames are padded. After the multiuser frame is transmitted to the three stations, block ACKs are used to confirm their successful transmission.

The AP then takes the next AC_VO frame for Station 1 and begins to construct multiuser frame 2. Again, the AP can take frames for the other stations and add them to the multiuser frame. In this instance, two frames destined for Station 2 are short enough that they can both be sent during the time needed to transmit the AC_VO frame to Station 1. Block ACKS are again used to confirm their successful transmission.

A third multiuser frame is constructed, transmitted, and acknowledged. During the construction of each of the multiuser frames, lower-priority frames can piggyback with the higher-priority frame, providing they do not increase the time needed to transmit the primary data and providing the stations they are being sent to are spatially distinct.

Infrastructure Requirements

When transitioning to newer technology, it is often necessary to update some of the infrastructure to support the newer technology. In the case of upgrading to 802.11ac, you will need to assess whether the current PoE equipment will support the new 802.11ac APs. You will also need to consider not if, but when to upgrade the Ethernet network that connects to the APs.

Ethernet

With the transition to the second phase of 802.11ac, the data throughput of the wireless network may exceed Gigabit Ethernet speeds. Currently, first phase 802.11ac APs support up to 450 Mbps of transmission speed on a 2.4 GHz radio (802.11n) and up to 1.3 Gbps of transmission speed on a 5 GHz radio. This works out to about 1.75 Gbps of total transmission speed. Actual maximum throughput will vary but is around two-thirds of the maximum calculated transmission speed, which works out to just slightly greater than a gigabit. Since these rates are maximums under perfect conditions, a single Gigabit Ethernet connection can support a phase one 802.11ac AP. Since 2.4 GHz networks are limited to three nonoverlapping channels, it is not likely that 40 MHz wide channels will be used in an enterprise environment. The realistic maximum transmission speed for 2.4 GHz 802.11n using 20 MHz wide channels is about 216 Mbps for first phase 802.11ac APs.

FIGURE 19.20   MU-MIMO and QoS

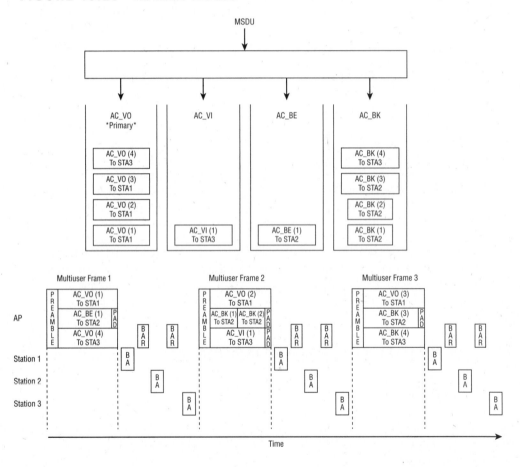

The second phase of 802.11ac may require faster uplink technology than Gigabit Ethernet. The second phase of 802.11ac is expected to support channel widths of up to 160 MHz and four spatial streams. Since the AP will support four spatial streams, the 2.4 GHz 802.11n maximum transmission speed will increase from 450 Mbps to 600 Mbps, with the realistic 20 MHz wide channel maximum transmission speed of about 289 Mbps. The maximum transmission speed for the 5 GHz radio will increase to just under 3.5 Gbps. Although some people will have a need for the wider 160 MHz channels, it is not likely that they will be used often. If we consider 80 MHz as the likely or typical maximum channel width, then the maximum transmission speed for the 5 GHz radio will be about 1.7 Gbps. Therefore, with the realistic 2.4 GHz (20 MHz wide channel) speed of 289 Mbps and the 5 GHz (80 MHz wide channel) speed of 1.7 Gbps, the maximum transmission speed is just under 2 Gbps, with maximum throughput of the AP of about 1.3 Gbps.

So, if second phase 802.11ac is capable of data rates of up to 1.3 Gbps, what options are available for providing this throughput on the distribution system? An initial thought may be to consider 10 Gbps Ethernet; however, 10 Gbps copper Ethernet is not commonly available, and at the time that we wrote this book, there was no PoE option available for 10 Gbps copper. Another option would be to use 10 Gbps fiber from the switch to the AP. The problem with using fiber is that it does not support PoE, and therefore if it is used, power would have to be provided using another method. The most obvious option is to equip the AP with two 1 Gbps Ethernet ports and to run two 1 Gbps Ethernet cables to each 802.11ac AP. AP vendors will likely bond the two Ethernet channels together to provide up to 2 Gbps of throughput. It is important to remember that these suggestions are based upon using a second phase AP, with four spatial streams. It is likely that second phase APs will be available that support fewer than four spatial streams and will function well with a single gigabit Ethernet connection.

802.11ac APs and Dual Ethernet Cables

Since the next phases of 802.11ac will eventually require more than 1 Gbps to backhaul the data, two Ethernet cables will be necessary to take advantage of the additional bandwidth requirements.

Power

When companies first began to install 802.11 APs, it was common to use power bricks or mid-span PoE injectors to provide power to the APs. By the time most companies had installed or upgraded to 802.11g or 802.11n, most of these APs were being powered by PoE-capable Ethernet switches. The majority of enterprise APs are able to be powered by 802.3af-compliant PoE.

As companies transition to 802.11ac APs, transitioning to PoE+ will be inevitable. The greater the performance of the AP, the more likely that additional power will be needed. The industry is transitioning to PoE+. Some 802.11ac APs can operate using 802.3af PoE, whereas other APs restrict some features if 802.3af is used instead of PoE+. Still other APs specify that PoE+ is mandatory.

With the second phase of 802.11ac, it is more likely that these APs will require PoE+ and that a single 802.3af-powered cable will not provide enough power. As future phases of 802.11ac are implemented, in addition to providing connectivity to an AP using two

Ethernet ports, the Ethernet cables could both be used to provide PoE to the AP. If the existing infrastructure only supports 802.3af power, each cable could carry the 15.4 watts of power that 802.3af PoE provides for a total of 30.8 watts. While this scenario may be possible by some vendors' 802.11ac APs, upgrading the network to provide 802.3at (PoE+) power of 30 watts is highly recommended and most likely will become a necessity.

802.11ac in a SOHO or Home

Since you are reading this book, it is likely that you are someone who likes technology toys—or you know someone who does. Or maybe you are someone (or know someone) who just wants the best or fastest of whatever they are buying. In the past, as newer 802.11 PHYs were introduced to the market, there typically has been a benefit to the SOHO or home user to upgrade to the newer PHY. 2 Mbps 802.11 was replaced by 11 Mbps 802.11b, which was replaced with 54 Mbps 802.11g, which was then replaced by 300 Mbps or 450 Mbps 802.11n. During each of these migrations, the faster transmission speed could often be justified and provided real increases in performance to the users. So, the question now is, Will installing or migrating to 802.11ac be beneficial in a SOHO or home environment? There is no right answer to this question, but there are numerous pieces to evaluate when considering migrating.

Although the following sections focus on the SOHO and home environment, much of the decision making is also valid for enterprise environments. We try to break out and summarize what you learned in this chapter, from a technology and practical perspective. Hopefully this will help you as you decide your 802.11ac migration path and timeline.

Device Radios

One of the first things to determine is whether the client devices that you will be using support 802.11ac. If you purchase a new laptop or phone, it is likely that they support 802.11ac. Do all of your other devices? Remember that 802.11ac uses only 5 GHz transmissions. This is not compatible with any 2.4 GHz 802.11b/g/n devices you may still be using. Printers, scanners, tablets, gaming devices, TVs, Blu-ray players, and many other devices that you already own probably do not support 5 GHz. Therefore, if you do plan to upgrade, you will need to purchase a dual-radio AP to continue to provide support for older 2.4 GHz devices.

Data Flow/Usage

Another consideration for whether or not to upgrade to 802.11ac is to determine if you will gain any benefit from the additional speed. Unless you have an unusual network configuration, your communications will be either between your client device and the Internet or between your client device and some type of server within your network. If your communication is out to the Internet, it is not likely that your Internet connection is fast enough to support the throughput that an 802.11ac AP can provide. If your communication is to a server within your network, you will need to find out whether the server can handle the faster data rates. If it can, you will need to ensure that the entire datapath between the AP and the server supports at least 1 Gbps Ethernet.

Spatial Streams

Many personal mobile devices do not support multiple spatial streams due to the power requirements. If you are operating 802.11ac multiple-spatial-stream devices along with single-spatial-stream devices, the single-stream devices will decrease the performance of the faster devices. You will need to consider how your faster devices are affected and whether the performance you achieve is worth the upgrade costs.

Wider 802.11ac Channels

With channel widths up to 80 MHz and 160 MHz with the second phase of 802.11ac, the wider channel width is a technology that all 802.11ac devices can benefit from. Although it takes more power to process the data that is transmitted across wider channels because more subcarriers are being transmitted, the faster data rates along with mandatory A-MPDU support actually reduces transmission time and power consumption. A single spatial stream device can achieve transmission speeds of up to 433 Mbps using an 80 MHz channel and up to 866 Mbps with 160 MHz channels.

MU-MIMO

MU-MIMO does have the potential of improving performance in the SOHO or home environment. With CSMA/CA technology, slower devices affect the overall performance of the network for all devices. With MU-MIMO, the AP can transmit to up to four devices simultaneously. Instead of four 433 Mbps single-stream devices splitting the transmission, MU-MIMO allows multiple downstream transmissions to occur simultaneously, theoretically providing up to four simultaneous 433 Mbps communications. You need to remember that this can only occur if the devices are spatially separated, since beamforming will not work properly if two devices are near each other.

Wi-Fi Alliance Certification

In June 2013, prior to the ratification of the 802.11ac amendment, the Wi-Fi Alliance published its vendor certification program for 802.11ac, Wi-Fi CERTIFIED ac. 802.11ac products are tested for both the mandatory and optional baseline capabilities listed in Table 19.5. As with Wi-Fi CERTIFIED n products, Wi-Fi CERTIFIED ac products must support both Wi-Fi Multimedia (WMM) quality-of-service mechanisms and WPA2/WPA2 security mechanisms. Unlike Wi-Fi CERTIFIED n devices, Wi-Fi CERTIFIED ac devices do not operate in both the 2.4 GHz and 5 GHz frequency bands. Wi-Fi CERTIFIED ac devices only operate in the 5 GHz frequency band. As stated earlier in this chapter, this is due to the limited frequency range available in the 2.4 GHz ISM band. Therefore, they only need to be backward compatible with 5 GHz 802.11a/n certified devices.

TABLE 19.5   Wi-Fi CERTIFIED ac baseline requirements (phase 1)

Feature	Mandatory	Optional
Channel width	20, 40, 80 MHz	80+80, 160 MHz
Modulation and coding	MCS 0–7	MCS 8,9
Spatial streams	One for clients, two for APs	Two to eight
Guard Interval	Long (800 nanoseconds)	Short (400 nanoseconds)
Beamforming feedback		Respond to beamforming sounding
Space-time block coding (STBC)		Transmit and receive STBC
Low-density parity check (LDPC)		Transmit and receive LDPC
Multiuser MIMO		Up to four spatial streams per client, using the same MCS

Summary

In this chapter, you learned about the 802.11ac amendment, how the amendment is currently implemented, and the migration path with future phases of the standard. We also discussed all the methods used by VHT radios to increase throughput and range at the Physical layer. We explained the evolutionary updates to 802.11ac: 5 GHz only, channel widths up to 160 MHz, enhanced modulation with 256-QAM, and mandatory A-MPDU for all frames. The most exciting part of 802.11ac (and the revolutionary aspect of the amendment) is the introduction of MU-MIMO, which allows an AP to transmit to multiple client stations simultaneously. Some of the technologies are being implemented in the first products released; others will follow in multiple phases of future implementation. 802.11ac has great potential.

If you are interested in learning more about 802.11ac, we recommend that you read *802.11ac: A Survival Guide* by Matthew Gast (O'Reilly Media, 2013). Matthew has done an excellent job of explaining the core technologies that make up 802.11ac, in an in-depth and concise format.

Exam Essentials

Define the differences between 802.11n and 802.11ac.   Understand how 802.11ac is similar and different than 802.11n. Know which 802.11ac technologies are evolutionary and which are revolutionary. Explain why 802.11ac is only being implemented in the 5 GHz band.

Understand 20 MHz, 40 MHz, 80 MHz, and 160 MHz channels.   Understand the differences between 20 MHz, 40 MHz, 80 MHz, and 160 MHz channels. Explain how 160 MHz channels are actually two 80 MHz channels. Explain how 802.11ac radios will dynamically switch to narrower channels if the wider channel is not available. Describe the importance of primary channel selection for each channel width.

Understand 64-QAM and 256-QAM.   Explain how 256-QAM is similar and how it is different than 64-QAM. Describe the significance of the constellation chart and the pros and cons of the denser 256-QAM.

Explain MCS.   Explain the transition from 77 MCSs in 802.11n and 10 MCSs in 802.11ac. Explain why 802.11ac does not allow individual data rates to be enabled or disabled.

Describe explicit beamforming.   Describe the communications between the AP and the client to perform explicit beamforming. Describe the benefits of explicit beamforming.

Explain the difference between SU-MIMO and MU-MIMO.   Explain how many spatial streams are supported by 802.11ac along with the additional resources necessary to implement more spatial streams. Explain the technological differences between sending a SU-MIMO signal and a MU-MIMO.

Explain MU-MIMO.   Explain the MU-MIMO process and the conditions under which it will be most successful. Explain how beamforming makes this possible. Explain the requirements for adding more spatial streams. Explain how QoS is implemented in a MU-MIMO environment.

Understand 802.11ac data rates.   Understand how MCS, spatial streams, and channel width determine the maximum data rate achievable by a device.

Understand the infrastructure requirements of 802.11ac.   Understand how the Ethernet and PoE requirements are affected by an 802.11ac deployment.

Describe the concerns when deploying 802.11ac in any environment.   Describe how user devices, data flow, spatial streams, channel width, and MU-MIMO need to be taken into consideration when evaluating whether to migrate to an 802.11ac environment.

Review Questions

1. Which of the following technologies was optional in 802.11n and now mandatory in 802.11ac?
   A. MIMO
   B. RIFS
   C. A-MPDU
   D. A-MSDU
   E. SU-MIMO

2. With the first phase of 802.11ac supporting three spatial streams, what is the maximum transmission speed?
   A. 600 Mbps
   B. 1.3 Gbps
   C. 3.5 Gbps
   D. 6.933 Gbps
   E. 7.0 Gbps

3. Which of the following modulation methods are supported with 802.11ac? (Choose all that apply.)
   A. BPSK
   B. BASK
   C. 32-QAM
   D. 64-QAM
   E. 256-QAM

4. Which of the following channel widths are supported in 802.11ac? (Choose all that apply.)
   A. 20 MHz
   B. 40 MHz
   C. 80 MHz
   D. 80+80 MHz
   E. 160 MHz

5. When a 160 MHz wide channel is used, how many primary channels are defined?
   A. 1
   B. 2
   C. 3
   D. 4
   E. None

6. Using 256-QAM, how many bits are represented by each subcarrier?

A. 1

B. 2

C. 4

D. 6

E. 8

7. How many modulation and coding schemes are defined in 802.11ac?

A. 8

B. 10

C. 64

D. 77

E. 256

8. Which 802.11ac MCS range defines all of the MCSs that are mandatory?

A. MCS 0–2

B. MCS 0–4

C. MCS 0–6

D. MCS 0–7

E. MCS 0–8

F. MCS 0–9

9. The 802.11ac amendment defines a maximum of how many spatial streams for an AP, and how many maximum devices can an AP communicate with at once?

A. One spatial stream, four devices

B. One spatial stream, eight devices

C. Four spatial streams, four devices

D. Eight spatial streams, four devices

E. Eight spatial streams, eight devices

10. Requiring all frames to be transmitted as A-MPDU frames increases performance due to which of the following? (Choose all that apply.)

A. Frame overhead is reduced.

B. Block ACK is required.

C. Frame information is shifted from the MPDU header to the PLCP header.

D. Reduced Interframe Space (RIFS) decreases the amount of time between frames.

E. A-MSDU is required; A-MPDU is optional.

11. Which of the following technologies is part of explicit beamforming? (Choose all that apply.)

  A. Channel sounding

  B. Feedback matrix

  C. Sounding matrix

  D. Steering matrix

  E. Null data packet

  F. Channel matrix

12. What is the main reason that many smartphones do not support multiple spatial streams?

  A. It is difficult to install multiple antennas in the smart phone.

  B. The size of the necessary technology would make the smartphone larger than desired.

  C. Battery consumption would be too great.

  D. Most smartphones actually do support four spatial streams.

13. Which of the following are QoS categories? (Choose all that apply.)

  A. AC_VO (access category voice)

  B. AC_DA (access category data)

  C. AC_VI (access category video)

  D. AC_BE (access category best effort)

  E. AC_BK (access category background)

14. When transmitting a QoS frame using MU-MIMO, which of the following statements is true? (Choose all that apply.)

  A. Voice frames are always transmitted before lower-priority frames.

  B. The category that is used to take control of the transmission is known as the primary access category.

  C. If a lower category frame is transmitted, only higher category frames can be transmitted using the other spatial streams.

  D. Lower category frames can be transmitted as long as they do not increase the transmission duration of the primary access category.

  E. Multiple lower category frames can be transmitted along with the primary access category frame.

15. Name some of the factors that a modulation and coding scheme (MCS) uses to define data rates for a VHT radio? (Choose all that apply.)

  A. Modulation method

  B. Equal/unequal modulation

  C. Number of spatial streams

  D. GI

  E. Channel size

  F. Code rate

16. Which of these capabilities are considered mandatory for a phase one 802.11ac access point as defined by the Wi-Fi Alliance's vendor certification program called Wi-Fi CERTIFIED ac? (Choose all that apply.)

    A. 20, 40, 80, 160 MHz channel

    B. MCS 0–7

    C. MCS 0–8

    D. Two spatial streams

    E. Long guard interval

17. VHT radios are backward compatible with which of the following type of 802.11 technology? (Choose all that apply.)

    A. Clause 17 radios (HR-DSSS)

    B. Clause 18 radios (OFDM)

    C. Clause 14 radios (FHSS)

    D. Clause 19 radios (ERP)

    E. Clause 20 radios (HT)

18. Which of the following statements is not true regarding the number of subcarriers in the following channels? (Choose all that apply.)

    A. 40 MHz subcarriers = 2 times 20 MHz subcarriers

    B. 40 MHz subcarriers > 2 times 20 MHz subcarriers

    C. 80 MHz subcarriers = 2 times 40 MHz subcarriers

    D. 80 MHz subcarriers > 2 times 40 MHz subcarriers

    E. 160 MHz subcarriers = 2 times 80 MHz subcarriers

    F. 160 MHz subcarriers > 2 times 80 MHz subcarriers

19. The 802.11ac amendment defines a maximum of how many spatial streams for client?

    A. One spatial stream

    B. Two spatial streams

    C. Four spatial streams

    D. Eight spatial streams

20. Which 802.11ac technology is the most revolutionary?

    A. 80 MHz and 160 MHz channel widths

    B. A-MPDU for all frames

    C. 256-QAM modulation

    D. 5 GHz only frequencies

    E. MU-MIMO

    F. Explicit beamforming

Chapter

20

Bring Your Own Device (BYOD)

IN THIS CHAPTER, YOU WILL LEARN ABOUT THE FOLLOWING:

✓ **Mobile Device Management**

- Company-issued devices versus personal devices
- MDM architecture
- MDM enrollment
- MDM profiles
- MDM agent software
- Over-the-air management
- Application management
- Wi-Fi client onboarding

✓ **Guest WLAN access**

- Guest SSID
- Guest VLAN
- Guest firewall policy
- Captive web portals
- Client isolation, rate limiting, and web content filtering
- Guest management
- Guest self-registration
- Employee sponsorship
- Social login
- Encrypted guest access

✓ **Network access control (NAC)**

- Posture
- NAC and BYOD
- OS fingerprinting
- AAA
- RADIUS change of authorization

For many years, the primary purpose of enterprise WLANs was to provide wireless access for company-owned laptop computers used by employees. Some vertical markets, such as healthcare, retail, and manufacturing, also required WLAN access for company-owned mobile devices such as VoWiFi phones and wireless bar code scanners. However, in recent years there has been a massive population explosion of Wi-Fi personal mobile devices. Wi-Fi radios are now a common component in smartphones, tablet PCs, and many other mobile devices.

Although mobile devices initially were intended for personal use, employees now want to use their personal mobile devices in the workplace. Employees have expectations of being able to connect to a corporate WLAN with multiple personal mobile devices. The catch-phrase of *bring your own device (BYOD)* refers to the policy of permitting employees to bring personally owned mobile devices such as smartphones, tablets, and laptops to their workplace. A BYOD policy dictates which corporate resources can or cannot be accessed when employees connect to the company WLAN with their personal devices.

The main focus of this chapter is BYOD and the *mobile device management (MDM)* solutions that are needed to supervise personal mobile Wi-Fi devices. This chapter will also cover the many components of WLAN guest access, which has evolved over the years. Finally, you will learn about *network access control (NAC)* for corporate Wi-Fi devices.

Mobile Device Management

Consumerization of IT is a phrase used to describe a shift in information technology (IT) that begins in the consumer market and moves into business and government facilities. It has become common for employees to introduce consumer market devices into the workplace after already embracing new technology at home. In the early days of Wi-Fi, most businesses did not provide wireless network access for their employees. However, because employees had Wi-Fi at home, they began to bring small office, home office (SOHO) wireless routers into the office and install them despite the objections of the IT department. Eventually, businesses and government agencies realized that they needed to deploy WLANs to take advantage of the technology as well as manage the technology.

Personal mobile Wi-Fi devices, such as smartphones and tablets, have been around for quite a few years. The Apple iPhone was first introduced in June 2007, and the first iPad debuted in April 2010. HTC introduced the first Android smartphone in October 2008. These devices were originally meant for personal use, but in a very short time, employees wanted to also use their personal devices on company WLANs. Additionally, software developers began to create enterprise mobile business applications for smartphones and tablets. Businesses began to purchase and deploy tablets and smartphones to take advantage of these mobile enterprise applications. Tablets and smartphones provided the true mobility that employees and businesses desired, and within a few years, the number of mobile devices connecting to corporate WLANs surpassed the number of laptop connections.

Because of the proliferation of personal mobile devices, a BYOD policy is needed to define how employees' personal devices may access the corporate WLAN. A mobile device management (MDM) solution might be needed for onboarding personal mobile devices as well as *company issued devices (CIDs)* to the WLAN. Corporate IT departments can deploy MDM servers to manage, secure, and monitor the mobile devices. An MDM solution can manage devices across multiple mobile operating systems and across multiple mobile service providers. Most MDM solutions are used to manage iOS and Android mobile devices. However, mobile devices that use other operating systems such as BlackBerry OS and Windows Phone can also be managed by MDM solutions. Although the main focus of an MDM solution is the management of smartphones and tablets, some MDM solutions can also be used to onboard personal Mac OS and Chromebook laptops. A few of the devices that can be managed by an MDM solution are shown in Figure 20.1.

FIGURE 20.1 Personal mobile devices with Wi-Fi radios

Some of the WLAN infrastructure vendors have developed small-scale MDM solutions that are specific to their WLAN controller and/or access point solution. However, the bigger MDM companies sell overlay solutions that can be used with any WLAN vendor's solution.

These are some of the major vendors selling overlay MDM solutions:

Airwatch—www.air-watch.com

Fiberlink—www.maaS360.com

JAMF Software—www.jamfsoftware.com

Mobile Iron—www.mobileiron.com

Company-Issued Devices vs. Personal Devices

An MDM solution can be used to manage both company-issued devices and personal devices. However, the management of CID and BYOD is quite different. A company mobile device was purchased by the company with the intent of enhancing employee performance. A tablet or smartphone might be issued to an individual employee or shared by employees on different shifts. Commercial business applications, and very often industry-specific applications, are deployed on these devices. Many companies even develop in-house applications unique to their own business needs. Very often company mobile devices are deployed to replace older hardware. For example, inventory control software running on a tablet might replace legacy handheld bar code scanners. A software Voice over Internet Protocol (VoIP) application running on a smartphone might be used to replace WLAN VoWiFi handsets. The IT department will usually choose one model of mobile device that runs the same operating system.

The management strategy for company mobile devices usually entails more in-depth security because very often the CIDs have company documents and information stored on them. When company devices are provisioned with an MDM solution, many configuration settings such as virtual private network (VPN) client access, email account settings, Wi-Fi profile settings, passwords, and encryption settings are enabled. The ability for employees to remove MDM profiles from a CID is disabled and the MDM administrator can remotely wipe company mobile devices if they are lost or stolen. The MDM solution is also used for hardware and software inventory control. Because these devices are not personal devices, the IT department can also dictate which applications can or cannot be installed on tablets and/or smartphones.

The concept of BYOD emerged because personal mobile devices are much more difficult to manage unless a proper MDM solution has been deployed. Employees, visitors, vendors, contractors, and consultants bring a wide range of personal devices—different makes and models loaded with a variety of operating systems and applications—to the workplace. Therefore, a different management strategy is needed for BYOD. Every company should have its own unique BYOD containment strategy while still allowing access to the corporate WLAN. For example, when the personal devices are provisioned with an MDM solution, the camera may be disabled so that pictures cannot be taken within the building. As shown in Figure 20.2, many restrictions can be enforced on a BYOD device after it has been enrolled in the MDM solution.

MDM Architecture

The basic architecture of any MDM solution consists of four main components:

Mobile Device   The mobile Wi-Fi device requires access to the corporate WLAN. The mobile device can be either a company-owned or employee-owned device. Depending on the MDM vendor, multiple operating systems may be supported, including iOS, Android, Chrome, Mac OS, and so forth. The mobile devices are not allowed onto the corporate network until an enrollment process has been completed and an MDM profile has been installed.

FIGURE 20.2 Device restrictions

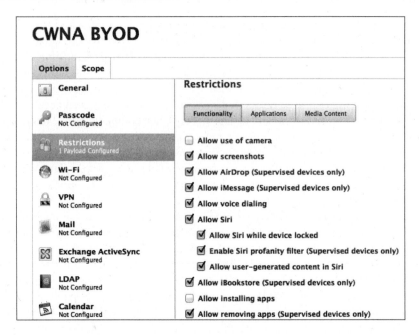

AP/WLAN Controller All Wi-Fi communications are between the mobile devices and the access point to which they connected. If the devices have not been enrolled via the MDM server, the AP or WLAN controller quarantines the mobile devices within a restricted area of the network known as a walled garden. Mobile devices that have been taken through the enrollment process are allowed outside of the walled garden.

MDM Server The MDM server is responsible for enrolling client devices. The MDM server provisions the mobile devices with MDM profiles that define client device restrictions as well as configuration settings. Certificates can be provisioned from the MDM server. MDM servers can also be configured for either enrollment whitelisting or blacklisting. Whitelisting policies restrict enrollment to a list of specific devices and operating systems. Blacklisting policies allow all devices and operating systems to enroll except for those that are specifically prohibited by the blacklist. Although the initial role of an MDM server is to provision and onboard mobile devices to the WLAN, the server is also used for client device monitoring. Device inventory control and application management are key components of any MDM solution. The MDM server usually is available as either a cloud-based service or as an on-premise server that is deployed in the company data center. On-premise MDM servers can be in the form of a hardware appliance or can run as software in a virtualized server environment.

Push Notification Servers The MDM server communicates with push notification servers such as *Apple Push Notification service (APNs)* and *Google Cloud Messaging (GCM)* for over-the-air management of mobile Wi-Fi devices. Over-the-air management will be discussed in greater detail later in this chapter.

There are other key components to an MDM architecture deployment. MDM servers can be configured to query Lightweight Directory Access Protocol (LDAP) databases, such as Active Directory. Typically, a corporate firewall also will be in place. Proper outbound ports need to be open to allow for communications between all of the various components of the MDM architecture. For example, Transmission Control Protocol (TCP) port 443 needs to be open for encrypted SSL communications between the AP and the MDM server as well as SSL communications between the mobile device and the MDM server. TCP port 5223 needs to be open so that mobile devices can communicate with APNs. TCP ports 2195 and 2196 are needed for traffic between the MDM server and APNs. TCP ports 443, 5223, 5229, and 5330 are required for communication between mobile devices and GCM. Communications between the MDM server and GCM require TCP port 443 to be open.

MDM Enrollment

When MDM architecture is in place, mobile devices must go through an enrollment process in order to access network resources. The enrollment process can be used to onboard both company-issued devices and personal devices. Figure 20.3 illustrates the initial steps of the MDM enrollment process.

FIGURE 20.3 MDM enrollment—initial steps

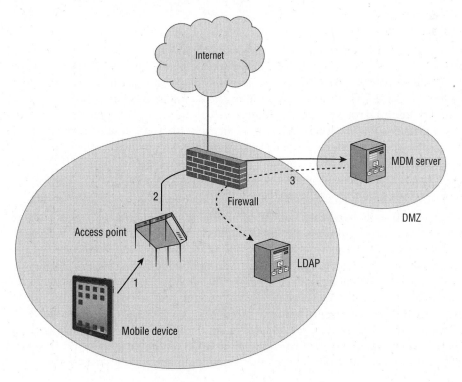

Step 1: Mobile device connects with the access point. The mobile device must first establish an association with an AP. The Wi-Fi security could be open, but usually the CID or personal devices are trying to establish a connection with a secure corporate SSID that is using 802.1X or preshared key (PSK) security. At this point, the AP holds the mobile client device inside a *walled garden*. Within a network deployment, a walled garden is a closed environment that restricts access to web content and network resources while still allowing access to some resources. A walled garden is a closed platform of network services provided for devices and/or users. While inside the walled garden designated by the AP, the only services that the mobile device can access are Dynamic Host Configuration Protocol (DHCP), Domain Name System (DNS), push notification services, and the MDM server. In order to escape from the walled garden, the mobile device must find the proper exit point, much like in a real walled garden. The designated exit point for a mobile device is the MDM enrollment process.

Step 2: AP checks if the device is enrolled. The next step is to determine if the mobile device has been enrolled. Depending on the WLAN vendor, the AP or a WLAN controller queries the MDM server to determine the enrollment status of the mobile device. If the MDM is provided as a cloud-based service, the enrollment query crosses a WAN link. (An on-premise MDM server typically will be deployed in a DMZ.) If the mobile device is already enrolled, the MDM server will send a message to the AP to release the device from the walled garden. Unenrolled devices will remain quarantined inside the walled garden.

Step 3: MDM server queries LDAP. Although an open enrollment process can be deployed, administrators often require authentication. The MDM server queries an existing LDAP database, such as Active Directory. The LDAP server responds to the query, and then the MDM enrollment can proceed.

Step 4: Device is redirected to the MDM server. Although the unenrolled device has access to DNS services, the quarantined device cannot access any web service other than the MDM server. When the user opens a browser on the mobile device, it is redirected to the captive web portal for the MDM server, as shown in Figure 20.4. The enrollment process can then proceed. For legal and privacy reasons, captive web portals contain a legal disclaimer agreement that gives the MDM administrator the ability to restrict settings and remotely change the capabilities of the mobile device. The legal disclaimer is particularly important for a BYOD situation where employees are onboarding their own personal devices. If the user does not agree to the legal disclaimer, they cannot proceed with the enrollment process and will not be released from the walled garden.

Step 5: Devices installs certificate and MDM profile. Once enrollment begins, a secure *over-the-air provisioning* process for installing the MDM profile is needed. Over-the-air provisioning differs between different device operating systems, but using trusted certificates and SSL encryption is the norm. For this example we will describe how iOS devices are provisioned. For iOS devices, the *Simple Certificate Enrollment Protocol (SCEP)* uses certificates and Secure Sockets Layer (SSL) encryption to protect the MDM profiles. The user of the mobile device accepts an initial profile that is installed on the device. After installation of the initial profile, device-specific identity information can be sent to the MDM server. The MDM server then sends a Simple Certificate Enrollment Protocol (SCEP) payload that instructs the mobile device about how to download a trusted certificate from the MDM certificate authority (CA) or a third-party CA. Once the certificate is installed on the mobile device, the encrypted MDM profile with the device configuration and restrictions payload is sent securely to the mobile device and installed. Figure 20.5 depicts the installation of MDM profiles using SCEP on an iOS device.

FIGURE 20.4   MDM server—enrollment captive web portal—step 4

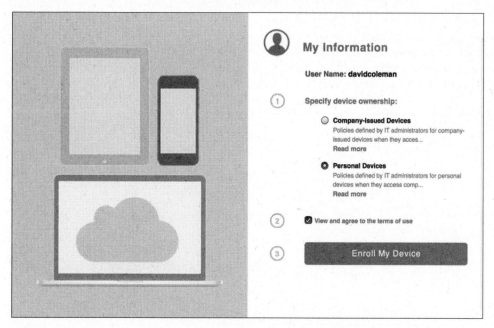

FIGURE 20.5   Certificate and MDM profile installation—step 5

Step 6: MDM server releases mobile device   As shown in Figure 20.6, once the device has completed the MDM enrollment, the MDM server sends a message to the AP or WLAN controller to release the mobile device from the walled garden.

Step 7: Mobile device exits the walled garden   The mobile device now abides by the restrictions and configuration settings defined by the MDM profile. For example, use of the mobile device's camera may no longer be allowed. Configuration settings, such as email or VPN settings, also may have been provisioned. The mobile device is now free to exit the walled garden and access the Internet and corporate network resources. Access to available network resources is dictated by the type of device or the identity of the user. For example, company-owned devices may have access to all network servers while personal devices may only access specific servers such as the email server.

FIGURE 20.6   Mobile device exits the walled garden–final steps

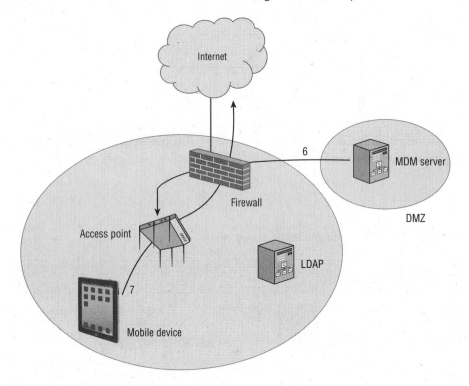

MDM Profiles

We have already learned that MDM profiles are used for mobile device restrictions. The MDM profiles can also be used to globally configure various components of a mobile device. MDM profiles are essentially configuration settings for a mobile device. As the example in Figure 20.7 shows, MDM profiles can include device restrictions, email settings, VPN settings, LDAP directory service settings, and Wi-Fi settings. MDM profiles can also include *webclips*, which are browser shortcuts that point to specific URLs. A webclip icon is automatically installed on the desktop screen of the mobile device. For example, a company-issued device could be provisioned with a webclip link to the company's internal intranet.

FIGURE 20.7   MDM profile settings

The configuration profiles used by Mac OS and iOS devices are *Extensible Markup Language (XML)* files. Apple has several tools to create profiles, including the Apple Configurator and the iPhone Configuration Utility. For manual installations, the XML profiles can be delivered via email or through a website. Manual installation and configuration is fine for a single device, but what about in an enterprise where thousands of devices might need to be configured? In the enterprise, a method is needed to automate the delivery of configuration profiles, and that is where an MDM solution comes into play. MDM configuration profiles are created on the MDM server and installed onto the mobile devices during the enrollment process.

As mentioned, one aspect of an MDM profile is that the Wi-Fi settings can be provisioned. Company-owned devices can be locked down with a specific Wi-Fi profile that designates the corporate SSID and proper security settings. If 802.1X/EAP is deployed, a root CA certificate must be installed on the supplicant mobile device. An MDM solution is the easiest way to provision root CA certificates on mobile devices. Client certificates can also be provisioned if EAP-TLS is the chosen 802.1X security protocol.

MDM profiles can be removed from the device locally or can be removed remotely through the Internet via the MDM server.

Can Employees Remove the MDM Profiles from the Mobile Device?

Once a mobile device has gone through an enrollment process, the MDM configuration profiles and related certificates are installed on the mobile device. The figure below shows the settings screen of an iPad with installed MDM profiles.

Can an employee remove the MDM profiles? The answer to this question is a matter of company policy. Company-owned mobile devices usually have the MDM profiles locked and they cannot be removed. This prevents the employee from making unauthorized changes to the device. If the mobile device is stolen and sensitive information resides on the device, the MDM administrator can remotely wipe the mobile device if it is connected to the Internet. The BYOD policy of personal devices is usually less restrictive. When employees enroll their personal devices through the corporate MDM solution, typically the employee retains the ability to remove the MDM profiles because they own the device. If the employee removes the MDM profiles, the device is no longer managed by the corporate MDM solution. The next time the employee tries to connect to the company's WLAN with the mobile device, the employee will have to once again go through the MDM enrollment process.

MDM Agent Software

The operating systems of some mobile devices require *MDM agent* application software. For example, Android devices require an MDM agent application like the one shown in Figure 20.8. The Android OS is an open-source operating system that can be customized by the various mobile device manufacturers. While this provides much more flexibility, managing and administering Android devices in the enterprise can be very challenging due to the sheer number of hardware manufacturers. An MDM agent application can report unique information about the Android device back to an MDM server, which can later be used in MDM restriction and configuration policies. An MDM agent must support multiple Android device manufacturers.

FIGURE 20.8   MDM agent application

An employee downloads the MDM agent from a public website or company website and installs it on their Android device. The MDM agent contacts the MDM server over the WLAN and is typically required to authenticate to the server. The MDM agent must give the MDM server permission to make changes to the device and function as the administrator of the device. Once this secure relationship has been established, the MDM agent software enforces the device restriction and configuration changes. MDM administration on an Android device is handled by the agent application on the device. Changes can however be

---

Stop Thief!

A stolen company-owned device can be remotely wiped. MDM vendors implement different types of remote wipes.

Enterprise Wipe   Wipes all corporate data from the selected device and removes the device from the MDM. All of the enterprise data contained on the device is removed, including MDM profiles, policies, and internal applications. The device will return to the state it was in prior to the enrollment with the MDM.

Device Wipe   Wipes all data from the device, including all data, email, profiles, and MDM capabilities and returns the device to factory default settings.

Application Management

Enterprise MDM solutions also offer various levels of management of the applications that run on mobile devices. Once an MDM profile is installed, all of the applications installed on the device can be viewed from the MDM server, as shown in Figure 20.11. The MDM server can manage applications by whitelisting and/or blacklisting specific applications that can be used on the mobile devices. Managing applications on company-owned devices is commonplace; however, application management on employee's personal devices is not as prevalent.

FIGURE 20.11   Mobile device applications

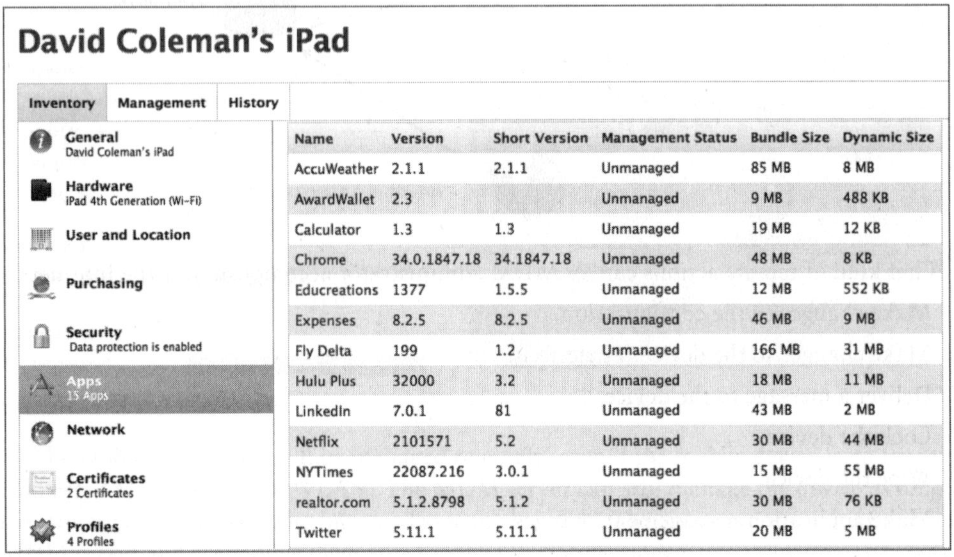

David Coleman's iPad

Inventory	Management	History

	Name	Version	Short Version	Management Status	Bundle Size	Dynamic Size
General David Coleman's iPad	AccuWeather	2.1.1	2.1.1	Unmanaged	85 MB	8 MB
Hardware iPad 4th Generation (Wi-Fi)	AwardWallet	2.3		Unmanaged	9 MB	488 KB
User and Location	Calculator	1.3	1.3	Unmanaged	19 MB	12 KB
	Chrome	34.0.1847.18	34.1847.18	Unmanaged	48 MB	8 KB
Purchasing	Educreations	1377	1.5.5	Unmanaged	12 MB	552 KB
	Expenses	8.2.5	8.2.5	Unmanaged	46 MB	9 MB
Security Data protection is enabled	Fly Delta	199	1.2	Unmanaged	166 MB	31 MB
Apps 15 Apps	Hulu Plus	32000	3.2	Unmanaged	18 MB	11 MB
	LinkedIn	7.0.1	81	Unmanaged	43 MB	2 MB
Network	Netflix	2101571	5.2	Unmanaged	30 MB	44 MB
	NYTimes	22087.216	3.0.1	Unmanaged	15 MB	55 MB
Certificates 2 Certificates	realtor.com	5.1.2.8798	5.1.2	Unmanaged	30 MB	76 KB
Profiles 4 Profiles	Twitter	5.11.1	5.11.1	Unmanaged	20 MB	5 MB

MDM solutions integrate with public application stores, such as iTunes and Google Play, in order to allow access to public applications. The MDM server communicates with the push notification servers, which then places an application icon on the mobile device. The mobile device user can then install the application. The Apple Volume Purchase Program (VPP) provides a way for businesses and educational institutions to purchase apps in bulk and distribute them across their organization. Applications can be purchased and pushed silently to the remote devices. An MDM server can also be configured to deliver custom in-house applications that might be unique to the company.

As shown in Figure 20.12, eBooks can also be managed and distributed to mobile devices via an MDM platform. We suggest that your company make a bulk purchase of the *CWNA Study Guide eBook*.

FIGURE 20.12   MDM distribution of the *CWNA Study Guide eBook*

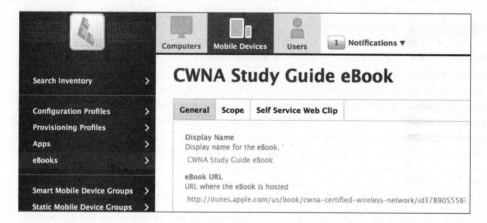

Wi-Fi Client Onboarding

As mentioned earlier in this chapter, several of the WLAN infrastructure vendors have developed small-scale MDM solutions that are specific to their WLAN controller and/or access point solution. However, most of the WLAN vendors offer these solutions more as a Wi-Fi client *onboarding* solution as opposed to a robust enterprise MDM. The main purpose of these onboarding solutions is to give the customer an inexpensive and simple way to provision mobile devices onto the secure corporate SSID.

802.1X/EAP requires that a root CA certificate be installed on the supplicant. Installing the root certificate onto Windows laptops can be easily automated using a *group policy object (GPO)*. However, a GPO cannot be used for Mac OS, iOS, or Android mobile devices. Manually installing certificates on mobile devices is an administrative nightmare. So, what is the easiest way to automate the installation of certificates onto mobile devices? Over-the-air provisioning.

Over-the-air provisioning is used to install Wi-Fi client profiles configured with the corporate SSID and security settings. By now you should know that the mobile device is the supplicant. The onboarding solution is most often used to install the root CA certificates on mobile devices to be used with an 802.1X/EAP-enabled SSID. Client certificates can also be provisioned with an onboarding solution. Some of the Wi-Fi vendors that offer dynamic PSK solutions also offer onboarding solutions that can provision mobile devices with Wi-Fi client profiles configured with unique individual PSKs.

Guest WLAN Access

Although the primary purpose for enterprise WLANs has always been to provide employees wireless mobility, WLAN access for company guests can be just as important. Customers, consultants, vendors, and contractors often need access to the Internet to accomplish job-related duties. When they are more productive, employees will also be more productive. Guest access can also be a value-added service and often breeds customer loyalty. In today's world, business customers have come to expect guest WLAN access. Free guest access is often considered a value-added service. There is a chance that your customers will move toward your competitors if you do not provide guest WLAN access. Retail, restaurants, and hotel chains are all prime examples of environments where wireless Internet access is often expected by customers.

The primary purpose of a guest WLAN is simply to provide a wireless gateway to the Internet for company visitors and/or customers. Generally, guest users do not need access to company network resources. Therefore, the most important security aspect of a guest WLAN is to protect the company network infrastructure from the guest users. In the early days of Wi-Fi, guest networks were not very common because of fears that the guest users might access corporate resources. Guest access was often provided on a separate infrastructure. Another common strategy was to send all guest traffic to a separate gateway that was different from the Internet gateway for company employees. For example, a T1 or T3 line might have been used for the corporate gateway, while all guest traffic was segmented on a separate DSL phone line.

WLAN guest access has grown in popularity over the years, and the various types of WLAN guest solutions have evolved to meet the need. In the following sections, we will discuss the security aspects of guest WLANs. At a minimum, there should be a separate guest SSID, a unique guest VLAN, a guest firewall policy, and a captive web portal. We will also discuss the many guest access options that are available, including guest self-registration.

Guest SSID

In the past, a common SSID strategy was to segment different types of users—even employees—on separate SSIDs; each SSID was mapped to an independent VLAN. For example, a hospital might have unique SSID/VLAN pairs for doctors, nurses, technicians, and administrators. That strategy is rarely recommended now because of the layer 2 overhead created by having many SSIDs. Today, the more common method is to place all employees on the same SSID and leverage Remote Authentication Dial-In User Service (RADIUS) attributes to assign different groups of users to different VLANS. What has not changed over time is the recommendation that all guest user traffic be segmented onto a separate SSID. The guest SSID will always have different security parameters than the employee SSID, and therefore the necessity of a separate guest SSID continues. For example, employee SSIDs commonly use 802.1X/EAP security, while guest SSIDs are most often an open network that uses a captive web portal for authentication. Although encryption is not usually provided for guest users, some WLAN vendors have begun to offer encrypted guest access and provide data privacy using dynamic PSK credentials. Encrypted guest access can also be provided with 802.1X/EAP with Hotspot 2.0, which is discussed later.

Like all SSIDs, a guest SSID should never be hidden and should have a simple name, such as CWNA-Guest. In most cases, the guest SSID is prominently displayed on a sign in the lobby or entrance of the company offices.

Guest VLAN

Guest user traffic should be segmented into a unique VLAN tied to an IP subnet that does not mix with the employee VLANs. Segmenting your guest users into a unique VLAN is a security and management best practice. The main debate about the guest VLAN is whether or not the guest VLAN should be supported at the edge of the network. As shown in Figure 20.13, a frequent design scenario is that the guest VLAN does not exist at the edge of the network and instead is isolated in what is known as a demilitarized zone (DMZ). As shown in Figure 20.13, the guest VLAN (VLAN 10) does not exist at the access layer, and therefore, all guest traffic must be tunneled from the AP back to the DMZ where the guest VLAN does exist. An IP tunnel, commonly using Generic Routing Encapsulation (GRE) protocol, transports the guest traffic from the edge of the network back to the isolated DMZ. Depending on the WLAN vendor solution, the tunnel destination in the DMZ can be either a WLAN controller or simply a layer 2 server appliance.

Although isolating the guest VLAN in a DMZ has been a common practice for many years, it is no longer necessary if guest firewall policies are being enforced at the edge of the network. Various WLAN vendors are now building enterprise-class firewalls into access points. If the guest firewall policy can be enforced at the edge of the network, the guest VLAN can also reside at the access layer and no tunneling is needed.

Guest Firewall Policy

The most important security component of a guest WLAN is the firewall policy. The guest WLAN firewall policy prevents guest user traffic from getting near the company network infrastructure and resources. Figure 20.14 shows a very simple guest firewall policy that allows DHCP and DNS but restricts access to private networks 10.0.0.0/8, 172.16.0.0/12, and 192.168.0.0/16. Guest users are not allowed on these private networks because corporate network servers and resources often reside on that private IP space. The guest firewall policy should simply route all guest traffic straight to an Internet gateway and away from the corporate network infrastructure.

FIGURE 20.13   GRE tunneling guest traffic to a DMZ

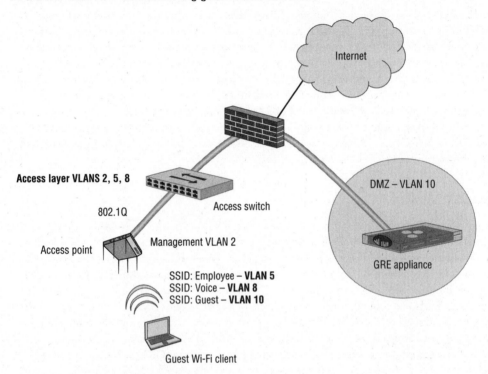

FIGURE 20.14   Guest firewall policy

Source IP	Destination IP	Service	Action
[-any-]	[-any-]	Network Service: DHCP-Server	Permit
[-any-]	[-any-]	Network Service: DNS	Permit
[-any-]	10.0.0.0/255.0.0.0	Network Service: [-any-]	Deny
[-any-]	172.16.0.0/255.240.0.0	Network Service: [-any-]	Deny
[-any-]	192.168.0.0/255.255.0.0	Network Service: [-any-]	Deny
[-any-]	[-any-]	Network Service: [-any-]	Permit

Firewall ports that should be permitted include the DHCP server (UDP port 67), DNS (UDP port 53), HTTP (TCP port 80), and HTTPS (TCP port 443). This allows the guest user's wireless device to receive an IP address, perform DNS queries, and browse the Web. Many companies require their employees to use a secure VPN connection when the employee is connected to an SSID other than the company SSID. Therefore, it is recommended that IPsec IKE (UDP port 500) and IPsec NAT-T (UDP port 4500) also be permitted.

The firewall policy shown in Figure 20.14 represents the minimum protection needed for a guest WLAN. The guest firewall policy can be much more restrictive. Depending on company policy, many more ports can be blocked. A good practice is to force the guest users to use webmail and block SMTP and other email ports so users cannot SPAM through the guest WLAN. It really is up to the security policy of the company to determine what ports need to be blocked on the guest VLAN. If the policy forbids the use of SSH on the guest WLAN, then TCP port 22 will need to be blocked. In addition to blocking UDP and TCP ports, several WLAN vendors now have the ability to block applications. In addition to stateful firewall capability, WLAN vendors have begun to build application-layer firewalls capable of *deep packet inspection (dpi)* into access points or WLAN controllers. An application-layer firewall can block specific applications or groups of applications. For example, some popular video streaming applications can be blocked on the guest SSID, as shown in Figure 20.15. The company security policy will also determine which applications should be blocked on a guest WLAN.

FIGURE 20.15   Application firewall policy

Source IP	Destination IP	Service	Action
[-any-]	[-any-]	Application Service: YOUTUBE	Deny
[-any-]	[-any-]	Application Service: PANDORA AUDIO	Deny
[-any-]	[-any-]	Application Service: PANDORA.TV	Deny
[-any-]	[-any-]	Application Service: GOOGLE VIDEO	Deny
[-any-]	[-any-]	Application Service: HULU	Deny
[-any-]	[-any-]	Application Service: ITUNES	Deny
[-any-]	[-any-]	Application Service: NETFLIX VIDEO STREAM	Deny

Captive Web Portals

Often, guest users must log in through a captive web portal page before they are provided access to the Internet. One of the most important aspects of the captive web portal page is the legal disclaimer. A good legal disclaimer informs the guest users about acceptable behavior when using the guest WLAN. Businesses are more likely to be legally protected if something bad, such as being infected by a computer virus, should happen to a guest user's WLAN device while connected through the portal. A *captive portal* solution effectively turns a web browser into an authentication service. To authenticate, the user must first connect to the WLAN and launch a web browser. After the browser is launched and the user attempts to go to a website, no matter what web page the user attempts to browse to, the user is redirected to a logon prompt on the captive portal logon web page. Captive portals can redirect unauthenticated users to a logon page using an IP redirect, DNS redirection, or redirection by HTTP. As shown in Figure 20.16, many captive web portals are triggered by

DNS redirection. The guest user attempts to browse to a web page but the DNS query redirects the browser to the IP address of the captive web portal.

FIGURE 20.16 Captive web portal—DNS redirect

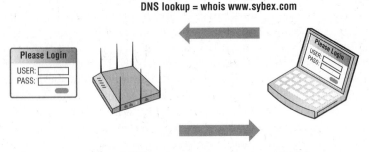

DNS lookup = whois www.sybex.com

DNS response = www.sybex.com = 1.1.1.1

Captive portals are available as standalone software solutions, but most WLAN vendors offer integrated captive portal solutions. The captive portal may exist within a WLAN controller, or it may be deployed at the edge within an access point. WLAN vendors that support captive portals provide the ability to customize the captive portal page. You can typically personalize the page by adding graphics such as a company logo, inserting an acceptable use policy, or configuring the logon requirements. As shown in Figure 20.17, depending on the chosen security of the guest WLAN, different types of captive web portal logon pages can be used. A user authentication logon page requires the AP or WLAN controller to query a RADIUS server with the guest user's name and password. The logon page may require the guest user to self-register or simply acknowledge a user policy acceptance agreement.

FIGURE 20.17 Captive web portal logon pages

User authentication   Self-registration   User policy acceptance

Client Isolation, Rate Limiting, and Web Content Filtering

When guest users are connected to the guest SSID, they are all in the same VLAN and the same IP subnet. Because they reside in the same VLAN, the guests can perform peer-to-peer attacks against each other. Client isolation is a feature that can be enabled on WLAN access points or controllers to block wireless clients from communicating directly with other wireless clients on the same wireless VLAN. *Client isolation* (or the various other terms used to describe this feature) usually means that packets arriving at the AP's wireless interface are not allowed to be forwarded back out of the wireless interface to other clients. This isolates each user on the wireless network to ensure that a wireless station cannot be used to gain layer 3 or higher access to another wireless station. The client isolation feature is usually a configurable setting per SSID linked to a unique VLAN. Client isolation is highly recommended on guest WLANs to prevent peer-to-peer attacks.

Enterprise WLAN vendors also offer the capability to throttle bandwidth of user traffic. Bandwidth throttling, which is also known as rate limiting, can be used to curb traffic at either the SSID level or user level. Rate limiting is recommended on guest WLANs. It can ensure that the majority of the wireless bandwidth is preserved for employees. Rate limiting the guest user traffic to 1024 Kbps is a common practice.

Enterprise companies often deploy web content filter solutions to restrict the type of websites that their employees can view while at the workplace. A web content filtering solution blocks employees from viewing websites based on content categories. Each category contains websites or web pages that have been assigned based on their primary web content. For example, the company might use a web content filter to block employees from viewing any websites that pertain to gambling or violence. While content filtering is most often used to block what employees can view on the Internet, web content filtering can also be used to block certain types of websites from guest users. All guest traffic might be routed through the company's web content filter.

Guest Management

As Wi-Fi has evolved, so have WLAN guest management solutions. Most guest WLANS require a guest user to authenticate with credentials via a captive web portal. Therefore, a database of user credentials must be created. Unlike a preexisting Active Directory database, guest user databases are normally created on-the-fly. Guest user information is usually collected when the guests arrive at company offices. Someone has to be in charge of managing the database and creating the guest user accounts. IT administrators are typically too busy to manage a guest database; therefore, the individual who manages the database is often a receptionist or the person who greets guests at the front door. This individual requires an administrative account to the guest management solution, which might be a RADIUS server or some type of other guest database server. The guest management administrators have the access rights to create guest user accounts on the database server and issue the guest credentials, which are usually usernames and passwords.

A guest management server can be cloud based or can reside as an on-premise server in the company data center. Although most guest management systems are built around a RADIUS server, the guest management solution offers features in addition to providing RADIUS services. Modern WLAN guest management solutions offer robust report generation capabilities for auditing and compliance requirements. As shown in Figure 20.18, a guest management solution can also be used as a 24/7 fulltime monitoring solution. An IT administrator usually configures the guest management solution initially; however, a company receptionist will have limited access rights to provision guest users. Guest management solutions can also be integrated with LDAP for employee sponsorships and usually have some method for guest users to self-register. Most often, guest management solutions are used for wireless guests, but they might also be used to authenticate guests connected to wired ports.

FIGURE 20.18   Guest management and monitoring

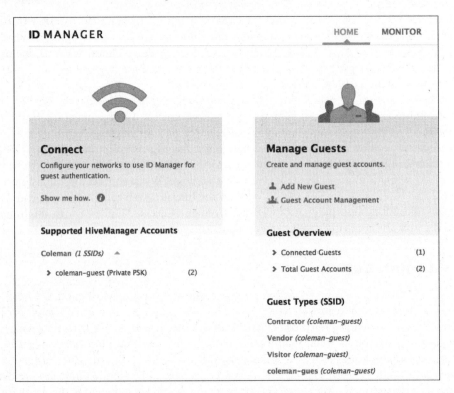

As shown in Figure 20.19, there can be multiple ways to deliver the guest credentials to the guest user. The credentials can be delivered via an SMS text message, an email message, or a printed receipt. The SMS, email, and receipt can also be customized with company information. The guest registration logon pages can all be customized with company logos and information.

FIGURE 20.19   Guest credential delivery methods

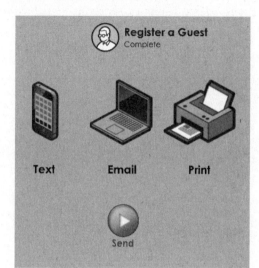

Guest Self-Registration

Guest management solutions have always relied on a company receptionist or lobby ambassador to register the guest users. A good guest management solution allows the receptionist to register a single guest user or groups of users. Over the past few years, there has also been a greater push for guest users to create their own account, what is commonly referred to as self-registration. When the guest is redirected to the captive web portal, if they do not already have a guest account, a link on the logon web page redirects the guest to a self-registration page. Simple self-registration pages allow the guest to simply fill out a form, and their guest account is created and displayed or printed for them. More advanced self-registration pages require the guest to enter an email or SMS address, which is then used by the registration system to send the user their logon credentials.

As shown in Figure 20.20, some of the better guest management solutions now offer a kiosk mode, where the self-registration logon page runs on an iPad or Android tablet that functions as the kiosk. Self-registration via a kiosk is quite useful when the kiosk is deployed in the main lobby or at the entrance to the company. An advantage of self-registration kiosks is that the receptionist does not have to provision the users and can concentrate on other work duties.

Employee Sponsorship

Guest users can also be required to enter the email address of an employee, who in turn must approve and sponsor the guest. The sponsor typically receives an email with a link that allows them to easily accept or reject the guest's request. Once the user is registered or sponsored, they can log on using their newly created credentials. A guest management solution with *employee sponsorship* capabilities can be integrated with an LDAP database, such as Active Directory.

FIGURE 20.20   Kiosk mode

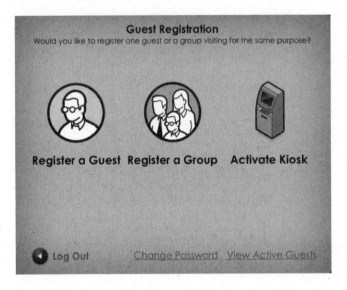

As you already learned, a receptionist can register guest users or a company may choose to use a registration kiosk so that guests can self-register. For larger or distributed organizations, a central registration kiosk does not scale well. Self-registration with employee sponsorship is becoming popular for many organizations.

When a guest user initially connects to the guest network, they are redirected to a captive portal page. The captive portal page prompts them to log on if they already have an account, or it allows them to click a link that allows them to create their own guest account. As shown in Figure 20.21, the guest must enter the email address of the employee that is sponsoring them. Typically, this is the person that they are meeting with.

When the registration form is completed and submitted, the sponsor receives an email notifying them that the guest would like network access. As shown in Figure 20.22, the email typically contains a link that the sponsor must click to approve network access. Once the link is clicked, the guest account is approved and the guest receives confirmation either by email or SMS, and they will then be allowed to log on to the network. If the sponsor does not click the link, the guest account is never created and the guest is denied access to the network.

Employee sponsorship ensures that only authorized guest users are allowed onto the guest WLAN and that the company employees are actively involved in the guest user authorization process.

FIGURE 20.21   Employee sponsorship registration

FIGURE 20.22   Employee sponsorship confirmation email

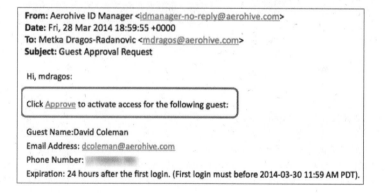

Social Login

A new trend in guest networks in retail and service industries is *social login*. Social login is a method of using existing logon credentials from a social networking service (such as Twitter, Facebook, or LinkedIn) to register on a third-party website. Social login allows a user to forgo the process of creating new registration credentials for the third-party website. Social login is often enabled using the *OAuth* protocol. OAuth is a secure authorization protocol that allows access tokens to be issued to third-party clients by an authorization server. The OAuth 2.0 authorization framework enables a third-party application to obtain limited access to an HTTP service and can be used for social login for Wi-Fi guest networks.

As shown in Figure 20.23, social login can be tied to an open guest SSID. The guest user is redirected to a captive web portal page and they can then log on to the guest WLAN using their existing social media logon credentials. Retail and service businesses like the idea of social login because it allows the business to obtain meaningful marketing information about the guest user from the social networking service. Businesses can then build a database of the type of customers that are using the guest Wi-Fi while shopping at the business. It should be noted that there are serious privacy concerns with social login and the logon captive web portal always has a legal disclaimer stating that customer information might be gathered if the customer agrees to use the social login registration to the guest WLAN.

FIGURE 20.23   Social login

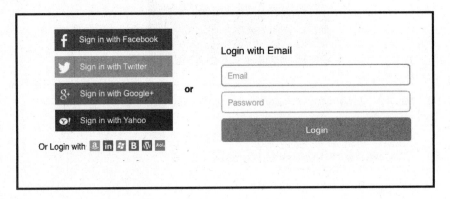

Encrypted Guest Access

Most guest networks are open networks that do not use encryption; thus there is no data privacy for guest users. In Chapter 14, "Wireless Attacks, Intrusion Monitoring, and Policy," you learned about the numerous wireless attacks that make unsecured Wi-Fi users vulnerable. Because no encryption is used on most guest WLANs, the guest users are low-hanging fruit and often targets of skilled hackers or attackers. For that reason, many corporations require that their employees use an IPsec VPN solution when connected to any kind of public or open guest SSID. Because the guest SSID does not provide protection, the guest user must bring their own security in the form of a VPN that provides encryption and data privacy.

The problem is that the many consumers and guest users are not savvy enough to know how to use a VPN solution when connected to an open guest WLAN. As a result, there is a recent trend to provide encryption and better authentication security for WLAN guest users. It should be noted that protecting the company network infrastructure from attacks from a guest user still remains the top security priority. However, if a company can also provide encryption on the guest SSID, the protection provided to the guest user is a value-added service.

One simple way to provide encryption on a guest SSID is to use a static PSK. Although encryption is provided when using static PSK, this is not ideal because of brute-force dictionary attacks and social engineering attacks. Some WLAN vendors offer cloud-based servers to distribute secure guest credentials in the form of unique dynamic PSKs. A guest management solution that utilizes unique PSKs as credentials also provides data privacy for guest users with WPA2 encryption.

Another growing trend with public access networks is the use of 802.1X/EAP with Hotspot 2.0. Hotspot 2.0 is a Wi-Fi Alliance technical specification that is supported by the Passpoint certification program. With Hotspot 2.0, the client device is equipped by an authentication provider with one or more credentials, such as a SIM card, username/password pair, or X.509 certificate. Passport devices can query the network prior to connecting in order to discover the authentication providers supported by the network. Though open networks are still the norm today, growing interest in security and automated connectivity in public access networks will motivate adoption and use of Hotspot 2.0.

Network Access Control (NAC)

Network access control (NAC) evaluates the capability or state of a computer to determine the potential risk of the computer on the network and to determine the level of access to allow. NAC has changed over the years from an environment that primarily assessed the virus and spyware health risk to an environment where checks and fingerprinting are performed on a computer, extensively identifying its capabilities and configuration.

Posture

Network access control (NAC) began as a response to computer viruses, worms, and malware that appeared in the early 2000s. The early NAC products date back to around 2003 and provided what is known as *posture assessment*. Posture is a process that applies a set of rules to check the health and configuration of a computer and determine whether it should be allowed access to the network. NAC products do not perform the health checks themselves but rather validate that the policy is adhered to. A key task of posture assessment is to verify that security software (antivirus, antispyware, and a firewall) is installed, up-to-date, and operational. Essentially, posture assessment "checks the checkers." In addition to checking security software status, posture assessment can check the state of the operating system. Posture policy can be configured to make sure that specific patches or updates are installed, verify that certain processes are running or not running, or even check to determine whether specific hardware (such as USB ports) is active or not.

A posture check is performed by a *persistent agent* (software that is permanently installed on the computer) or by a *dissolvable agent* (software that is temporarily installed). If a company deploys posture software, a persistent agent will likely be installed on all of the corporate laptops to make sure that they are healthy. The company may also want to check guest computers that are trying to connect to the network; however, the guest is not likely to allow your company to install software on their computer. When the guest connects to the captive portal, a posture assessment process can temporarily run and check the guest computer for compliance.

After the posture check is performed, if a computer is considered unhealthy, the ideal scenario would be for the posture agent to automatically fix or remediate the problem so that the computer can pass the check and gain network access. Since the persistent agent is installed on the corporate computer and typically has permissions to make changes, automatic remediation can be performed. Computers that are running dissolvable agents typically cannot be automatically updated. The guest user must resolve the problems before network access will be allowed.

NAC and BYOD

With the proliferation of personal Wi-Fi-enabled devices, enterprises were forced to decide if these devices would be allowed to connect to the enterprise network and if so, what type of access would be allowed. After an organization determined what type of access users would be allowed on the network, the organization was faced with the task of how to identify the different types of user equipment that was being connected to the network. Consider this scenario: Jeff logs in to the enterprise network as an employee from his corporate computer using 802.1X/EAP. His username is verified in the LDAP database using RADIUS. In this scenario, Jeff is trusted as the user because his username and password are valid. His corporate laptop is trusted because his machine can be validated. However, Jeff using his corporate laptop is different from Jeff using his smartphone, Jeff using his personal laptop, or Jeff using his tablet. With all of these new devices, enterprises are faced with the task of identifying and discerning the different types of devices. NAC uses various monitoring and fingerprinting techniques to identify different devices so that access can be controlled.

OS Fingerprinting

The operating system of WLAN client devices can be determined by a variety of fingerprinting methods, including DHCP snooping. After a client successfully establishes a layer 2 connection, the next action is to send a DHCP request to obtain an IP address. As part of the DHCP request, the client device includes DHCP option information and requests a list of DHCP parameters or options from the DHCP server. These options may include subnet mask, domain name, default gateway, and the like. When a client sends DHCP Discover and request messages, each type of client requests different parameters under DHCP option 55. The parameters within DHCP option 55 create a fingerprint that can be used to identify the operating system of the client. For example, iOS devices use a common set of parameters when performing a DHCP request, thus making it possible to identify that the device is most likely an iOS device but not making it possible to discern the difference between an iPod, an iPhone, or an iPad. An extensive list of DHCP fingerprints can be found at www.fingerbank.org. Although the parameter request list is not guaranteed to be unique, it can typically be used along with other fingerprinting techniques to identify devices. Another OS detection method is HTTP fingerprinting. The user-agent header within an HTTP packet identifies the client operating system.

AAA

Earlier in the book we mentioned authentication, authorization, and accounting (AAA). AAA is a key component of NAC. Authentication obviously is used to identify the user who is connecting to the network. We often refer to this as identifying "who you are." Although "who you are" is a very important piece of the process for allowing access to the network, an equally important component of the connection is authorization. We often refer to this as identifying "what you are." Authorization is used to process information such as the following:

- User type (admin, help desk, staff)
- Location, connection type (wireless, wired, VPN)
- Time of day
- Device type (smartphone, tablet, computer)
- Operating system
- Posture

By utilizing both authentication and authorization, a NAC can distinguish between Jeff using his smartphone and Jeff using his personal laptop. From this information, the NAC can control what Jeff can do with each device on the network.

RADIUS Change of Authorization

Prior to RADIUS Change of Authorization (CoA), if a client was authenticated and assigned a set of permissions on the network, the client authorization would not change until the client logged out and logged back in.

RADIUS accounting (the final *A* in *AAA*) is used to monitor the user connection. It can track resources such as time and bytes used for the connection. If the user exceeds the allowed limits of resources, RADIUS CoA can dynamically change the permissions that the user has on the network. RADIUS CoA was originally defined by RFC3576 and later updated in RFC5176. Before you begin to worry, no you do not need to know this for the CWNA exam. We are mentioning it because many of the AAA servers, NAC servers, and enterprise wireless equipment reference RADIUS RFC3576 on configuration menus. Therefore, from a practical perspective, you should be aware that if you see RFC3576 on any configuration menus, that is the section where RADIUS CoA is configured.

Summary

In this chapter, we discussed BYOD policy and the MDM solutions that are needed to manage company-issued mobile devices as well as employee personal mobile devices. We examined the differences between CID and BYOD devices and the MDM policy considerations for both. We discussed the various components of an MDM architecture and how the components interact. We explained the MDM enrollment process and over-the-air provisioning. We reviewed the types of mobile devices that use MDM profiles and those that use MDM agent software. We also discussed over-the-air management and application management when using an MDM solution for mobile devices.

We reviewed guest WLAN access and the key security components needed to protect corporate network infrastructure from guest users. We examined the various methods of guest management, including employee sponsorship, self-registration, and social login. Finally, we discussed how NAC can be used to provide access control by monitoring posture and by fingerprinting the client device prior to it connecting to the network. AAA services can authenticate the user connecting to the network and can authorize the device onto the network. RADIUS CoA can be used to modify the authorization of a user if a new set of permissions needs to be assigned.

Although MDM, WLAN guest management, and NAC are separate components of a WLAN, we choose to write about all three together in this chapter because several WLAN vendors package these security solutions together as one application suite. MDM, WLAN guest management, and NAC can be deployed as separate components or can be deployed in unison to provide mobile device security management, guest user security, and network access security.

Exam Essentials

Define the differences between company-issued devices and personal mobile devices.   Be able to explain the MDM policy concerns for both CID and BYOD devices.

Describe the four main components of an MDM architecture.   Define the roles of a mobile device, an MDM server, an AP, and push notification servers. Explain how they interact.

Explain how MDM profiles and MDM agents are used within an MDM solution.   Describe how MDM profiles can be used for restrictions and mobile device configurations. Describe the role of MDM agents and which mobile devices require MDM agent software.

Discuss MDM over-the-air management and MDM application management.   Be able to explain how push notification servers are used to manage mobile devices across the Internet. Explain how an MDM can manage mobile device applications.

Define the four main security objectives of a guest WLAN.   Discuss the importance of guest SSIDs, guest VLANs, guest firewall policies, and captive web portals.

Explain the many components and methods of WLAN guest management.   Be able to explain self-registration, employee sponsorship, social login, and other ingredients of guest management.

Explain NAC and how it is used to control access to the network.   Describe how posture, RADIUS attributes, and DHCP fingerprinting are used along with AAA to authenticate and authorize a user and device onto the network. Describe how RADIUS CoA can be used to modify the authorization of the user.

Review Questions

1. In a guest firewall policy, what are some of the ports that are recommended to be permitted? (Choose all that apply.)

   A. TCP 22

   B. UDP 53

   C. TCP 443

   D. TCP 110

   E. UDP 4500

2. In a guest firewall policy, which IP networks should be restricted? (Choose all that apply.)

   A. 172.16.0.0/12

   B. 20.0.0.0/8

   C. 192.16.0.0/16

   D. 172.10.0.0/24

   E. 10.0.0.0/8

3. What are some the components within an MDM architecture? (Choose all that apply.)

   A. AP

   B. RADIUS

   C. BYOD

   D. APNs

   E. GCM

4. What are some the methods that can be used to provision a root certificate onto Wi-Fi clients that function as 802.1X supplicants? (Choose all that apply.)

   A. GPO

   B. RADIUS

   C. MDM

   D. APNs

   E. GCM

5. What type of files are used by the MDM profiles for Apple Mac OS and iOS devices? (Choose all that apply.)

   A. HTTP

   B. XML

   C. JAVA

   D. PHP

   E. Python

6. What type of information can be seen on a mobile device that is monitored by an MDM server? (Choose all that apply.)

A. SMS messages

B. Battery life

C. Web browsing history

D. Installed applications

E. Device capacity

7. Which of these is used to report back to an MDM server unique information about mobile devices that can later be used in MDM restriction and configuration policies?

A. MDM profile

B. Push notification service

C. Captive web portal

D. MDM agent

E. Access point

8. What are some of the methods that can be used by a captive web portal to redirect a user to the captive portal logon page? (Choose all that apply.)

A. HTTP redirection

B. IP redirection

C. UDP redirection

D. TCP redirection

E. DNS redirection

9. During the MDM enrollment process, what resources can a mobile client reach while quarantined inside a walled garden? (Choose all that apply.)

A. SMTP

B. DHCP

C. DNS

D. MDM server

E. LDAP server

10. What is the protocol used by iOS and Mac OS devices for over-the-air provisioning of MDM profiles using certificates and SSL encryption?

A. OAuth

B. GRE

C. SCEP

D. XML

E. HTTPS

11. What mechanism can be used if the guest VLAN is not supported at the edge of the network and only resides in A DMZ?

    A. GRE

    B. VPN

    C. STP

    D. RTSP

    E. IGMP

12. Which type of guest management solution needs to integrate with LDAP?

    A. Social login

    B. Kiosk mode

    C. Receptionist registration

    D. Self-registration

    E. Employee sponsorship

13. Given: An employee has enrolled a personal device with an MDM server over the corporate WLAN. The employee removes the MDM profile while at home. What will happen with the employee's personal device the next time the employee tries to connect to the company SSID?

    A. The MDM server will reprovision the MDM profile over the air.

    B. The push notification service will reprovision the MDM profile over the air.

    C. The device will be quarantined in the walled garden and will have to reenroll.

    D. The device will be free to access all resources because the certificate is still on the mobile device.

14. Which phrase best describes a policy of permitting employees to bring personally owned mobile devices such as smartphones, tablets, and laptops to their workplace?

    A. MDM

    B. NAC

    C. DMZ

    D. BYOD

15. Which method of guest management can be used by a company to gather valuable personal information about guest users?

    A. Social login

    B. Kiosk mode

    C. Receptionist registration

    D. Self-registration

    E. Employee sponsorship

16. What kind of remote actions can an MDM administrator send to the mobile device over the Internet?

    A. Configuration changes

    B. Restrictions changes

    C. Locking the device

    D. Wiping the device

    E. Application changes

    F. All of the above

17. What are some extra restrictions that can be placed on a guest user other than the restrictions defined by the guest firewall policy? (Choose all that apply.)

    A. Encryption

    B. Web content filtering

    C. DHCP snooping

    D. Rate limiting

    E. Client isolation

18. With a WLAN infrastructure, where can the guest captive web portal operate? (Choose the best answer.)

    A. AP

    B. WLAN controller

    C. Third-party server

    D. All of the above

19. When an MDM solution is deployed, after a mobile device connects to an access point, where does the mobile device remain until the MDM enrollment process is complete?

    A. DMZ

    B. Walled garden

    C. Quarantine VLAN

    D. IT sandbox

    E. None of the above

20. In order to calculate the capability Jeff should have on the network, which of the following can the NAC server use to initially identify and set his permission? (Choose all that apply.)

    A. Posture

    B. DHCP fingerprinting

    C. RADIUS attributes

    D. RADIUS CoA

    E. MDM profiles

Appendix A

Answers to Review Questions

Chapter 1: Overview of Wireless Standards, Organizations, and Fundamentals

1. C. 802.11 wireless networking is typically used to connect client stations to the network via an access point. Autonomous and lightweight access points are deployed at the access layer, not the core or distribution layer. The Physical layer is a layer of the OSI model, not a network architecture layer.

2. E. RF communications are regulated differently in many regions and countries. The local regulatory domain authorities of individual countries or regions define the spectrum policies and transmit power rules.

3. B. 802.11 wireless bridge links are typically used to perform distribution layer services. Core layer devices are usually much faster than 802.11 wireless devices, and bridges are not used to provide access layer services. The Network layer is a layer of the OSI model, not a network architecture layer.

4. A. The Institute of Electrical and Electronics Engineers (IEEE) is responsible for the creation of all of the 802 standards.

5. D. The Wi-Fi Alliance provides certification testing, and when a product passes the test, it receives a Wi-Fi Interoperability Certificate.

6. C. A carrier signal is a modulated signal that is used to transmit binary data.

7. B. Because of the effects of noise on the amplitude of a signal, amplitude-shift keying (ASK) has to be used cautiously.

8. C. The IEEE 802.11-2012 standard defines communication mechanisms at only the Physical layer and MAC sublayer of the Data-Link layer of the OSI model. The Logical Link Control (LLC) sublayer of the Data-Link layer is not defined by the 802.11-2012 standard. WPA is a security certification. FSK is a modulation method.

9. E. The IETF is responsible for creation of RFC documents. The IEEE is responsible for the 802 standards. The Wi-Fi Alliance is responsible for certification tests. The Wi-Fi Alliance used to be known as WECA but changed its name to Wi-Fi Alliance in 2002. The FCC is responsible for RF regulatory rules in the United States.

10. D. Wi-Fi Multimedia (WMM) is a Wi-Fi Alliance certification program that enables Wi-Fi networks to prioritize traffic generated by different applications. 802.11-2012 is

the IEEE standard, and WEP (Wired Equivalent Privacy) is defined as part of the IEEE 802.11-2012 standard. 802.11i was the IEEE amendment that defined robust security network (RSN) and is also part of the 802.11-2012 standard. PSK is not a standard; it is an encoding technique.

11. A, B and C. The three keying methods that can be used to encode data are amplitude-shift keying (ASK), frequency-shift keying (FSK), and phase-shift keying (PSK).

12. B and E. The IEEE 802.11-2012 standard defines communication mechanisms at only the Physical layer and MAC sublayer of the Data-Link layer of the OSI model.

13. C. *Height* and *power* are two terms that describe the amplitude of a wave. Frequency is how often a wave repeats itself. Wavelength is the actual length of the wave, typically measured from peak to peak. Phase refers to the starting point of a wave in relation to another wave.

14. B. Wi-Fi Direct is designed to provide easy setup for communications directly between wireless devices. Wi-Fi Personal does not exist. 802.11n will likely provide connectivity, but setup could be easy or difficult depending on the environment. CWG-RF is designed for Wi-Fi and cellular radios in a converged handset. Wi-Fi Protected Setup is designed to simplify security setup.

15. A, C and E. Voice Enterprise offers enhanced support for voice applications in enterprise Wi-Fi networks. Voice Enterprise equipment must also support seamless roaming between APs, WPA2-Enterprise security, optimization of power through the WMM-Power Save mechanism, and traffic management through WMM-Admission Control.

16. A, B, C, D and E. All of these are typically regulated by the local or regional RF regulatory authority.

17. B and E. The Wi-Fi Alliance maintains certification programs to ensure vendor interoperability. Voice Personal is a certification program that defines enhanced support for voice applications in residential and small-business Wi-Fi networks. WMM-PS is a certification program that defines methods to conserve battery power for devices using Wi-Fi radios by managing the time the client device spends in sleep mode.

18. D. A wave is divided into 360 degrees.

19. B and C. The main advantages of an unlicensed frequency are that permission to transmit on the frequency is free and that anyone can use the unlicensed frequency. Although there are no additional financial costs, you still must abide by transmission regulations and other restrictions. The fact that anyone can use the frequency band is also a disadvantage because of overcrowding.

20. C. The OSI model is sometimes referred to as the seven-layer model.

Chapter 2: Radio Frequency Fundamentals

1. B and C. Multipath may result in attenuation, amplification, signal loss, or data corruption. If two signals arrive together in phase, the result is an increase in signal strength called upfade. The delay spread may also be too significant and cause data bits to be corrupted, resulting in excessive layer 2 retransmissions.

2. D. The wavelength is the linear distance between the repeating crests (peaks) or repeating troughs (valleys) of a single cycle of a wave pattern.

3. B and C. RF amplifiers introduce active gain with the help of an outside power source. Passive gain is typically created by antennas that focus the energy of a signal without the use of an outside power source.

4. A. The standard measurement of the number of times a signal cycles per second is hertz (Hz). One Hz is equal to one cycle in 1 second.

5. D. Often confused with refraction, the diffraction propagation is the bending of the wave front around an obstacle. Diffraction is caused by some sort of partial blockage of the RF signal, such as a small hill or a building that sits between a transmitting radio and a receiver.

6. F. Nulling, or cancellation, can occur when multiple RF signals arrive at the receiver at the same time and are 180 degrees out of phase with the primary wave.

7. B and C. When the multiple RF signals arrive at the receiver at the same time and are in phase or partially out of phase with the primary wave, the result is an increase in signal strength (amplitude). However, the final received signal, whether affected by upfade or downfade, will never be stronger than the original transmitted signal because of free space path loss.

8. B. 802.11 wireless LANs operate in the 5 GHz and 2.4 GHz frequency range. However, 2.4 GHz is equal to 2.4 billion cycles per second. The frequency of 2.4 million cycles per second is 2.4 MHz.

9. A. An oscilloscope is a time domain tool that can be used to measure how a signal's amplitude changes over time. A frequency domain tool called a spectrum analyzer is a more commonplace tool most often used during site surveys.

10. A, C and D. This is a tough question to answer because many of the same mediums can cause several different propagation behaviors. Metal will always bring about reflection. Water is a major source of absorption; however, large bodies of water can also cause reflection. Flat surfaces such as asphalt roads, ceilings, and walls will also result in reflection behavior.

11. A, B, C and D. Multipath is a propagation phenomenon that results in two or more paths of a signal arriving at a receiving antenna at the same time or within nanoseconds of each other. Because of the natural broadening of the waves, the propagation behaviors of reflection, scattering, diffraction, and refraction can all result in multiple paths of the same signal. The propagation behavior of reflection is usually considered to be the main cause of high-multipath environments.

12. B. Scattering, or scatter, is defined as an RF signal reflecting in multiple directions when encountering an uneven surface.

13. A, B and C. High multipath environments can have a destructive impact on legacy 802.11a/b/g radio transmissions. Multipath has a constructive effect with 802.11n and 802.11ac transmissions that utilize MIMO antenna diversity and maximum ratio combining (MRC) signal processing techniques. Multipath does not affect the security mechanisms defined by 802.11i.

14. A, B, C and D. Air stratification is a leading cause of refraction of an RF signal. Changes in air temperature, changes in air pressure, and water vapor are all causes of refraction. Smog can cause a density change in the air pressure as well as increased moisture.

15. A and D. Because of the natural broadening of the wave front, electromagnetic signals lose amplitude as they travel away from the transmitter. The rate of free space path loss is logarithmic and not linear. Attenuation of RF signals as they pass through different mediums does occur but is not a function of FSPL.

16. D. The time difference due to a reflected signal taking a longer path is known as the delay spread. The delay spread can cause intersymbol interference, which results in data corruption and layer 2 retransmissions.

17. C. A spectrum analyzer is a frequency domain tool that can be used to measure amplitude in a finite frequency spectrum. An oscilloscope is a time domain tool.

18. A and C. Brick walls are very dense and will significantly attenuate a 2.4 GHz and 5 GHz signal. Older structures that are constructed with wood-lath plaster walls often have wire mesh in the walls, which was used to help hold the plaster to the walls. Wire mesh is notorious for disrupting and preventing RF signals from passing through walls. Wire mesh is also used on stucco exteriors. Drywall will attenuate a signal but not to the extent of water, cinder blocks, or other dense mediums. Air temperature has no significance during an indoor site survey.

19. A. There is an inverse relationship between frequency and wavelength. A simplified explanation is that the higher the frequency of an RF signal, the shorter the wavelength will be of that signal. The longer the wavelength of an RF signal, the lower the frequency of that signal.

20. A. Refraction is the bending of an RF signal when it encounters a medium.

Chapter 3: Radio Frequency Components, Measurements, and Mathematics

1. C. The transmitter generates the AC signal and modifies it by using a modulation technique to encode the data into the signal.

2. E. An isotropic radiator is also known as a point source.

3. A, B, C, E and F. When radio communications are deployed, a link budget is the sum of all gains and losses from the transmitting radio, through the RF medium, to the receiver radio. Link budget calculations include original transmit gain and passive antenna gain. All losses must be accounted for, including free space path loss. Frequency and distance are needed to calculate free space path loss. The height of an antenna has no significance when calculating a link budget; however, the height could affect the Fresnel and blockage to it.

4. A and D. *IR* is the abbreviation for *intentional radiator*. The components making up the IR include the transmitter, all cables and connectors, and any other equipment (grounding, lightning arrestors, amplifiers, attenuators, and so forth) between the transmitter and the antenna. The power of the IR is measured at the connecter that provides the input to the antenna.

5. A. Equivalent isotropically radiated power, also known as EIRP, is a measure of the strongest signal that is radiated from an antenna.

6. A, B and D. Watts, milliwatts, and dBms are all absolute power measurements. One watt is equal to 1 ampere (amp) of current flowing at 1 volt. A milliwatt is 1/1,000 of 1 watt. dBm is decibels relative to 1 milliwatt.

7. B, C, D and E. The unit of measurement known as a bel is a relative expression and a measurement of change in power. A decibel (dB) is equal to one-tenth of a bel. Antenna gain measurements of dBi and dBd are relative measurements. dBi is defined as decibels referenced to an isotropic radiator. dBd is defined as decibels referenced to a dipole.

8. C. To convert any dBd value to dBi, simply add 2.14 to the dBd value.

9. A. To convert to mW, first calculate how many 10s and 3s are needed to add up to 23, which is 0 + 10 + 10 + 3. To calculate the mW, you must multiply $1 \times 10 \times 10 \times 2$, which calculates to 200 mW. The file ReviewQuestion9.ppt, available for download from www.sybex.com/go/cwna4e, shows the process in detail.

10. C. To reach 100 mW, you can use 10s and 2s and multiplication and division. Multiplying by two 10s will accomplish this. This means that on the dBm side, you must add two 10s, which equals 20 dBm. Then subtract the 3 dB of cable loss for a dBm of 17. Because you subtracted 3 from the dBm side, you must divide the 100 mW by 2, giving

you a value of 50 mW. Now add in the 16 dBi by adding a 10 and two 3s to the dBm column, giving a total dBm of 33. Because you added a 10 and two 3s, you must multiply the mW column by 10 and two 2s, giving a total of 2,000 mW, or 2 W. Since the cable and connector loss is 3 dB and the antenna gain is 16 dBi, you can add the two together for a cumulative gain of 13 dB; then apply that gain to the 100 mW transmit signal to calculate an EIRP of 2,000 mW, or 2 W. The file ReviewQuestion10.ppt, available for download from www.sybex.com/go/cwna4e, shows the process in detail.

11. A. If the original transmit power is 400 mW and cabling induces a 9 dB loss, the power at the opposite end of the cable will be 50 mW. The first 3 dB of cable loss halved the absolute power to 200 mW. The second 3 dB of cable loss halved the absolute power to 100 mW. The final 3 dB of cable loss halved the power to 50 mW. The antenna with 19 dBi of gain passively amplified the 50 mW signal to 4,000 mW. The first 10 dBi of antenna boosts the signal to 500 mW. The next 9 dBi of antenna gain doubles the signal three times to a total of 4 watts. Since the cable loss is 9 dB and the antenna gain is 19 dBi, you could add the two together for a cumulative gain of 10 dB and then apply that gain to the 400 mW transmit signal to calculate an EIRP of 4,000 mW, or 4 W.

12. B and D. RSSI thresholds are a key factor for clients when they initiate the roaming handoff. RSSI thresholds are also used by vendors to implement dynamic rate switching, which is a process used by 802.11 radios to shift between data rates.

13. A. The received signal strength indicator (RSSI) is a metric used by 802.11 radio cards to measure signal strength (amplitude). Some vendors use a proprietary scale to also correlate to signal quality. Most vendors erroneously define signal quality as the signal-to-noise ratio (SNR). The signal-to-noise ratio is the difference in decibels between the received signal and the background noise (noise floor).

14. B. dBi is defined as "decibel gain referenced to an isotropic radiator" or "change in power relative to an antenna." dBi is the most common measurement of antenna gain.

15. A and F. The four rules of the 10s and 3s are as follows: For every 3 dB of gain (relative), double the absolute power (mW). For every 3 dB of loss (relative), halve the absolute power (mW). For every 10 dB of gain (relative), multiply the absolute power (mW) by a factor of 10. For every 10 dB of loss (relative), divide the absolute power (mW) by a factor of 10.

16. B. If the original transmit power is 100 mW and cabling induces a 3 dB loss, the power at the opposite end of the cable will be 50 mW. The 3 dB of cable loss halved the absolute power to 50 mW. An antenna with 10 dBi of gain would boost the signal to 500 mW. We also know that 3 dB of loss halves the absolute power. Therefore, an antenna with 7 dBi of gain would amplify the signal to half that of a 10 dBi antenna. The antenna with 7 dBi of gain passively amplified the 50 mW signal to 250 mW.

17. D. A distance of as little as 100 meters will cause FSPL of 80 dB, far greater than any other component. RF components such as connectors, lightning arrestors, and cabling all introduce insertion loss. However, FSPL will always be the reason for the greatest amount of loss.

18. B. The 6 dB rule states that increasing the amplitude by 6 decibels will double the usable distance of an RF signal. The 6 dB rule is very useful for understanding antenna gain because every 6 dBi of extra antenna gain will double the usable distance of an RF signal.

19. D. In a high-multipath or noisy environment, a common best practice is to add a 5 dB fade margin when designing for coverage based on a vendor's recommended received signal strength or the noise floor, whichever is louder.

20. D. WLAN vendors execute RSSI metrics in a proprietary manner. The actual range of the RSSI value is from 0 to a maximum value (less than or equal to 255) that each vendor can choose on its own (known as RSSI_Max). Therefore, RSSI metrics should not be used to compare different WLAN vendor radios because there is no standard for the range of values or a consistent scale.

Chapter 4: Radio Frequency Signal and Antenna Concepts

1. A, C and F. The Azimuth chart is the top-down view of an antenna's radiation pattern, also known as the H-plane, or horizontal. The size view is known as the Elevation chart, vertical view, or E-plane.

2. A. The azimuth is the top-down view of an antenna's radiation pattern, also known as the H-plane.

3. C. The beamwidth is the distance in degrees between the –3 dB (half-power) point on one side of the main signal and the –3 dB point on the other side of the main signal, measured along the horizontal axis. These are sometimes known as half-power points.

4. D and E. A parabolic dish and a grid are highly directional. The rest of the antennas are semidirectional, and the sector antenna is a special type of semidirectional antenna.

5. A, C and D. Semidirectional antennas provide too wide of a beamwidth to support long-distance communications but will work for short distances. They are also useful for providing unidirectional coverage from the access point to clients in an indoor environment. They can also minimize reflections and thus the negative effects of multipath.

6. B. Any more than 40 percent encroachment into the Fresnel zone is likely to make a link unreliable. The clearer the Fresnel zone, the better, and ideally it should not be blocked at all.

7. C and D. The distance and frequency determine the size of the Fresnel zone; these are the only variables in the Fresnel zone formula.

8. B. The distance when the curvature of the earth should be considered is 7 miles.

9. A and C. Installing a shorter cable of the same grade will result in less loss and thus more amplitude being transmitted out the antenna. A higher-grade cable rated for less dB loss will have the same result.

10. C and D. A transceiver using antenna diversity can transmit from only one antenna at a time. If it transmitted from both antennas, the two signals would interfere with each other. A transceiver can also interpret only one signal at a time, so it samples the signals received by both antennas and chooses the better signal to be received.

11. A and D. Point-to-point bridge links require a minimum Fresnel zone clearance of 60 percent. Semidirectional antennas such as patch antennas or Yagi antennas are used for short-to-medium-distance bridge links. Highly directional antennas are used for long-distance bridge links. Compensating for earth bulge is not a factor until 7 miles.

12. C. Voltage standing wave ratio (VSWR) is the difference between these voltages and is represented as a ratio, such as, for example, 1.5:1.

13. A, C, D and E. The reflected voltage caused by an impedance mismatch can result in a decrease in power or amplitude (loss) of the signal that is supposed to be transmitted. If the transmitter is not protected from excessive reflected power or large voltage peaks, it can overheat and fail. Understand that VSWR may cause decreased signal strength, erratic signal strength, or even transmitter failure.

14. A, B, D and F. Frequency and distance are needed to determine the Fresnel zone. Visual line of sight is not needed as long as you have RF line of sight. You may not be able to see the antenna because of fog, but the fog will not prevent RF line of sight. Earth bulge will need to be considered. The beamwidth is not needed to determine the height, although it is useful when aiming the antenna.

15. A and D. Cables must be selected that support the frequency you are using. Attenuation actually increases with frequency.

16. A, B, C and D. These are all possible capabilities of RF amplifiers.

17. A, B and D. Adding an attenuator is an intentional act to add loss to the signal. Since cable adds loss, increasing the length will add more loss, whereas shortening the length will reduce the loss. Better-quality cables produce less signal loss.

18. C. Lightning arrestors will not stand up to a direct lightning strike, only transient currents caused by nearby lightning strikes.

19. A and D. The first Fresnel zone is in phase with the point source. The second Fresnel zone begins at the point where the signals transition from being in phase to being out of phase. Because the second Fresnel zone begins where the first Fresnel zone ends, the radius of the second Fresnel zone is larger than the radius of the first Fresnel zone.

20. D. Side lobes are areas of coverage (other than the coverage provided by the main signal) that have a stronger signal than would be expected when compared with the areas around them. Side lobes are best seen on an azimuth chart. Side bands and frequency harmonics have nothing to do with antenna coverage.

Chapter 5: IEEE 802.11 Standards

1. A and D. Support for both Extended Rate Physical DSSS (ERP-DSSS/CCK) and Extended Rate Physical Orthogonal Frequency Division Multiplexing (ERP-OFDM) are required in an ERP WLAN, also known as an 802.11g WLAN. Support for ERP-PBCC and DSSS-OFDM PHYs are optional in an ERP WLAN.

2. E. ERP (802.11g) radios mandate the support for both ERP-DSSS/CCK and ERP-OFDM spread spectrum technologies. ERP-DSSS/CCK supports data rates of 1, 2, 5.5, and 11 Mbps and is backward compatible with HR-DSSS (802.11b) and DSSS (802.11 legacy).

3. B, D and E. The original 802.11 standard defines three Physical layer specifications. An 802.11 legacy network could use FHSS, DSSS, or infrared. 802.11b defined the use of HR-DSSS, 802.11a defined the use of OFDM, and 802.11g defined ERP.

4. C. The 802.11 Task Groups (TGs) has set forth the pursuit of standardizing mesh networking using the IEEE 802.11 MAC/PHY layers. The 802.11s amendment defines the use of mesh points, which are 802.11 QoS stations that support mesh services. A mesh point (MP) is capable of using a mandatory mesh routing protocol called Hybrid Wireless Mesh Protocol (HWMP) that uses a default path selection metric. Vendors may also use proprietary mesh routing protocols and metrics.

5. D and F. The required encryption method defined by an RSN wireless network (802.11i) is Counter Mode with Cipher Block Chaining Message Authentication Code Protocol (CCMP), which uses the Advanced Encryption Standard (AES) algorithm. An optional choice of encryption is the Temporal Key Integrity Protocol (TKIP). The 802.11i amendment also requires the use of an 802.1X/EAP authentication solution or the use of preshared keys.

6. D. 802.11a radio cards operate in the 5 GHz Unlicensed National Information Infrastructure (U-NII) 1–3 frequency bands using Orthogonal Frequency Division Multiplexing (OFDM).

7. D. The IEEE 802.11-2012 standard requires data rates of 6, 12, and 24 Mbps for both OFDM and ERP-OFDM radios. Data rates of 6, 9, 12, 18, 24, 36, 48, and 54 Mbps are typically supported. 54 Mbps is the maximum defined rate.

8. B. Fast basic service set transition (FT), also known as fast secure roaming, defines fast handoffs when roaming occurs between cells in a WLAN using the strong security defined in a robust security network (RSN). Applications such as VoIP that necessitate timely delivery of packets require the roaming handoff to occur in 150ms or less.

9. B, C and E. The 802.11ac amendment debuted and defined the use of 256-QAM modulation, eight spatial streams, multi-user MIMO, 80 MHz channels, and 160 MHz

channels. 802.11 MIMO technology and 40 MHz channels debuted with the ratification of the 802.11n amendment.

10. D. Both 802.11a and 802.11g use OFDM technology, but because they operate at different frequencies, they cannot communicate with each other. 802.11a equipment operates in the 5 GHz U-NII bands, whereas 802.11g equipment operates in the 2.4 GHz ISM band.

11. A and E. The 802.11-2012 standard defines mechanisms for dynamic frequency selection (DFS) and transmit power control (TPC) that may be used to satisfy regulatory requirements for operation in the 5 GHz band. This technology was originally defined in the 802.11h amendment, which is now part of the 802.11-2012 standard.

12. C and D. The 802.11ac and 802.11ad amendments are often referred to as the "gigabit Wi-Fi" amendments because they define data rates of greater than 1 Gbps. The 802.11ac and 802.11ad Very High Throughput (VHT) task groups define transmission rates of up to 7 Gbps in an 802.11 environment.

13. A, D and E. ERP (802.11g) requires the use of ERP-OFDM and ERP-DSSS/CCK in the 2.4 GHz ISM band and is backward compatible with 802.11b HR-DSSS and DSSS equipment. 802.11b uses HR-DSSS in the 2.4 GHz ISM band and is backward compatible with only legacy DSSS equipment and not legacy FHSS equipment. The 802.11h amendment defines use of TPC and DFS in the 5 GHz U-NII bands and is an enhancement of the 802.11a amendment. OFDM technology is used with all 802.11a- and 802.11h-compliant radios.

14. D. The 802.11-2012 standard using OFDM or ERP-OFDM radios requires data rates of 6, 12, and 24 Mbps. Data rates of 6, 9, 12, 18, 24, 36, 48, and 54 Mbps are typically supported. 54 Mbps is the maximum defined rate.

15. B, D and E. The original 802.11 standard defined the use of WEP for encryption. The original 802.11 standard also defined two methods of authentication: Open System authentication and Shared Key authentication.

16. A. The 802.11u draft amendment defines integration of IEEE 802.11 access networks with external networks in a generic and standardized manner. 802.11u is often referred to as Wireless Interworking with External Networks (WIEN).

17. A and C. The 802.11e amendment (now part of the 802.11-2012 standard) defined two enhanced medium access methods to support quality of service (QoS) requirements. Enhanced Distributed Channel Access (EDCA) is an extension to DCF. Hybrid Coordination Function Controlled Channel Access (HCCA) is an extension to PCF. In the real world, only EDCA is implemented.

18. A and C. The 802.11h amendment effectively introduced two major enhancements: more frequency space in the U-NII-2 extended band and radar avoidance and detection technologies. All aspects of the 802.11h ratified amendment can now be found in Clause 10.8 and Clause 10.9 of the 802.11-2012 standard.

19. A. The 802.11b amendment defined systems that can transmit at data rates of 5.5 Mbps and 11 Mbps using High-Rate DSSS (HR-DSSS). 802.11b devices are also compatible with 802.11 DSSS devices and can transmit at data rates of 1 and 2 Mbps.

20. B and D. The IEEE specifically defines 802.11 technologies at the Physical layer and the MAC sublayer of the Data-Link layer. By design, anything that occurs at the upper layers of the OSI model is insignificant to 802.11 communications.

Chapter 6: Wireless Networks and Spread Spectrum Technologies

1. A, B and D. The ISM bands are 902 MHz – 928 MHz, 2.4 GHz – 2.5 GHz, and 5.725 GHz – 5.875 GHz. 5.725 GHz – 5.85 GHz is the U-NII-3 band.

2. A, B and C. The four current U-NII bands are 5.15 GHz – 5.25 GHz, 5.25 GHz – 5.35 GHz, 5.47 GHz – 5.725 GHz, and 5.725 GHz – 5.85 GHz.

3. A, B, C and D. The 802.11-2012 standard allows for the use of legacy FHSS radios (802.11), legacy DSSS radios (802.11), HR-DSSS radios (802.11b), and ERP radios (802.11g).

4. A, B and D. The 802.11-2012 standard specifies that 802.11n HT radios can transmit in the 2.4 GHz ISM band and all four of the current 5 GHz U-NII bands.

5. A. The U-NII-1 band is between 5.15 GHz and 5.25 GHz, 5,150 MHz to 5,250 MHz. To calculate the frequency in MHz from the channel, multiply the channel by 5 (200) and then add 5,000 for a center frequency of 5,200 MHz, or 5.2 GHz.

6. D. To calculate the channel, first take the frequency in MHz (5,300 MHz). Subtract 5,000 from the number (300) and then divide the number by 5, resulting in channel 60.The U-NII-2 band is between 5.25 GHz and 5.35 GHz.

7. B. HR-DSSS was introduced under the 802.11b amendment, which states that channels need a minimum of 25 MHz of separation between the center frequencies to be considered nonoverlapping.

8. C. The time that the transmitter waits before hopping to the next frequency is known as the dwell time. The hop time is not a required time but rather a measurement of how long the hop takes.

9. B. The 802.11a amendment, which originally defined the use of OFDM, required only 20 MHz of separation between the center frequencies for channels to be considered nonoverlapping. All 25 channels in the 5 GHz U-NII bands use OFDM and have 20 MHz of separation. Therefore, all 5 GHz OFDM channels are considered nonoverlapping by the IEEE. However, it should be noted that adjacent 5 GHz channels do have some sideband carrier frequency overlap.

10. C and D. In order for two ERP or HR-DSSS channels to be considered nonoverlapping, they require 25 MHz of separation between the center frequencies. Therefore, any two channels must have at least a five-channel separation. The simplest way to determine what other channels are valid is to add 5 or subtract 5 from the channel you want to use. If you added 5, then the number you calculated or any channel above that number is valid. If you subtracted 5, then the number you calculated or any channel below that number is valid. Deployments of three or more access points in the 2.4 GHz ISM band normally use channels 1, 6, and 11, which are all considered nonoverlapping.

11. B. Extended Rate Physical Packet Binary Convolutional Code (ERP-PBCC) is the optional modulation technique that specifies data rates of 22 and 33 Mbps.

12. B. The cause of the problem is delay spread resulting in intersymbol interference (ISI), which causes data corruption.

13. D. The 802.11-2012 standard states that "the OFDM PHY shall operate in the 5 GHz band, as allocated by a regulatory body in its operational region." A total of twenty-five 20 MHz wide channels are available in the U-NII bands.

14. D. Because of the lower subcarrier data rates, delay spread is a smaller percentage of the symbol period, which means that ISI is less likely to occur. In other words, OFDM technology is more resistant to the negative effects of multipath than DSSS and FHSS spread spectrum technologies.

15. C. A medium access method known as Carrier Sense Multiple Access with Collision Avoidance (CSMA/CA) helps to ensure that only one radio can be transmitting on the medium at any given time. Because of the half-duplex nature of the medium and the overhead generated by CSMA/CA, the actual aggregate throughput is typically 50 percent or less of the data rate when using legacy 802.11a/b/g radios. The aggregate throughput of 802.11n/ac radios is about 65 percent.

16. C and F. The FCC has proposed two new U-NII bands. A new 120 MHz wide band called U-NII-2B occupies the frequency space of 5.35 GHz – 5.47 GHz with six potential 20 MHz channels. Another new 75 MHz wide band called U-NII-4 occupies the 5.85 GHz – 5.925 GHz frequency space with the potential of four more 20 MHz channels.

17. C. In 2009, the Federal Aviation Authority (FAA) reported interference to Terminal Doppler Weather Radar (TDWR) systems. As a result, the FCC suspended certification of 802.11 devices in the U-NII-2 and U-NII-2E bands that require DFS. Eventually certification was re-established, however, the rules changed and 802.11 radios are currently were not allowed to transmit in the 5.60 - 5.65 GHz frequency space where TDWR operates. Channels 120 -128 were not available for a number of years. As of April 2014, the TDWR frequency space is once again available for 802.11 transmissions in the United States.

18. A and B. OFDM uses BPSK and QPSK modulation for the lower ODFM data rates. The higher OFDM data rates use 16-QAM, 64-QAM, and 256-QAM modulation. QAM modulation is a hybrid of phase and amplitude modulation.

19. B. When a data bit is converted to a series of bits, these bits that represent the data are known as chips.

20. C. A 20 MHz OFDM channel uses 52 subcarriers, but only 48 of them are used to transport data. The other 4 subcarriers are used as pilot carriers.

Chapter 7: Wireless LAN Topologies

1. D and E. The service set identifier (SSID) is a 32-character, case-sensitive, logical name used to identify a wireless network. An extended service set identifier (ESSID) is the logical network name used in an extended service set. ESSID is often synonymous with SSID.

2. C and E. The 802.11 standard defines four service sets, or topologies. A basic service set (BSS) is defined as one AP and associated clients. An extended service set (ESS) is defined as one or more basic service sets connected by a distribution system medium. An independent basic service set (IBSS) does not use an AP and consists solely of client stations (STAs).

3. E. By design, the 802.11 standard does not specify a medium to be used in the distribution system. The distribution system medium (DSM) may be an 802.3 Ethernet backbone, an 802.5 token ring network, a wireless medium, or any other medium.

4. D. A wireless personal area network (WPAN) is a short-distance wireless topology. Bluetooth and ZigBee are technologies that are often used in WPANs.

5. A. The most common implementation of an extended service set (ESS) has access points with partially overlapping coverage cells. The purpose behind an ESS with partially overlapping coverage cells is seamless roaming.

6. A, C and D. The size and shape of a basic service area can depend on many variables, including AP transmit power, antenna gain, and physical surroundings.

7. C. The normal default setting of an access point is root mode, which allows the AP to transfer data back and forth between the DS and the 802.11 wireless medium. The default root configuration of an AP allows it to operate inside a basic service set (BSS).

8. B, E and F. The 802.11 standard defines an independent basic service set (IBSS) as a service set using client peer-to-peer communications without the use of an AP. Other names for an IBSS include ad hoc and peer-to-peer.

9. A and D. Clients that are configured in Infrastructure mode may communicate via the AP with other wireless client stations within a BSS. Clients may also communicate through the AP with other networking devices that exist on the distribution system medium, such as a server or a wired desktop.

10. B, C and D. The four topologies, or service sets, defined by the 802.11-2012 standard are basic service set (BSS), extended service set (ESS), independent basic service set (IBSS), and mesh basic service set (MBSS). DSSS and FHSS are spread spectrum technologies.

11. A. A wireless metropolitan area network (WMAN) provides coverage to a metropolitan area such as a city and the surrounding suburbs.

12. D. The basic service set identifier (BSSID) is a 48-bit (6-octet) MAC address. MAC addresses exist at the MAC sublayer of the Data-Link layer of the OSI model.

13. B, C and E. The BSSID is the layer 2 identifier of either a BSS or an IBSS service set. The 48-bit (6-octet) MAC address of an access point's radio is the basic service set identifier (BSSID) within a BSS. An ESS topology utilizes multiple access points, thus the existence of multiple BSSIDs. In an IBSS network, the first station that powers up randomly generates a virtual BSSID in the MAC address format. FHSS and HR-DSSS are spread spectrum technologies.

14. D. The 802.11s-2011 amendment, which is now part of the 802.11-2012 standard, defined a new service set for an 802.11 mesh topology. When access points support mesh functions, they may be deployed where wired network access is not possible. The mesh functions are used to provide wireless distribution of network traffic, and the set of APs that provide mesh distribution form a mesh basic service set (MBSS).

15. B. In half-duplex communications, both devices are capable of transmitting and receiving; however, only one device can transmit at a time. Walkie-talkies, or two-way radios, are examples of half-duplex devices. IEEE 802.11 wireless networks use half-duplex communications.

16. A, B, C, D and E. The default standard mode for an access point is root mode. Other operational modes include bridge, workgroup bridge, mesh, scanner, and repeater modes.

17. A and C. An extended service set (ESS) is two or more basic service sets connected by a distribution system. An ESS is a collection of multiple access points and their associated client stations, all united by a single distribution system medium.

18. A. A wireless distribution system (WDS) can connect access points together using a wireless backhaul while allowing clients to also associate to the radios in the access points.

19. B and C. The distribution system consists of two main components. The distribution system medium (DSM) is a logical physical medium used to connect access points. Distribution system services (DSS) consist of services built inside an access point, usually in the form of software.

20. B. The 802.11 standard is considered a wireless local area network (WLAN) standard. 802.11 hardware can, however, be utilized in other wireless topologies.

Chapter 8: 802.11 Medium Access

1. B and D. DCF is an abbreviation for Distributed Coordination Function. CSMA/CA is an 802.11 media access control method that is part of DCF. CSMA/CD is used by 802.3, not 802.11. There is no such thing as Data Control Function.

2. E. 802.11 technology does not use collision detection. If an ACK frame is not received by the original transmitting radio, the unicast frame is not acknowledged and will have to be retransmitted. This process does not specifically determine whether a collision occurs. Failure to receive an ACK frame from the receiver means that either a unicast frame was not received by the destination station or the ACK frame was not received, but it cannot positively determine the cause. It may be due to collision or to other reasons such as high noise level. All of the other options are used to help prevent collisions.

3. D. ACK frames and CTS-to-self frames follow a SIFS. LIFS do not exist.

4. A, B and D. The NAV timer maintains a prediction of future traffic on the medium based on duration value information seen in a previous frame transmission. Virtual carrier sense uses the NAV to determine medium availability. Physical carrier sense checks the RF medium for carrier availability. Clear channel assessment is another name for physical carrier sense. Channel sense window does not exist.

5. C. The first step is to select a random backoff value. After the value is selected, it is multiplied by the slot time. The random backoff timer then begins counting down the number of slot times. When the number reaches 0, the station can begin transmitting.

6. B and D. PCF requires an access point. Ad hoc mode and an independent basic service set (IBSS) are the same and do not use an access point. A basic service set (BSS) is a WLAN topology, where 802.11 client stations communicate through an access point. Infrastructure mode is the default client station mode that allows clients to communicate via an access point. Basic service area (BSA) is the area of coverage of a basic service set.

7. B and D. The Duration/ID field is used to set the network allocation vector (NAV), which is a part of the virtual carrier sense process. The contention window and random backoff time are part of the backoff process that is performed after the carrier sense process.

8. D. The goal of airtime fairness is to allocate equal time, as opposed to equal opportunity. Access fairness and opportunistic media access do not exist. CSMA/CA is the normal media access control mode for Wi-Fi devices.

9. A, B, D and E. DCF defines four checks and balances of CSMA/CA and DCF to ensure that only one 802.11 radio is transmitting on the half-duplex medium. Virtual carrier sense (NAV), physical carrier sense (CCA), interframe spacing, and the random backoff timer all work together. CCMP is the encryption protocol that was introduced with 802.11i.

10. C. Currently, WMM is based on EDCA mechanisms defined by the 802.11e amendment, which is now part of the 802.11-2012 standard. The WMM certification provides for traffic prioritization via four access categories. EDCA is a subfunction of Hybrid Coordination Function (HCF). The other subfunction of HCF is HCCA.

11. E. HCF defines the ability for an 802.11 radio to send multiple frames when transmitting on the RF medium. When an HCF-compliant radio contends for the medium, it receives an allotted amount of time to send frames called a transmit opportunity (TXOP). During this TXOP, an 802.11 radio may send multiple frames in what is called a frame burst.

12. A, B, D and E. WMM Audio priority does not exist. The WMM certification provides for traffic prioritization via the four access categories of Voice, Video, Best Effort, and Background.

13. B, C and E. DCF and PCF were defined in the original 802.11 standard. The 802.11e quality of service amendment added a new coordination function to 802.11 medium contention, known as Hybrid Coordination Function (HCF). The 802.11e amendment and HCF have since been incorporated into the 802.11-2012 standard. HCF combines capabilities from both DCF and PCF and adds enhancements to them to create two channel access methods, HCF Controller Channel Access (HCCA) and Enhanced Distributed Channel Access (EDCA).

14. B. The EDCA medium access method provides for the prioritization of traffic via the use of 802.1D priority tags. 802.1D tags provide a mechanism for implementing quality of service (QoS) at the MAC level. Different classes of service are available, represented in a 3-bit user priority field in an IEEE 802.1Q header added to an Ethernet frame. 802.1D priority tags from the Ethernet side are used to direct traffic to different access-category queues.

15. A and E. The first purpose is to determine whether a frame transmission is inbound for a station to receive. If the medium is busy, the radio will attempt to synchronize with the transmission. The second purpose is to determine whether the medium is busy before transmitting. This is known as the clear channel assessment (CCA). The CCA involves listening for 802.11 RF transmissions at the Physical layer. The medium must be clear before a station can transmit.

16. A, B, C and D. An 802.11 radio uses a random backoff algorithm to contend for the medium during a window of time known as the contention window. The contention window is essentially a final countdown timer and is also known as the random backoff timer. The NAV timer and the clear channel assessment (CCA) are also used in the medium contention process to determine the availability of the medium.

17. C. When the listening radio hears a frame transmission from another station, it looks at the header of the frame and determines whether the Duration/ID field contains a Duration value or an ID value. If the field contains a Duration value, the listening station will set its NAV timer to this value.

18. B. Enhanced Distributed Channel Access provides differentiated access for stations by using four access categories The EDCA medium access method provides for the prioritization of traffic via the four access categories that are aligned to eight 802.1D priority tags.

19. A. ACKS are used for delivery verification of unicast 802.11 frames. Broadcast and multicast frames do not require an acknowledgment. Anycast frames do not exist.

20. E. A Block ACK improves channel efficiency by aggregating several acknowledgments into one single acknowledgment frame. There are two types of Block ACK mechanisms: immediate and delayed. The immediate Block ACK is designed for use with low-latency traffic, whereas the delayed Block ACK is more suitable for latency-tolerant traffic.

Chapter 9: 802.11 MAC Architecture

1. D. Both frames are used to join a BSS. Reassociation frames are used during the roaming process. The reassociation frame contains an additional field called Current AP Address. This address is the BSSID of the original AP that the client is leaving.

2. D. An IP packet consists of layer 3–7 information. The MAC Service Data Unit (MSDU) contains data from the LLC sublayer and/or any number of layers above the Data-Link layer. The MSDU is the payload found inside the body of 802.11 data frames.

3. B and D. RTS/CTS and CTS-to-Self provide 802.11g protection mechanisms, sometimes referred to as mixed-mode support. NAV back-off and RTS-to-Self do not exist. WEP encryption provides data security.

4. A, C and D. An ERP AP signals for the use of the protection mechanism in the ERP information element in the beacon frame. If a non-ERP STA associates to an ERP AP, the ERP AP will enable the NonERP_Present bit in its own beacons, enabling protection mechanisms in its BSS. In other words, an HR-DSSS (802.11b) client association will trigger protection. If an ERP AP hears a beacon with only an 802.11b or 802.11 supported rate set from another AP or an IBSS STA, it will enable the NonERP_Present bit in its own beacons, enabling protection mechanisms in its BSS.

5. A, B, C and D. The probe response contains the same information as the beacon frame, with the exception of the traffic indication map.

6. B and D. Beacons cannot be disabled. Clients use the time-stamp information from the beacon to synchronize with the other stations on the wireless network. Only APs send beacons in a BSS; client stations send beacons in an IBSS. Beacons can contain proprietary information.

7. B. If a station finds its AID in the TIM, there is unicast data on the AP that the station needs to stay awake for and request to have downloaded. This request is performed by a PS-Poll frame.

8. D. When the RTS frame is sent, the value of the Duration/ID field is equal to the time necessary for the CTS, DATA, and ACK frames to be transmitted.

9. B. When the client station transmits a frame with the Power Management field set to 1, it is enabling Power Save mode. The DTIM does not enable Power Save mode; it only notifies clients to stay awake in preparation for a multicast or broadcast.

10. A and B. The receiving station may have received the data, but the returning ACK frame may have become corrupted and the original unicast frame will have to be retransmitted. If the unicast frame becomes corrupted for any reason, the receiving station will not send an ACK.

11. B. The PS-Poll frame is used by the station to request cached data. The ATIM is used to notify stations in an IBSS of cached data. The Power Management bit is used by the station to notify the AP that the station is going into Power Save mode. The DTIM is used to indicate to client stations how often to wake up to receive buffered broadcast and multicast frames. The traffic indication map (TIM) is a field in the beacon frame used by the AP to indicate that there are buffered unicast frames for clients in Power Save mode.

12. A and E. All 802.11 APs are required to respond to directed probe request frames that contain the correct SSID value. The AP must also respond to null probe request frames that contain a blank SSID value. Some vendors offer the capability to respond to null probe requests with a null probe response.

13. A and D. There are two types of scanning: passive, which occurs when a station listens to the beacons to discover an AP, and active, which occurs when a station sends probe requests looking for APs. Stations send probe requests only if they are performing an active scan. After a station is associated, it is common for the station to continue to learn about nearby APs. All client stations maintain a "known AP" list that is constantly updated by active scanning.

14. B, D and E. Although there are similarities, the addressing used by 802.11 MAC frames is much more complex than Ethernet frames. 802.3 frames have only a source address (SA) and destination address (DA) in the layer 2 header. The four MAC addresses used by an 802.11 frame can be used as five different types of addresses: receiver address (RA), transmitter address (TA), basic service set identifier (BSSID), destination address (DA), and source address (SA).

15. B. When the client first attempts to connect to an AP, it will first send a probe request and listen for a probe response. After it receives a probe response, it will attempt to authenticate to the AP and then associate to the network.

16. B. The delivery traffic indication message (DTIM) is used to ensure that all stations using power management are awake when multicast or broadcast traffic is sent. The DTIM interval is important for any application that uses multicasting. For example, many VoWiFi vendors support push-to-talk capabilities that send VoIP traffic to a multicast address. A misconfigured DTIM interval would cause performance issues during a push-to-talk multicast.

17. A and C. An ERP (802.11g) AP is backward compatible with HR-DSSS and supports the data rates of 1, 2, 5.5, and 11 Mbps as well as the ERP-OFDM data rates of 6, 9, 12, 18, 24, 36, 48, and 54 Mbps. If a WLAN admin disabled the 1, 2, 5.5, and 11 Mbps data rates, backward compatibility will effectively be disabled and the HR-DSSS clients will not be able to connect. The 802.11-2012 standard defines the use of basic rates, which are required rates. If a client station does not support any of the basic rates used by an AP, the client station will be denied association to the BSS. If a WLAN admin configured the ERP-OFDM data rates of 6 and 9 Mbps as basic rates, the HR-DSSS clients would be denied association because they do not support those rates.

18. A and C. The amplitude of the received signals from the APs is usually the main variable when clients make a roaming decision. Client roaming mechanisms are often based on RSSI values, including received signal levels and signal-to-noise ratio (SNR). Distance and WMM access categories have nothing to do with the client's decision to roam to a new AP.

19. A, C, D and E. Applications now control the power-save management behavior by setting doze periods and sending trigger frames. Clients using time-sensitive applications will send triggers to the AP frequently, while clients using more latency-tolerant applications will have a longer doze period. The trigger and delivery method eliminates the need for PS-Poll frames. The client can request to download buffered traffic and does not have to wait for a beacon frame. All the downlink application traffic is sent in a faster frame burst during the AP's TXOP.

20. B. The IEEE 802.11-2007 standard defines an enhanced power-management method called automatic power save delivery (APSD). The two APSD methods that are defined are scheduled automatic power save delivery (S-APSD) and unscheduled automatic power save delivery (U-APSD). The Wi-Fi Alliance's WMM Power Save (WMM-PS) certification is based on U-APSD.

Chapter 10: WLAN Architecture

1. A. In recent years there has been a handheld client population explosion of mobile devices such as smartphones and tablets. Most users now expect Wi-Fi connectivity with numerous handheld mobile devices as well as their laptops. Almost all mobile devices use a single chip form factor that is embedded on the device's motherboard.

2. B. All bridge links can have only one root bridge. A PtP link will have only one root bridge, and a PtMP link will also have only one root bridge.

3. G. The 802.11 standard does not mandate what type of form factor must be used by an 802.11 radio. Although PCMCIA and Mini PCI client adapters are the most common, 802.11 radios exist in many other formats, such as CompactFlash cards, Secure Digital cards, USB dongles, ExpressCards, and other proprietary formats.

4. B. Controller-based access points normally forward user traffic to a centralized WLAN controller via an encapsulated IP tunnel. Autonomous and cooperative access points normally use local data forwarding. Controller-based APs are also capable of local data forwarding. Although the whole point of a cooperative and distributed WLAN model is to avoid centrally forwarding user traffic to the core, the access points may also have IP-tunneling capabilities.

5. A, B, D and E. WLAN controllers support the VRRP redundancy protocol. HSRP is a proprietary redundancy protocol. WLAN controllers have a captive portal option and support user management via role-based access control. WLAN controllers may also have an integrated IDS server.

6. A, D and E. An IP-encapsulated tunnel is needed for 802.11 frames to be able to traverse between a lightweight AP and a WLAN controller over a wired medium. Each 802.11 frame is encapsulated entirely within the body of an IP packet. Many WLAN vendors use Generic Routing Encapsulation (GRE), a commonly used network tunneling protocol. WLAN vendors that do not use GRE use other proprietary protocols for the IP tunneling. Although CAPWAP is used as a management protocol, it can also be used for IP encapsulation of traffic.

7. D. One major disadvantage of using the traditional autonomous access point is that there is no central point of management. Any autonomous WLAN architecture with 25 or more access points is going to require some sort of network management system (NMS). Although a WLAN controller can be used to manage the WLAN in a centralized WLAN architecture, if multiple controllers are deployed, an NMS may be needed to manage multiple controllers. Although the control plane and management plane have moved back to the APs in a distributed WLAN architecture, the management plane remains centralized. Configuration and monitoring of all access points in the distributed model is still handled by an NMS.

8. F. WLAN controllers support layer 3 roaming capabilities, bandwidth policies, and stateful packet inspection. Dynamic RF and AP management are also supported on a controller.

9. D. Telecommunication networks are often defined as three logical planes of operation. The control plane consists of control or signaling information and is often defined as network intelligence or protocols.

10. B. A wireless workgroup bridge (WGB) is a wireless device that provides wireless connectivity for wired infrastructure devices that do not have radio cards.

11. A and E. In the centralized WLAN architecture, autonomous APs have been replaced with controller-based access points. All the intelligence resides on the centralized device known as a WLAN controller.

12. B and D. The control plane mechanisms are enabled in the system with inter-AP communication via cooperative protocols in a distributed WLAN architecture. In a distributed architecture, each individual access point is responsible for local forwarding of user traffic; therefore, the data plane resides in the APs. The management plane resides in an NMS that is used to manage and monitor the distributed WLAN.

13. B. In a point-to-point bridge link, one bridge must be the root bridge and the other must be a nonroot bridge. Although they are on separate subnets, this factor does not come into account during the association process. Typically, the IP address of the bridges is purely for management purposes and has no impact on the traffic being passed.

14. D. Because of performance issues, repeater mode is not a recommended mode for wireless bridging. If at all possible, a better bridge deployment practice is to use two separate bridge links as opposed to repeating the link of a root bridge to a nonroot bridge.

15. A and C. All three WLAN infrastructure designs support the use of VLANs and 802.1Q tagging. However, the centralized WLAN architecture usually encapsulates user VLANs between the controller-based AP and the WLAN controllers; therefore, only a single VLAN is normally required at the edge. An 802.1Q trunk is, however, usually required between the WLAN controller and a core switch. Both the autonomous and distributed WLAN architectures do not use a controller. Noncontroller architectures require support for 802.1Q tagging if multiple VLANs are to be supported at the edge of the network. The access point is connected to an 802.1Q trunk port on an edge switch that supports VLAN tagging.

16. E. The majority of WLAN controller vendors implement what is known as a split MAC architecture. With this type of WLAN architecture, some of the MAC services are handled by the WLAN controller and some are handled by the controller-based access point.

17. B. In a centralized WLAN architecture, traffic is tunneled from controller-based access points deployed at the access layer to a WLAN controller that is typically deployed at the core of the network. Standard network design suggests redundancy at the core, and redundant WLAN controllers should be deployed so there is no single point of network failure. If all user traffic is being tunneled to a WLAN controller and it fails without a redundant solution, effectively the WLAN is down.

18. A, B and C. Most WLAN APs have the capability of supporting multiple virtual BSSIDs. Within each AP's coverage area, multiple virtual WLANs can exist. Each virtual WLAN has a logical name (SSID) and a unique virtual layer 2 identifier (BSSID), and each WLAN is mapped to a unique virtual local area network (VLAN) that is mapped to a subnet (layer 3). Multiple layer 2 and 3 domains can exist within one layer 1 domain.

19. A, C, D and E. WLAN controllers introduced the concept of virtual WLANs, which are often called WLAN profiles. Different groups of 802.11 clients exist in a virtual WLAN. The WLAN profile is a set of configuration parameters that are configured on the WLAN controller. The profile parameters can include the WLAN logical name (SSID), WLAN security settings, VLAN assignment, and QoS parameters. Do not confuse the WLAN profile with an AP group profile. Multiple WLAN profiles can

be supported by a single AP; however, an AP can alone belong to one AP group. An AP group profile defines the configuration settings for a single AP or group of access points. Settings such as channel, transmit power, and supported data rates are examples of settings configured in an AP group profile.

20. A, C and E. VoWiFi phones are 802.11 client stations that communicate through most WLAN architecture. The PBX is needed to make connections among the internal telephones of a private company and also connect them to the public switched telephone network (PSTN) via trunk lines. WMM quality-of-service capabilities must be supported by both the VoWiFi phone and WLAN infrastructure. Currently most VoWiFi solutions use the Session Initiation Protocol (SIP) as the signaling protocol for voice communications over an IP network, but others protocols can be used instead.

Chapter 11: WLAN Deployment and Vertical Markets

1. A, B, C and D. The goal of fixed mobile convergence is to enable the user to have a single device with a single phone number and to enable the user to roam between different networks, taking advantage of the least expensive and best performing network that is available.

2. C and D. Municipal and transportation networks are both specific types of public hotspots. Law enforcement and first-responder networks are hotspot-type networks, but they are not intended for public use.

3. C. Because of the potential for interference and the importance of preventing it, hospitals often have a person responsible for keeping track of frequencies used within the organization. Some municipalities are starting to do this as well—not just for law enforcement, but for all of their wireless needs, because they often use wireless technologies for SCADA networks, traffic cameras, traffic lights, two-way radios, point-to-point bridging, hotspots, and more.

4. D. Since cruise ships are often not near land where cellular or WiMAX uplink is available, it is necessary to use a satellite uplink to connect the ship to the Internet.

5. B and D. Fixed mobile convergence allows roaming between Wi-Fi networks and cellular phone networks, choosing the available network that is least expensive.

6. D. When designing a warehouse network, the networking devices are often barcode scanners that do not capture much data, so high capacity and throughput are not typically needed. Because the data-transfer requirements are so low, these networks are typically designed to provide coverage for large areas. Security is always a concern; however, it is not usually a design criterion.

7. A, C and D. Corporations typically install a WLAN to provide easy mobility and/or access to areas that are difficult or extremely expensive to connect via wired networks. Although providing connectivity to the Internet is a service that the corporate wireless network offers, it is not the driving reason for installing the wireless network.

8. A, C and D. The phone company, cable providers, and WISPs are all examples of companies that provide last-mile services to users and businesses.

9. B. The main purpose of SOHO networks is to provide a gateway to the Internet.

10. A, B and D. Mobile office networking solutions are temporary solutions that include all of the options listed except for the remote sales office, which would more likely be classified as a SOHO installation.

11. A and D. Warehousing and manufacturing environments typically have a need for mobility, but their data transfers are typically very small. Therefore, their networks are often designed for high coverage rather than high capacity.

12. D. Hotspot providers are not likely to provide data encryption. It is more difficult to deploy, and there is no benefit or business reason for them to provide it.

13. A, B and C. Manufacturing plants are typically fixed environments and are better served by installing permanent access points.

14. C and D. Point-to-multipoint, hub and spoke, and star all describe the same communication technology, which connects multiple devices by using a central device. Point-to-point communications connects two devices. Mesh networks do not have a defined central device.

15. C. Most of the 802.11 implementations used FHSS, with industrial (warehousing and manufacturing) companies being some of the biggest implementers. Their requirement of mobility with low data-transfer speeds was ideal for using the technology.

16. C. To make wireless access easy for the subscriber, hotspot vendors typically deploy authentication methods that are easy to use but that do not provide data encryption. Therefore, to ensure security back to your corporate network, the use of an IPsec VPN is necessary.

17. A, C and D. VoWiFi is a common use of 802.11 technology in a medical environment, providing immediate access to personnel no matter where they are in the hospital. Real-time location service (RTLS) solutions using 802.11 RFID tags for inventory control are also commonplace. WLAN medical carts are used to monitor patient information and vital signs.

18. A and C. The installation of multiple point-to-point bridges is either to provide higher throughput or to prevent a single point of failure. Care must be taken in arranging channel and antenna installations to prevent self-inflicted interference.

19. A, B and C. Healthcare providers often have many other devices that use RF communications, and therefore, RF interference is a concern. Fast access along with secure and accurate access is critical in healthcare environments. Faster access can be performed without faster speed. The mobility of the technology will satisfy the faster access that is typically needed.

20. D. Public hotspots are most concerned about ensuring that only valid users are allowed access to the hotspot. This is performed using authentication; however, this only secures the network from nonauthorized users.

Chapter 12: WLAN Troubleshooting and Design

1. A, C and D. Unidirectional MIMO patch antennas can be mounted in the ceiling to provide sectorized coverage in a high-density WLAN. Load balancing clients between multiple APs will help with capacity. Lowering the AP transmit power effectively reduces the cell size and minimizes co-channel interference. Band steering can be useful if used to balance the clients between both the 2.4 and 5 GHz radios. Steering all the clients only to 5 GHz is not necessarily ideal in a high-density environment. Layer 3 roaming is not part of high client capacity design.

2. E. In an MCA architecture, if all the access points are mistakenly configured on the same channel, unnecessary medium contention overhead is the result. If an AP is transmitting, all nearby access points and clients on the same channel will defer transmissions. The result is that throughput is adversely affected. Nearby APs and clients have to wait much longer to transmit because they have to take their turn. The unnecessary medium contention overhead that occurs because all the APs are on the same channel is called co-channel interference (CCI). In reality, the 802.11 radios are operating exactly as defined by the CSMA/CA mechanisms, and this behavior should really be called co-channel cooperation.

3. A, D and E. The original transmission amplitude will have an impact on the range of an RF cell. Antennas amplify signal strength and can increase range. Walls and other obstacles will attenuate an RF signal and affect range. CSMA/CA and encryption do not affect range but do affect throughput.

4. B, C and D. The hidden node problem arises when client stations cannot hear the RF transmissions of another client station. Increasing the transmission power of client stations will increase the transmission range of each station, resulting in increased likelihood of all the stations hearing each other. Increasing client power is not a recommended fix because best practice dictates that client stations use the same transmit power used by all other radios in the BSS, including the AP. Moving the hidden node station within transmission range of the other stations also results in stations hearing each other. Removing an obstacle that prevents stations from hearing each other also fixes the problem. The best fix to the hidden node problem is to add another access point in the area that the hidden node resides.

5. B, D and E. If any portion of a unicast frame is corrupted, the cyclic redundancy check (CRC) will fail and the receiving 802.11 radio will not return an ACK frame to the transmitting 802.11 radio. If an ACK frame is not received by the original transmitting radio, the unicast frame is not acknowledged and will have to be retransmitted. RF interference, low SNR, hidden nodes, mismatched power settings, near/far problems, and adjacent channel interference may all cause layer 2 retransmissions. Co-channel interference does not cause retries but does add unnecessary medium contention overhead.

6. A, B and D. The hidden node problem arises when client stations cannot hear the RF transmissions of another client station. Distributed antenna systems with multiple antenna elements are notorious for causing the hidden node problem. When coverage cells are too large as a result of the access point's radio transmitting at too much power, client stations at opposite ends of an RF coverage cell often cannot hear each other. Obstructions such as a newly constructed wall can also result in stations not hearing each other.

7. B, D and E. Excessive layer 2 retransmissions adversely affect the WLAN in two ways. First, layer 2 retransmissions increase MAC overhead and therefore decrease throughput. Second, if application data has to be retransmitted at layer 2, the timely delivery of application traffic becomes delayed or inconsistent. Applications such as VoIP depend on the timely and consistent delivery of the IP packet. Excessive layer 2 retransmissions usually result in increased latency and jitter problems for time-sensitive applications such as voice and video.

8. E. An often overlooked cause of layer 2 retransmissions is mismatched transmit power settings between an access point and a client radio. Communications can break down if a client station's transmit power level is less than the transmit power level of the access point. As a client moves to the outer edges of the coverage cell, the client can "hear" the AP; however, the AP cannot "hear" the client. If the client station's frames are corrupted near the AP but not near the client, the most likely cause is mismatched power settings.

9. D. If an end user complains of a degradation of throughput, one possible cause is a hidden node. A protocol analyzer is a useful tool in determining hidden node issues. If the protocol analyzer indicates a higher retransmission rate for the MAC address of one station when compared to the other client stations, chances are a hidden node has been found. Some protocol analyzers even have hidden node alarms based on retransmission thresholds.

10. B. Overlapping coverage cells with overlapping frequencies cause adjacent channel interference, which causes a severe degradation in latency, jitter, and throughput. If overlapping coverage cells also have frequency overlap, frames will become corrupt, retransmissions will increase, and performance will suffer significantly.

11. B. As client station radios move away from an access point, they will shift down to lower bandwidth capabilities by using a process known as dynamic rate switching (DRS). The objective of DRS is upshifting and downshifting for rate optimization and

improved performance. Although dynamic rate switching is the proper name for this process, all these terms refer to the method of speed fallback that a wireless LAN client uses as distance increases from the access point.

12. E. Highly directional antennas are susceptible to what is known as antenna wind loading, which is antenna movement or shifting caused by wind. Grid antennas may be needed to alleviate the problem. Rain and fog can attenuate an RF signal; therefore, a system operating margin (also known as fade margin) of 20 dB is necessary. A change in air temperature is also known as air stratification, which causes refraction. K-factor calculations may also be necessary to compensate for refraction.

13. E. Higher frequency signals have a smaller wavelength property and will attenuate faster than a lower frequency signal with a larger wavelength. Higher frequency signals therefore will have shorter range. In any RF environment, free space path loss (FSPL) attenuates the signal as a function of distance. Loss in signal strength affects range. Brick walls exist in an indoor physical environment, while trees exist in an outdoor physical environment. Both will attenuate an RF signal, thereby affecting range.

14. D. A mobile client receives an IP address also known as a home address on the original subnet. The mobile client must register its home address with a device called a home agent (HA). The original access point on the client's home network serves as the home agent. The home agent is a single point of contact for a client when it roams across layer 3 boundaries. Any traffic that is sent to the client's home address is intercepted by the home agent access point and sent through a Mobile IP tunnel to the foreign agent AP on the new subnet. The client is therefore able to retain its original IP address when roaming across layer 3 boundaries.

15. A and B. Although overlap cell coverage is a fallacy, cell overlap is often used to refer to the duplicate cell coverage heard from a client perspective. Roaming problems will occur if there is not enough overlap in cell coverage. Too little overlap will effectively create a roaming dead zone, and connectivity may even temporarily be lost. If two RF cells have too much overlap, a station may stay associated with its original AP and not connect to a second access point even though the station is directly underneath the second access point.

16. A, B and C. A mistake often made when deploying access points is to have the APs transmitting at full power. Effectively, this extends the range of the access point but causes many problems that have been discussed throughout this chapter. Oversized coverage usually will not meet your capacity needs. Oversized coverage cells can cause hidden node problems. Access points at full power may not be able to hear the transmissions of client stations with lower transmit power. Access points at full power will most likely also increase the odds of co-channel interference due to bleed-over transmissions. If the access point's coverage and range is a concern, the best method of extending range is to increase the AP's antenna gain instead of increasing transmit power.

17. A and C. Medium contention, also known as CSMA/CA, requires that all radios access the medium in a pseudorandom fashion. Radios transmitting at slower data

rates will occupy the medium much longer, while faster radios have to wait. Data rates of 1 and 2 Mbps can create very large coverage cells, which may prevent a hidden node station at one edge of the cell from being heard by other client stations at the opposite side of the coverage cell.

18. A. Multipath can cause intersymbol interference (ISI), which causes data corruption. Because of the difference in time between the primary signal and the reflected signals, known as the delay spread, the receiver can have problems demodulating the RF signal's information. The delay spread time differential results in corrupted data and therefore layer 2 retransmissions.

19. A. HR-DSSS (802.11b) and ERP (802.11g) channels require 25 MHz of separation between the center frequencies to be considered nonoverlapping. The three channels of 1, 6, and 11 meet these requirements in the United States. In other countries, three-channel plans such as 2, 7, and 12; 3, 8, and 13; and 4, 9, and 14 would work as well. Traditionally, 1, 6, and 11 are chosen almost universally.

20. A, D and E. Several factors should be considered when planning a 5 GHz channel reuse pattern. One factor is what channels are available legally in your country or region. Another factor to consider is what channels the client population supports. Wi-Fi radios must be certified to transmit in the dynamic frequency selection (DFS) channels to avoid interference with radar. A high likelihood exists that the client population may not be certified for dynamic frequency selection (DFS) channels in the UNII-2 and UNII-2e bands. Additionally, many 5 GHz access points might also not be certified to transmit in the DFS channels.

Chapter 13: 802.11 Network Security Architecture

1. B. As required by an 802.1X security solution, the supplicant is a WLAN client requesting authentication and access to network resources. Each supplicant has unique authentication credentials that are verified by the authentication server.

2. B and D. The 802.11-2012 standard defines CCMP/AES encryption as the default encryption method, and TKIP/RC4 is the optional encryption method. This was originally defined by the 802.11i amendment, which is now part of the 802.11-2012 standard. The Wi-Fi Alliance created the WPA2 security certification, which mirrors the robust security defined by the IEEE. WPA2 supports both CCMP/AES and TKIP/RC4 dynamic encryption-key management.

3. E. 128-bit WEP encryption uses a secret 104-bit static key that is provided by the user (26 hex characters) and combined with a 24-bit initialization vector (IV) for an effective key strength of 128 bits.

4. A, C and E. The supplicant, authenticator, and authentication server work together to provide the framework for an 802.1X/EAP solution. The supplicant requests access to network resources. The authentication server authenticates the identity of the supplicant, and the authenticator allows or denies access to network resources via virtual ports.

5. C. The original 802.11 standard ratified in 1997 defined the use of a 64-bit or 128-bit static encryption solution called Wired Equivalent Privacy (WEP). Dynamic WEP was never defined under any wireless security standard. The use of 802.1X/EAP, TKIP/RC4, and CCMP/AES are all defined under the current 802.11-2012 standard.

6. A, D and E. Access points may be mounted in lockable enclosure units to provide theft protection. All access points should be configured from the wired side and never wirelessly. Encrypted management interfaces such as HTTPS and SSH should be used instead of HTTP or Telnet. An 802.1X/EAP solution guarantees that only authorized users will receive an IP address. Attackers can get an IP address prior to setting up an IPsec VPN tunnel and potentially attack the access points.

7. A and C. Virtual LANs are used to segment wireless users at layer 3. The most common wireless segmentation strategy often used in 802.11 enterprise WLANs is segmentation using VLANS combined with role-based access control (RBAC) mechanisms. CCMP/AES, TKIP/RC4, and WEP are encryption solutions.

8. A and C. The Wi-Fi Protected Access (WPA) certification was a snapshot of the not-yet-released 802.11i amendment, supporting only the TKIP/RC4 dynamic encryption-key generation. 802.1X/EAP authentication was required in the enterprise, and passphrase authentication was required in a SOHO or home environment. LEAP is Cisco proprietary and is not specifically defined by WPA. Neither dynamic WEP nor CCMP/AES was defined for encryption. CCMP/AES dynamic encryption is mandatory under the WPA2 certification.

9. B, D and E. Role-based access control (RBAC) is an approach to restricting system access to authorized users. The three main components of an RBAC approach are users, roles, and permissions.

10. A, D and E. The purpose of 802.1X/EAP is authentication of user credentials and authorization to network resources. Although the 802.1X/EAP framework does not require encryption, it highly suggests the use of encryption. A by-product of 802.1X/EAP is the generation and distribution of dynamic encryption keys.

11. A, B, D and E. All forms of WEP encryption use the Rivest Cipher 4 (RC4) algorithm. TKIP is WEP that has been enhanced and also uses the RC4 cipher. PPTP uses 128-bit Microsoft Point-to-Point Encryption (MPPE), which uses the RC4 algorithm. CCMP uses the AES cipher.

12. B and D. Shared Key authentication is a legacy authentication method that does not provide seeding material to generate dynamic encryption keys. Static WEP uses static keys. A robust security network association requires a four-frame EAP exchange known as the 4-Way Handshake that is used to generate dynamic TKIP or CCMP keys. The handshake may occur either after an 802.1X/EAP exchange or as a result of PSK authentication.

13. A and D. An 802.1X/EAP solution requires that both the supplicant and the authentication server support the same type of EAP. The authenticator must be configured for 802.1X/EAP authentication but does not care which EAP type passes through. The authenticator and the supplicant must support the same type of encryption.

14. C. WLAN controllers use lightweight access points, which are dumb terminals with radio cards and antennas. The WLAN controller is the authenticator. When an 802.1X/EAP solution is deployed in a wireless controller environment, the virtual controlled and uncontrolled ports exist on the WLAN controller.

15. A, C and D. TKIP starts with a 128-bit temporal key that is combined with a 48-bit initialization vector (IV) and source and destination MAC addresses in a process known as per-packet key mixing. TKIP uses an additional data integrity check known as the message integrity check (MIC).

16. A. The root bridge would be the authenticator, and the nonroot bridge would be the supplicant if 802.1X/EAP security is used in a WLAN bridged network.

17. D. The AES algorithm encrypts data in fixed data blocks with choices in encryption-key strength of 128, 192, or 256 bits. CCMP/AES uses a 128-bit encryption-key size and encrypts in 128-bit fixed-length blocks.

18. A and D. The WPA2 certification requires the use of an 802.1X/EAP authentication method in the enterprise and the use of a preshared key or a passphrase in a SOHO environment. The WPA2 certification also requires the use of stronger dynamic encryption-key generation methods. CCMP/AES encryption is the mandatory encryption method, and TKIP/RC4 is the optional encryption method.

19. E. The 802.11-2012 standard defines what is known as a robust security network (RSN) and robust security network associations (RSNAs). CCMP/AES encryption is the mandated encryption method, and TKIP/RC4 is an optional encryption method.

20. C. The supplicant, authenticator, and authentication server work together to provide the framework for 802.1X port-based access control, and an authentication protocol is needed to assist in the authentication process. The Extensible Authentication Protocol (EAP) is used to provide user authentication.

Chapter 14: Wireless Attacks, Intrusion Monitoring, and Policy

1. B and C. Denial-of-service (DoS) attacks can occur at either layer 1 or layer 2 of the OSI model. Layer 1 attacks are known as RF jamming attacks. A wide variety of layer 2 DoS attacks exist that are a result of tampering with 802.11 frames, including the spoofing of deauthentication frames.

2. C and D. Malicious eavesdropping is achieved with the unauthorized use of protocol analyzers to capture wireless communications. Any unencrypted 802.11 frame transmission can be reassembled at the upper layers of the OSI model.

3. D. A protocol analyzer is a passive device that captures 802.11 traffic and can be used for malicious eavesdropping. A WIDS cannot detect a passive device. Strong encryption is the solution to prevent a malicious eavesdropping attack.

4. C and D. The only way to prevent a wireless hijacking, man-in-the-middle, and/or Wi-Fi phishing attack is to use a mutual authentication solution. 802.1X/EAP authentication solutions require that mutual authentication credentials be exchanged before a user can be authorized.

5. A and C. The radios inside the WIPS sensors monitor the 2.4 GHz ISM band and the 5 GHz U-NII bands. Older legacy wireless networking equipment exists that transmits in the 900 MHz ISM band, and these devices will not be detected. The radios inside the WIPS sensors also use only DSSS and OFDM technologies. Wireless networking equipment exists that uses frequency hopping spread spectrum (FHSS) transmissions in the 2.4 GHz ISM band and will go undetected. The only tool that can detect either a 900 MHz or frequency hopping rogue access point is a spectrum analyzer.

6. A and B. The general wireless security policy establishes why a wireless security policy is needed for an organization. Even if a company has no plans for deploying a wireless network, there should be at a minimum a policy detailing how to deal with rogue wireless devices. The functional security policy establishes how to secure the wireless network in terms of what solutions and actions are needed.

7. A and E. After obtaining the passphrase, an attacker can also associate to the WPA/WPA2 access point and thereby access network resources. The encryption technology is not cracked, but the key can be re-created. If a hacker has the passphrase and captures the 4-Way Handshake, they can re-create the dynamic encryption keys and therefore decrypt traffic. WPA/WPA2-Personal is not considered a strong security solution for the enterprise because if the passphrase is compromised, the attacker can access network resources and decrypt traffic.

8. A, C, D and E. Numerous types of layer 2 DoS attacks exist, including association floods, deauthentication spoofing, disassociation spoofing, authentication floods, PS-Poll floods, and virtual carrier attacks. RF jamming is a layer 1 DoS attack.

9. A and C. Microwave ovens operate in the 2.4 GHz ISM band and are often a source of unintentional interference. 2.4 GHz cordless phones can also cause unintentional jamming. A signal generator is typically going to be used as a jamming device, which would be considered intentional jamming. 900 MHz cordless phones will not interfere with 802.11 equipment that operates in either the 2.4 GHz ISM band or the 5 GHz U-NII bands. There is no such thing as a deauthentication transmitter.

10. A and B. The radios inside the WIPS/WIDS sensors currently use only DSSS and OFDM technologies. Wireless networking equipment exists that uses frequency hopping spread spectrum (FHSS) transmissions in the 2.4 GHz ISM and will go undetected by layer 2 WIPS/WIDS sensors. The only tool that can detect either a 900 MHz

or a frequency hopping rogue AP is a spectrum analyzer. Some WIPS/WIDS vendors offer layer 1 distributed spectrum analysis system (DSAS) solutions.

11. A and B. Client isolation is a feature that can be enabled on WLAN access points or WLAN controllers to block wireless clients from communicating with other wireless clients on the same wireless segment. The use of a personal firewall can also be used to mitigate peer-to peer attacks.

12. C. A wireless intrusion prevention system (WIPS) is capable of mitigating attacks from rogue APs. A WIPS sensor can use layer 2 DoS attacks as a countermeasure against a rogue device. SNMP may be used to shut down ports that a rogue AP has been connected to. WIPS vendors also use unpublished methods for mitigating rogue attacks.

13. A, B, E and F. Most WIPS solutions label 802.11 radios into four or more classifications. An infrastructure device refers to any client station or AP that is an authorized member of the company's wireless network. An unknown device is any new 802.11 radio that has been detected but not classified as a rogue. A known device refers to any client station or AP that is detected by the WIPS and has been identified as an interfering device but is not considered a threat. A rogue device refers to any client station or AP that is considered an interfering device and a potential threat.

14. A and E. Every company should have a policy forbidding installation of wireless devices by employees. Every company should also have a policy on how to respond to all wireless attacks, including the discovery of a rogue AP. If a WIPS discovers a rogue AP, temporarily implementing layer 2 rogue containment abilities is advisable until the rogue device can be physically located. After the device is found, immediately unplug it from the data port but not from the electrical outlet. It would be advisable to leave the rogue AP on so that the administrator can do some forensics and look at the association tables and log files to possibly determine who installed it.

15. A, C, D, F and G. Currently, there is no such thing as a Happy AP attack or an 802.11 sky monkey attack. Wireless users are especially vulnerable to attacks at public-use hotspots because there is no security. Because no encryption is used, the wireless users are vulnerable to malicious eavesdropping. Because no mutual authentication solution is in place, they are vulnerable to hijacking, man-in-the-middle, and phishing attacks. The hotspot AP might also be allowing peer-to-peer communications, making the users vulnerable to peer-to-peer attacks. Every company should have a remote access wireless security policy to protect their end users when they leave company grounds.

16. A and C. Public-access hotspots have absolutely no security in place, and it is imperative that a remote access WLAN policy be strictly enforced. This policy should include the required use of an IPsec or SSL VPN solution to provide device authentication, user authentication, and strong encryption of all wireless data traffic. Hotspots are prime targets for malicious eavesdropping attacks. Personal firewalls should also be installed on all remote computers to prevent peer-to-peer attacks.

17. B. MAC filters are configured to apply restrictions that will allow only traffic from specific client stations to pass through based on their unique MAC addresses.

MAC addresses can be spoofed, or impersonated, and any amateur hacker can easily bypass any MAC filter by spoofing an allowed client station's address.

18. A. The integrated WIDS is by far the most widely deployed. Overlay WIDS are usually cost prohibitive for most WLAN customers. The more robust overlay WIDS solutions are usually deployed in defense, finance, and retail vertical markets where the budget for an overlay solution may be available.

19. A, D and E. Wired Equivalent Privacy (WEP) encryption has been cracked, and currently available tools may be able to derive the secret key within a matter of minutes. The size of the key makes no difference, and both 64-bit WEP and 128-bit WEP can be cracked. TKIP/RC4 and CCMP/AES encryption have not been cracked.

20. D. An attack that often generates a lot of press is wireless hijacking, also known as the evil twin attack. The attacker hijacks wireless clients at layer 2 and layer 3 by using an evil twin access point and a DHCP server. The hacker may take the attack several steps further and initiate a man-in-the-middle attack and/or a Wi-Fi phishing attack.

Chapter 15: Radio Frequency Site Survey Fundamentals

1. C and D. It is a highly recommended practice to conduct the site survey by using equipment from the same vendor who will supply the equipment that will later be deployed on site. Mixing vendors during the survey is not recommended. Mixing a standalone AP solution with a controller-based AP solution is also not recommended in most cases. Security is not implemented during the survey.

2. B. Although all the options are issues that may need addressing when deploying a WLAN in a hospitality environment, aesthetics is usually a top priority. The majority of customer service businesses prefer that all wireless hardware remain completely out of sight. Note that most enclosure units are lockable and help prevent theft of expensive Wi-Fi hardware. However, theft prevention is not unique to the hospitality business.

3. A, B and C. Although security in itself is not part of the WLAN site survey, network management should be interviewed about security expectations. The surveying company will make comprehensive wireless security recommendations. An addendum to the security recommendations might be corporate wireless policy recommendations. Authentication and encryption solutions are not usually implemented during the physical survey.

4. C. Segmentation, authentication, authorization, and encryption should all be considered during the site survey interview. In Chapter 13, "802.11 Network Security Architecture," you learned about the necessary components of wireless security.

Segmenting three types of users into separate VLANs with separate security solutions is the best recommendation. The data users using 802.1X/EAP and CCMP/AES will have the strongest solution available. WPA-2 provides the voice users with CCMP/AES encryption as well but avoids using an 802.1X/EAP solution that will cause latency problems. The guest user VLAN requires a minimum of a captive web portal and a strong guest firewall policy for security.

5. A and B. Training, security, and choice of vendor are extra recommendations that may also accompany the site survey report. The site survey report should already be addressing coverage, capacity, and roaming requirements.

6. A and C. Blueprints will be needed for the site survey interview to discuss coverage and capacity needs. A network topology map will be useful to assist in the design of integrating the wireless network into the current wired infrastructure.

7. B and D. Latency is an important consideration whenever any time-sensitive application such as voice or video is to be deployed. A layer 3 roaming solution will be needed if layer 3 boundaries are crossed during roaming.

8. A, D and E. The final site survey report known as the deliverable will contain spectrum analysis information identifying potential sources of interference. Coverage analysis will also define RF cell boundaries. The final report also contains recommended access point placement, configuration settings, and antenna orientation. Application throughput testing is often an optional analysis report included in the final survey report. Firewall settings and router access control lists are not included in a site survey report.

9. A, B and E. Roaming problems may be interference related or caused by a lack of adequate coverage and/or cell overlap. In Chapter 12, "WLAN Troubleshooting," you learned that duplicate cell coverage is needed for roaming. Roaming problems will occur if there is not enough duplicate cell coverage. Too little duplicate coverage will effectively create a roaming dead zone, and connectivity may even temporarily be lost. On the flip side, too much duplicate coverage will also cause roaming problems. For example, a client station may stay associated with its original AP and not connect to a second access point even though the station is directly underneath the second access point. This can also create a situation in which the client device is constantly switching back and forth between the two or more APs on different channels. If a client station can also hear dozens of APs on the same channel with very strong signals, a degradation in performance will occur due to medium contention overhead. 2.4 GHz portable phones may be a source of interference. Cell phones operate in a frequency space that will not interfere with the existing WLAN.

10. D. Although option C is a possible solution, the best recommendation is to deploy hardware that operates at 5 GHz, and interference from the neighboring businesses' 2.4 GHz network will never be an issue.

11. A. The cheapest and most efficient solution will be to replace the older edge switches with newer switches that have inline power that can provide PoE to the access points.

A core switch will not be used to provide PoE because of cabling distance limitations. Deploying single-port injectors is not practical, and hiring an electrician will be extremely expensive.

12. A, B and D. Co-channel interference is a common cause of poor performance. Inadequate capacity planning can result in too many users per access point, leading to throughput problems. Multipath interference can also be destructive in an 802.11a/b/g environment where MIMO radios have yet to be deployed.

13. A, B, C and D. User density, data applications, and peak usage levels are all considerations when capacity planning for an 802.11a/b/g/n network. When designing a 5 GHZ WLAN, a proper channel plan must be designed. Legacy clients may not support DFS channels.

14. E. Multiple questions are related to infrastructure integration. How will the access points be powered? How will the WLAN and/or users of the WLAN be segmented from the wired network? How will the WLAN remote access points be managed? Considerations such as role-based access control (RBAC), bandwidth throttling, and load balancing should also be discussed.

15. A, B and C. Network management will be consulted during most of the site survey and deployment process for proper integration of the WLAN. The biomedical department will be consulted about possible RF interference issues. Hospital security will be contacted in order to obtain proper security passes and an possible escort.

16. B, C and D. Coverage, not capacity, is the main objective when designing a wireless network in a warehouse. Seamless roaming is also mandatory because handheld devices are typically deployed. Security is a major requirement for all WLAN enterprise installations.

17. A, C and D. Outdoor equipment must ultimately be protected from the weather elements by using either hardened APs or enclosure units rated by the National Electrical Manufacturers Association (NEMA). NEMA weatherproof enclosures are available with a wide range of options, including heating, cooling, and PoE interfaces. Parabolic dishes and patch antennas are usually used with APs for outdoor bridge links.

18. C. Probabilistic traffic formulas use a telecommunications unit of measurement known as an Erlang. An Erlang is equal to 1 hour of telephone traffic in 1 hour of time.

19. A, B and D. Based on information collected during the site survey, a final design diagram will be presented to the customer. Along with the implementation diagrams will be a detailed bill of materials (BOM) that itemizes every hardware and software component necessary for the final installation of the wireless network. A detailed deployment schedule should be drafted that outlines all timelines, equipment costs, and labor costs.

20. C and E. Many hotspots are small, and care should be taken to limit the RF coverage area using a single access point at a lower power setting. Security solutions at hotspots are usually limited to a captive portal solution for user authentication against a customer database.

Chapter 16: Site Survey Systems and Devices

1. **A, B, C and E.** First a forecast model is created with the predictive software and then the site survey engineer conducts a manual site survey to validate the projections. Modeling forecasts that can be validated include channel reuse patterns, coverage cell boundaries, access point placement, access point power settings, number of access points, and data rates. Testing of throughput and roaming will then validate that the design will support the requirements of the environment.

2. **A and C.** Lightning can cause damage to Wi-Fi bridging equipment and the network infrastructure equipment that resides behind the 802.11 bridges. Strong winds can cause instability between long-distance bridge links and a loss of RF line of sight. Potential weather conditions should be noted during the outdoor site survey. Proper protection against lightning, such as lightning arrestors and/or copper-fiber transceivers, must be recommended for deployment. In high-wind areas, consider the use of grid antennas. Dew point, cloud cover, and thunder have no effect on an 802.11 outdoor deployment and therefore need not be considered during a site survey.

3. **C and E.** Manual site surveys are usually conducted for coverage analysis using a signal strength measurement tool. Predictive analysis tools can create a model of RF coverage cells.

4. **A, B and E.** Any type of RF interference could cause a denial of service to the WLAN. A spectrum analysis survey should be performed to determine if any of the hospital's medical equipment will cause interference in the 2.4 GHz ISM band or the 5 GHz U-NII bands. Dead zones or loss of coverage can also disrupt WLAN communications. Many hospitals use metal mesh safety glass in many areas. The metal mesh will cause scattering and potentially create lost coverage on the opposite side of the glass. Elevator shafts are made of metal and often are dead zones if not properly covered with an RF signal.

5. **E.** During an active manual survey, the radio card is associated to the access point and has upper layer connectivity, allowing for low-level frame transmissions while RF measurements are also taken. The main purpose of the active site survey is to look at the percentage of layer 2 retransmissions.

6. **A, C and D.** A measuring wheel can be used to measure the distance from the wiring closet to the proposed access point location. A ladder or forklift might be needed when temporarily mounting an access point. Battery packs are used to power the access point. GPS devices are used outdoors and do not properly work indoors. Microwave ovens are sources of interference.

7. **A, B, C and D.** Outdoor site surveys are usually wireless bridge surveys; however, outdoor access points and mesh routers can also be deployed. Outdoor site surveys are

conducted using either outdoor access points or mesh routers, which are the devices typically used to provide access for client stations in an outdoor environment. These outdoor Wi-Fi surveys will use most of the same tools as an indoor site survey but may also use a global positioning system (GPS) device to record latitude and longitude coordinates.

8. B and D. Cordless phones that operate in the same space as the 5GHz U-NII bands may cause interference. Radar is also a potential source of interference at 5 GHz. Microwave ovens and 802.11b/g WLANs transmit in the 2.4 GHz ISM band. FM radios use narrowband transmissions in a lower-frequency licensed band.

9. A and C. During a passive manual survey, the radio card is collecting RF measurements, including received signal strength (dBm), noise level (dBm), and signal-to-noise ratio (dB). The SNR is a measurement of the difference in decibels (dB) between the received signal and the background noise. Received signal strength is an absolute measured in dBm. Antenna manufacturers predetermine gain using either dBi or dBd values.

10. C. An outdoor bridge network would not require blueprints since the wireless connection is a bridge link and is not inside the building.

11. A, B, C and D. Outdoor bridging site surveys require many calculations that are not necessary during an indoor survey. Calculations for a link budget, FSPL, Fresnel zone clearance, and fade margin are all necessary for any bridge link.

12. B, C, D and E. Spectrum analysis for an 802.11b/g/n site survey should scan the 2.4 GHz ISM band. Bluetooth radios, plasma cutters, 2.4 GHz video cameras, and legacy 802.11 FHSS access points are all potential interfering devices.

13. A, C, D and E. Every indoor wireless site survey should use at least one access point and multiple antennas. A client radio card will be needed for coverage analysis as well as a floor plan to record measurements. A spectrum analyzer is needed that sweeps the 2.4 GHz ISM band and 5 GHz U-NII bands.

14. D. If the survey was performed manually, the 5 GHz coverage analysis should be done first because of shorter range due to the smaller size 5 GHz wavelength. When performing a site survey for dual-radio access points, perform the initial site survey for the radios that provide the smallest coverage area, in this case the higher-frequency 5 GHz radios. The 2.4 GHz radios that provide the larger coverage area should be able to use the same access point location at a lower power setting to provide a similar coverage area as the 5 GHz radios. It may also be necessary to turn off some of the 2.4 GHz radios.

15. A and E. The number one source of RF interference in a multitenant environment is other WLANs. The odds are that most neighboring businesses will have deployed 2.4 GHz WLANs, and special consideration should be given to deploying a 5 GHz WLAN. Because RF propagates in all directions, it is necessary to always think three-dimensionally when designing a channel reuse pattern.

16. A, B and E. Temporary access point mounting gear is a necessity. A digital camera and colored electrical tape may also be used to record the locations of AP placement. Grid antennas are used outdoors for long-distance bridge links. An access point enclosure unit is used for permanent mounting.

17. B and D. Generically, this is known as a self-organizing wireless LAN, and technically, it is known as radio resource management (RRM). In the example, Jane was installing a controller-based system. This type of technology can also be found in cooperative WLAN products.

18. A and D. Wherever an access point is placed during a site survey, the power and channel settings should be noted. Security settings and IP address are not necessary.

19. B. During a passive manual survey, the radio card is collecting RF measurements, including received signal strength (dBm), noise level (dBm), signal-to-noise ratio (dB), and bandwidth data rates. The client adapter, however, is not associated to the access point during a passive survey.

20. C. Predictive coverage analysis is accomplished using software that creates visual models of RF coverage cells, bypassing the need for actually capturing RF measurements. Projected cell coverage zones are created using modeling algorithms and attenuation values.

Chapter 17: Power over Ethernet (PoE)

1. D. Even when 802.3af and 802.3at were amendments, PoE was defined in Clause 33. PoE is still defined in Clause 33, as defined in the updated 802.3 standard. When an amendment is incorporated into a revised standard, the clause numbering remains the same.

2. A. Any device that does not provide a classification signature (which is optional) is automatically considered a Class 0 device, and the PSE will provide 15.4 watts of power to that device.

3. A and C. The PoE standard defines two types of devices: powered devices (PDs) and power-sourcing equipment (PSE).

4. D. The power supplied to the PD is at a nominal 48 volts; however, the PD must be capable of accepting up to 57 volts.

5. A, B and C. The PD must be able to accept power over either the data pairs or the unused pairs if it is a 10BaseT or 100BaseTX device and over the 1-2, 3-6 data pairs, or the 4-5, 7-8 data pairs if it is a 1000BaseT device. The PD must also reply to the PSE with a detection signature. The PD must accept power with either polarity. Replying to the PSE with a classification signature is optional.

6. D. Providing a classification signature is optional for the PD. If the PD does not provide a classification signature, the device is considered a Class 0 device, and the PSE will allocate the maximum power, or 15.4 watts.

7. A, B and C. Alternative B devices, either endpoint or midspan, provide power to the unused data pairs when using 10BaseT or 100BaseTX connections. Prior to the 802.3at amendment, 1000BaseT devices were only compatible with endpoint PSE devices that supported Alternative A. With the ratification of 802.3at, 1000BaseT devices could now be powered using either Alternative A or Alternative B. 100BaseFX uses fiber-optic cable and is not compatible with PoE.

8. D. Class 4 devices are defined in the 802.3at amendment. The maximum power that a class 4 PD requires is between 12.95 and 25.5 watts.

9. C. At maximum power, each PoE device will be provided with 30 watts of power from the PSE. If all 24 ports have PDs connected to them, then a total of just under 720 watts (30 watts × 24 ports = 720 watts) is needed.

10. D. The power-sourcing equipment (PSE) provides five potential levels of power: Class 0 = 15.4 watts, Class 1 = 4.0 watts, Class 2 = 7.0 watts, Class 3 = 15.4 watts, and Class 4 = 30.0 watts. Because this device requires 7.5 watts of power, the PSE would be required to provide it with 15.4 watts.

11. D. The PSE provides power within a range of 44 volts to 57 volts, with a nominal power of 48 volts.

12. A. The maximum distance of 100 meters is an Ethernet limitation, not a PoE limitation. At 90 meters, this is not an issue. Although not specifically mentioned in the PoE standard, Category 5e cables support 1000BaseT communications and are therefore capable of also providing PoE. The large number of PoE VoIP telephones could be requiring more power than the switch is capable of providing, thus causing the APs to randomly reboot.

13. B. The switch will provide the Class 0 devices with 15.4 W of power each and the Class 1 devices with 4.0 W of power each. So the 10 VoIP phones will require 40 W of power, the 10 APs will require 154 W of power, and the switch will need 500 W—for a total of 694 W (40 W + 154 W + 500 W).

14. B. The switch will provide the Class 2 devices with 7.0 W of power each and the Class 3 devices with 15.4 W of power each. So the 10 cameras will require 70 W of power, the 10 APs will require 154 W of power, and the switch will need 1,000 W—for a total of 1,224 W (70 W + 154 W + 1,000 W).

15. B and D. Implementing PoE does not affect the distances supported by Ethernet, with is 100 meters or 328 feet.

16. D. An 802.3at powered device (PD) will draw up to 25.5 watts of power.

17. C. The maximum power used by a Class 0 PD is 12.95 W. The PSE provides 15.4 W to account for a worst-case scenario, in which there may be power loss due to the cables and connectors between the PSE and the PD. The maximum power used by a Class 1 PD is 3.84 W, and the maximum power used by a Class 2 PD is 6.49 W.

18. E. The different class and range values are as follows:

> Class 0: 0 to 4 mA
>
> Class 1: 9 to 12 mA
>
> Class 2: 17 to 20 mA
>
> Class 3: 26 to 30 mA
>
> Class 4: 36 to 44 mA

19. C. Mode A accepts power with either polarity from the power supply on wires 1, 2, 3, and 6. With mode B, the wires used are 4, 5, 7, and 8.

20. C. Type 2 devices will perform a two-event Physical layer classification or Data-Linklayer classification, which allows a Type 2 PD to identify whether it is connected to a Type 1 or a Type 2 PSE. If mutual identification cannot be completed, then the device can only operate as a Type 1 device.

Chapter 18: 802.11n

1. B. The majority of enterprise 802.1n access points are either 2×2:2 or 3×3:3. However, most 802.11n mobile devices, such as smartphones and tablets, only have a 1×1:1 MIMO radio because the addition of more radio chains would drain the battery life of the mobile device too quickly. In the described scenario, the highest available data rate for 1×1:1 communications is 65 Mbps. Please refer to Table 18.2.

2. A, C and D. Spatial multiplexing transmits multiple streams of unique data at the same time. If a MIMO access point sends two unique data streams to a MIMO client who receives both streams, the throughput is effectively doubled. If a MIMO access point sends three unique data streams to a MIMO client who receives all three streams, the throughput is effectively tripled. Because transmit beamforming results in constructive multipath communication, the result is a higher signal-to-noise ratio and greater received amplitude. Transmit beamforming will result in higher throughput because of the higher SNR that allows for the use of more complex modulation methods that can encode more data bits. 40 MHz HT channels effectively double the frequency bandwidth, which results in greater throughput. A-MPDU and Dual-CTS protection are MAC layer mechanisms.

3. D. Spatial multiplexing power save (SM power save) allows a MIMO 802.11n device to power down all but one of its radios. For example, a 4×4 MIMO device with four radio chains would power down three of the four radios, thus conserving power. SM power save defines two methods of operation: static and dynamic.

4. E. The guard interval acts as a buffer for the delay spread, and the normal guard interval is an 800-nanosecond buffer between symbol transmissions. The guard interval will compensate for the delay spread and help prevent intersymbol interference. If the guard interval is too short, intersymbol interference will still occur. HT radios also have the capability of using a shorter 400-nanosecond GI.

5. A, B, C, D and E. HT radios use modulation and coding schemes to define data rates based on numerous factors, including modulation type, the number of spatial streams, channel size, guard interval, equal/unequal modulation, and other factors. Each modulation and coding scheme (MCS) is a variation of these multiple factors. A total of 77 modulation and coding schemes exist for both 20 MHz HT channels and 40 MHz HT channels.

6. A, B, C and E. The 802.11n amendment introduces two new methods of frame aggregation to help reduce overhead and increase throughput. Frame aggregation is a method of combining multiple frames into a single frame transmission. The two types of frame aggregation are A-MSDU and A-MPDU. Multiple traffic ID block acknowledgment (MTBA) frames are used to acknowledge A-MPDUs. Block ACKs result in less overhead. RIFS is a 2-microsecond interframe space that can be used in an HT Greenfield network during frame bursts. The 2-microsecond interframe space is less overhead than the more commonly used SIFS. Guard intervals are used at the Physical layer.

7. C. An 802.11n transmitter that uses beamforming will try to adjust the phase of the signals based on feedback from the receiver using sounding frames. The transmitter is considered the beamformer, and the receiver is considered the beamformee. The beamformer and the beamformee work together to educate each other about the characteristics of the MIMO channel.

8. A. MIMO radios transmit multiple radio signals at the same time and take advantage of multipath. Each individual radio signal is transmitted by a unique radio and antenna of the MIMO system. Each independent signal is known as a spatial stream, and each stream can contain different data than the other streams transmitted by one or more of the other radios. A 3×3:2 MIMO system can transmit two unique data streams. A 3×3:2 MIMO system would use three transmitters and three receivers; however, only two unique data streams are utilized.

9. A. Multiple MPDUs can be aggregated into one frame. The individual MPDUs within an A-MPDU must all have the same receiver address. However, individual MPDUs must all be of the same 802.11e quality-of-service access category.

10. A, B and C. Modes 0, 1, and 2 all define protection to be used in various situations where only HT stations are allowed to associate to an HT access point. Mode 3—HT Mixed mode—defines the use of protection when both HT and non-HT radios are associated to an HT access point.

11. B, C and D. Some of the mandatory baseline requirements of Wi-Fi CERTIFIED n include WPA/WPA2 certification, WMM certification, and support for 40 MHz

channels in the 5 GHz U-NII bands. 40 MHz channels in 2.4 GHz are not required. 802.11n access points must support at least two spatial streams in both transmit and receive mode. Client stations must support one spatial stream or better.

12. C and D. Cyclic shift diversity (CSD) is a method of transmit diversity technique specified in the 802.11n standard. Unlike STBC, a signal from a transmitter that uses CSD can be received by legacy 802.11g and 802.11a devices. Maximum ratio combining (MRC) is a method of receive diversity.

13. A, B and D. 802.11n (HT) radios are backward compatible with older 802.11b radios (HR-DSSS), 802.11a radios (OFDM), and 802.11g radios (ERP). HT radios are not backward compatible with legacy frequency hopping radios.

14. B. Transmit beamforming is a method that allows a MIMO transmitter using multiple antennas to adjust the phase of the outgoing transmissions in a coordinated method. If the transmitter (TX) knows about the receiver's location, the phase of the multiple signals sent by a MIMO transmitter can be adjusted. When the multiple signals arrive at the receiver, they are in phase, resulting in constructive multipath instead of the destructive multipath caused by out-of-phase signals. Beamsteering and dynamic beamforming use smart antenna technology to create directional beams.

15. C and D. The HT Mixed format is considered mandatory, and transmissions can occur in both 20 MHz and 40 MHz channels. Support for the HT Greenfield format is optional, and the HT radios can transmit by using both 20 MHz and 40 MHz channels. Support for the non-HT legacy format is mandatory for 802.11n radios, and transmissions can occur in only 20 MHz channels. PCO is not a PPDU format.

16. C. Deploying 40 MHz HT channels at 2.4 GHz does not scale properly in multiple channel architecture. Although 14 channels are available at 2.4 GHz, there are only 3 nonoverlapping 20 MHz channels available in the 2.4 GHz ISM band. When the smaller channels are bonded together to form 40 MHz channels in the 2.4 GHz ISM band, any two 40 MHz channels will overlap. Channel reuse patterns are not possible with 40 MHz channels in the 2.4 GHz ISM band.

17. C. Non-HT duplicate transmissions will be sent using 802.11a data rates in the 5 GHz band or 802.11g data rates in the 2.4 GHz band. Non-HT duplicate transmissions are just sending the same data on two adjacent 20 MHz (52 subcarriers) OFDM channels at the same time. This will cause STAs operating in either the primary or secondary channel to update their NAVs and defer their transmissions. Non-HT duplicate mode improves error rate performance but is not widely implemented by WLAN vendors.

18. B and C. Other 802.11 technologies are frequency dependent on a single RF band. For example, 802.11b/g radios can transmit in only the 2.4 GHz ISM band. 802.11a are restricted to the 5 GHz U-NII bands. 802.11n radios are not locked to a single frequency band and can transmit on both the 2.4 GHz ISM band and the 5 GHz U-NII bands.

19. B. 802.11n also uses an 800-nanosecond guard interval; however, a shorter 400-nanosecond guard interval is optional. A shorter guard interval results in a

shorter symbol time, which has the effect of increasing data rates by about 10 percent. If the optional shorter 400-nanosecond guard interval is used with an 802.11n radio, throughput should increase. However, if intersymbol interference occurs because of multipath, the result is data corruption. If data corruption occurs, layer 2 retransmissions will increase and the throughput will be adversely affected. Therefore, a 400-nanosecond guard interval should be used in only good RF environments. If throughput goes down because of a shorter GI setting, the default guard interval setting of 800 nanoseconds should be used instead.

20. A and C. As the distance between a transmitter and receiver increases, the received signal amplitude decreases to levels closer to the noise floor. Maximum ratio combining (MRC) algorithms are used to combine multiple received signals by looking at each unique signal and optimally combining the signals in a method that is additive as opposed to destructive. MIMO systems using both switched diversity and MRC together will effectively raise the SNR level of the received signal. Because transmit beamforming results in constructive multipath communication, the result is a higher signal-to-noise ratio and greater received amplitude. Therefore, transmit beamforming will result in greater range for individual clients communicating with an access point.

Chapter 19: Very High Throughput (VHT) and 802.11ac

1. C. 802.11ac requires that all frames are transmitted as A-MPDU. MIMO and SU-MIMO are synonymous with each other and supported in both 802.11n and 802.11ac. A-MSDU is optional with both technologies. RIFS is no longer supported and is obsolete.

2. B. The first phase of 802.11ac supporting three spatials streams introduced transmission speeds up to 1.3 Gbps. 600 Mbps is the maximum transmission speed for the 802.11n amendment. 3.5 Gbps is the expected maximum transmission speed of the second phase of 802.11ac, which is expected to support four spatial streams. 6.933 Gbps is the maximum transmission speed for the 802.11ac amendment.

3. A, D and E. The 802.11ac amendment supports BPSK, QPSK, 16-QAM, 64-QAM, and 256-QAM. BASK and 32-QAM do not exist.

4. A, B, C, D and E. All of these are supported channel widths. The 160 MHz channel is actually made up of two 80 MHz channels that can be side by side or separated.

5. C. When a 160 MHz wide channel is used, an 80 MHz, 40 MHz, and 20 MHz primary channel are defined.

6. E. With 256-QAM, 256 distinct values can be represented, with each subcarrier is capable of representing 8 bits.

7. B. 802.11ac defines only 10 MCSs, unlike 802.11n, which defined 77. 802.11n defined MCSs based on modulation, coding method, the number of spatial streams, channel size, and guard interval. 802.11ac defines 10 MCSs based upon modulation and code rate.

8. D. MCS 0–7 are mandatory. MCS 8 and MCS 9 use 256-QAM, which is optional but will most likely be supported by most vendors.

9. D. The amendment defines a maximum of eight spatial streams and only allows MU-MIMO communications with a maximum of four devices.

10. A and B. A-MPDU is mandatory for all frames in 802.11ac. It reduces the per-frame overhead and requires only a single block ACK. Frame information is shifted from the slow PLCP header to the faster MPDU header. RIFS is no longer supported.

11. B, D and E. The beamformer transmits an NDP announcement frame followed by an NDP frame. The beamformee processes this information and creates and transmits a feedback matrix. The AP uses the feedback matrices to calculate a steering matrix that is used to direct the transmission.

12. C. Due to technology costs and battery consumption, many smartphones only support a single stream of data.

13. A, C, D and E. AC_DA is not a QoS category.

14. B, D and E. The AP will initiate a transmission from whichever access category is next in line. This is known as the primary access category, and all others are known as secondary access categories. The AP can transmit additional frames (one or more) from primary or secondary access categories, providing that the frames are shorter than the primary frame.

15. A and F. VHT radios use modulation and coding schemes to define data rates based on modulation and code rate. This is different from HT radios that used modulation type, the number of spatial streams, channel size, guard interval, equal/unequal modulation, and other factors.

16. B, D and E. Wi-Fi CERTIFIED ac access points require 20, 40, and 80 MHz channel widths, MCS 0-7, two spatial streams, and 800 nanosecond long guard interval.

17. B and E. VHT radios are backward compatible with all previous 5 GHz compliant radios. This include 802.11a (OFDM) radios and 5 GHz 802.11n (HT) radios.

18. B, D and E. A 20 MHz channel uses 64 subcarriers. A 40 MHz channel uses 128 subcarriers. An 80 MHz channel uses 256 subcarriers. A 160 MHz channel is made of two 80 MHz channels that can be either side by side or separated from each other. The number of subcarriers in a 160 MHz channel is exactly two times the number of 80 MHz subcarriers, 512 subcarriers.

19. C. The amendment defines a maximum of four spatial streams for a client and eight for an AP.

20. E. MU-MIMO is the most revolutionary technology. 802.11 APs will now be able to transmit to multiple client stations at the same time. 80 MHz and 160 MHz channels are an expansion of the 40 MHz bonded channel introduced in 802.11n.

A-MPDU was introduced with 802.11n and made mandatory in 802.11ac. 5 GHz only is a necessity since the 2.4 GHz band cannot support the wider channels. Explicit beamforming itself was introduced with 802.11n and is a necessity for MU-MIMO to be successful but by itself is an upgrade from the earlier technology.

Chapter 20: Bring Your Own Device (BYOD)

1. B, C and E. Firewall ports that should be permitted include DHCP server UDP port 67, DNS UDP port 53, HTTP TCP port 80, and HTTPS TCP port 443. This allows the guest user's wireless device to receive an IP address, perform DNS queries, and browse the Web. Many companies require their employees to use a secure VPN connection when they are connected to a SSID other than the company SSID. Therefore, it is recommended that IPsec IKE UDP port 500 and IPsec NAT-T UDP port 4500 also be permitted.

2. A and E. The guest firewall policy should allow for DHCP and DNS but restrict access to private networks 10.0.0.0/8, 172.16.0.0/12, and 192.168.0.0/16. Guest users are not allowed on these private networks because corporate network servers and resources usually reside on the private IP space. The guest firewall policy should simply route all guest traffic straight to an Internet gateway and away from corporate network infrastructure.

3. A, D and E. The four main components of an MDM architecture are the mobile device, an AP and/or WLAN controller, an MDM server, and a push notification service. The mobile Wi-Fi device requires access to the corporate WLAN. The AP or WLAN controller quarantines the mobile devices inside a walled garden if the devices have not been enrolled via the MDM server. The MDM server is responsible for enrolling client devices. The push notification services such as Apple Push Notification Service (APNs) and Google Cloud Messaging (GCM) communicate with the mobile devices and the MDM servers for over-the-air management.

4. A and C. 802.1X/EAP requires that a root CA certificate be installed on the supplicant. Installing the root certificate onto Windows laptops can be easily automated using a group policy object (GPO). An MDM uses over-the-air provisioning to onboard mobile devices and provision root CA certificates onto the mobile devices that are using 802.1X/EAP security.

5. B. The MDM profiles used by Mac OS and iOS devices are Extensible Markup Language (XML) files.

6. B, D and E. An MDM server can monitor mobile device information including device name, serial number, capacity, battery life, and applications that are installed on the

device. Information that cannot be seen includes SMS messages, personal emails, calendars, and browser history.

7. D. The operating systems of some mobile devices require MDM agent application software. An MDM agent application can report back to an MDM server unique information about mobile devices that can later be used in MDM restriction and configuration policies.

8. A, B and E. A captive portal solution effectively turns a web browser into an authentication service. To authenticate, the user must launch a web browser. After the browser is launched and the user attempts to go to a website, no matter what web page the user attempts to browse, the user is redirected to a logon prompt, which is the captive portal logon web page. Captive portals can redirect unauthenticated users to a logon page using an IP redirect, DNS redirection, or redirection by HTTP.

9. B, C and D. The AP holds the mobile client device inside a walled garden. Within a network deployment, a walled garden is a closed environment that restricts access to web content and network resources while still allowing access to some resources. A walled garden is a closed platform of network services provided for devices and/ or users. While inside the walled garden designated by the AP, the only services that the mobile device can access include DHCP, DNS, push notification services, and the MDM server. In order to escape from the walled garden, the mobile device must find the proper exit point, much like a real walled garden. The designated exit point for a mobile device is the MDM enrollment process.

10. C. Over-the-air provisioning differs between different device operating systems; however, using trusted certificates and SSL encryption is the norm. iOS devices use the Simple Certificate Enrollment Protocol (SCEP), which uses certificates and SSL encryption to protect the MDM profiles. The MDM server then sends a SCEP payload, which instructs the mobile device about how to download a trusted certificate from the MDM's certificate authority (CA) or a third-party CA. Once the certificate is installed on the mobile device, the encrypted MDM profile with the device configuration and restrictions payload is sent to the mobile device securely and installed.

11. A. An IP tunnel normally using Generic Routing Encapsulation (GRE) can transport guest traffic from the edge of the network back to the isolated DMZ. Depending on the WLAN vendor solution, the tunnel destination in the DMZ can be either a WLAN controller or simply a layer 2 server appliance. The source of the GRE tunnel is the AP.

12. E. A guest management solution with employee sponsorship capabilities will integrate with an LDAP database such as Active Directory. Guest users can also be required to enter the email address of an employee, who must approve and sponsor the guest prior to allowing the guest access on the network. The sponsor typically receives an email requesting access for the guest, with a link in the email that allows the sponsor to easily accept or reject the request. Once the user has registered or been sponsored, they can log on using their newly created credentials.

13. C. When employees enroll their personal devices though the corporate MDM solution, typically the employee will still have the ability to remove the MDM profiles because they own the device. If the employee removes the MDM profiles, the device is no longer managed by the corporate MDM solution. However, the next time the employee tries to connect to the company's WLAN with the mobile device, they will have to once again go through the MDM enrollment process.

14. D. The phrase bring your own device (BYOD) refers to the policy of permitting employees to bring personally owned mobile devices such as smartphones, tablets, and laptops to their workplace. A BYOD policy dictates which corporate resources can or cannot be accessed when employees access the company WLAN with their personal devices.

15. A. Social login is a method of using existing logon credentials from a social networking service such as Twitter, Facebook, or LinkedIn to register into a third-party website. Social login allows a user to forgo the process of creating new registration credentials for the third-party website. Retail and service businesses like the idea of social login because it allows the business to obtain meaningful marketing information about the guest user from the social networking service. Businesses can then build a database of the type of customers that are using the guest Wi-Fi while shopping.

16. F. A mobile device can still be managed remotely even if the mobile device is no longer connected to the corporate WLAN. The MDM servers can still manage the devices as long as the devices as connected to the Internet from any location. The communication between the MDM server and the mobile devices requires push notifications from a third-party service. Push notification services will send a message to a mobile device telling the device to contact the MDM server. The MDM server can then take remote actions over a secure connection.

17. B, D and E. Client isolation is a feature that can often be enabled on WLAN access points or controllers to block wireless clients from communicating with other wireless clients on the same wireless VLAN. Client isolation is highly recommended on guest WLANs to prevent peer-to-peer attacks. Enterprise WLAN vendors also offer the capability to throttle bandwidth of user traffic. Bandwidth throttling, which is also known as rate limiting, can be used to curb traffic at either the SSID level or user level. Rate limiting the guest user traffic to 1024 Kbps is a common practice. A web content filtering solution can block guest users from viewing websites based on content categories. Each category contains websites or web pages that have been assigned based on their prevalent web content.

18. D. Captive portals are available as standalone software solutions, but most WLAN vendors offer integrated captive portal solutions. The captive portal may exist within a WLAN controller, or it may be deployed at the edge within an access point.

19. B. The mobile device must first establish an association with an AP. The AP holds the mobile client device inside a walled garden. Within a network deployment, a walled garden is a closed environment that restricts access to web content and network resources while still allowing access to some resources. A walled garden is a closed platform of network services provided for devices and/or users. While the mobile device is inside the walled garden designated by the AP, the only services it can access are DHCP, DNS, push notification services, and the MDM server. After the mobile device completes the MDM enrollment process, the device is released from the walled garden.

20. A, B and C. A NAC server will use system health information, as reported by a posture agent, to identify if the device is healthy. DHCP fingerprinting is used to help identify the hardware and operating system. RADIUS attributes can be used to identify if the client is connected wirelessly or wired, along with other connection parameters. RADIUS CoA is used to disconnect or change the privileges of a client connection.

Appendix
B

Abbreviations and Acronyms

Certifications

CWAP   Certified Wireless Analysis Professional

CWDP   Certified Wireless Design Professional

CWNA   Certified Wireless Network Administrator

CWNE   Certified Wireless Network Expert

CWNT   Certified Wireless Network Trainer

CWSP   Certified Wireless Security Professional

CWTS   Certified Wireless Technology Specialist

Organizations and Regulations

ACMA   Australian Communications and Media Authority

ARIB   Association of Radio Industries and Businesses (Japan)

ATU   African Telecommunications Union

CEPT   European Conference of Postal and Telecommunications Administrations

CITEL   Inter-American Telecommunication Commission

CTIA   Cellular Telecommunications and Internet Association

ERC   European Radiocommunications Committee

EWC   Enhanced Wireless Consortium

FCC   Federal Communications Commission

FIPS   Federal Information Processing Standards

GLBA   Gramm-Leach-Bliley Act

HIPAA   Health Insurance Portability and Accountability Act

IAB   Internet Architecture Board

ICANN   Internet Corporation for Assigned Names and Numbers

IEC   International Electrotechnical Commission

IEEE   Institute of Electrical and Electronics Engineers

IESG   Internet Engineering Steering Group

IETF   Internet Engineering Task Force

IRTF   Internet Research Task Force

ISO   International Organization for Standardization

ISOC   Internet Society

NEMA   National Electrical Manufacturers Association

NIST   National Institute of Standards and Technology

NTIA   National Telecommunication and Information Agency

PCI   Payment Card Industry

RCC   Regional Commonwealth in the field of communications

SEEMesh   Simple, Efficient, and Extensible Mesh

TGn Sync   Task Group n Sync

WECA   Wireless Ethernet Compatibility Alliance

WIEN   Wireless InterWorking with External Networks

Wi-Fi Alliance   Wi-Fi Alliance

WiMA   Wi-Mesh Alliance

WWiSE   World-Wide Spectrum Efficiency

Measurements

dB   decibel

dBd   decibel referenced to a dipole antenna

dBi   decibel referenced to an isotropic radiator

dBm   decibel referenced to 1 milliwatt

GHz   gigahertz

Hz   hertz

KHz   kilohertz

mA   milliampere

MHz   megahertz

mW   milliwatt

SNR   signal-to-noise ratio

V   volt

VDC   voltage direct current

W   watt

Technical Terms

AAA   authentication, authorization, and accounting

AC   access category (802.11)

   alternating current (electricity)

ACK   acknowledgment

AES   Advanced Encryption Standard

AGL   above ground level

AID   association identifier

AIFS   arbitration interframe space

AKM   Authentication and Key Management

AM   amplitude modulation

A-MPDU   Aggregate MAC Protocol Data Unit

A-MSDU   Aggregate MAC Service Data Unit

AP   access point

APNs   Apple Push Notification services

APSD   automatic power save delivery

ARS   adaptive rate selection

ARS   automatic rate selection

AS   authentication server

DBPSK   Differential binary phase shift keying

DQPSK   Differential quadrature phase shift keying

BPSK   Binary phase shift keying

QPSK   Quadrature phase shift keying

ASK   amplitude-shift keying

ATEX   Atmosphères Explosives

ATF   airtime fairness

ATIM   announcement traffic indication message

AVP   attribute-value pair

BA   Block acknowledgment

BER   bit error rate

BPSK   binary phase shift keying

BOM   bill of materials

BSA   basic service area

BSS   basic service set

BSSID   basic service set identifier

BT   Bluetooth

BVI   bridged virtual interface

BYOD   bring your own device

CA   certificate authority

CAD   computer-aided design

CAM   content-addressable memory

CAM   Continuous Aware mode

CAPWAP   Control and Provisioning of Wireless Access Points

CBN   cloud-based networking

CCA   clear channel assessment

CC-AP   cooperative control access point

CCI   co-channel interference

CCK   Complementary Code Keying

CCMP   Counter Mode with Cipher Block Chaining Message Authentication Code Protocol

CCX   Cisco Compatible Extensions

CEN   cloud-enabled network

CF   CompactFlash (memory)
        contention free (802.11)

CFP   contention-free period

CID   company issued device

CLI   command-line interface

CoA   Change of Authorization

CP   contention period

CRC   cyclic redundancy check

CSMA/CA   Carrier Sense Multiple Access with Collision Avoidance

CSMA/CD   Carrier Sense Multiple Access with Collision Detection

CTS   clear-to-send

CW   contention window

CWG-RF   Converged Wireless Group–RF Profile

DA   destination address

DBPSK   differential binary phase shift keying

DC   direct current

DCF   Distributed Coordination Function

DDF   distributed data forwarding

DFS   dynamic frequency selection

DHCP   Dynamic Host Configuration Protocol

DIFS   Distributed Coordination Function interframe space

DoS   denial of service

DPI   deep packet inspection

DQPSK   differential quadrature phase shift keying

DRS   dynamic rate switching

DS   distribution system

DSAS   distributed spectrum analysis system

DSCP   differentiated services code point

DSM   distribution system medium

DSP   digital signal processing

DSRC   Dedicated Short Range Communications

DSS   distribution system services

DSSS   direct sequence spread spectrum

DTIM   delivery traffic indication message

EAP   Extensible Authentication Protocol

EDCA   Enhanced Distributed Channel Access

EIFS   extended interframe space

EIRP   equivalent isotropically radiated power

EM   electromagnetic

EQM   equal modulation

ERP   Extended Rate Physical

ERP-CCK   Extended Rate Physical–Complementary Code Keying

ERP-DSSS   Extended Rate Physical–Direct Sequence Spread Spectrum

ERP-OFDM   Extended Rate Physical–Orthogonal Frequency Division Multiplexing

ERP-PBCC   Extended Rate Physical–Packet Binary Convolutional Code

ESA   extended service area

ESS   extended service set

ESSID   extended service set identifier

EUI   extended unique identifier

EWG   enterprise wireless gateway

FA   foreign agent

FAST   Flexible Authentication via Secure Tunnel

FCS   frame check sequence

FEC   forward error correction

FHSS   frequency hopping spread spectrum

FILS   fast initial link setup

FM   frequency modulation

FMC   fixed mobile convergence

FSK   frequency-shift keying

FSPL   free space path loss

FSR   fast secure roaming

FT   fast BSS transition

FZ   Fresnel zone

GCM   Google Cloud Messaging

GCMP   Galois/Counter Mode Protocol

GCR   GroupCast with retries

GFSK   Gaussian frequency shift keying

GI   guard interval

GLK   General Link

GMK   Group Master Key

GCM   Google Cloud Messaging

GPO   group policy object

GPS   global positioning system

GRE   Generic Routing Encapsulation

GSM   Global System for Mobile Communications

GTC   Generic Token Card

GTK   Group Temporal Key

GUI   graphical user interface

HA   home agent

HAT   home agent table

HC   hybrid coordinator

HCCA   Hybrid Coordination Function Controlled Channel Access

HCF   Hybrid Coordination Function

HR-DSSS   High-Rate Direct Sequence Spread Spectrum

HSRP   Hot Standby Router Protocol

HT   High Throughput

HT-GF-STF   high-throughput Greenfield short training field

HT-LTF   high-throughput long training field

HT-SIG   high-throughput SIGNAL field

HT-STF   high-throughput short training field

HTTPS   Hypertext Transfer Protocol Secure

HWMP   Hybrid Wireless Mesh Protocol

IAPP   Inter-Access Point Protocol

IBSS   independent basic service set

ICMP   Internet Control Message Protocol

ICV   Integrity Check Value

IDS   intrusion detection system

IE   Information Element

IFS   interframe space

IoT   Internet of Things

IP   Internet Protocol

IP Code   Ingress Protection Code

IPsec   Internet Protocol Security

IR   infrared

IR   intentional radiator

IS   integration service

ISI   intersymbol interference

ISM   Industrial, Scientific, and Medical

ITS   Intelligent Transportation Systems

IV   initialization vector

L2TP   Layer 2 Tunneling Protocol

LAN   local area network

LEAP   Lightweight Extensible Authentication Protocol

LLDP   Link Layer Discovery Protocol

LLC   Logical Link Control

L-LTF   legacy (non-HT) long training field

LOS   line of sight

L-SIG   legacy (non-HT) signal

L-STF   legacy (non-HT) short training field

LWAPP   Lightweight Access Point Protocol

M2M   machine-to-machine

MAC   media access control

MAHO   Mobile Assisted Handover

MAN   metropolitan area network

MAP   mesh access point

MCA   multiple-channel architecture

MCS   modulation and coding scheme

MD5   Message Digest 5

MDI   media dependent interface

MDM   mobile device management

MFP   management frame protection

MIB   Management Information Base

MIC   message integrity check

MIMO   multiple-input, multiple-output

MMPDU   Management MAC Protocol Data Unit

MP   mesh point

MPDU   MAC Protocol Data Unit

MPP   mesh point portal

MPPE   Microsoft Point-to-Point Encryption

MRC   maximal ratio combining

MSDU   MAC Service Data Unit

MSSID   Mesh Service Set Identifier

MTBA   multiple traffic ID block acknowledgment

MTU   maximum transmission unit

MU-MIMO   multiuser MIMO

NAC   network access control

NAT   Network Address Translation

NAV   network allocation vector

NDP   null data packet

NEC   National Electrical Code

NMS   network management server

OAuth   open standard for authorization

OFDM   Orthogonal Frequency Division Multiplexing

OKC   opportunistic key caching

OS   operating system

OSI model   Open Systems Interconnection model

OUI   Organizationally Unique Identifier

PAN   personal area network

PAT   Port Address Translation

PBCC   Packet Binary Convolutional Code

PBX   private branch exchange

PC   point coordinator

PCF   Point Coordination Function

PCI   Peripheral Component Interconnect

PCMCIA   Personal Computer Memory Card International Association (PC Card)

PCO   phased coexistence operation

PD   powered device

PEAP   Protected Extensible Authentication Protocol

PHY   physical

PIFS   Point Coordination Function interframe space

PLCP   Physical Layer Convergence Procedure

PMD   Physical Medium Dependent

PMK   pairwise master key

PN   pseudo-random number

PoE   Power over Ethernet

POP   Post Office Protocol

PPDU   PLCP Protocol Data Unit

PPP   Point-to-Point Protocol

PPTP   Point-to-Point Tunneling Protocol

PSE   power-sourcing equipment

PSK   phase-shift keying

PSK   preshared key

PSMP   Power Save Multi-Poll

PSPF   Public Secure Packet Forwarding

PS-Poll   Power Save Poll

PSTN   public switched telephone network

PTK   pairwise transient key

PtMP   point-to-multipoint

PtP   point-to-point

QAM   quadrature amplitude modulation

QAP   quality-of-service access point

QBSS   quality-of-service basic service set

QoS   quality of service

QSTA   quality-of-service station

QPSK   quadrature phase shift keying

RA   receiver address

RADIUS   Remote Authentication Dial-In User Service

RBAC   role-based access control

RF   radio frequency

RFC   request for comment

RFSM   radio frequency spectrum management

RIFS   reduced interframe space

RRM   radio resource measurement

RSL   received signal level

RSN   robust security network

RSNA   robust security network association

RSSI   received signal strength indicator

RTLS   real-time location system

RTS   request to send

RTS/CTS   request to send/clear to send

RX   receive or receiver

SA   source address

SaaS   software as a service

S-APSD   scheduled automatic power save delivery

SCA   single-channel architecture

SCEP   Simple Certificate Enrollment Protocol

SD   Secure Digital

SDR   software defined radio

SIFS   short interframe space

SISO   single-input, single-output

SM   spatial multiplexing

SMTP   Simple Mail Transfer Protocol

SNMP   Simple Network Management Protocol

SNR   signal-to-noise ratio

SOHO   small office, home office

SOM   system operating margin

SQ   signal quality

SSH   Secure Shell

SSID   service set identifier

SSL   Secure Sockets Layer

STA   station

STBC   space-time block coding

STP   Spanning Tree Protocol

TA   transmitter address

TBTT   target beacon transmission time

TCP/IP   Transmission Control Protocol/Internet Protocol

TDLS   Tunneled Direct Link Setup

TDWR   Terminal Doppler Weather Radar

TIM   traffic indication map

TKIP   Temporal Key Integrity Protocol

TLS   Transport Layer Security

TPC   transmit power control

TS   traffic stream

TSN   transition security network

TTLS   Tunneled Transport Layer Security

TX   transmit or transmitter

TxBF   transmit beamforming

TXOP   transmit opportunity

U-APSD   unscheduled automatic power save delivery

UEQM   unequal modulation

U-NII   Unlicensed National Information Infrastructure

UP   user priority

USB   Universal Serial Bus

VHT   Very High Throughput

VLAN   virtual local area network

VoIP   Voice over IP

VoWiFi   Voice over Wi-Fi

VoWIP   Voice over Wireless IP

VPN   virtual private network

VRRP   Virtual Router Redundancy Protocol

VSWR   voltage standing wave ratio

WAN   wide area network

WAVE   Wireless Access in Vehicular Environments

WDS   wireless distribution system

WEP   Wired Equivalent Privacy

WGB   workgroup bridge

WIDS   wireless instruction detection system

Wi-Fi   Sometimes said to be an acronym for *wireless fidelity*, a term that has no formal definition; *Wi-Fi* is a general marketing term used to define 802.11 technologies.

WIGLE   Wireless Geographic Logging Engine

WiMAX   Worldwide Interoperability for Microwave Access

WIPS   wireless intrusion prevention system

WISP   wireless internet service provider

WLAN   wireless local area network

WM   wireless medium

WMAN   wireless metropolitan area network

WMM   Wi-Fi Multimedia

WMM-AC   Wi-Fi Multimedia Access Control

WMM-PS   Wi-Fi Multimedia Power Save

WNMS   wireless network management system

WPA   Wi-Fi Protected Access

WPAN   wireless personal area network

WPP   Wireless Performance Prediction

WWAN   wireless wide area network

WZC   Wireless Zero Configuration

XML   Extensible Markup Language

XOR   exclusive or

Appendix C

About the Additional Study Tools

IN THIS APPENDIX:

✓ Additional Study Tools

✓ System Requirements

✓ Using the Study Tools

✓ Troubleshooting

Additional Study Tools

The following sections are arranged by category and summarize the software and other goodies you'll find on the companion website. If you need help with installing the items, refer to the installation instructions in the "Using the Study Tools" section of this appendix.

 The additional study tools can be found at www.sybex.com/go/cwna4e. Here, you will get instructions on how to download the files to your hard drive.

Sybex Test Engine

The files contain the Sybex test engine, which includes three bonus practice exams, as well as the Assessment Test and the Chapter Review Questions, which are also included in the book itself.

Electronic Flashcards

These handy electronic flashcards are just what they sound like. One side contains a question, and the other side shows the answer.

PDF of Glossary of Terms

We have included an electronic version of the Glossary in PDF format. You can view the electronic version of the Glossary with Adobe Reader.

Adobe Reader

We've also included a copy of Adobe Reader so you can view PDF files that accompany the book's content. For more information on Adobe Reader or to check for a newer version, visit Adobe's website at www.adobe.com/products/reader/.

System Requirements

Make sure your computer meets the minimum system requirements shown in the following list. If your computer doesn't match up to most of these requirements, you may have problems using the software and files. For the latest and greatest information, please refer to the ReadMe file located at the book's website.

- A PC running Microsoft Windows 98, Windows 2000, Windows NT4 (with SP4 or later), Windows Me, Windows XP, Windows Vista, or Windows 7
- An Internet connection

Using the Study Tools

To install the items, follow these steps:

1. Download the ZIP file to your hard drive, and unzip to an appropriate location. Instructions on where to download this file can be found here: `www.sybex.com/go/cwna4e`.

2. Click the `Start.exe` file to open the study tools file.

3. Read the license agreement, and then click the Accept button if you want to use the study tools.

   The main interface appears. The interface allows you to access the content with just one or two clicks.

Troubleshooting

Wiley has attempted to provide programs that work on most computers with the minimum system requirements. Alas, your computer may differ, and some programs may not work properly for some reason.

The two likeliest problems are that you don't have enough memory (RAM) for the programs you want to use or you have other programs running that are affecting installation or running of a program. If you get an error message such as "Not enough memory" or "Setup cannot continue," try one or more of the following suggestions and then try using the software again:

Turn off any antivirus software running on your computer.   Installation programs sometimes mimic virus activity and may make your computer incorrectly believe that it's being infected by a virus.

Close all running programs.   The more programs you have running, the less memory is available to other programs. Installation programs typically update files and programs; so if you keep other programs running, installation may not work properly.

Have your local computer store add more RAM to your computer.   This is, admittedly, a drastic and somewhat expensive step. However, adding more memory can really help the speed of your computer and allow more programs to run at the same time.

Customer Care

If you have trouble with the book's companion study tools, please call the Wiley Product Technical Support toll-free phone number at (877) 762-2974, or email them at http:// sybex.custhelp.com/.

Index

Note to Reader: **Bolded** page references indicate main discussions of a topic. *Italicized* page references indicate illustrations.

B

Free Online Study Tools

Register on Sybex.com to gain access to a complete set of study tools to help you prepare for your CWNA Exam

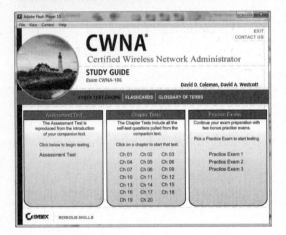

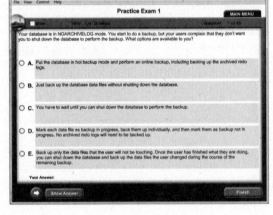

Comprehensive Study Tool Package Includes:

- **Assessment Test** to help you focus your study to specific objectives

- **Chapter Review Questions** to reinforce what you learned

- **Three CWNA Practice Exams** to test your knowledge of the material

- **Electronic Flashcards** to reinforce your learning and give you that last-minute test prep before the exam

- **Searchable Glossary** gives you instant access to the key terms you'll need to know for the exam

Go to www.sybex.com/go/cwna4e to register and gain access to this comprehensive study tool package.